Music in American Life

A list of books in the series appears
at the end of this book.

Opera on the Road

∽ Opera ∽
on the Road

Traveling Opera Troupes in the United States, 1825–60

Katherine K. Preston

UNIVERSITY OF ILLINOIS PRESS
Urbana and Chicago

Publication of this work has been supported by a grant from the National Endowment for the Humanities, an independent federal agency, and is also made possible through a gift in memory of Lois Ashbeck McClure.

This book is printed on acid-free paper.

Library of Congress Cataloging-in-Publication Data

Preston, Katherine E.
    Opera on the road : traveling opera troupes in the United
States. 1825–60 / Katherine K. Preston.
        p.   cm. — (Music in American life)
    Includes bibliographical references and index.
    ISBN 0-252-01974-1
    1. Opera—United States—19th century.   I. Title.   II. Series.
ML 1711.4.P73 1993
782.1′0973′09034 — dc20   92–20644
                                                                CIP
                                                                MN

We are apt, in America, to look forward too exclusively, — to think we have no history. We forget that we have had a culture in the past, of which we may be proud for its own sake, from which we may gather encouragement and inspiration.

—Louis Madeira, Preface to *Annals of Music in Philadelphia* (1896)

Contents

Appendixes:
319

Notes
377

Bibilography
431

Index
455

Preface

My fascination with the history of early nineteenth-century opera performance in the United States constitutes a broad spinoff from my research into the lives and work of professional musicians active in Washington, D.C., in the 1870s, 1880s, and 1890s. While engaged in that research, I noticed that compositions from the musical stage kept cropping up in the repertories of the hired musicians whose activities I was investigating. Works from musical comedies, operettas, and—more interesting, I thought—Italian, French, English, and German operas appeared over and over again: on programs from instrumental and vocal concerts, to be sure, but also among the entre-act compositions performed by theater orchestras; on dance cards from masquerade balls, hops, and soirées; among the works played by brass bands marching in parades; as part of the repertory for college commencement ceremonies; as music performed by wind and string ensembles to entertain excursionists on Potomac River steamers. My curiosity was piqued, and I fell into the habit of counting the instances of operatic-derived compositions whenever I saw a nineteenth-century American musical program of any sort. I remember sitting in a darkened hall at one scholarly conference, listening to a colleague read a paper on some aspect of American musical life of the early nineteenth century, and losing the train of his thought whenever he flashed on the screen a slide of a concert program. I could not resist counting the works that came from operas, operettas, or musical comedies. This penchant for musical/theatrical composition-counting continued for several years. Over time, my observations were confirmed again and again: numbers from stage productions—including numerous compositions from European operas—generally constituted at least half of the repertory on published American music programs from the nineteenth century.

I found this to be curious. If journeymen musicians of the late nineteenth century were performing operatic music, the only logical conclusion I could draw from this observation is that middle-class Americans—the people who hired the musicians—must have been familiar with the music of European operas. In fact, the evidence suggested that they preferred this style of music to many other styles.

The so-called golden age of opera in the United States, however—at least according to most opera aficionados—did not occur until the early part of the twentieth century, during the careers of Enrico Caruso and others of his generation. Where did this nineteenth-century American love of operatic music come from? How far back into the century did it go? How familiar were Americans with European operas? Did they know just the arranged music, or were they conversant with the staged operas as well? Was there perhaps an earlier golden era of opera performance in the United States? These were some of the early questions I had in mind when I embarked on the research for this study. In the process of finding the answers for this first set of questions, I discovered many more questions and answers. This book is the result of my piqued curiosity.

The story of opera performance in North America during the colonial and revolutionary periods has been well documented by Oscar Sonneck in his indispensable work *Early Opera in America*. The story of opera in the United States during the nineteenth century, however, has been limited almost entirely to events that occurred during the final twenty-five years: John Cone's study of the James Mapleson Company is one of the earliest in subject matter, and it commences with the arrival of that impresario in America in 1878. The other seventy-five years of the century have been for the most part neglected; investigations of antebellum opera productions (in particular) have been limited to chapters in surveys of music in the United States (such as Charles Hamm's valuable chapter on Italian opera as popular song in *Yesterdays*) and to studies of opera production in particular cities (Henry Kmen's work on New Orleans, for example) or geographical areas (Ronald Davis's study of opera in the West). The lack of in-depth scholarship on this subject has led some historians (and most opera aficionados) to believe that opera was an unimportant and inconsequential part of American musical culture, especially during the antebellum period. The purpose of this book is to dispel that incorrect belief.

The history of opera in nineteenth-century America—especially during the antebellum period—is inextricably intertwined with the history of American theater. Opera, as musical theater, was a normal part of the American theatrical repertory of the time. As a consequence, I have relied for much of my material on sources that normally fall within the purview of theater historians: playbills, prompt books, theatrical periodicals of the nineteenth and twentieth centuries, memoirs, and theses, dissertations, and books on the history of the theater in specific American cities and regions. Musical materials have included similar secondary and primary sources: regional studies, contemporary music periodicals, reviews, memoirs, concert and operatic programs, biographical source materials, libretti and scores of the operas, and operatic sheet-music publications. For background material and for information about the American audience I have examined newspaper articles and advertisements, personal letters, diaries, letters to the editors of periodicals and newspapers, memoirs, and photographs. The result is a combination of information from secondary sources (there are, for example, copious numbers of books, theses, and dissertations on the history of music or theater in specific American cities and towns) combined with an abundance of primary source materials. The sum of all this information is an overall picture of the place of opera and opera performance in American culture of the antebellum period.

The book is quite straightforward in organization. The Prologue sets the scene by providing background information on American and British theater practices in the early nineteenth century. Chapters 1, 3, and 5 survey specific types of troupes: vocal-star, Italian, and English opera companies, respectively. No individual troupes are examined in detail in these chapters; the point is to demonstrate the ubiquity and pervasiveness of itinerant opera performers in the United States during the period and to provide the cultural context for the other three chapters. Chapters 2, 4, and 6 are detailed examinations of particular seasons by specific companies chosen as prototypes of the three kinds of troupes active at different times. In the short Epilogue, I discuss briefly other aspects of operatic-music popularity in antebellum America: the appeal of this music to amateur musicians; its pervasiveness in the instrumental concert and band repertories; its status as standard material performed by such "low-brow" musicians as street organ-grinders; its use as parody material by minstrel troupes and burlesque-opera companies. The Epilogue also includes some perceptions about the general appeal of opera and operatic stars to antebellum Americans of wide-ranging socioeconomic status.

I have deliberately excluded French and German opera companies from this study. The French troupes were very important, especially in the early antebellum period; John Davis's French Opera Company of New Orleans, in fact, was the second troupe to visit the East Coast. The only other scholarly study of itinerant opera companies in the United States, however, focuses on precisely this troupe: Sylvie Chevalley's article on the tours of the New Orleans company from 1827 to 1833 covers the subject of French troupes fairly well; her coverage is particularly valuable because itinerant French companies ceased to be important in the United States after the mid–1840s. I have excluded German companies for a much simpler reason: most, if not all, were short-lived resident troupes (primarily in New York), not itinerant companies.

I have not attempted to write the definitive history of opera performance in the antebellum United States. Our knowledge of the history of music in America of this period is still too incomplete to attempt such a task. A major contribution of this study, however, is to make available to scholars of American music, history, and culture a large body of information that can be expanded and built upon. In the late twentieth century, our general knowledge of the history of music in nineteenth-century America is still so incomplete that it can be compared to the partially drawn map of an unexplored region. This work might be thought of as a mass of detail that can be used to fill in a blank portion of that figurative map. Then again, perhaps a different— but similar—metaphor might be more appropriate. As a detailed description of one specific aspect of the history of music in the United States, this book can be likened to the illustrative narration of a journey: a trip taken, perhaps, by an itinerant group of singers, performing European operas for audiences comprised of nineteenth-century Americans—who became, over time, increasingly fascinated with and enamored of operatic melody.

Acknowledgments

It is impossible to undertake and complete a project of this scope without the help of many institutions and individuals; all deserve my sincere gratitude. I was in residence at the National Museum of American History of the Smithsonian Institution in Washington, D.C., as a Fellow from 1985 through 1988, and the tenure greatly facilitated my completion of this study. In particular, John Hasse and Cynthia Hoover of the Division of Musical History provided encouragement and moral support, and Jim Rose of the museum's library was always willing to process yet another in a seemingly endless series of interlibrary loan requests. I also benefited from and had my intellectual horizons expanded by working closely with other Fellows from a variety of disciplines, all of whom were engaged in research and writing on interesting scholarly projects, most about some aspect of American history and culture.

I was privileged to be in residence as a Peterson Fellow at the American Antiquarian Society in Worcester, Massachusetts, on two separate occasions. A full month's tenure at that remarkable archive during the summer of 1985 proved to be an insufficient amount of time, and I had to return for another full month in 1986 before exhausting the relevant materials. The entire genial staff of the society deserves my thanks; in particular, however, I am grateful for the friendship and help of Georgia Barnhill, curator of the Graphic Arts Collection. I also spent a fruitful month as a Fellow at the Newberry Library in Chicago. In addition, I received financial and travel support for research from the Sinfonia Foundation, the Philadelphia Center for Early American Studies, and the Ph.D. Alumni Association of the Graduate Center, City University of New York. The book is being published with the generous assistance of a subvention award from the National Endowment for the Humanities. It is also supported by a grant from the H. Earle Johnson Fund of the Sonneck Society for American Music and by a Minor Research Grant from the College of William and Mary. I am extremely grateful for this assistance.

The staffs of the Music, Rare Books, and Newspapers and Current Serials Divisions of the Library of Congress put up with my constant presence (and countless call slips) for several years. I am grateful for their help. In particular, my thanks to the resident genius of the Music Division, Wayne Shirley, for his suggestions, good humor, encouragement, moral support, and editing recommendations. Wayne surely went beyond the call of duty. I also thank the Reader Services Division of the library for the study desk I occupied for two years in an alcove above the Main Reading Room of the Jefferson Building. The staffs of numerous other libraries and archives, including the Theatre Department of the Philadelphia Free Library, Manuscripts Division of the Historical Society of Pennsylvania, Music Department of the Boston Public Library, Harvard Theatre Collection of Houghton Library, Billy Rose Theatre Collection of the New York Public Library, and many other repositories in San Francisco, Chicago, Philadelphia, Boston, New York, and Washington all deserve my thanks.

I benefited greatly from the help and advice of many scholars. I first thank H. Wiley Hitchcock for hours spent carefully reading and editing my manuscript and—in particular—for words of encouragement and enthusiasm that helped to keep me going. Lawrence Levine gave freely of his time, advice, and friendship, and his interest and enthusiasm were invaluable. John Graziano and Charles Hamm also read and commented on various drafts. I also bent the ear of many other friends and colleagues during the course of this project. In particular, William Brooks gave me copies of the research notes to articles he wrote on several nineteenth-century figures for the *New Grove Dictionary of American Music,* and he also read and commented on several of the chapters. He was always sympathetic, supportive, and forthcoming with good advice; his enthusiasm for and curiosity about the history of music in nineteenth-century America continues to be a source of inspiration. Harlan Jennings of Michigan, Robert Commanday of San Francisco, Bruce Carr of Pittsburgh, Kathryn Reed-Maxfield of Ann Arbor, and Thomas Kaufman of New Jersey all generously lent me copies of research notes for their own opera-related projects; this material was invaluable. I constantly marvel at my luck to be in a discipline in which scholars—even near-strangers—support and trust each other to such an extent. To Allen Lott, whose work on traveling virtuoso pianists is closely related to my own research, my thanks for encouragement and occasional nuggets of information. Betsy Sanford was always willing to read copy and act as a sounding board; I sincerely appreciate her enthusiasm and interest for a subject that is leagues away from her normal discourse.

I also took advantage of the generous hospitality of numerous friends who put me up while I was conducting research away from home. In particular, I wish to thank my sister Teresa Imfeld, who lives in San Francisco; Mary Lee and Steven Ledbetter and Anne Dhu McLucas, who live (or lived) near Boston; and Christine Niehaus and Barbara Heyman, both residents of New York City. My parents, Mary Elizabeth Imfeld and the late Clem Imfeld, Jr., also provided much moral support.

To my students and colleagues at the College of William and Mary, my thanks for patience and forbearance. In particular, Dale Cockrell, William DeFotis, and Edgar Williams—friends as well as colleagues—were particularly understanding and thoughtful in one of the earlier stages of this project when I was dealing with a looming deadline, a balky printer, cumbersome software, and discs with mysteriously missing blocks of text. Loretta Early and Brewer Eddy of the College Computer Center and Donna Wilson of the Educational Media Center lent computer-related assistance, and two other friends also helped with these marvelous—and sometimes infuriating—machines. John Holdway created several maps, and Johanna Pfund spent hours helping convert my files from one word-processing program to another. There was a time when book acknowledgments did not include thanks for help with machines, but that time is long past— at least for me. I would also like to mention three professionals who helped greatly in the production of the book: Mary Giles (editing), Teresa Imfeld (proofreading), and Beth McNeer (indexing). My grateful thanks to all three.

My bicycling buddies and good friends—in particular John Holdway, Susan Hartman, and Jeff Travis—helped to keep me sane and healthy by dragging me away from my computer and making me forget about nineteenth-century opera companies while traversing the roads of rural and suburban Maryland, Virginia, and Washington, D.C. I appreciate their forbearance.

Finally, my husband Daniel—the most musically knowledgeable American historian I know—went far beyond the call of duty in keeping our lives together, especially during several of the earlier stages of this project. This work is dedicated to him.

Prologue

England and America carry on, undoubtedly, a most thriving and
multifarious traffick. Not only do they exchange cotton, tobacco,
turpentine, laces, silks, cloths, cutlery, fashions, frippery, and a
thousand other *et ceteras* . . . but a more intellectual barter of authors, travellers, artists, and actors, is most spirited and unceasingly
kept up. In the latter department the United States are insatiable
in their demands. They have absorbed nearly all the talent of Great
Britain.[1]

The history of touring opera troupes in the United States begins in
the 1820s, with the appearance first of Manuel García's Italian
Opera Company in 1825 and, two years later, with the first East Coast
tour of John Davis's French Opera Company of New Orleans. These
two troupes, however, were only the vanguard of a whole host of
opera companies of different types and sizes that would have a significant role in the development of American musical culture during
the antebellum period. The touring opera company was, above all, a
type of theatrical troupe; as a consequence, a study of their activities
during the antebellum period must have as its foundation an understanding of the theatrical system of which they were a part.

It is of paramount importance to understand that to American theater-goers of the early nineteenth century music was a normal and
important part of all dramatic productions. As a matter of course
theaters employed orchestras, singing actors and actresses, and musical
directors and relied heavily upon them in their productions. A standard
theatrical bill of fare from either the late eighteenth or the early nineteenth century consisted of an instrumental overture (often from an
opera), a full-length dramatic piece with added songs and dances (either
interpolated into the action or performed between the acts), and an
afterpiece (a farce, burletta, one-act opera, dance, pantomime, or masque)
that often was musical in nature. In addition, dances or musical compositions were frequently performed before and after either the dra-

matic work or the afterpiece.[2] The musical interpolations into "straight" dramatic works were far more than superfluous window-dressing. Theater historian Julian Mates cites as one example a production (in the mid-eighteenth century) of Shakespeare's *The Tempest* that contained no fewer than thirty-two interpolated songs and duets (25). So pervasive was music on the stage, in fact, that by the late eighteenth century it was difficult for American or British audiences to differentiate between English operas (with spoken dialogue) and "straight" drama.[3]

English comic and ballad operas were themselves an important part of the standard theatrical repertory in both Britain and America, and they became increasingly so as the eighteenth century turned into the nineteenth.[4] By then, scholars estimate, almost 50 percent of the theatrical works performed in the United States were musical in nature.[5] Both resident and itinerant dramatic troupes included in their standard repertories a large number of operatic works such as *Love in a Village* and *Thomas and Sally* (by Thomas Arne), *The Padlock* and *The Quaker* (Charles Dibdin), *The Poor Soldier, Rosina,* and *The Woodman* (William Shield), *No Song, No Supper* and *The Haunted Tower* (Stephen Storace), and *The Duenna* (Thomas Linley). By 1820 these same companies had incorporated Italian operas into their repertories for the first time; the works were adapted for the English stage by British composers such as Henry Rowley Bishop. At this time, "adapting" meant making these operas closer in musical style to English comic operas. Bishop's versions of Mozart's *Don Giovanni* (as *The Libertine*) and Rossini's *Il barbiere di Siviglia* (*The Barber of Seville*) were first performed in the United States by the stock company of New York's Park Theatre on 7 November 1817 and 3 May 1819, respectively.[6] Subsequently, these two works (and many others similarly adapted) entered the American theatrical repertory, where some remained well into the middle of the nineteenth century.[7] To American audiences, then, opera—as first performed by García's Italian and Davis's French companies in the mid to late 1820s—was significantly different from other theatrical repertory primarily because of the language. The fact that all the action of the drama (including the dialogue) was set to music was more of an exaggeration of an already popular style (drama suffused with music) than the introduction of an entirely new genre.[8]

The introduction of operas by Rossini and Mozart into the American theatrical repertory coincided—serendipitously—with the first appearances in this country of visiting British singers of true stellar rank. Most notable among these were Charles Incledon (1757–1826) of Vauxhall and Covent Garden, and Thomas Philipps (d. 1841) of Dublin. Both men arrived in the United States in 1817 and both performed (in separate, consecutive engagements) at the Park Theatre in New York shortly thereafter. Each subsequently appeared in opera and concert performances in New York, Boston, Philadelphia, and elsewhere. Incledon, at the time the most renowned of English vocalists, toured the East Coast fairly extensively from October 1817 through August 1818.[9] Philipps returned to Dublin sometime after the autumn of 1819, and then made a second visit to the United States from October 1821 through June 1823.[10] In part through their choice of concert repertory, these two singers (along with other vocalists who performed in opera and on the concert circuit during the 1820s and 1830s) helped to create in American audiences a taste for Italian melody. Philipps was the more successful of the two, for he was younger, a better actor, and closer to his prime than Incledon; by late 1819, when he performed in the Park Theatre's premiere of *The Barber of Seville,* he had become the "supreme public idol" of New York audiences.[11]

Although Incledon and Philipps were not the first touring vocal stars to visit this country, they were among the best of the early singers who came to America to perform both in playhouses and on the concert circuit. As visiting theatrical stars, they were but a small part of a multitude of British dramatic stars (including Edmund and Charles Kean, William Charles Macready, Junius Brutus Booth, and Charles and Fanny Kemble) who by the early 1820s appeared in increasing numbers on the American theatrical circuit. The appearance of these big-name itinerant performers in the United States illustrates two important—and closely related—aspects of the American theater during the early years of the antebellum period. First, Americans continued to depend on the theatrical culture (including the repertory) of Great Britain, a dependence that would not begin to break down until the late 1840s. Second, British and European stars, whose performances in this country were made possible by the "star system," increasingly dominated American theatrical culture.

Well into the middle of the nineteenth century, American theaters continued to operate—as they had during the colonial, post-revolutionary, and federal periods—as cultural outposts of London. "Our theatre came to us from England," observed the theater historian Alfred Bernheim about the eighteenth-century American stage, "not merely ideologically but materially as well, in the shape of plays, actors, managers, and even of costumes and sets. Everything was imported except the buildings which housed the performances."[12] By the early years of the nineteenth century, many British actors, actresses, theater musicians, and managers had emigrated to the United States, and most sets, costumes, and scenery were also manufactured here. Well into the 1840s, however—and, in some respects, much later—little had changed culturally. American theaters, although admittedly much more distant, still operated as minor outposts of the London cultural sphere, somewhat on a par with the provincial theaters of Manchester, Leeds, Dublin, Edinburgh, and Glasgow. Although a constant—and increasing—influx of German, Italian, and French musicians occurred in the 1820s, 1830s, and well into the 1840s, a majority of the singers and singer/actors who appeared in the United States, on both the dramatic and the concert stages, were from Great Britain. American managers kept close tabs on theatrical and musical failures and successes on the London boards and—like all provincial managers—eschewed the former and quickly produced the latter. As American cities grew in the first years of the nineteenth century, and as local theaters became more thoroughly established and profitable, English dramatic and vocal stars (who regularly toured in the provinces) began increasingly to look further west, across the Atlantic, for work.

The first actor of international reputation to appear in an American theater was George Frederick Cooke, who was engaged at New York's Park Theatre in late 1810. Cooke was not the first "star" to be imported, for the star system had been evolving gradually in American theaters from the late 1790s.[13] He was, however, the first to be imported by Stephen Price (d. 1840). A theatrical speculator and the manager of the Park, Price was responsible not only for Cooke's visit but also for visits by numerous other famous British and European stars over the course of the next thirty years. Price can be credited with—and blamed for—helping to establish in the United States the star system, a managerial modus operandi that, by 1810, had been in operation in Great Britain for some time.[14] Under this system, dramatic or vocal "stars"—including some of the most prominent, popular, and talented performers of England, the Continent, and (slightly later) the United States—were free agents. They were attached to no particular company and hence were free to travel around the theatrical circuit and make their own contracts for short- or long-term (but nonpermanent) engagements with theater managers.[15] As visiting performers, they typically assumed the major roles in plays or operas; the actors and actresses of the theater's stock company filled in the supporting roles. Dramatic stars generally toured alone or, occasionally, in pairs. Vocal stars, however, more often toured as pairs, trios, or sometimes quartets in order to better insure that all the principal roles in the operas they performed were adequately covered.

Stock companies of local theaters were self-sufficient and capable of mounting plays or operas by themselves, which they did during the periods when no stars were visiting. As the century wore on, however, the stream of stars (and would-be stars) traversing the American theatrical circuit became almost unceasing. As a result, by the 1830s and 1840s, stock companies on the East Coast or in New Orleans rarely performed without the services (and the drawing power) of a big-name actor, actress, or singer.

The star system met with little resistance when it was first introduced into this country, primarily because it was already well established in Great Britain. American actors and actresses gradually joined the ranks of the itinerant stars; over the course of the next several decades, all aspiring actors and actresses—both native and imported—eschewed performing with stock companies in favor of the greater acclaim and wealth of stardom. Stock companies disbanded, and managers, faced with the exorbitant salary demands of the stars, went bankrupt. After the Civil War the star system was replaced by the "combination system," under which entire companies (instead of stars) toured the theatrical circuit.[16] A detailed examination of the rise and fall of the star system in the United States is not central to this study. It is important, however, to understand that during the antebellum period a theatrical method existed in the United States that allowed—even encouraged—performances by itinerant musical and dramatic stars. Under that system, first-rank performers (who, had they been required to join a local theatrical or operatic company in order to perform in the United States would have had little incentive to come here) were free to visit and perform in America for as long or as short a period as they wished.

The star system was a flexible one that gradually changed over the years to meet the altered needs and tastes of the theatrical and musical audience. Throughout the 1820s American audiences were satisfied with operatic fare that consisted almost entirely of English comic operas and translations of a handful of Italian, French, and German works. By the 1830s, Americans began to develop a taste for foreign-language operas. As this taste grew, American audiences gradually concluded that performances of the more technically demanding operas were no longer adequate or acceptable if done by the combination of vocal stars and stock companies. As a consequence, by the mid and late 1840s American theaters hosted larger numbers of visiting opera companies, and fewer individual vocal stars or vocal-star troupes. By the mid 1850s, in fact, vocal-star troupes had disappeared almost entirely from the American theatrical circuit, especially in the East. They had been replaced by itinerant English, French, and Italian opera companies.

The transformation of itinerant opera companies from vocal-star troupes to full-fledged traveling opera companies was gradual. For a long time and in many areas the two kinds of companies overlapped, especially those troupes that performed in English. The change was fairly complete by the 1850s, however, and a theatrical system that had accommodated a constantly changing stream of visiting operatic stars early in the antebellum period had shifted to the accommodation instead of a constantly changing stream of operatic companies.

1

Vocal-star Troupes

During the 1820s, 1830s, and 1840s, numerous British vocal stars, following in the footsteps of Charles Incledon and Thomas Philipps, made the trek from the stages of England to the theaters of the East Coast of the United States. Some of these singers performed in America for several years before returning home, while others spent the rest of their lives in their adopted country. Some were first-rank stars and toured as such, while others worked, at different times, as both stars and members of stock companies. Most of them—even the most popular and successful—have been forgotten. During the antebellum period, however, they not only were celebrities, but they also played a crucial role in the success of the full-fledged opera troupes, Italian as well as English, that appeared and flourished during the 1840s and 1850s. This role was so significant that any study of itinerant opera companies must commence with a thorough discussion of vocal stars and their activities—despite the fact that they were individuals rather than companies.

When Inclecon and Philipps visited America—during the late 1810s and early 1820s—many of the best singers active on the East Coast were closely affiliated with the stock companies of theaters in New York and Philadelphia; many, in fact, had been recruited by those theaters. Because of the large amount of music in the standard repertory, theatrical managers often were eager to hire talented singer/actors for their companies. Managers, however, were more interested in actors who could sing than in singers who could act. "Let your singer be a gentleman and capable of playing the parts of opera," the agent of Philadelphia's Chestnut Street Theatre was instructed before a recruiting trip to London in 1827. "A good singer who will maintain with respectability his parts in opera will have much to do next season." Even so, he was cautioned, "high musical attainments are not so essential as expression, feeling, and vivacity."[1] In the early 1820s it was somewhat difficult to convince an actor or a singer to cross the Atlantic—and the more successful the performer, the less inclined he or she was to undertake the lengthy and dangerous crossing. It did not help matters that few British players knew about theatrical conditions in the United

States. London colleagues of the actor Francis Courtney Wemyss, for example, teased him about his impending retirement "into banishment" after he signed on as a member of the Chestnut Street Theatre Company in Philadelphia in 1822.[2] But some actors believed that the advantages offered by the New World outweighed the obvious disadvantages. First and foremost was the lure of a quick fortune that—reportedly—could be made in the land of the unsophisticated Yankee.

Americans commonly believed that foreign performers came to the United States for the sole purpose of "acquiring rapidly a fortune," and to a certain extent this was true.[3] Many a performer's dreams of exorbitant financial reward did indeed materialize. The vocal stars Jane Shirreff and John Wilson were quite successful monetarily (chapter 2), and the singer Thomas Philipps was sufficiently pleased with the gains from his first visit that he returned for a second. In addition to the desire for quick riches, however, was a related craving for easy professional success. Some ambitious actors (especially footloose young performers, or those who had not reached the first rank in London) considered the new and expanding dramatic market of the United States a golden opportunity and believed that theatrical triumph would be a foregone conclusion. Francis Wemyss, for example, considered his chances for success much higher in the New World than they had been in England. "My plain calculation," he later wrote, "was having been considered a respectable actor in my own country, surrounded by competitors of every grade, I may be considered something more than respectable in America." Wemyss, however—whose beliefs probably were shared by many other performers—realized upon arrival that he had underestimated both the caliber of actors in the United States and the sophistication of American audiences. He discovered that at Philadelphia's Chestnut Street Theatre "every part was filled by an actor fully competent to sustain the reputation of the theatre"; furthermore, the company itself was made up of "veteran actors, who understood their profession, and whose exertions were fully appreciated by a discriminating audience." He quickly concluded that "I had a harder task before me, to insure success, than I [had] hitherto suffered myself to suppose."[4]

As the theatrical traffic between Great Britain and the United States increased throughout the 1820s, the reputation of American theaters steadily improved. Visiting actors sent reports to England that the United States was not a theatrical wilderness; this helped enhance the reputation of dramatic life here. This improvement—coupled with an increased level of prosperity in American theaters—helped convince a larger number of higher-caliber actors and singers to give the United States a try. By the middle and late 1820s, in fact, American theaters were attracting a more talented class of singers; some of them were stars, many were stock-company performers.

It was not unusual for singers who later toured the United States as stars to commence their American careers as members of stock companies. One such performer was a Mrs. Sharpe, a well-known contralto active here during the 1820s and 1830s, who started her American career in 1825 as a member of the company at New York's Park Theatre.[5] Equally versatile in dramatic and musical roles, Sharpe was "as useful a stock actress as ever graced the Park boards."[6] She performed with that company for five years, playing dramatic parts in both comedies and tragedies in such works as *The Rivals, The School for Scandal, The Beaux' Stratagem, William Tell,* and *Hamlet* as well as in many less familiar plays; she also performed vocal roles in such operas as William Shield's *Rosina* and *The Poor Soldier* and Carl Maria von Weber's *Oberon*.[7] When the Park management engaged true vocal stars for opera appearances, Sharpe sang secondary roles. In 1828, for example, she performed in *The Marriage of Figaro* (as Susannah), *Oberon,* and Henry Bishop's *Native Land* during Elizabeth Austin's engagement; she also later appeared in supporting roles in Boieldieu's *The Caliph of Bagdad* in 1829 and Arne's *Artaxerxes* in 1831.[8] Sharpe left the Park company after the 1830 season, and thereafter traversed the American theatrical circuit as a secondary star, usually singing in support of other, more talented, vocal stars with whom she traveled. Even as seconda donna, however, she enjoyed a great deal of success, for she continued singing here until 1839.[9]

Although the pattern of Sharpe's career was not particularly unusual for a vocal star, it was not uncommon for the progression to be in the opposite direction. There always were numerous singers who moved back and forth from the ranks of stock companies to the ranks of the stars—the exceptions being those who were indisputably first-rate. An example of a singer who commenced her American career as a star and who later "retired" to a stock company is Mrs. Edward (Mary Ann) Knight (1804–61). Knight (née Povey), a veteran of Drury Lane, made her New York debut as a vocal star in the fall of 1826, and for more than a year—until her popularity was eclipsed by the appearance of Elizabeth Austin—reigned as the operatic favorite of East Coast audiences.[10] Knight's popularity in the United States suggests that in the 1820s the American concept of vocal beauty continued to be more heavily influenced by the musical demands of Thomas Moore than by those of Italian bel canto composers. Her voice, according to the *New-York Mirror* on 20 October 1827, could be likened "to a plaintive Scotch melody—simple and unostentatious, the touching beauty of whose tones, however, cling to our memory, and will not pass away."[11]

The theater historian Joseph Ireland likewise suggests that Knight's voice was better suited to ballad singing than to opera. "Had [Knight] first appeared in 1866," he explained, writing that year, "probably she would never have been regarded as a great singer, but the public taste forty years ago had not its present cultivation, nor its present fastidiousness, and consequently Mrs. Knight for a while stood at the very summit of popular regard, and her songs were certainly given with a spirit and expressiveness at that time entirely unrivaled."[12]

Knight's success during the mid–1820s indicates how much and how quickly audience taste changed—and, in fact, broadened—over the next several decades. Although she was soon replaced by the more florid Austin as the country's ranking soprano, she nevertheless remained a popular singer. She toured the United States successfully as a star for almost fifteen years, performing in the Northeast as well as in Charleston, Augusta, Mobile, and New Orleans.[13] In the early 1840s she joined the stock company at the Park Theatre and remained there until 1848. She returned to England in 1849.[14]

Numerous singers similar to Mrs. Sharpe and Mary Ann Knight were active in the United States in the late 1820s and early 1830s. Although neither of these women was of true stellar quality, both were better than average stock-company singers. Their presence and success in North America indicates an overall improvement in the quality of opera performances at the best theaters in the country. Furthermore, singers of this caliber helped to raise performance standards in places other than New York or Philadelphia because they toured the country and performed with stock companies not as strong as those of the Park or the Chestnut Street theaters.

As performance quality gradually improved in American theaters in the 1820s, so did the expectations of American audiences. Heightened audience expectations, in turn, added to the pressure on theater managers to recruit even better singers. Partly in response to this pressure, Francis Wemyss (the former actor now turned acting and stage manager for William Warren's Chestnut Street Theatre) achieved a major coup in 1827 by luring to the United States a singer of true stellar rank, Elizabeth Austin (ca. 1800 until after 1835). Mrs. Austin, as she was known, was the first English prima donna to capture the imagination of Americans, and the first vocal star to maintain her status as the "queen of song" in the United States for more than a year (Figure 1). It is significant that she was an excellent singer but a mediocre actress.[15]

In August 1827, Austin, a popular singer at Drury Lane, Vauxhall, and the English Opera House, signed a contract in London with Wemyss, who was on a recruiting trip.[16] She arrived in the United States late the following November, accompanied by her own musical director

1. Engraving of Elizabeth Austin. After a portrait by
H. P. Briggs. (*Century Illustrated Monthly Magazine,*
March 1882)

and agent, F. H. F. Berkeley. She made her American debut at the
Chestnut Street Theatre in Philadelphia as Rosetta in Arne's *Love in
a Village* on 10 December 1827; her New York debut was a month
later, on 2 January 1828.[17] As would be typical of many vocal stars in
the 1820s and 1830s, Austin's contract with Warren and Wemyss stip-
ulated a guaranteed number of performances: in her case a month-long
engagement of three performances a week at the Chestnut Street Theatre and an engagement of undisclosed length at Warren's Holliday
Street Theatre in Baltimore. At the conclusion of her original engagement, she was free to make her own arrangements for performances
elsewhere, which she did.[18]

Elizabeth Austin's success in the United States was pronounced.
Possessing a soprano voice of "perfect bird-like softness, sweetness,

and wonderful flexibility," with a range "of nearly three octaves, and . . . [of] remarkable purity and sweetness," she was more accomplished in the Italian school than any English vocalist who had yet visited the United States.[19] She replaced Mary Ann Knight as America's reigning prima donna almost overnight.

Austin performed in the United States for more than seven years. During that time she toured all over the eastern half of the country, singing in concerts in small towns and in operas with the stock companies of theaters in larger cities. Berkeley served as her agent, making all the necessary arrangements with the various theaters in which she appeared. Occasionally she performed as the single featured star in operas mounted by stock companies. More often, however, she teamed up with other popular singers to form a vocal-star troupe of two, three, or four stars, which traveled as an ensemble and performed with local stock companies. During her tenure in the United States, Austin toured in a succession of such troupes comprised of popular singers like Charles Edward Horn, Mrs. Sharpe, Mary Ann Knight, Elizabeth Feron, John Sinclair, Elizabeth Hughes, John Jones, and Thomas Reynoldson. Scanty information makes a reconstruction of her journeys difficult, but it is clear that she performed principally in the Northeast (in New York, Boston, Providence, Philadelphia, Baltimore, and Washington) and made at least one trip to the South, appearing at the Camp Street Theatre in New Orleans in January and February 1834.[20]

Mrs. Austin sang in many of the same English-language operas that had been seen on American stages for years: *The Beggar's Opera* (Gay), *Love in a Village* (Arne), *The Duenna* (Linley), *Guy Mannering* (Bishop), *Rob Roy* (Davy), *Lionel and Clarissa* (Dibdin), and *No Song, No Supper* (Storace). But she also starred in the American premieres of a significant number of works, including Arne's *Artaxerxes* (Philadelphia, 28 December 1827), and the English versions of Auber's *Fra Diavolo* (New York, 20 June 1833) and Boieldieu's *The White Lady* (New York, 23 April 1828) and *The Caliph of Bagdad* (New York, 14 October 1829).[21] Furthermore, she helped to popularize many other European operas, including *The Marriage of Figaro* (she sang the role of the Countess) and *The Magic Flute* (Pamina), *Masaniello* and *Gustavus III* (by Auber), *The Maid of Judah* (with music by Rossini), *The Barber of Seville,* and *Der Freischütz*. She was identified most closely, however, with Michael Rophino Lacy's *Cinderella; or, The Fairy and the Little Glass Slipper,* an adaptation of Rossini's *La Cenerentola* that included music from three of his other operas, *Armida, Maometto II,* and *Guillaume Tell*. She sang in the U.S. premiere of this opera at the Park Theatre on 24 January 1831, and performed in it countless times during her subsequent American tours. The work was mounted so often, in fact, that in

October 1834 the critic from the *American Musical Journal* described it as the "much worn, but ever attractive opera of *Cinderella*" (18). According to Charles Hamm, it was destined to become "one of the most popular works of musical theater in the history of the American stage."[22]

All of the foreign-language operas—like *Cinderella*—in which Austin and other vocal stars appeared were translated and adapted for the English stage. Recitative, when present, was changed into dialogue, the more difficult ensemble numbers were eliminated, and many of the complex arias were turned into strophic songs. The works essentially became English comic operas. Some "adapted" operas included a great deal of extra musical material, either newly composed or borrowed from other operas, making them musical pastiches (see, for example, the playbill for Lacy's *Cinderella* in Figure 2). Critics sometimes complained about the nature of the adaptations, especially when favorite arias or concerted pieces were removed, or when a work was "adapted" almost beyond recognition. In July 1832, for example, a reviewer for the *New-York Mirror* described a version of Auber's *La Fiancée* as "sadly mutilated" and "shorn of much of its original beauty" (22). In June 1833, a critic from the *Spirit* complained that the "adapted" version of *Fra Diavolo* as performed by Austin was "stuffed with the stolen pieces of a dozen other [operas] . . . among them a duett from 'Tancredi'—an Aria from 'Jean de Paris,'—an English ballad,—a buffa aria from 'La Gazza Ladra,'—and a bravura from 'Robert le Diable.' " Some critics, on the other hand, defended the practice of adapting works. A reporter for the *Mirror*, presumably writing about the same version of *Fra Diavolo* ("with additions by Rossini, &c.") so disparaged by his colleague at the *Spirit*, commented at length on the issue on 6 July 1833. "Hypercriticism may affect to call in question the propriety of strengthening the work of one master by additions from others," he wrote,

> but, in our poor thinking, all translations are fair subjects for improvement, for it is self-evident, that, as many parts of an opera which might please a French audience, would not be effective if literally given to Englishmen or Americans, so it is fair to strengthen the weak part from other sources. The Italians constantly do this . . . the Germans likewise do it. . . . [W]hy we, who have not much claim to a regular or severe school of dramatic music, are to cavil at that which other nations admit, we cannot very well comprehend. Indeed we laugh at the idea, and profess ourselves ready to doff our hats to any gentleman who will serve us up so rich and melodious a dish of harmony as that found in "Fra Diavolo," without being over nice as to its ingredients. (3)

Although a fair amount of such controversy is found in the musical

Theatre.

For the Benefit of

MRS. AUSTIN

AND HER

LAST APPEARANCE

The celebrated Romantic Opera of

DON GIOVANNI;

OR,

The Spectre.

The Music by Mozart.

Will this Evening be produced

With New Scenery, &c.

The Public is most respectfully informed that in consequence of
the unprecedented success of the New Opera and the enthusiastic
applause with which

CINDERELLA

Has been nightly received by crowded houses, this splendid piece
will this Evening be repeated, for the 16th time.

The Orchestra and Chorus

Have both been encreased and no expense or pains spared to
render the

SPLENDID OPERA

OF

CINDERELLA,

Worthy of the Patronage of the Public.

The Overture will commence precisely at 7 o'clock.

On Monday Evening, March 7, 1831.

Will be performed, 16th time, the new comic Opera of

CINDERELLA;

OR,

The Fairy and the Little Glass Slipper.

The Music composed - - - - by Rossini.
Containing selections from
"Cenerentola," "Armida," "Maometto Secondo," and
"Guillaume Tell."
The whole arranged and adapted to the English Stage, by
Rophino Lacy.
The Piece produced under the direction of MR. BARRY
Stage Manager.

Leader of the Orchestra, : : Mr. De Luce
Chorus Master, : : Metz
With new Scenery, : : by Mr. Evers
Dresses, : : : : by Mead.
Machinery, , : : , by Dunn
Properties, : : : : by Chambers.
Felix, (Prince of Salerno,) - Mr. Jones
Baron Pumpolino, (of Montefiesco.) Placide
Alidoro, (The Prince's Tutor,) - Richings
Dandini, (The Prince's Valet,) Thorne
Pedro, (Servant to the Baron,) T. Placide
Hunters and Attendants, Messrs. Blakeley, Povey, Field. Collet.
Hayden, Thornton, Pearson, Nott, Bissett, Ford, Singleton,
Weight &c.

CINDERELLA, ⎫ ⎧ Mrs. AUSTIN
Clorinda. ⎬ Daughters of the Baron ⎨ Blake,
Thisbe. ⎭ ⎩ Vernon.
Fairy Queen, Mrs. Wallack
1st. Fairy, Godey
2nd Fairy, - - - - Durie
Fairies,—Mesdames Benjamin, Jessop, Rogers, Turnbull, J. Turn
bull, Wheatley, E. Wheatley, Simms, &c.

2. Playbill from a performance of Mozart's *Don Giovanni* and the Rossini/Lacy opera *Cinderella; or, The Fairy and the Little Glass Slipper,* at New York's Park Theatre on 7 March 1831. Elizabeth Austin was the star and the beneficiary of this performance. (Theatre Collection, Museum of the City of New York)

and theatrical press of the time, adapted operas generally were accepted at face value. The author of an article about Elizabeth Austin matter-of-factly stated that "during her different engagements she has produced the 'Caliph of Bagdad,' Boieldieu's splendid opera, translated purposely for her; 'Cinderella,' as adapted by Lacy . . . taken from the original score, and got up expressly for her; and Boieldieu's 'White Lady' "; in the same issue the critic noted that *The Beggar's Opera,* "completely revised and re-scored," would soon be mounted at the Park Theatre.[23] Indeed, the fact that an opera was presented in a translated or adapted version was frequently not mentioned in contemporary reviews. On 1 October 1830, during one of Austin's engagements at the Park Theatre, for example, the *Euterpiad* reported simply that *"The Tempest* and *John of Paris,* the *Barber of Seville,* and the *Caliph of Bagdad,* have followed in succession, and were all got up with a care and attention which do honour to the management" (102). That the operas were performed in English was taken for granted. However, although it was possible for companies to perform drastically altered versions of operas without eliciting press comment, this does not necessarily indicate acquiescence by knowledgable members of the audience. Joseph Sill, a Philadelphia merchant and a native Londoner, complained bitterly about an 1832 performance of *The Beggar's Opera.* "The Opera," he noted in his diary in January, "was miserably curtail'd: Gay would scarcely have known the mutilated farce of the night, as the intended representation of his own wit & humour."

Musical interpolations were treated similarly. Often, additions were unnoted in reviews, although the fact that playbills frequently include lists of added songs indicates that interpolations were an accepted performance practice. A playbill for an 1831 performance of *John of Paris* at the Holliday Street Theatre in Baltimore, for example, points out that "in addition to the music of the Opera," the prima donna would sing " 'Cupid Hear Me'; 'The Arab Steed'; and 'Strike for Tyrol and Liberty' (from the opera *William Tell*)." Another, from a perfor-mance of *Cinderella* at Philadelphia's Chestnut Street Theatre in 1833, points out that "in the course of the opera [the vocal star] Miss Hughes will sing 'Away to the Mountain's Brow' and 'Savourneen Deelish.' "[24] Reviewers sometimes took umbrage at the additions, as did one critic for the *Euterpiad,* who complained on 1 February 1831 that "incessant interpolations" are "intrusions" that disturb "the peace of dialogue and cue . . . destroying the fine concert of *general effect*" (203). Just as frequently, however, interpolations were treated as ordinary occur-rences. In 1829, for example, Elizabeth Austin was reported (without comment) to have introduced into *The Beggar's Opera* the songs "We're a Noddin' " and "The Genius of Freedom."[25] In April 1835, the *Amer-*

ican Musical Journal reported that the same singer performed Bellini's
"Dalla gioja" during *Cinderella,* an interpolation that was "encored
most enthusiastically . . . in a decided and unanimous demand for repetition" (116). The interpolations that tended to rouse the critics' ire
were songs that were less "elevated" than the Bellini aria Austin introduced. A reviewer in the *Euterpiad* on 1 October 1830, for example,
took Mary Ann Knight severely to task for introducing into *The Marriage of Figaro* ballads and other "drum and fife-like compositions" by
such composers as Alexander Lee. " 'The Bonnets of Blue'—'The Blue
Bonnets'—the 'Charlie's Over the Water'—and 'Over the Waters with
Charlie,' " he argued, "are [not] otherwise than trash, fit only to amuse
gentlemen and ladies of colour in the gallery" (103).[26] Other, more
spontaneous liberties taken with the text likewise elicited criticism and,
more important, offer similar glimpses into the composition of the
audience itself. In a 14 January 1832 *New-York Mirror* review of a
performance of the Lacy/Rossini *Cinderella* in Philadelphia, a critic
sharply (and ironically) reprimanded one of the stock company actors
for making "a dialogue of his own, with no respect or regard to that
written by Mr. Rophino Lacy." The actor's improvised lines, the critic
continued, were no more than "a tissue of witless unmeaning epi-
thets . . . [which were] duly appreciated by the colored gentlemen in
the gallery" (219).

This presence of "gentlemen and ladies of colour" at opera productions is a startling revelation if one is accustomed to thinking of
attendance at operas during the nineteenth century as an activity limited
to the wealthy and socially elite. But the American theater of the
antebellum period was not the exclusive resort of that segment of the
population. On the contrary, the theater was a democratizing institution. In the words of the actor and manager Lewis Hallam, theaters
were egalitarian because they could "draw all [the] ranks of the people
together."[27] Most American theaters of the early nineteenth century
were physically divided into three separate sections—the boxes, the
pit, and the gallery.[28] The cost of admission to each of the sections
was different, and sometimes there were even separate entrances. The
New National Theatre that opened in Philadelphia in 1840, for example, advertised that "Separate entrances have been arranged to different sections [of the house] to avoid the mingling of the classes."[29]
Because each section of the theater was occupied by a different segment
of the population, the audience was consistently divided along fairly
clear economic and class lines. Nevertheless, all segments of the population attended theatrical productions on a regular basis.

The gallery, then as now, was the highest balcony in the theater.
There, as noted, sat the "colored," who were proscribed from sitting

in any other part of the house. Southern blacks had the gallery to themselves. The St. Charles Theatre, for example, reserved one entire section for free blacks and another for slaves, indicating clearly that African Americans formed an important part of the New Orleans theater audience.[30] In the North, some theaters also featured "colored galleries," while in others blacks shared this area—the cheapest section of the house—with apprentices, servants, and others who were young, rowdy, or of limited economic means.[31] The pit, which corresponds with the orchestra section of a modern theater, ranked next in price of admission; it attracted primarily the "middling classes" and "honest folks"—although only of the male gender. The same New National Theatre announcement quoted previously stated explicitly, "No females allowed in the pit," and Thomas Chamberlain, a recent immigrant to New York from London, noted in his diary in the mid–1830s that "it is not the custom [here] for females to go in the pit."[32] Because the stage could best be seen from this section, many of the more serious (male) theater-goers joined the "unclassified miscellany" seated on the rough benches in the pit.[33] In Walt Whitman's words, this segment of the audience consisted of the "alert, well-dress'd, full-blooded young and middle-aged men, the best average of American born mechanics." Another writer, in less grandiloquent terms, described the denizens of the pit in 1820 as "a mixed multitude of the lower orders of all sorts, sizes, ages and deportments."[34] The most expensive seats in the house, the boxes, were located above the pit, arranged in several tiers around the circumference of the theater's interior. Boxes offered privacy, prestige, and comfort. Generally they were reserved for the socially elite of the community, but they were also the only section where women who wished to retain their respectability could sit, especially before the 1840s, when some theaters transformed their pits into "parquets," thereby opening up another section to females.[35] Until the early 1850s, many theaters' third tier of boxes (that located just below the gallery) was given over to prostitutes, hence its common contemporary designation as the "notorious third tier."

Reviewers of opera almost never mention any portion of the audience beyond the "fashionable and elite." By definition, however, any house described as "crammed," "overflowing," "crowded from top to bottom," or "filled to its utmost capacity" had to include significant numbers of auditors who were neither wealthy nor elite—all those individuals who occupied either the gallery or the pit.[36] According to Grimsted, the numbers of people in the pit and gallery—compared to those in boxes—did not change significantly from performance to performance. "The proportion of pit and gallery attendance to that in the boxes of Boston's National Theatre or Philadelphia's Chestnut

Theatre," he wrote in his study of antebellum American theater and culture, "remained fairly constant whether *Hamlet* or *The Six Degrees of Crime* was the attraction" (1968, 57). As this study will show, Grimsted could easily have used as his examples *Cinderella* and *The Beggar's Opera*, or, for that matter, *Cinderella* and *The Six Degrees of Crime* or *The Beggar's Opera* and *Hamlet.* All of these works, in addition to ballet, pantomime, melodrama, farce, minstrelsy, and acrobatics, were part and parcel of the antebellum American theater.

The denizens of the pit and the gallery are mentioned so rarely in contemporary opera reviews that they are (at least from the vantage point of the twentieth century) invisible members of the audience. Lower- and middle-class theater-goers were ignored by contemporary journalists because they were not important or influential. One must search long and hard for the occasional acknowledgment of their presence. Hence the importance of the disparaging remarks about the tastes of the "colored" inhabitants of the gallery, or the observation by one critic on 11 November 1828 in the *Theatrical Censor and Musical Review* that for a performance by Elizabeth Austin in Philadelphia "the pit was well filled but the boxes were thin," or the admission in print that opera was enjoyed by all segments of the theater-going public. One such rare comment was made on 4 April 1829 by a reviewer in the *New-York Mirror* about a performance of *The Marriage of Figaro* at the Park Theatre. *Figaro* "as an opera . . . is without a rival in the English language," he wrote, for it is "equally fitted to all tastes, whether the box, pit, or gallery."

In the early 1830s ever-increasing numbers of vocal stars appeared on the stages of the United States, in part because of Elizabeth Austin's phenomenal success. According to Francis Wemyss, the soprano's reception here "induced others, of higher talent, to cross the Atlantic in search of fame."[37] Austin's popularity in this country remained unthreatened and undiminished for a full six years—until the arrival of one of those "others, of higher talent": Mary Anne Paton Wood. In 1833, Wood (1802–64), a Scottish soprano, was in the midst of a triumphant career at Covent Garden and the Italian Opera in London when she left to come to the United States. At the time, she was acclaimed as the finest and most celebrated female vocalist in England.[38] She traveled and performed with her husband Joseph (1801–90), who was an excellent actor, a passable tenor, and a shrewd manager.[39] Soon after their arrival, Mary Anne Wood eclipsed Austin in both popularity and fame.

Much of the Woods' success in this country was a result of the foundation laid down by Elizabeth Austin, who had "laboured hard, and successfully too, to establish a taste for English opera."[40] A critic in the *New-York Mirror* commented on 28 September 1833 that "we are more indebted to Mrs. Austin for the great improvement in our musical taste than to any other professional lady whatever" (103). But by 1833 Austin's period of influence in the United States was nearing an end; she would retire to England in May 1835. The torch was about to be passed to the Woods, who also contributed mightily to the tradition of opera performance in this country. As Wemyss observed in 1847, "To Mr. and Mrs. Wood belongs the credit of establishing what Mrs. Austin and Mr. Berkeley commenced—a taste for English opera. They made the citizens of these United States [fall] in love with music" (236). The English opera to which Wemyss referred included "Englished" operas. British vocal stars sang as much Italian as English repertory, and the Woods contributed to this trend toward the performance of Italian music by introducing American audiences to even more Italian operas, in particular works by Bellini.

The new singers made their joint American debut in New York on 9 September 1833, and as if in deliberate challenge to the reigning American prima donna, Mary Anne Wood chose for her first role one that Elizabeth Austin had claimed for her own: Cinderella in the Rossini/Lacy opera.[41] The Woods' repertory was similar to that of Mrs. Austin, but their inclusion of additional Italian operas and their heavier reliance upon the Italian works in their repertory is further indication of Americans' growing taste for Italian melody. Particularly notable were the Woods' North American premieres of Bellini's *La Sonnambula* in New York on 13 November 1835 and *Norma* on 11 January 1841.[42] Both operas were destined to become long-term American favorites in both Italian and in English, but *Sonnambula* quickly became the most successful opera on the American stage since *Cinderella* (Figure 3).

Indeed, it would eventually prove to be one of the most enduringly popular operas in the United States during the entire first half of the nineteenth century.[43] A review of one of the Woods' performances of this opera in Philadelphia in the 7 May 1836 *Gentlemen's Vade-Mecum* gives an idea of the work's popularity. "The *Sonnambula*," wrote the critic, "is, as usual, doing a tremendous business at the Arch Street Theatre, the house being filled to its utmost capacity whenever that opera is performed. The two first tiers are nightly so completely crowded with ladies that the male sex are almost banished to the pit and to the lobbies." And the Philadelphia merchant Joseph Sill wrote revealingly about the opera in his diary on 26 October 1840: "In the evening I went to the Chestnut St. Theatre to see Mr & Mrs Wood in the Sonnambula. They were both welcomed by a very full & fashionable house in a very enthusiastic manner. . . . The Opera throughout was well perform'd—It is very delightful in both the plot and music, and

3. Illustration from sheet-music cover of the aria "Ah! non giunge uman pensiero" (Ah, don't mingle) from Vincenzo Bellini's *La Sonnambula,* as sung by Mary Anne Wood. Lithograph by J. H. Bufford (New York: Atwill's Music Saloon, 1835). (Music Division, Library of Congress)

never tires in repetition. I have seen it, I suppose, twenty times, and could see it twenty times more."[44]

The Woods' incorporation of more Italian works was spurred in part by a sudden (and short-lived) flurry of competition from Italian opera companies on the East Coast, singing in Italian. The Montresor and Rivafinoli companies performed in New York and Philadelphia during 1832, 1833, and 1834, and the Porto Sacchi troupe was active in New York from late 1834 through spring 1835 (chapter 3). As soon as the Italians disappeared, however, English opera once again regained its fashionable allure. "The departure of the Italian company from our city," wrote a critic for the *New-York Mirror* on 28 November 1835, "has had a very sensible influence upon the success of the English opera at the Park, and we hardly need say a favourable one. Our musical *dilettanti,* who had lounged away some seasons in the privileged circle of the Opera House . . . were at first reluctant to desert the beautiful temple which they had themselves erected to *la belle science* for the common and unfashionable boxes of a theatre. . . . But the restraint has at last worn off, the Park has now become the rage, and upon each successive opera-night [it] is filled with lovely women, as gay and brilliant as ever" (174). On 21 November, the critic for the *Spirit* observed that "The fashionables and dilettanti are returning to their first love, and are seen night after night flocking to the Park. English Opera now 'reigns lord of the ascendant,' and long may it flourish."

The return of the "fashionables and dilettanti" to the Park was undoubtedly cause for great rejoicing by the management, but the house had hardly been empty during their absence. Odell reports that despite competition from "the new fashionable toy of the Italian Opera" the Woods had attracted very strong houses, especially for their benefit performances (3:673–74). The *Spirit*'s critic also made note of the singers' wide appeal. "The present engagement of Mr. and Mrs. Wood," he wrote on 14 November 1835, "has been exceedingly profitable to all concerned. They have for some time been playing four nights per week, and their attraction, instead of retrograding, seems actually to have increased with each performance. English opera is so much the rage among our fashionables, *as well as other classes of society,* that the unfortunate Italians and their beautiful house are apparently forgotten" (emphasis added).

If the Woods' success had been impaired by the presence of the Italian companies, as the *New-York Mirror* seems to suggest, their box-office receipts elsewhere clearly indicate that this temporary setback was felt only in New York. In his history of the Chestnut Street Theatre, Reese James reported that for their first engagement in Philadelphia the Woods attracted audiences well above normal, comparable in size to those for performances by the extremely popular dramatic stars Fanny and Charles Kemble, whose engagement followed that of the Woods in October 1833. The receipts for the singers' second engagement in February 1834 were also larger than usual.[45] Furthermore, Clapp provides lists of the Woods' receipts from December 1834–January 1835 and December 1835–January 1836 that indicate the resounding success of the vocal stars in Boston, and Weldon Durham claims that the "greatest success" at the Tremont Street Theatre from 1833 through 1836 were the Woods' "starring appearances" in English opera.[46]

Mary Anne Wood (Figure 4) thrilled American audiences as much by her acting, in which she far outstripped Elizabeth Austin, as by her singing. "Somebody said that the New York audiences have at last been astonished," wrote a critic in the *Spirit* on 28 September 1833, shortly after the Woods' debut at the Park. "The praise was applied to her singing; but it properly belongs equally to her acting." A reporter for *Knickerbocker* magazine concurred. "As an actress," he wrote in November 1840, "her powers are sufficient to entitle her to a proud

4. Mary Anne Paton Wood. After the engraving on
steel by R. Newton from a miniature by W. J. Newton.
(*Century Illustrated Monthly Magazine*, March 1882)

rank in the histrionic art. We can safely say, that we have never beheld
a great singer possessing such attractions as an actress."[47] Philadelphia
diarist Joseph Sill, writing on 13 February 1836 about Wood's performance in *La Sonnambula,* likewise attested to her dramatic skill: "In
the last [scene] when the Sleep Walker crosses the plank Bridge, & it
cracks under her, the effect is awful, and it created a thrill within me
which I shall never forget."

    Although Wood was a skilled actress, her rank as America's reigning
prima donna during the mid and late 1830s was due principally to her
musical ability. "Mrs. Wood," wrote a critic for the *New-York Mirror*
on 21 September 1833, "possesses one of the most extraordinary voices
we ever remember to have heard"; according to William Husk, it was
"powerful, sweet-toned, and brilliant," and ranged from a to d‴ or
e‴.[48] In November 1840, a critic for *Knickerbocker* likened her voice

to that of a singing bird, and in 1853 William Clapp described it as "of extraordinary compass, excellent quality and great power . . . [with] remarkable cultivation and scientific attainment [and with] that command of feeling and expression which touches and moves the mass."[49] In 1881 one of Wood's erstwhile competitors, the soprano Mary Ann Horton, remembered her with admiration. "She could sing everything," Horton said in an interview, "from the simplest English ballads to grand opera. Her voice was full, round and rich. The only artist I have heard in recent years who could approach her as a singer was [Euphrosine] Parepa, and Parepa could not compare with Mrs. Wood as an actress."[50]

Wood's husband Joseph (Figure 5), although not universally praised, was described by the *New-York Mirror*'s critic on 21 September 1833 as "certainly the best singing actor we have had for some time"; Clapp observed that he "agreeably surprised" the Boston audience by "the grace and fluency of his execution, the sweet mellow and full tones of a voice ranging from the upper bass to high tenor, and the manly elegance of his person" (318).[51] It was in duets with his wife, however, that Joseph Wood most pleased the American audience. "Nothing like their duets has ever been heard in [Boston] since," wrote Clapp in 1853, "excepting perhaps the occasional hit of Madame [Anna] Bishop and [William] Reeves in *Linda,* and the exquisite blending of voice by [Fortunata] Tedesco and [Natale] Perelli. With the Woods, however, this fusion and blending of voice and soul in song, was the rule and constant practice" (319).

Comments by diarists in both Philadelphia and New York confirm the Woods' American popularity. Sill frequently attended their performances and often commented on his pleasure at listening to them. "The House was crowded . . . and the audience delighted with their exquisite Singing," he wrote on 22 January 1836, "I have never heard them in better voice, & they exerted themselves to please—I have heard many of the Prima Donnas of Europe, but none pleases me more, if as much as Mrs. Wood." Four years later, on 23 October 1840, Thomas Chamberlain noted "this was the last night of [Mrs. Wood's] engagement, and if she appears no more whilst I am in New York it will be a few dollars in my pocket, for I cannot resist going to see her."

The Woods made two separate tours of the eastern United States. They appeared in New York, Boston, Philadelphia, and elsewhere from September 1833 through May 1836, when they returned to England. They came back to America in September 1840 for a second tour, which lasted only through January 1841. Like Austin, the two singers often teamed with other British singers to form (generally short-lived) vocal-star troupes, sometimes with the same singers who earlier had

5. Joseph Wood. From an india-ink drawing in possession of Thomas J. McKee. (*Century Illustrated
Monthly Magazine*, March 1882)

traveled with Austin. Although the Woods were extremely successful
in this country, both of their visits were cut short by controversies
(evidently the result of misunderstandings), and an announced visit to
New Orleans had to be abandoned. The censure of American audiences,
however, was directed toward Joseph Wood, who was blunt and short-
tempered; Mary Anne Wood's popularity remained undiminished.[52]

Numerous other singers, most of them British, were active in the
United States during the tenures of Elizabeth Austin and the Woods;
a few of them have been mentioned previously as performing occasionally in vocal-star troupes with Austin. Some of these performers
played important enough roles in the early history of opera performance
in America to merit brief mention.

Two vocalists typical of "secondary" singers who performed with
Austin and the Woods (and, later, with other vocal stars) were the

tenor Charles Edward Horn (1786–1849) and the soprano Elizabeth Feron (1797–1853); both first appeared in America during the late 1820s. Horn is best known to scholars of American music as a composer and a theater musician, but he also was a renowned itinerant vocal star during the 1820s and 1830s. After his debut in New York in 1827, he toured extensively, performing in operas in New York, Philadelphia, Boston, Albany, New Orleans, Baltimore, Washington, and elsewhere. He also made a concert tour of the Northeast in 1832 (including appearances in Boston, Portland, Providence, and Halifax) and one in the South in 1834.[53]

Feron, who made her American debut (also in New York) in 1828, was a "brilliant soprano" described by one prominent London critic as "second to no English singer and inferior to no Italian but [Giuditta] Pasta," the reigning European prima donna.[54] She was a secondary singer in the United States only because of insurmountable competition from Elizabeth Austin. In 1828 Madame Feron was the most internationally renowned singer yet to appear in this country. Evidently, however, she was not as physically attractive as Elizabeth Austin, and despite her stature as "a brilliant singer of the most florid Italian school, with a voice of equal power and melody," she was unable to overcome the year-long head start that Austin had in the affections of American audiences; she also lacked, according to Joseph Ireland, "the graceful form, the face divine, and the inexpressible charm of girlhood, which rendered her fair predecessor so irresistible" (1:593–94). As a result, although Feron remained in this country until 1833 and appeared in New York, Philadelphia, Boston, Baltimore, Charleston, and New Orleans, her pecuniary success did not approach that of her contemporary.[55] Feron performed at various times, either in vocal-star troupes or in joint engagements by the same theaters, with Mary Ann Knight, John Sinclair, Elizabeth Hughes, Elizabeth Austin, Charles Horn, and others.[56]

A number of other more-or-less prominent secondary vocal stars arrived in the United States slightly later than Feron and Horn. In contemporary sources, their names are linked with those of Austin, Horn, Feron, and the Woods. John Sinclair (1790–1857) was a Scottish tenor who toured here for eleven years (1831–42), performing in Boston, New York, Philadelphia, New Orleans, Charleston, St. Louis, and points in between. Elizabeth Hughes, who sang in the United States for only two theatrical seasons (1831–33), was considered by many (before Wood's appearance) to be second only to Mrs. Austin in vocal skill.[57] Charlotte Watson (b. 1817), who after her marriage in 1837 was known as Mrs. Bailey, made her American debut in 1834 and remained here until 1847. She performed all over the country, including St. Louis

and Cincinnati as well as the usual locations. She sang with the Woods
and with William Brough in the 1830s and, during the next decade,
with many of the vocal stars who first appeared here in 1838 and 1839,
including Jane Shirreff, John Wilson, and Edward and Anne Seguin.
Another soprano, Antoinette Otto, a German, started her American
career in the chorus of the Park Theatre Company. By 1833 she was
singing her first small name roles, and from 1836 or 1837 until 1846
when she returned to Europe, she performed all over the eastern half
of the country as a member of various vocal-star troupes.[58]

The bass William F. Brough was another secondary English vocal
star who performed widely in North America during this period. Brough
came to the United States with the Woods in 1833, but did not make
his American debut until September 1835, when he appeared with them
in *Cinderella* (as Dandini) in New York.[59] Brough performed with the
Woods during both of their visits to this country (Figure 6), made at
least two different tours to the South as a member of vocal-star troupes
(the first, from November 1838 through May 1839, the second, from
November 1839 through the spring of 1840), and also sang and toured
with Jane Shirreff and John Wilson in 1839 (chapter 2). His extensive
travels during the late 1830s were typical of those of vocal stars in
general; also typical is the extent to which his path crossed those of
other itinerant singers. Table 1 charts Brough's travels from September
1835 through April 1841, when he returned to England temporarily.
Although incomplete (the information has been extracted from secondary sources and contemporary periodicals, not from newspapers),
the table clearly demonstrates that vocal-star activity was not limited
to the Northeast. Like Charles Horn, Brough became a major musical
and theatrical influence in this country. After a lengthy first career as
a singer, he embarked upon a successful second one as an operatic
impresario and manager. Brough's American career, interrupted by
several trips back to England, continued through the 1850s (Figure 7).
By the mid–1840s, however, his activities were principally with English
opera companies rather than with vocal-star troupes (chapters 5 and
6).

The first-rank British vocal stars who traveled and performed in the
United States during the 1820s, 1830s, and 1840s relied heavily upon
such singers as Brough, Otto, and Sinclair. Even more important to
the success of vocal-star troupes, however, was an entirely different
group of performers: the actors, singers, and instrumentalists connected
with the stock companies of theaters all over the eastern and southern
portions of North America. The activities of these performers were
little noticed in the press, but the support they provided to visiting
singers was essential. A vocal-star troupe, no matter how good, could

THEATRE.

Eighth night of LA SOMNAMBULA! in which

MRS. WOOD, MR. WOOD,
—AND—
MR. BROUGH.

WILL APPEAR.

Doors open at 6.   Curtain will rise at 1-2 past 6.

Wednesday Evening, Jan. 6th

Will be presented the celebrated Opera (Music by BELLINI, adapted to the English Stage by BISHOP) called

LA SOMNAMBULA

WITH NEW SCENERY BY MR. STOCKWELL.

COUNT RHODOLPHO	- - - - - - - - - - - - - -		MR. BROUGH
ELVINO	- - - - - - - - - - - - - - - -		MR. WOOD
Alessio	Mr Andrews	Joanno	Mr Rice
Notary	Lewis	Pedro	Whiting
AMINA	- - - - - - - - - - - - -		MRS. WOOD
Teresa	Miss A. Fisher	Louise	Madame Otto
Liza	Mrs. Smith		

CHORUS—Messrs. Addams, Stedman, Hall, Lothrop, J. Hall, Sowerby, Denton, Mesdames Campbell, Brown, Leman, Holden, Misses McBride, Kerr, Hurley, Whitmore, &c.

IN THE COURSE OF THE OPERA THE FOLLOWING MUSIC.

Chorus, Live Amina.
Cavatina, Sounds so joyful - - - Louise
The Wedding Song, - Alessio and Chorus
Chorus, May fortune's fairy power.
Recitativo, Dearest Companions, - Amina
Air, Oh ! Love, - - - - Amina
Duetto, Take now this ring, - Elvino, Amina
Air, As I view these scenes, - Rhodolpho
Dialogue Chorus, Who is he ?
Chorus, Then gently gliding.
Recitativo, From my toilsome journey, Rhodolpho.
Chorus, Good Repose.
Recitativo and Duetto, Surely this must be the Nocturnal Phantom.
Chorus, Nothing fearing, let us enter.
Dialogue Duett and Chorus, Go Guilty Traitress, - - - Elvino and Amina
Duett and Chorus, We disdain thee, Alessio and Liza.

Air, I am not guilty, - - - Amina
Duett, Such return for love according, Elvino and Amina.
Concerted Piece, See him dear mother, Amina, Elvino, Principals and Chorus.
Song, Still so gently e'er me stealing, Elvino
Chorus, Liza the chosen is.
Air, These sounds of joy, - - Louise
Quartette and Chorus, If I saw it, I could believe you, Elvino, Rhodolpho, Principals and Chorus.
Chorus, Oh ! guide her wanderings now.
Dialogue Music, Once more could I now see him, - Amina, Principals and Chorus
Recitative, The ring he gave me, - Amina
Air, Yes for thee, - - - Amina
Duetto and Recitativo, Do not restrain me, Elvino and Amina.
Dialogue Music, Where am I ? Amina and Principals.

THE MUSIC UNDER THE DIRECTION OF MR. COMER.

To conclude with the admired Farce of

THE DUMB BELLE !

Capt. Vivian	Mr. G. Barrett	Janus	Mr. Benson
O'Smirk	Comer	Mr. Manvers	Sarzedas
Eliza	Mrs. G. Barrett	Mary	Miss McBride

EASTBURN'S PRESS, 18 STATE STREET.

6. Playbill from a performance of Vincenzo Bellini's *La Sonnambula* (as adapted by Henry Rowley Bishop) given by the Woods and William Brough at the Park Theatre, 6 January 1836. The visiting vocalists were given star billing. (American Antiquarian Society)

Table 1. Vocal-star Activities of William F. Brough, 1835–41

Dates	Location	Other Singers Named
Sept.–Oct. 1835	Park Theatre, New York City	Mr. & Mrs. Wood. *Also* Walton, Latham, Richings, Conduit
Oct.–Nov. 1835	Tremont Street Theatre [?], Boston	Woods
Nov.–Dec. 1835	Park Theatre	Woods
Jan. 1836	Tremont Street Theatre [?]	Woods
Jan.–Feb. 1836	Chestnut Street Theatre, Philadelphia	Woods, Thomas Walton
March–April 1836	Park Theatre	Woods
April 1836	Chatham Street Theatre, New York City	Woods
April–May 1836	Arch Street Theatre, Philadelphia	Woods
May 1836	Park Theatre	Woods
Sept. 1837	Park Theatre	Mary Ann Horton, Charles Horn
Nov. 1837	Chestnut Street Theatre	
Dec. 1837	Holliday Street Theatre [?], Baltimore	C. E. Horn, M. A. Horton, T. Walton
Jan. 1838	Philadelphia	Antoinette Otto, Pearson
Jan.–Feb. 1838	Park Theatre	Caradori-Allan, J. Jones, P. Richings, Miss Hughes, Mrs. Bailey
Feb. 1838	Philadelphia	Caradori-Allan
April 1838	New York City	Caradori-Allan, Mrs. Hughes, J. Jones
June 1838	Philadelphia	Concert
Nov. 1838	Philadelphia	A. Otto, T. Bishop
Jan. 1839	National Theatre, New York City	Mrs. Bailey, P. Richings
Feb. 1839	Charleston	A. Otto, T. Bishop
March 1839	Augusta	A. Otto, T. Bishop, Hardwick
March 1839	Charleston	A. Otto, T. Bishop, Thomas A'Beckett
May 1839	Charleston	
Sept. 1839	Philadelphia	Jane Shirreff, John Wilson
Sept.–Oct. 1839	Baltimore	Jane Shirreff, John Wilson
Nov. 1839	Pittsburgh	Brough benefit

Table 1. Continued

Dates	Location	Other Singers Named
Feb. 1840	Savannah	A. Otto, John Jones
April 1840	New Orleans	A. Otto, John Sinclair
May 1840	Mobile	A. Otto, John Sinclair
1840 (when?)	St. Louis	A. Otto, John Sinclair
June 1840	New York City to Buffalo (concert tour)	
Summer 1840	Buffalo, Syracuse, Canada (concert tour)	
Sept.–Oct. 1840	Park Theatre	Woods, Leffler, Mrs. Bailey, A. Andrews
Oct. 1840	Chestnut Street Theatre	Woods
Nov.–Dec. 1840	Park Theatre	Woods, Clara Maeder, John Jones
Dec. 1840	Tremont Theatre [?], Boston	Woods
Feb. 1841	Charleston?	Martyn, Inverarity
April 1841	Richmond	Mr. and Mrs. Martyn

not mount an opera by itself. Operatic stars such as Austin or the Woods (or luminaries who appeared later, such as Jane Shirreff, Anne and Edward Seguin, and John Wilson), and such dramatic stars as Edwin Forrest, Junius Brutus Booth, Edmund Kean, Charlotte Cushman, or William Charles Macready, played only the most important roles. Subordinate players and—in opera—the chorus were all members of local theaters' stock companies. When stars were hired, these players (even those who normally took leading roles when the company performed alone) assumed secondary parts in such works as *Richard III, Hamlet, The School for Scandal,* or *The Six Degrees of Crime* for dramatic stars or *Cinderella, Fra Diavolo, The Beggar's Opera,* and *The Marriage of Figaro* for vocal stars. This reliance upon stock-company performers is the most significant difference between vocal-star troupes and the full-fledged English opera companies of the 1840s, 1850s, and later.

A great deal of evidence illustrates the relationship between vocal-star troupes and local stock companies. Advertisements for productions by vocal-star troupes, for example, occasionally read like the following, which appeared in the *New York Daily Express* on 21 October 1839

7. William Brough, photographed as an older man.
(George C. D. Odell Collection, Columbia University)

in reference to the Shirreff/Wilson/Seguin troupe: "To-night, Gustavus the III . . . will be played. The entire company will assist in it, and the principal characters will be sustained by *all* the vocal talent of the theater." The vocal star Anne Seguin, interviewed in 1881, remembered that "in those days it was the rule for everybody to go on when opera was given—that is, everybody in the regular company of a theater was required to assist in dressing the stage on opera nights."[60] Stephen Massett, an actor who wrote in his memoirs of being a member of a stock company, gave an account from the other side. He described working at the Charleston, South Carolina, theater in 1841 when the Seguin Opera Company (an expanded vocal-star troupe) arrived for an engagement. *La Sonnambula* was the scheduled opera, and Massett was assigned the part of one of the male peasants. "My duties," he related, were "simply to come on and go off with one of the female ditto, joining in the chorus loud or soft as the case might be" (42–43).

Massett had additional experience as a subordinate actor in another opera mounted by the Charleston company. In a production of *Fra Diavolo,* again with the Seguins as stars, he was assigned the minor role of Matteo, the innkeeper. There were only two days for "getting [the opera] up," and Edward Seguin eventually decided that the part was too difficult for the inexperienced Massett to learn on short notice. Consequently, it was reassigned as a spoken role to another actor (42–43). Many of the operas regularly performed by vocal-star troupes, like *Fra Diavolo, La Sonnambula,* or *The Bohemian Girl,* have a limited number of principal singing roles—few enough, in fact, that the most important parts were all taken by the visiting vocalists; *The Marriage of Figaro* is a notable exception to this rule, for its performance requires a large number of strong vocalists. In any case, however, if the theater's manager discovered that he did not have a sufficient number of musically skilled actors to cover all of the secondary roles, as happened in Charleston, the parts often were simply spoken, and any songs normally performed by the characters omitted.[61] Although the two-day rehearsal period Massett mentions might seem grossly inadequate, vocal-star troupes generally performed only operas that were a normal part of the repertory. Stock-company actors and instrumentalists, consequently, were familiar with the roles, staging conventions, and chorus numbers of these works; most of the chorus parts in this repertory, in any case, are relatively simple. Furthermore, theaters already owned appropriate scenery and costumes.[62]

Stephen Massett did not complain about having to perform in opera choruses, but he was a singer as well as an actor. Some actors in stock companies, however, were not pleased at the prospect of being drafted into an opera chorus or of "dressing the stage," as Anne Seguin put it. Members of the Chestnut Street Theatre company in Philadelphia threatened to quit in November 1845 when ordered to perform in the chorus for *The Bohemian Girl.* One indignant actress reportedly wailed in protest, "it is too much, to ask the Lady MacBeths and the Juliets to suddenly drop to singing in opera choruses."[63] In this particular incident most of the company players eventually capitulated, and the threatened rebellion was averted. Such dissatisfaction among stock players, however, would become more noticeable in the late 1840s and 1850s, as opera performance, especially in the larger cities, became increasingly regarded as the domain of "specialty" troupes—itinerant opera companies.

Reviewers of performances by vocal-star troupes and stock companies sometimes complained mightily about the ability of the supporting actors and actresses. In October 1834, the critic for the *American Musical Journal* was particularly caustic about performances by stock-company actors during an engagement of the Woods at the Park Theatre. "The inability of the available vocal talent, which the Theatre possesses, to do justice to any opera containing much concerted music," he wrote,

> [was] painfully apparent [last evening]. We have no wish to hurt the feelings of the musical persons who were engaged in the matter, by giving names; suffice it, therefore, to say that all the secondary parts in [*The Maid of Judah*] and also in *Fra Diavolo,* were shamefully given. . . . To this lack of *tone* and *ensemble,* by the way, do we in a great measure attribute the want of success which characterizes one or two of Mr. and Mrs. Wood's engagements. How, in fact, could it possibly turn out otherwise, when Mr. Blakely and Mr. Fisher—two persons useful enough in their line, but utterly ignorant of music—how, we repeat, could it be otherwise, when these gentlemen were respectively charged with difficult and intricate tenor and bass parts, in Trios, Quintettos, &c. &c. (18)

In October 1835, during another engagement of the Woods, a critic for the same journal was similarly harsh in his judgment of a performance of *Cinderella*. "It has appeared to us," he commented, "that the manager of the Park has studiously, for the last few years, kept his second women for the purpose of setting off with greater brilliancy the qualities of his prima donnas; for we doubt whether a more incompetent set of ladies for operatic business could be found in any theatre in the country than has usually been cast in these parts" (261). By 1846 the situation had not changed much. In a review of a performance of *The Bohemian Girl* by the Seguin Opera Company in Philadelphia, a critic for the *Spirit* commented sardonically on 7 November that "the subordinate characters were, as usual, very badly filled" (439).

Not all efforts by stock-company actors, however, were mediocre or poor. Although the quality of stock companies tended to fluctuate from year to year, theaters in the larger cities, especially those in New York, Philadelphia, and New Orleans, often had strong troupes whose players could hold their own in dramatic and operatic performances alike. On 19 May 1832, for example, a writer for the *Spirit,* commenting on performances by Mrs. Austin and Miss Hughes, suggested that "*The Marriage of Figaro* and *Masaniello* were . . . selected by [the manager] . . . as giving scope to the entire display of the varied talents of his excellent company of stock actors." On 24 March 1832, a critic for the *New York Mirror,* writing about a performance of *Cinderella,* noted that the choruses of Boston's Tremont Street Theatre "were admirably drilled . . . [and] completely perfect in their business." Three years later, on 3 January 1835, the chorus at one of the Philadelphia theaters was described in the same journal as "the most effective in the United States for its size . . . its business is always perfect" (211); and on 27 June 1838 a writer in the *Musical Review* offered "great praise . . . to the Ladies and Gentlemen of the Chorus" of the Park Theatre, for not only was "their portion of the music . . . given with great precision and effect," but "they are improving daily" (95). Finally, Thomas Chamberlain, writing in his diary on 9 October 1840 about *La Sonnambula*, simultaneously praised the chorus of the Park Theatre company and confirmed the opera's popularity. "The choruses in this piece," he wrote, "are remarkably well performed, as indeed they ought to be, with the practice they have had in [it]." However, he continued parenthetically, "it is about the only piece [at the Park] in which they are [well performed]." On 19 November and 5 December, on the other hand, he waxed enthusiastic about performances at New York's National Theatre, noting that "the choruses were splendid" in Donizetti's *The Elixir of Love* and describing the choral singers as both "first rate" and "splendid" for a production of *Don Giovanni*.

A theatrical company's choice of repertory was a major factor in its success or failure; some operas simply were too ambitious to be tackled by stock troupes, even with the assistance of visiting vocal stars. In 1832, for example, the Park Theatre company mounted, among other works, productions of the Lacy/Rossini pastiche *The Maid of Judah* and Boieldieu's *The White Lady*. The *New-York Mirror*'s critic had nothing good to say about the performance of the former. "This opera contains beautiful music," he wrote on 22 July,

> but there are so many concerted pieces in it, which require to be filled by professed singers, that it is no less than a mockery to entrust them to singing actors, or chorus singers. Here again we see Mr. [Peter] Richings thrust into a part expressly arranged for [Henry] Phillips, the best bass singer in England, and taking part with the prima donna of the piece, Miss Hughes, in a duet which, on the Italian stage, was thought to tax the powers of [Matteo] Porto or [Filippo] Galli; and which, without any disparagement to Mr. Richings, with no knowledge of music, and with a baritone voice of inferior quality, he ought not to have had fastened on him. (22)

The same critic's evaluation of the company's production of the lighter Boieldieu opera, however, was quite different. "The cast of this piece, on the contrary, displayed the *elite* of the Park company," he judged, also in July 1832. "Jones, Placide, Mrs. Sharpe, Thorne, and Richings— all have parts within the scope of their talents, and the adapter of the music most freely offers his testimony, that the opera has been cast with all the strength and all the talent he could desire" (22).

The quality of a theater's company undoubtedly had a major influence on the decision of a vocal star or vocal-star troupe to accept or reject an engagement, no matter how tantalizing the terms offered by the manager. Once engaged, the stars' success or failure depended on the ability of the theater's stock performers to mount the production. As one critic for the *Spirit* pointed out on 17 November 1849, "a good chorus may aid inferior principals, but principals can very rarely supply or cover the defects of bad choristers" (468). Occasionally, if local talent proved to be particularly deficient, visiting singers were forced to change their performance plans. The soprano Mary Ann (Horton) Horn, for example, remembered traveling in a vocal-star troupe with her husband Charles Edward Horn in the mid 1830s. They had an engagement at a theater in New Orleans, she related, but "the [stock] company, was so bad that we could not give opera. Instead we gave concerts."[64]

The other important group of performers on which vocal-star troupes depended was the theater orchestra. It was indispensable for the performance of opera, and both vocal-star and English opera troupes relied heavily on the instrumental musicians attached to the theaters where the performers were engaged.[65] During the 1830s and 1840s, the standing orchestras of local theaters were often augmented for opera performances given by vocal-star troupes (apparently by hiring additional local instrumentalists). A playbill from a performance of Auber's *Masaniello* at the Walnut Street Theatre in Philadelphia on 19 May 1832, for example, announced that "in order to give all possible effect to the music, the Orchestra will be augmented." Another playbill, from a performance of *Amilie; or, The Love Test* (William Rooke) at the Tremont Theatre in Boston on 5 November 1838, likewise noted that "the Orchestra will be increased."[66]

Consistent information on the size and make-up of theater orchestras is difficult to find. During this period four theaters—the Tremont (Boston), St. Charles (New Orleans), Park (New York), and Chestnut Street (Philadelphia)—maintained the largest orchestras in the country.[67] As early as 1828 the Tremont Theatre had an orchestra of twenty-eight instrumentalists (of unknown combination).[68] Despite the fact that this was a very small orchestra for the performance of Bellini or Donizetti operas, the author of a 3 January 1835 article in the *New-York Mirror* titled "The Orchestras," judged the ensemble to be "the best in America" (211). This author, however, admitted that he did not include "the orchestras of the south" in his article and so awarded

first-place honors to the wrong group of instrumentalists: the orchestra
of the St. Charles Theatre was almost certainly a stronger ensemble.

The St. Charles, a splendid new theater, had first opened its doors
in 1835, and the large orchestra that owner and manager James Caldwell
engaged for his inaugural season consisted of "at least twenty-nine
instrumentalists plus the conductor." It included seventeen strings (ten
violins, two violas, three cellos, two double basses), six winds (two
clarinets, two flutes, one oboe, one bassoon), five brasses (two trumpets,
one trombone, and two horns), and harp.[69] (Even this ensemble, impressive as it was for the time and place, was slightly smaller than the
orchestra employed at the Théâtre d'Orléans.) The St. Charles orchestra
also could boast of several skilled virtuosos, including James Kendall
(clarinet), Felippe Cioffi (trombone), and John T. Norton (trumpet).[70]
During this same year the orchestra at the Park numbered only eighteen.
Six years later, however, that New York theater's ensemble had grown
considerably, to twenty-seven musicians, including eleven strings (three
first violins, two second violins, two violas, two cellos, two double
basses); seven winds (two clarinets, one oboe, two flutes, and two
bassoons); six brass (two horns, two trombones, and two trumpets);
and three percussion instruments (double drums, grande casse, and
cymbals).[71] In 1841, according to a 3 May playbill at the Library
Company of Philadelphia, the regular orchestra at the Chestnut Street
Theatre included twenty-three instrumentalists: eleven strings (seven
violins, two violas, two cellos); six winds (two clarinets, two flutes, one
oboe, one bassoon); five brass (two horns, two trombones, one trumpet);
and drums. Several of these orchestras could have performed *La Sonnambula,* for example, without too much tinkering with the orchestral
parts. Bellini's score calls for two flutes, two oboes, two clarinets, two
bassoons, four horns, two trumpets, three trombones, timpani, percussion, and strings. None, however, could have handled *The Marriage
of Figaro* without significant orchestral rewriting.[72]

Occasionally, orchestras were augmented for special performances.
For example, according to the *Spirit* of 16 January 1841, the orchestra
of the Chestnut Street Theatre was augmented for one of the Woods'
engagements by "a goodly number of amateurs [who] volunteered their
services," reportedly increasing the size of the ensemble to forty-seven
musicians. For a truly special event, a theater would assemble an ex-
ceptionally large ensemble, such as the orchestra of fifty-five hired by
the Chestnut Street Theatre for the premiere of William Henry Fry's
Leonora by the Seguins in June 1845.[73] Even at the largest theaters in
the country, however, the cost of such extraordinarily large ensembles
was prohibitive for all but the most exceptional events.

Orchestras of other American theaters were almost invariably smaller than those of the St. Charles or the major theaters on the East Coast. According to the 25 March *Spirit,* the theater in Mobile, Alabama, mustered only fourteen musicians for performances by the Woods in 1837; during that same year, the St. Louis theater engaged an orchestra of only eleven: four violins, one viola, cello, double bass, one flute, two horns, and one trumpet, reported the *Spirit* on 22 July. In 1838 the ensemble at the theater in Providence, Rhode Island, numbered nine, and its composition—two violins, double bass, two clarinets, two horns, trumpet, and trombone—indicates that it was closer in sound to a band than to a regular string-dominated theater orchestra. This ensemble nonetheless was a source of pride for residents of the city and was described as "the largest and best drilled orchestral band that had ever been heard in Providence."[74] In New Orleans in 1841, the English-language American Theatre had an orchestra of eighteen. The only thing known about the Charleston Theatre's orchestra for the same year is that it was "the best, by far the best" ever heard in the city.[75]

Little is known about the quality of orchestras' performances for vocal-star opera productions; at best, written comments in the press are conflicting, ranging from utter damnation to high praise. A correspondent to the *American Musical Journal* in November 1835, for example, complained bitterly about the performance of the Park Theatre orchestra during one of the Woods' engagements. "At the orchestra I was perfectly astonished," he wrote, "for by placing myself in the pit near the music desks, I perceived [that players of] some instruments never even attempt the passages that were written. I am told, and indeed I do not doubt it, that the present is the most inefficient orchestra that this theater has had for years past" (278–79).

More often, critics were less strident in their censure. On 21 March 1833, a critic for the *Spirit,* writing about a performance of *The Marriage of Figaro* by Elizabeth Austin at the Park, commented mildly that "the Opera could not have been in better hands—though some of the fiddles could—." Seven years later, in 1840, after attending a performance of Donizetti's *The Elixir of Love* at the National Theatre, Thomas Chamberlain wrote in his diary on 19 November that "the band [was] but so-so."

Most frequently, critics and other auditors praised theater instrumentalists. The same Park Theatre orchestra that was attacked so vehemently in the *American Musical Journal* in 1835 was highly praised by a critic for the *New-York Mirror,* who wrote on 28 November that the ensemble's leader, William Penson, "has brought his orchestra into an excellent state, [one] that for once gives satisfaction to the critics of the daily press" (174). On 22 February 1840, the *Corsair* described the Park Theatre orchestra as "in excellent training" (796). That of the Tremont Theatre in Boston, variously under the direction of Louis Ostinelli and Thomas Comer, was frequently praised as "excellent," as in the *Spirit* on 1 December 1832, and "very good, much better than [New York] can boast of at present" in the November 1835 *American Musical Journal* (287).

The discrepancies in perception probably can be blamed on widely divergent levels of experience with orchestral performance. The *Musical Magazine* reported on 5 January 1839 that "instruments and instrumental music are as yet very little understood, and consequently not properly appreciated, in this country" (15). This same source again suggests that pecuniary gain was a principal motivation for touring musicians, for the writer pointed out that "first rate performers can do much better by remaining in Europe; and therefore, we rarely, if ever, see them here." Because many auditors, including critics, had little experience listening to instrumental ensembles, an orchestra that played reasonably in tune and together probably would have been considered satisfactory. Awareness of instrumental timbre and color, or even of missing or substituted parts, after all, requires a somewhat discriminating ear. A writer for the *New-York Mirror* addressed this issue on 17 January 1835. Secondary instruments, as opposed to principals, he pointed out,

> are generally awfully deficient in this country. . . . Let us take the opera of *Masaniello* for instance, and the *Maid of Judah,* as played at the Park theatre. In both of these operas the first clarionet has to play the first hautboy part, and the second clarionet the part of the first, and consequently the second parts of either instrument are not represented. The bassoon has to play a part written for two bassoons, and consequently plays notes which, as they were intended in many parts to produce the effect of a duet, are so much nonsense when played by one instrument. All this might have been remedied by the parts being properly condensed; but the London resident of the Park management, whose musical knowledge may be limited to an imperfect acquaintance with the tunes of Yankee Doodle and God Save the King, sent them out as *real* Drury-Lane parts; and the New York resident ordered them to be played, and so they are played. (231)

The most common complaint was theater orchestras' tendencies to play too loudly, which either destroyed the ensemble's balance or drowned out the singers. On 4 May 1839, the Park Theatre orchestra was mildly criticized in the *Spirit* because "the brass instruments are occasionally a little too loud for the rest of the band." Whatever the perceived strengths and weaknesses of theater orchestras during the 1830s, critics seemed to agree that overall quality of performance had improved dramatically since the 1810s and 1820s. According to some sources, vocal stars were responsible for this improvement. The musical profession, wrote one critic in the April 1835 *American Musical Journal,* is "indebted to Mrs. Austin. To her may the Park orchestra attribute their being paid full salaries during the whole season; through her means have managers of the principal theatres found out the necessity of maintaining full bands" (115).

The obvious success of Elizabeth Austin in the late 1820s and early 1830s, and the even more pronounced triumphs of the Woods on their first visit from 1833 through 1836, had not gone unnoticed in the business offices of American theaters. As Francis Wemyss pointed out, by the mid–1830s the successes of both Austin and the Woods had so thoroughly established English opera in the United States that the genre had become "essential to the success of a theatrical season."[76] Managers had learned well that audiences were ready and willing to pay good money for performances of English and "Englished" opera by top-notch vocal stars. In the waning years of the decade, two managers in particular—James Wallack of New York's National Theatre, and Edmund Simpson of the Park—attempted to capitalize on this popularity. Because of Wallack and Simpson's competition, more and more British vocal stars came to the United States, and the level of overall operatic activity around the country in 1838, 1839, and 1840 was enhanced considerably.[77]

Wallack (1794–1864) was a successful theatrical star, active in both Britain and the United States during the 1820s and 1830s; in 1837 he decided to try his hand at management. He took over direction of the National Theatre at Leonard and Church Streets (Figure 8) in New York and assembled a strong stock company for its reopening in September 1837.[78] To help fill out the operatic division of this troupe (which eventually included, among others, the vocal stars Charlotte Watson, Antoinette Otto, Charles Horn, and Mary Ann Horton), Wallack recruited several new singers from London.[79] The principal newcomers were the soprano Miss Turpin, a fair singer from Covent Garden who would make little impact on the United States, and Henry Horncastle, a respectable and successful buffo from Drury Lane and the theaters of Dublin and Liverpool.[80] Horncastle was quite influential in America; he toured America widely as a vocal star from 1838 through 1840 and again in the 1850s as a member of a variety of English opera companies.[81] As manager, Wallack got the opera portion of his inaugural season (1837–38) off to a quick start. Both of his new singers, along with Mr. Morley (a bass) and Antoinette Otto, performed in *La Sonnambula* on the second night of the season.[82] During the year the

8. James Wallack's National Theatre, formerly the Italian Opera House. (*Century Illustrated Monthly Magazine*, March 1882)

company gave a large number of performances of the usual repertory, including both older English works (*Guy Mannering, The Poor Soldier, The Waterman,* and *The Devil's Bridge*) and "newer" Italian ones (*The Marriage of Figaro* and *La Sonnambula*).[83] In November the operatic spectacle *The Two Figaros,* a mélange of music by Rossini and Mozart, was introduced and enjoyed "great success."[84]

Simpson (1784–1848), as manager of the Park Theatre — Wallack's competition — was not to be outdone. A scant two weeks into his company's 1837–38 season, he engaged a vocal-star troupe comprised of William Brough, Charles Horn, and Mary Ann Horton (the latter two would shortly join Wallack's company) for several weeks of performances.[85] Some New Yorkers had hoped that Simpson would be able to lure Mary Anne Wood back across the Atlantic, but this was not to happen for several more years. In lieu of Wood, the Park engaged a new vocal star: Maria Caradori-Allan (1800–65), a soprano, who had an established continental reputation and was considered by many to be Wood's equal.[86]

Caradori-Allan was one of the more influential singers to appear in the United States during the period. Richard Grant White described her voice as a "delicious soprano of unusual compass." According to one of her contemporaries (writing in 1827), it was "sweet, but not strong, her knowledge of music very great, [and] her taste and style excellent, full of delicacy and expression." Furthermore, she was beautiful, with "large liquid blue eyes and golden hair, and a complexion of milk and roses."[87] Her engagement at the Park was a triumph; Philip Hone, who attended her debut (as Rosina, in *The Barber of Seville*) on 31 October 1837, recorded in his diary that she was a "decided hit."[88] In addition to the usual repertory, Allan also performed in two American premieres, Michael William Balfe's *The Siege of Rochelle* (9 April 1838, with Brough, John Jones, Elizabeth Hughes, and others) and *The Elixir of Love,* an adaptation of Donizetti's *L'Elisir d'amore* (18 June 1838, with Jones, Hughes, Mr. Morley, and the actor Henry Placide).[89] The latter production, which evidently included a jumble of pilfered numbers from *Le Pré aux clercs* (Hérold), *Anna Bolena* (Donizetti), and *Maometto secondo, Otello,* and *Tancredi* (Rossini), was very successful.[90] The English opera by Balfe, however, was a failure, probably because the politics of the libretto meant nothing to Americans. Allan thereafter successfully toured the United States as a vocal star, performing in concerts and in operas with William Brough, Antoinette Otto, Elizabeth Hughes, John Jones, Charlotte Bailey, and others, traveling as far afield in an 1839 tour as Louisville and St. Louis. She returned to London in July 1839.[91]

For his next season, James Wallack imported more—and better— vocal stars. On 18 September 1838 he introduced his first new celebrity, Giuseppe de Begnis (1795–1849), a native of Rome and the greatest buffo yet to appear on the American stage.[92] Then, less than a month after de Begnis's debut, Wallack triumphantly raised the National Theatre's curtain on a trio of vocal stars: Jane Shirreff, John Wilson, and Edward Seguin. The manager had recruited the three in the hope that they and Michael Rooke's *Amilie; or, The Love Test,* a new opera they brought from London, could successfully lure New York audiences away from the Park and into his house. His gamble paid off. The Shirreff/Wilson/Seguin vocal-star troupe was the triumph of the season at Wallack's National Theatre (chapter 2). To make Wallack's victory over Simpson even more lopsided, the Park manager had no operatic novelties of his own with which to counteract the seemingly irresistible draw of the singers at the National.

Simpson was determined not to misjudge the public's seemingly ravenous appetite for opera two years in a row, and in the fall of 1839 he imported his own new vocal stars, a quintet of singers that included Charles T. Martyn, a baritone, his wife, Mrs. Martyn (née Inverarity), a soprano, and the tenor Charles Manvers, all from Covent Garden; Signor Theodore Victor Giubilei (1801–45), a bass from Drury Lane; and—the surprise success of the company—a young contralto named

Clara Poole.[93] Simpson's stars chose for their debut performance *Fidelio* in English translation, an unfortunate choice from the manager's point of view, for the work puzzled both audiences and critics. Despite its unpopularity, however, the "serious and sometimes heavy" opera was performed fourteen times before the company moved on to more familiar fare, which included *Cinderella, La Sonnambula, La Gazza Ladra, The Love Spell, Guy Mannering, Rob Roy,* and other works.[94] Simpson was dismayed, however, to discover that his new vocal-star troupe did not begin to duplicate the success that Wallack's singers had enjoyed at the National Theatre during the previous season.

As a result of this spate of activity, within a single year—from autumn 1838 to fall 1839—the two managers were responsible for introducing ten new vocalists to the American public. Wallack's five singers (de Begnis, Shirreff, Wilson, Seguin, and Seguin's wife Anne) all arrived in 1838, Simpson's five (Mr. and Mrs. Martyn, Manvers, Poole, and Giubilei) in 1839. The long-term American success of Simpson's singers, and hence their overall impact on American musical culture, was varied. Although Mrs. Martyn was a favorite artist in Britain, by the time she came to the United States her voice was worn and her success as a consequence was limited. Her husband was barely tolerated in New York; both returned to England in the fall of 1840.[95] Clara Poole arrived as an unknown and as a subordinate to Martyn, and her success with the New York and Philadelphia public was a surprise.[96] She was described in the New York press as "a lively, plump, pretty little actress, [with] a strong, musical [contralto] voice, as clear as crystal."[97] After the break-up of the 1839–40 Park Theatre troupe, she performed during the following theatrical season in New York and Philadelphia with the Seguins, Giubilei, and Manvers; her final American appearance was in April 1841.[98] Giubilei (1801–45), a native of London despite his Italianate name, was a skilled actor and an accomplished bass singer who also apparently left the United States after the 1840–41 season.[99] During his second season in North America, however, he performed widely and appeared at different times with Shirreff and Wilson and the Seguins. Charles Manvers, unlike the three co-stars of his Park Theatre troupe, remained in the United States until 1851; he traveled as a vocal star for a short period of time and then sang in a number of English opera companies (chapter 5).

Two of Wallack's singers (Shirreff and Wilson) likewise left the United States within two years of their arrival. The other three, however, remained here until their deaths, and played important roles in the development of opera in the United States. The activities of the Seguins are discussed in detail in chapter 5; de Begnis, however, merits additional mention here. According to White, he was "indisputably the great *buffo* of his time." He apparently remained in the United States only because of his terror of the ocean: "The voyage over here," writes White, "filled him with such fear that he never returned [to Europe]."[100] De Begnis traveled widely and performed at different times with Jane Shirreff, John Wilson, the Seguins, Charlotte Bailey, Charles Manvers, Clara Poole, William Brough, Charles Horn, Henry Horncastle, Theodore Giubilei, and Joseph and Mary Anne Wood (during their second visit). He also managed and sang with an Italian opera company at Palmo's Opera House in New York in 1844 (chapter 3) and with the Anna Bishop English Opera Company in 1847 (chapter 5). His significant influence on the cultivation of opera in the United States continued undiminished until his death by cholera in New York in 1849.

The increased number of stellar vocalists active in the United States in 1838, 1839, and 1840 clearly indicates the growing popularity of opera among American audiences. The very presence of these vocalists and the sheer numbers of their numerous concert and opera performances from 1838 to 1840 and afterward stimulated the development of American musical culture. Viewed together, this cluster of singers, some of whom continued to perform in the United States until the early 1850s, represent the final, large influx of British vocal stars in the nineteenth century. For in the next decade, a nationwide economic slump (caused by a shortage of currency in the United States and a depression in Europe, and first manifested in the Panic of 1837) would close American theaters all over the country, throwing actors, orchestra musicians, and singers out of work and discouraging many British stars who otherwise might have entertained the notion of traveling to the United States. By the time the nation's theaters recovered from effects of the Panic, the heyday of vocal-star troupes was past. By 1847, Italian opera companies were in the ascendant, and the performance of English opera in North America was in the hands of full-fledged English opera companies.

Solid information about the careers of these vocal stars—especially those who were journeymen singers—is elusive. Names pop up in secondary sources—for example in studies of the history of music or the theater in specific American cities, and in such primary sources as playbills or music and theater periodicals. Only by accumulating such isolated bits of information—and by fleshing out the resulting itinerary with additional data—can we begin to understand just how active these singers were, how their careers constantly converged and diverged, how frequently they performed, how widely they traveled, and how important their activities were in American life during the 1820s, 1830s, and 1840s. An in-depth look at the extensive travels of one such pair of singers—Jane Shirreff and John Wilson—is the focus of the next chapter.

2

Jane Shirreff and John Wilson, Vocal Stars, 1838–40

During the summer of 1838, James Wallack sent his elder brother Henry to London to undertake the serious task of recruiting stars for the 1838–39 season.[1] The younger Wallack, a well-known actor and former star of the Park Theatre, had taken over management of the National the previous year. The theater was not a new one. Ironically—especially in view of the repertory that Wallack was destined to offer during his second season—it was the old Italian Opera House, which had been constructed largely through the efforts of Lorenzo da Ponte and had opened in 1833 with a lengthy run of performances by the Italian opera company of Cavaliere Vincenzo Rivafinoli.[2] After the failure of that troupe, the house had fallen on hard times, for it was situated in an inconvenient and poor neighborhood.[3] When Wallack took over in 1837, his aim was to turn around the fortunes of the theater and, in the process, compete successfully with the Park, the dominant theater in New York since the beginning of the century (Figure 9).

To almost everyone's astonishment, Wallack managed to do just that, in part by assembling a stock company "so full and effective in every department" that its equal "had never before been gathered together in New York."[4] A critic for the *Knickerbocker,* in October 1838 called Wallack's troupe "the best stock company in the United States" (381). Fresh on the heels of his first successful theatrical campaign, Wallack, in the summer of 1838, was eager to import strong reinforcements for his new season. His brother's task was fairly clear-cut: he was to find some stars who were successful and somehow lure them to the United States.

Henry Wallack did not limit his perusal of the theatrical field to actors and actresses. Well-known dancers, and opera stars in particular, were also fair game. Opera had been an important part of the National's repertory during its premiere season. Besides, as veterans of the Amer-

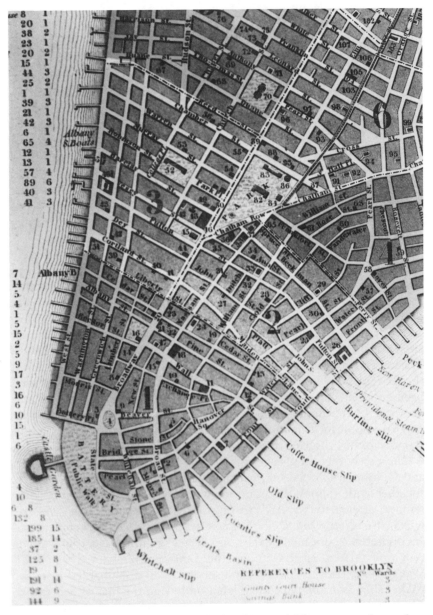

9. Map of lower Manhattan. Wallack's National Theatre was located at Church and Leonard streets (in the center near the top of this image). The Park Theatre was located on Park Row, about two hundred feet east of Ann Street (center). From H. S. Tanner, *New Universal Atlas* (Philadelphia: Carey & Hart, 1844). (Manuscripts and Rare Books Department, Swem Library, College of William and Mary)

ican stage, both Wallacks were familiar with the opera productions of vocal-star troupes and stock companies.[5] Thus, in the summer of 1839, a pair of opera singers and a new and popular opera attracted Wallack's attention.

The previous December two well-known English singers, Jane Shirreff and John Wilson, had created major roles in the Covent Garden premiere of the three-act opera *Amilie; or, The Love Test,* by William Michael Rooke.[6] The London musical press had praised the opera for having "much pleasing melody" and orchestral accompaniments that were "full and appropriate." The reviewer for the London *Musical World,* who admitted having low expectations of the performance, pronounced *Amilie* "one of the most successful works that has been produced since the young days of Mr. [Henry Rowley] Bishop."[7] The opera had also received decided audience approval, which presumably piqued Wallack's interest.[8]

After some inquiries, Wallack learned that Wilson and Shirreff were amenable to an American tour. The third star of the opera, Henry Phillips, either was not asked or could not be convinced to make the crossing.[9] For a while it appeared that the National intended to hire only two new singers, for on 15 September 1838, the *Musical Review* announced that "a fine operatic corps, among whom are Miss Shirreff and Mr. Wilson, English vocalists, have been engaged for the [National] Theatre" (203). By late summer, however, Wallack had added a third: the Covent Garden bass Arthur Edward Seguin. Seguin, furthermore, brought along yet another vocalist, his wife Anne, a soprano who was not part of the original trio hired by Wallack, but who would later play an important role in the history of opera performances by vocal-star troupes in the United States.

The newly recruited singers arrived in New York during September and October 1838. Shirreff, her mother, and a friend, Mary Blundell, together with John Wilson and his wife Mary, all landed on 24 September, after a sixteen-day crossing on the steamship *Great Western,* which, the *New York Daily Express* reported on 25 September, had encountered "continual squalls and heavy weather" en route. Some two weeks later, on 9 October, the *Daily Express* noted that "Mr. Seguine [*sic*], Lady, 3 children, and servant" had disembarked from the packet ship *Samson,* which had left London on the first of September. The arrival of the National's new stars and their impending appearance at the theater was quietly announced in the New York daily newspapers in early October.

Wallack's three vocal stars have been almost completely forgotten, as has their vehicle, *Amilie.* Their operatic and concert performances during the 1838–39 and 1839–40 seasons, however, created a musical and theatrical furor in this country, for the three became great American favorites. According to Joseph Ireland, writing in the mid–1860s, Jane Shirreff was America's "most admired English prima donna between the days of Mrs. Wood and those of Louisa Pyne" (2:276).[10] She and Wilson remained in North America for more than a year and a half, traveling and performing widely before returning to England in 1840. Shirreff toured as a member of several vocal-star troupes and, in the company of Wilson, as a concert artist, giving vocal concerts in both small towns and large cities in an area bounded by Detroit to the west, Montreal to the north, and Savannah to the south.

Her activities during her sojourn are typical of the pattern many vocal stars followed during the 1820s, 1830s, and 1840s. The reason for choosing her tour as a prototype (rather than one of Elizabeth Austin's or Joseph and Mary Anne Wood's) is compelling. Shirreff left a remarkable collection of materials that document her stay in the United States. These make possible a detailed account of her activity, including her itinerary, repertory, financial remuneration, and reception by and reaction to American audiences. It is a perfect illustration of the activities of dozens of other English vocal stars who toured the United States singly or as members of vocal-star troupes during the period.[11]

The Characters

Many early nineteenth-century Americans were fascinated with theatrical goings-on in London. Consequently, managers in this country made sure to publicize any connections that visiting celebrities had with the London theater. As "stars of the London stage," all of Wallack's new singers had excellent credentials. Jane Shirreff (1811–83) made an auspicious debut at Covent Garden in December 1831, and subsequently sang regularly either there or at Drury Lane. She also had appeared with the Concerts of Antient Music, the Philharmonic concerts, and at various provincial festivals.[12] A soprano, she possessed perfect intonation and a full-toned, powerful voice. One critic, writing in 1838, described her upper notes as "clear and bell-like"; another wrote that same year that her voice was "clear, full, and bird-like."[13] Shirreff also was a superior actress, and in this skill surpassed even Mary Anne Wood. Miss Shirreff, wrote the critic for the *Boston Morning Post* on 26 November 1838, shortly after her debut in that city, "has not the wonderful volume and richness of sound of Mrs. Wood, but in every other respect she is, as an actress, incomparably her superior."[14] Others also praised her skills as a performer. In a *New York Morning Herald* review on 15 October following the troupe's debut in New

York, one critic wrote that "Miss Shirreff . . . is a finely formed woman, with an expressive eye—and an admirable theatrical face. But more than form, color, or complexion—she has soul, heart, mind, intellect, and genius in her music and style of acting." The critic for the *Knickerbocker* described her acting as "natural and graceful," and a Philadelphia reviewer wrote in the *National Gazette* that she "possesses an interesting face and figure, a fine, well disciplined voice and taste, and a racy and delightful appreciation of the character she represented" (Amina, in *La Sonnambula*).[15]

According to Joseph Ireland, Shirreff "fairly bewitched half the young men of the city by her engaging naîveté of manner" (2:277). This was a decidedly appealing and marketable quality; a critic for a Philadelphia newspaper praised the "naivete and . . . earnestness about her representation of the character" of Amilie (Figure 10), and his counterpart at the *Boston Morning Post* commented on her "unembarrassed and graceful" motions and her "simple and naive" manner.[16] Such artlessness was an important part of the image that Shirreff wished to convey, and the fact that American critics frequently commented on her "modest demeanor" and the "purity of her life" and pointed out that she enjoyed an "unblemished reputation in private life" contributed to her success with an American public still somewhat suspicious of the morality of women on the stage.[17] After twenty successful months in North America, Jane Shirreff returned to London, married, and retired from professional life.

During their travels and performances together, John Wilson (1801–49) apparently regarded the soprano as his protégé or even his ward. He looked after her interests and managed her financial affairs throughout the tour.[18] Wilson (Figure 11) was a well-known performer in his own right. A tenor of Scottish birth, he first appeared in concerts and opera in Edinburgh. After his operatic debut in 1830, he sang in English opera at both Covent Garden and Drury Lane, where he performed with Shirreff, the Seguins, and many others.[19] He was described in 1866 as of "fine, open, [and] manly countenance"; his voice was "pure, sweet, vigorous, and highly cultivated" and, according to a Philadelphia critic, "clear, rich, and fresh."[20] Wilson took advantage of the craze for national song and became one of the most successful Scottish singers in the nineteenth century. He traveled extensively on the concert circuit, giving "Songs of Scotland" entertainments, and in 1842 published *Wilson's Edition of the Songs of Scotland,* a two-volume compendium of piano-vocal arrangements of traditional Scottish tunes. Like Shirreff, he remained in the United States for twenty months. He returned to North America for a second tour in 1849 but was stricken

10. Jane Shirreff, in costume as Amilie. From a lithograph published by J. Mitchell, London, 1838. (Billy Rose Theatre Collection, New York Public Library)

11. John Wilson in *Amilie,* as portrayed in an illustration on a sheet-music publication of the air "Yes, Methinks I See Her Smiling." Note the Tyrolean costume and set for the opera. Lithograph by Sanford. (Music Division, Library of Congress)

with cholera while performing in Quebec City and died there on 9 July 1849.[21]

Edward and Anne Seguin commenced their American careers in the company of Shirreff and Wilson—Mr. Seguin in October 1838, Mrs. Seguin in February 1839. Both Seguins were also well known to the London opera-going public. A product of the Royal Academy of Music, Arthur Edward Seguin (1809–52) began his singing career in 1828. He fashioned a highly successful career on the London stage, where he sang at Covent Garden, Drury Lane, the King's Theatre, and the English Opera House; he also performed with the Concerts of Antient Music and at various festivals.[22] He had a deep, rich, bass voice of extensive compass and precise intonation and was considered a superlative actor. After his debut in Boston in November 1838, the critic for the *Morning Post* was rhapsodic: "The moment Mr. Seguin opened his mouth," he wrote on 7 November, "the corresponding feature of his auditory assumed the same appearance; one universal gape seemed to infect all; such was the astonishment produced by his magnificent organ." Seguin, whose voice was a "pure, legitimate and ponderous bass, of large and even quality," was, according to this critic, "beyond all comparison, the finest singer of his class we have yet heard in America." Stephen Massett, writing in 1863, also remembered the strong impression that Seguin made when he first appeared in this country. The actor described the dress rehearsal at the National Theatre for *Amilie* before that opera's premiere. "The stage was lighted up, and chairs were placed for the 'principals,'" he wrote, "and when the time came for the aria 'My boyhood's home,' on walked Mr. Seguin, in his rough pea jacket, as if just from sea, and with his magnificent voice charmed every one present by the rendering of this popular melody" (25).

Anne Childe Seguin (1814–88), a soprano, also received her musical training at the Royal Academy; she sang at Covent Garden, Drury Lane, and the Concerts of Antient Music and performed with both Malibran and Grisi at Her Majesty's Theatre in the Haymarket.[23] Although Mrs. Seguin did not elicit such universally laudatory praise as did Austin, Wood, or Shirreff, she was described as a "pleasing and accomplished singer" and as a "correct" and "very beautiful musician." Americans, according to Nicholas Tawa, found her "handsome, graceful, and vivacious, as well as an accomplished actress."[24] After the Seguins concluded their various engagements with James Wallack following 1840, they formed the Seguin Opera Company, a well-traveled vocal-star troupe that performed English opera in the United States until shortly before Edward Seguin's death in 1852.[25] The Seguins played an important role in the cultivation of English opera in this country during the 1840s (chapter 5).

Amilie in New York

The Shirreff/Wilson/Seguin troupe made its debut at the National Theatre in precisely the opera that had caught Henry Wallack's eye in London—Rooke's *Amilie; or, The Love Test*. The National's manager spared no expense and neglected no detail in mounting the work. The theater was to be closed on Saturday evening, 13 October, "in consequence of the preparations for the grand new opera," the *New-York American* reported on 12 October; this was the dress rehearsal at which Massett first encountered Seguin's singing. *Amilie* opened on Monday, 15 October with new scenery and costumes, a chorus of more than two dozen, and an "expanded" orchestra (Figure 12).

The Wallacks had gauged their public well, for the opera was a success from the beginning. A critic for the *Morning Herald,* after experiencing the rush of opening night, wrote on 16 October, "last night we attempted to get a peep into the National Theatre, but such was the crowd, the thing was utterly impossible. So popular is the Opera—so popular the *prima donna*—the tenor—the bass—the all, that we know not when we can have a chance of seeing it."

Subsequent enthusiasm was no less marked. According to the November *Knickerbocker,* audiences crowded the National "nightly, from pit to gallery" and made the theater "resound with round after round of the most enthusiastic applause" (470). The same critic noted that the performance was "unmarked by a single blemish"; Joseph Ireland described the success of *Amilie* as "brilliant in the extreme."[26] All three stars were soundly praised, as were Wallack's stock players, who sang in numerous "delightful and spirited choruses [that] . . . were admirably given," according to the *Knickerbocker* (470). Secondary roles were taken by several of the National's better singers, including Henry Horncastle, the buffo whom Wallack had imported the previous year; W. H. Williams; Andrew Andrews, a well-known singing actor and light comedian; and Mrs. William Penson, wife of the orchestra leader. *Amilie* was so successful that it ran for the entire duration of the troupe's initial two-week engagement at the National.[27] Each performance also featured a farce (given by the stock company) that changed nightly and an instrumental composition (often an operatic overture) played by the orchestra between the two dramatic works.

The author of the opera's text was one John Thomas Haines, who wrote the libretti for both of Rooke's operas. The story, in the words of a London critic, "consists in a young girl remaining faithful to her lover through the persecutions and machinations of a rejected suitor," hence the subtitle "Love Test." The young woman, Amilie, is rewarded by being reunited with her lover at the end of the third act.[28] Although

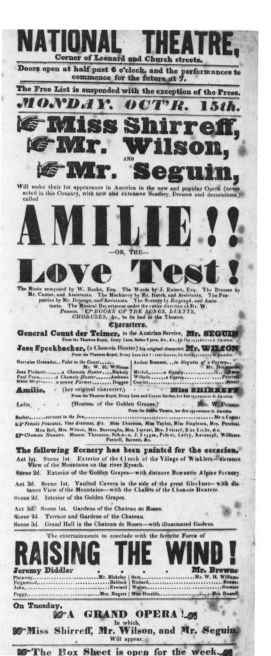

12. Playbill from the American premiere performance of William Michael Rooke's *Amilie,* on 15 October 1838 at the National Theatre in New York. The opera, featuring Jane Shirreff, John Wilson, and Edward Seguin, was followed by a farce performed by the theater's stock company. (Billy Rose Theatre Collection, New York Public Library)

the opera is in the English style, with dialogue rather than recitative, the *Knickerbocker*'s critic pointed out that it had little spoken dialogue (November 1838, 470). The musical numbers include arias and short recitatives, ensemble works (duos, trios, and some fairly complex finales), choruses (described as "some of the most delightful and spirited . . . we ever heard wreaked upon music"), and a potpourri overture (470). On 9 December 1837, the critic of the *Athenaeum* praised Rooke's orchestral writing and suggested that the composer had "taken the benefit of his situation, as a member of the [London] Philharmonic orchestra . . . he has enriched his mind, but brought away nothing which belonged to another" (900).

Amilie is set in the mountains of Switzerland, and Rooke filled it with fetching, folklike melodies. According to a critic in the *Philadelphia Pennsylvanian* on 21 January 1839, the opera's popularity could be attributed to "the Alpine melodies which belong naturally to the story and prevail throughout the piece. Such themes as these," he explained, "are always sure to gratify both cultivated and uncultivated auditors." Rooke's score is full of folk-music references to both Alpine and non-Alpine music, including drone basses, "Scotch-snap" rhythms, horn calls, and yodel-like melodies. The soprano aria "To the Vine Feast," performed by Mrs. Penson in New York and, later, by Mary Ann Knight in Philadelphia, illustrates many of these musical techniques. A distinctly ländler-like song in ternary form, it commences with a brief solo for horn, which foreshadows the opening gesture of the soprano's melody. Midway through the A section, there is a drone in the accompaniment, and close to the end of this section the vocal line, replete with "tra-la-las," is decidedly like a yodel. The song is appealing and tuneful, and Rooke demonstrates both skill in modulation and a sound sense of drama in its construction.

Much of *Amilie*'s popularity can be attributed to this evocation of folk music. The American public had been fascinated with Scotch tunes since the late eighteenth century, and a mania for Irish melody had started in 1818, when Thomas Phillips, one of the first British vocal stars, introduced the songs of Thomas Moore to the United States. American audiences of 1838 were also ready to succumb to the charms of "Tyrolean" melody: the Rainer Family would soon enjoy phenomenal success in this country. These self-billed "Tyrolese minstrels," who performed harmonized native songs in folk costumes, were the first of many singing families to tour the United States; their American debut would be in New York in November 1839, slightly over a year after the premiere of *Amilie*.[29] Americans were also enamored of Italian melody, and *Amilie* features numerous arias that are florid and Italianate in style. The ten extant sheet-music publications of solo arias from

Amilie include at least one—sometimes more—florid song for each of the three stars. The recitative and aria "O Love Thou Art Near Me," sung by Jane Shirreff, is a good example. Melodically, the song is both "birdlike" and full of Rossini-like fioritura, allowing the soprano to show off her vocal dexterity in a manner much loved during the period. Another of Shirreff's florid arias, even more evocative of songbirds, is "When the Morning First Dawns." It is strophic in form and tells of lovers wandering in the woods, listening to nightingales in the early morning and larks in the evening—with obvious possibilities for vocal pyrotechnics.

The stylistic contrast typical of Rooke's opera can be readily seen in a comparison of two arias sung by Edward Seguin. The first, "What Is the Spell?," is full of the triplets and broken-chord melodic gestures typical of Bellini. It is in a fairly straightforward rounded binary form, and toward the end of each A section a sequence occurs that is particularly full of fioritura. The second song, "My Boyhood's Home," is a simple, balladlike tune in ternary form. Although it has none of the folkish characteristics of "To the Vine Feast," its melody in the A section is pleasant, somewhat plaintive, and eminently "hummable." The middle section, in strong contrast, is dramatic, marchlike, and overtly militaristic, complete with thunderous octaves and chords in snare-drum rhythms in the accompaniment. If the number of different sheet-music editions of a work is any indication, "My Boyhood's Home" was one of the most popular songs in the opera, and it must have retained its appeal. Stephen Massett referred to it as a "popular melody" twenty-five years after its American premiere. "What Is the Spell?," on the other hand, became one of the songs that Seguin performed frequently throughout 1838 and 1839, in concert and interpolated into other operas, which suggests that American audiences were also fond of the more florid style.

The juxtaposition in the same opera of simple, tuneful, and folklike songs with florid and Italianate arias might seem jarring to some modern listeners. In fact, however, the same thing happens in both *The Magic Flute* and *Der Freischütz*. Furthermore, in the 1830s and 1840s, the combination apparently was just what American audiences wanted. In his study of American popular song, Charles Hamm describes *The Social Choir* (1835) as a "typical collection of the time" and points out that it includes selections from English, French, and Italian opera, along with Scotch and Irish songs. He further relates that slightly later in the century, in personal collections of sheet music—the individual pieces of which have been bound together—"Bellini is found side by side with Thomas Moore, Henry Bishop, Henry Russell, the Hutchinsons, and Stephen Foster."[30] One might think that Rooke had written

Amilie precisely for American audiences of the 1830s and 1840s, had it not been composed twenty years earlier.

Shirreff, Wilson, and Seguin on Tour:
Boston, Providence, and New York

When Elizabeth Austin came to the United States in 1828, she agreed to perform at the Chestnut Street Theatre in Philadelphia for a specific length of time; she then was free to make engagements elsewhere. Evidently Shirreff, Wilson, and Seguin had a similar arrangement with James Wallack, for at the end of their initial two-week engagement they left New York. Undoubtedly, Wallack would have been perfectly happy to keep his trio performing opera at the National for as long as they were drawing paying houses, but there had been no way for the manager to predict the extent of their success in New York, and he had allotted them the conventional two-week slot in his fall schedule. The numerous contracts for engagements that he had made with other artists for the fall and winter season had to be honored.[31] Under the circumstances, the best that Wallack could do was to book the singers into the remaining free time in the National's 1838–39 schedule (three weeks in December 1838, seven weeks in February–March 1839, and a block of eight weeks in April, May, and June 1839) and hope that the vocal stars would continue to draw "large and fashionable" audiences when they returned to New York.

Itinerant vocal stars and vocal-star troupes did not limit their appearances to the northeastern part of the country, although most visiting artists did concentrate their performances in the Northeast when they first arrived, branching out only later to include the South or the "West" (the Ohio-Mississippi river basin). This pattern was both logical and practical. A majority of the population was concentrated in the Northeast, cities were closer in that area, and the transportation network connecting the cities was well established. Furthermore, it was imperative that performers establish their reputations firmly in the public mind before heading away from populous areas. Because the American musical and theatrical press was based in the Northeast, it made sense to commence with a tour of that region. Finally, major stars generally arrived in this country under the aegis of theater managers who were often based in New York or Philadelphia, and such obligations had to be met before going elsewhere. Thus it is not surprising that Wallack's vocal stars, who had engagements at his theater in October and December 1838 and February–March and April–June 1839, stayed fairly close to New York City during the 1838–39 theatrical season (15 October 1838 through 22 June 1839). Between their appearances in

New York, however, they performed in Philadelphia, Boston, Baltimore, and Washington. Shirreff and Wilson, without Seguin, also performed in Providence, Rhode Island, for a week (Table 2).

The first city the vocal stars visited after their tumultuous reception in New York was Boston, where they opened in *Amilie* at the Tremont Theatre on 5 November. Bostonians, although they approved of the vocal stars, evidently disliked *Amilie* from the beginning. Midway through the first week of the troupe's run, a local critic hinted in the *Daily Evening Transcript* that Bostonians had not been overwhelmed by the new opera. "We do not think that *Amilie* is an Opera well calculated to display [the vocalists'] powers to the best advantage," he wrote on 7 November. "It is good and new, but we should much prefer, old as the piece is, to hear them in *La Sonnambula*." At the beginning of their second week, the troupe did bring out the tried-and-true Bellini, and response improved markedly. "*La Sonnambula* went off gloriously at the Tremont [Theatre] last evening," wrote the same critic on 13 November. "We never heard such loud and so frequent applause. . . . It is not a gem, but a casket of gems . . . it throws that thing of shreds and patches, the opera of *Amilie*, far into the back ground. It is no secret that the house was not well filled last week. The fault was with the piece, and not the performers. The energetic applause bestowed on *La Sonnambula* last evening is proof enough of the assertion." The vocal stars had learned their lesson well. Excepting benefits, they performed Bellini's opera exclusively for the remainder of the Boston engagement.

Boston's negative response to *Amilie* is somewhat puzzling; perhaps it is evidence of the musical and theatrical conservatism for which the city enjoyed a solid reputation. The opera was a smash hit in New York, and would continue to be so throughout the year. It also was well received in Washington, Baltimore, and, with some reservations, in Philadelphia.[32] Many of the work's arias were disseminated in sheet-music form, with numerous editions of the more popular selections; tunes from *Amilie* were fashioned into grand waltzes, marches, quadrilles, and "brilliant divertimentos" for performance on the piano, flute, and Spanish guitar.[33]

That the opera did not succeed in Boston is not particularly significant in itself, however, except for what it indicates about operatic repertory. The overall repertories of itinerant vocal-star troupes in the United States were fairly consistent from city to city. The Boston reaction to *Amilie*, however, suggests that musical taste was apparently not universal; an opera that played well in one city evidently was not guaranteed to succeed in another. Furthermore, this discrepancy indicates that a large number of performances of a particular work is

Table 2. Itinerary of the Shirreff/Wilson/Seguin Vocal-star Troupe,
15 Oct. 1838–22 June 1839

15 Oct.–31 Oct. 1838	National Theatre, New York	14 opera performances
5 Nov.–23 Nov. 1838	Tremont Street Theatre, Boston	15 opera performances
10, 17 Nov. 1838	Masonic Temple, Boston	2 concerts
26 Nov.–30 Nov. 1838	Providence, R.I.	5 opera performances[a]
3 Dec.–21 Dec. 1838	National Theatre, New York	17 opera performances
24 Dec.–29 Dec. 1838	National Theatre, Washington	6 opera performances
31 Dec.–12 Jan. 1839	Holliday Street Theatre, Baltimore	12 opera performances
14 Jan.–9 Feb. 1839	Chestnut Street Theatre, Philadelphia	24 opera performances[b]
11 Feb.–30 March 1839	National Theatre, New York	41 opera performances[c]
1 April–28 April 1839	Chestnut Street Theatre, Philadelphia	22 opera performances[d]
19 April 1839	New York	1 concert
29 April–22 June 1839	National Theatre, New York	48 opera performances[e]
Total opera performances by troupe, 1838–39		199[f]
Additional opera performances by Shirreff and Wilson		5
Concerts		2

[a] The Providence engagement was of Shirreff and Wilson and did not include either Edward or Anne Seguin.
[b] Because of illness, Shirreff appeared in only nineteen of these performances.
[c] Because of continued illness, Shirreff apeared in thirty-one performances.
[d] Shirreff appeared in nineteen of these performances.
[e] Shirreff appeared in thirty-four of these performances.
[f] Jane Shirreff missed thirty-two performances during the 1838–39 season.

not by itself an adequate gauge of popularity. In Boston, after all, the troupe presented *Amilie* for five of its fifteen performances at the Tremont Theatre before the management withdrew it.

After leaving Massachusetts, the Seguins headed back to New York, while Shirreff and Wilson made a brief, one-week stop in Providence. Their engagement there was a last-minute arrangement. The previous week (21 November), the editor of the *Republican Herald,* on behalf of "our Theatre-going community," had urged that the "distinguished vocalists" Shirreff, Wilson, and Sequin "be engaged by our spirited managers, after the [current] engagement."

Shirreff and Wilson were receptive to the overtures of the "spirited managers," although apparently the Seguins were not, and the two stars gave five performances with the stock company of the Providence Theatre. The operas they chose to mount were familiar works from the old comic-opera repertory: *Love in a Village* (Arne), *Clari; or, The Maid of Milan* and *Guy Mannering* (Bishop), and *Rob Roy* (Davy). The singers' choice of repertory is probably a measure of the type of opera the local stock company could mount on short notice, rather than a reflection of the operatic tastes of Providence. The troupe was well received in Rhode Island. Its second performance, *Guy Mannering*, drew a "crowded audience" that was presumably mixed socially, economically, and racially although (as in most theaters) the Providence house restricted "colored persons" to "a division in the Gallery," according to the *Republican Herald* of 26 November and 1 December.

The trio reunited in early December for a return engagement at the National, where they performed for three weeks (3–21 December), adding Auber's *Fra Diavolo* to their repertory of *Amilie* and *La Sonnambula*. Their first several engagements of the 1838–39 season, in New York and Boston—and the manner in which the singers introduced their operas—are good examples of the standard scheduling practices that most vocal-star troupes and theatrical companies followed. If the first work a troupe offered attracted large crowds, the manager and the company kept it on the boards. If that meant that the same opera or drama was performed every evening for the duration of a star's or a troupe's engagement, so be it. When the production began to wane in popularity, it was replaced with something else, and that work continued for as long as it drew large audiences.

Today, the population on the East Coast is immense, and one can generally assume that theater audiences are comprised of entirely different individuals for each performance. In the early nineteenth century, however, it was not at all unusual for individuals to attend several performances of the same dramatic work during a single engagement. On 25 March 1837, for example, one theater-goer in Mobile, Alabama, commented in a letter to the *Spirit* that he had attended four out of six of the local stock company's performances of *Cinderella* within a short period; he did not indicate that this was by any means extraordinary. Three years later, on 26 October 1840, the Philadelphia merchant Joseph Sill noted in his diary that he had seen *La Sonnambula* some twenty times since the opera's Philadelphia premiere in 1836. And a critic writing in the *Spirit* on 16 January 1841 about a recent run of *Don Giovanni* in New York City (mounted by an unknown company) pointed out—probably with some exaggeration—that the opera "was performed to the same audience each night; that there was but the slightest change of faces—the same seats being occupied by the same individuals night after night." The tendency for audiences to attend repeated performances of the same work was common, especially if the visiting star was a celebrity or the work was either old and a favorite (as with *La Sonnambula* or *Cinderella*) or new and unfamiliar (as with *Amilie*). Managers were aware that many patrons returned night after night, and, as a consequence, frequently changed the farce that concluded each evening's performance.

The added complexity of music (a play can be read, after all) meant that a new opera required numerous hearings before an auditor became sufficiently familiar with it. People in the 1840s who wished to learn a new opera had two options: they could purchase and learn the sheet-music publications of the more popular arias, or they could attend multiple performances when the opera was produced locally. Once the popularity of an opera was established, piano transcriptions—along with piano potpourris, fantasias, and variations based on operatic melodies—also became familiarizing agents.

The performance patterns for both of Shirreff's new operas reflect this tendency. Both *Amilie* and Adolph Adam's *The Postillion of Longjumeau* were performed for two entire weeks to the total—or, in the case of *Postillion,* almost total—exclusion of other operas.[34] Clearly, some patrons attended more than one performance. A New York critic for the *Daily Express,* after noting on 16 October 1839 that Rooke's opera "gives great pleasure to the [New York] audience," pointed out that "some of [Miss Shirreff's] hearers have been present at the performance of [*Amilie*] ten or fifteen times, and always with the same satisfaction." Contemporary critics often viewed an opera's ability to withstand repeated hearings as a mark of its quality. One reviewer in Philadelphia remarked that "the many beautiful melodies and combinations of [*Amilie*] improve much on repetition"; another, after the Philadelphia premiere of *The Postillion of Longjumeau,* wrote that "the music can be heard many times with increased pleasure,—with every fresh hearing new designs and effects are developed." He added, "an opera to be worth hearing should bear successfully many repetitions."[35] Finally, Joseph Sill, the reliable source of behind-the-scenes attitudes toward opera, made similar comments in 1841. "In the evening," he wrote on 29 January, "a large party of us went to see the Opera of 'Norma' and were more delighted than on our last Visit—Every representation develops new beauties in the orchestra, in the Songs, Duetts, & Chorusses that we did [not] discover before."

If a performer's engagement was for more than one or two weeks, as was the Shirreff/Wilson/Seguin troupe's December reengagement in New York, the management would mount several additional "new" operas or a combination of the works already introduced, to be performed on alternate evenings (Table 3). The company usually chose as its second or third opera one that was a guaranteed favorite, especially if the first production was of a new work. This had certainly been the case in Boston, where even the newspaper critic called for *La Sonnambula*, "old as the piece is." A typical performance pattern was that of Wallack's star troupe during its second visit to New York in December 1838. For the first two nights the singers performed *Amilie*; for the next three nights a "new" opera, *Fra Diavolo*; then *Amilie* again on Saturday. For the entire second week the troupe produced *La Sonnambula*, and during the third week gave all three operas on different nights. Although Shirreff did not keep records of the financial receipts for each of these performances, her records of 1839 generally support managerial decisions to change operas. Extraneous circumstances, for example, weather, the night of the week, and whether or not the performance was a benefit, affected attendance, but almost invariably (excepting benefits) the first performance of a work drew the largest crowd, with subsequent performances attracting ever-smaller ones.[36]

The Tour Continues:
Baltimore, Washington, and Philadelphia

At the conclusion of their December reengagement at the National, the trio of vocal stars took to the road once again (Table 4). This time they headed south to Washington for one week, Baltimore for two weeks, and Philadelphia for four weeks. Their reception in all three cities was enthusiastic. "Some of the choicest songs" from *Amilie* were encored the night of its second performance in Washington, where the final appearance ended with a "tumult of applause" from a "numerous and brilliant" audience, according to the *National Intelligencer* of 28–29 December 1838. In Baltimore, where *Amilie* elicited "unqualified approbation," the "musical public" was "thrown into ecstasies by the performances of the most delightful cantatrice that has ever charmed the ear" reported the *American and Commercial Daily Advertiser* and the *Baltimore Sun* on 5 January 1839.

In Philadelphia, the singers—although well received in general—ran into some difficulties with *Amilie*, but of a different sort than they had encountered in Boston. In October, when the stars had made their successful American debut in New York, Francis Wemyss, by then the manager of Philadelphia's Walnut Street Theatre, watched carefully. *Amilie*'s popularity so impressed him that he quickly engaged several

Table 3. Repertory Performed by the Shirreff/Wilson/Seguin Vocal-star
Troupe, Oct.–Dec. 1838

National Theatre, New York City, 15–31 Oct. 1838:

  15 Oct. (Monday): *Amilie/Raising the Wind* (farce)
  16 Oct.: *Amilie/The Spoil'd Child!* (farce)
  17 Oct.: *Amilie/Robert Macaire* (drama)
  18 Oct.: *Amilie/Luke the Laborer* (drama)
  19 Oct.: *Amilie/Naval Engagements* (farce)
  20 Oct.: *Amilie/Robert Macaire* (first act)
  22 Oct. (Monday): *Amilie/Naval Engagements*
  23 Oct.: *Amilie/The Waterman* (Wilson benefit)
  24 Oct.: *Amilie/Naval Engagements*
  25 Oct.: *Amilie/The Waterman* (Shirreff benefit)
  26 Oct.: *Amilie/Robert Macaire* (entire)
  27 Oct.: *Amilie/*Musical Pasticcio*/Sudden Thoughts! or, Fashionable Society*
        (farce)
  30 Oct. (Tuesday): *Amilie/Sudden Thoughts*
  31 Oct.: *Amilie/*Musical Pasticcio*/My Young Wife and Old Umbrella* (farce)

Tremont Street Theatre, Boston, 5–23 Nov. 1838:

  5 Nov. (Monday): *Amilie/State Secrets* (farce)
  6 Nov.: *Amilie/The Citizen* (burletta)
  7 Nov.: *Amilie/Irish Tutor* (farce)
  8 Nov.: *Amilie/Young Widow* (comedy)
  9 Nov.: *Amilie/Truth! or, A Glass too Much* (drama)
  12 Nov. (Monday): *La Sonnambula/Truth!*
  13 Nov.: *La Sonnambula/Does Your Mother Know You're Out?*
  14 Nov.: *La Sonnambula/Truth!*
  15 Nov.: *La Sonnambula/Little Sins and Pretty Sinners* (farce)
  16 Nov.: *La Sonnambula/Truth!*
  19 Nov. (Monday): *Guy Mannering/The Waterman* (Wilson benefit)
  20 Nov.: *La Sonnambula/Little Sins*
  21 Nov.: *La Sonnambula/*Musical Pasticcio (Seguin benefit)
  22 Nov.: *State Secrets/La Sonnambula*
  23 Nov.: *La Sonnambula/*Vocal Concert (Shirreff benefit)

Providence Theatre, Providence, R.I., 26–30 Nov. 1838:

  26 Nov. (Monday): *Love in a Village/Lady and the Devil*
  27 Nov.: *Guy Mannering/Perfection; or, The Lady of Munsrer*
  28 Nov.: *Clari; or, The Maid of Milan/No Song, No Supper*
  29 Nov.: *Guy Mannering/*comic dance, Mr. Burns*/Miller's Maid*
  30 Nov.: *Rob Roy/No Song, No Supper* (Shirreff and Wilson benefit)

Table 3. Continued

National Theatre, New York, 3–21 Dec. 1838:

3 Dec. (Monday): *Amilie/Valet de Sham* (farce)
4 Dec.: *Amilie/Modern Antiques!* (farce)
5 Dec.: *Fra Diavolo/Valet de Sham*
6 Dec.: *Fra Diavolo/Shocking Events!* (farce)
7 Dec.: *Fra Diavolo/The Spoil'd Child!*
8 Dec.: *Amilie/The Dead Shot* (farce)
10 Dec. (Monday): *La Sonnambula*
11 Dec.: *La Sonnambula/Deaf as a Post!*
12 Dec.: *La Sonnambula/The Bengal Tiger* (farce)
13 Dec.: *La Sonnambula/Illustrious Stranger* (farce)
14 Dec.: *La Sonnambula/Stranger*
15 Dec.: *La Sonnambula/Uncle John* (farce)
17 Dec. (Monday): *La Sonnambula/Miller and His Men*
18 Dec.: *Amilie/Uncle John*
19 Dec.: *Fra Diavolo/Crammond Brig* (burletta) (Wilson benefit)
20 Dec.: *Amilie/Une bonne bouche musicale* (Seguin benefit)
21 Dec.: *La Sonnambula/No Song, No Supper* (Shirreff benefit)

vocal stars and a number of New York choristers to mount a production of his own in November. Starring Antoinette Otto, William Brough, and the singer-actor Thomas Bishop, *Amilie* had been received, according to Wemyss, with "cheers, and such applause as rewards a manager . . . by the knowledge that the receipts of his treasury will be increased." The opera ran for two weeks at the Walnut Theatre and was judged a great success.[37]

The Shirreff/Wilson/Seguin troupe did not open at Wemyss's competition, the Chestnut Street Theatre, until January 1839, a full three months after their debut performance in New York. The fact that Wemyss had stolen much of their thunder by preempting their new opera, however, quickly became apparent. The singers opened their month-long engagement with a crowd-pleaser, *La Sonnambula*, probably in order to give the Chestnut Theatre Company time to rehearse the new opera. They unveiled *Amilie* on the fifth night of their engagement, and for the first few performances the new work drew fairly well. Even local critics expressed enthusiasm. Two days after *Amilie*'s second presentation on 19 January, the *Pennsylvanian*'s critic commented positively on the opera's "pleasing melodies and effective choruses" and concluded that it "cannot fail" in Philadelphia. It seems,

Table 4. Repertory Performed by the Shirreff/Wilson/Seguin Vocal-star
Troupe, 24 Dec. 1838–9 Feb. 1839

National Theatre, Washington, 24–29 Dec. 1838:

24 Dec. (Monday): *La Sonnambula/Love in Humble Life* (afterpiece)
25 Dec.: *La Sonnambula/The Vagrant, the Workman and the Manufacturer*
(new drama)
26 Dec.: *Amilie/Bee Hive* (afterpiece)
27 Dec.: *Amilie/Songs/Fish Out of Water* (afterpiece) (Shirreff benefit)
28 Dec.: *Fra Diavolo*/Musical Pasticcio (Seguin benefit)
29 Dec.: *Fra Diavolo*/Musical Pasticcio

Holliday Street Theatre, Baltimore, 31 Dec.–12 Jan. 1839:

31 Dec. (Monday): *Amilie/Sudden Thoughts! or, Fashionable Society* (farce)
1 Jan.: *La Sonnambula/Love in Humble Life* (afterpiece)
2 Jan.: *Fra Diavolo/A Quiet Day* (afterpiece)
3 Jan.: *Amilie/The Bath Road* (afterpiece)
4 Jan.: *Amilie*/Musical Pasticcio
5 Jan.: *La Sonnambula*
7 Jan. (Monday): *Amilie*/Musical Pasticcio/Favorite Farce
8 Jan.: *La Sonnambula*/Concert (Seguin benefit)
9 Jan.: *Fra Diavolo/Crammond Brig* (Wilson benefit)
10 Jan.: *Cinderella*/Favorite Farce
11 Jan.: *Cinderella*/Favorite Selection of Vocal Music (Shirreff benefit)
12 Jan.: *La Sonnambula/Crammond Brig*

Chestnut Street Theatre, Philadelphia, 14 Jan.–9 Feb. 1839:

14 Jan. (Monday): *La Sonnambula/Katharine and Petruchio*
15 Jan.: *La Sonnambula/General Bertrand's Farewell to France*/favorite song/
The Spitfire (farce)
16 Jan.: *La Sonnambula*/Gallopade/*State Secrets* (farce)
17 Jan.: *La Sonnambula/The Wandering Minstrel* (farce)
18 Jan.: *Amilie*/"A New Cotillion" (orchestra) from *Robert le Diable/Fish Out
of Water*
19 Jan.: *Amilie/Robert le Diable* Cotillion/*The Mummy* (farce)
21 Jan. (Monday): *La Sonnambula*/Miscellaneous Concert (Shirreff benefit)
22 Jan.: *Amilie/Dead Shot* (entertainment)
23 Jan.: *Amilie/My Friend the Governor* (drama)
24 Jan.: *Amilie/The Spitfire*
25 Jan.: *La Sonnambula*/"New Wiener Gallopade" (orchestra)/*Comfortable
Service* (entertainment)
26 Jan.: *Amilie*/"New Wiener Gallopade"/*Fish Out of Water*
28 Jan. (Monday): *La Sonnambula*/Miscellaneous Concert (Wilson benefit)
29 Jan.: *Fra Diavolo/My Friend the Governor*

Table 4. Continued

---

30 Jan.: *Fra Diavolo*/*Barbers at Court* (entertainment)

31 Jan.: *Fra Diavolo*/*The Mummy*

1 Feb.: *Fra Diavolo*/"New Trumpet Gallopade" (orchestra)/*Comfortable Service* (entertainment)

2 Feb.: *Fra Diavolo*/"New Trumpet Gallopade"/*Turning the Tables*

4 Feb. (Monday): *La Sonnambula*/"New Trumpet Gallopade"/*Perfection* (musical entertainment) [Shirreff ill]

5 Feb.: *La Sonnambula*

6 Feb.: *Cinderella*/Vocal and Instrumental Concert (Seguin benefit) [Shirreff ill]

7 Feb.: *Cinderella*/*Young Widow* (farce) [Shirreff ill]

8 Feb.: *Guy Mannering*/"New French Cotillion" (orchestra)/*A Day after the Wedding* (farce) [Shirreff ill]

---

however, that the Philadelphians who flocked to the Chestnut Street Theatre for the first two nights of the opera wished primarily to see and to hear the celebrated new prima donna and compare her performance of Amilie with that by Madame Otto. After this wish was fulfilled, however, the audiences melted away. By the company's third presentation, Philadelphia's enthusiasm for the work had declined precipitously. Shirreff noted in her diary on 22 January that the company had attracted a "bad house" that evening. The next day she recorded, "not a very good house—seems this opera will not do as much here as in New York," and on the twenty-fourth she wrote, "confirmed in my opinion about this opera [in Philadelphia]." Information from Shirreff's financial ledger likewise portrays a marked decline in the opera's popularity. On its opening night the house take was $676 in paid admissions; on the second night the theater took in $607. The subsequent three performances, however, netted $455 on Tuesday, 22 January, $302 on Wednesday, and $230 on Thursday. The audience for the final performance was slightly larger, but the critic for the *National Gazette* was blunt in his evaluation of the opera's reception. "We had intended to have prepared an analysis of the music [of *Amilie*]," he wrote on 26 January, during the company's second week, "but as the production has entirely failed, we deem the matter not worth while."

Wemyss, who wrote about his theatrical coup in his memoirs, pointed out that although "the opera was better done at the Chestnut Street Theatre as a whole," his own presentation had been sufficient "to destroy any great excitement; the airs had become familiar, and notwithstanding the full force of the chorus from the National Theatre, [the Chestnut Street production] failed to draw money" (1847:315–16). Wemyss admitted cheerfully that his ploy had been "one of those fair (unfair) movements in management, which frequently overthrow well-laid schemes" (316). When the Shirreff/Wilson/Seguin troupe returned to Philadelphia two months later in early April 1839, they gave *Amilie* another try, and the results were much more gratifying. Shirreff concluded in her diary on 18 April that Philadelphians "seemed to like it better than on our former visit."[38] For the remainder of this engagement, however, the stars gave performances of *Fra Diavolo* and the perennials *La Sonnambula* and *Cinderella*. Auber's opera met with "great success," and the Bellini, which Shirreff astutely chose for her benefit performance on 21 January, attracted the largest house of the engagement.[39]

Wemyss's comment that the Chestnut Street Theatre production of *Amilie* in January had included "the full force of the chorus from the National Theatre" raises an important issue about vocal-star troupes in general and about the Shirreff/Wilson/Seguin troupe of 1838–39 in particular. As Wemyss's statement suggests, vocal stars of the 1820s and 1830s—who usually traveled singly or in troupes of two, three, or four—occasionally toured with larger contingents comprised of members of the stock company of a particular theater. The latter took secondary roles and functioned as a chorus in an arrangement that temporarily transformed a vocal-star troupe into something much closer to the English opera companies of the late 1840s and 1850s.

American theaters in Boston, Philadelphia, New York, and New Orleans were the most likely houses to engage vocal-star troupes in the 1820s and 1830s, because their stock companies generally were strong enough to support opera productions adequately. Theaters in smaller towns such as Providence, Washington, and Baltimore, however, occasionally also wished to hire vocal stars for limited engagements, especially if a particular combination of singers was creating a major stir elsewhere. When the manager of such a theater engaged stars, it usually was for performances of the old-fashioned repertory, such as those performed by Shirreff and Wilson in Providence, because stock-company players already knew these works. If a local theater wished to produce a more elaborate opera or a popular new work, the manager was forced to hire additional musicians to supplement his stock-company performers.

Occasionally, even managers in the larger cities such as Boston and Philadelphia found their interest piqued by a successful new group of performers or a particularly celebrated new work, and they, too, often wished to engage such popular attractions. In the case of a new opera, however, some were unwilling to absorb the significant overhead costs associated with its production; these included the manufacture of new costumes and scenery and the training of the chorus and the orchestra. In both small theaters that wished to mount a work not in the comic-opera repertory and larger theaters whose management balked at the additional costs incurred by the production of a new opera, a theater was more likely to engage a vocal-star troupe if the troupe was closer to a real opera company—that is, including singers for all the important roles, a chorus, and (occasionally) instrumentalists to augment the orchestra.

For short engagements, the manager of the theater where a new opera had premiered could sometimes be prevailed upon to "lend" members of his stock company to other theaters. This practice benefited the manager who had mounted the original production, for by lend-ing—or, more likely, "renting"—his already-trained chorus and singing actors he ensured that the opera would remain in the public eye until the stars could return to his own theater for additional performances. It also provided work for the extra singing actors and actresses he had hired for the production and kept them employed in the interim while nonoperatic stars performed at his theater. It is also possible that vocal stars themselves occasionally arranged to borrow their manager's stock-company players for a short tour, perhaps in exchange for a percentage of their profits on the road.

In any case, during the 1838–39 season, James Wallack made an arrangement of one or the other type regarding the disposition of the chorus and singing actors he had trained for *Amilie*. Over the course of their first six months in this country, Shirreff, Wilson, and Seguin toured with players from the National Theatre. Cast lists from playbills of performances in Boston, Philadelphia, Washington, and Baltimore include the names of various actors not in the ranks of the local stock companies.[40]

On 25 December 1839, the Baltimore *American and Commercial Daily Advertiser* noted that several singers, all described as employees of the National Theatre in New York, had been permitted "by James Wallack, Esq. . . . to accept the engagement" in Baltimore. In both Baltimore and Washington, the local newspapers reported that the visiting troupe's performances were "sustained and supported by . . . the CHORUS of the National Theatre, N. Y." in Baltimore and assisted by "the whole of the Operatic Corps of the National Theatre, in New York" in Washington.[41] The number of additional singer-actors who performed with the vocal stars varied from theater to theater. A larger number of National Theatre actors performed with the stars during their engagements at the smaller theaters in Washington and Baltimore, for example, than when they appeared with the more complete local companies of Philadelphia and Boston.[42]

Whether Wallack had agreed to lend part of his stock company to the three vocal stars as part of his original contract with them, or whether this arrangement was made after the singers and *Amilie* had proven to be so successful in New York in October, is unknown.[43] The arrangement itself, however, was rather uncommon for vocal stars. During the subsequent theatrical season (1839–40), Shirreff, Wilson, and the Seguins traveled only with other principal singers. All the other parts in the operas in which they performed—including the chorus— were taken by members of the stock companies of the theaters where they were engaged.

The identity of the singers' business agent during the 1838–39 season is unknown; it is possible that Wallack or his business manager worked on their behalf to set up engagements at the major theaters in the Northeast. Extant correspondence between performers and managers active during the antebellum period suggests that although some engagements, especially those at the more prominent theaters, were set up months in advance, it was certainly possible to make last-minute arrangements.[44] That Shirreff, Wilson, and Seguin successfully negotiated contracts to perform at such important theaters as the Tremont in Boston and the Chestnut Street in Philadelphia indicates that someone was doing advance work. The last-minute engagement of Shirreff and Wilson in Providence, however, also suggests that, at least in the autumn, their schedule was still flexible.

Disagreements, Illnesses, and Economic Triumphs

Toward the end of their engagement at the Chestnut Street Theatre in February 1839, the vocal-star troupe began to fray around the edges. By that time, the singers had worked together for three and a half months, and the pressure of daily performances and constant travel began to take its toll. No information in the public press hints of discord, but several incidents during and shortly after the Philadelphia engagement—as recorded by Shirreff—indicate that rapport among the singers was no longer particularly good. This personal discord may have been the result of a serious crisis that occurred in early February: during the first week of the month, the troupe's star soprano fell seriously ill.

Overall, February and early March was a bad time for Jane Shirreff. She first mentioned not feeling well on Wednesday, 30 January, when she complained in her diary of a "frightful cold"; nevertheless, she appeared in *Fra Diavolo* that night. On the thirty-first she was confined to bed all day but again performed that evening. On Sunday, she complained of a "very sore" throat and on Monday, despite being "very ill," participated in the company's rehearsal for *Cinderella*, in which she was to appear that evening. She left the rehearsal feeling "much worse." After consultation with a physician and the manager of the theater, it was decided to have an apology printed and distributed to the public and to substitute the familiar and less demanding *La Sonnambula* for that evening's performance. Shirreff noted in her diary that she "got through [*La Sonnambula*] wonderfully," but as a result she felt "much worse," and on Tuesday was confined to bed, unable to sing. This threw the troupe's plans for the remainder of the Philadelphia engagement into disarray; evidently Mrs. Sharpe took over Shirreff's roles for the rest of the week.[45]

In retrospect, the soprano's attempt to continue performing backfired. Instead of taking time off to recover, she persisted, and consequently aggravated her illness. Shirreff never stated the reasons for her persistence; perhaps she simply underestimated the seriousness of her illness. The financial incentive for her to continue was always present, however. If she did not perform, she was not paid. More intriguing is the speculation that Shirreff pushed herself for reasons of professional competition and jealousy. The company had another fully competent soprano in the wings; Anne Seguin was ready to take over should Shirreff falter. Edward Seguin wished to boost his wife's career—she had performed very little in the four months since their arrival in the United States—and had been lobbying on her behalf. Francis Wemyss later wrote that the troupe eventually fell apart because Seguin wished to "bring his wife more prominently before the audience" (1847, 327).

Shirreff's illness during the first week of February gave Seguin his first opportunity to urge that his wife be hired as a temporary substitute, and the fact that Shirreff continued must have been frustrating and infuriating. That the soprano's persistence negatively colored Edward Seguin's behavior toward her is clear, for Shirreff began to note disagreements with him at precisely this time. On 1 February, for example, when Shirreff performed despite having a "frightful cold," she noted in her diary being "provoked with Seguin." The next day she was much more than provoked, for she indignantly wrote, "Mr. Seguin behaved so ill during the whole of my character scene [in *Fra Diavolo*] that I resolved never to play in that opera again with him—told [manager] Maywood &c"; the threat, of course, was not carried out. The nature of Seguin's alleged poor conduct is a mystery, for no reviews mention any abnormalities in the performance.

When Shirreff was unable to continue, the Chestnut Theatre management turned to Mrs. Sharpe, an established vocal star and stock-company singer, rather than to Anne Seguin, an unknown. Perhaps Seguin blamed this on Shirreff, for by early spring Shirreff and the bass were barely amicable. On 26 February in New York Shirreff once again expressed outrage in her diary at "shameful conduct on the part of Seguin," and in April her written comments clearly reveal animosity toward the bass. The troupe was performing in Philadelphia, and Seguin, who had returned to New York for the weekend, fell ill himself and was unable to perform, according to a report on 10 April in the *Pennsylvanian*. Shirreff noted his absence: "4/8. Marriage of Figaro—splendid house—Mr. Seguin not from New York—ill—him!!"

Shirreff missed five performances in Philadelphia, and the entire first week of the subsequent New York engagement (Table 5). She attempted to resume performing on Monday, 18 February and managed to sing well enough that week, but still was not fully recovered, for on 21 February a *Daily Express* critic urged "the friends of Miss Shirreff" to "advise her [to] withdraw for a few nights, for her exertions under the indisposition through which she labors are sufficient to prove permanently injurious to the voice." Shirreff persevered, however, and as a consequence suffered a relapse. During the last week of February she noted in her diary that she felt "weak and languid" and "very poorly—hoarse and ill"; on the twenty-seventh she was "too weak and ill to attend rehearsal." Somehow she managed to perform for the remainder of the week, but finally approached Wallack and "arranged to have a week's cessation" (1 March). Altogether, Shirreff missed three weeks of performances—one in Philadelphia and two in New York. During this time she was sufficiently ill to have had sixty leeches applied on 11 February and her throat lanced on 3 March. According to her diary, she was unable to resume a regular performance schedule until 11 March.

As a result of Shirreff's sickness, Wallack allowed Anne Seguin to make her American debut at the National on 11 February, as Rosina in *The Barber of Seville*. After February, in fact, the National's vocal-star troupe consisted of all four singers. Wallack, skilled manager that he was, used both sopranos to his best advantage: spotlighting Seguin while Shirreff was ill, featuring the latter upon her recovery, and mounting operas throughout March—in particular *The Marriage of Figaro*—that used the talents of both. Anne Seguin's connection with the company must have been on an ad hoc basis, for the economic terms to which Wallack and the vocal stars had agreed earlier in the year did not change after her debut, according to Shirreff's financial ledger. Playbills in the Shirreff Collection indicate that Seguin sang regularly with the troupe until it disbanded at the conclusion of the 1838–39 season.

Table 5. Performances by the Shirreff/Wilson/Seguin Vocal-star Troupe,
11 Feb.–22 June 1839

National Theatre, New York, 11 Feb.–30 March 1839:

11 Feb. (Monday): *The Barber of Seville/Nicholas Nickleby*
12 Feb.: Same
13 Feb.: Same
14 Feb.: *The Barber of Seville/The Spitfire*
15 Feb.: Drama
16 Feb.: *Il Fanatico per la Musica/The Barber of Seville/Gentleman in Difficulties*/Musical Pasticcio (De Begnis benefit)
18 Feb. (Monday): *Amilie/The Spitfire*
19 Feb.: *Amilie/Deaf as a Post*
20 Feb.: *La Sonnambula/Nicolas Nickleby*
21 Feb.: *Fra Diavolo/The Spitfire*
22 Feb.: *Amilie/Nicholas Nickleby*
23 Feb.: *Fra Diavolo/The Spitfire*
25 Feb. (Monday): *Amilie/Crammond Brig*
26 Feb.: *La Sonnambula/The Waterman*
27 Feb.: *Amilie/Crammond Brig*
28 Feb.: *Conrad and Medora/Nicholas Nickleby*
 1 March: *Conrad and Medora/The Spitfire*
 2 March: *Amilie/Turning the Tables*
 4 March (Monday): *Rob Roy/Falls of the Clyde* [Shirreff ill]
 5 March: *Cinderella/Uncle John* [Shirreff ill]
 6 March: *Cinderella/Deep as a Post* [Shirreff ill]
 7 March: *Rob Roy/Nicholas Nickleby* [Shirreff ill]
 8 March: *Cinderella/The Spitfire* [Shirreff ill]
11 March (Monday): *Amilie/LaFitte*
12 March: *La Sonnambula/LaFitte*
13 March: *Amilie/LaFitte*
14 March: *Fra Diavolo/LaFitte*
15 March: *Love in a Village/LaFitte* (Shirreff benefit)
16 March: *Guy Mannering/LaFitte* (Wilson benefit)
18 March (Monday): *Amilie/LaFitte*
19 March: *The Marriage of Figaro*
20 March: *The Marriage of Figaro*/Concert (Seguin benefit)
21 March: *La Sonnambula/LaFitte*
22 March: *Amilie/LaFitte*
23 March: *The Marriage of Figaro/LaFitte*
25 March (Monday): *The Marriage of Figaro*/Instrumental Concert (Mitchell benefit)
26 March: *The Marriage of Figaro/The Poor Soldier*
27 March: *The Marriage of Figaro/LaFitte*

Table 5. Continued

28 March: *Amilie/Musical Pasticcio/Cinderella*
29 March: *La Sonnambula* (act 1)/*Amilie* (act 3)/*Clari; or, The Maid of Milan*
30 March: *Fra Diavolo*/Concert/*Clari; or, The Maid of Milan* (Wilson benefit)

Chestnut Street Theatre, Philadelphia, 1–27 April 1838:

1 April (Monday): *La Sonnambula*/Pas de Deux by Misses J. and H. Vallee/
  "New Fancy Gallopade" (orchestra)/*Touch and Take*
2 April: *Fra Diavolo*/Pas de Deux/*Fortune's Frolic*
3 April: *La Sonnambula*/Pas de Deux/*The Married Rake*
4 April: *Fra Diavolo*/Pas de Deux/"Parisian Gallopade" (orchestra)/*The Secret*
5 April: *La Sonnambula*/Pas de Deux/"Parisian Gallopade"/*A Day after the
  Wedding*
6 April: *Fra Diavolo*/Pas de Deux/"Parisian Gallopade"/*The Dumb Belle*
8 April (Monday): *The Marriage of Figaro*/Pas de Deux/*Raising the Wind*
9 April: *The Marriage of Figaro*/Pas de Deux/*Fortune's Frolic*
10 April: *The Marriage of Figaro*/Grand Concert (Wilson benefit)
13 April: *The Marriage of Figaro*/Pas de Deux/*The Secret*
15 April (Monday): *Cinderella*/Pas de Deux/*The Married Rake* (Shirreff benefit)
16 April: *Cinderella*/*'Twas I; or, The Truth a Lie*
17 April: *Cinderella*/*The Weathercock*
18 April: *Amilie*/Pas de Deux/*The Rival Valets*
20 April: *Amilie*/"New Fancy Gallopade"/*'Twas I; or, The Truth a Lie*
22 April (Monday): *Love in a Village*/*La Sonnambula* (act 1)/"New Fancy
  Gallopade"
23 April: *Amilie*/*The Waterman*
24 April: *The Marriage of Figaro*/*The Unfinished Gentleman*
27 April: *La Sonnambula*/*Crammond Brig* (Shirreff and Wilson benefit)

National Theatre, New York, 29 April–22 June 1839:

29 April (Monday): *The Mountain Sylph*/*John Dibbs*
30 April: *The Mountain Sylph*/*The Dumb Belle*
 1 May: *The Mountain Sylph*/*The Spitfire*
 2 May: *The Mountain Sylph*/*My Neighbor's Wife*
 3 May: *The Mountain Sylph*/*What Have I Done?*
 4 May: *The Mountain Sylph*/*What Have I Done?*
 6 May (Monday): *Amilie*/*The Original*
 7 May: *The Mountain Sylph*/*The Original*
 8 May: *La Sonnambula*/*The Original*
 9 May: *Amilie*/*What Have I Done?*
10 May: *The Mountain Sylph*/*The Original*
11 May: *The Mountain Sylph*/*The Middy Ashore*

Table 5. Continued

---

13 May (Monday): *Cinderella/The Middy Ashore*
14 May: *Cinderella/No* (operetta)
15 May: *Cinderella/The Original*
16 May: *Amilie*/Musical Pasticcio (Shirreff benefit)
17 May: *Cinderella/Gilderoy* (Wilson benefit)
20 May (Monday): *John of Paris/The Peasant Neighbor/Gilderoy*
21 May: *Amilie/The Middy Ashore*
24 May: *La Sonnambula* [in diary]/*Amilie/What Have I Done?* [in newspaper]
25 May: *Amilie/The Original*
27 May (Monday): *Amilie/The Middy Ashore*
28 May: *Fra Diavolo/The Original* (Seguin benefit)
31 May: *La Sonnambula*
 6 June: *La Gazza Ladra*
 7 June: *La Gazza Ladra*
 8 June: *La Gazza Ladra*
21 June: Wilson benefit

The National's manager took advantage of a second soprano when his first one fell ill for a simple reason: he was a businessman and was making money hand-over-fist with opera performances. No other kind of dramatic fare attracted theatrical audiences of any size. "It would be more characteristic," commented a critic in *Corsair* on 23 March 1839, "if [the National] theatre were called the Opera House, for it is to the refined and elevating entertainments which music affords, that it owes all its prosperity" (30). The comment surely was ironic; the National Theatre, of course, had been built as New York's first Italian Opera House. A writer for the *Spirit* had expressed a similar view earlier that same month. "The entertainment which is most universal and absorbing in its attractions," he wrote on 9 March, "is with us [the] Opera." So successful was the opera—and so moribund everything else Wallack tried—that he must have rued the day that he allowed his stars to leave for Philadelphia during April. When they finally returned to the National, the *Corsair*'s critic welcomed them back with open arms. "Most gladly did we read the announcement that the vocalists of the opera [have] returned to us," he wrote on 4 May. "Another week without them and the National would have been as lifeless as a dead lion. It was pleasant to witness with what alacrity the lovers of music responded to the call, and filled the house on Monday evening" (123).

The extent of the vocal stars' success at the National Theatre had taken almost everyone by surprise. Not only was *Amilie* a stunning

triumph in New York, but Wallack's operatic forces also were clearly
responsible for keeping his theater open. That his vocal stars found a
financial bonanza in the United States — and that Wallack and the other
theater managers who had engaged the singers shared in this prosperity — is obvious not only from contemporary critical acclaim published in newspapers (information that is often unreliable), but also
from the daily figures Shirreff meticulously recorded in her financial
ledger in 1839.[46]

The financial arrangement between the vocal stars and Wallack and
other theater managers was standard. The theater was guaranteed a
certain amount of each evening's take, generally between $150 and
$300, the figure varying from theater to theater depending on the size
of the house and the negotiating skills of the parties involved.[47] Daily
receipts in excess of that amount were split four ways: one part for
the theater and one for each of the three singers. In addition, each
star was allowed a benefit performance, the total proceeds of which
were split between the beneficiary and the theater management.[48]

The final engagement of the Shirreff/Wilson/Seguin vocal-star troupe
during the 1838–39 season lasted eight weeks, from 29 April through
22 June, and the amount Jane Shirreff earned during that period clearly
demonstrates the success the singers enjoyed. Because of the scheduling
of various benefit performances — hers and those of the others — her
weekly earnings varied wildly, ranging from a low of $83.56 (during a
week when there were several benefits) to a high of $481.75 (the week
of her own benefit). Her share of the earnings overall, however, was
enviable, totaling $1,165.25, roughly the 1992 equivalent of $15,250.
Shirreff and Wilson also gave three concerts in Philadelphia on 23 and
30 May and 13 June, and her earnings amounted to $252.62, or $3,307.
Jane Shirreff's total income for the eight weeks of 29 April through
22 June was $1,417.87, or $18,560 in contemporary reckoning. Over
the course of the entire 1838–39 season, during which the vocal stars
performed operas almost to the exclusion of concerts, Shirreff — despite
missing three full weeks of work — netted the handsome sum of $13,098,
approximately the equivalent of $171,450.[49]

In its 27 July 1839 issue, the *Corsair* assessed the theatrical season
just finished:

> Tragedy and the higher comedy have not lately had charms for [New
> York] audiences. . . . The tact of the manager at the National Theatre
> induced him to dash boldly into Opera, with a larger accession of vocal
> strength, all the members of which [were] entirely new to American
> hearers; to this novelty he added an Opera, not a bar of which had
> been heard in this side of the Atlantic; and to complete the charm he
> embellished his stage with fine scenery, and his actors with costly and

appropriate costumes. The public were fascinated at once; an impulse was given, in the direction of Opera, and every species of performance that could be brought to bear against it, was deeply injured in the collision. The *petite comedie,* and the *vaudeville* . . . could not stand before it. Tragedy was helpless against it; the Ballet, at the beginning of the season, sank in its opposition. . . . Even the amusements proposed by the manager of the National itself, as reliefs to opera, only served to remove the superfluity of coin from his own treasury, and proved to him that he had been another Frankenstein—had effected a creation, the force of which he had not only under-calculated, but which presently became beyond his own control. 'Amilie! Amilie!' was the universal cry, and for a while was not merely paramount, but it reigned *alone.*

Lovers of legitimate drama were not thrilled with what had happened in their theaters in 1838 and 1839. "The sweet but senseless warblings of the Rossini music," this same critic lamented on 27 July 1839, "are listened to with real or affected rapture by thousands, whilst the lofty sentiment, the pure morality, the speaking *nature* of Shakespeare, drops silently and unregarded on the dull ear of man." This was not the first time that disgruntled drama critics used the increasing popularity of opera as incontrovertible evidence of degraded public taste. During the preceding fifteen years, the public triumph of any particular vocal star had elicited similar cries of warning that public taste in general and serious drama in particular were in critical danger. After a particularly successful engagement by a vocal-star troupe that included Elizabeth Austin, Elizabeth Feron, and Charles Horn at the Park Theatre in 1829, for example, the *New-York Mirror* had observed on 11 April that "Although the fine old tragedies and comedies are found too solid and substantial fare for the light and fluttering intellects of the worthy denizens of New-York, yet opera, with its airy and graceful attractions, has found favour in their eyes, and they have flocked in considerable quantities . . . to listen to the stream of song that has been nightly poured forth at the Park theatre for this week past."

Several months later, on 13 October, the same periodical published a letter to the editor decrying the Park's engagement of vocal stars. "There is always a small number in every Community," the writer pointed out, "who prefer what some term light entertainment, consisting of Farce, low Comedy and Opera. . . . We would fain hope the wishes of those who are partial to something more intellectual and solid will now be consulted [and that] therefore, after Mrs. Knight's present engagement is concluded, there will not be another Opera produced, at least for two months."

This attitude toward opera as "light entertainment" is perhaps the best explanation for the success that the Shirreff/Wilson/Seguin troupe enjoyed in the Northeast, particularly in New York, during the 1838–39 theatrical season. Their success is even better understood given the fact that during this year parts of the Northeast, including New York, were encountering the severe economic depression that had been looming since the Panic of 1837. The fact that people generally prefer lighter entertainment to heavier dramatic fare during times of depression is a truism. What is revealing, however—especially in view of modern attitudes toward opera as serious art music—is that during this period of economic distress many Americans did indeed turn to opera. It is clear that to many Americans of the antebellum period, opera was an enjoyable, lightweight, and—above all—popular theatrical entertainment.

Shirreff and Wilson, 1839–40

At the conclusion of the final National Theatre engagement in June, Shirreff and Wilson left New York almost immediately for a summer concert tour. It was normal for singers to make concert tours in the summer months because most American theaters were dark in July and August. Performers also tended to fall back on concert tours when other engagements fell through. Shirreff and Wilson mounted concert tours during 1839 for both reasons. Their first tour, which lasted eight weeks, from 2 July through 28 August, took them through upper New York state, northern Ohio, southern Michigan, and into Canada (Table 6).

The world of a stage performer was small in the late 1830s, and North America was still part of London's cultural sphere. In July and August 1839, numerous other British artists were touring the United States and Canada, and Shirreff recorded meetings with several, including the British actress Ellen Tree; Elizabeth Richardson, the eldest daughter of the elder Joseph Jefferson and a highly esteemed singer and actress with the Park Company; and the tenor Frederick Lyster, also on a concert tour. Shirreff and Wilson probably knew all of these performers well.

Anne and Edward Seguin, along with W. H. Latham, a popular buffo singer, likewise took to the concert circuit.[50] They performed in a number of the same cities as Shirreff and Wilson, sometimes within a week of their competitors' concerts.[51] The troupes actually crossed paths in Quebec City on the last weekend in August, much to the consternation of Shirreff. When she and Wilson arrived in Quebec the morning of Friday, 30 August, they discovered that their scheduled concert had been postponed from Friday to Saturday because the Seguins, who were singing in the same hall, had changed their night

Table 6. Concert Tour of Jane Shirreff
and John Wilson, 2 July–2 Sept. 1839

2 July	Albany
8 July	Troy
9 July	Albany
12 July	Utica
13 July	Syracuse
15 July	Auburn
16 July	Syracuse
17 July	Geneva
18 July	Canandaigua
19 July	Rochester
25 July	Buffalo
30 July	Toronto
2 Aug.	Buffalo
5 Aug.	Toronto
8 Aug.	Cleveland
9 Aug.	Cleveland
12 Aug.	Detroit
13 Aug.	Detroit
16 Aug.	Buffalo
19 Aug.	Toronto
23 Aug.	Kingston
28 Aug.	Montreal
2 Sept.	Montreal

from Thursday to Friday. Before they left Montreal for Quebec, however, Shirreff and Wilson had scheduled a concert in the former city for Monday, 2 September. No transportation was available between the two cities on Sunday, and thus Shirreff and Wilson were forced to cancel their concert in Quebec and leave the city without having performed. The soprano was understandably miffed. She and Wilson ran into the Seguins in the hotel lobby on Saturday morning, and Anne Seguin "had the arrogance," Shirreff recorded in her diary on 31 August, "to speak to me as tho' nothing had happened—bah!"

Shirreff traveled with her dog, her mother, and her friend Mary Blundell; Wilson had the companionship of his wife, Mary.[52] Most of their transportation was by steamboat. Their route took them up the Hudson from New York City, then to Troy and by rail to Utica, then by canal to Syracuse and Auburn, New York. After returning to Syracuse from Auburn they continued by stage to Geneva, Canandaigua, Rochester, Niagara, and Buffalo. They traveled between Buffalo and Toronto several times by steamboat, traversed the entire length of Lake Erie, stopping for concerts in both Cleveland and Detroit, and then turned east and went the entire length of Lake Ontario, stopping for a concert in Kingston, Ontario, before heading up the St. Lawrence River to Montreal and Quebec City. From Montreal, they took a steamer down Lake Champlain; when they disembarked, they took rail cars to Whitehall, New York. From there, in Shirreff's words, they "took a canal boat and finished the journey by coach—to Saratoga . . . a lovely place" (4 September 1839). From the Springs, they went on to Troy, New York, and then by boat down the river and back to their starting point, New York City (Figure 13).

Shirreff found parts of the trip quite enjoyable. She visited the falls in Trenton Falls Gorge near modern Berneveld, New York, and was delighted by the "splendid sight." She also enjoyed the "very beautiful scenery" around Geneva at the top of Seneca Lake, one of the Finger Lakes, and spent several days at Niagara Falls, where she and her companion were enthralled at the magnificent sight.[53] The steamer trips on the Great Lakes also must have been relaxing and enjoyable. Traveling by stage was hot, dusty, and fatiguing, however, and Shirreff repeatedly noted in her diary that she was very tired, ill, hoarse, or nervous. In Niagara on 20 July she recorded that the weather was "oppressively hot" and the "room [was] so warm that [I] could not sleep"; in Kingston, Ontario, on 21 August it was still "intensely hot." Much of the singers' time during these two months was actually spent traveling. If they arrived a day or two before a concert, Shirreff spent the extra time practicing, reading, or sight-seeing.

After a week-long rest in New York in September, Shirreff and Wilson left for Philadelphia, where their operatic activities for the 1839–40 season commenced at the Chestnut Street Theatre on 16 September.[54] They sang there for two weeks, then went to Baltimore for seven performances. They performed in a vocal-star troupe with the bass William F. Brough for these two engagements (chapters 1 and 6).[55] The singers' next engagement was at the National, where they and the manager hoped to duplicate their success of the previous season. James Wallack wanted to engage his original trio of vocal stars, so Shirreff and Wilson parted company with Brough and teamed with Edward Seguin again.

Considering the extent of their success during the 1838–39 season, Shirreff and Wilson can be forgiven for expecting another triumph in 1839–40. This was not to be, however, for the 1839–40 theatrical season—to the misfortune of Shirreff, Wilson, Brough, the Seguins, Wallack, and the rest of the American theatrical community—was an unmitigated disaster. It marked the beginning of what one theater

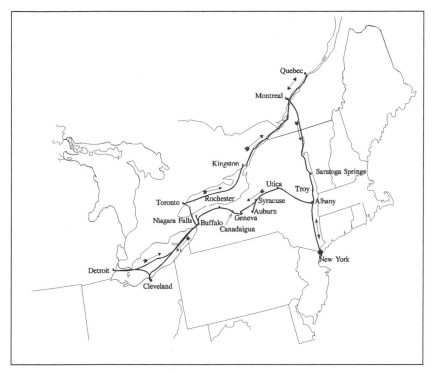

13. Itinerary of concert tour by Jane Shirreff and John Wilson, 2 July–2 September 1839. The arrows indicate the singers' travels. Shirreff and Wilson traveled from Buffalo to Toronto and back; they then journeyed by lake steamer to Cleveland and Detroit before returning to Albany. After a second stop in Toronto, they headed north. (Map by Brewer Eddy, College of William and Mary)

historian has termed "perhaps the most grievous [period] in the history of the American stage."[56] The depression that had threatened the nation for several years affected different parts of the country at different times; by late 1839, however, the economic downswing had caught up with the Northeast. Imports were down, currency was scarce, and people lost jobs. Theatrical activity, which typically flourishes during times of prosperity, came to a halt. By 16 November 1839, only two months into the season, the *New York Morning Herald* reported that "theatricals are at a low ebb in this country—[with] every principal theatre losing money, including the Park and National in New York, the Chestnut in Philadelphia, and the Tremont in Boston." Nor was the grim theatrical situation destined to be short-lived. A full year later, on 26 December 1840, the *Spirit* apologized for the dearth of theatrical news and expressed despair about the situation in general: "How all the difficulties of Managers—not in New York alone, but in Philadelphia, Boston, New Orleans, &c.—will terminate it is impossible to conjecture. It cannot be that the taste for pleasures of this kind has suddenly become extinct; but it is very sure that the conduct of a theatre is now the most disastrous business that one can attempt."

Despite the grim economic situation, the trio remained guardedly optimistic about their immediate professional future. After all, they had enjoyed unprecedented success the previous year—much of it at the National—and in the middle of October they were to reopen at the same house. Fate intervened, however, while Shirreff, Wilson, and Brough were in Philadelphia: on 23 September, Wallack's National Theatre burned to the ground. As a consequence, when Shirreff and Wilson returned to New York following the conclusion of their Baltimore engagement, they opened—again with Edward Seguin—not at the National but at Niblo's Theatre, which Wallack had rented the week after his house was consumed by flames.[57] The manager's attempt to continue his season in rented quarters, however, hampered as it was by the general theatrical malaise, ended in failure. Wallack closed his theater on 18 November. All the members of his company—and all the visiting artists engaged to appear during the upcoming season—were thrown out of work. Shirreff and Wilson did what all singers tended to do when faced with similar circumstances: they mounted another concert tour (Table 7).

The two singers probably did not set up a definite itinerary for either of their concert tours before they left New York. Both schedules were somewhat flexible so concerts could be repeated in towns where bad weather interfered with a good turn-out, or when it looked as though a second performance might draw a large crowd. After their first concert appearance in Syracuse on 13 July, for example, Shirreff noted in her diary that they had been "persuaded to return on Tuesday to give another [concert]." This lack of prior planning also had drawbacks, however, for when the two singers arrived in Boston for a concert they had planned to give on 7 November, they were unable to secure a hall and had to leave the city without giving a performance.

Whether or not the singers' itinerary was carefully arranged ahead of time, someone had to do advance work. In particular, a suitable hall had to be rented, a competent accompanist engaged, and the concert advertised. Wilson probably managed both tours; Shirreff was not bothered by such managerial details and never mentioned them in her diary. Wilson could either have traveled a day or so ahead of Shirreff to take care of arrangements or hired someone by mail to do so. Extant correspondence among performers and theater managers

Table 7. Jane Shirreff and John Wilson's Itinerary, Sept. 1839–May 1840

16–28 Sept. 1839	Chestnut Street Theatre, Philadelphia (12 opera performances)
30 Sept.–7 Oct.	Holliday Street Theatre, Baltimore (7 opera performances)
14–26 Oct.	National Theatre/Niblo's, New York City (12 opera performances)
31 Oct.	New Haven (concert)
1 Nov.	New Haven (concert)
2 Nov.	Hartford (concert)
4 Nov.	Hartford (concert)
5 Nov.	Springfield (concert)
6 Nov.	Worcester (concert)
11 Nov.	New York City (concert)
15 Nov.	New York City (concert)
21 Nov.	New York City (concert)
25 Nov.	New York City (concert)
27 Nov.	Philadelphia (concert)
29 Nov.	Philadelphia (concert)
2 Dec.	Philadelphia (concert)
4 Dec.	Baltimore (concert)
14–27 Dec.	Charleston Theatre, Charleston, S.C. (10 opera performances)
30 Dec.	Augusta (concert)
1 Jan. 1840	Augusta (concert)
3 Jan.	Augusta (concert)
6 Jan.	Savannah (concert)
7 Jan.	Savannah (concert)
8 Jan.	Savannah (concert)
9 Jan.	Savannah (concert)
10 Jan.	Savannah (concert)
11 Jan.	Savannah (concert)
18 Jan.	Charleston (concert)
22 Jan.	Norfolk (concert)
[?] Jan.	Norfolk (concert)
28 Jan.	Baltimore (concert)
29 Jan.	Washington, D.C. (concert)
30 Jan.	Baltimore (concert)
31 Jan.	Washington (concert)
1 Feb.	Baltimore (concert)
7 Feb.	Philadelphia (concert)
10 Feb.	Philadelphia (concert)
11 Feb. [?]	Philadelphia (concert)
18 Feb.	New York City (concert)
21 Feb.	New York City (concert)
26 Feb.	New York City (concert)
2 March	New York City (concert)

Table 7. Continued

6 March	New York City (concert)
13 March	New York City (concert)
30 March–13 April	Park Theatre, New York City (11 opera performances)
20 April–2 May	Chestnut Street Theatre, Philadelphia (12 opera performances)
22 May	Park Theatre (1 opera performance: Shirreff's farewell appearance and final American performance)

suggests that the latter was an accepted method of operation and was probably used by Wilson, at least for some of the necessary arrangements. Publicity for upcoming concerts never appeared in newspapers more than several days in advance, which also suggests that the singers did not work from a firm itinerary. In many towns the vocalists did not announce their concert in the newspaper at all. This was not unusual, however. In small towns during the antebellum period most publicity for public performances was accomplished by the posting of handbills.[58] Someone had to have the handbills printed and distributed, and Wilson either made such arrangements by mail or traveled to the town beforehand to take care of the task himself. Occasionally, the two singers arrived several days in advance of their planned concert date, or left to give a concert in a nearby town and then returned to the first location for a second or third performance. In either of these cases they had plenty of time to publicize an upcoming appearance.

Despite the economic depression, the popular pair of singers drew huge crowds to their fall concerts in New York and Philadelphia. According to Shirreff's financial records, they grossed $2,190 for their four New York performances and $1,927 for the three in Philadelphia. Because the price of admission to their concerts was $1, these figures translate into average crowds of 550 in New York and 640 in Philadelphia (not taking into account the inevitable deadheads, complimentary admissions, and tickets for the press). On 16 November the *New York Morning Herald* reported that "Miss Shirreff and Mr. Wilson are making immense sums by their concerts in this city." Shirreff's figures from her financial ledger confirm this statement. For the seven concerts the two singers earned $2,875 (in 1992 dollars, $37,634) after paying expenses; Shirreff's half came to $1,437 ($18,810).

The vocalists attracted these large crowds with concert repertory that was a mixture of operatic arias and popular and Scotch ballads. Their programs typically included almost equal proportions of ballads and selections from the musical stage, either English or translated Italian or French operas. A typical program—from the singers' final concert at Niblo's Grand Saloon—was printed in the *New York Morning Herald* on 25 November 1839:

PART I

Duett, "Love like a shadow flies" (Parry)	Shirreff/Wilson
Song "Who hath not mark'd?" (Rooke)	Wilson
Polacca, "Trifler, forbear" (Bishop)	Shirreff
Song, "The Flowers of the Forest" (Old Scotch Melody)	Wilson
Song, "Meet me in the Willow Glen" (A. Lee)	Shirreff
"The Meeting of the Waters" (Irish Melody) Harmonized for three voices by Maeder	Wilson, Shirreff, Maeder
"Savourneen Deelish" (Irish Ballad, S. Lover)	Wilson
Rondo, "The Rapture Dwelling" (Balfe)	Shirreff
Irish Song, "Rory O'Moore" (Lover)	Wilson
Duett, "Birks of Aberfeldie" (Old Scotch Melodie harmonized by Mr. Wilson)	Wilson, Shirreff

PART II

Scena—From the Opera of Fra Diavolo, descriptive of the life of a Brigand (Auber)	Wilson
Recitative, "My Companions are Warn'd"	
Air, "Proudly and Wide My Standard Flies"	
Recitative, "Now a poor and simple maid appears"	
Cantabile, "We never aught demand from the fair"	
Allegro, "Then since time flies so fast away"	
Scotch Song, "I'm o'er young to marry yet"	Shirreff
Song, "The land far away" (Maeder)	Wilson
Song, "Bid me discourse" (Bishop)	Shirreff
Scotch ballad, "My Boy Tammie"	Wilson
Scotch song, "The bonnie briar bush"	Shirreff

Trio, "The Last Rose of Summer" (Maeder)	Wilson, Shirreff, Maeder
Scotch song, "John Anderson, My Joe"	Wilson
Scotch song, "Oh whistle and I'll come to you my lad"	Shirreff
Old Scotch Ballad, "Tak yer auld cloak about ye"	Wilson
Duett, "Though I leave now in sorrow" (Scotch melody)	Wilson, Shirreff

Of the twenty-five selections on this concert program, nine—more than one-third—are from operas: "Who Hath not Mark'd" from *Amilie;* "Trifler, Forbear," a recitative and polacca from Henry Bishop's comic opera *The Farmer's Wife;* "The Rapture Dwelling" from Michael Balfe's *The Maid of Artois;* "Bid Me Discourse" from *Twelfth Night,* also by Bishop; and the lengthy scena from Auber's *Fra Diavolo.* Three compositions—"Meet Me in the Willow Glen" by George Alexander Lee, "Love Like a Shadow Flies" by John Parry, and James G. Maeder's "The Land Far Away"—are the only nonoperatic composed songs on the program. The other thirteen are contemporary arrangements of traditional songs, mostly Scotch or Irish. The British composers Samuel Lover and George Alexander Lee and the Bohemian Leopold Kozeluch arranged four of the songs: "Savourneen Deelish" and "Rory O'Moore" (Lover), "I'm O'er Young to Marry Yet" (Lee), and "Flowers of the Forest" (Kozeluch). For the remainder, the singers probably used either Wilson's arrangements or those by James Maeder, their accompanist for this and their other New York concerts.[59] Six of the songs later appeared in *Wilson's Edition of the Songs of Scotland,* although with slightly altered titles: "The Birks of Aberfeldy," "My Boy Tammy," "The Bonnie Briar Bush," "John Anderson, My Jo," "Whistle and I'll Come to Ye, My Lad," and "Tak' Yer Auld Cloak Aboot Ye." Maeder already had published an arrangement of Parry's "Love Like a Shadow Flies" in 1833, and his arrangements of the traditional "Meeting of the Waters" and "The Last Rose of Summer" would be published in 1840 in a collection titled *Six Irish Melodies by Thomas Moore Esq As Sung by ... Miss Shirreff, Mr. Wilson & Mr. Maeder, Harmonized for Three Voices ... by James G. Maeder.*[60] All twenty-five of the selections on the concert program are vocal works. Wilson and Shirreff included instrumental compositions on their concert programs only when they were accompanied by an orchestra, which usually occurred when the concert was in conjunction with an operatic performance. In the majority of their concert appearances, however, their accompanist was a local pianist, who almost never performed a solo instrumental work as part of the program.

Although concert selections changed from town to town, the relative percentages of opera, traditional, and nonoperatic, nontraditional songs on the program are typical. The singers chose operatic selections by Rossini ("Rapture Fills My Joyful Heart" from *La Gazza Ladra* and "Let Thine Eyes on Mine Mildly Beaming" from *Cinderella*), Balfe ("Well if I Must Speak My Mind" from *The Siege of Rochelle,* "O'er Shepherd Pipe & Rustic Dell" from *Joan of Arc,* and "Oh Hasten, Dearest Lady," from *Diadeste*), Bellini ("Goodnight, Love" from *La Sonnambula*), Donizetti ("Barcarole" from *Marino Faliero*), Adam ("Romance" and "Pastoral Aria" from *Postillion of Longjumeau*), and Hérold ("Lovely Lady Mine" from *La Pré Aux Clercs*).[61] The list includes a fair sample of Italian composers; by far, however, the majority of operatic selections included in the Shirreff and Wilson concerts were from works by Balfe, Rooke (especially from *Amilie*), and Auber (*Fra Diavolo*). A large number of the songs on this and similar concert programs were published in sheet-music form in the United States in the late 1830s and early 1840s. Many, as was usual, carry such tags as "As Sung by Miss Shirreff & Mr. Seguin"; "As Sung with Enthusiastic Applause by Mr. Wilson"; and "As Sung by Mr. Wilson in the Opera of Fra Diavolo."[62]

The vocalists' mixed bag of concert repertory met with audience approval in most places; in only one city did newspaper reports indicate otherwise. In Savannah in the winter of 1840, Shirreff and Wilson gave a series of six concerts that at first were not well patronized. The repertory of the first two concerts was similar to the program quoted previously, and after the second the reviewer from the *Savannah Republican* scolded his fellow citizens on 8 January for their poor showing. He also expressed distress that "none of the pieces were much applauded, except some of the popular street ballads." Wilson and Shirreff knew how to gauge the taste of their public, however, and henceforth gave the Savannah audiences a slightly larger dose of ballads, attracting larger audiences. On 10 January, they evidently decided that most Savannahans preferred ballads and popular tunes to operatic selections and offered a concert comprised entirely of the former. (Apparently no program from this concert survives.) The *Republican*'s critic was mortified. "We regret the selection of pieces for to-night," he wrote.

> That Mr. Wilson and Miss Shirreff are better appreciated now, than at first, is entirely owing to the influence of those who have taste enough to discriminate in such matters. When [the size of the audience is] obviously in a state of improvement, why select a whole bill of popular ballads? However, the plan will no doubt fill the house, for these ballads

have been all the go, at previous concerts, and if these distinguished strangers cannot give us the delightful strains of Rooke, Bellini, and Auber, then we are content to take such songs as Lover's 'Rory O'More.' The many-headed monster has decreed it, and it is sovereign in this country, but this same democracy is a horrid tyrant in all matters of polite accomplishments. For ourselves, we would rather hear Miss Shirreff and Mr. Wilson in their operatic selections, than all the ballads that were ever sung.

It is unclear whether musical tastes in Savannah were different from those around the country. In no other cities where Shirreff and Wilson gave concerts were such sentiments expressed in print; in no other cities, however, did they offer such unusual concert fare. For most of their concerts in the Northeast the singers performed the usual mixture of repertory and attracted audiences that were "large and fashionable," according to the *Hartford Courant* on 5 November 1839, or "very numerous and fashionable," as noted in the *Montreal Gazette* on 29 August. In New York and Philadelphia, the singers had no trouble whatsoever attracting "most crowded" houses as reported the *New York Morning Herald* on 12 November and "immense numbers of persons" according to the *Philadelphia National Gazette* on 28 November. Even in the small towns of upper New York state—Utica, Syracuse, Geneva, Canandaigua, and Rochester—the vocalists regularly attracted between fifty and a hundred paid audience members for each concert, according to Shirreff's financial records. All of these audiences—residents of both large cities and small towns—were attracted by programs that regularly included both operatic airs and ballads.

The Operatic Repertory of Jane Shirreff and John Wilson

Jane Shirreff and John Wilson sang in more than 230 opera productions in this country over the course of some eleven months. They relied on a repertory of twenty-one operas (Table 8). This number is deceptively high, however, for in reality the singers used only a half-dozen works as war-horses: *Amilie* (sixty-one productions), *La Sonnambula* (fifty-five), *Fra Diavolo* (thirty-one), *Cinderella* (twenty-two), *The Postillion of Longjumeau* (twenty-two), and *The Marriage of Figaro* (thirteen). The remaining fifteen works—including ballad, English comic, French, and Italian operas—were performed fewer than ten times each, sometimes as afterpieces (Tables 9 and 10.)

A limited repertory was typical for vocal-star troupes. In 1838 a critic in the *Spirit* had praised Maria Caradori-Allan for limiting her performances during a New York engagement to three operas, *Cinderella, The Barber of Seville,* and *La Sonnambula.* "In thus circum-

Table 8. Repertory Performed by the Various Vocal-star Troupes of Jane Shirreff and John Wilson, 1839–40 Theatrical Season

Chestnut Street Theatre, Philadelphia, 16–28 Sept. 1839:

16 Sept. (Monday): *La Sonnambula/Gretna Green*
17 Sept.: *La Sonnambula/Perfection*
18 Sept.: *Fra Diavolo/The Secret*
19 Sept.: *Cinderella/The Wedding Day*
20 Sept.: *Fra Diavolo/The Rival Valets*
21 Sept.: *Cinderella/Chaos Is Come Again*
23 Sept. (Monday): *The Marriage of Figaro/Luke the Laborer*
[?] Sept.: *Love in a Village/*Vocal Concert*/The Married Rake* (Brough benefit)
25 Sept.: *The Marriage of Figaro/Chaos Is Come Again*
26 Sept.: *Native Land/*Vocal Concert (Shirreff benefit)
27 Sept.: *Native Land/The Spoil'd Child!*
28 Sept.: *Fra Diavolo/Crammond Brig* (Wilson benefit)

Holliday Street Theatre, Baltimore, 30 Sept.–8 Oct. 1839

30 Sept. (Monday): *La Sonnambula/Oh, What Fun*
 1 Oct.: *Cinderella/*Miss Gannon (dancer)*/The Handsome Husband*
 2 Oct.: *Fra Diavolo/Bottle Imp*
 3 Oct.: *Fra Diavolo/Maid of Croissey*
 4 Oct.: *La Sonnambula/Loan of a Lover*
 5 Oct.: *Native Land/Crammond Brig* (Wilson benefit)
 6 Oct.: *The Marriage of Figaro/*Miscellaneous Concert*/Fra Diavolo* (last act) (Shirreff benefit)
 8 Oct. (Monday): *Maid of Croissey/Tom and Jerry* (Wilson benefit)

National Theatre (at Niblo's), New York City, 14–26 Oct. 1839:

14 Oct. (Monday): *Amilie/Schoolfellow*
15 Oct.: *Amilie/Raising the Wind*
16 Oct.: *Amilie/Robert Macaire*
17 Oct.: *La Sonnambula/My Young Wife and Old Umbrella*
18 Oct.: *La Sonnambula/Schoolfellow*
19 Oct.: *La Sonnambula/My Young Wife and Old Umbrella*
21 Oct. (Monday): *Gustavus III/My Young Wife and Old Umbrella*
22 Oct.: *Gustavus III/Middy Ashore*
23 Oct.: *Gustavus III/What Have I Done?*
24 Oct.: *Gustavus III/*Vocal Concert (Seguin benefit?)
25 Oct.: *Gustavus III/*Vocal Concert (Wilson benefit)
26 Oct.: *Gustavus III/*Vocal Concert (Shirreff benefit)

Charleston Theatre, Charleston, S.C., 14–27 Dec. 1839:

14 Dec.: *La Sonnambula*
16 Dec. (Monday): *La Sonnambula/The Handsome Husband*

Table 8. Continued

17 Dec.: *Fra Diavolo/Rendezvous*
18 Dec.: *Fra Diavolo/The Dumb Belle*
19 Dec.: *Cinderella/The Lottery Ticket*
20 Dec.: *La Sonnambula/Crammond Brig*
21 Dec.: *Rob Roy/Married Rake*
23 Dec. (Monday): *Cinderella/The Dumb Belle*
24 Dec.: *Fra Diavolo/Crammond Brig*
26 Dec.: *Native Land/The Lottery Ticket*
27 Dec.: *Native Land*/Songs from *Amilie* (Shirreff benefit)

Park Theatre, New York City, 30 March–13 April 1840:

30 March (Monday): *Postillion of Longjumeau/Katherine and Petruchio*
31 March: *The Postillion of Longjumeau/A Roland for an Oliver*
 1 April: *The Postillion of Longjumeau/Dancing Barber*
 2 April: *The Postillion of Longjumeau/Young Widow*
 3 April: *The Postillion of Longjumeau/Court of Old Fritz*
 4 April: *The Postillion of Longjumeau/Court of Old Fritz*
 6 April (Monday): *The Postillion of Longjumeau/Crammond Brig* (Wilson benefit)
 8 April: *La Sonnambula*/Dancers/ Instrumental Concert/*M. P.* (Giubilei benefit)
 9 April: *The Postillion of Longjumeau/The Review*
10 April: *The Postillion of Longjumeau/Clari; or, The Maid of Milan* (Shirreff benefit)
13 April (Monday): *La Sonnambula/State Secrets*

Chestnut Street Theatre, Philadelphia, 20 April–2 May 1840:

20 April: *The Postillion of Longjumeau/The Dumb Belle*
21 April: *The Postillion of Longjumeau/Little Black Parlour*
22 April: *The Postillion of Longjumeau/Mrs. White*
23 April: *The Postillion of Longjumeau/My Uncle John*
24 April: *The Postillion of Longjumeau/A Day After the Wedding*
25 April: *The Postillion of Longjumeau/The Maid of Croissey*
27 April (Monday): *The Postillion of Longjumeau/Touch and Take*
28 April: *Fra Diavolo/Turning the Tables*
29 April: *La Sonnambula/My Uncle John*
30 April: *The Postillion of Longjumeau/Loan of a Lover* (Shirreff benefit)
 1 May: *The Postillion of Longjumeau/Midas* (Giubilei benefit)
 2 May: *The Postillion of Longjumeau/Crammond Brig* (Wilson benefit)

Park Theatre, New York City, 21 May 1840:

21 May: *The Postillion of Longjumeau/Loan of a Lover* (Shirreff farewell benefit)

Table 9. Operatic Repertory of Jane Shirreff and John Wilson

1838–39 Season:

	New York City Oct.	Boston Nov.	Rhode Island Nov.	New York City Dec.	Washington, D.C. Dec.	Baltimore Jan.	Philadelphia Jan.	New York City Feb.-March	Philadelphia April	New York City May-June	Total [as of June 1839]
Amilie; or, The Love Test	14	5	—	5	2	4	6	11	3	7	57
La Sonnambula	—	8	—	8	2	4	8	5	5	2	42
Clari; or, The Maid of Milan	—	1	1	—	—	—	—	2[a]	—	—	1(2[a])
Guy Mannering	—	1	2	—	—	—	[1]	1	—	—	4[1]
The Waterman	2[a]	1	1	—	—	—	—	2[a]	1[a]	—	1(5[a])
Love in a Village	—	—	1	—	—	—	—	—	—	1	2
Rob Roy	—	—	1	—	—	—	—	[2]	—	—	1[2]
Fra Diavolo	—	—	—	4	2	2	5	4	3	1	21
Crammond Brig	—	—	—	1[a]	—	2[a]	—	2[a]	1[a]	—	6[a]
Cinderella	—	—	—	—	—	2	[4]	[3],1[a]	3	4	9[7](1[a])
The Mountain Sylph	—	—	—	—	—	—	—	—	—	9	9
La Gazza Ladra	—	—	—	—	—	—	—	—	—	3	3
The Barber of Seville	—	—	—	—	—	—	—	[5]	—	—	[5]
Conrad and Medora	—	—	—	—	—	—	—	2	—	—	2
John of Paris	—	—	—	—	—	—	—	—	—	1	1
Il Fanatico	—	—	—	—	—	—	—	[1]	—	—	[1]
The Marriage of Figaro	—	—	—	—	—	—	—	6	5	—	11
The Poor Soldier	—	—	—	—	—	—	—	1[a]	—	—	1[a]
Total performances	14(2[a])	15	5	17(1[a])	6	12	19[5](2[a])	29[11](8[a])	19(2[a])	27	164[16](15[a])

Table 9. Continued.

	Phila-delphia Sept.	Balti-more Oct.	New York City Oct.	Charles-ton Dec.	New York City March-April	Phila-delphia April-May	New York City May	Total [as of May 1840]
1839–40 Season:								
Amilie; or, The Love Test	—	—	3	1	—	—	—	4
La Sonnambula	2	3	3	2	2	1	—	13
Clari; or, The Maid of Milan	—	—	—	—	1[a]	—	—	1[a]
Love in a Village	1	—	—	—	—	—	—	1
Rob Roy	—	—	—	1	—	—	—	1
The Elixir of Love	—	—	—	—	1	—	—	1
Fra Diavolo	3	3	—	3	—	1	—	10
Crammond Brig	1[a]	—	—	1[a]	1[a]	1[a]	—	4[a]
Cinderella	2	1	—	2	—	—	—	5
The Postillion of Longjumeau	—	—	—	—	11	10	1	22
Gustavus III	—	—	6	—	—	—	—	6
The Marriage of Figaro	2	—	—	—	—	—	—	2
Native Land	2	1	—	2	—	—	—	5
Total performances	12(1[a])	8	12	11(1[a])	13(2[a])	12(1[a])	1	69(5[a])

[ ] = Performances in which Jane Shirreff did not participate because of illness.
[a] = Afterpieces.

Table 10. Total Number of Performances of Operatic Repertory,
1838–40

Amilie; or, The Love Test (Rooke)	61
La Sonnambula (Bellini)	55
Clari; or, The Maid of Milan (Bishop)	1(3ª)
Guy Mannering (La dame blanche)	4(1ª)
Rob Roy (Davy)	[2]
The Waterman (Dibdin)	1(5ª)
Love in a Village (Arne)	3
The Elixir of Love (Donizetti)	1
Fra Diavolo (Auber)	31
Crammond Brig	10ª
Cinderella (Rossini)	14(1ª)[7]
The Postillion of Longjumeau (Adam)	22
The Mountain Sylph (Barnett)	9
Gustavus III (Auber)	6
La Gazza Ladra (Rossini)	3
The Barber of Seville (Rossini)	[5]
Conrad and Medora	2
Native Land (Bishop)	4
John of Paris (Boieldieu)	1
Il Fanatico (Mayr)	[1]
The Marriage of Figaro (Mozart)	13
The Poor Soldier (Shield)	1ª
Total	233(21ª)[15]

[ ] = Performances in which Jane Shirreff did not participate because of illness.
ª = Afterpieces.

scribing the range of the entertainments," he explained on 27 January,
"they become vastly more pleasing. The choruses are more perfect,
each subordinate more familiar with his part, and above all, the audience
become familiar with the music."

The all-important role of the stock company was critical in the
question of repertory, for most theatrical troupes knew only a limited
number of operatic works. Furthermore, the fewer the number of
operas that a visiting troup mounted during an engagement, the easier
it was for the local company. A relatively small repertory meant fewer
opera choruses for the stock-company players to rehearse, less scenery
and stage machinery for the theater to have painted or built, and fewer
costumes for the stage manager to dredge up for the stock-company
performers to wear. (The vocal stars traveled with their own costumes.)
On the other hand, although the stock companies' repertories were

small, they usually included the most popular operas—the works the vocal-star troupes were most likely to perform. Visiting performers, whether dramatic or musical, did not come to the United States to educate or edify the American public or to raise musical or theatrical standards. They came to make money, and the Shirreff/Wilson repertory of crowd-pleasing works reflects this goal. Two of the singers' six war-horses were new operas, each produced as a calculated risk that it might turn into a big hit. A third work, *The Marriage of Figaro,* was familiar to Americans, although it did not enjoy nearly the popularity of *Cinderella, La Sonnambula,* and *Fra Diavolo.*[63]

Taken as a whole, Shirreff and Wilson's total repertory appears to be an odd mixture of different operatic styles, especially the combination of Italian operas (with sung recitative) and French and English comic operas (which had spoken dialogue). As mentioned previously, however, all the foreign-language works produced by vocal-star troupes were given in versions adapted to the English stage by such composers as Sir Henry Rowley Bishop and Michael Rophino Lacy (chapter 1). Few contemporary reviews or advertisements mention any translator or adaptor, but the versions the vocal stars used in the United States undoubtedly were the same adaptations in which they had performed in London. The six operas performed most frequently by Wallack's troupe included five translation-adaptations by Bishop (*Sonnambula* and *The Marriage of Figaro*), Lacy (*Fra Diavolo* and *La Cenerentola,* renamed *Cinderella; or, The Fairy Queen and the Little Glass Slipper*), and J. B. Phillips (*The Postillion of Longjumeau*). *Amilie,* of course, was written in English.

Americans, like the British, were fond of songs with their plays, especially songs that could be hummed or sung and played on parlor pianos. Too much concerted music was frowned upon, and adaptors either frequently eliminated long concerted pieces or turned them into strophic songs. The comments of some critics suggest, however, that even concerted pieces were popular, especially if the melodies were pleasing and singable. Writing about *Amilie* on 31 December 1838, for example, a Baltimore journalist predicted in the *American and Commercial Daily Advertiser* that the new opera would prove popular with audiences because, like *La Sonnambula* (which he called "overwhelmingly popular"), it was "so filled with concerted music, that the chorusses are hardly for an instant off the stage through the entire course." Most Americans were fond of operas with "lively and melodious music" or operas whose melodies they could "hum, sing, or whistle . . . as they return to their respective homes."[64] Whether the source of that melody was an aria, a chorus, or an instrumental piece seems to have been unimportant.

Other than frequency of performance, another ready gauge of an opera's popularity was whether singers used it for their benefits. During the 1838–39 season, each of the three stars in the Shirreff/Wilson/ Seguin troupe usually had one benefit performance per engagement. The beneficiary split half the evening's take with the theater, and the other star artists volunteered their services in exchange for reciprocal treatment for their own benefits. If an opera was in the midst of a successful run, a singer normally used that work for his or her benefit. During the troupe's opening engagement in New York, when *Amilie* was drawing such good houses, all three of the stars chose that opera for their benefits. Likewise, in Boston the following month both Shirreff and Seguin used *La Sonnambula*. During other engagements, however, their choices varied. A singer's identity with a particular opera or character, such as Shirreff's with *Amilie,* was an important factor in the choice, as was the track record of that work in a particular theater. The operas that the singers chose during the 1838–39 season, not surprisingly, had proved their popularity by frequency of performance. Shirreff used *La Sonnambula* four times, *Amilie* three, *Cinderella* twice, and *Love in a Village* once. Seguin twice chose *Amilie, La Sonnambula, Fra Diavolo,* and *The Marriage of Figaro* and once used *Cinderella;* Wilson performed in *Fra Diavolo* three times, *Guy Mannering* twice, and *Amilie, Cinderella,* and *La Sonnambula* once each.

For a benefit performance, the farce by the stock company generally was omitted, and either an English comic opera (such as *Crammond Brig, Clari; or, The Maid of Milan,* or *The Waterman*) or a vocal concert or "musical pasticcio" was performed instead. Vocal selections also sometimes were added to a normal evening's entertainment as added attractions performed after the opera, interpolated into it, or sung between the opera and the farce. Each singer had a standard repertory, for he or she performed the same songs over and over, regardless of whether the selections were sung in post-opera concerts or interpolated into the operas themselves. Most of the extra songs that Shirreff and Wilson sang as part of their operatic performances also appeared on their concert programs.

John Wilson was well known for his Scottish songs and often sang such traditional tunes as "John Anderson, My Jo," "My Boy Tammie," "The Lass of Gowrie," and "Tak Yer Auld Cloak Aboot Ye."[65] All four of these pieces were in his *Songs of Scotland* (1842), and he also included them in "Songs of Scotland" entertainments. Although most of his songs were Scotch, Irish, or English ballads, he did occasionally perform operatic selections, such as the "Celebrated Cavatina of 'Vivi tu' " from Donizetti's *Anna Bolena,* which he introduced in English into a performance of *Cinderella* in Philadelphia, according to the *Pennsylvanian*

on 5 February 1839. Most of the songs that Jane Shirreff sang in
connection with opera performances were likewise popular ballads, for
example, "Comin' thru the Rye." The songs that she performed most
frequently in the United States, however, were "I'm O'er Young to
Marry Yet" and "Whistle and I'll Come to Thee, My Lad," both Scotch
songs in contemporary arrangements. She also occasionally sang selections from the operatic stage, such as "Pappataci" from Rossini's *L'Italiana in Algeri* and "The Rapture Dwelling," a "Grand Scene" from
Balfe's *The Maid of Artois*.[66]

Edward Seguin's song choices tended to be more from the musical
stage and less from the ballad repertory. Although during the 1838–
39 season he did not become readily identified with any one particular
selection, he frequently performed the aria "Non più andrai" from
Mozart's *The Marriage of Figaro* and "Qui sdegno" ("In diesen heilgen
Hallen") from *The Magic Flute*.[67] Because he sang in these operas, it
is safe to assume that he performed the selections in translation despite
the fact that they were always identified in advertisements and on
playbills in Italian. Seguin also frequently performed selections from
La Sonnambula ("As I View These Scenes so Charming") and *Amilie*
("What Is the Spell?").[68] When the stars sang joint vocal selections as
duos or trios, they also tended to use repertory from the operatic stage,
such as "Donque oi Sono" (probably "Dunque io son" from *The Barber
of Seville*), "Sir, a Secret," from *Cinderella*, and "Vadasi via di qua,"
the "Laughing Trio" from a Terzetto by the French opera composer
Jean Paul Egide Martini (1741–1816).

The following program is typical of after-opera fare as performed
by the Shirreff/Wilson/Seguin troupe during the 1838–39 season. The
artists, with the help of Mr. Walton of the National Theatre in New
York, gave this concert to benefit Jane Shirreff after a performance of
Amilie in Philadelphia on 21 January 1839, as reported in the *Pennsylvanian*.

CONCERT

Grand Overture [orchestra]	
"Non Piu andre" by Mozart	Mr. Seguin
Finale—"The Rapture Dwelling" from	
the Opera of The Maid of Artois	Miss Shirreff
The admired Scotch Ballad of "John	
Anderson, My Joe"	Mr. Wilson
"I'm o'er young to marry yet"	Miss Shirreff
"Life on the Ocean Wave"	Mr. Walton
Laughing Trio, "Vadasi Via di Qua"	Miss Shirreff, Mr. Wilson, Mr. Seguin

Concerts that followed opera productions often included some in-strumental music, such as the unidentified "Grand Overture" mentioned above. Most instrumental works are identified only vaguely on playbills or in advertisements. During the company's first Philadelphia engage-ment in 1839, for example, the Chestnut Street Theatre's orchestra performed "General Bertrand's Farewell to France, a favorite song arranged as a Gallopade, by F. Wieland," the "New Cotillion from Robert le Diable," a "New Wiener Gallopade," and a "Trumpet Gal-lopade."[69] During their second New York engagement, the stars gave a concert to conclude a performance at the National Theatre on 20 December. The selections included Strauss's "Waltz Apollo," "as ar-ranged by the orchestra leader William Penson," an unidentified clarinet concerto, and "National Air and Variations for Violin as composed and played by Sig. Bassini" of the theater's orchestra.[70] Occasionally, a program even included a piece of chamber music, for example, the "Quintetto composed by J. Kiffner, for cor de basset, clarinet, flute, horn, and trombone, to be performed by members of the orchestra" that was part of the evening's entertainment in Philadelphia on 8 January 1839.[71] Overtures, however, were by far the most common instrumental selections performed as part of an operatic production. By the late 1820s and early 1830s these overtures, entirely severed from the operas for which they had been written, had been appropriated by American theater orchestras as an ordinary part of their repertories. An overture frequently was performed between an opera and the farce that con-cluded the evening's performance, and also before the commencement of a dramatic work. Critics complained about the overuse of operatic overtures. As early as 1830, the overtures from *The Caliph of Bagdad* (Boieldieu), *The Marriage of Figaro, Masaniello* (Auber), *Der Freischütz,* and *The Barber of Seville,* according to a critic for the *Dramatic Mirror* on 23 October, had become "worn out" because of "continual and hacknied use" (126).

It was normal performance practice during the period for vocal stars to interpolate songs into whatever opera was being produced (chapter 1). Playbills often include the information that extra songs would be introduced, but it is almost impossible to fathom which songs were introduced, and when and where. Most playbills and advertisements are no more specific than the Shirreff playbill from the National Theatre in New York for 19 December 1838, which informed the audience that "during the evening and in the course of the Burletta [*Crammond Brig*] the following [listed] songs" would be sung. Only rarely is a playbill or an advertisement more explicit. It is safe to conclude, how-ever, that songs were freely interpolated into opera performances, especially in view of the lengthy lists of extra songs named in advertisements and on playbills.

Conclusion

Many of the entries that Jane Shirreff made in her diary show clearly that the 1839–40 tour—especially the southern part—was fraught with inconveniences and irritations from its very beginning. The concert room in Baltimore was unsuitable, as was the accompanist ("such an accompanist, ye Gods! defend me!" Shirreff wrote on 4 December). Transportation south from Maryland was uncomfortable, dirty, and unpleasant, especially the portion by stage over corduroy roads between Portsmouth, Virginia, and Wilmington, North Carolina, and the food available en route was "nasty," "nauseous," and "disgusting."[72] To heap insult on injury, the artists' baggage, music and costumes arrived in Charleston almost a week late, causing cancellation of five opera performances (Figure 14).

The theater audiences in Charleston, according to Shirreff, were not only meagre, but they were also the "dull[est] and most uninteresting and disagreeable . . . I have ever played to in America" (16 December 1839). Shirreff's complaints, in fact, were endless. The hotel in Augusta, Georgia, was "cheerless, cold and comfortless" (30 December), the climate in the South was "unhealthy" (23 December), and the weather cold, rainy, or just plain "cold and wretched in the extreme" (31 December). It is clear that by late 1839 Jane Shirreff was more than ready to pack her bags and head home to London; several times during December she expressed a sentiment she had first voiced on 7 August: "Oh, how I long to end my exile!"

The two singers concluded their stay in the United States as they had begun it, with opera performances in New York and Philadelphia. Their twenty months in North America had been busy and full of both success and failure, of good luck and bad. Shirreff and Wilson had arrived in this country at the beginning of a severe national economic depression. The soprano had fallen seriously ill in the middle of her first dramatic season, and at the beginning of the second the theater in which she and Wilson had given most of their performances had burned to the ground. Despite such troubles, the tour was an artistic and financial success. Jane Shirreff performed in 237 operas, and Wilson, who had not missed any due to illness, appeared in 253. The two gave a total of seventy concert performances. They sang in eleven states, two Canadian provinces, and the District of Columbia, and covered approximately nine thousand miles. The various concert and opera tours differed in repertory, itinerary, length, personnel, fi-

Theatre.

FRA DIAVOLO

Will be repeated This Evening, for the Last Time.

Miss Shirreff

AS ZERLINA.

Mr. Wilson

AS FRA DIAVOLO.

MR. LATHAM
AS LORD ALLCASH.

This Evening, Wednesday, Dec. 18th,

Will be performed Auber's Grand Opera of

FRA DIAVOLO:

OR, THE

INN OF TERRACINA!

Fra Diavolo, Disguised as Marquis San Carlo,	-	*Mr. Wilson.*
Lord Allcash,	-	*Mr. Latham.*
Lorenzo,	-	Mr. A'Becket.
Beppo,	-	Mr. Sherman.
Giacomo,	-	Mr. Sprague.
Matteo,	-	Mr. McCann.
1st Carbineer,	-	Mr. Reed.
2d do.	-	Mr. Merceron.
3d do.	-	Mr. Beck.
Francesco,	-	Mr. Clifford.
Zerlina,	-	*Miss Shirreff.*
Lady Allcash,	-	Mrs. Timm.

Bridesmaids, Peasants, &c. by

A POWERFUL CHORUS!

Previous to the Opera.

Auber's Splendid Overture!

To conclude with, first time this season, the Farce of THE

DUMB BELLE!

Vivian,	-	Mr. Weston.
Smirk,	-	Mr. Hautonville.
Mr. Manvers,	-	Mr. McCann.
James,	-	Mr. Clifford.
Eliza,	-	Mrs. Timm.
Mary,	-	Mrs. Hautonville.

Leader of the Orchestra, Mr. Marks.

Director of Music, - Mr. Timm.

MISS SHIRREFF, MR. WILSON
And MR. LATHAM
WILL APPEAR TO-MORROW EVENING.

Stage Manager, - Mr. Fuller.

Places for the BOXES and PARQUET, to be had of Mr. Melton, at the
Office of the Theatre daily, from 10 till 2 o'clock.
Boxes and Parquet, $1; Third Tier, 50 Cents. Entrance at the north side
door. Doors to be opened at half past 6, the performance to commence at
7, o'clock, precisely. Tickets admissible only on the Night they are issued.

Printed at the Office of BURGES & JAMES, Charleston.

14. Playbill from a performance of Auber's *Fra Diavolo* at the Charleston (S.C.) Theatre on 18 December 1839. Jane Shirreff and John Wilson, along with W. H. Latham, who was associated with the Charleston Theatre, took the starring roles in this performance. (Billy Rose Theatre Collection, New York Public Library)

nances, and incidental circumstances, but, as a whole, they represent the experiences of vocal-star troupes active during the period.

During the final eleven months of their visit, from summer 1839 through spring 1840, the two singers each earned $4,675 ($61,196 in 1992 dollars) from concerts and $3,975 ($52,032) from opera performances, for a combined amount of $8,650 ($113,228). Jane Shirreff's total earnings for her twenty months' work in the United States (in 1992 dollars) was $284,678. If the 1839–40 theatrical season had not been such an economic disaster, it is plausible that the singers might have earned even more Yankee dollars to take back to London in the spring of 1840. As it was, the influence of these two vocalists on the development of American musical culture during the 1840s must have been significant. They were an important part of an opera craze that was centered in New York, and their success at the National Theatre in 1838–39 spurred the Park Theatre to import its own troupe. Furthermore, Shirreff and Wilson's phenomenal financial success in North America undoubtedly encouraged other British musicians to try their luck on American audiences during the 1840s and 1850s, thereby increasing the number of professional musical performers and performances in the United States.

The artistic and financial success that Jane Shirreff and John Wilson enjoyed is a strong indication of how important entertainment was to Americans of the antebellum period and how important staged operas and operatic-ballad concerts were within the arena of entertainment. Their success demonstrates clearly that operas and operatic music were important to Americans all over the eastern part of the United States in the late 1830s and early 1840s, even during times of economic hardship.

3

Italian Opera Companies, 1825–60

"Of making opera troupes there is no end." So would Mrs. Browning be likely to say if she lived in America and witnessed the many vain and impotent attempts to establish here a permanent and creditable institution of opera. Five and forty times at least within the recollection of the past few years, have the leading operatic managers of the land been utterly undone, ruined, swamped and devoted to everlasting disgrace. Five and forty times, at least, have broken-hearted paragraphs been scattered through the newspapers, announcing the fatal fact that Maximilian Maretzek, B. Ullman, Esq. or some equally eminent master of the art of humbug has at length retired in a disordered mental condition to the seclusion of private life and the mortification of sackcloth and ashes. Experience lessens all great evils. It is said the eels become in time accustomed to the skinning process. Just so must it be with operatic managers.[1]

The history of the performance of Italian opera in Italian in the United States during the antebellum period is a story of both failure and success. It is a tale of shattered dreams, lost fortunes, failed individuals, bankrupt managers, and disbanded companies. But it also is a chronicle of successful premieres, debuts, and gala benefits, of fame and adulation won, of reputations enhanced, and of fortunes made. It is a history of perseverance and determination, a story of singers, instrumentalists, and impresarios who banded together again and again in new versions of the same troupes, always in search of the magical combination of big-name stars, popular repertory, favorable performing conditions, and receptive audiences, all in search of that elusive goal, the successful season.

The story of the gradual emergence of opera in Italian in the antebellum period is also bound up with a related issue: the slow but almost insidious expropriation of this musical-theatrical form by the

wealthy and elite of American society, and the increasing exclusion
from these performances of the other social classes that traditionally
had been a normal part of the American theater audience. How the
wealthy undertook the task of transforming opera from an ordinary
component of the popular theater repertory into an art form widely
identified as aristocratic and exclusive—and to a certain extent succeeded in doing so—is a complex story that will be addressed in this
chapter. That the elite did not entirely succeed in this goal—or, at
least, did not entirely succeed during the antebellum period—is a lesser-
known side of that development. It, too, will form an important part
of this discussion of Italian opera companies in antebellum America.

From 1825 through 1846, Italian operatic activity in the United States
was rather sparse and intermittent. The situation changed considerably
after 1847, for by that watershed year (although it was not apparent
at the time) the fight to establish foreign-language opera in the United
States was well on its way to being won. During each year after 1846—
usually simultaneously—three to six different companies were performing staged operas in Italian somewhere in the United States. All
of these troupes were itinerant (the establishment of the first resident
Italian troupe had to wait until 1883, with the founding of the New
York Metropolitan Opera Company), and the personnel of each company changed constantly.[2] The troupes existed, however, and not only
were they active, but they also mounted staged performances of operas
in Italian in numbers almost incomprehensible today.

The wealth of activity after 1847 was a direct result of the foundation
built by the earlier companies. Consequently, it is important to examine
in some detail the troupes that toured during the period from 1825
though 1847. This approach, however, is impossible for each of the
many companies active from 1848 through 1860. The sheer number
of troupes, their wide-ranging and overlapping itineraries, the changing
names under which they appeared, and the constantly fluctuating nature
of their personnel make the operatic history of this period an almost
hopeless jumble.

Although I have detailed the activities of the several companies in
1847, the latter part of this chapter is principally a brief summary of
operatic performances by itinerant troupes during the period from 1848
through 1860. The basis for the summary—the hard data assembled
about Italian troupes active in this country during those years—is
presented in tabular form in Appendix C. The second part of this
chapter, then, should be read in the context of this voluminous sup-
plementary information.

1825–46: Laying the Groundwork

The Garcías

Manuel García's Italian Opera Company, the first Italian opera troupe to perform in the United States, was a traveling company only in the broadest terms; in 1825 the singers traveled here from London, performed exclusively in New York for a year, and then left for Mexico. Because the influence of this troupe on subsequent itinerant Italian opera companies in the United States was significant, however, it is appropriate to commence this discussion with the arrival of the García Company.

In the summer of 1825, one Dominick Lynch, a wealthy New York wine merchant, member of the bon ton, and a music lover, traveled to London to recruit opera singers. Lynch was a prominent member of a group of wealthy New York socialites who were interested in promoting elite cultural activities. His trip to London was on their behalf, but he also had the essential backing of Stephen Price, the manager of the Park Theatre.[3] Price (1782–1840), who had become manager of that house in 1808, made frequent recruiting trips to London himself, and he made a point to keep himself informed about the theatrical attractions, including Italian opera, that drew fashionable audiences in England.[4] In 1825, he and his partner Edmund Simpson had ample reason to be interested in novel theatrical fare, for the previous year their house had faced some serious competition from an upstart rival, the Chatham Theatre. Although a season of Italian opera in New York was something of a financial long shot in 1825—two years before the arrival of Elizabeth Austin—Lynch discovered that Price and Simpson were amenable to the idea of bringing a troupe to the United States, especially because the proposal had the support of a least a portion of New York's high society.[5]

In London, Lynch attempted, unsuccessfully, to interest a number of prominent singers, including Maria Caradori-Allan and Giuditta Pasta, in a New York opera season.[6] Although originally rebuffed, Lynch eventually managed to recruit an entire troupe, albeit a small one, the leader and patriarch of which was the prolific composer, distinguished teacher, and excellent and well-known Spanish singer and actor Manuel del Popolo Vicente Rodriguez García (1775–1832).

How Lynch induced García to forsake London for New York is unknown; Lawrence suggests that the great Italian soprano Giuditta Pasta, a friend of the Garcías, had a hand in the negotiations.[7] Whether or not this allegation is true, it is certain that practical considerations played a major part in García's decision. The tenor himself, for example, was not enjoying a particularly successful season in London that year. He was fifty years old, and his voice, according to the London *Harmonicon*, was "half worn out"[8] Although nearing the end of his own performing days, García was a shrewd businessman and opera manager. He also had two offspring who were fledgling operatic performers: Manuel, Jr., a bass, and Maria Felicità, a contralto. He knew that the standards of New York audiences were lower than those of their London counterparts and that a season of performances in America would provide excellent training for his son and daughter. Furthermore, because his projected company included three members of his own family, the overhead costs of the troupe were extraordinarily low. The risks seemed reasonable, and the terms offered by Lynch and Price acceptable. So García signed a contract, gathered his company together, and boarded a ship headed west.

The Italian Opera Company arrived in New York on 6 November 1825.[9] The principal singers of the troupe numbered eight: the manager, Manuel García, a tenor; his wife, Maria Joaquina Stiches, a soprano; Manuel García, Jr. (1805–1906), a twenty-year-old bass; the seventeen-year-old mezzo-soprano Maria Felicità (1808–36), who later would be renowned as Maria Malibran; Madame Barbieri (or Barbiere), a soprano; Giovanni (or Domenico) Crivelli, second tenor and chorus master; Felix Angrisani, a distinguished bass; and Paolo Rosich, basso buffo and librettist. Several other Italians who were listed on the ship's passenger list as "of the Italian Opera" served as support crew and chorus. These included Don Fabian, Giovanni Cardini, Cristoforo Constantini, Giuseppe Pasta (a tenor and the husband of Giuditta Pasta), and Signor Ferri (a singer and set designer) and his wife.[10] Although García brought no instrumental musicians, the orchestra of the Park Theatre was expanded to assist in the opera performances. As early as September, the theater's management had announced the engagement of a "double band" for the season.[11] For the performances by the García Company, the orchestra numbered twenty-six: seven violins (six, according to Nelson), two violas, three cellos, two double-basses, two flutes, two clarinets, one bassoon, two horns, two trumpets, two timpani, and piano. The ensemble was one of the largest and most complete orchestras that had ever been assembled in the United States.[12]

The company made its debut on 29 November 1825 in *Il barbiere di Siviglia*. García's choice of an opening opera indicates his astute business sense. The work had an extraordinary personal advertising value for the vocalist—Rossini had written the part of Almaviva for García, and the tenor had created the role in the opera's premiere in

Rome in 1816—and the music was already familiar to New York audiences. The English version had been premiered at the Park Theatre in 1819 (chapter 1), and the opera had not only been performed in New York every season until 1824, but it had also had been heard elsewhere around the country. As the critic of the *New-York Review and Athenaeum Magazine* commented in December 1825, "The music of 'Il Barbiere di Siviglia' has always been extremely popular, and Signor García has shewn great judgment in [its] selection [as] the first opera" of the season.[13]

The company limited its repertory almost exclusively to proven European favorites; five of their nine operas were by Rossini, the reigning operatic composer. Over the course of the season they mounted seventy-nine performances of nine different works, including Rossini's *Il barbiere di Siviglia, La Cenerentola, Tancredi, Il Turco in Italia,* and *Otello; Giulietta e Romeo* (by Niccolò Zingarelli); Mozart's *Don Giovanni* (at the instigation of Lorenzo da Ponte, then a resident of New York); and two operas by García himself (to libretti by Rosich): *L'amato astuto* and *La figlia dell' aria.* García's company was responsible for the North American premieres of all these works in Italian.[14] As a rule, the troupe performed twice a week at the Park, repeating each new opera after its introduction for as many times as possible before moving on to another work. By June, the company was rotating its repertory on a regular basis.[15] The other nights were occupied by dramatic performances given by the Park's company, the members of which were not particularly pleased that two of their evening performances each week were preempted by the foreigners.[16]

At first, the troupe drew well. The aristocratic nature of the opening night audience in particular was widely lauded in the contemporary press, and this commentary—especially references to "the galaxy of fashion and beauty" or the "elegant and well-dressed females" present in the theater—has been cited frequently in secondary sources.[17] That the Park's management was encouraging a wealthier audience is clear from the doubled ticket prices (to $2 for boxes and $1 for the pit), the more-fashionable curtain time (8 P.M., rather than the usual 6:30 or 7 P.M.), and the availability of subscriptions for the entire series.[18] Furthermore, shortly after the appearance of the García troupe, New York newspapers became filled, according to Lawrence, with a "veritable deluge of advertisements of hitherto unknown items," including opera hats, opera cloaks, and opera hoods (Figures 15–16).[19] This indicates clearly that the fashionable and wealthy—those who could afford to purchase such luxuries—were attracted in large numbers to the novel theatrical performances.

Evidence that is often overlooked, however, just as clearly suggests

15 and 16. Examples of advertisements for clothing designed to be worn at opera performances. (Figure 15 from *Godey's Magazine and Ladies' Book*, May 1850; Figure 16 from *Harper's New Monthly Magazine*, November 1850.)

that the Italian troupe attracted attention and paid admissions from average New Yorkers. What most modern commentators fail to mention about ticket prices, for example, is that the Park Theatre managers held the admission cost in the gallery to the usual 25 cents. They did so for a practical reason. As McConachie points out, Price and Simpson knew that New York "craftsmen, servants, and other 'gallery gods'" could be counted on to "patronize Italian opera as they had English musical performances and plays."[20] That the troupe did indeed attract both wealthy and working-class New Yorkers is also illustrated, perhaps inadvertently, by a charming story in the *New-York Mirror* on 21 January 1826. "Opera Cloaks" is about elite, opera-going apparel. A local merchant, so the author related, imported a number of "beautiful silk cloaks for ladies" during the autumn of 1825. Despite numerous advertisements, he was unable to sell them. "Well, things went on in this manner," the writer continued,

> until Signor García and the Italian company set themselves down among us and began *una voce-ing* and *poco fa-ing* until every one's head was turned. Joe [the clerk of the store] rummaged his pockets — picked out a couple of shillings — went up among the [gallery] gods — was in ecstasy

and rapture—and next morning was directed to put into the newspapers another advertisement about the ever-lasting cloaks. Joe's head being full of the opera, wrote out in fair and legible characters, *Opera cloaks—a brand new importation*, &c.

Next morning Joe was standing, as usual, behind the counter, and behold! a blue-eyed beauty came in—"have you any *opera cloaks*, sweet sir?" Joe down with the opera cloaks, and Blue-eyes fitted herself in a trice, and paid the price without a single frudge. Another fair lady came in—"you have opera cloaks," said she. "To be sure we have," said Joe. Away went another opera cloak, and Joe laid violent hands on the cash. By this time, many others came in, and it was—"have you any opera cloaks?" "have you any opera cloaks?" "have you any opera cloaks?" until the whole importation was gone, and Joe had secured the proceeds in the till.

The obvious message of the story—that merchants could capitalize on the current operatic craze—confirms the appeal of opera to the fashion-conscious and wealthy. Just as clear, however, is that clerks like Joe (who "ever since . . . has made his appearance on the second seat in the pit on the opera nights") were likewise attracted to performances by the visiting Italians.

The fascination of the New York public with García's troupe was short-lived. A great deal of their early success apparently was due to the sheer novelty of their undertaking, for after only two months of performances, it was apparent that New Yorkers were not yet prepared to support an Italian company on a regular basis. The *American* reported in February that García was barely able to pay expenses; neither he nor the members of his family, he reported, had received any compensation.[21] But the company's fortunes must have waxed as well as waned, for on 17 June 1826 a critic for the *New-York Mirror* complained that "the Italian opera threatens to exclude the English from the stage." Everyone was surprised, he continued, at the enthusiastic reception the company had enjoyed; no one had expected to see the Italian opera "so wholly engross the attention of the public, as to leave the music of our own language neglected" (375). Some lovers of the drama also dissented, complaining—as they would do later during successful runs of English opera—that the musical form was an inferior one and unworthy to take the place of "the old English tragedy and comedy" on the American stage. "We have always looked on farce, melo-drama, and opera, with dissatisfaction," one writer grumbled. "Let us [re]turn to the good old time when Shakespeare played."[22]

Dominick Lynch and a committee of several other wealthy New Yorkers refused to be discouraged by the on-again, off-again nature of the public's support and tried in the spring of 1826 to drum up enthusiasm for the construction of an opera house where the Italian troupe would be the resident ensemble. The project, however, was abandoned, and García and his company gave their final North American performance on 30 September 1826, just eleven months after their New York debut. Shortly thereafter, they left for Mexico, where they performed for some eighteen months before returning to Paris.[23] The manager left behind in New York, however, several members of his company, including Felix Angrisani, Paolo Rosich, Signor Ferri, and the troupe's star soprano, his daughter Maria, who in March 1826 had ill-advisedly married Eugene-Louis Malibran, who was more than twice her age and, although reportedly wealthy, turned out to be almost penniless.[24]

The Montresor, Rivafinoli, Porto-Sacchi, and Havana Companies

American audiences had no opera in Italian for five years after the García troupe left New York in the autumn of 1826. Elizabeth Austin's first appearance was in 1827, and her repertory of "Englished" Italian works guaranteed that Americans continued to hear Italian melody. There was little Italian music in Italian, however, during the late 1820s and early 1830s, other than for a few isolated instances. The concerts given by vocal stars and by the several singers left behind in New York by the García troupe, for example, continued to include numerous selections from the Italian operatic repertory. A handful of incidental productions of staged operas were also sung in Italian. In April 1829, for example, the vocal stars Elizabeth Feron and Charles Horn banded together with the Italians Angrisani, Rosich, and a new vocal star, Frances Brichta, to mount four performances of *Il Trionfo della musica,* a pasticcio from Mayr's opera *Il Fanatico per la musica,* at the Bowery Theatre in New York. In May the same singers traveled to Philadelphia to perform that work, the first opera in Italian given there, at the Chestnut Street Theatre.[25] A year later, in April 1830, Giulia da Ponte, the librettist's niece, and a number of other singers including Angrisani, Rosich, and Ferri, mounted two performances of Cimarosa's *Il Matrimonio segreto* and da Ponte's pasticcio *L'Ape musicale,* with music by Cimarosa, Salieri, Zingarelli, and—predominantly—Rossini, at the Park Theatre in New York.[26] Except for these isolated instances, however, no opera was performed in Italian, at least by professional companies, in the United States from the late 1820s to the early 1830s. This dearth was interrupted in the early and mid–1830s by the appearance of three different troupes in the North and two in the South. The northern companies performed principally in New York and Philadelphia from 1832 through 1835; the southern troupes appeared in New Orleans and Louisville, Kentucky, in 1836 and 1837. All five companies were linked, to a certain extent, by shared personnel.

The first troupe to appear in North America during the 1830s was headed by the tenor Giacomo Montresor. The company had been recruited in Italy during the fall of 1831 by Lorenzo da Ponte, an indefatigable proselytizer for Italian language and culture, who reportedly was acting on behalf of "a number of gentlemen of N. York and Philadelphia," according the *Spirit* on 3 March 1832 (335). The troupe arrived in New York late in the summer of 1832.[27] The Montresor Company numbered thirty-six individuals, not counting spouses, children, servants, and other hangers-on. The total included fifteen principal singers (five sopranos, two contraltos, four tenors, three basses, and one bass-buffo), six choristers, seven instrumental musicians (two oboists, a harpist, a trombonist, and string principals), a director of the opera, a chorus director, a scene painter and three assistants, a chief costumer, and Montresor himself (Appendix A).[28] According to the *New-York Mirror* of 13 October 1832, the orchestra was "chiefly collected in New York"; it numbered nineteen: five violins, two violas, one cello, one bass, two each of oboes, clarinets, and horns, and one each of bassoon, flute, trombone, and trumpet (119). Although smaller than García's ensemble, the orchestra had two oboists (both had arrived with Montresor), which undoubtedly effected an overall improvement. Oboes had been conspicuously absent from García's orchestra, unless the clarinetists could also play the double-reed instrument.

The Montresor Company was the first Italian troupe to attempt a true season of opera in this country, for the García Company's performances had been grafted onto a theatrical season. The musical climate in the United States had changed a great deal in the years since Manuel García left the country. According to the *New-York Mirror* on 18 July 1829, García and his "inimitable corps" had commenced the change, which a critic for that journal described as nothing short of a musical revolution. "The sweet sound of the Italian [had] no sooner reached the American ear," he wrote, "than it became a convert." The writer somewhat grandiosely continued, "After the Garcías left, the musical excitement was threatened with extinction, when a Knight renewed it. . . . Austin, Feron, Horn, and Pearson have lately been stars of the ascendant. A great change has been effected. Pianos . . . are manufactured without number, at as high a price as you please; and no house is without one. Music is every where cultivated" (15).

Montresor undoubtedly hoped that his troupe could exploit the growing taste for Italian melody. He also hoped that his singers would satisfy and please Americans, whose expectations had been heightened in the intervening years by performances of such superior vocal stars as Elizabeth Austin and the others mentioned by the *Mirror*'s critic. "Operas have become so fashionable in New York," the editor of the *Spirit* explained on 1 August 1832, just before the opening of Montresor's season, "and Five years of listening to the scientific performances of various Prima Donnas, has perfected a taste that will require first rate execution, fully to gratify."

The Montresor Company opened in New York at the Richmond Hill Theatre (renamed the Italian Opera House) to much acclaim. On 10 November, the *Spirit* reported that the opera house "continues to be fashionably attended" and that the company was enjoying "unequalled success"; on 12 January the same journal noted that the "beauty and fashion of the city" packed the theater, which—significantly—was "crowded from pit to gallery." The company mounted two seasons in New York and one in Philadelphia during 1832–33, giving thirty-five performances in the former city and twenty-three in the latter, of a repertory of eight operas: *La Cenerentola, L'Italiana in Algieri, Mosè in Egitto, L'Inganno felice, Il barbiere di Siviglia,* and *Otello* by Rossini; *Il Pirata* by Bellini; and *Elisa e Claudio* by Mercadante.[29] All these works, excepting *La Cenerentola* and *Il barbiere,* were new to the North American stage.

Montresor undoubtedly calculated that his troupe's performances of *La Cenerentola* would attract some of the same enthusiastic audiences that had flocked to Elizabeth Austin's performances of *Cinderella;* in this expectation, however, he was disappointed. Joseph Sill, who attended several of the Montresor Company's performances in Philadelphia, commented favorably on the musical and dramatic abilities of various members of the troupe on 13 February 1833. But he was unfavorably impressed with *La Cenerentola.* "As a whole," he wrote, "we infinitely preferr'd the performance of Mrs. Austin and Mr. [John] Jones in the English version." In this judgment Sill evidently was not alone, and American taste reflected that of British audiences. In an 1830 article from the London *Harmonicon*—later quoted in the September issue of the *Euterpiad*—praising Rophino Lacy's version of *Cinderella,* the author noted that "Rossini's Opera, *La Cenerentola,* has never, as a whole, been popular even on our Italian stage" (86). *Cinderella* without a fairy godmother is a story sadly bereft to audiences, English or French, used to the more-familiar fairy-tale version.

At the end of his first season in New York, Montresor found himself slightly in debt to the committee that had sponsored his performances there. He remained confident of eventual success, however, and was certain that subsequent profitable seasons would help defray the heavy expenses incurred during the first year, which included the formidable cost of transporting the troupe from Italy. Toward the end of the company's visit to Philadelphia (during which engagement they drew large houses but, according to Curtis, lost money), Montresor was dismayed to discover that the Italian Opera Association in the City of New York, which was building an Italian Opera House at Leonard and Church streets in Manhattan, had awarded the first lease of the facility not to him, but to one Cavaliere Vincenzo Rivafinoli.[30] This development threw his plans and hopes for the subsequent 1833–34 season into serious disarray. Faced with significant debts and no future source of income, Montresor appealed to the good citizens of Philadelphia for assistance. "The Italian Opera, who have been here about 5 or 6 weeks," Joseph Sill wrote on 7 March, "have been compelled by their misfortunes to make application to the Community for relief, in consequence of the want of sufficient support." Five or six hundred dollars were raised by subscription, and further assistance was promised. At the conclusion of their engagement in Pennsylvania, the troupe returned to New York and disbanded after a final performance there on 11 May.

A large number of Montresor's musicians elected to remain in New York. This significant enlargement of the city's pool of competent singers constituted the principal long-term contribution of the Montresor Company to opera in the United States, for their one-year tenure had little lasting impact. Rivafinoli hired many of the Montresor performers for his own company, but he pointedly did not hire either Giacomo Montresor or most of the principal singers of the former troupe, despite being publicly urged to do so, according to the *New-York Mirror* on 7 December. Sometime after the beginning of the new year, Montresor and his unemployed compatriots (including Luciano Fornasari, a bass; the leader's son, Giovanni Battista Montresor, a tenor; the soprano Adelaide Pedrotti; Giuseppe Corsetti, a bass; and the orchestra director and violinist Michele Rapetti) left New York and went south. They next are mentioned in the American musical-theatrical press in the *Spirit* on 29 August 1835 as members of the Havana Opera Company.

Vincenzo Rivafinoli's company, the first resident troupe of the newly opened, short-lived Italian Opera House, shared a number of similarities (besides personnel) with the Montresor Company. It performed in both New York and Philadelphia, it had a small repertory heavily weighted toward Rossini, and it was in existence for but a year. In New York, the company performed in the brand-new, luxurious facilities that the Italian Opera Association had built earlier that year. The backers of the venture, apparently inspired by da Ponte, were a number of wealthy New Yorkers.

The house itself, observed Richard Grant White in 1882, was "of an exquisiteness and a splendor as has not since been seen in New York" (1:702). The theater had a different arrangement from any other house built in the United States up to that point. The first tier, where the seats were mahogany sofas, was connected to the old "pit," which had been transformed into a "parterre" (or "parquette"); this section, also furnished with upholstered sofas, was now open to women.[31] The second balcony was occupied by private boxes, for which the stockholders drew lots. This was the first theater in New York to sell private boxes for the entire season, and most of them went to the members of the Italian Opera Association.[32] The prices of admission to the rest of the house were high: sofa-seats, $2; parterre, $1; and gallery, 75 cents.[33]

The troupe gave approximately eighty performances—fourteen in Philadelphia, the rest in New York—of eight operas, including Rossini's *La Gazza Ladra, La Cenerentola, La Donna del Lago, Il Turco in Italia,* and *Matilde de Shabran;* Cimarosa's *Il Matrimonio segreto;* Pacini's *Gli arabi nelle Gallie;* and *La Casa da Vendere* by Carlo Salvioni, the chorus master of both the Montresor and Rivafinoli troupes.[34] Overall, however, the public's reception lacked enthusiasm. A critic for the *American Musical Journal* wrote in October 1834 that "as a whole, the company was very mediocre," inferior, he claimed, to both the García and the Montresor troupes (17). The troupe ended its season disastrously, closing during July 1834 with an astonishing deficit of $30,000 ($411,000 in 1992 terms). Da Ponte and others subsequently accused Rivafinoli of dishonesty, but an itemized account of his expenditures suggests that the manager was not a crook, just an inept businessman.[35]

The overall impact of the company—beyond the importation of several additional singers—was minimal. "It produced no very strong impression upon the American public," White pointed out, "and, indeed, left no mark, in our musical experience, but that of its appearance and its extinction" (1:703). The underlying reasons for its failure, however—beyond artistic mediocrity and poor management—reveal a great deal about New York opera and theater audiences of the 1830s. First, the continued, growing popularity of English (or translated Italian) opera and the tremendous box-office draw of Joseph and Mary Anne Wood at the Park Theatre provided almost insurmountable competition to the Italians. "The immense houses which Mr. and Mrs. Wood bring nightly to the Park," wrote Philip Hone in his diary, "prove that the New Yorkers are not devoid of musical taste, notwithstanding that the Italian opera does not succeed."[36] Just as damaging as the Woods' popularity, however, was the high cost of admission to the Italians' performances. "The Opera was placed beyond the reach of the great body of the people," lectured a critic for the *American Musical Journal* in October 1834, "and that class from whom support was mainly expected are not yet sufficiently numerous to be the exclusive supporters of an Opera House" (18). The ready availability of opera performances by an overwhelmingly popular vocal-star troupe—performing in English, and at significantly lower admission prices, at the Park Theatre—spelled almost-certain doom for the Rivafinoli Company. Finally, and in the long run perhaps more important, was the negative impression of exclusivity created by the sumptuous surroundings and private boxes of the new opera house. Because the wealthy and elite of New York City were not yet "sufficiently numerous" to support an opera company, this deliberate attempt to exclude the other parts of the traditional theater audience simply backfired. Philip Hone, an aristocrat and one of the box-holders at the Italian Opera, commented in his diary about the majority of New Yorkers who stayed away from the Rivafinoli performances and expressed admiration for this "spirit of independence which refuses to countenance to anything exclusive."[37]

The critic for the *American Musical Journal* perhaps voiced the thoughts (and severe disapprobation, to use a contemporary term) of many New York theater-goers when he pointed out that the division of the opera house created "distinctions offensive to our republican notions" and gave "an impression that the Opera is intended to be exclusive." He solicitously advised the managers of the enterprise to "recollect that musical pieces have been the main support of the Park Theatre for several years past" and suggested that "no permanency will be given to [opera] until it draws its support from the great mass of people in middling circumstances" (18). The tone of this criticism, however, suggests strongly that the reviewer had not yet caught on to the fact that the "impression" created by the new opera house was not inadvertent; exclusivity was one of the goals of the Italian Opera Association. Wealthy New Yorkers were not interested in importing Italian opera because of their innate love of music, but because it could be transformed into an exclusive and elite pastime that could lend to its auditors—merely by attendance—some of those attributes. An obvious model was the British aristocracy's patronage of the Italian Opera House in London. That this attempt at exclusivity failed in 1834 indicates that the American theater still depended on the patronage of all social classes; the development of an exclusive audience for a particular segment of the theatrical repertory (opera) would have to wait until the future, when the upper class was "sufficiently numerous."

The final Italian troupe to appear in the North in the 1830s was the second group to attempt to mount a successful season at the Italian Opera House. The Italian Opera Association—undaunted in spite of

the Rivafinoli fiasco—resolved in September 1834 to lease the facility
to the partnership of Antonio Porto, a singer from Rivafinoli's troupe,
and Signor G. A. Sacchi, that company's treasurer. The troupe opened
its season on 10 November 1834, again in the new Opera House. By
24 December, however, the *American Musical Journal* was predicting
the demise of a company it characterized as "unquestionably . . . the
most destitute of vocal talent, of any that has essayed the performance
of Italian Operas in this country" (42). Apparently, the troupe's single
redeeming feature, at least according to the February 1835 issue of the
American Musical Journal, was its orchestra of twenty-seven musicians:
seven violins, two violas, two cellos, two basses, one oboe, one bassoon,
two each of horns, trumpets, clarinets, and flutes, three trombones,
and drums (66–67).

Despite dire predictions, the company limped through its first season
(10 November–24? December 1834) and, after some reorganization,
mounted a second one (23 January–3 April 1835). Lowered prices,
suggested the *New-York Mirror* on 7 February, had "brought about a
change in feeling" toward the troupe; even the *American Musical
Journal* admitted in its February issue—although somewhat grudg-
ingly—that although the company "is not so good as is desirable, still
they form the nucleus of a better [troupe], and should therefore be
kept together." Repertory carefully chosen to highlight the company's
strengths also helped. The *Mirror*'s critic suggested on 28 February
that they perform works "full of concerted pieces," for the troupe "is
woefully inadequate in strong soloists." By the end of March, the
company's management felt that the troupe was strong enough to make
a short out-of-town trip—to Albany, New York, where they performed
Mosè in Egitto, L'Inganno felice, and the second act of *Eduardo e
Christina* in early April.[38] The visit, according to the *American Musical
Journal* in May 1835, "appears to have given the liveliest satisfaction
to the Albanians, and to have been a profitable one to the company"
(144). The troupe returned once again to New York City and performed
there from 22 April until sometime in May, when their season petered
out. In October 1835 the Italian Opera Association realized that "the
object for which the Opera House was built cannot be effected";
consequently, they authorized its sale.[39] Eventually the theater was
purchased by James Hackett, renamed the National Theatre, and leased
to James Wallack, who mounted the successful opera-dominated season
of 1838–39.

Two Italian companies performed in the southern United States
during 1836 and 1837. The first brings the discussion of Italian troupes
active in North America during the 1830s full circle, for it was none
other than the Montresor Opera Company, now under the direction

of Giovanni Battista Montresor, Giacomo's son.[40] A precise chronicle of the whereabouts or activities of the principal singers from the Montresor troupe (those left unhired by Rivafinoli) from May 1833, when the company disbanded in New York, to March 1836, when the troupe resurfaced in New Orleans, is not possible. A general sketch of the singers' activities, however, is both feasible and of interest, for it clearly illustrates how resourceful musicians had to be to eke out a living as performers and how widely traveled they were, despite the relatively undeveloped transportation system of the 1830s.

In 1833, one Francesco Brichta engaged Pedrotti, Montresor, Fornasari, Corsetti, Rapetti, and other members of the defunct Montresor troupe as the nucleus of the first resident opera company in Havana, Cuba.[41] The Montresor musicians evidently performed for Brichta for only one season (fall and winter 1834), however, for by April 1835 all (with the exception of the violinist Rapetti) had left Havana as a result of a dispute over wages with Brichta.[42] Apparently by fall even Rapetti joined the ranks of the disaffected, for in September 1835 the *American Musical Journal* reported that Montresor, Pedrotti, and Rapetti had just arrived in New York and that Fornasari was "daily expected" (239). Montresor and his colleagues did not remain in New York long; by March 1836, his company was in New Orleans, performing at James Caldwell's resplendent new St. Charles Theatre.[43] While in New York, however, Montresor had enlisted for his new troupe a number of the singers from his old one, most of whom had sung in the interim with the Rivafinoli Company. He also hired several performers who had come to the United States at the behest of that former competitor.[44] Undoubtedly, many of these singers eagerly signed on with Montresor despite the distance they had to travel for the engagement. After the Rivafinoli Company folded in July 1834, the Italian operatic pickings in New York had become slim indeed. Only a small number of the stranded singers had been hired for the Porto-Sacchi venture which, in any case, was past history by May 1835. Whether Montresor paid the singers' travel expenses to New Orleans or whether they had to make their own way south is not known.

The Montresor Company opened its season on 6 March 1836 with the New Orleans premiere of Bellini's *Il Pirata*. During the next three months they gave thirty-five performances, usually three a week, of seven different operas.[45] The company's repertory during this New Orleans engagement clearly indicates a gradual substitution of Bellini for Rossini in the affections of American opera lovers; of the seven works performed, four were by Rossini (*Otello, La Cenerentola, Zelmira,* and *Il barbiere di Siviglia*) and three by Bellini (*Il Pirata, Norma,* and *La Straniera*).[46] Four operas besides *Il Pirata* were presented for the first time in New Orleans, including *Otello, La Straniera, Zelmira,* and *Norma;* the latter two were also U.S. premieres.[47] The troupe closed its very successful St. Charles season on 31 May 1836; they had attracted good audiences for almost four months.[48] The nascent elitism that was beginning to be associated with Italian opera in New York seems to have been entirely absent in the Crescent City for two reasons. First, foreign-language opera had been a part of the city's cultural fabric since as early as the 1790s. The first resident opera company, that of Louis Tabary at the St. Peter Street Theatre, had given more than three hundred and fifty opera performances (in French) of seventy-six operas between 1806 and 1810. Other companies, including that of John Davis (who arrived in New Orleans in 1809) had provided such a steady diet of French opera that by the 1830s the genre was firmly established.[49] As the *New Orleans Bee* pointed out on 26 April 1836, operas "amuse our citizens more than any other form of public amusement—except balls."[50] Second, it was a matter of national pride for English-speaking residents to support Caldwell and his St. Charles Theatre, even when the featured artists were performing in Italian. Caldwell's engagement of the Montresor troupe represented a serious challenge to the operatic preeminence of the city's French theater, the Théâtre d'Orléans, and the residents of the American sector—elite and nonelite alike—were delighted at the prospect of some real competition. "For those Americans who had resented French superiority in opera," Henry Kmen wrote, "it was a happy time."[51]

After closing their season in New Orleans, the singers—excepting Montresor and Pedrotti, who went back to Havana—traveled to Louisville, Kentucky, where they spent the summer performing *L'Inganno felice, La Cenerentola,* and *Il barbiere di Siviglia* in the American Theatre, which was also owned by Caldwell. The manager later claimed that he kept the entire company on his payroll throughout the summer to ensure its return during the 1836–37 season.[52] The troupe, or at least part of it, did indeed return to New Orleans in late 1836, and opened at the St. Charles Theatre on 4 December in *La Cenerentola.* This ensemble, however, was but a remnant of the Montresor troupe, to which some local singers had been added. It now was known as the de Rosa Opera Company, with Antonio de Rosa, a bass with Montresor, as its new head.[53] They performed intermittently at the St. Charles until 27 February 1837.[54]

Caldwell evidently was not satisfied with the caliber of this makeshift de Rosa Company, for sometime before the end of their engagement he sent an emissary to Havana to persuade Francesco Brichta to bring his Havana Opera Company to New Orleans after the conclusion of the season there.[55] Caldwell's terms were acceptable to Brichta, and his troupe arrived on 1 April 1837. Brichta brought with him soloists, chorus, an orchestra conductor, and three string principals to augment the already large orchestra of the St. Charles. Apparently, he also absorbed into his troupe some of the singers of the now-disbanded de Rosa Company.[56] This was the first of numerous visits that various Havana opera companies would make to the United States during the antebellum period, and the troupe, even this early in its history, already had a formidable reputation in North America. "The Havana Company [is] one of the best that has ever crossed the Atlantic," a reporter for the *New York Evening Star* would explain the following spring, "because operatic singers have been always well paid by the rich and music-loving Spaniards."[57]

The Havana Opera Company performed at the St. Charles for slightly more than two months, from 4 April through 6 June 1837. Their repertory of eight operas was much more varied than the Montresor troupe's had been. It included three works by Rossini (*Tancredi, Il barbiere di Siviglia,* and *Semiramide*); two by Bellini (*I Capuleti e i Montecchi* and *Norma*); and one each by Saverio Mercadante (*Donna Caritea*), Luigi Ricci (*Chiara di Rosembergh*), and Gaetano Donizetti (*Parisina*). Six of these works were new to audiences in the Crescent City; four of them were given their North American premieres.[58]

The musical sophistication, knowledge, and expectations of the New Orleans audience is demonstrated by a remarkable occurrence that took place during the second performance of *Semiramide,* one of the new operas, on 21 May. The work was performed without incident up until the last act, when the management attempted—without explanation—to curtail the opera by omitting the final scene. When the audience realized that the curtain was not to be raised for the opera's conclusion, they were indignant. "The *falling* of the green curtain was the signal for *raising* a most tremendous racket," wrote the critic for the *Picayune* the next day. The pit "became uproarious," and when no explanation was forthcoming from the management, the audience "became tumultuous. Such a din," he continued, "we have rarely heard. Hissing, howling, whistling, kicking and screaming reigned in that temple where, but a few moments before, all was harmony." The management attempted to subdue the auditors by dousing the house lights; this enraged the citizens even further (the more so because ladies were present), and a full-fledged riot ensued. Canes and other missiles were thrown, drapery around the boxes torn, cushions ripped open, seats broken, chairs sent flying in all directions. "The house," wrote the critic, "presented more the appearance of a brothel, in the midst of a row, than a respectable resort for amusement." The rioters were not subdued until the management finally sent someone out to explain that the company's soprano, Lorenza Marozzi, who was singing the title role, had suddenly been taken ill. The New Orleaneans' outrage was fueled by a strong suspicion that the Italians had attempted to cut the opera only because they were tired or lazy and had done so on the assumption that the American audience would not know the difference. That they did know the difference suggests that many individuals in the audience either had attended the opera's first performance two days previous, had read the libretto ahead of time, or—at the least— knew the basic plot.[59]

This attempt by the Havana Company to alter the opera significantly from the written version was probably common performance practice during the entire antebellum period; it certainly was an accepted practice in Europe. Unfortunately, the theatrical and musical press of the 1830s and early 1840s contains little information about specific changes made for performances mounted in the United States. Most journalistic complaints about "mutilations" to the scores of operas during this time are directed at English adaptations; only occasionally are journalistic critiques of Italian performances sufficiently specific to give a clear idea of what was performed. This situation, however, would change significantly by the mid to late 1840s. As performances of Italian opera became more numerous and the operas themselves more familiar to both audiences and critics, complaints about alterations, transpositions, deletions, and interpolations—indicating widespread practice—would become more commonplace.

The riot over changes in *Semiramide* was only a harbinger of further difficulties for Manager Caldwell. The Havana Company's St. Charles engagement ended abruptly on 6 June when a managerial disagreement that had been smoldering during most of the run between Brichta and Caldwell broke into open conflict. After Caldwell almost literally kicked the opera singers out of his theater on 7 June, Brichta adroitly transferred his troupe to Caldwell's arch-rival, the Théâtre d'Orléans, where the engagement extended from 10 June through 14 July.[60] The American manager was satisfied to see the Italians leave. "I have known nothing but trouble, annoyance and loss since my first unfortunate introduction of the Italian Opera last year," he grumbled to the *Picayune* after Brichta's company left. "For my own part," he continued, "I am not now, nor shall I ever be disposed to try it again."[61] It was a vow that Caldwell would not keep for long.

Havana Opera Companies, 1842–44

No Italian opera troupes were active in North America for the next five years; the economic situation in the United States during the late

1830s and early 1840s was not conducive to expensive theatrical undertakings. James Caldwell, his earlier declaration evidently forgotten, appears to have been the first American manager to attempt to bring back Italian opera, for he tried to engage the Havana Company in the spring of 1841. Despite the "good terms" Caldwell offered he was refused; the *Spirit* reported on 1 May that the company had other commitments. The next year, however, Caldwell's bid was successful, and the Havana Company, now managed by the impresario Francisco Marti y Torrens, arrived in New Orleans in late February 1842.[62]

The company, which numbered fifty-seven, included principal singers, orchestra, and a chorus of thirty. Their engagement at the St. Charles commenced on 22 February and was a resounding success. The troupe's stars, as well as its ensemble, were highly praised. "Of the chorus we must say a word," wrote a correspondent to the *Spirit* on 12 March, "and that word must be one of the very highest commendation. They are good voices, every one of them, and are drilled with admirable nicety in all their duties." Two weeks later, another correspondent wrote to describe the troupe's reception and to sing the praises of the company's prima donna, Ober Rossi. The theater, he wrote, "was 'jam up' with beauties of the first grade, and fashionables, mustached like monkeys of the last grade." He continued:

> Of the performances I dare not speak—I am fearful of being carried away by the enthusiasm they created in my bosom. When I 'offered' myself to my wife, I don't believe my heart palpitated more than it did when the *divine* Ober Rossi burst first upon my view—then wiled [beguiled] my ear—then stole my homage. The piece was Marino Faliero, by Donizetti—a beautiful and touching composition—full of rich melodies that stole through the instrumentation like a soft sweet river through a meadow, and fraught with harmonies that ran parallel to each other like threads in a skein of golden wire![63]

By this time it had become abundantly clear that the Italian opera at the St. Charles was a viable competitor to the long-established French opera at the Théâtre d'Orléans; whether mounted in English by vocal stars or in the original language, the Italian style was a musical and theatrical force of great appeal in the Crescent City. "The opera is eminently successful," wrote the *Spirit*'s critic on 26 March, "and the San Carlos [St. Charles] averages $2,600 every night! 'Damn the times,' say good looking men, 'and let's enjoy the opera *before* going to the other world!'" The same correspondent wrote on 16 July that "the taste of this community has entirely changed within the last five years. Everybody except flat boatmen and steamboat hands love the opera. Music is our goddess."

Despite their resounding success, the Havana Company's season came to an abrupt halt after only ten performances, when the St. Charles Theatre burned to the ground on 13 March.[64] Luckily, no lives were lost, and the troupe, which had stored its costumes and properties elsewhere, lost only those costumes that had been used in that evening's performance.[65] Marti quickly reached an agreement with the management of the Théâtre d'Orléans and moved his troupe there, where they performed for another month.[66] During their visit to New Orleans, the Havana Company mounted seven operas by three composers. As before, the troupe's repertory reflects changing operatic tastes; it included one work by Ricci (*Chiara di Rosembergh*), two by Bellini (*La Sonnambula* and *Beatrice di Tenda*), and four by Donizetti (*Marino Faliero, Il Furioso nell' isola di San Domingo, Belisario,* and *L'Elisir d'amore*). All of these works but one (*Chiara di Rosembergh*) were new to New Orleans audiences; four were new to the United States. All were relatively recent compositions, dating from the 1830s.[67]

The next spring, in April 1843, the Havana Company returned to New Orleans to perform again, this time in the American Theatre. Their engagement lasted for a month, and during that time they presented the U.S. premieres of three operas, one by Bellini and two by Donizetti.[68] The company's personnel had changed almost completely from the troupe of the previous year, however, and Crescent City critics were quick to judge this version inferior to the former one. According to the historian Giovanni Schiavo, the company could boast of only two vocalists, the tenor Cirillo Antognini and the bass Attilio Valtellina, who "amounted to anything"; the rest of the singers "were all minor ones."[69] Despite its mediocrity, however, it is useful to examine this troupe in some detail, for it was the first Italian company to undertake a lengthy and extended tour of the United States. The journey lasted nine months and included visits to Cincinnati, Pittsburgh, Philadelphia, New York, Baltimore, Washington, and (again) New Orleans.

Shortly after ending their New Orleans engagement on 17 May, the Havana musicians embarked via steamboat for Cincinnati. Several theater and music periodicals of the time carried regular reports on the travels of itinerant performers, and the company's departure was duly noted by the *Spirit* on 3 June. "The Italian troupe," the reporter commented in rather a gossipy vein, "has gone to Porkopolis to give some melting strains." Cincinnati was a major port on the Ohio-Mississippi River network, and the city had had opera performances before 1843. The Havana Company, however, was the first Italian troupe to appear there; it also was the city's first experience with a fully appointed traveling opera company—in this case, a troupe that numbered thirty.[70] A reporter for the *Cincinnati Daily Gazette,* explaining the difference between this ensemble and the more common vocal-star troupes, pointed out on 14 June that the Havana Opera Company traveled not only with stars, but also with a chorus and an orchestra. "This," he emphasized, "is not the old story of one or two stars for the leading parts, and all the rest 'mere leather and prunella.' "[71]

The company performed seven times over the course of three weeks at the National Theatre, mounting productions of *Norma, I Puritani, Gemma di Vergy,* and *Lucia di Lammermoor;* according to the *Daily Gazette,* the troupe's principal singers "astonished" the citizens of the Queen City by the "exquisite skill and wonderful power in their divine art."[72] After their last performance on 21 June, the musicians headed up the Ohio River, making a brief stop in Pittsburgh before crossing the mountains to settle in for an extended stay on the East Coast.

The Havana Company opened at the Chestnut Street Theatre on 15 July 1843, one of the few times during the entire antebellum period that a traveling opera troupe opened in Philadelphia before New York. During the Philadelphia engagement, and later in New York, a musician long associated with the New York musical scene, Signor La Manna, conducted the orchestra; the Havana troupe's conductor had resigned in New Orleans in May.[73] The company performed in Philadelphia for two weeks (15–31 July), limiting itself to four operas by Donizetti and Bellini (*Lucia di Lammermoor, Belisario, I Puritani,* and *Norma*).[74] Joseph Sill and a friend attended one of the performances of *I Puritani,* and he commented on 22 July that "as [this] was [the opera's] first representation in this City, it was not so well understood, and of course not so well appreciated as [Bellini's] other works, the 'Sonnambula' and 'Norma.' " The performance nevertheless attracted "a fashionable & tolerably well-fill'd house," and an interpolated song by the company's bass Valtellina, "Song to the Flag of Liberty," was "very spiritedly sung & brot down thunders of applause." Sill recorded that overall he was "much pleased" with the evening's entertainment, but that he wanted to "get better acquainted" with the new opera.

Where the company went during the next three weeks is unknown. Theaters often closed during July and August, so it is possible that the singers disbanded for the duration and enjoyed the summer months, blessedly away from the heat and miasma (and yellow fever) of Cuba. By the last week of August they were engaged at the Holliday Street Theatre in Baltimore, where they mounted productions of *Norma, Lucia di Lammermoor, I Puritani,* and *Gemma di Vergy* from 21 August through 2 September.[75] In September, fortified with some local singers, the troupe opened at Niblo's Garden in Manhattan. "Mr. Niblo," commented the *Spirit* on 16 September, "has wisely determined to take advantage of the prevailing taste for music by engaging the Italian Company from Havana and New Orleans." Their performances of

"Grand Opera," the critic continued, "will be quite a novelty, as it has not been played in this city for some time past."

Staged Italian opera may have been a novelty, but the music was not. Even much of *Lucia di Lammermoor*—the New York premiere performance of which this company mounted on its opening night—recently had become familiar to New York concert-goers. As Odell pointed out, "Italian singers flitting to and fro from Havana, had whetted the appetite [of New Yorkers] by [giving] concerts during the moments of transit through New York." Lawrence indicates that "arias and ensembles" from *Lucia* had formed an important component of these singers' concert repertory.[76]

At first, the Havana troupe did not meet with resounding success at Niblo's; just a week into the engagement one critic for the *Spirit* reported on 23 September that several of the company's principal singers had "comparatively failed." Yet, he commented philosophically, "it is very fair Italian Opera for fifty cents." Thereafter the troupe's fortunes must have improved, for the singers were rehired at the end of their original engagement. During their tenure at Niblo's—their season lasted from 15 September to 23 October—they performed two nights a week, alternating with the popular (and perennial) Ravel Company of acrobats and dancers (Figure 17).[77] For the entire duration of their stay at Niblo's they mounted only three operas: *Gemma di Vergy*, *Norma*, and *Lucia*, all in New York premieres (in Italian).[78]

Performances at Niblo's popular summer garden theater were anything but exclusive. In 1840 Thomas Chamberlain described the casual atmosphere of the establishment. "Niblo's," he observed in his diary on 7 July, "is a first rate place altogether for the summer, the [best of] any of [the] theaters, [with] beautiful walks and promenades all defended from the weather, and a spacious saloon" (Figure 18). A critic for the *Spirit* agreed with this assessment. "The gardens are now in beautiful order," he wrote on 10 June 1843, "and the whole place, with its trees, and fountains, and flowers, harmonizes pleasingly with the attractions presented by the music and mirth of the saloon."

Although the atmosphere was casual and relaxed—or perhaps because it was so—the importance of William Niblo's establishment on the development of American musical taste was marked. A critic for the *Musical Review*, for example, wrote on 25 July 1838 that "thousands go there who would not go to the theatre; and thousands of others go there because the admission is but fifty cents." Furthermore, he pointed out, because Niblo's attracted "thousands . . . of strangers who are passing through [New York], or [who] are temporarily here on business," in the end "not only this city, but this entire country is greatly affected in regard to musical taste" (134). One review of a

NIBLO'S.

BENEFIT OF Signor RAPETTI.

☞ FRIDAY, OCTOBER 6th. ☜

The performance to commence at half past SEVEN precisely, with the
Overture to "Lucia di Lammermoor," - - - *Donizetti
To be led and conducted by Signor Rapetti.

After which, for the **Last time**, a grand Opera, in 3 acts, Music by Donizetti, composer of "Belisario,
La Fille du Regiment, and Gemma di Vergy," called

☞ LUCIA DI LAMMERMOOR!!

Lord Henry Ashton,	- -	Signor Attilio Valtellina
Lucia, sister of Lord Ashton,		Signora Amelia Majocchi
Lord Edgar, of Ravenwood,		Signor Cirillo Antognina
Lord Arthur Bucklaw,	- -	Signor Albertazzi
Raimond, Tutor of Lucia,	- - -	Signor Magiori
Norman,	- - - -	Signor Thamesi
Alisa, lady of honor to Lucia,	- - -	Signora Coad

Between the first and second acts,

☞ SIGNOR RAPETTI

Will play on the Violin a GRAND SOLO!

**Fantasia, with variations, on Bellini's Thema, Il Pirata!
Arranged by Signor Rapetti.**

BETWEEN THE SECOND AND THIRD ACTS OF THE OPERA
An Intermission of a quarter of an Hour.

The Evening's entertainments to conclude with an
☞ *Instrumental Concert!*
IN THE
☞ REFRESHMENT SALOON!

To-morrow, Saturday, Third Night of the gorgeous Comic Pantomime, entitled the
CONJUROR'S GIFT!
(Received on Tuesday, by a crowded Saloon, with shouts and peals of laughter,) in which the whole force of
the
RAVEL FAMILY,
And company, will be brought into active display.

Manager,..............John Sefton

☞ TICKETS 50 CENTS.

THOMAS SNOWDEN, PRINTER 58 WALL STREET, FOURTH STORY

17. Playbill from a performance of Gaetano Donizetti's *Lucia de Lammermoor* at Niblo's Garden on 6 October 1843. Note the written comment at the top: "The music was splendid—better than that at the Park Theatre. The singing very good—." (American Antiquarian Society)

foreign-language opera production at Niblo's during the summer of 1843 sheds light on what attracted Americans to such performances. "Although a large portion of the audience were unable to understand the language," wrote the critic for the *Spirit* on 27 May, "still the frequent introduction of bits of most agreeable music amply repaid them and drew forth their applause." Of course, performances at Niblo's also attracted individuals such as Thomas Chamberlain who did go to the theater regularly and were musically knowledgable. Furthermore, at least some of these patrons were pleased with the quality of the presentations. A playbill from a performance of *Lucia di Lammermoor* on 6 October 1843, for example, has inscribed across the top, "The music was splendid — Better than that at the Park Theatre. The singing was very good — " (Figure 17).

From late October through early November, the Havana Company again disappears from modern view. They resurface in Philadelphia for another two-week engagement, during which they added *Gemma di Vergy* to the repertory already performed at the Chestnut Street Theatre.[79] At the conclusion of this run, the troupe went south. They stopped in early December for short engagements in Baltimore and Washington, D.C., but evidently gave no other performances en route. They began another short run at the American Theatre in New Orleans on 13 December and then returned to Havana.[80] How many of the original singers were left with the troupe by the time it reached Cuba is unknown; at least four performers — Cirillo Antognini, Amalia Majocchi, Attilio Valtellina, and Luigi Perozzi — either stayed on the East Coast when the troupe headed south or returned to New York by February 1844.

New York: Palmo's Opera Company

In the mid–1840s, the center of Italian opera performance in the United States once again shifted to New York (Figure 19). The credit for operatic activity in 1844 and early 1845 goes without qualification to Ferdinando Palmo (1785–1869), an Italian who over the course of some twenty years (starting about 1823) had amassed a considerable fortune as the proprietor of fashionable cafes in New York.[81] Palmo was an inveterate lover of opera, and in 1843, encouraged by Niblo's success in attracting Americans of all social classes to opera performances, he decided to invest his fortune in an opera house so that, as Ireland put it, "the music of his own beloved Italy should once more thrill the soul of himself and [his] countrymen" (2:423). Palmo leased a former public bathhouse located on a convenient site on Chambers Street opposite City Hall Park and refurbished the place into an intimate little

18. Exterior view of Niblo's Garden and Theatre, from *Valentine's Manual,*
1865. (New-York Historical Society)

opera house (Figure 20). His was not an exclusive establishment. The
seats, which numbered a mere eight hundred, ran all around the house,
without private boxes; admission to all parts of the theater was a
uniform $1; and curtain time was 7:30 P.M., according to the *Spirit*
on 27 January 1844.[82] The *New York Herald* praised the arrangement
as "republican" and suggested on 14 December that it would "work
as well as our own beautiful democratic system." By abolishing the
gallery as well as private boxes, Palmo apparently was aiming at a
middle-class clientele.[83]

While refurbishing and decorating the theater, the restaurateur-turned-
impresario went about assembling an opera troupe. He did not import
any new stars. On the contrary, all of the singers he hired were already
well known to New York audiences through concert and opera appearances. Many had been part of the Havana Company that had
performed at Niblo's the previous fall, these included the four Havana
troupe "stars": Antognini, Majocchi, Valtellina, and Perozzi. For a new
prima donna, Palmo hired Eufrasia Borghese, a fine singer and an
excellent actress who had sung in Havana for the previous two years
but was known to New York audiences only through concert appearances.[84] To this company of mostly second-rate singers, Palmo
added a chorus of twenty-four and an orchestra of thirty-two of the
best instrumental musicians in New York, under the direction of the

19. Portion of an 1850 street map of Manhattan. 1. Niblo's Gardens, Broadway and Prince streets (est. 1822); 2. Palmo's Opera House, Chambers Street (1844–47); 3. Astor Place Opera House, 8th and Lafayette streets (1847–52); 4. New York Academy of Music, 14th Street and Irving Place (1854–86). (Manuscripts and Rare Books Department, Swem Library, College of William and Mary)

20. Exterior, Palmo's Opera House, Chambers Street. Unattributed print.
(New-York Historical Society)

inverterate Michele Rapetti.[85] Finally, the neophyte impresario hired
Attilio Valtellina, a respected performer, to serve both as the troupe's
primo basso and as its director.

Palmo's season opened on 3 February 1844 with the New York
premiere of *I Puritani*. The troupe performed regularly on Monday,
Wednesday, and Friday evenings until 25 March, giving twenty performances of four operas (*Lucia di Lammermoor, I Puritani, Belisario,*
and *Beatrice di Tenda,* the last two also in New York premieres).[86]
Despite the acknowledged mediocrity of the company, it drew large
audiences. Apparently, many New Yorkers shared the attitude of a
critic for the *Spirit,* who counseled patience. "Let us not be so foolish,"
he advised on 14 February, "to refuse to sustain this attempt to establish
a stage for fuller and richer enjoyment hereafter [simply] because we
cannot at the first command all the talent the world affords. In the
language of another, 'let us not kill our canary, because we cannot get
a nightingale.' " To many listeners the mediocrity of the troupe was
an irrelevant issue. The fashionables found the house neither as elegant

nor as comfortable as they wished; a critic for the *New World* complained on 10 February that the armless seats were "miserably uncomfortable." Nevertheless, they attended the performances in droves.[87] As the *Spirit*'s critic pointed out on 24 February, Palmo's functioned as "an elegant salon . . . where friends meet friends, acquaintance, acquaintance, without the bore of over-crowded and over-heated drawing rooms, and with none of the disagreements of party-giving and party-going. The entertainments are precisely the same, so far as seeing and being seen, enjoying the chit-chattery of themselves and of each other, and keeping on terms with society, are concerned." The critic—lest his readers consider the habitués of the opera to be completely indifferent to the charms of the music—hastened to add that the musical offerings did function as an added attraction. He pointed out that instead of being forced to listen to the "dolorous bangings and twangings of unlucky piano fortes, which are occasionally heard between the comparative lulls of universal conversation at an evening party,— at the Opera House, one has a chance, at least, of listening to the grandest compositions of the best masters, not only excellently sung, but with all their beauties impressed upon the soul by the potent aid of scenic and histrionic effects." He concluded that "the addition of accessories like these [to the] social and fashionable assembly . . . cannot be considered a drawback upon its pleasure."

If the large numbers of opera-lovers and fashionables who thronged the theater at every performance were any indication, Palmo should have been making money hand-over-fist. It soon became clear, however, that the manager had struck what Lawrence calls a "disastrous bargain" with his bass-director Valtellina. The financial terms to which he had agreed were impossible to meet, especially considering the size of the theater. Even with full houses, Palmo was unable to show a profit after paying the star singers' exorbitant salaries. As a result, only a month after opening night, he was well on his way to bankruptcy.[88]

To make matters worse, the company soon found itself beset with other serious difficulties, many of which were symptomatic of the problems that would cause the failure of scores of Italian troupes during the 1840s and 1850s. The star tenor Antognini, for example, repeatedly pleaded indisposition. As a result, Palmo was forced to send in a substitute for him night after night, which irritated critics and alienated members of the audience. The tenor's first appearance was not until 20 March, almost seven weeks into the season.[89] Furthermore, a war erupted between the rival partisans of the two sopranos, Majocchi and Borghese, in which the press joined whole-heartedly. By March, according to Lawrence, a "general explosion of public accusations, counter-accusations, mutual recriminations, self-glorifying justifications, conflicting financial statements, and angry rebuttals" filled the newspapers.[90] It was clear that the company was being torn apart by internal dissension, and New Yorkers rapidly became weary of the internecine war among visiting Italian "professors of harmony" whose "habit of quarrelling, overreaching, factionary intriguing, indulgence in ungenerous feeling, and moral discords of the most violent descriptions" was "the plague and shame of the musical—and particularly the vocal—profession."[91] Not surprisingly, the season collapsed in late March, and it soon was clear that the genial Palmo was the heavy loser in the enterprise. The *Anglo American* reported on 6 April that of a net profit of $14,000 (approximately $209,580 in 1992 currency), the principal singers had made off with $7,500 ($112,275). Each of the stars had made several thousand dollars in the venture; Palmo was left with a loss of $1,500 ($22,455).[92]

The company reformed almost immediately for an additional twelve performances, this time under the management of Giuseppe de Begnis, the Italian buffo who had come to the United States in 1838 as a vocal star. This second season, including all the benefit performances, lasted from 29 April through 10 June.[93] It was somewhat more successful than the first season, perhaps because this troupe performed a different repertory than had Palmo's, one that included the Italian versions of some familiar and popular works (*Il barbiere di Siviglia, Lucia di Lammermoor, La Sonnambula,* and *L'Elisir d'amore,* the New York premieres—in Italian—of the latter two).[94]

In September 1845, the same troupe was back, again under the aegis of Palmo.[95] The company played for a month, giving performances of *Lucia, L'Elisir d'amore,* and *Il Pirata,* only to collapse spectacularly in renewed dissension and chaos in October. The troupe fell apart quite literally; during the last act of *Il Pirata* on 18 October the tenor refused to continue, and half of the orchestra walked out over a wage dispute.[96] The New York press was both scandalized and thoroughly disgusted by the behavior of the troupe as a whole.[97] A month later, however, phoenixlike, the company commenced yet another season with a new prima donna, the Italian contralto Rosina Pico, and apparently with the serious collective intention to turn over a new leaf. This time they managed to stay together for almost two months and gave performances of five works: *Belisario, La Cenerentola, Semiramide, Chiara di Rosembergh,* and *Lucrezia Borgia,* the last three in New York premieres.[98] At the end of the run of scheduled performances, the *Spirit's* critic wryly congratulated the singers on 11 January 1845 for having brought a season to a successful conclusion without a single serious public squabble, fight, or letter of accusation or explanation to the newspapers. By the mid 1840s, however, the image of Italian opera performers as greedy, contentious, lazy, and dishonest individuals—a stereotype that would be widespread among Americans during the late 1840s and 1850s—was already in full bloom; its source should be clear.[99]

Because of the long string of benefits that inevitably was tacked onto the end of each season, the company's last performance was on 25 January. The troupe must have been reasonably successful during this season, for they attracted large enough audiences that drama critics were once again prompted to complain about the dubious taste of New Yorkers, who were so interested in pleasure and entertainment that they would neglect the theater in favor of seating themselves "night after night . . . in the Opera House," according to the *Spirit* on 25 January (576). After their final performance, the company was faced with three choices: mount another season in New York, mount a season elsewhere, or disband. It was unclear at first what the musicians would do. The previous 7 December, the *Spirit* had announced that the ensemble was engaged to appear in March and April at the American Theatre in New Orleans, and many expected the singers to leave (492). By January, however, the southern trip was in doubt. "No definite information can be furnished with regard to the Italian Troupe," wrote the reporter for the *Spirit* on 25 January, "as they seem all to be pulling in contrary directions. Borghese signed, on their behalf, articles to perform at New Orleans, but the Signora Pico is determined to concertize in Boston. . . . The truth is," he concluded, "they are going, through their own folly and wilfulness, but to destruction." This level of uncertainty about a company's intentions is typical of attempts by journalists of the time to predict, or by present historians to unravel, the movements of such troupes.

By early February, it was clear that the company had split at least in half. On 8 February, four singers (Borghese, Luigi Perozzi, Signor Tomasi, and Amalia Ricci, the first three erstwhile members of Palmo's troupe) were reportedly "progressing slowly southward, giving concerts at Philadelphia &c, with marked success"; at the same time, Pico was giving concerts in New York.[100] From 3 March through 2 May, the southern branch of the troupe did appear at the American Theatre in New Orleans, where they gave performances of seven operas (*I Puritani, Belisario, Lucrezia Borgia, Marino Faliero, L'Elisir d'amore, Lucia di Lammermoor,* and *Semiramide*).[101] The company's reception in New Orleans is not mentioned in contemporary musical or theatrical journals, but according to reviews in March and April in the *Daily Picayune,* they enjoyed a great deal of success. The enthusiasm of New Orleans for opera had not abated. As a correspondent to the *Spirit* had reported the previous 14 September, "we are persuaded that nothing is so popular as opera with all classes" (348).

The subsequent travels of this company are unknown; perhaps they simply disbanded. A reference to "the Borghese troupe" in the *Spirit* on 29 August 1846, however, suggests that at least the soprano continued to tour with some kind of an opera company. Borghese and Perozzi both eventually resurfaced in New York, the former in 1849 after some time spent in Havana, the latter in 1847.[102] The other two — because of a dearth of information in contemporary periodicals — seem to have vanished. Italian opera, too, seems to have vanished from the United States for the rest of 1845 and for all of 1846. This situation, however, changed significantly — and permanently — in January 1847.

1847–60: Social and Economic Background

1847–48: Palmo's, the Havana Company, and the Astor Place Opera Company

The year 1847 was a watershed in the annals of Italian opera performance in the United States. During that year Americans witnessed the final demise of Ferdinando Palmo's ill-fated opera house, attended performances in New York and Philadelphia of the Astor Place Opera Company (the troupe organized to perform in the new Astor Place Opera House in New York), and enthusiastically welcomed a truly stellar company from Havana that was making the first of several lengthy visits to North America.[103] Although the last ensemble in residence at Palmo's was not an itinerant company, its tale is nevertheless relevant to this study, for the initial success of that company led to the construction of the Astor Place Opera House, a theater that would serve as the New York home of many itinerant troupes from 1847 through 1852.[104] Because all three companies were important — and their activities, to a certain extent, typical of those of many later troupes — it is useful to review the history of each.

The man behind the new company at Palmo's was the buffo Antonio Sanquirico. He had first appeared in New York as a member of Palmo's second company, then subsequently returned to Europe, where he intended to stay.[105] During the summer of 1846, however, he became associated with a troupe of vocalists in Europe; remembering Palmo's delightful little opera house, he decided to try to take this company to New York. After securing (by mail) a subscription list of thirty at $100 each, the company announced a season at Palmo's and left Liverpool for the United States in November 1846.[106] The troupe was under the joint management of Sanquirico, the tenor Salvatore Patti, and one C. Pogliani. At the conclusion of this enterprise the latter would rapidly fade from view; Sanquirico and Patti, however, would remain active as members of opera companies in the United States well into the 1850s. Salvatore Patti has a further claim on music history as the father of Adelina Patti, one of the legendary singers of the nineteenth century.[107]

The *Spirit* reported on 21 November 1846 that Sanquirico had engaged "a remarkably fine troupe"; this, in truth, was no mere puffery. The company had two major stars. The prima donna was the young Clotilda Barili, step-daughter of Salvatore Patti, a soprano who overwhelmed Manhattan critics and audiences with her teen-age good looks and angelic singing. The principal tenor was Sesto Benedetti who, according to White, had "in the tone and quality of his voice something to which the public could not say no."[108] Within several weeks of the season's opening, "La Barili" had become the "toast of New York," and the *New York Herald* had proclaimed Benedetti a "full-fledged public idol."[109]

By the time the troupe opened its season on 4 January 1847 with the U.S. premiere of Donizetti's *Linda di Chamounix,* New Yorkers had been almost two full years without performances of Italian opera. They greeted the termination of this enforced abstinence with delight. Audiences flocked to Palmo's on opening night and continued to do so for the duration of the first season, which lasted until 31 March. Certainly, the esteem in which New Yorkers held "La Barili" and Benedetti did nothing to dampen the public's enthusiasm for the troupe; the presence of a favored star or two in the cast never hurt box-office receipts. The company's repertory also worked in its favor. According to Lawrence, the production of *Lucia di Lammermoor,* their second choice, was a "spectacular hit." They also successfully mounted performances of two other new operas during these twelve weeks: Pier Antonio Copolla's *Nina, la pazza per amore* and Verdi's *I Lombardi.*[110] The latter, significantly, was the first work by Giuseppe Verdi to be performed in the United States. By the time the season closed in March, the Sanquirico-Patti Company discovered that their run had been, in Ireland's rather dry assessment, "more than ordinarily successful" (2:481). Subsequently, however, the company would not be able to sustain this level of support.

During its second season, the troupe was plagued by a rash of illnesses among its principal singers; with no stars to serve as box-office draws, audiences quickly melted away. To make matters worse, in April the Sanquirico-Patti Company found itself in direct competition with another Italian troupe—the first time in the history of the United States that this had happened. This competition, furthermore, came from no upstart neophyte troupe, but from Marti's Havana Opera Company, which in 1847 was a huge, formidable, and star-studded ensemble. The company paused in New York only briefly in April, giving two operas and one concert before heading on to Boston. The mere presence in the United States of this brilliant ensemble, however, coupled with the publicity and excitement it generated, was enough to destroy completely any remaining enthusiasm left in New York for the Sanquirico-Patti troupe. The *Spirit*'s critic wrote on 24 April, for example, that the Cuban troupe was "equal to if not superior to any company that ever came to this city, and [is] certainly better than [the company] at Palmo's." The Palmo troupe attempted to entice audiences back by adding four new operas to its repertory (*Lucrezia Borgia, L'Elisir d'amore, Semiramide,* and *Il barbiere di Siviglia*), but even operatic novelty did not help. The season, which officially closed on 26 May but dribbled on until 7 June with sundry benefit performances, was a financial disaster.[111] At its end, the company, in a pattern already drearily familiar, disbanded.

The 1847 Havana Opera Company was not the first ensemble of that name to visit the United States. Although this version of the Cuban company was vastly superior to the others in both size and quality of performers, it would be surpassed in overall skill by the Havana Company of 1849–51 (chapter 4). Yet the 1847 troupe easily outclassed any other opera company that had performed in North America up to that point. The impresario Marti represented the power — and the money — behind the impressive succession of opera companies in residence at the Gran Teatro de Tacon, an opulent theater he had built in the Cuban capital in 1838.[112] A number of the celebrities in this particular Havana troupe had joined the company at the beginning of the 1846–47 season. They included the troupe's co-directors and instrumental superstars, the doublebass and violin virtuosi Giovanni Bottesini (1821–89) and Luigi Arditi (1822–1903). The latter musician's reputation as the composer of the popular waltz "Il Baccio" has survived into the twentieth century.[113]

Marti's Havana companies were primarily resident ensembles at the Tacon Theatre; only secondarily were they touring groups. Because it was to the musicians' advantage to leave Cuba during yellow-fever season, the visits of Havana companies to the United States almost invariably occurred during the spring and summer months, after the conclusion of the Cuban opera season in late February or early March. The companies in 1837 and 1843 had followed this pattern, as did the 1847 troupe that toured North America and mounted seasons in Boston, Philadelphia, and New York from mid-April through early October.[114]

When the company arrived in the United States it numbered seventy-three; by July its ranks had swollen to eighty-three.[115] They traveled with a complete contingent of singers, instrumentalists, and support crew. "From the *prima donna assoluta* down to the youngest chorister," reported the *New York Herald* on 15 April 1847, "everything is comprised in its ranks—an entire orchestra, a magnificent wardrobe, in fact everything, save a theatre, they carry with them."[116] The twenty-member chorus (four sopranos, three altos, six tenors, and seven basses) was small but well rehearsed; according to the critics, it was better than any opera chorus yet heard in North America. "So powerful and melodious were the voices, and so perfectly were the tones delivered," marveled one reporter for the *Boston Musical Gazette* on 25 October, "that one could scarcely believe less than a hundred were singing." The critic for the *Spirit* agreed. "The choruses [in *Ernani*] were admirably, nay deliciously given," he wrote on 24 April. "Indeed, [they sang] in such a style as never greeted our ears by any efforts of any choristers we ever listened to." (Of course, the fact that the choruses in *Ernani* are more significant as choruses than any Italian opera choral parts previously heard in New York may have contributed to the enthusiasm.)

Even more astonishing were the instrumentalists who traveled with the troupe. The company's orchestra reportedly numbered between twenty-five and thirty, an ensemble described by the *Spirit* as "very perfect in its arrangement and disposition, and most favorable to the singers because [it is] constantly with them."[117] Furthermore, the co-directors Bottesini and Arditi were both virtuosos, and they stunned audiences with their feats of instrumental prowess. The skill of the two instrumentalists is well documented. Bottessini, in particular, was a true virtuoso: in Europe, he was known as "the Paganini of the double bass." New Yorkers, according to Lawrence, found performances by both men to be "nothing short of miraculous."[118] The two performed duets of their own composition, either during intermissions or after the evening's opera. Their repertory consisted of variations on operatic tunes or on other works.

During their North American visit the company performed ten works by five composers: *I due Foscari* (the U.S. premiere), *Ernani,* and *I Lombardi* (Verdi); *I Capuleti e i Montecchi, Norma,* and *La Sonnambula* (Bellini); *Mosè in Egitto* and *Il barbiere di Siviglia* (Rossini); *Linda di Chamounix* (Donizetti); and *Saffo* (Pacini, Figure 21). The company also gave concert performances in each of the cities; *Mosè in Egitto,* for example, was mounted as an oratorio in both Philadelphia and Boston concert halls.[119] Furthermore, during the troupe's second Boston visit, the musicians gave operatic concerts for an entire week, from 11 to 15 October, performing the music (without acting or scenery) of *Norma, La Sonnambula, Ernani, Linda di Chamounix,* and *I Capuleti*

HOWARD ATHENÆUM

8TH NIGHT OF THE SEASON!

—OF THE—

ITALIAN OPERA COMPANY

FROM HAVANA,

CONSISTING OF 73 PERSONS.

Second Night of Giovanni Pacini's Grand Opera of

SAFFO,

Which was received with enthusiastic favor, on its first representation.

SIGNA. FORTUNATA TEDESCO
will appear. ☞ Second appearance of
SIGNOR L. PEROZZI.

Wednesday Eve'g, May 5, 1847

Will be produced, for the 2nd time in the United States, Signor Giovanni Pacini's
Grand Lyrical Tragedy, in three acts, entitled

SAFFO!

ALCANDRO, Priest of Apollo	Sig. L. BATAGLINI
FAON	Sig. L. PEROZZI
IPPIA, Chief of the Priests	Sig. I. PIAMONTESI
LISIMACO	Sig. PIETRO CANDI
SAFFO	Signorina FORTUNATA TEDESCO
CLIMENE, Alcandro's daughter	Signorina SOFIA MARINI
DIRCE	Signorina THEODOLINDA GERLI

Chorus of both sexes—Priests, Attendants, Greek Citizens, Natives of Leucarde,
Secret Guards, Musicians.

The action is in Greece—First part in Olympia; the rest in Leucarde.

☞ Parquette Boxes $1; Parquette 50 cents; Boxes 50 cents; Second Circle 50 cents.
☞ Doors open at 7 o'clock; the Opera will commence at 1·4 to 8 o'clock. ☜
☞ Books, containing an English version of the Opera, can be had at the Box Door.
Price 12½ cents.

☞ The Choice of Boxes will be sold at Public Auction, in the Vestibule of
the Athenæum, WEDNESDAY MORNING, at 10 o'clock.
CLARK & HATCH, Auctioneers.

☞ FRIDAY—Ninth Night of the Opera Season.

EASTBURN'S PRESS—STATE STREET.

21. Playbill for a performance of Giovanni Pacini's opera *Saffo* by the
Havana Opera Company at the Howard Athenaeum in Boston, 5 May
1847. (American Antiquarian Society)

e i Montecchi at the Tremont Temple "for the benefit of those whose consciences will not allow them to attend the opera."[120]

The company made a strong impression on East Coast audiences. As Lawrence observes, "with their fine singing stars, well-rehearsed chorus and orchestra, luminous musical direction by Arditi and Bottesini, elaborate staging, wardrobe of costumes 'worth $30,000,' and impeccable ensemble," the troupe "exhibited a degree of professionalism previously unknown" in New York—or, for that matter, in the rest of the Northeast.[121] By the time the troupe left for Havana in mid-October, the *Boston Musical Gazette* reported on 25 October that its performances—like those of the vocal stars of the late 1820s and 1830s—had helped to heighten the expectations of American opera audiences. The Sanquirico-Patti troupe already had fallen victim to the impact of this company; during the autumn of 1847 the company of the new Astor Place Opera House in New York (Figure 22) would also have to contend with the continuing reverberations from Marti's departed musicians.[122]

In the spring of 1847, a group of 150 wealthy New Yorkers decided to form yet another Italian opera association. There had already been two: the group that imported Manuel García's troupe in 1825 and the association that built the first New York Italian Opera House in 1833. According to both White and Schiavo, New York socialites were impressed by the initial pecuniary success of the Sanquirico-Patti troupe; certainly the enthusiasm generated by the Havana Company during the spring and summer was encouraging.[123] The association arranged to have the Astor Place Opera House built; at the same time the directors sent Sanquirico and Patti back to Italy to recruit a company "capable of performing all the operas now being sung in Europe."[124] Because a growing cadre of Italian singers now lived in New York (including those left over from Sanquirico and Patti's own recently disintegrated company), the singer-managers did not have to recruit an entire troupe. They signed contracts, however, with a large group of singers and brought them back to New York in the fall.[125] They also hired some singers from their own defunct company, but apparently newcomers outnumbered veterans by almost two to one. The overall impression was of an entirely new company.[126]

The construction of the Astor Place Opera House and the organization of the new company represents yet another in a continuing series of attempts by New York's bon ton to commandeer Italian opera for themselves. This time, for a variety of reasons, their efforts met with a great deal more success than had previous ventures. The very segregation of opera from the popular theater—by its removal to a house built exclusively for its performance—was the first and most obvious step in the process of expropriation. Removal to this particular house loudly broadcast to New Yorkers of all classes the message of intended exclusivity. Especially marked was the contrast with Palmo's deliberate attempt at egalitarianism. Even the location of the Astor Place Opera House—at Eighth and Lafayette streets in a remote but very fashionable section of (then) uptown Manhattan—discouraged attendance by the everyday, nonsubscribing, impulsive, theater-going public.

If location itself was not sufficient to frustrate ordinary theater-goers, the physical layout of the house certainly helped. Those individuals who could afford the 50 cent admission to only the old upper gallery, now renamed the "amphitheatre," found that section of the house to be "the most uncomfortable and ill-contrived place imaginable." Even worse, the view of the stage from the gallery was almost completely blocked by a huge, ornate chandelier.[127] Furthermore, a dress code requiring "freshly shaven faces, evening dress, fresh waistcoats, and kid gloves for gentlemen" discriminated against audience members who were not wealthy.[128] Finally, in case the rabble still did not understand, the critic for the *New York Herald* spelled the message out in plain American English in the 23 November 1847 review of the opening-night performance: "The fashionable world is now completely organized—the opera is successful—white kid gloves are all the go—and the *canaille* must keep themselves a respectful distance from Astor Place hereafter. Read and obey."[129]

According to White, the intimidations worked. "It may safely be said," he wrote, "that there was hardly a person present [on opening night] who was not known, by name, at least, to a very considerable number of his or her fellow auditors." His clear implication is that the audience of 1,500 or so in the theater for the company's debut on 22 November was comprised exclusively of the close-knit New York social elite.[130] But White's observations—he was the critic for the *Courier and Enquirer*—like those of many of his colleagues, were selective. On opening night, in fact, the house was crowded with both the bon ton and the general public.[131] The critic for the *Sunday Age,* who did not have aristocratic blinders on, observed on 28 November that above the "very hotbed of Upper Tendom exclusiveness" were seated the "vulgar wretches, low creatures, [and] *canaille,*" some five hundred of them "piled up [in the third tier], one above the other, and striving in vain to catch a glimpse of the stage."[132]

The Astor Place Company was well received, although critics disagreed about its merits in comparison with the recently departed Havana Company.[133] Despite the lingering memories of that troupe's overwhelming success, however, by the end of the first six weeks of the season (during which the company had mounted productions of *Ernani,*

22. Astor Place Opera House, 8th and Lafayette streets. This drawing illustrates the aristocratic mien of the theater. (New York: Henry Hoff, 1850) (New-York Historical Society)

Beatrice di Tenda, La Sonnambula, Lucia, and *I Puritani*), the Astor Place troupe was proclaimed a "solid and complete success."[134] The *Spirit*'s critic was optimistic. "If none of those unfortunate disagreements, which have heretofore occurred in connexion with every Italian company in this city, should occur with this [troupe]," he wrote on 23 January 1848, "we feel assured of its undoubted success." This, however, was not to be. Sanquirico and Patti were doomed to watch the early success of the Astor Place Company turn to disaster, just as they had watched their previous troupe fail in spite of its early promise. Although the company added new works to its repertory during the second season (*I Capuleti e i Montecchi* and, on 14 February, the North American premiere of Mercadante's *Il Giuramento*), by mid-February it was clear that the ensemble was in serious financial trouble. The "unfortunate disagreements" so common to Italian troupes had cropped up: singers became—or claimed to be—ill, and jealousies, competition, and backbiting were rife among the performers. The vocalists, to a large extent, sabotaged their own performances by alienating the audience. The season, only two-thirds finished, ground to an ignominious halt in early March.[135]

The management, claiming merely to be taking a two- or three-week recess, put the company on the train and went south in search of an audience in Philadelphia. The troupe carried on more or less successfully at the Chestnut Street Theatre, giving a total of twenty-one performances of *Lucia di Lammermoor, Lucrezia Borgia, Ernani,* and *Il Giuramento* over the course of four weeks.[136] According to Joseph Sill, the Italians attracted reasonably good houses; on 3 March the theater "was well filled by a fashionable and intelligent audience," and on 10 March "the House was well fill'd." At the end of the final week of the season, however, the company—at least according to Curtis—"went broke" and returned home.[137] The New York critics, who thought that they had seen the last of the Italians, were surprised when the troupe reopened at the Astor Place House in late March.[138] They mounted one new opera (the North American premiere of Verdi's *Nabucco*), but thereafter gave only additional performances of *Lucia di Lammermoor* and *Lucrezia Borgia;* by the second week of April the end was clearly in sight.[139] Sanquirico and Patti eventually relinquished management of the rapidly failing troupe, and Michele Rapetti and the Barilis and Pattis split off and went south on their own to perform in Philadelphia. A final, last-ditch attempt by the three remaining stars (Truffi, Benedetti, and Beneventano) to keep the disintegrating company afloat failed, and the troupe fell apart completely in late April.[140]

Although the troupe disintegrated in April and relinquished control of the Astor Place House to New York pleasure-garden operator William Niblo, it was not long before new companies—three of them—formed from the rubble. Several singers joined forces with some of the artists from the 1847 Havana Opera Company, who were back in the United States again after the completion of the Tacon season. This group opened at the Chestnut Street Theatre and performed for slightly over a week, then fell apart.[141] After reorganizing under the direction of Luigi Arditi, also recently arrived from Cuba, the company mounted a two-week season from 14 to 26 August at Philadelphia's Walnut Street Theatre before disbanding again.[142] A different group of vocalists that continued to cling to the name "New York Astor Place Company" (the group, in fact, was comprised primarily of Astor Place singers) mounted a season at the Howard Athenaeum in Boston in May and June. They performed a repertory of four operas (*Lucrezia Borgia, Nabucco, Ernani,* and *Il Giuramento*) before disbanding.[143] Finally, a third group of survivors, the Barili-Patti contingent, formed a concert troupe and performed in Philadelphia and New York; they were assisted in this endeavor by the pianist and impresario-to-be Maurice Strakosch.[144]

The reasons for the failure of the Astor Place troupe itself were numerous. Some of the company's familiar problems included stars'

23. Interior, Boston Theatre, site of many performances by Italian opera companies in the 1850s. (*Ballou's Pictorial Drawing-Book Companion*, November 1855)

exorbitant salary demands and bickering among the singers.[145] A number of individuals, however, suggested that the New York critics were also to blame for the demise of the ensemble. Many of the journalists had endeavored to prove their own musical sophistication by picking apart the company's performances and repertory, by comparing the troupe unflatteringly to the departed Cuban ensemble, and even by cruelly attacking individual singers. Most of those who were interested in assigning blame, however, placed responsibility squarely on the managers. "The management was conducted by too many," complained a critic in the *Spirit* on 6 May, "and authority [was] exercised by persons having no idea of what they were doing." Furthermore, he continued, "there were too many stars, and too little brilliancy. The materials were possessed but so badly put together that there was discord behind the scenes and grumbling before them. The great variety that could have been presented was neglected, and two or three operas forced upon the subscribers. The *bon ton,* or the *dilettanti,* or both, were *ennuied* to death."

Perhaps a more serious problem—and one that most critics seem to have ignored—was the deliberate alienation of the popular audience by the Astor Place subscribers and directors. The bon ton, by 1847, evidently believed themselves to be sufficiently numerous to support opera without the help of the middle and working classes. The failure of the Astor Place troupe, however, seems to suggest that this judgment was erroneous. Erroneous or not, the wealthy had set out to exclude what they thought of as riff-raff, and, to a great extent, they had succeeded. Large numbers of "vulgar wretches, low creatures, [and] *canaille*" had been in the audience on opening night, but it did not take middle- and working-class New Yorkers long to discover, and be thoroughly insulted by, the egregious discrimination built into the physical arrangement of the Opera House. Not only was there a marked and obvious contrast between the inferior gallery seats and the plush sofas in the boxes and comfortable armchairs in the "parquette," but opera lovers who were not wealthy, as nonsubscribers, were also completely excluded from that more comfortable section of the house — and they knew it. In November, Philip Hone, who had predicted the eventual failure of the Astor Place Company, based his forecast on precisely these social inequities. "I apprehend the danger [to the Astor Place enterprise]," he observed in his diary on 23 November 1847, "to be the same which has hitherto operated against the opera and occasioned its failure, namely the aristocratic exclusiveness of assigning the principal seats to the subscribers." He continued, "The *public*, strangers, and other entertainment-seekers, will not consent to an arrangement by which certain fashionables are helped first to the best cuts. There is nothing of which the sovereign people are so tenacious as their equality in matters relating to their amusements. The Declaration of Independence on political rights is not more precious to us freeborn Americans (as we love to call ourselves) than our right to demand for a (few) poor dollars the privilege of 'first come, first served.' "[146]

The contribution of middle- or working-class audience alienation to the demise of the first Astor Place troupe is less critical an issue than the development of this alienation itself and the significant role that the Astor Place elite had in its growth. Partly as a result of the Astor Place Opera House, the New York public, as the wealthy had intended, began to be chary of patronizing a form of entertainment that was gradually taking on some of the trappings of the elite. The upper-class social rituals that McConachie rightly suggests were becoming a part of opera-going (for example, proper dress and proper behavior) were starting to be associated in the minds of the middle- and working-class public — at least in New York — with Italian opera. As a result, ordinary New York theater-goers did not just avoid performances of the Astor Place Opera Company. By the late 1840s many were also beginning to experience feelings of antipathy toward Italian opera itself. A backlash was in the making.

In the United States there had always been an undercurrent of disapproval toward foreigners and foreign entertainments, especially among Americans with strong nativist leanings. Animosity toward Europeans in general increased during the 1840s, as levels of immigration climbed dramatically.[147] In New York, this xenophobia became intertwined with the increasing identification of Italian opera as an entertainment with aristocratic trappings. The combination gave fresh impetus and, in the eyes of many, legitimacy to the expression of nativist sentiment. Evidence of this attitude began to appear in the pages of musical and theatrical periodicals. "Everyone in the city but myself has heard 'Lucia di Lammermoor' and the other performances of the troupe now engaged at Palmo's," one such individual wrote to the *Spirit* on 10 April 1847.

> I am very fond of music, but (may I be forgiven for it!) I have some prejudices as strong, and no doubt as unreasonable, as those of blunt John Bull. I hate Italians! Like the war-horse towards the battle, I "scent" them "afar off." They look so greasy and are so redolent of pomatum, and bear's oil, olives, and sardines. And then the varlets are so vain! ... the poorest supernumerary of an Italian company deems himself the wonder of men, and the idol of women. What superb voices the rascals have! How they do excel in music! And yet, beyond this ... what is left of the land that produced Cicero and Petrarch. Oh! Monkeys and hand organs! (73)

Even Walt Whitman, who was later to find one of his great sources of inspiration in Italian opera, had difficulties with the growing elitism associated with the genre. His well-known plea to the democratic masses to throw off the yoke of European cultural domination dates from 1847. "We have long enough followed obedient and child-like in the track of the Old World," he wrote in the *Brooklyn Daily Eagle* on 8 September. "We have received her tenors and her buffos, her operatic troupes and her vocalists, of all grades and complexions; listened to and applauded the songs made for a different state of society — made perhaps by royal genius, but made to please royal ears likewise; and it is time that such listening and receiving should cease."[148]

The appearance of such contrary opinions — and of such stereotypical and overtly anti-Italian sentiments — suggests that the New York elite had made some progress by the late 1840s in their quest to remove Italian opera from the domain of the popular theater.[149] This progress, however, was incomplete and, to a certain extent, transitory. The Astor Place Opera Company, after all, had failed. Furthermore, the succeeding Astor Place troupes did not cater so exclusively and overtly to the wealthy (chapter 4). But the snobbish attitudes of the Astor Place elite, so much in evidence during 1847, elicited a response from many working- and middle-class opera lovers. The so-called *canaille* avenged their wounded pride in May 1849 by the infamous Astor Place Riot, an altercation ostensibly prompted by a feud between the British actor William Charles Macready and the American star Edwin Forrest but in reality a class conflict: the rich versus the poor, the aristocracy versus American democrats.[150] "Elite operagoing had successfully excluded the people," McConachie observed about the riot, "but clearly it failed to mystify them" (185).

But had the New York elite really succeeded in excluding the people other than temporarily? Certainly, the elite did not exclude ordinary people from performances of Italian opera in English translation (chapters 1 and 2). But what of Italian opera? McConachie points out that by the late 1840s most of the elements that would eventually help the New York elite claim Italian opera-going as an exclusive and fashionable activity were solidly in place (187). During the 1850s, the New York elite used their opera-going rituals to make progress in their social endeavors. Furthermore, they would use the primarily New York-based musical and theatrical press to communicate the image of opera as entertainment for the wealthy to Americans in the rest of the country. This conquest by the elite, however—even in New York and even as late as 1860—was anything but a fait accompli.[151]

1848–60: Social, Political, Economic, and Cultural Considerations

There is little question that 1847 marked a turning point for Italian opera in the United States. As the last year during which the entire aggregate of national Italian-opera performance can be summarized in narrative form, it marked the end of an on-again, off-again period of the accessability of Italian music. From 1847 through 1860 and later, there would be no lengthy periods of hiatus in the performance of Italian opera in this country. Although it was not clear at the time, the genre had finally become firmly established in the United States. The latter part of the antebellum period is characterized by a multiplicity of Italian troupes. From 1847 through 1860, between three and six Italian companies were active somewhere in this country during any single year (Appendix C). Increasingly wide-ranging itineraries took companies away from the East Coast and the cities on the Ohio-Mississippi River network and deeper and deeper into the American interior. Finally, the personnel of the numerous troupes tended to be in a constant state of flux. Even more than English vocal-star companies,

Italian troupes were so volatile that they formed, broke down, and reformed with a dismaying frequency.

The activity of Italian opera companies in North America grew steadily after 1847 for a number of economic, political, social, and artistic reasons. By the end of the 1840s, the United States had finally recovered from the devastating nationwide recession caused by the Panic of 1837. By 1847 and 1848, exports were up, citizens were again employed, cities were growing and prospering, and theaters were back in business. On the other hand, economic conditions in Europe during the same period were increasingly unstable; the political situation on the Continent was in a state of extreme crisis. Such circumstances were unconducive to the support of theatrical or musical business-as-usual. Consequently, many working musicians, singers, and instrumentalists — Italians, Germans, and French — immigrated to the United States during the late 1840s. As *Saroni's Musical Times* noted on 17 November 1849, "there is at this moment an unusual activity in the musical world. Every vessel that furrows the broad Atlantic brings with it its precious load of musical genius and talent" (86). The immigration continued throughout the 1850s, and the increased pool of Italian singers living in the United States naturally affected the number of opera troupes being formed. As early as the late 1840s, theater managers and impresarios no longer had to send to Europe for entire troupes. It was sufficient to import a new star or two and then build around them a company comprised largely of singers who lived in New York or elsewhere in the United States. Because this pool of competent Italian vocalists continued to grow during the 1850s, the formation of numerous companies became increasingly feasible as the decade wore on.

Another, more personal, economic lure attracted operatic stars to the United States. By the late 1840s and early 1850s, most prominent European performers were well aware of the monetary windfall that awaited them with an American tour. Certainly the fortune that Jenny Lind made during her phenomenally successful 1850–52 tour was common knowledge. Even before Lind's arrival, however, the United States had earned a reputation as a gold mine for European performers; numerous vocal stars returned to England in the 1830s with their pockets bulging. Jane Shirreff and John Wilson's North American tour, which had taken place at the beginning of the recession, had been lucrative, and visits during the 1840s by such virtuoso instrumentalists as Henry Vieuxtemps, Ole Bull, Leopold de Meyer, and Henri Herz likewise had been pecuniarily successful. By 17 August 1854, the *Musical Review* was observing that the United States was known to Europeans as the "El Dorado of the musical world" (289). And no wonder. Countless complaints published in musical and theatrical journals in the United States during the 1850s blame the failure of Italian companies on the outrageous salaries demanded by, and paid to, European operatic stars (or supposed-stars). "The people of the United States," wrote the editor of the *Musical World* in 1852, "cannot afford (and ought not if they could) to pay the . . . exorbitant and unjust . . . sums which are nightly expended, often on an ambiguous Prima Donna or an ordinary Tenor." Three years later, the *Musical Gazette* wondered why all the principal singers in the company of the New York Academy of Music were being paid "twice as much as they can command in any European city."[152]

Fair or unfair, excessive or not, the exorbitant salary demands of European vocalists were often met, especially if the star was truly first-rank. As a result, the quantity of Italian stars who visited the United States during the 1850s increased considerably; their quality also rose markedly. On 7 May 1853, the *Musical World* gleefully observed, "Europe is being deserted altogether of its great stars," and, to a certain extent, hyperbole aside, this was true (289). Theodore Thomas, who performed as a violinist in several itinerant opera companies during the 1850s, later wrote, "I doubt if there were ever brought together in any part of the world a larger number of talented vocalists than were gathered in New York between 1850 and the early sixties."[153] During that decade American audiences, and not just those in New York, could attend performances by many near-great and some truly great European operatic stars, including Henriette Sontag (1806–54), Anna de la Grange, Domenico Lorini, Angiolina Bosio (1830–59), Lorenzo Salvi (1810–79), Felicita Vestvali, Cesare Badiali (1810–65), Ignazio Marini (1815–73), Marietta Alboni (1826–94), Pasquale Brignoli (1824–84), and Marietta Gazzaniga (1824–84).[154] From September 1854 through February 1855, two of the greatest singers of the century—Giulia Grisi (1811–69) and her husband Giovanni Matteo Mario (1810–83)—performed in operas in New York, Boston, Philadelphia, Baltimore, and Washington (Appendix C). According to the *Musical Review,* their tour was so successful that James Hackett, the American actor-manager who had engaged them, earned some $20,000 after expenses (roughly $310,400 in modern terms) despite the "somewhat extravagant" salaries the stars had demanded to come to the United States.[155]

The social factors involved in the increased numbers of Italian companies active in North America during the 1850s are also, to a certain extent, bound up with economic conditions. The return of prosperity in the late 1840s brought about a renewed effort to expand the nationwide transportation system, as well as a significant growth in the size, number, and prosperity of cities and towns all over the country. Both the expanded transportation network and the increased size of cities in the interior meant that the days were numbered when an opera company would limit its activities almost exclusively to major urban areas of the East Coast or to New Orleans and its environs. Even in the early 1850s, Italian opera troupes could be found performing in cities as far-flung and as diverse as Richmond, Charleston, and Savannah (the Astor Place Company of 1850–51); San Francisco (the Pellegrini Opera Company in 1851 and 1853 and the Catherine Hayes Opera Company in 1854); as well as Montreal, Buffalo, Cincinnati, Louisville, St. Louis, Pittsburgh, Milwaukee, Chicago, Washington, Richmond, Charleston, Savannah, Augusta, Mobile, Memphis, Nashville, Toronto, Cleveland, Detroit, and Rochester (the Arditi Italian Opera Company tour of 1853–54) (Appendix C).

The potential audience for opera grew significantly during the period, which also contributed to the success of itinerant companies. The population of the United States itself increased by a third between 1840 and 1850, and again by the same factor between 1850 and 1860. The country grew by eight million—from twenty-three to thirty-one million—during the 1850s, the result of a high birth rate coupled with huge increases in immigration. Many newcomers, in particular Germans fleeing political repression after the failed revolution of 1848, were middle-class urban dwellers who settled in towns and cities on the East Coast and in the interior of the country. The overall growth— and the increased wealth—of the American middle class during the 1850s created an ever-expanding population of individuals with leisure time and disposable income, ready and waiting to be enticed into theaters and concert halls by touring European musical stars.

The number of wealthy people, especially in New York and Phila-delphia, likewise increased during this same time, and the opera-related activities of this segment of the population perhaps inadvertently ben-efited the rest of the country. The wealthy and elite of New York had set out to exclude those people who were not aristocrats from opera audiences, in part by the physical layout of the Astor Place Opera House itself. That they succeeded in New York to a certain extent is clear. What they perhaps had not considered when building their ex-clusive theater, however, was the subsequent use of the Astor Place House as the home base for a number of itinerant companies that traveled extensively in the United States and Mexico from 1848 through 1852, performing Italian opera elsewhere in the country for audiences comprised of elite as well as nonelite (chapter 4).

The existence of an opera house in New York or in Philadelphia to serve as a home base obviously greatly facilitated the formation of traveling companies. After the demise of the Astor Place House in 1852, the New York Academy of Music took over as the East Coast headquarters of numerous troupes that traveled around North America.[156] The academy first opened its doors in October 1854 with a performance of *Norma* by the Mario and Grisi Opera Company. It served for the next thirty years as New York's center for opera performance.[157] Philadelphia's elite finally made its contribution to the cultivation of opera by building the Philadelphia Academy of Music, which opened in 1857. This house served a similar function as the headquarters of touring companies; during the three-year period of 1857 to 1860, it was the home base of troupes managed primarily by Max Maretzek.

The final factor in the proliferation of Italian opera performance during the 1850s was an artistic one: the presence in this country after 1848 of operatic and concert impresarios, in particular, Bernard Ullman, Maurice Strakosch, and Max Maretzek, each of whom had a significant impact on the cultivation of Italian opera in North America. Ullman (?1817–85) arrived in this country sometime around 1842. During the 1840s he successfully managed American concert tours by various artists, and in the early years of the 1850s was associated with the opera companies of the German soprano Henriette Sontag and the French coloratura soprano Anna de la Grange. From 1856 through 1860 he managed a variety of other opera troupes, either on his own (the Ullman Opera Company) or jointly with Maurice Strakosch (the Ullman and Strakosch Opera Company). The Ullman Opera Company, and those Ullman managed with Strakosch, were generally affiliated with the New York Academy of Music. Ullman returned to Europe in 1862.[158]

Strakosch (1825–87) arrived in the United States in the spring of 1848. He quickly became closely associated with the family of Salvatore and Caterina Barili-Patti and in 1852 married their daughter Amalia, a contralto. During his thirteen years in the United States, Strakosch toured widely as a pianist, composer, and the manager of both full-blown opera companies and operatic concert troupes featuring such artists as Amalia and Adelina Patti, Ole Bull, Teresa Parodi, Miska Hauser, and others. In 1855 he entered into a short-lived partnership with Maretzek and Ole Bull to manage the Academy of Music Opera Company and from 1856 to 1857 managed his own opera troupe (Figure 24), which in February 1857 merged with Bernard Ullman's company.[159] The Ullman and Strakosch Opera Company (also identified variously as the Academy of Music Opera Company, the Ullman Company, and the Strakosch Company) toured the East Coast until 1860. Strakosch is best known for his artistic association with his sister-in-law, the great coloratura soprano Adelina Patti. He managed her operatic career from

24. Playbill from a performance by the Strakosch Opera Company at McVicker's Theatre in Chicago, 11 March 1857. This program is a good example of the potpourri nature of many benefit performances. (Chicago Historical Society)

1860 through 1868, but they quit the United States and returned to Paris in 1861.[160]

Maretzek (1821–97) also arrived in the United States in 1848. He served as the musical director for the second Astor Place Opera House Company under the management of Edward Fry. He became manager of that company in March 1849 when Fry relinquished control; he later served as the manager of various Astor Place companies, also identified widely as "Maretzek Opera Companies," until 1852 (chapter 4). During the mid to late 1850s, Maretzek managed his own troupe, the Maretzek Opera Company, which toured extensively in the United States, Mexico, and Cuba. He was also associated with a number of the companies that performed at the Philadelphia Academy of Music.[161] Unlike Strakosch or Ullman, Maretzek remained active as an impresario in the United States until well after the Civil War. He retired from management in 1878.[162]

Although Ullman, Strakosch, and Maretzek dominated Italian opera performance and management in the United States during the 1850s, they did not act alone (Appendix C). Numerous other individuals, including some singers, managed their own opera troupes. The soprano Felicita Vestvali, for example, managed a company that performed extensively in Mexico during 1856 and visited the United States for five months in 1857, appearing in New Orleans, St. Louis, Cincinnati, Pittsburgh, and New York before returning to Cuba and Mexico. Teresa Parodi (the prima donna of Maretzek's 1850–51 company), Balbina Steffanone, and Mariette Piccolomini, as other examples, at least nominally headed their own opera companies in the mid and late 1850s. One other important competitor with the Strakosch/Maretzek/Ullman triumvirate was Luigi Arditi, the virtuoso violinist and orchestra leader for Marti's 1846–51 Havana opera companies and the musical director for Maretzek's Astor Place troupe during part of 1851.[163] From December 1852 through June 1855, Arditi was associated with a succession of opera troupes, including those identified variously in contemporary sources as the Alboni, Le Grand Smith, Marshall, Grand Combination, Arditi, DeVries, and Sontag Opera companies. It would be easy to assume that these were different and distinct troupes; this, however, was not necessarily the case. It is not always easy to ferret out just which troupe was which, in part because the identification of an Italian opera company in contemporary newspapers, periodicals, or even on playbills, depended on the manager's or a critic's perception of how the troupe was best known to the public. As a result, a particular troupe was frequently referred to, sometimes simultaneously, by different names. Conversely, the personnel of a company that was well known by a specific title — the Astor Place or Havana opera companies,

for example—was often significantly different from season to season.
The rampant confusion connected with the various Arditi companies,
much of which—at least for the 1853–54 tour—has been sorted out
by Thomas Kaufman, is typical. It is similarly difficult to sort out
companies that toured and performed slightly later in the decade.[164]

It would be impossible to make an intelligible narrative summary of
the activities, personnel, repertories, and itineraries of all the Italian
troupes active in the United States from 1848 through 1860. The survey
of activity during the first part of the antebellum period and the over-
view of the succeeding years, however, should be an adequate background for an examination of one prototype troupe active during the
second part. This close examination of a single troupe, Max Maretzek's
Astor Place Opera Company of 1850–51, will illustrate the astonishing
complexities of opera management during the period and reveal the
fluctuation of personnel from company to company, choice of repertory,
managerial tactics, frequency of performance, and composition of audience. Such insights can be applied to other Italian opera troupes of
the period. In order to understand the pervasiveness of Italian operatic
activity in the United States during the 1850s, it is necessary to consider
the large numbers and varied itineraries of opera companies listed in
Appendix C as well as the documentation concerning a single season
of a single company reported in chapter 4. Through such extrapolation
an approximate picture of the sheer quantity of Italian operatic activity
in this country during the 1850s begins to emerge, and the importance
of this genre to the development of American musical culture becomes
clear.

4

Max Maretzek and His
Astor Place Opera Company,
1850–51

In October 1850, New York's Astor Place Opera House opened for its fourth year of operation. Max Maretzek, the man in charge of the Italian Opera Company in residence, was the third person to attempt to manage an opera company at the Astor Place House since it had first opened in November 1847.[1] With the start of this new season, it was clear that Maretzek was becoming a man to be reckoned with in the production of opera in the United States, for this was his third year of association with an Astor Place company and his second as manager. Maretzek had survived the pitfalls and financial tribulations of two seasons mounted during 1849–50, as well as a short season in April 1849.[2] He also would survive afflictions, catastrophes, crises, and mishaps of all varieties for many years to come. When the 1850–51 season opened, Maretzek was at the start of an illustrious thirty-year career as an operatic impresario in North America. He would become one of the most influential individuals connected with the performance of Italian opera in the United States.

Maximilian Maretzek (né Mareczek) (1821–97, Figure 25) was a native of Brno, Moravia (in modern Czechoslovakia). Although he began his musical career as a violinist and composer, he quickly made a name for himself as a conductor, and in 1842 was invited to Paris, where he conducted opera and ballet for several years.[3] In 1844, he was hired by George Lumley as choral director and assistant conductor at Covent Garden, and three years later, Louis Antoine Jullien engaged him as chorus master in a grandiose but unsuccessful attempt to produce English opera at Drury Lane Theatre in London.[4] After the collapse of Jullien's project, Maretzek was hired as a choral director for a London concert series organized by Hector Berlioz.

During the summer of 1848, Edward P. Fry (1815–89), the new manager of the Astor Place Opera House Company, contacted Maretzek (possibly through his brother, William Henry Fry, who was in Europe)

25. Maximilian Maretzek, operatic impresario. (*Glea-son's Pictorial Drawing-Room Companion*, March 1852)

and offered him a position as musical director and conductor of his company.[5] Edward Fry evidently was an ardent supporter of his brother, who was a composer and would later be a critic. The previous winter the young Fry had paid a substantial sum to Sanquirico and Patti to help underwrite a New York production of his brother's opera *Leonora* by the first Astor Place Company.[6] The troupe had fallen apart before the performance, however, and Fry, who was determined to carry out his mission at any cost, purchased the costumes and music of the defunct company, instructed his brother in Europe to hire new singers, rehired most of the old ones, and announced that he would assume management.[7]

When Fry's representative approached Maretzek with the offer, the conductor apparently was out of work; Berlioz had gone back to Paris in July. Because of the political turmoil in France, Maretzek was reluctant to return to Paris, his previous place of employment, and the situation in Italy was equally bad. Fry's offer, as a consequence, must have seemed a godsend.[8] The always-ambitious young conductor regarded the virgin operatic territory of the United States as a plum ripe for picking, and he responded favorably to what he called Fry's " 'engaging' inducement . . . to quit Europe."[9] In August he boarded a steamer headed west, leaving behind without regret the thick fog of late-summer London. Even the climate of his newly adopted country favorably impressed Maretzek. Gazing out at New York Harbor from the deck of his steamer, he was so pleased at the "bright, clear and blue sky" — a sky such as he "had not seen since [he] last left Naples" — that he determined at once, he later wrote to Berlioz, "to remain in America, supposing it were possible and (this is for your private ear) profitable."[10]

Meanwhile, the Astor Place House had been leased for the summer by William Niblo for his summer season (Niblo's theater, on the grounds of his Manhattan pleasure gardens, had burned in September 1846).[11] In an attempt to ameliorate the unfavorable conditions of the amphitheater (gallery), Niblo had made several important structural changes to the Astor Place House, including the addition of a grand staircase that connected this formerly segregated area to the rest of the theater. (Whether Niblo did something about the view-obstructing chandelier is not known.) Niblo's alterations evidently helped make the house less frigidly aristocratic, as did his uniform admission price of 50 cents and his usual menu of highly varied theatrical productions, including drama, acrobatics, farce, concerts, opera, and ballet. His very successful summer operation helped remove some of the theater's aura of exclusivity.

When the opera season opened on 1 November, it was apparent that Fry also wished to avoid the charge of elitism. Although he ran the season on a subscription basis, the seats in the amphitheater — now, because of Niblo's alterations, described as the "best in the house" — cost only 25 cents; furthermore, operas were also mounted on off-nights (Tuesdays, Thursdays, and Saturdays), when the entire theater was open to nonsubscribers.[12] Despite his good intentions, however, Fry was totally unsuited to the task that he had so blithely undertaken. Maretzek later wrote that the neophyte manager "knew nothing whatever of the business he had entered upon."[13] The season, which Lawrence described as a "bottomless quagmire of Byzantine intrigue, factional animosities, personal vendettas, and extempore illnesses," was a disaster. When it was over, Fry — who had lost a great deal of money — wisely gave up operatic management forever; Maretzek claimed that Fry had "ruined himself" economically.[14]

The managerial committee of the Astor Place House immediately attempted to persuade Maretzek to take over the idle opera company and to lease the hall. After a few weeks of vacillation he agreed to do so, although he later described himself at the time as "very young, very unwise, and very enthusiastic."[15] He presided over a short season in the spring of 1849, then—after a summer spent recruiting singers in Europe—organized and managed another company that performed in New York and Boston during 1849–50.[16] In June 1850, this troupe disbanded until fall.

Maretzek had been pleased with his 1849–1850 troupe, which he described as a "decidedly good Operatic Company." He judged the troupe vastly superior to the ensemble he had directed under Fry.[17] The public had been satisfied, and the season was deemed an artistic, if not financial, success. Furthermore, evidence suggests that the company had been successful in attracting a more varied audience to its performances than had the original Astor Place troupe. The *Spirit*'s critic on 1 December 1849 wrote a tongue-in-cheek description of the attire of various segments of the Astor Place audience and mentioned that "clerks, dry goods and others—wine dealers—students, medical and otherwise, are usually known by the immensity of the bows on their cravats." Maretzek himself wrote that *Don Giovanni* saved the season financially; the opera, he claimed, "brought support from all classes, and attracted persons of all professions and every description to the Opera House."[18] Although Odell can find no evidence to support Maretzek's claim of fourteen consecutive performances of this opera, other sources corroborate the manager's description of the audience.[19] A critic for *Saroni's* wrote on 17 August 1850 that "if any one had ever doubted the growing taste of this community for Music of an elevated character, a visit to the Opera House on Tuesday night, would have convinced him of his error. The parquette and amphitheater were crowded, while the boxes were by no means indifferently filled. We are gratified, that it was *Don Giovanni,* an opera by Mozart, which called together so vast an assemblage" (556).

Through natural attrition the 1849–50 company lost the services of several singers who returned to Europe, and they had to be replaced before the start of the 1850–51 season. Maretzek fulfilled an essential managerial duty, one that was almost a requirement for antebellum American opera company managers or agents, by sending his brother, Albert, and the company's tenor, Giuseppe Forti, on a summer recruiting trip to Europe. The two were to search for new contralto and bass singers.[20]

It quickly become obvious that their task was much more difficult than the simple replacement of departed vocalists with singers of similar caliber. Maretzek had to upgrade the quality of his troupe. The American musical press concurred. "Let us hope," wrote one critic in *Figaro* on 31 August, "that this [1850–51 company] may be a considerably better assortment of musical notabilities than those which were given us during the past year.... [It] is absolutely necessary for Maretzek, if he would make another and more profitable season than the last one, that he should give us something better than [last year's] artists."

The 1849–50 company had been successful in part because of lack of competition. "The public of New York," Maretzek later observed, "had not yet been accustomed to the Jenny Linds, Sontags, Albonis, Grisis, Marios and Lagranges," all operatic superstars who would appear in the United States during the 1850s.[21] The level of operatic competition, and the public's exposure to artists of "planetary proportion" (Maretzek's term), were both crucial factors in the success or failure of a season. During the summer of 1850 it became increasingly clear to anyone familiar with the Astor Place troupe that the level of competition during the coming season was going to be significantly higher than it had been the previous year.[22]

The competition that loomed on the operatic horizon, and which had no little influence on how Maretzek would conduct his season, came from two separate quarters. The first was Marti's Havana Opera Company, back in the United States after an eighteen-month hiatus. This troupe had arrived in New York in April for a month-long engagement, gone briefly to Boston, then returned to New York and settled in for the summer at Castle Garden, performing Italian repertory in Italian. The second source of competition was the superstar Jenny Lind (Figure 26). The "Swedish Nightingale," whose impending arrival in the United States had aroused much excitement and anticipation during the summer, landed in New York in September 1850. The concert tour managed by P. T. Barnum on which she subsequently embarked has been described as "arguably the most successful [musical tour] in American history."[23]

The Havana Company was never in direct competition with the Astor Place troupe, for it left New York after its final performance at Castle Garden on 7 September 1850.[24] The legacy it left behind was competition enough, however. Marti's ensemble, by Maretzek's own description, was "the greatest troupe which had ever been heard in America." This company, he later wrote to the Austrian pianist Joseph Fischof, was a troupe that "has seldom been excelled in any part of the Old World." He continued, "It would be useless, my old friend, to attempt to indicate the excellence of this Company. You have long since known their names, or been aware of their standing as artists, in the World of Music. The greater portion of them enjoy a wide and

26. Jenny Lind in concert at Castle Garden. This view shows the voluminous size of the hall. (*Gleason's Pictorial Drawing-Room Companion*, May 1851)

well-deserved European reputation, and their re-union, anywhere, would form an almost incomparable Operatic *troupe*."[25]

Maretzek's high opinion of the company was echoed almost universally in the American musical press.[26] Furthermore, Luigi Arditi, the leader of the Havana Company and later an important conductor of various opera troupes in England and the United States, including Maretzek's own company in 1851, concurred. "When I look back to those *ensembles*," he wrote in his memoirs, "I have no hesitation in saying that never for the time and place, would it have been possible to secure more admirable operatic performances than those rendered by this particular company."[27] In case Maretzek had failed to see the handwriting on the wall, American critics made sure to point it out to him. "After hearing [Havana Company singers] Marini, Salvi, and Badiali," wrote one journalist in the *Message Bird* on 15 July, "we shall hardly be contented with fourth or fifth rate artists, and unless Maretzek engages some really talented artists, we very much fear that he will be often greeted with the *beggarly account of empty boxes.* [Maretzek's principal soprano Teresa] Truffi, indeed, would not suffer by a comparison with any of the prime donne of the Havana Troupe, but the stars of [tenor Sesto] Benedetti and [bass Pietro] Novelli have waned before the brilliancy of [tenor Lorenzo] Salvi and [bass Ignazio] Marini;

and as to comparing [the baritone G. F.] Beneventano with [Cesare] Badiali—Hyperion to Satyr" (394).

It obviously was going to be difficult for Maretzek's singers to compete with Marti's stars. To make matters worse, it was hopelessly impractical for the Astor Place troupe to attempt to compete with the Havana Company economically. Marti was a wealthy businessman whose principal employment was not as an impresario, so his fortune did not depend on the success or failure of his company. His troupe furthermore was supported by both a substantial number of Havanese subscribers and a hefty government subvention.[28] The Cuban impresario sent his singers to New York for several practical reasons. First, he knew that their performances there would create a furor, which could only enhance their reputations in Havana. Second, as usual, he wished to remove his singers from Cuba during the torrid, yellow fever-plagued summer months. Finally, because prominent Italian artists were understandably reluctant to travel to Cuba to sing for only one season, Marti had been obliged to engage them for a two-year period (1849–51).[29] Consequently, the singers were under contract to him for the intervening summer, and Marti vastly preferred for them to be singing anywhere than to be idle during those months.[30] Thus, according to Maretzek, it was "purely a matter of the most perfect indifference to Marty . . . whether [the Havana troupe] made him money, or whether they did not make him money, during their summer season."[31] The Havana Company performed in New York at Castle Garden at what Maretzek called "something less than half the usual price," 50 cents, which put the local company at a distinct disadvantage.[32] When Maretzek opened the season at the Astor Place House in October, his company was not only inferior to that of the just-departed Havanese, but he also had to charge significantly higher admission prices for its performances: $1 and $1.50 for unreserved and reserved parquet seats and boxes and 25 cents for the amphitheater, according to the *Figaro* of 19 October.

Maretzek, however, had several factors in his favor in this competition with Marti. First was the simple law of supply and demand. During the theatrical season of 1850–51, Maretzek's audiences, wealthy and non-wealthy alike, wished to attend opera performances, and the Astor Place Company was the only show in town. Music critics might complain, criticize, and unfavorably compare the Astor Place singers with those in Marti's departed company, but Marti's company was just that—departed—safely ensconced at the Tacon Theatre in Havana. A second factor, which Maretzek failed to mention, is that lowering theatrical prices during the summer was a common practice, especially when performances were held in an facility that could accommodate thousands, as could Castle Garden. The first opera company to perform in the Castle Garden auditorium when it opened in 1845 also had charged an admission price of 50 cents, and Maretzek, during the summer of 1851, would do the same.[33] Therefore, it was hardly a matter for raised eyebrows that Maretzek had to charge prices to the Astor Place House that were appreciably higher than those Marti had charged during the summer. Finally, the Havana Company made its biggest impression in New York while performing in June, July, and August. Because many of the subscribers to the opera season at the Astor Place House were out of town, visiting resorts or summer homes, few even heard the highly touted singers of the Havana Company. Any unfavorable comparisons, as a consequence, were so much hearsay.

This last factor—that the Havana Company performed before audiences of thousands of working- and middle-class individuals—would eventually benefit Maretzek. The performances at Castle Garden and earlier in the summer at Niblo's were decidedly neither exclusive nor elite, and seasons at both places must have attracted many ordinary Americans who heard their first performances of foreign-language opera. According to the *Message Bird* of 15 August, performances at Castle Garden also attracted many foreign auditors (434). At Niblo's new theater, which had reopened in July 1849, the Havana Company attracted huge crowds.[34] The last night of their engagement there, reported the *Message Bird* on 15 May, "was a bumper. Every nook and corner of that spacious theater was crowded to suffocation, and hundreds went away unable even to obtain a standing place" (335). The troupe attracted even larger crowds at Castle Garden. This resort (Figure 27), located on a tiny island just off the Battery and connected to Manhattan by a two-hundred-foot causeway was, like Niblo's, a place to lounge, eat Italian ices, visit with friends, promenade along the gallery overlooking the bay, watch ships and boats, catch a cool summer breeze, and listen to the evening's musical entertainment. (For the location of Castle Garden, see the map reproduced in Figure 9.)[35] Philip Hone described the interior of the theater (Figures 26 and 28) shortly after it opened: "when I entered I found myself on the floor of the most splendid and the largest theatre I ever saw, a place capable of seating comfortably six or eight thousand persons. The pit, or area of the pavilion, is handsomely floored, with some hundred small white tables and movable stools. . . . In front of the stage is a beautiful fountain which plays when the performers do not. The whole of this area is surrounded by circular benches above and below, from every point of which the view is enchanting."[36]

The size of the audiences that the Havana Company attracted to Castle Garden surprised some critics. Many expected the troupe to

27. Exterior view of Castle Garden. Sheet-music cover, "Castle Garden Schottisch." Lithograph by G. W. Lewis (New York: J. Jaques and Brother, 1852). (New-York Historical Society)

28. Interior, Castle Garden, illustrating a benefit opera performance for Max Maretzek. (*Gleason's Pictorial Drawing-Room Companion*, March 1852)

fail because New York's fashionables were out of town and the Garden itself was a "miserably unsuitable place for the proper reception of sight and sound in either operatic or dramatic representations."[37] Their expectations, however, were unfounded. The troupe attracted nearly five thousand on the night of their opening performance of *I Puritani*, and attendance on subsequent evenings also numbered in the thousands.[38] Perfect acoustics and unencumbered sight-lines obviously were not of paramount concern to individuals attracted to the Castle. Enjoyable and pleasant entertainment was important, and evidently opera performances fit the bill. "We are rejoiced," wrote one critic in the *Spirit* on 13 July, "that the million, who have music in their souls, but little in their pockets, have now an opportunity to enjoy delicious music" (252). Enjoyment of the music was indeed possible despite the immense size of the hall. As the *Message Bird* reported in September, "the doubts as to whether the voices of the Company would be able to fill [the] vast area [of the Castle] have been triumphantly dissipated. The voices of . . . all the principals, and the chorus, completely fill every nook of the interior; even above the full power of the most powerful orchestras, they can be heard distinctly in every part of the amphitheatre."[39]

Audiences could also enjoy an instrumental concert along with the vocal music, for a band performed between the acts of the operas. These instrumentalists, according to *Saroni's* on 27 July, "discourse the choicest of music, undisturbed by the moving tide of humanity that, let loose from the spell thrown upon them by the singers, throng through the large area of the Castle and climb its broad staircases, to enjoy the grateful embrace of the ocean breeze, the still music of the calmly sleeping bay, and the poetry of the dancing star-beams" (518).

Surely the performance of Italian opera in such enjoyable and non-aristocratic surroundings helped to reinforce the genre's image as a pleasant, accessible form of entertainment. It also dispelled some of the negative connotations created by the attempts of the Astor Place elite to make opera performance an exclusive pastime. Furthermore, some of the thousands of Americans who were first introduced to Italian opera (in Italian) at the Castle or at Niblo's must have enjoyed the experience enough to attend performances by Maretzek's company or other troupes during the regular season. At the same time that the Havana Company singers threatened Maretzek because of the quality of their performances, then, they helped create a portion of his future audience.

Because the Havana Company left New York in early September, Maretzek's immediate competition from the troupe consisted primarily of the remembered glory of departed singers. The competition from

Jenny Lind was something else entirely. The Swedish Nightingale arrived in New York in September to a veritable frenzy of excitement orchestrated by the shrewd P. T. Barnum. The commotion was similar to her reception by London audiences from 1847 through 1849, and was to continue almost undiminished until her departure from North America in May 1852. Lind sang her first concert in New York on 11 September at Castle Garden, less than a week after Marti's company closed its season there, and excitement was at such a fever pitch that George Odell wondered in 1931 if the performance was not perhaps "the most thrilling [experience] in the history of American musical activities" (5:592). Not the finest performance, Odell cautioned, but the most thrilling because "never before and possibly never since were so many human hearts beating in unison, in almost tragic expectation of the first notes from a human throat or indeed from any other musical instrument."[40]

Lind's European reputation, coupled with Barnum's massive exploitation of it, prompted some critics to predict that her appearances would "teach our public what good vocal melody really is," according to *Figaro* on 31 August. Americans had heard world-class singers before Lind; never, however, had they been subjected to the kind of hyperbole about a singer that Barnum unleashed. Lind's name became a household word, and people began to believe what they were being told—that she was a "matchless" singer and the "Queen of Song."[41] Her performances in New York were in direct competition with the Astor Place Company, despite the fact that she sang in concert rather than in staged operas. Her first six concerts at Castle Garden, between 11 and 24 September, were sold out despite a minimum $3 ticket cost.[42] In late October, when Lind returned to New York after a month-long engagement in Boston, it was for a series of fifteen concerts at the newly opened Jenny Lind (later Tripler) Hall, a series that coincided precisely with the opening weeks of Maretzek's season.[43] When Lind finally left town for an extended American tour on 25 November, the damage— so Maretzek feared—had been done.[44]

Long before Lind's arrival, however, Maretzek had leased the Astor Place Opera House for much of the 1850–51 season. Because he was legally obligated to pay rent on the hall whether he used it or not, it was disastrous for his troupe to try to sit out the season despite the likelihood of economic failure. "Figure to yourself," he later wrote, "the position of a luckless *impresario* with a company of Truffis and Beneventanos upon his hands, and the lease of the Astor Place Opera House upon his shoulders, with Jenny Lind and Barnum, real genius and undoubted 'humbug,' in a strange copartnership, staring ominously in his face." He would have been perfectly happy, he continued, "to give up the whole concern" except for his legal obligations and the sobering realization, as he confessed, that "I had not . . . the means to do anything else."[45] In August and September 1850, then, faced with the real possibility of economic ruin, Maretzek prepared to stand up to the competition as best he could. His plan was simple: to go to work "in the same manner I had seen practiced by Barnum."[46]

The troupe that Maretzek had assembled for the 1850–51 season was fairly strong; for name singers he had four sopranos, three tenors, two baritones, and four basses.[47] The chorus and orchestra were presumably similar in size and make-up to those of previous Astor Place troupes. The only available information about choral or orchestral musicians connected with the Astor Place establishment is from Edward Fry's 1848–49 company. That orchestra numbered forty-three: fourteen violins, four violas, three cellos, four contrabasses, two each of flutes, oboes, clarinets, bassoons, trumpets, and horns, three trombones, one ophicleide, one bass drum and cymbals, and timpani. This is the most complete opera orchestra discussed to this point in this study; it was the first ensemble that could perform, for example, *Le Nozze di Figaro* without alterations. Fry's company also boasted a chorus of forty-four, some of whom functioned as minor name artists in the troupe.[48]

In order to use Barnum's tactics properly, however, Maretzek needed more than a well-rounded troupe with a well-appointed orchestra and sizable chorus. He also needed stars whose reputations he could "puff," and he relied on his brother and Giuseppe Forti to bring at least one such artist from Europe. The recruiting trip, however, had failed. Forti and Albert Maretzek—who had been sent overseas to recruit bass and contralto singers—had come back with only one artist, the bass Settimo Rossi (or Rosi). Even Rossi was not really a newcomer, for he been a member of the first two companies of the Astor Place House and was returning to the United States after a year spent in Europe.[49] Furthermore, Maretzek and Forti had been unable to sign any contraltos to replace the two who had left. For the performance of contralto roles, the troupe would have to rely at first on the services of Amalia Patti, one of its sopranos; later in the year a true contralto, Caroline Vietti, would join the company.

Despite the failure of the recruiting trip, when the season commenced in October the company included two other newcomers, both recruited in New York. The first, the baritone Antonio Avignone, like Rossi, had been a member of the first Astor Place Company; thus his was not a new face to the New York public. The second, also a familiar artist, had an even higher cachet with New York audiences than either Rossi or Avignone, for he was the tenor Domenico Lorini, whom Maretzek had lured away from the Havana troupe.[50] The rest of Maretzek's star singers were familiar from the previous season. Some were quite good and well liked by Americans; others were second- and third-rate artists. All, in any case, were much too well known to be the successful objects of any extensive puffing. As Maretzek later wrote, "my old artists were impossible cards, for me to attempt playing in Barnum's manner. They were, alas! too well known."[51]

Evidently few first-class European singers were willing to risk a season in the United States at the same time as the Lind-Barnum extravaganza, or so the failure of the Forti-Maretzek recruiting trip seems to indicate. By early fall Maretzek was desperate. Finally, by pulling some trans-atlantic strings and calling in some favors, he was able to engage a new prima donna, the soprano Teresa Parodi (Figure 29). She was, Maretzek recalled, "an artist of sufficient talent to realize the expectations which I might raise upon her behalf."[52] Parodi had been a favorite pupil of the great mezzo-soprano Giuditta Pasta and was fairly well known and respected, especially in southern Italy and London, where she was under contract to Benjamin Lumley at Her Majesty's Theatre. Lumley was willing to release her to Maretzek—for a financial consideration, of course. Once that deal was made and Parodi was on her way to New York, Maretzek was ready. At last he had a viable star for his season, and he intended to exploit her to the hilt.

The Fall Campaign in New York

Maretzek's troupe opened its New York season with performances of Weber's *Der Freischütz* (as *Il Franco Archiero* and billed as the New York premiere of the Italian version) on 21, 23, and 25 October at the Astor Place Opera House.[53] Because the company usually performed on Monday, Wednesday, and Friday evenings early in the season, the Weber opera occupied the entire first week. The *Daily Tribune* assured its readers on 22 October that "a brilliant audience filled the house" and that Maretzek "could not have selected an opera better fitted to inaugurate his second season." Another local critic, however, who admitted later that he "stood alone among the Press in [his] strictures on the Freyschütz [performance]," vehemently disagreed. The vocal portion of the opera, he complained, "was no more like Weber's opera of *Der Freyschütz,* as [he had] heard it when Weber himself conducted it, than a Dutch cheese is like a diamond."[54] Apparently Maretzek himself also disagreed with the laudatory verdict, for the opera was withdrawn after the third performance. During the troupe's second week Maretzek trotted out two old favorites: Donizetti's *Lucia di Lammermoor* and Verdi's *Ernani.*[55] The reaction of the critics, although favorable, was not overwhelmingly enthusiastic. The Havana Company

29. Teresa Parodi. From the cover of a sheet-music publication of an aria from Maurice Strakosch's opera *Giovanna Prima di Napoli* (New York: William Hall, 1851). (Music Division, Library of Congress)

had recently performed both of these works with greatly superior singers, to large audiences and much acclaim. The company, it appears, was biding its time until Parodi's arrival.

Meanwhile, Maretzek's Barnum-like campaign to build Parodi's American reputation was already well underway. With single-minded determination he manufactured "foreign" letters and biographies, wrote public-relations puffs, and obtained lithographs and engravings of her likeness, which he distributed to newspapers and periodicals. All of these efforts were for naught. According to Maretzek, the American public was so bedazzled with Barnum's overwhelming promotion of Lind that the editors of newspapers and music journals indicated no interest at all in Teresa Parodi. "Whatever I did," he wrote later, "was against the pyramidal puffing of Barnum. [My efforts were] no more than the murmuring of a garden streamlet as compared with the roar and thunder of Niagara."[56] George Upton later agreed with this assessment: Maretzek "was no match for Barnum in [inventing] short stories. The people had caught Jenny Lind fever."[57]

Undaunted, Maretzek tried a new tack. He fabricated and circulated a story that Parodi (who was already en route to New York) had decided to renege on her Astor Place contract. The Duke of Devonshire, so the tale went, had secretly been in love with the soprano for years, and at the announcement of her imminent departure for the United States had asked her hand in marriage. She had accepted and now had no intention to come to New York; Maretzek — poor fellow — faced certain ruin. The story, according to the manager, had been leaked under strict pledge of secrecy. As expected, and precisely according to plan, it was published in its entirety almost immediately. The day after it broke, Maretzek related, the tale could be seen on the pages of every daily paper in New York, and within three weeks it had "found its way into almost every newspaper from Maine to Texas. In a fortnight more [it] had completed its travels by one huge stride from New York to San Francisco."[58]

Maretzek was delighted; the newspapers even began to print the biographies, anecdotes, and portraits they had previously ignored. The unknown Teresa Parodi, according to Maretzek, suddenly became the object of a great deal of interest and curiosity in the United States. Although this tale is interesting, however, Maretzek apparently exaggerated it. Newspapers and periodicals certainly mentioned Parodi — and with greater frequency as the season progressed and her reputation grew — but nothing remotely resembling the great flood of attention Maretzek described seems to have occurred. Maretzek probably manufactured much of the tale out of whole cloth; as Odell noted wryly, "the good Max dealt ever in superlatives" (5:573).

Parodi, of course, did arrive during the middle of the troupe's first week. If Maretzek's story is true, he undoubtedly made a great show of relief when the supposed "Duchess of Devonshire" disembarked from the steamer *Pacific*. Parodi was astonished at the "rumor." The wily manager, however, was not finished, for he had yet another astute public-relations move up his sleeve. On the very day of Parodi's arrival, he closed the company's subscription list, forcing any nonsubscribers to purchase tickets to individual performances, and doubled his admission prices to $2 ($2.50 for reserved seats).[59] This "dispelled all doubts of [Parodi's] superiority, as it was supposed that I could not have dared to do this, with such a rival attraction as Jenny Lind in the market, if I had not been morally certain of her success."[60]

By this point, Maretzek had the New York media in his pocket. They seemed more than happy to help him augment excitement even further for the prima donna's debut, which was scheduled for the third week of the season. "PARODI. The Singer of the South, PARODI, will be heard for the first time in America, on Monday evening next," exclaimed the *Tribune* on 31 October.[61] "Expectation is already on the rise," the columnist continued, "and the debut in New-York of the pupil of Pasta and the rival of [Giulia] Grisi will be greeted with the largest and most brilliant audience which the Opera House ever enclosed within its walls." Maretzek's choice of *Norma* as the soprano's debut vehicle was a stroke of managerial genius. By 1850, Bellini's masterpiece had become one of the most popular operas in America.[62] Furthermore, it was a role in which Jenny Lind had failed in England; it exploited Parodi's remarkable strength as a dramatic actress; it was itself "revolutionary," as a tale of good Druids against evil Roman colonial oppressors; and it reminded American audiences of the singer's close relationship with the great Pasta, who had created the title role.[63] Finally, although Parodi excelled in the part (Figure 30), it was not her strongest role. This made it ideal for a debut; the hordes who would flock to the three performances of *Norma* could easily be lured back again the following week when Maretzek featured his new star in a role for which she was renowned and that would become her American tour de force: Lucrezia Borgia in Donizetti's opera.[64]

The New York audience behaved precisely as Maretzek had hoped: during Parodi's first week, they mobbed all three performances of *Norma*. "At the rising of the curtain," wrote *Figaro*'s critic on 9 November of the soprano's debut performance, "every seat in the opera house had an occupant. . . . The audience in the body of the house, was fashionable; in the amphitheatre, highly respectable." Furthermore, according to the *Tribune* on 5 November, "all the entrances and steps were occupied by those who were only too glad, at such inconvenience, to see and hear the Queen of the evening." The critical reaction, however, was mixed. Most agreed that Parodi's dramatic powers were great, but some had serious reservations about her singing. "She is physically and dramatically the greatest tragic singing actress we have ever heard in America," wrote the critic for *Figaro* on 9 November. "Her face and voice . . . are truly grand; the first in expression, and the last in quality, but artistically, she has been greatly surpassed here; her execution is mediocre, never in any one instance (on this occasion) rising to great excellence, or reaching the expectations naturally awakened by so loudly bruited a celebrity as she has acquired."

The reservations about her *Norma* did not carry much weight in the long run, however, for during her second week Parodi performed as Lucrezia, and many of the critics became converts. After her first portrayal of the tragic role, the reviewer for *Figaro* gushed that the performance was the "greatest triumph ever witnessed in the Astor Place Opera House"; he continued by describing her on 12 November as "the greatest tragic singer that has yet been in America." Another

30. Teresa Parodi as Norma. This illustration was accompanied by a biographical sketch of the singer that was typical of public-relations hyperbole distributed by Maretzek and others to the American press for advertising purposes. By the time this material appeared, Parodi's reputation in this country was well established. (*Gleason's Pictorial Drawing-Room Companion,* October 1851)

critic concurred: "As a vocalist, Parodi appears to us almost fault-less. . . . Her voice is pure and sympathetic; it has a great range — over two octaves . . . it has been so carefully cultivated, that she exercises over it the most perfect control. . . . Her vocalizing is perfect; devoid of trickery or machinery, pure as nature assisted by art can make it."[65]

Maretzek was delighted with the reaction, for the popularity of at least one of the principal singers — preferably the prima donna — was crucial to a troupe's success. As the author of a letter to the *Musical World* pointed out on 20 June 1857, "nobody goes to hear an opera. They go to hear the *prima donna*" (388). Even those critics who were not entirely convinced of the soprano's artistic virtues may have helped Maretzek's cause by calling attention to Parodi. The reviewer for the *Spirit,* for example, commented that there was "much diversity of thought" about her. He later observed, "we never saw an artiste about whose dramatic excellence such contrarity of opinion exists, nor have we ever [seen] one whose acting has created among [so] many such a furore."[66] Although comments of this nature are hardly unmitigated praise, they did nothing to dampen curiosity about the new singer.

Parodi appeared as Lucrezia three times, sang the lead female role of *Ernani* the following week, then took several days off. To maintain the troupe's momentum, the manager had his company mount the New York premiere (incorrectly advertised as the "first time in America") of Donizetti's *Parisina* on Friday, 22 November and again on Monday the twenth-fifth.[67] Teresa Truffi, the troupe's other, much respected, soprano, sang the title role. Because Parodi did not appear, prices were reduced for both performances.[68]

Between the two productions of *Parisina,* Maretzek and the company produced a "Grand Gala Night at the Opera House" on Saturday, 23 November. Because it was a nonsubscription performance, all seats were sold individually; because the gala featured both Parodi and the American debut of Maretzek's Parisian danseuse Mlle. Nathalie Fitz-james ("of the Grand Opera, Paris, and other theatres"), the prices were the same as those charged for Parodi's opera appearances. The house was the largest of the season, according to the *Tribune* on 25 November. A critic for *Figaro* reported that such gala concerts usually attracted audiences made up almost exclusively of the general public; "the 'upper tendom,' " he wrote on 30 November, "does not come to such extra concerts, while the Public . . . crowd the house, and liberality for once is seated on the sofas usually dedicated to meanness."

By this time — the end of the fifth week of the season — Maretzek knew that he had the ingredients for a financially successful run, barring disaster. As early as the third week he had successfully orchestrated a ferment of public interest in his company and its star prima donna, even in the face of direct competition from the Swedish Nightingale, who was singing simultaneously at Jenny Lind Hall. This interest, furthermore, had continued unabated for two additional weeks, outlasting the initial burst of natural curiosity about a new and highly touted artist. Now, Maretzek's task was to maintain—and build upon—this interest and enthusiasm over an extended season.

An essential element for maintaining audience interest was variety. The company had to present a constantly changing bill of fare so attractive that large numbers of the New York public would continue to attend performances regularly. This turned out not to be a serious problem for the Astor Place troupe, for Maretzek already was showing evidence of remarkable managerial ability. Major elements of his technique throughout the 1850–51 season included stringing out novelties over as long a period as possible by arranging, for example, that singers' debuts occur on different nights; ceaselessly varying the appearances of such special guest artists as dancers; shuffling the combination of singers; and changing bills of fare as often as necessary.

Maretzek's method of juggling his company's repertory at the Astor Place House is illustrative. The troupe mounted a New York premiere and one world premiere during this time. The former was of Donizetti's *Parisina;* the latter was of the opera *Giovanna Prima di Napoli* by Maurice Strakosch (in January 1851).[69] The troupe also added three other works new to New York (*Semiramide, Der Freischütz,* and *Gemma di Vergy*) and performed yet another three operas that had not been heard in the city (at least in Italian) for some time: *La Sonnambula; I Capuleti e i Montecchi* (billed as *Romeo e Giulietta*) (Bellini), and *Il Giuramento* (Mercadante). More than half of a total repertory of fifteen operas were relatively fresh to the company's audiences in New York and elsewhere.

This significant number of new (or relatively new) works, however, is misleading. The eight operas account for fewer than one-third (40 of 132) of the company's total performances (Table 11). The other two-thirds of the troupe's productions were of older, more familiar works; six of these seven had become, even by 1850, a bit shopworn, especially considering the numerous repetitions common in any one season.[70] During the four-year period from 1847 to 1851 (Table 12), *Ernani, Norma, Il barbiere di Siviglia, Lucia di Lammermoor, La Favorita,* and *Lucrezia Borgia* all had been performed during at least four of the six previous seasons. *Ernani, Norma, Lucia di Lammermoor,* and *Lucrezia Borgia,* were rapidly becoming operatic chestnuts and constituted more than 55 percent of the Astor Place Company's 1850–51 performances. (Of course, the most-performed operas of the season, *Ernani* and *Lucrezia Borgia,* were the *Cats* and *Phantom of the Opera*

Table 11. Repertory of the 1850–51 Astor Place Company, Ranked by Frequency of Performance

	New York City	Phila-delphia	Balti-more	Boston	South Boston	Total
Ernani	7	5	1	1	3	3	20
Lucrezia Borgia	9	2	—	1	2	2	16
Norma	7	2	—	2	2	—	13
La Favorita	5	5	—	1	2	3	16
Lucia di Lammermoor	4	1	1	—	2	3	11
Parisina	4	2	2	—	1	—	9
Don Giovanni	2	3	—	—	—	4	9
Il Giuramento	2	1	1	—	2	1	7
Il barbiere di Siviglia	2	—	—	1	2	2	7
Romeo e Giulietta	4	—	—	1	—	1	6
Gemma di Vergy	4	1	—	—	—	—	5
Giovanna Prima di Napoli	4	—	—	—	—	—	4
Semiramide	2	—	—	1	—	—	3
La Sonnambula	1	1	1	—	—	—	3
Der Freischütz	3	—	—	—	—	—	3
Total	60	23	6	8	16	19	132

of the early 1850s in terms of sheer popularity.) This overreliance on a handful of operas, however, was not obvious during Maretzek's season because he was so skillful at juggling the repertory and using the company's novelties to the best advantage. The eight fresh works were introduced carefully and sparingly over the course of the eighteen-week New York season in weeks one (*Der Freischütz*), five (*Parisina*), six (*Gemma di Vergy*), nine (*La Sonnambula*), ten (*Il Giuramento*), twelve (*Giovanna Prima*), fifteen (*Romeo e Giulietta*), and seventeen (*Semiramide*).

Such incessant juggling of repertory should clearly indicate that by the 1850s the earlier common practice of repeating performances of the same opera for weeks on end, as had been the case for the Shirreff/Wilson/Seguin troupe, had fallen out of favor. By the late 1840s the American public, especially on the East Coast and in New Orleans, had been introduced to a rather large repertory; repetition for the sake of fostering familiarity was no longer necessary. Now, however, even such new works as *Parisina* and *Giovanna Prima* were not usually

Table 12. Italian Repertory in New York

| 1847 | 1847–48 | 1848–49 | 1849–50 | 1850 | 1850–51 |
Havana Opera Company	Astor Place Opera Company	Astor Place Opera Company	Astor Place Opera Company	Havana Opera Company	Astor Place Opera Company
Ernani	*Ernani*	*Ernani*	*Ernani*	*Ernani*	*Ernani*
Foscari[a]				*Foscari*	
Saffo					
Norma		*Norma*	*Norma*	*Norma*	*Norma*
Sonnam	*Sonnam*	*Sonnam*			*Sonnam*
Mosè					
Linda		*Linda*			
Romeo	*Romeo*				*Romeo*
Barbiere		*Barbiere*	*Barbiere*		*Barbiere*
	Beatrice				
	Lucia	*Lucia*	*Lucia*	*Lucia*	*Lucia*
	Puritani			*Puritani*	
	Lucrezia	*Lucrezia*	*Lucrezia*	*Lucrezia*	*Lucrezia*
	Giura[a]	*Giura*			*Giura*
	Nabucco				
		L'Elisir		*L'Elisir*	
		Favorita	*Favorita*	*Favorita*	*Favorita*
		Roberto			
		I Lombardi			
			Otello		
			Maria[a]		
			Don Pasquale		
			Anna B.[a]		*Giovanni*
			Giovanni		
			Parisina[a]		
		Huguenots[a]			

Abbreviations:

Foscari	*I Due Foscari*	*Mosè*	*Mosè in Egitto*
Linda	*Linda di Chamounix*	*Romeo*	*Romeo e Giulietta*
Barbiere	*Il barbiere di Siviglia*	*Lucia*	*Lucia di Lammermoor*
Lucrezia	*Lucrezia Borgia*	*L'Elisir*	*L'Elisir d'amore*
Roberto	*Roberto Devereux*	*Maria*	*Maria di Rohan*
Beatrice	*Beatrice di Tenda*	*Sonnam*	*La Sonnambula*
Puritani	*I Puritani*	*Giura*	*Il Giuramento*
Anna B.	*Anna Bolena*	*Giovanni*	*Don Giovanni*

[a] = *The New York premiere of an opera.*

repeated more than twice in a row. Some critics decried this practice. "The great mistake that opera managers are too apt to make," wrote one, "is to *change* one new opera for another, just as the public are getting familiar with [it], and begin to like it. The WOODS understood this better when they gave us English opera, many years since. Sonnambula was repeated over a hundred nights successively, and the enthusiasm of their packed house increased with every performance."[71]

Others, however, pointed out that the public demanded constant change; besides, it was closer to the general practice followed in the dramatic world. "The object of the opera-going public appears to be to find out how many operas they can gulp down in a season," J. S. Dwight complained on 16 January 1858, "and not how much lyrical instruction they can derive from a repeated consideration of the same work." The audience, to Dwight's evident sorrow, was not particularly interested in getting a musical education; they wanted to be entertained. By midcentury, a skillful juggling of all the elements of a season — not only repertory, but also singers, dancers, and special attractions — was a characteristic tactic not only of Maretzek, but also of other opera and theater impresarios and managers. It was also essential if a season were to succeed in the face of strong competition.

As is the case with most theatrical productions during the nineteenth century, it is almost impossible to know with any certainty just what the audience saw and heard. Cuts, interpolations, transpositions, and ornamentation were all common performance practice in Europe as well as in the United States; this did not begin to change until well into the century. Specific information on modifications made to a particular opera generally can be obtained from performance parts, but precious few can be linked to American performances during this time. Even fewer contain marginalia or specific instructions to singers or instrumentalists. Furthermore, contemporary evidence suggests that even the hundreds of extant libretti published for and distributed by opera companies in the United States are of little help in resolving this issue. "It is well known to all but the hopelessly simple," wrote one critic in the *Boston Musical Times* on 16 June 1860, "that the prompter pays as little attention to the 'only authentic edition' [of the libretto] as to the Koran." He continued, "consequently, there is [much] discussion in the auditorium. . . . Some charming daughter, being quicker than the rest of the family, first discovers the place, points it out to paterfamilias, who settles his spectacles and prepares to read; but before he has taken the thumb off the first word, the entire corps operatic has leaped several pages" (134). One frustrated opera-goer "from the country," after attending a performance of *Don Giovanni* in New York, wrote a letter of complaint to the *Musical World*. "Is it often the case that operas are much altered in the performance without due notice of the same?" he asked, perhaps rhetorically, on 28 March 1857. "If so, what shall we poor fellows do, who know nothing in the 'Book of the Opera?' It is a little hard upon us" (197).

Such comments demonstrate that changes were frequent; the precise nature of the alterations, however, remains unclear. The overall reaction by critics to modifications in the text—like the earlier reactions to changes made in vocal-star productions—range from calm acceptance to violent disapproval. The *Spirit*'s critic, when discussing a performance of *Norma* by the Astor Place troupe, conceded on 18 January 1851 that although "there was a little 'scene' not set down in the bills, and 'supplimentaria' to the composer's ideas," these were simply "vagaries [of the] Prima Donna" that added "a new excitement" to the work (576). A month later, after Parodi's first appearance in Boston, also in *Norma*, a reporter commented matter-of-factly in the *Boston Post* on 19 February that "she gave some fine runs most admirably in an interpolated piece." And when Maretzek's company performed Rossini's *William Tell* in 1855, even John Sullivan Dwight reported on 26 May that "the inordinate length of the opera . . . necessitated large omissions. . . . The whole of the ballet . . . was cut out. Entire choruses and songs in every Act were left out, and others [were] much abridged." Although Dwight decried some of the modifications, he nevertheless concluded, "it was quite important that it should be shortened somewhat. . . . The parts omitted were, in the main, those which could best be spared" (62). *William Tell*, of course, is quite long, and parts of it, notably the scenery choruses and dances, can be cut without harm to the opera itself.[72]

Other critics, however, although no more specific, were much less acquiescent. The reporter who so vehemently lambasted the Astor Place troupe's version of *Der Freischütz* at the opening of the season is one example. Others, especially later in the decade, complained that *Don Giovanni* was produced "in a ridiculous manner," that alterations to Verdi's *Il Trovatore* "so changed and marred [the work] . . . as fairly to deserve a sign of disapprobation from the public," and that the Italian repertory in general was "mutilated in the most absurd manner" or "recklessly cut to pieces."[73]

At the same time that Maretzek was grappling with the challenge of varied bills-of-fare at the Astor Place House, he was looking for audiences elsewhere. His promotional techniques and his star prima donna had raised bumper crops of audiences in New York; logically, they should do likewise in other American cities. In early November, it became clear that Maretzek intended to open a theater of operations in Philadelphia. The plan was to alternate performances between Philadelphia and New York; the size and quality of the troupe, one journalist noted in the *Tribune* on 13 November, "[should] enable him to do this very effectively." Arrangements for the season in Philadelphia, where performances were to take place at the Chestnut Street Theatre, were handled by one Edward L. Walker, who owned a music store there.[74] Maretzek was announced as the director of the fifteen performances, and the entire production was to be "in the same style and grandeur and magnificence displayed at the Astor Place Opera House, New York."[75] The new season commenced on Tuesday, 10 December.

Meanwhile, before the departure of the Philadelphia wing of the company, and along with all the necessary preseason preparations, there was much to occupy Maretzek's attention in New York. During the final two and one-half weeks before the anticipated split, the company shifted into overdrive. Beginning with 2 December and (with a few exceptions) extending through February, there were performances five nights of the week rather than three. Furthermore, the variety of repertory offered during any one week increased markedly (Table 13). There were premieres of new operas, and a single work was no longer regarded as sufficient for an entire week's performances.

Maretzek used techniques other than changes in repertory to increase variety in his offerings. Regular subscription performances were increasingly interspersed with benefits and "Grand Gala" events featuring the dancers Mlle. Fitzjames and Mons. Carrese, whose ballet repertory also changed to further vary the bills. Furthermore, whenever possible, the manager took advantage of the presence in New York of visiting musicians; if he could engage a renowned individual for a night or two, he featured that artist as a guest performer. Maretzek constantly tinkered with his evening's programs; he was always looking for different ways to sweeten the pot. When a new opera was produced—or when a new and particularly successful combination of repertory and artists was achieved—the company typically presented the same bill for several performances before moving on to something else. Whether a performance was repeated depended entirely on the size of the audience it attracted. Otherwise, the bills were always varying, always featuring different combinations of performers and different combinations of repertory to attract a large, paying audience.

The activities of the week commencing Monday, 2 December provide good examples of Maretzek's operating techniques. On Monday, the company gave its second performance of Donizetti's *Gemma di Vergy* (Figure 31), an opera new to the troupe's repertory, with Parodi in the title role (its first performance had taken place the previous Saturday).[76] The opera was repeated on Wednesday, 4 December after an off-night.

Table 13. Astor Place Opera Company Calendar of Performances,
21 Oct. 1850–11 March 1851

	New York:	Philadelphia:
21 Oct. (Monday)	Der Freischütz	
23 Oct.	Der Freischütz	
25 Oct.	Der Freischütz	
28 Oct. (Monday)	Lucia di Lammermoor	
30 Oct.	Ernani	
1 Nov.	Ernani	
4 Nov. (Monday)	Norma	
6 Nov.	Lucia di Lammermoor	
7 Nov.	Norma	
9 Nov.	Norma	
11 Nov. (Monday)	Lucrezia Borgia	
13 Nov.	Lucrezia Borgia	
15 Nov.	Lucrezia Borgia	
18 Nov. (Monday)	Ernani	
20 Nov.	Ernani	
22 Nov.	Parisina	
23 Nov.	Lucrezia Borgia (gala night)	
25 Nov. (Monday)	Parisina	
26 Nov.	Norma	
27 Nov.	Lucrezia Borgia	
29 Nov.	Don Giovanni	
30 Nov.	Gemma di Vergy	
2 Dec. (Monday)	Gemma di Vergy	
4 Dec.	Gemma di Vergy	
5 Dec.	Lucia di Lammermoor	
6 Dec.	Don Giovanni	
7 Dec.	Lucrezia Borgia (gala benefit)	
9 Dec. (Monday)	Norma	
10 Dec.		Lucia di Lammermoor
11 Dec.	Lucrezia Borgia	
13 Dec.	Ernani	Don Giovanni
14 Dec.	Concert	Don Giovanni
16 Dec. (Monday)	Gemma di Vergy	
17 Dec.	Concert	Ernani
18 Dec.	La Sonnambula	
20 Dec.	Parisina	Lucrezia Borgia
23 Dec. (Monday)	Lucia di Lammermoor	Norma
26 Dec.	Il Giuramento	Ernani
27 Dec.	Il Giuramento	

Table 13. Continued

28 Dec.		*Gemma di Vergy*
30 Dec. (Monday)	*La Favorita*	*Norma*
1 Jan. 1851		Concert: Musical Fund Hall
2 Jan.	*La Favorita*	*Ernani*
4 Jan.		*Parisina*
6 Jan. (Monday)	*Giovanna Prima*	*Parisina*
8 Jan.	*Giovanna Prima*	*Il Giuramento*
10 Jan.	*Giovanna Prima*	*Ernani*
11 Jan.	Concert (postponed)	
13 Jan. (Monday)	*Norma*	*La Favorita*
14 Jan.	Concert	*Don Giovanni*
15 Jan.	*Lucrezia Borgia*	*Ernani*
17 Jan.	*Giovanna Prima*	*La Sonnambula* (benefit)
18 Jan.	Concert	*La Favorita*
20 Jan. (Monday)	*Norma*	Benefit
21 Jan.	Concert	
22 Jan.	*La Favorita*	**Baltimore:**
23 Jan.	Concert	*Ernani*
24 Jan.	*La Favorita*	
25 Jan.		*Parisina*
27 Jan. (Monday)		*Lucia di Lammermoor*
28 Jan.	*Romeo et Giulietta*	*La Sonnambula*
29 Jan.	*Romeo et Giulietta*	
30 Jan.	*Romeo et Giulietta*	*Parisina*
31 Jan.	*Romeo et Giulietta*	
1 Feb.		*Il Giuramento*
3 Feb. (Monday)	*Il barbiere di Siviglia*	
4 Feb.		Benefit
5 Feb.	*Il barbiere di Siviglia*	
6 Feb.	Benefit	
7 Feb.	*La Favorita*	Concert
10 Feb. (Monday)	*Lucrezia Borgia*	
12 Feb.	*Semiramide*	Concert
14 Feb.	*Semiramide*	
		Boston:
17 Feb. (Monday)	*Ernani*	*Lucrezia Borgia*
19 Feb.	*Parisina*	*Norma*
21 Feb.	*Ernani*	*Il barbiere di Siviglia*
22 Feb.		Concert (Providence, R.I.)
24 Feb. (Monday)	*La Favorita*	*Romeo et Giulietta*
26 Feb.		*La Favorita*
28 Feb.		Benefit

Table 13. Continued

1 March		Concert
3 March (Monday)		*Semiramide*
4 March	*Philadelphia:*	*Norma*
6 March	Concert	Concert (Whiting, post-poned)
7 March	*Ernani*	
8 March	Concert	
11 March	Concert (benefit for Bertucca-Maretzek, New York City)	

On Thursday, Maretzek thought that he had a treat for his audience. The "celebrated tenor" Alessandro Bettini had arrived in New York on 30 November en route from Paris to Havana where he had been engaged by Marti. Bettini was to be in New York for several days while awaiting a steamer to Cuba.[77] Maretzek recognized a golden opportunity and immediately approached the tenor to offer him a short engagement. On 3 December, he triumphantly announced in the *Tribune* that Bettini had agreed to sing for "a few nights only."

The tenor's first appearance was on Thursday, 5 December in *Lucia di Lammermoor* as Edgardo, Bettini's "favorite character," according to the playbill.[78] The dancers Fitzjames and Carrese also were scheduled to appear. Unfortunately, however, Bettini was hoarse at the beginning of the performance and became increasingly indisposed as the opera progressed. Maretzek was forced to halt the production at the end of the first act, and the audience was dismissed after being given the choice of a refund or an exchange for the next night (Friday), when the company would try the same bill again.[79] Bettini was still hoarse on Friday, so the troupe offered *Don Giovanni,* which had been very popular during the 1849–50 season.[80] On Saturday, Bettini again was advertised, again along with the dancers, again to perform in *Lucia di Lammermoor.* That evening a huge crowd appeared at the Opera House. As ill luck (or ill singers) would have it, however, the audience once again was disappointed. When the curtain rose, Maretzek came forward and announced that although the tenor had assured him repeatedly throughout the day that he would be able to sing, he had changed his mind a scant hour before curtain time. By then, of course, it was much too late to post playbills with that announcement. Maretzek, who gave

ITALIAN
OPERA HOUSE
ASTOR PLACE

New Machinery.................by.............Mr. Tunison
New Dresses..................by.......... ....Mr. Debeurre
Properties....................by....... ..... A. K. Gilbert
New Scenery and Decorations.......by...................F. Grain
Secured Seats, Parquet & Boxes $2 50
Admission to Parquet and Boxes, on the
evening of Performance..........$2 00
Amphitheatre.....................50 Cents

LAST WEEK
BUT ONE OF
SIGNORINA TERESA
PARODI
IN NEW YORK.

2nd performance of Donizetti's celebrated Opera
in 3 acts, of
GEMMA DI VERGY
Signorina Teresa Parodi........as........Gemma

19th Subscription Night

MONDAY EVENING, DECEMBER 2, 1850
Will be performed, 2d time, Donizetti's Grand Opera, in 3 acts, of

GEMMA
DI VERGY

Gemma............Sig'na Parodi
Conte di Vergy..................Sig. Avignone
Ida.....................Signorina A. Patti
Tamas....................Signor Lorini
Guido ....Sig. Novelli
Rolando.....................Signor. Guibelei
Leaders...........Mr. Kreutzer and Sig. Lietti
Chorus Master.....................Mr. Hensler
Doors open at a quarter before 7.
            To commence at half-uast 7 o'clock.

No Free List. No Orders

31. Playbill from a performance of Gaetano Donizetti's *Gemma di Vergy* at the Astor Place Opera House on 2 December 1850. This playbill illustrates the techniques Maretzek used to announce the forthcoming departure of his star prima donna, Teresa Parodi. (Courtesy of the Trustees of the Boston Public Library)

his little speech "evidently with great feeling," threw himself "upon the indulgence of the audience" and offered as a substitution Teresa Parodi in *Lucrezia Borgia*. The audience, undoubtedly to Maretzek's great relief, reacted to this offer with "shouts of applause," according to the 9 December *Tribune*.

The manager astutely mollified his potentially irate audience by offering as a substitute the star of the season in her most popular role. But Bettini himself came under attack in the New York press for his total lack of consideration for the public. "Tenor voices, we all know, are very delicate affairs," the *Figaro*'s critic wrote sarcastically on 14 December, "and in such weather as Bettini encountered on his arrival here, very apt to get out of order. But Bettini surely must have known whether he could or could not sing before the audience had assembled to hear him."

The sarcasm and suspicion expressed by this journalist were not unusual during the late 1840s and 1850s; Americans were increasingly hostile toward and distrustful of Italian vocalists. To any kind of itinerant performer during this period, serious illness meant no performance. And no performance meant no pay. But a decade had passed since Jane Shirreff had attempted to continue singing despite a serious malady, and the circumstances of singers' illnesses — or purported illnesses — had changed. Choral or orchestral members of large troupes still found "no pay" to be a serious matter, for these musicians were paid by the performance.[81] For the stars of large Italian troupes, however, the story was different. Many were paid so handsomely that an occasional missed performance meant no economic hardship whatsoever. Furthermore, a star of sufficient reputation could demand — and get — payment in advance. Under such circumstances, a missed performance meant little or nothing financially.[82]

Illness seems to have been endemic to all traveling singers, but American critics increasingly viewed Italian artists as particularly unpredictable, undependable, and susceptible to maladies of various kinds. "These people always seem to be afflicted with some indisposition, and to demand much waiting for and caresses," wrote one individual in 1852 about an Italian company performing in Dresden, Germany. "One night Pozzolani, the tenor, was sick — no opera; — on another, Tamburini, the basso — no opera again; and last [night] Persiani, the soprano — again no opera."[83] The maligned company was performing in Europe, but the sentiments closely echoed those of many Americans. By the mid 1840s, many Americans had decided that Italian performers were greedy, contentious, lazy, and dishonest (chapter 3). The negative attitude had been fueled by the behavior of singers associated with various companies assembled to perform in New York. The stereotype eventually included the conviction that most of the illnesses that befell Italian singers were feigned, and that the supposed indispositions were simply matters of convenience for either the singers or their managers. In 1853 a critic for the *New York Daily Times* expressed a prevailing attitude toward Italian stars:

> The great singer in the present day...can do precisely what he likes. Get largely paid beforehand for services which he has it in his power to render or not as he chooses. Treat everybody from his manager down to his audience with insufferable impertinence. Have a new whim every hour in the day, and a fresh cold every time that his presence is required by the public. Sow sedition in the establishment with which he is connected, and make fools of two or three thousand respectable people half an hour before the raising of the curtain with a "sudden indisposition."[84]

A critic for the *Cincinnati Enquirer* perhaps best summed up the skepticism Americans felt toward the members of Italian opera companies. Reviewing a just-completed, successful season by the Grau Opera Company in the Queen City, he marveled, "they did what they agreed to do—which is very remarkable for Italian vocalists—The prime donne were not suddenly and mysteriously indisposed; the bassi did not refuse to sing; the tenori did not become unmanageable at the very moment they were needed most, and the artists were upon their good behavior unquestionably."[85]

This resentment is completely understandable in view of the drawing power (and managers' exploitation of it) of the same star singers who were so prone to maladies. American audiences of the nineteenth century—in this respect no different from their descendants in the twentieth—were attracted like flies to the honey of celebrity status and reputation. Managers, of course, knew and capitalized on this: hence Maretzek's frantic search in the late summer and fall of 1850 for a star singer whose reputation he could puff, and his remarkable success in doing so. Audiences were drawn by the promised appearance of a favorite star, perhaps singing in a favorite role. A last-minute substitution often resulted in ill-will directed at both the star and the manager: toward the singer if the illness was believed feigned; toward the manager if the entire incident was considered a nineteenth-century style bait and switch operation.

After the fiasco of Bettini's failure to appear, the Astor Place Company entered its seventh week, and Maretzek began to use for the first time during the season a standard managerial trick: the inevitable promotional build-up before a star's departure. Although Parodi had another three weeks of performances in New York, Maretzek announced that the removal to Philadelphia of the new favorite was imminent. Playbills and newspaper advertisements issued during the week carried the following announcement (Figure 31):

LAST WEEK
but one of
SIGNORINA TERESA
PARODI
In New York

This style of subtle deception was such a standard technique, used by most impresarios and theater managers, that the public undoubtedly had become accustomed to it and learned not to be taken in. As the public became more sophisticated, however, managers and impresarios grew more devious. Messages on playbills sometimes were so misleading that even experienced play-, opera-, and concert-goers could be caught unaware. For example, an Astor House playbill announced that on 9 December:

Signorina Teresa
PARODI
Will perform for the
LAST TIME
Bellini's Grand Opera of
NORMA

The message could have two quite different interpretations: that Parodi's performance on 9 December in *Norma* would be her last in New York; or that this performance on 9 December would be Parodi's last appearance in the opera *Norma* during her remaining time in New York. As might be suspected, the latter message was the correct one; Parodi had yet another five performances after 9 December before leaving for Philadelphia.

Expansion to Philadelphia

When the troupe mounted *Norma* on 9 December, the performance was not under the baton of Maretzek. The impresario had split his company and headed south to Philadelphia, apparently leaving the New York division under the direction of Sesto Benedetti, as the *Tribune* reported. Two Astor Place companies now performed simultaneously in different cities; it is inaccurate, however, to describe the troupe as being split into two separate wings. Because New York and Philadelphia are close geographically and were linked by reliable and relatively cheap transportation, Maretzek could shuttle singers back and forth readily if not particularly easily. This, in fact, is what he did. Rather than

splitting into two separate companies, the Astor Place troupe expanded
to encompass two theaters of operation.

Almost all of the name singers (those mentioned in advertisements
or on playbills) who performed during the Philadelphia engagement
also appeared in New York during the same period. The several artists
who sang in Philadelphia but not in New York were newcomers who
evidently had been added for the expansion: the basses Francesco
Giubernao and Domenico Locatelli and Napoleone Parozzi, a tenor.
Furthermore, during the Philadelphia run, all of the stars who sang in
New York also appeared in Pennsylvania. It was perfectly accurate,
then, for the manager to name each star singer in the preseason Philadelphia advertisements. The roster of the company actually in Philadelphia at any one time, however, fluctuated from week to week as
singers came from and returned to New York.[86]

Maretzek arranged his Philadelphia performance dates, at least at
the beginning of the season, to best use his limited number of stars.
During each of the first two weeks in Philadelphia the company mounted
performances on Tuesday, Friday, and Saturday evenings. In New York,
the troupe performed on Monday, Wednesday, Friday, and Saturday
evenings during the week of 9 December and added Tuesday the
subsequent week. Maretzek chose his Philadelphia evenings based on
his New York schedule. During the week of 9 December, for example,
three vocalists (G. F. Beneventano, August Giubilei, and Amalia Patti)
sang in New York in *Lucrezia Borgia* on Wednesday; two days later
the trio performed in *Don Giovanni* in Philadelphia. If Mozart's opera
had been mounted on the normal Thursday evening, the singers would
have been fatigued, hence the change of the Philadelphia opera night
to Friday.

Information is nonexistent about orchestral and choral musicians
employed for the Philadelphia engagement. It is obvious, however, that
the manager had to hire an additional chorus and another orchestra,
despite the schedule-juggling, for there were simultaneous performances
in the two cities. Maretzek probably used the Chestnut Street Theatre
orchestra as the nucleus for his accompanying ensemble and augmented
it with other Philadelphia or New York musicians. The 10 December
North American and United States Gazette noted only that "the Orchestra will be a strong and talented one . . . and will be under the
masterly conduct of the Prince of leaders—Max Maretzek." No other
contemporary sources mention the instrumental or choral musicians
connected with the company's Philadelphia engagement.

The task of shuttling star singers back and forth from city to city
and ensuring that the right singers were in the right places at the right
times fell, undoubtedly, to Maretzek himself.[87] And what a gargantuan

logistical headache it must have been. The opening of an entirely new venue more than doubled the necessary decisions. In addition to choosing the repertory, juggling joint appearances by various singers and dancers, and calculating the drawing power of each evening's bill of fare, the manager now had to deal with railroad schedules, travel time, and accommodations for his performers. He also had to weigh travel costs against a star's potential draw in a particular opera and somehow determine whether it was more cost-effective to pay the transportation expenses or to make do with a secondary singer, who would have a smaller audience draw, to cover the part.

In Philadelphia, Maretzek followed the same general managerial method of operation that he had established in New York. He ensured that far in advance the local newspapers published advertisements and puffs to inform the Philadelphia public of the troupe's impending arrival. The first Philadelphia advertisement appeared in the *North American and United States Gazette* on 27 November, almost two full weeks before the season began. On opening night, 10 December, the same paper predicted "undoubted success" for the troupe, reiterated the "great reputations" of the singers, and shrewdly reported the large number of seats that had already been taken. The *Philadelphia Public Ledger*, furthermore, informed its readers that the troupe's local manager (Walker) had taken great pains to improve the physical condition of the Chestnut Street Theatre by installing two additional stoves and by removing the liquor bars from the building. These improvements, the *Ledger* suggested on 13 December, made the theater a "place for the enjoyment of pure and refined pleasure, without any drawbacks." No opera-lover, in other words, need fear discomfort or embarrassment by attending a performance.

For the first four performances in Philadelphia Maretzek relied on three well-known and popular operas: *Lucia di Lammermoor, Don Giovanni,* and *Ernani.* The manager counted on the anticipation, excitement, and glitter associated with the season's opening week to attract substantial crowds; "large and brilliant" and "large and fashionable" audiences obligingly attended these performances, at least according to the local newspapers.[88] The opening night of the season featured the Philadelphia debut of the contralto Apollonia Bertucca-Maretzek, Maretzek's wife, in *Lucia.* On the other three nights Teresa Truffi was featured in both *Don Giovanni* and *Ernani.* The *Public Ledger*, on 14 December, the day of Truffi's second performance, pointed out that she was soon "to leave for New York, to remain there for some time." The clear implication was that if Philadelphia music lovers intended to hear her sing, they should not procrastinate.

Although the company apparently attracted full houses in its first two weeks of performances, the commencement of the Philadelphia season was remarkably similar to the beginning of the New York season in one respect: it was again compared, unfavorably, with the Havana Company's performances. John Hill Martin, a Philadelphia resident, witnessed the troupe in *Lucia di Lammermoor* on 10 December. "Bertucca, Avignone, Forti, and Rossi [are] all good singers," he wrote in his diary, "but [they are] not equal to the previous troupe."[89] For the time being, however, the company had to make do without Parodi, who had not yet finished her performances in New York. The northern branch of the troupe was in the eighth week of its season, offering *Norma, Lucrezia Borgia,* and *Ernani* and featuring Parodi's last appearance in each. On Saturday, 14 December, the prima donna sang in a grand gala concert at Jenny Lind Hall that was advertised incorrectly in the 14 December *Tribune* as "Parodi's only concert appearance in New York."

Maretzek stalled as long as possible before introducing his big attraction to Philadelphia. Parodi's debut in *Lucrezia Borgia* was on Friday, 20 December, at almost the end of the company's second week. Before her appearance, the manager had widely puffed her pending arrival, making sure to include lavish reports of her success in New York. When Parodi finally came, he doubled his admission prices, which had been $1 for unreserved box and parquet—50 cents extra for reserved—and 25 cents for the amphitheater. Both tactics had been successful in New York.[90] After her Philadelphia debut, Parodi sang in the next seven consecutive performances, receiving great acclaim and attracting large audiences. The critic for the *North American and United States Gazette* pointed out that her success was all the more remarkable, coming as it did on the heels of Jenny Lind's triumphant engagement. Diarist Joseph Sill confirmed that the Chestnut Street Theatre—at least at Parodi's debut performance on 20 December—was packed; "I went to the Parquette," he wrote, "& could only get a 'stool' as the house was filled.—Parodi filled the character admirably, and has great musical power; tho' she is not so perfect as many others whom I have heard—Still, I was exceedingly pleased both with the performances & the opera; and also with the appearance of the house, which was very brilliant with people." Because of the truncated nature of the Philadelphia season, the operas in which Parodi performed changed much more frequently than they had in New York. She sang, in quick succession, in *Lucrezia Borgia* (twice), *Norma* (twice), *Ernani, Gemma di Vergy,* and, for her benefit and last performance, once again in *Lucrezia Borgia* (Table 13).

By the prima donna's fourth appearance, her magic appeared to be wearing somewhat thin. On 27 December, the *Gazette* commented rather disapprovingly that the audience the previous evening was "not such a one, in point of numbers, as the occasion deserved."[91] In quick response to the low turn-out, Maretzek added as another attraction to his Saturday offering of *Gemma di Vergy,* the debut performances — for "This Night Only" — of the sisters Caroline, Teresina, Adelaide, and Clementine Rousset, "Première Danseuses . . . from the Grand Theatres of St. Petersburg, Brussels and Italy."[92] The combination of ballet and opera did the trick; a review that appeared on 30 December described the resulting house as "crowded from parquet to dome" with an audience that was "the most splendid . . . of the season."[93] The attraction was so successful that the management featured the Rousset sisters again the following Monday, along with Parodi's second appearance in *Norma.*[94]

The Philadelphia branch of the troupe had entered its fourth week, and momentum was building. Parodi's departure was fast approaching, a fact prominently noted on playbills and in advertisements. Meanwhile in New York, the northern branch was doing fairly well without either Parodi or Maretzek. The troupe had filled the vacuum left by the departure of the star prima donna with performances of *Parisina* — still novel enough to draw substantial audiences — and *Lucia di Lammermoor,* both featuring Truffi, who had returned from Philadelphia. After these productions, the company mounted two operas that were new neither to the troupe nor to New York audiences but that had not yet been mounted this season: Mercadante's *Il Giuramento* (the first New York performance in two years) and Donizetti's *La Favorita.*[95] Both operas featured Truffi in prominent roles and were evidently well received.

Back in Philadelphia, Maretzek was orchestrating Parodi's final appearances. After her second performance of *Norma* on Monday, 30 December with the Rousset sisters, the prima donna had one last scheduled appearance in that city. On 1 January, however, Walker announced in the *North American and United States Gazette* that he was "unwilling that the popular Parodi should leave Philadelphia without being seen and heard by the many who are prevented from attending the theatre." Consequently, he arranged for her appearance in a "Festival Concert" that evening at Musical Fund Hall, assisted by a "Celebrated Violinist" (one Herr Griebel), the chorus of the Italian Opera Company, a "Grand Orchestra of Fifty Performers," and most of the members of the Astor Place troupe who were in Philadelphia. The concert consisted almost entirely of operatic selections from works by Rossini, Donizetti, Bellini, Verdi, Mercadante, and Halévy; even the single work for violin was a "Fantasie on Themes of 'Pirata' for the Violin." According to the *Public Ledger,* the performance was a great success.

Presumably, it attracted those individuals whose religious convictions would not allow them to enter a theater, as well as music lovers who preferred to hear operatic stars in the less-fettered context of a concert. The next evening, Thursday, 2 January, Parodi chose for her benefit and last Philadelphia appearance the reliable *Lucrezia Borgia*. Because this was the third performance of the opera within a two-week period, however, the management decided to add the Philadelphia debut of Maretzek's dancers, Fitzjames and Carrese.[96]

At this point, the middle of the eleventh week in New York and the fourth in Philadelphia, the company's two sopranos changed places: Parodi went north and Truffi south. With the departure of Parodi, the number of weekly performances at the Chestnut Street Theatre increased, just as the momentum at the Astor Place House had increased as the season progressed there. During the fourth and fifth weeks there were four performances each, and during the final, benefit week there were five (Table 13). In addition, Maretzek boosted the levels of variety and novelty offered in Philadelphia and decreased his admission prices.[97] After Parodi's departure, the Philadelphia troupe used a new opera to attract audiences, presenting, as had the New York branch, Truffi in the Philadelphia premiere of *Parisina*. During the fifth and sixth weeks, the troupe offered *Parisina* (its second performance), *Il Giuramento*, *Ernani* (twice), *La Favorita* (twice), *Don Giovanni*, *La Sonnambula*, and—in the troupe's final appearance—a benefit performance comprised of parts of various operas. In addition, two groups of dancers, the duo of Fitzjames and Carrese and the Rousset sisters, also appeared during these two weeks to add variety.

The only additional information about the Philadelphia audience during this engagement is from Joseph Sill's diary, but that is instructive. He attended five performances during the season and in general was pleased with the company, although on 10 January he noted disliking *Ernani* and on 4 January described the plot of *Parisina* as "disagreeable, but the Music . . . often very sweet and expressive." He took his daughter to one performance, his son to another, and his wife, his daughter, and a woman who worked at his store to a third. "Mrs. Sill," he noted on 13 January, "had not attended the Theatre for about 2 years, & I thought that a visit there would be agreeable & pleasant to her." The trip on 10 January had been a casual, spur-of-the-moment affair. As he related, "in the Evening Mr. Wilton call'd, and after chatting with us for a length of time, presented us with 3 tickets of admission to the 'opera'—[my son] Willy & I accompanied him there & the other ticket we presented to Mr. Richter, the Musical Teacher."

Sill's attendance at both dramatic and operatic performances during the twenty-year period covered by his diaries was remarkably consistent.

His numerous comments do not indicate musical literacy, but he had a discriminating ear. The fact that he frequently took his young children to opera performances suggests that he did not consider it inappropriate fare for them, and—as the diary entry quoted above indicates—he sometimes attended performances on the spur of the moment.[98] Furthermore, he did not seem to make a distinction among English, French, or Italian varieties of opera, but attended performances of all three types. All of these factors suggest that to Joseph Sill, and perhaps to other Philadelphians, Italian opera was still a normal part of the theatrical repertory. Comments found in a Philadelphia monthly, *Graham's Magazine,* furthermore indicate that some Philadelphians were resisting the attempts by the elite, particularly New Yorkers, to claim Italian opera for their own. "The small circle of fashionable people may subscribe and talk," wrote the editor, "but they can do little in this opera matter, without the support of the plain, unpretending portion of the inhabitants, who, after all, make up the audience, and bring in the money."[99]

As the Philadelphia engagement drew to a climactic finish, excitement was building once again in New York. By 3 January, Maretzek had returned to the Astor Place House, leaving Benedetti in charge at Chestnut Street.[100] In early January there was a temporary lull in New York, for no performances were given at the Astor Place House for the remainder of the week following Truffi's departure. There were, however, a spate of rehearsals and a general air of anticipation, for the company was preparing for its world premiere production of *Giovanna Prima di Napoli,* a new opera by the pianist, impresario, and composer Maurice Strakosch (Figure 32), who was well known and well liked by New York audiences and music professionals.

The opera's premiere had been anticipated from the very beginning of the season. The *Message Bird* had announced on 15 July that the Astor Place troupe would give the debut performance during the year, and several journals had occasionally published reports on the progress of rehearsals (395). The three-act opera was written to a libretto by Agostino Pendola; Strakosch composed it, according to the published libretto, "expressly . . . for the Italian Opera Company of New York, Under the Management and Direction of Max Maretzek."[101] This is the only known opera by Strakosch, who is better known as a pianist and a composer of works for the piano.

The opera was well received at its premiere on 6 January. One critic called it "the work of a most devoted and appreciating student of [the Italian] style." He was quick to point out that the opera "has no original melody or treatment" but obviously did not consider this cause

32. Opera and concert impresario, pianist, and composer Maurice Strakosch. From the illustration on a sheet-music publication titled "Oeuvres choisies de Maurice Strakosch" (New York: William Hall & Son, 1848). (Music Division, Library of Congress)

for censure, for he wrote in the *Tribune* on 8 January that the work "recalls the pleasantest parts of the pleasantest operas as its sweet, full stream flows on." Strakosch evidently was adept at writing in the style of the most popular contemporary continental opera composers. The critic for the *Message Bird* commented on 1 February that "of course it is not to be disguised, that some of [its] themes are first cousins to something, *somewhere* heard before," and the same *Tribune* reporter quoted previously pointed out similarities to works by Verdi (especially *Ernani*), Weber, and Meyerbeer (610). Overall, however, *Giovanna Prima* won unqualified approval from local critics. One reviewer concluded that Strakosch had "done himself great credit" in the composition of his first opera, and another wrote that the work was "of a remarkable uniformity of excellence" and praised the opera's "unflagging sense of melody," rejoicing in the absence of "those dreamy desert patches of monotonous and meaningless recitative which disfigure most . . . contemporary Italian Operas."

Although the last comment seems to imply the use of spoken dialogue in place of recitative, the libretto clearly indicates that the entire work was sung. The opera evidently was never published in score; if it was, no copies have been located. Some of the extant sheet music publications from it, however, contain occasional sections of recitative that are melodious and dramatic and have instrumental interjections.[102] It is possible that Strakosch, aware of the distaste his audience had for long stretches of dry recitative sung in a language incomprehensible to most Americans, kept these sections as short and as interesting as possible. A reduction in the amount of recitative in operas, in any case, was a general trend among Italian composers.

The aria "I Greet Thee Gentle Flowers" ("Io vi saluto"), written for Parodi, is a good example. It commences with an introductory recitative section for soprano and orchestra that is at first dramatic, then ariosolike: pleasing and melodious. This segment is decidedly not "monotonous," but neither is it particularly remarkable. Stylistically, it is garden-variety late Donizetti or early Verdi introductory material.

If a new work were judged today to have "no original melody or treatment," most composers would consider the critique a damning insult. Strakosch, however, was probably not disturbed by the assessment. In writing a work for the musical stage, his goal undoubtedly had been to compose a pleasant, sweet, melodious—and thoroughly conventional—opera. Maretzek, after all, had commissioned the work, and the impresario's goal was to please his American audiences, who seemed to prefer the conventional and the familiar. As the *Message Bird*'s reviewer noted of the opera on 1 February: "[It] is written in the most approved modern Italian style; the aim of the composer being, apparently, to invent a series of pleasing and brilliant melodies, and present them to the public in the most palatable and acceptable way" (609). All six extant numbers from Strakosch's opera are in standard forms (most are ternary), and the tonal treatment likewise is rather commonplace, with modulatory movement either to the dominant, the subdominant, or the relative minor or major.

Both "I Greet Thee Gentle Flowers" and "While My Thoughts Still Turn to Thee" ("Tornera nel mis core") are in bel canto style, with numerous examples of *fioritura*, again evidently in response to American taste. In the second of these, which consists of a ternary aria (*Allegro con spirito*) repeated in its entirety after an extended instrumental interlude, Strakosch provides the soprano with two florid, written-out cadenzas. One of the most appealing of the six arias is a standard cabaletta and includes a part for chorus. This composition, "For Our Queen and Liberty" ("Combattim per nostra Regina"), is a stirring martial work and was written for the company's tenor Domenico Lorini. The composition is harmonically simple, as befits a military call-to-arms; the harmonic simplicity, however, belies a work that is deftly constructed dramatically. The melody is stirring, and Strakosch's handling of chorus, soloist, and accompaniment is skillful. The audience must have left the theater humming the tunes.

The Astor Place Company repeated *Giovanna Prima* twice during the week of 6 January and once more the following week before withdrawing it.[103] With the relative success of Strakosch's work, Maretzek's season appears to have been going swimmingly. The logistical complications of managing simultaneous seasons in two cities had not proven insurmountable, and the engagements in both Philadelphia and New York had proceeded with no noticeable hitches. Just after the third performance of *Giovanna Prima*, however, Maretzek's delicate two-city balancing act began to wobble dangerously, and the manager had to administer emergency personal attention to both troupes in order to avert further crises. The resulting temporary near-chaos exemplifies both the precarious nature of Maretzek's enterprise and the absolute necessity of a firm managerial hand at the helm of an Italian opera company. It also illustrates some of the unexpected problems that occasionally blew up in the faces of opera company managers.

On Saturday evening, 11 January, a "Grand Musical Festival" was scheduled at Jenny Lind Hall in New York, and Teresa Parodi was to be joined by the Austrian violinist Miska Hauser (1822–87) in his American debut, as well as by the pianist Strakosch. Maretzek was to be the orchestra conductor. On Saturday morning, however, the manager received a telegram from Philadelphia informing him that "some screw was loose in the difficult mechanism of the Philadelphia branch of his company," as reported in the *Tribune* on 13 January. The precise nature of this problem was not described by New York journalists, and the difficulty was never alluded to in the Philadelphia press. Whatever the trouble, however, it was serious enough that Maretzek's "immediate departure" for Philadelphia was required, and the manager, according to the *Tribune* on 15 January, "rush[ed] on to the City of Brotherly Love . . . [to] pour on such oil of healing as he could command."

Maretzek had no sooner left for Philadelphia when arrangements for the Saturday concert in New York began to unravel with a dizzying rapidity. He had left the duties of conducting the orchestra at the concert in the capable hands of his New York deputy, Herr I. Kreutzer.[104] Parodi, however, suddenly was seized with serious misgivings about performing her new arias—which she had rehearsed under Maretzek—under Kreutzer. Apparently her fears were primarily nationalistic, for she announced that although she could not possibly sing under the German Kreutzer, she could bring herself to perform under the baton of an Italian conductor if one could be found. The orchestra staged a mutiny of its own and refused to play under anyone but Kreutzer, especially under an unknown Italian.[105] As a result, the concert was postponed to Tuesday, disappointing the audience of three or four thousand that had assembled for the Saturday performance. Order was fully restored only when Maretzek returned, and the make-up concert transpired without incident. But according to a report in the *Tribune* on 15 January, Tuesday's audience, although large, was not nearly the size of the Saturday gathering. All the stars, and the management, were financial losers in a fiasco that apparently had been initiated by the whim of a prima donna.

Maretzek does not mention this imbroglio in his memoirs; it was, after all, a relatively minor incident. He does, however, detail a sufficient number of similar difficulties: problems caused by singers' "quarrels, jealousies and intrigues" as well as various and sundry "tricks, plots and conspiracies" inflicted upon opera managers by "capricious, conceited, egotistical, rapacious, intriguing, cheating, troublesome, mischievous and malicious . . . vocalists."[106] All of this suggests that the inconveniences that Teresa Parodi caused were not particularly extraordinary. Such behavior, of course, contributed no end to the increasingly widespread and negative stereotype about Italian opera singers. Even a skeptical reading of Maretzek's tales, which George Odell describes as the "doubtless exaggerated accounts of his sufferings," makes it clear that the lot of a manager of an Italian opera company was not an easy one.[107] More often than not, he seems to have been at the mercy of his "charges."

Sideshow in Baltimore

The Philadelphia season of 1850–51 concluded on Monday, 20 January. The New York engagement had yet another five weeks to run, and Maretzek summoned back to Manhattan six of the thirteen singers who had appeared during the final week in Philadelphia: Beneventano, Bosio, Giubilei, Amalia and Salvatore Patti, and Sanquirico. For the other seven—Avignone, Avogadro, Bertucca, Forti, Parozzi, Rosi, and Truffi—he had different plans. They were sent, along with the baritone

Biondi and the bass Locatelli, south to Baltimore, where this new itinerant branch of the company was engaged for a run at the Holliday Street Theatre.

This ensemble, unlike the artists who had appeared in Philadelphia and New York, was really a separate branch of the New York troupe. Under the direction of Benedetti, the Baltimore company was independent of the New Yorkers, and its season featured none of the shuttling back and forth between cities that had characterized the Philadelphia engagement. The visiting company was advertised in the *Baltimore Sun* of 23 January as including "all the distinguished performers of the great troupe now at the Astor Place Opera [House]." This was, however, hyperbole. Except for Truffi, none of the troupe's big-name stars—Bosio, Beneventano, Giubilei, the two Pattis, or Parodi—sang in Baltimore.

The Maryland season was advertised in the *Sun* of 15 January to last "Positively Six Nights Only," and they gave precisely that many performances. The troupe mounted six operas: *Ernani, Parisina, Lucia di Lammermoor, La Sonnambula, La Favorita,* and *Il Giuramento.* There was no time for repeat performances; besides, the management did not want to risk a small audience for an opera's second night. Under the circumstances, this policy made good managerial sense. Benedetti left little to chance at the Holliday Street Theatre. When the old favorite *La Sonnambula* was performed on 28 January ("the first time in Italian in Baltimore"), he also featured the dancers Fitzjames and Carrese; the performance was advertised as a "Grand Gala Night."[108]

According to reviews, the Baltimore public received the troupe favorably. Critics mention "fashionable," "brilliant," and "overflowing and highly fashionable" audiences, and one critic described the theater as "resplendent with beauty and fashion throughout." The "appearance . . . animation, and sociability" of the audience suggested to this critic the gathering of Baltimoreans who earlier in the year had assembled to pay homage to Jenny Lind.[109] Reviews of the quality of the performance are also overwhelmingly—and exclusively—positive; as usual, this tends to cast some doubt on the objectivity of the critics. In fact, when Maretzek's troupe returned to Baltimore in the fall of 1851, a Baltimore correspondent to *Saroni's* described "the production of opera here last winter, under Maretzek's name, but without his presence" as being "in a style utterly beneath serious criticism." He furthermore mentioned that performances by the troupe under Benedetti had left such a negative impression about Maretzek's company that the manager had to work hard to overcome it when his troupe revisited Baltimore in the fall.[110] It is possible, however, that the latter writer was as biased as the former, in this instance with a negative rather than a positive slant.

The Baltimore season lingered into a third week with a benefit performance for Truffi, who chose the second act of *Lucrezia Borgia* and the first, second, and third acts of *Ernani,* which is a good indication that the latter opera probably had drawn a large crowd during the first week of the run. On Friday, 7 February and again on Wednesday, 12 February, the company joined forces with the Germania Society Orchestra, then visiting Baltimore, for two "Grand Musical Festivals."[111] Like the earlier concert in Philadelphia, the works performed consisted almost entirely of operatic selections; the concert on the twelfth, for example, included overtures by Auber (*Zannetto*), Verdi (*Nabucco*), and Rossini (*Guillaume Tell*), as well as works by Donizetti (Duet from *Marino Faliero;* the Aria, Grand Finale from Act II, and Romanza from *La Favorita;* the Terzetto from *Lucrezia Borgia,* and Duet and Quintette from *Lucia di Lammermoor*). The "Quintette" from *Lucia* was undoubtedly the Sextet from that opera; evidently the singers omitted the mezzo's part.

While the Baltimore branch of the company was performing, the main body of the Astor Place troupe in New York had been busy wrapping up their extended season by mounting four operas a week. Parodi, whose contract was soon to expire, sang in every performance; her final New York appearance, her benefit, occurred on 14 February in *Semiramide.* It was not unusual for benefit performances to include guest appearances by additional artists willing to "kindly volunteer their services"; on this occasion Maurice Strakosch, Miska Hauser, and the violinist Mr. Griebel performed various instrumental works between the acts of the opera. This was to be Parodi's final appearance of the season with the troupe in New York, and the advertising made careful note of that fact.[112] The public came in droves and responded enthusiastically to the singer's appearance, throwing on the stage at the close of the first act "enough bouquets to stock an ordinary florist," according to the *Tribune* of 18 February. The *Tribune* also reported that the receipts of the evening amounted to $1,967, of which Parodi received $1,200 outright and divided the balance with Maretzek. If this division was an equal one, she took home $1,583 for the evening's work, roughly the equivalent of $26,550 in 1992.[113]

The Road Company

The conclusion of Parodi's New York engagement also marked the end of the New York season for the Astor Place Company. A skeleton crew, most of them singers returned from Baltimore, remained in New

York to perform during the final week of benefits. The majority of the company, however, took to the road.[114] From the middle of February until the end of May the whole Astor Place Company was transformed into an itinerant troupe, performing in Boston, Charleston, Augusta, and (again) Boston. Not until the conclusion of the second Boston engagement would the company return to New York, and then it would perform, as had the Havana Company during the previous summer, at Castle Garden.

During the four months that Maretzek's company was on the road, its personnel fluctuated. Some singers joined the troupe, performed for a while, then disappeared. Others, who had been with the company in New York or Philadelphia, rejoined the ensemble in Charleston or during the second Boston engagement. Still others, newcomers to the country or artists who had left another troupe, signed on with Maretzek's ensemble for the duration. Parodi performed with the company for a short while more before taking her final leave, and Maretzek and Benedetti apparently traded responsibilities as acting managers. The repertory performed during the four seasons was fairly consistent; most of the other circumstances, however, were different.

Boston

The season in Boston, which commenced on 17 February, was held at the Federal Street Theatre. Advertisements note that the visiting troupe featured the "Casts, Costumes, Grand Orchestra, and Chorus of the Astor Place Opera House, New York."[115] As this suggests, itinerant opera companies traveled with their own costumes; whether they were the property of the troupe or of individual singers or a combination of both—stars wearing their own clothing, chorus singers wearing the troupe's costumes—is unknown. By omission, the advertisement also alludes to the fact that most traveling companies did not take along scenery. Newspaper critics occasionally comment on new scenery painted for a particular opera production, but such references suggest that the painters were individuals associated with the local theater. This situation seems to be the same for all types of opera troupes active during the period.[116] The size of the chorus or the orchestra mentioned in the advertisement—or how many musicians Maretzek had left behind for the final three performances in New York—is also unknown.

Maretzek hired as his business manager in Boston the same Edward Walker who had served in that capacity in Philadelphia. Walker arrived in Boston on 12 February and set about sprucing up the slightly ratty interior of the theater: he had boxes reconstructed, worn carpets replaced, additional gas lights installed, and the number of stoves increased.[117] The hall had been allowed to deteriorate into a shabby and soiled state during the preceding several years, when it had been leased out to pantomime companies and equestrian groups as well as to dramatic stars; it was not an elite and exclusive house.[118] This state of affairs was cause for some concern; one individual wrote to the *Evening Transcript* on 13 February with a warning that "lovers of the opera" would not attend performances at the Federal Street Theatre until after a "thorough cleansing of the *dirt* and *dust* which has been allowed to lie unmolested on its floors for three seasons past, and which only requires the peculiar manner of Yankee applause to raise into an atmosphere sufficient to stifle the most enthusiastic opera-goer." The editor responded with an assurance that Walker would indeed put the theater into a "comfortable condition."

Walker also managed publicity efforts. He ran numerous advertisements in the newspapers and made sure that they included the information that Parodi's Boston performances were the last of her lengthy engagement with Maretzek. He probably was aware of the soprano's intentions to form a concert company at the completion of the Boston season, so he worded his advertisements very carefully: "Signorina Parodi Will Appear in Six Different Operas. Being the Last Nights of Her Engagement with Max Maretzek, and positively her last and ONLY APPEARANCE in *Opera* in America, previous to her departure for Europe."[119] Walker also had a local printer run off playbills, which were soon plastered all over the city.

Finally, in order to properly whet the appetite of the public, Walker provided puffing material about Parodi to the local dailies. The *Evening Transcript* of 12 February obligingly ran one such article, a lengthy biographical essay titled "A Sketch of Parodi." This public relations tour de force covered everything about the soprano that might appeal to Americans: the singer's humble origins in Genoa; the attempts of her respectable parents to dissuade her pursuit of a public career; her discovery by and study with the renowned Madame Pasta; the "wonderful display of [her] musical genius" on various European stages; her deep sympathies for the "struggling patriots" of Sicily and the consequent necessity for her to flee that island once the "friends of liberty" were "finally compelled to succumb to the overwhelming power of despotism"; her triumphant success in London; her arrival in the United States; and last but hardly least — and reminiscent of Jenny Lind — her generous and selfless nature, unspoiled youth, and cheerful willingness to assume the heavy responsibility of financial support for her parents and siblings back in Italy. Some of these biographical facts were mentioned in a calculated attempt to counteract the negative stereotype about Italian performers to which Parodi herself had contributed. The portrayal of the vocalist as a woman with documented sympathies toward the common folk spoke to Americans' well-known support for European revolutionaries; it was also a veiled allusion to the unresolved social issues raised by the Astor Place Riot (still very much in the American consciousness) that had occurred just two years earlier.[120]

The Boston engagement was advertised to be of six nights; in reality, the company gave eleven performances, nine operas and two concerts. It was easy for Maretzek to vary each evening's bill of fare; as in Baltimore, the troupe simply produced a different opera each night (see Table 14). The Boston public was gratifyingly enthusiastic. On opening night, according to the *Evening Transcript* of 18 February, the audience was "large, brilliant and enthusiastic, [it] filled all [the] seats, and crowded the lobbies." Parodi, according to the same newspaper, carried the night, surpassed all expectations, and was "applauded to an extent rarely witnessed in Boston." As further proof of the soprano's triumph, the critic pointed out that by press time the next day all seats in the parquet and first tier of boxes had been sold for the company's second performance, of *Norma,* on the nineteenth. "We might add," continued the reviewer, "that these were all bona fide sales, not hypothetical or made for purposes of effect, as in other instances that might be named." The target of the critic's rather snide remark is unknown. Others, however, concurred with this assessment of Parodi's appeal. A reviewer for the *Boston Post,* for example, wrote on 19 February that "as far as the popular favor is concerned there can be no question of [Parodi's] success. The applause from her crowded audience was frequent and cordial, and whether from the comparative novelty of opera [during] the present season . . . [or] from the belief in the European reputation of the vocalist, or from the genuine appreciation of actual excellence, her hearers seemed well satisfied with her efforts to please and to interest."

Subsequent performances by the company likewise attracted both large audiences and favorable reaction from the Boston press. The receipts for the first performance of *Norma,* for example, amounted to $2,500 (roughly $41,900 in 1992 terms).[121] Furthermore, at the beginning of the second week the *Courier* reported on 25 February that in spite of bad weather there had been a large audience at the previous evening's performance. The theater's "lower and upper portions" (the pit and the gallery), this critic wrote, "were crowded, and the second tier was two-thirds full."[122]

In addition to opera performances, the troupe also gave three concerts during the engagement: two in Boston, both at the Tremont Temple, and one in Providence, Rhode Island. As usual, the repertory of all three concerts was almost entirely operatic. For the 1 March

Table 14. Calendar of Performances, 17 Feb.–30 May 1851

Boston:

17 Feb. (Monday)	*Lucrezia Borgia*
19 Feb.	*Norma*
21 Feb.	*Il barbiere di Siviglia*
22 Feb.	Concert in Providence, R.I.
24 Feb. (Monday)	*Romeo e Giulietta*
26 Feb.	*La Favorita*
28 Feb.	Benefit
1 March	Concert
3 March (Monday)	*Semiramide*
4 March	*Norma*
6 March	Benefit concert (cancelled)
7 March	*Ernani*
8 March	Concert

Charleston:

21 March	*Ernani*
22 March	*La Favorita*
24 March (Monday)	*Parisina*
25 March	*Ernani*
27 March	*Lucrezia Borgia*
28 March	*La Favorita*
29 March	*Il Giuramento*
1 April	*Lucrezia Borgia*
5 April	*Norma*
7 April (Monday)	*Lucia di Lammermoor*
9 April	*Norma*
10 April	Concert
12 April	Concert

Augusta:

14 April (Monday)	*Ernani*
15 April	*Lucrezia Borgia*
17 April	*Il Giuramento*
19 April	*Il barbiere di Siviglia*
21 April (Monday)	*Norma*

Charleston:

22 April	*Il barbiere di Siviglia*

Boston:

28 April (Monday)	*Ernani* (postponed)
29 April	*Ernani*
1 May	*La Favorita*
2 May	*Il Giuramento*
3 May	Concert

Table 14. Continued

5 May (Monday)	*Lucia di Lammermoor*
7 May	*Lucrezia Borgia*
8 May	*Il barbiere di Siviglia*
9 May	*Ernani*
10 May	Concert
12 May (Monday)	*Lucia di Lammermoor*
14 May	*La Favorita*
16 May	*Don Giovanni*
17 May	Concert
19 May (Monday)	*Don Giovanni*
21 May	*Lucia di Lammermoor*
22 May	*Ernani*
23 May	*Don Giovanni*
26 May (Monday)	*Lucrezia Borgia*
27 May	*Romeo e Giulietta*
28 May	*Don Giovanni*
30 May	*La Favorita*

performance the singers were once again joined by Hauser and Strakosch for a "Grand Monstre Concert." In addition to various sung
operatic numbers by Rossini, Bellini, Donizetti, and Halévy, the concert
featured Hauser performing his "Fantasie Dramatique for Violin on
Lucia di Lammermoor" and the "Bird on the Tree Fable" (a program-
matic work for violin and piano that is his Opus 34); Strakosch playing
the Boston premiere of his "Fantasia de Concert on *Figlia del Regi-
mento*"; and the orchestra performing Maretzek's "Promenade Quadrilles" and "Tip Top Polka."[123]

The Rhode Island performance on 22 February was billed as a "Grand
Parodi Concert"; several other singers from the opera company and
the troupe's orchestra also appeared, according to the *Providence Daily
Journal.* Comments published in the local newspaper illustrate once
again the overwhelming impression that Lind, who had appeared in
Providence the previous October, had made on the American public.[124]
Parodi's performance was described in the *Providence Daily Post* on
24 February as a "greater feast to our music-loving people than they
have ever before enjoyed" excepting, of course, "the entertainment in
which the world famed Jenny Lind made her first and last appearance."
The critic hastened to mollify Lind enthusiasts by explaining that
although Parodi was "not . . . so charming a singer as Jenny," one could
listen to her without making undue and unfavorable comparisons with

the Swedish Nightingale because by late February Lind's October performance was a distant, albeit still pleasant, memory.

On 3 March the company completed its advertised run of six opera performances in Boston; this was also the date of Parodi's final appearance with the troupe. The overall critical verdict on the season was favorable. "The manner in which [the operas] were got up," wrote the reviewer for the *Boston Courier* on 27 February, "has given entire satisfaction . . . [and] it has been a favor to witness the excellent performances at the Federal Street Theatre." The critic added, "it is to be regretted that [Maretzek] has limited himself to six performances [especially as] we have had so little of opera lately." Evidently, Maretzek came to the same conclusion: an announcement appeared the following Monday that the manager had changed his mind about ending the season and had sent to New York for reinforcements—Truffi, Forti and the dancers Fitzjames and Carrese—to replace the departed Parodi. The *Evening Transcript* was delighted with this development. "We have pleasure," the editor wrote on 3 March, "in learning that all our operatic enjoyment for the season is not over yet. Truffi, ever a great favorite in Boston, is expected to protract the engagement of Max Maretzek's excellent company with Mr. Walker." The soprano, her husband Sesto Benedetti, and probably the other performers arrived in Boston on 4 March, according to the *Transcript* of the following day.

Whether Maretzek envisioned a lengthy reengagement in Boston or just a short one is unknown. The *Evening Transcript,* however, announced on 5 March that the troupe planned to mount four additional operas during the season: *Ernani* (Figure 33), *Don Giovanni, Parisina,* and *Il Giuramento,* all works they had not yet performed in Boston. It came as a surprise, then, that at the end of the first week the company abruptly announced the conclusion of the extended season. The critic for the *Evening Transcript* was dismayed at the sudden change of plans. "We had hoped," he observed on 6 March, "[that] sufficient encouragement would have been extended to induce Maretzek to keep [his company] here another week." The reason for the sudden change of plans would become clear later, when the troupe returned to Boston in April. For the time being, however, Maretzek simply changed the bill for the concert on Saturday, 8 March to read "Grand Farewell" performance. On Monday the tenth, the company members packed up their instruments, costumes, and music and boarded trains for New York, from there to depart for Charleston, South Carolina.[125]

Charleston and Augusta

The Astor Place Company, identified in the playbills of the Charleston Theatre simply as the "Italian Opera," traveled south by sea, arriving

ITALIAN OPERA!
FEDERAL STREET THEATRE.

MAX MARETZEK, LESSEE, DIRECTOR & CONDUCTOR.

☞ Owing to the desire of numerous families to witness

SIGNOR MARINI

In his great character of **SYLVA**, the opera

ERNANI!

Will be given, being the **LAST TIME THIS SEASON**.

ON FRIDAY EVENING, MAY 9TH, 1851.

Will be performed Verdi's favorite opera of

ERNANI

ELVIRA	Signora TRUFFI-BENEDETTI
ERNANI	Signor LORINI
DON CARLO	Signor BENEVENTANO
SYLVA	Signor MARINI

PRICES OF ADMISSION.
Parquet, first and second Tier of Boxes, $1,00.
Family Circle, 50 Cents; Gallery 25 Cents.

Doors open at 7, Performance commence at 8 o'clock

J. H. & F. F. Farwell, Printers, 3 and 5 State Street.

33. Playbill from a performance of Giuseppe Verdi's *Ernani* at Boston's Federal Street Theatre on 9 May 1851. (Courtesy of the Trustees of the Boston Public Library)

in Charleston on 18 March.[126] The troupe's first performance at the Charleston Theatre (Figure 34) was scheduled for Thursday the twentieth, but Truffi fell ill en route, and opening night was postponed until Friday.[127]

There was almost no advance publicity in the Charleston newspapers. The first advertisement appeared on the nineteenth, when "The Managers" announced the troupe's arrival and the date of its first appearance. This lack of advance publicity, however, is understandable in view of the company's abrupt departure from Boston and its sudden arrival in Charleston. The notice in the *Mercury* that the troupe's debut performance had to be postponed, however, suggests that the citizens of Charleston had some advance warning that the troupe was expected, as does the fact that by 17 March a subscription list for the opera season already had been assembled.[128] Evidently, F. L. Adams, the manager of the Charleston Theatre, relied heavily on the posting of playbills—rather than newspaper advertisements—for the dissemination of information about coming attractions.

This time-honored method of theatrical publicity would have been perfectly adequate in the South Carolina city, for in 1850 Charleston was a small town with a dense population concentrated almost entirely within limited confines.[129] Excepting Augusta, Charleston was by far the smallest town in which Maretzek's troupe mounted a season during the year: in 1850 its population was only 42,985, of whom 19,523 (slightly more than 45 percent) were slaves. The city occupied an area significantly less than a square mile. The other cities in which the company performed were much larger: New York (654,429, including Brooklyn), Philadelphia (340,045, including the suburbs), Boston (208,335, including suburbs), and Baltimore (169,054).[130] Although the troupe did perform in Providence (41,500), Maretzek deemed that town large or important enough for only one concert. In contrast, although Charleston was in the process of losing its long-held position as a major American cultural center, he felt sufficiently confident of Charlestonians' support that he mounted a full season there.

Maretzek depended on Adams to handle miscellaneous preliminary details because the entire troupe—including acting manager, stage manager, chorus master, prompter, conductor, leader of the orchestra, instrumentalists, and singers—all arrived at the same time.[131] Maretzek himself apparently acted as general manager on this trip, for both advertisements and playbills from Charleston identify Benedetti as "acting manager" of the troupe and Signor G. Lietti as the orchestra conductor.[132] After Benedetti's presumably unsatisfactory handling of the company in Baltimore, Maretzek perhaps had decided that his second-in-command needed some additional supervised managerial ex-

34. The New Charleston Theatre, where Maretzek's Astor Place Opera Company performed in March and April 1851. (South Carolina Historical Society)

perience. In addition, Maretzek had other business to attend to in Charleston.

The make-up of the troupe was admirably economical: numerous company members served in several capacities. In addition to his major singers, the manager used in name roles several relatively unfamiliar vocalists who probably were normally members of the chorus.[133] Conversely, at least one singer who had appeared in name roles elsewhere (the contralto Avogadro) sang in the chorus on this trip.[134] The doubling-up of duties must have been a standard practice, especially for a road company. Certainly all the secondary singers in the Astor Place troupe helped to fill out the ranks of the chorus when otherwise unoccupied.

The company included many of the name singers who had appeared in Boston, with the exception of Parodi. The five principals were Truffi, Forti, Beneventano (baritone), Rosi (bass), and Giubilei (bass); all had sung in Boston. Midway through the Charleston engagement the management added two other name singers: the contralto Caroline Vietti and the Boston soprano Virginia Whiting, whose Charleston debut was on 5 April. Whiting and the buffo Antonio Sanquirico came south on the steamer *Southerner* on its next trip from New York to Charleston; according to the *Daily Courier* of 28 March, they arrived on 27 March. Passenger lists published in newspapers provide further proof that many itinerant performers traveled with next-of-kin. In 1850, of course, it would have been unseemly for a young unmarried woman like Virginia Whiting, who had made her professional debut only several months earlier under Maretzek, to travel alone, so her mother accompanied her to Charleston.[135]

According to newspaper puffs this particular version of the Astor Place Company numbered some seventy performers, with "upwards of forty persons" in the orchestra and chorus.[136] It is impossible to determine the actual size and make-up of either chorus or orchestra, however, or to know whether musicians associated with the Charleston Theatre or other local musicians were engaged to augment either. It is likewise impossible to corroborate the figure of seventy performers. If the company had been noticeably smaller, however, one of the critics in either Charleston or Augusta probably would have mentioned it. Whatever the size of the company, Maretzek conducted the Charleston season in precisely the same manner that had previously proven successful—with variety as the governing principle. Over the course of three weeks the troupe performed eight different operas (*Ernani, La Favorita, Parisina, Lucrezia Borgia, Il Giuramento, Norma, Lucia di Lammermoor,* and *Il barbiere di Siviglia*), giving two performances of four: *Ernani, La Favorita, Lucrezia Borgia,* and *Norma.* Despite the repeats, each of the fifteen bills presented was different, the result of a varied slate of dances performed by Fitzjames and Carrese and the introduction of the new singers Whiting and Vietti at crucial points (Table 15).

Apparently, the company was well received. The only available commentary on the make-up of the Charleston audience, however, is from a diary entry by an individual who had attended an opera performance the previous spring. Elizabeth West Nevins, a Philadelphian who kept a journal of a trip to the South during 1850, was in Charleston when Marti's Havana Company, en route to New York, stopped there in March and April. Nevins and her party attended four of the five performances (the night they did not go she played whist). On the final evening, she noted that the theater was "crowded from pit to dome," a significant comment, especially for a segregated theater in a town with a slave population of 45 percent.[137] Newspaper commentary during the Astor Place Company's season suggests similarly large audiences.

Neither of the critics for the two newspapers seems to have been particularly knowledgable musically. The reviewer for the *Mercury* apparently possessed a modicum of musical discernment; "the chorus was well-drilled," he wrote on 22 March about the first performance, "but it lacked a little efficiency on the female side. . . . The Orchestra was full and efficient, every instrument harmonizing to the echo." The critic for the *Daily Courier,* however, wrote remarkably vacuous reviews. His "critique" of the opening night performance included the following very puff-like comments: "We have no desire, even if time

Table 15. Bills of the Astor Place Opera Company, Charleston Season,
21 March–12 April 1851

21 March (Friday)	*Ernani* (Truffi)
	Pas des tambourine and *La Manola* (Fitzjames and Carrese)
22 March (Saturday)	*La Favorita* (Truffi)
	Grand pas de deux and *La Zingarella* (Fitzjames and Carrese)
24 March (Monday)	*Parisina* (Truffi)
	Pas des tambourine and *La Manola* (Fitzjames and Carrese)
25 March (Tuesday)	*Ernani* (Truffi)
	Pas de deux and *La Sicilienne* (Fitzjames and Carrese)
27 March (Tursday)	*Lucrezia Borgia* (Truffi, Vietti)
	"First Appearance of the Celebrated Contralto Singer, Signora Vietti"
	La Zingarella and *La Manola* (Fitzjames and Carrese)
28 March (Friday)	*La Favorita* (Truffi)
	"Second and Positively Last Night of *Favorita*"
	Grand pas de deux and *La Sicilienne* (Fitzjames and Carrese)
31 March (Monday)	*Il Giuramento* (Truffi and Vietti; Truffi's benefit)
	"Two Prime Donne in One Opera!"
	La Sicilienne (Fitzjames and Carrese)
1 April (Tuesday)	*Lucrezia Borgia* (Truffi, Vietti)
	"For the Last Time This Season"
	Las Malaquenas (Fitzjames only)
4 April (Friday)	Truffi ill; no opera
5 April (Saturday)	*Norma* (Truffi, debut of Virginia Whiting)
	"Tip Top Polka" by Maretzek (Fitzjames)
7 April (Monday)	*Lucia di Lammermoor* (Whiting)
	"Second Appearance of Miss Virginia Whiting"
	(Dancers have gone to Augusta)
9 April (Wednesday)	*Norma* (Truffi, Whiting)
	"Last Appearance of Miss Virginia Whiting"
10 April (Thursday)	Concert
12 April (Saturday)	Concert
	(14–21 April, in Augusta)
22 April (Tuesday)	*Il barbiere di Siviglia* (Vietti)
	"Positively The Last Night that the Italian Opera Company Can Perform in Charleston"
	Unnamed Dance (Fitzjames and Carrese)

and space allowed, to criticize or discriminate between the respective performers. It is sufficient to say that the whole was harmony itself, and that never before within the walls of the new Theatre has an audience been more gratified at an Operatic performance." The citizens of Charleston deserved better; evidently they patronized the company's performances for the entire duration of their season.

Ironically, Maretzek and his troupe faced some significant competition in Charleston. Caroline Vietti and Fortunata Tedesco (one of Marti's most luminous stars) had arrived on 11 March and gave a grand concert on the fifteenth, three days before the Astor Place Company arrived.[138] It is likely that much of the audience was comprised of the same individuals Maretzek hoped to lure to his performances. Much more serious — and, under the circumstances, ironic — was competition from the concert company of Strakosch and Parodi (Figure 35). Their troupe arrived via steamer from Wilmington, North Carolina, on 1 April. It now numbered seven: Parodi, Strakosch, Amalia Patti, Avignone, Hauser, Salvatore Patti, and a Sig. Mustna. Four of the seven had once been members of Maretzek's company, and both Strakosch and Hauser had performed with the opera troupe on numerous occasions.[139] Advertisements for Parodi's two concert appearances in Charleston preceded her actual arrival there by about a month, attesting to Strakosch's remarkable organizational efficiency. Small advertisements announcing her imminent appearance "towards the end of the month" appeared in the *Daily Courier* as early as 10 March; starting on 24 March, the week before the concert, large, impressive advertisements were published listing full concert programs.[140]

The concert troupe was scheduled to give two performances, on Wednesday and Saturday, 2 and 5 April. Strakosch and Maretzek apparently were not interested in cut-throat competition. Maretzek also must have realized that many of his subscribers wished to hear Parodi, and that they would not be happy about sacrificing an opera ticket, for which they had paid, in order to attend one of her performances. It was bad enough, most Charleston music lovers thought, that they had to be satisfied with hearing Parodi in concert and not in opera. At least one of the city's critics noted, in a favorable review of Parodi's first performance, a "shade of disappointment" in the audience "not because [Parodi's] performance was not brilliant and full of the loftiest inspirations of genius, but because she could not help giving indications, under all the restraints of the concert room, of those wonderful dramatic powers which have made her the glory of the stage."[141]

Rumors that Maretzek himself was maliciously preventing an opera appearance by Parodi apparently were rife throughout the community,

M. STRAKOSCH'S GRAND CONCERT COMPANY.

Offering a Combination of Illustrious Names never yet Equaled.

M'LLE TERESA

PARODI

Begs leave to announce that she will give in WORCESTER her

First, and Positively only One Grand Concert!

— AT —

BRINLEY HALL,

WEDNESDAY EVENING, OCTOBER 15, 1856,

On which occasion she will be assisted by

Signor M. TIBERINI, The Great Roman Tenor.

M. STRAKOSCH is happy to inform the public that he has effected an arrangement with the Wonderful Violinist,

PAUL JULLIEN,

Who has been able to delay his departure for the Court of France, and consented to play a Farewell Engagement, for a limited number of nights, in M'lle PARODI'S Grand Concerts. The whole under the direction of

MAURICE STRAKOSCH.

The Programme will include Gems from Great Masters of Operatic, Sacred, Popular and Instrumental Music

M'LLE TERESA PARODI will Sing on this occasion, for the FIRST and ONLY time, the
CELEBRATED FRENCH NATIONAL HYMN,

LA MARSEILLAISE!

This Musical Gem has produced the most intense sensation wherever Sang by her.

PART I.

1. Duetto Concertante on Airs from "Guilaume Tell" by Rossini, composed by OSBORN & DE
   Performed by **PAUL JULLIEN** and **MAURICE STRAKOSCH.** [BERIOT.
2. The Gipsy Song from "L'Etoile du Nord," - - - - - - MAYERBEER
   Sung by **M'lle TERESA PARODI.** See Concert Book, No. 26
3. Aria from "Othello," - - - - - - ROSSINI
   Sung by **Signor TIBERINI.** See Concert Book, No. 48.
4. "Jerusalem, thou that killest the Prophets,"Aria from the Oratorio St. Paul, MENDELSSOHN
   Sung by **M'lle TERESA PARODI.** See Concert Book, No. 97.
5. "Marcelin,' Prayer from "Massaniello," - - - - - HAUMAN
   Performed by **PAUL JULLIEN.**
6. "Tu, perfida," Duetto from "Ernani," - - - - - VERDI
   Sung by **M'lle TERESA PARODI** and **Signor TIBERINI.** See Concert Book No. 116

PART II.

7. "Musical Rockets," composed and executed by
   MAURICE STRAKOSCH.
8. "La Donna e Mobile," Aria from "Rigoletto," - - - - VERDI
   Sung by **Signor TIBERINI.** See Concert Book, No. 80.
9. "Rataplan," composed by - - - - - MALIBRAN
   Sung by **M'lle TERESA PARODI.** See Concert Book, No. 15
10. The Witches Dance, - - - - - PAGANINI
    Performed by **PAUL JULLIEN.**
11. "LA MARSEILLAISE," the celebrated French National Hymn
    Sung by **M'lle TERESA PARODI.**
    See Concert Book, No. 23

35. Portion of a playbill for a performance by the Strakosch Grand Concert Company in 1856 at Brinley Hall in Worcester, Massachusetts. By the time of this concert, Teresa Parodi was again a member of Strakosch's well-traveled and successful troupe. The cost of admission was a uniform 50 cents. (American Antiquarian Society)

for he felt compelled to add a disclaimer to one of the company's playbills:

> The Managers would respectfully inform the citizens of Charleston that they have no connection with, or interest in, the Concerts to be given by Madame Parodi; nor has the Opera Company now performing under their management, nor Mr. Maretzek, any control over or interest in them whatever.
>
> The Managers have deemed it their duty to make this explanation, in consequence of a misapprehension which, they have been repeatedly informed, exists in the public mind, that they had prevented her from appearing in Opera, to protect their own interests.[142]

Whether to avoid the appearance of competition with Strakosch and Parodi or to accommodate the wishes of his subscribers, Maretzek announced on 1 April that the "Opera at the Theatre" was "suspended until Friday evening"; this development was reported in the *Daily Courier* on 2 April. Maretzek evidently did not want to compete with the concert singers on either of their two nights. The company's prima donna Truffi, however, fell ill on Friday and the performance had to be postponed to Saturday, putting it in direct competition with Parodi's concert after all. Apparently both performances attracted sizable audiences, which delighted the *Mercury*'s critic. "It is a gratifying evidence of the musical taste of our City," he wrote on 7 April, "that it can furnish in one night two such audiences as that of the Opera and that of the Concert, and equally gratifying that Charleston can attract the musical talent to furnish forth two such splendid entertainments."

Flush with the successful season in Charleston, the joint management of the Astor Place Company and the Charleston Theatre decided to attempt a short season in Augusta, Georgia. The smaller city of 11,753 is located about 140 miles inland from Charleston, and the two towns were linked by rail.[143] By the last week of the opera company's Charleston season, the dancers Fitzjames and Carrese had already been performing for a week in Augusta with a dramatic troupe, and perhaps a favorable reaction to their performances encouraged Maretzek to undertake the side trip to Augusta. The first opera company advertisement, however, appeared in the *Augusta Daily Chronicle and Sentinel* on 3 April, indicating that the managers had been thinking about Augusta at least since the middle week of the Charleston season. After the fact, Maretzek probably wished that his troupe had remained in Charleston, for the engagement in Georgia was almost a disaster.

The company announced a one-week season of five performances and billed it as the "First Italian Opera in Augusta" in the *Daily Chronicle* on 13 April. The run would last from Monday to Monday (14–21 April), with performances on Monday, Tuesday, Thursday, and

Friday evenings; a different opera would be mounted each night. The audience at the first performance, however, was so disappointingly small—the local critic termed it "very thin, though elite and discriminating"—that Maretzek immediately decided to retreat to friendlier territory in South Carolina, at least so he announced in the 15 April *Daily Chronicle*. He altered the billing of the troupe's second performance to "Last Night of the Season" and had playbills printed to announce the change.[144] The critical reaction in Augusta was predictable. "It is a matter of sincere regret to us," wrote a local reporter in the *Daily Chronicle* on 15 April, "that the Manager . . . has in consequence of the apparent indifference of the community to the merits of the Opera, determined to close after to-night. We wish it were otherwise," he lamented, "but [the manager] cannot continue without too great a [financial] sacrifice."

The music lovers of Augusta reacted logically to this announcement; the cultural reputation of their city, after all, had been seriously besmirched by the apparent "indifference of the community to the merits of the Opera." Galvanized into action, they flocked to the company's second performance. Maretzek was so pleased at this turnabout that he changed his mind about leaving and announced to "the citizens of Augusta" that, owing to the large Tuesday night audience and to "the assurances which he [had] received from several sources," the company would give another opera on Thursday. "The Opera—Another Night!" triumphantly crowed the headline in the *Daily Chronicle* on 17 April. All of this posturing might have been just another of Maretzek's many managerial tricks. Whether a bluff or a genuine act of desperation, however, the ploy apparently worked, for the troupe completed its entire season of five appearances as originally planned.

Following the final performance on 21 March, the Astor Place Company quit Augusta, traveled to Charleston, and gave another final performance, this one on the twenty-second.[145] The next afternoon they left Charleston and traveled north by land, headed back to Boston.

The company that left Charleston in late April, however, was much altered from the troupe that had arrived a month earlier. But the changes would not become apparent until the ensemble commenced its second season in Boston. By then it would be clear that Maretzek had added to his company a number of superstars, all of whom had the ability and celebrity to make Boston and New York forget about the departed Teresa Parodi. The changes were the result of circumstances that were in part fortuitous, in part calculated risk and careful planning; the essential final negotiations had taken place in Charleston. A reconstruction of the various steps Maretzek went through in order to acquire his new singers provides a satisfactory explanation for the company's rather odd and abrupt departure from Boston in early March and its sudden arrival in Charleston shortly thereafter. More important, it tells a great deal about the behind-the-scenes strategies, schemes, and machinations in which opera-troupe managers of the period dealt. The chain of events that ended in the spring of 1851 had commenced, according to Maretzek, in New York eight or nine months earlier, during the summer of 1850.

When Maretzek witnessed the performances of Marti's Havana Company at Castle Garden in August and September 1850, he realized immediately that his company—and any troupe that could be assembled in the United States—was hopelessly outclassed. Furthermore, as long as this particularly stellar group of singers was under Marti's management, and as long as that impresario, because of the circumstances under which he operated, could continue to charge low prices for their performances in New York, the Havana Company would represent "a most dangerous and effective opposition to the New York management." Consequently, that summer Maretzek "made up [his] mind" about Marti's stars: he would use "any means possible, to secure them for [New York]."[146]

Maretzek was aware that most of Marti's vocalists were under contract until the conclusion of the 1850–51 Havana season. He immediately embarked on a campaign to sign them to his own management at the expiration of their engagement to Marti. As he later wrote, "I decided [to] enter into immediate communication with the ... artists composing the [Havana] *troupe*."[147] How smooth were the various negotiations is impossible to know. It is likely, however, that Maretzek knew that his best chance for engaging these artists—and the only chance he had to avoid being upstaged by his rivals Ullman or Strakosch—was to be in personal contact with the singers as soon as they set foot in the United States; most could be expected to travel back to Europe via New York. Timing was of the essence, so he maintained close contact with individuals in Havana throughout the course of the opera season there and played a waiting game in Boston when the traditional end of the season at the Tacon rolled around in March.

The most convenient route from Cuba to New York was by way of Charleston, and Maretzek intended to be there when Marti's former singers disembarked. Because Charleston also was a good music and theater city, the manager could take his whole company with him. The Astor Place troupe could be performing under the direction of Benedetti while Maretzek awaited the arrival of, and then negotiated with, the Havana singers. Presumably, then, Maretzek made an arrangement by mail with the management of the Charleston Theatre for an opera season there, but left the beginning date somewhat flexible. Then he waited. By the time the Astor Place troupe concluded its scheduled run in Boston, Maretzek had heard nothing from Havana. He did not want to take the troupe prematurely to Charleston, so he sent to New York for reinforcements to replace the departed Parodi and announced a continuation of the Boston season. No sooner had the reinforcements arrived in Massachusetts when Maretzek heard from Havana that the Tacon Theatre season had ended, and that Marti's singers were soon to be leaving for South Carolina. The waiting game over, Maretzek dashed off a telegram to the manager of the Charleston Theatre announcing his anticipated date of arrival and brought the engagement in Boston to an abrupt halt. By 10 March the whole troupe had left for New York, and then on to Charleston.

Just as expected, Marti's former singers arrived in Charleston while the Astor Place Company was there. Tedesco and Vietti had appeared a week before the New York troupe, and Maretzek must have engaged Vietti almost immediately. The rest of the Havana singers landed in Charleston two weeks later, and Maretzek set to work.[148] Altogether, he managed to sign seven of the former Havana Company artists, including the troupe's star basso Ignazio Marini and one of the sopranos, Angiolina Bosio (Figure 36). As a consequence of his managerial coup, when the Astor Place Opera Company reopened at the Federal Street Theatre in Boston on 29 April, Maretzek not only had six new singers in his troupe, whose "first" and "second appearances" he could—and would—string out to glorious lengths, but he also had seven of the stars from the company that had so outclassed his own troupe the previous year.[149] The Astor Place Company now was a solid troupe with real talent rather than a mediocre company with one shining star.

Boston (Again)

When Maretzek's company had cut short its extended season and abruptly quit Boston on 10 March, they left behind a number of disappointed opera lovers. The newspapers attempted to appease Bostonians by publishing reports that the troupe planned to return in late April. On the very day the company left, 10 March, the *Evening Transcript* reported the "rumor" that "a number of gentlemen" had approached Maretzek and promised him "certain profits" if he would return and produce another opera season. A week later, this rumor had turned to reality, or, at least, a possibility. The same journal announced that Maretzek would stage another three-week season in Boston sometime in April, if two hundred and fifty subscribers at $1 per night for twelve nights could be found. The *Transcript*'s editor judiciously pointed out that the amount of financial security Maretzek

36. Illustration from topical material about the Astor Place Opera Company, titled "Celebrated Trio in Lucrezia Borgia." The singers portrayed here (Angiolina Bosio as Lucrezia Borgia, Ignazio Marini as the Duke, and Domenico Lorini as Gennaro) are three of the former Havana Opera Company stars Maretzek added to his troupe in the spring of 1851. The caption that accompanies the illustration reads in part, "Our readers are too familiar with this beautiful opera to require praise for its excellence from our pen." (*Gleason's Pictorial Drawing-Room Companion*, June 1851)

wanted in the form of pledged subscriptions came to less than half the amount Barnum had required for Jenny Lind's concerts, and Maretzek's proposal for a "much superior entertainment" was for twelve performances. "It would be mortifying indeed," he warned on 17 March, "if such a proposition is allowed to fail." By 11 April, the newspaper proudly announced that the subscription had succeeded and the company would be back in Boston by 23 April. A week later the public was informed that the company had been delayed, and their first performance would not occur until 28 April.[150]

For his new season in Boston, Maretzek charged significantly lower admission prices than he had throughout the company's first engagement. During the earlier visit the prices had been $2 for boxes and parquet seats and 50 cents for the third tier and gallery; for this engagement, the management charged $1 for parquet and first and second tier of boxes, 50 cents for the family circle, and 50 cents for the gallery.[151] This change in policy could have been the result of several factors. First, Maretzek's company had the luxury of a large block of subscribers (there is no evidence that subscriptions had been sold for the earlier season). Second, by April 1851 the Lind- and Parodi-mania had diminished somewhat, and Maretzek realized that the public was no longer as willing to pay prices inflated through hyperbole. Finally, Maretzek had dispensed with at least one overhead expense; Edward Walker no longer was associated with the troupe. All the improvements that Walker had made to the Federal Street Theatre, however, were still there, and the new, improved Astor Place troupe could benefit from them.

The repertory of the company on this visit to Boston was essentially the same as during the troupe's first engagement; there were many more repetitions, but the season was almost twice as long.[152] Maretzek did not try so hard to vary each night's bill through repertory; his company now was sufficiently talented musically that novelty was not such an overriding concern. Furthermore, he had the added advantage of six new singers whose first, second, and last performances he could use to add variety.[153]

The troupe had advertised a three-week season in Boston. In fact, the engagement lasted for five. Evidently, most of the performances were well attended. The *Evening Transcript* reported on 8 May that receipts for one performance, which featured the renowned soprano Angiolina Bosio, were "over $1500," roughly the equivalent of $25,155 in 1992.[154] Critical reception was so enthusiastic and appreciative that one critic felt that Bostonians had vindicated themselves as lovers of music. "The artists of the operatic corps must be aware by this time," he wrote somewhat smugly in the *Evening Transcript* on 22 May, "that Bostonians may be warmed up by genuine merit to something very like enthusiasm." A week later on 31 May the same critic offered a succinct assessment of the troupe's Boston season: "Last night saw the brilliant termination of the most brilliant operatic season we have ever had in Boston."

Postseason Activities

When the members of the Astor Place Opera Company took their bows after the final performance on 31 May, they concluded both their Boston engagement and the operatic season of 1850–51. The year had been a good one. It was so successful financially that at its conclusion Maretzek not only was able to pay off debts from the previous season, but he could also "close [his] campaign with some profit."[155] Although Maretzek himself gave credit to Teresa Parodi, much of the troupe's success could be traced directly to his own hard work and excellent managerial instincts.

From Boston, the company returned to New York, where they commenced a summer season, briefly at the Astor Place House, then at Castle Garden. The manager hoped to duplicate Marti's phenomenally successful season of the previous summer. His hopes for artistic excellence and financial success were justifiably high, for by June he had added to his troupe the rest of Marti's former stars—with the single exception of Tedesco. The future of opera in the United States, as a consequence, was looking quite rosy. "With the acquisition of this [Havana] company," Maretzek later remembered, "I began firmly to believe that Italian Opera would be perpetually domiciled in my new country."[156]

This fond dream, however, wilted in the summer heat. Like the Havana troupe of the previous summer, Maretzek's company attracted huge crowds to Castle Garden; the *Message Bird* noted on 1 September that "the Italian Opera, as it is now conducted under Mareztek [sic] seems to be extremely popular." But the company failed nonetheless, the victim, like so many other Italian troupes, of greed, bickering, duplicity, and general misbehavior by the singers. As Maretzek explained in some detail in *Crotchets and Quavers,* those singers whose vocal and artistic abilities were so remarkable, and whose contracts he had so coveted, had temperaments of equal magnitude. Individually, despite their "restless duplicity, their ungracious treatment of [the management], and the want of wisdom shown in the conduct of their relations with the public," the singers would have been manageable.[157] But the strength of this troupe was its remarkable ensemble and its depth. And as a group, the former Havana stars managed to live up—or down— to the stereotype of Italian artists that had become widespread among Americans. They simply overwhelmed Max Maretzek.

"The perfect liberty they enjoyed in New York," he explained later, "without the strict police regulations of either Italy or Havana, soon degenerated into impudence, insolence, and the most audacious contempt both for the public who came to listen to, and the management which paid them."[158] Maretzek described some of the problems that resulted in his near-bankruptcy: excessive demands for salaries, benefits, and bonuses; extra expenses for housing and feeding of spouses, servants, dogs, and parrots; demands that the management hire friends and acquaintances; and demands that the management provide season tickets for friends, relatives, and acquaintances. Behind many of these demands, according to Maretzek, was the very real threat of blackmail: feigned illness, drunkenness on stage, sudden nonappearances, and sabotaged performances.[159]

An attempt to detail what Maretzek called "all [his singers'] quarrels, jealousies and intrigues amongst themselves, or their tricks, plots and conspiracies against their Manager" would have to rely almost entirely on the presumably biased testimony of Maretzek himself. Very little in the New York newspapers corroborates the impresario's story. In any case, such detail, as Maretzek also wrote, would "take up far too much time and space."[160] By the end of the summer the Astor Place Company had collapsed utterly, its artists were scattered to the winds, and its manager was in deep financial trouble. After a scant three months of operations, the troupe had amassed, according to Maretzek, a "clear and unmistakable deficit of $22,000," the rather sobering sum of $368,940 in 1992 terms.[161]

Despite the financially and artistically successful season of 1850–51, and despite the high hopes at the beginning of the summer, by the fall the Astor Place Company was no more. It had become one of the first of many opera troupes that Americans in the 1850s, 1860s, and 1870s would see rise and fall in the "vain and impotent attempt to establish here a permanent and creditable institution of opera."[162] Despite its eventual failure, however, a great deal can be learned from the activities of the Astor Place troupe during the 1850–51 season. Maretzek's various managerial techniques presumably were typical of those of other Italian opera impresarios active during the 1850s; certainly they were typical of the techniques he used with his own later troupes. His heavy dependence on the transportation system in the Northeast, especially between Philadelphia and New York, indicates the importance of the nation's expanding railroad network to theatrical and operatic companies during the 1850s. The ability of his company to travel quickly from Charleston to Augusta by rail foreshadows the huge expansion of opera-troupe itineraries into the American interior that would occur early in the new decade. The competition from Marti's troupe, and especially from operatic concert companies, is typical of competition that many troupes faced in the 1850s, and the fluctuating personnel — from branch to branch of Maretzek's company, from Maretzek's troupe to Strakosch's concert company, and from Marti's company to Maretzek's — is characteristic. Furthermore, the varied problems that Maretzek had with his singers, and the crises he was required to resolve, were the same kinds of problems and crises managers faced over and over again during the 1850s.

The repertory performed by the Astor Place Company during 1850–51 is likewise typical. It is an excellent example of the Italian operas that Americans heard between the late 1840s and the late 1850s. As the decade wore on, Italian opera repertory became more and more stagnant, and critics complained increasingly of "thread-bare Italian operas," "old and worn-out Italian operas," and a "repertoire which has already been drawn upon well-nigh *ad nauseum*."[163] This dependence on many of the same operas that had been introduced in the late 1840s and early 1850s did not change significantly during the decade, except for the addition of more works by Verdi, especially *La Traviata* (1853), *Il Trovatore* (1855), and *Rigoletto* (1855). Although this was indeed a staggering change in operatic repertory, American critics soon so lamented the overreliance on these few works (in particular *Il Trovatore*) that by 1857 or 1858 John Sullivan Dwight began to refer to itinerant opera troupes as "Trovatopera companies."[164]

Finally, the audiences that Maretzek's company attracted in New York and elsewhere were similar to audiences that Italian troupes attracted throughout the 1850s. The attempts of wealthy, elite patrons to claim Italian opera for themselves would continue and increasingly succeed in large East Coast cities such as New York, Philadelphia, and Boston. At the same time, however, Italian troupes — the same singers performing the same repertory as they did for the elite — continued to perform at Niblo's and Castle Garden in New York, attracting thousands of the *canaille* and introducing them to some of Europe's best vocalists. Even more important, the same singers performing the same repertory used the aristocrats' opera houses in New York and Philadelphia as home bases. From them, the artists traveled around the country, performing in regular theaters as an accepted and normal part of the theater before audiences comprised of all segments of American society.

5

English Opera Companies, 1841–60

During the five-year period from June 1837 through February 1842, no professional company mounted a season of opera in Italian in the United States. Outside of New Orleans and, briefly, Louisville, this hiatus was even more prolonged, for it extended from May 1835, with the demise of the Porto-Sacchi Company in New York, through June 1843, when the first Havana Company arrived in Cincinnati. This dearth of Italian companies, however, does not indicate a lack of interest in Italian opera among Americans, nor does it suggest that U.S. audiences did not hear the music of Bellini, Donizetti, and Rossini during the period. On the contrary, Americans of the 1830s and 1840s were increasingly enamored of Italian melody, as is suggested by the ruthless Italianism of operas written in the United States by such composers as William Henry Fry and Maurice Strakosch. Americans' fascination with opera is also clearly reflected both in the success of the numerous English vocal stars and in the operatic repertory they performed. Skilled vocal stars such as Shirreff, Wilson, and the Woods neatly stepped into the breach and gave Americans plenty of Italian opera, albeit translated into English. These same vocalists increasingly replaced the erstwhile performers of opera in English—the singing actors and actresses of local stock companies.

During the 1840s, the pattern intensified toward reliance upon highly skilled artists. Vocal stars continued to be active throughout the 1840s, especially in theaters on the American frontier, but as early as 1842 fewer plied the theatrical circuit alone or in duos or trios. It now became the norm for singers to form themselves into small companies of four, five, or six. The movement to larger ensembles was a continuation of two related trends apparent in the late 1830s: higher performance expectations by audiences and the ever-growing popularity of the more-difficult bel canto repertory. Both were exacerbated by the appearance after 1843 of large, self-sufficient, and glamorous Italian opera companies that traveled and performed widely.

The increased size of vocal-star ensembles also was a response to developments in the American theatrical world. By the early 1840s, the star system was at its height, and the resulting deleterious effect on stock companies was pronounced. Because the public was no longer willing to patronize performances by stock company players alone, managers were forced to continue the practice of engaging high-priced stars. The managers, who competed for the services of performers, agreed to exorbitant salaries demanded by the stars—demands that sometimes, at the end of an engagement, left managers with nothing to pay house expenses. To stave off bankruptcy, theater owners cut expenses by slashing the salaries of their actors and actresses. Furthermore, many competent thespians were dismissed from stock companies and replaced by inferior performers whose salaries were lower. This accelerated a decline in the overall quality of stock companies, many of which had already lost some of their best performers to the lure of "stardom."[1] As a result, many companies that in the 1830s could have mounted an acceptable production of, for example, *Cinderella* with the assistance of one or two vocal stars were no longer capable of doing so by the early 1840s. Traveling singers could no longer rely on local actor-singers to perform even the secondary roles in the operatic repertory. In response to this situation, vocal stars banded together into larger troupes of five or six singers to cover the vocal roles of most works in the repertory and to serve as a small nucleus of a chorus.

English opera companies of the mid and late 1840s remained fairly small; they were basically expanded vocal-star troupes. By the 1850s, however, most English troupes were larger, numbering between fifteen and thirty performers—principal and secondary singers, chorus, and orchestra leader. To a great extent, however, these larger English companies were a compromise, a middle ground between the small, highly mobile, and heavily dependent vocal-star troupes and the large, unwieldy, and self-sufficient Italian companies. Their similarities to the earlier vocal-star ensembles were numerous. First, all English troupes continued to rely on stock companies: some on stock company actor-singers, almost all on the orchestra of the theater in which they performed. Second, English companies, like vocal stars, performed in the vernacular. Third, even in the late 1850s English troupes still occasionally performed works that had been mainstays in the older vocal-star repertory: eighteenth- and early nineteenth-century English operas by Dibdin, Storace, Arne, and Bishop, now generally chosen for benefit performances or as afterpieces rather than as the principal bill of fare.

English opera troupes also shared some of the characteristics of the flashier, more self-sufficient Italian companies. Most obvious was the incorporation of numerous works from the Italian repertory. Almost as soon as an Italian company would successfully introduce a new opera to Americans, it was translated, adapted, and happily appropriated by the English troupes. Among these adapted works were operas by Rossini, Bellini, Donizetti, and Verdi. Finally, the increased size of English companies, especially those of the 1850s, was to a great extent an imitation of the size and polish of the large Italian troupes. English stars who wished to compete with the foreign-language troupes—or even to satisfy audiences whose expectations of performance standards had been heightened—were forced to surround themselves with larger companies of better-skilled singers.

The Seguin Operatic Troupe

From 1841 through 1847, Anne and Edward Seguin dominated the performance of opera in English in the United States. The Seguins, who were among the sizable group of vocal stars that arrived in the late 1830s and early 1840s, came in 1838 with Jane Shirreff and John Wilson. Edward (and later Anne) Seguin toured with those two very successful singers during their first year in America. By mid 1841, however, the Seguins were almost the sole representatives of the group still left in the United States. Shirreff and Wilson had departed in 1840; the Woods left for the final time in January 1841; and Theodore Giubilei and Clara Poole, who sang with the Seguins in Philadelphia and New York during 1840–41, sailed at the conclusion of that season, reportedly to engagements at Drury Lane Theatre, according to the *Spirit* on 3 July. The rash of departures left the field of English opera wide open; even more convenient for the Seguins was the absence of any newly arrived high-caliber vocal stars to replace those who had departed. The dearth of competition was probably a principal factor in the couple's decision to stay in this country.

Both of the Seguins had been successful in London before their arrival in North America, and both presumably could have resumed their careers there had they returned. Edward sang regularly throughout the 1830s at Covent Garden and Drury Lane; Anne Seguin (née Childe) had also appeared in opera at the King's Theatre and at Drury Lane before crossing the Atlantic. Apparently, both were successful during their first three years in this country; certainly, during the time that Edward Seguin was closely associated with Shirreff and Wilson, his pecuniary success was equal to theirs (chapter 2).[2] Because none of the Seguins' business records are known to have survived, we can only guess at their earnings after they parted ways with Shirreff. The fact that they remained in the United States, however, strongly suggests at least moderate success despite the national economic slump. Furthermore, they must have believed that their artistic and financial future appeared to be more promising in North America than in England.

The Seguins' gamble evidently paid off, for they never returned permanently to Britain. For much of the 1840s, they enjoyed a virtual monopoly on English opera in the United States. Three related factors contributed to the dearth of rival companies. First, the prolonged economic depression in the United States during the 1840s, and the continued dismal fortunes of American theaters, meant that fewer singers were tempted to make the huge investment in time and expense of crossing the Atlantic in search of fame and fortune.[3] Second, although opera continued to be a popular performance medium among Americans through the mid 1840s, English opera, rather than Italian, was the dominant style, and most of the demand could be satisfied by the Seguins, whose firmly established base of operations was an obvious deterrent to British vocal stars who may have harbored dreams of quick riches in the New World. Finally, the trend toward the formation of larger itinerant companies meant that many of the singers who did come to the United States became part of the Seguins' company.[4]

Lack of competition, however, is not in itself sufficient explanation for the Seguins' remarkable success. In the 1840s and early 1850s these two British stars attracted audiences with such consistency that to many Americans the very name *Seguin* was all but synonymous with *English opera*. Their triumph was due both to their performing skill and to American theater-goers' continued widespread interest in opera. Opera in English, which had rescued the dramatic season at the National Theatre in 1838 and 1839, continued to attract otherwise-reluctant audiences for several years thereafter, despite the disastrous condition of theaters nationwide. Joseph Sill noted this phenomenon in his diary on 5 December 1842 after attending several of the Seguins' performances. "The house was quite crowded in every part," he wrote, "and presented a cheering sight, in contrast to the thin empty houses we have been accustom'd to for these few months past. The audience seem'd glad to listen again to the sweet tones of Bellini's music; and gave frequent tokens of their approbation during the performance of [*La Sonnambula*]."

According to theater manager F. C. Wemyss, this particular Philadelphia engagement, which ran well into February 1843, was the "longest opera season ever continued [in Philadelphia] by an English company."[5] Later that same year, when the Seguins appeared in Charleston, South Carolina, the response was similar. The singers visited the city in both March and April and, according to the theater historian W. Stanley Hoole, both engagements "swelled the manager's pocket-

37 and 38. Anne Childe Seguin and Edward Seguin. (*Century Illustrated Monthly Magazine*, April 1882)

book."[6] In fact, the Seguins' appearances in Charleston helped to make the 1842–43 season one of the theater's "most lucrative."[7]

Such success ensured that the Seguins had little trouble convincing managers around the country to engage them and the other singers with whom they toured. As a result, they traveled extensively for the next eleven years. Beginning with a lengthy southern excursion, including stops in Richmond, Charleston, Augusta, Mobile, and New Orleans in 1841, and continuing with tours each year until 1852, they took English opera—or at least opera in English—all over eastern North America. They traveled to the American "West," performing in St. Louis and Cincinnati in 1843 and 1851, and made three visits to Canada, appearing in Montreal in 1840, 1841, and 1847. They also journeyed to the American South regularly; the troupe performed in Charleston so often during the 1840s that Hoole referred to them as "the inevitable Seguins."[8]

Although the Seguins were active through 1852, the time of their greatest American impact was from 1841 through 1847.[9] Most American theater-goers and opera lovers of the 1840s regarded the Seguins in much the same light as they regarded Edwin Forrest, James Hackett, or William Charles Macready: as the best performers of opera or drama in the United States. Americans also continued to think of the Seguins and their associates as vocal stars rather than as an opera company. Over the course of the 1841–42 season, for example, the two singers toured extensively with the tenor Charles Manvers; the *Spirit,* which closely followed their movements around the country, invariably referred to them either as "the Seguins" or as "the Seguins and Manvers."[10] The following year, when the same trio performed in Mobile, the *Advertiser and Chronicle* called them "our vocal 'stars.' "[11] Furthermore, playbills from the Seguins' performances — some as late as 1847 — follow the same pattern as that used to identify itinerant dramatic stars: the visitors are given prominent individual billing and are rarely referred to as an opera or theatrical "troupe" or "company."[12]

The Seguins' persistent identity as vocal stars, although seemingly a minor issue, is nevertheless important. It tells us something about the American opera audience of the 1840s. The enduring vocal-star image of these singers suggests that English opera continued to be a normal and ordinary part of the American theatrical repertory throughout the 1840s. Vocal stars, after all, were a specialized subset of dramatic stars; as such, they were an accepted part of the English-speaking theater. As long as vocal stars could attract typical, mixed American theater audiences of widely varying social and economic background, and as long as opera itself was integrated into the rest of the theatrical repertory by virtue of shared vernacular language, then the genre retained its position as a part of American popular culture.

What was the make-up of the Seguins' audience from 1841 through 1847? According to the *Spirit,* the singers drew "immense houses" to their performances in New Orleans in 1841; the large crowds they attracted in Charleston in 1843 included the "fashion and beauty of the city."[13] In the spring of 1844, performances by Palmo's Italian company in New York posed a brief threat to their popularity there. On 11 May the *Spirit* blamed a poor turn-out for a Seguin performance of *Anna Boleyn* (the fashionables were notably absent) on "the establishment of the Italian Opera, at which place the public are instructed to believe Italian music can alone be performed" (132). Although perhaps an unsettling omen of the future, this Italian threat was short-lived. The following autumn, on 25 November 1844, the Seguins matched — and overwhelmed — the Italian competition by mounting the American premiere of a new English opera, Michael Balfe's *The Bohemian Girl.* The novelty not only became an instant hit, but it also remained extraordinarily popular for years. Its introduction, furthermore, guaranteed the success of the Seguins' 1844–45 season. For the moment, it ensured the triumph of English opera in the face of competition from Italians, even in New York. As the *Spirit* observed on 7 December, "the continued and increasing success which has attended the [Seguin] opera [company] conclusively shows a strong disposition on the part of the public to patronize any opera, avowedly of the English school of music" (492).

Even this small skirmish was limited to New York; outside of Manhattan and New Orleans, American performance of opera in Italian — and its challenge to opera in English — was nonexistent between 1844 and 1847. The Seguins' success, as a consequence, continued apace. In Boston in 1845, according to William Clapp (who wrote in 1853), the Seguins enjoyed "the most successful and brilliant English opera season in this city [since] the days of 'The Woods' " (435). The following year, again in Boston, the *Spirit* reported on 26 September that "every seat in the private boxes and first and second tiers" of the Federal Street Theatre had been taken even before the singers commenced their engagement. After the performers left town, the verdict on 17 October was that their season had been "most brilliant," with the house "literally jammed." Clapp also commented on the troupe's success during this 1846 season. "So potent was the spell that bound old Boston to English opera then," he wrote, "that almost every [Seguin] performance had a good house, and many were honored with overflows. Two benefits were awarded to Mrs. Seguin, and both had 1400 auditors within the walls, besides many unable to obtain admission, that remained upon the side-walks content with catching a strain at intervals" (439).

The Seguins' success was not limited to Boston, nor is the information on the audiences they attracted. In 1845, the singers were reported doing "a spirited business" at Baltimore's Holliday Street Theatre; two years later the troupe did "a great business" in Charleston in March and "an excellent business" in Philadelphia in May.[14] Finally, Joseph Sill, who frequently attended the company's performances, made numerous comments in his diary on Philadelphia's audiences. In April 1846, for example, the Chestnut Street Theatre "was cramm'd" for a performance of *Don Pasquale;* two years later the Seguins attracted a "large and fashionable" audience for a performance of *Masaniello;* later that same year the theater was "fill'd by the beauty and fashion of the City" for *Norma.*[15]

Published descriptions of opera and theater audiences from the antebellum period generally note the presence of only the wealthy, to the neglect of the denizens of the gallery, the pit, and the notorious third tier. But just as there is evidence that performances by vocal stars or Italian opera companies attracted mixed audiences, so, too, is there information to suggest that the Seguins were popular among ordinary Americans, and that the music of the operas they mounted was well known even to those who did not attend the theater.

Much of the evidence of the Seguins' widespread popularity is associated with music from one of the most favored and enduring works in their repertory, *The Bohemian Girl*. Even before they gave the American premiere of this English opera, its melodies were familiar to many. Its tunes had been "heard at some miscellaneous concert, or introduced by singers into a meagre operetta, and still are strummed on some jingling piano forte, or rendered discordant by practising songsters," according to the *Spirit* on 2 December 1844. After the opera's first performance, its most fetching melodies permeated the culture. "The gems of this opera," wrote Clapp, "were soon the rage in saloons, and ground upon organs, or hummed in the streets. 'I dreamt that I dwelt in marble halls,' absolutely possessed, as with an enchanter's spell, the female population . . . and [it] was *the* all-engrossing idea of amateur singers" (438). Richard Grant White, from the vantage point of the early 1880s, sourly remembered the opera's widespread popularity almost forty years earlier. The "trivial airs" of the work, he wrote, "with their vulgar rhythms and hideous intervals, were sung, and whistled, and thrummed, and hand-organed all day and all night the country over. One could not read or eat without hearing, in some form, 'I dreamt that I dwelt in marble halls,' and sleep was disturbed, if not by the dream, at least by the musical telling of it, the echoes of which have hardly yet died away" (2:876).

In 1846 or 1847, one William G. Bell attended a performance of *The Bohemian Girl* in Philadelphia. Bell, who by his own admission did not attend the opera regularly, found the performance so entertaining that the next day he went out and purchased the sheet music to the opera and sent it to a young woman friend. "I heard the *Seguins* Together with Mes[srs] Harrison & Frazier [*sic*] last night at the Walnut St. Theatre," he wrote on the title page, "My views of the '*opera*' have undergone quite a change—I was highly delighted with some portions of the '*Bohemian Girl*' and have accordingly sent it to you—whether I have selected the pretty pieces or not, I am unable to say—I trust however, that you will find some of the pieces worthy [of] your attention—The words to 'I dreamt that I dwelt in marble halls' are considered pretty and would certainly be quite agreeable to a growing lady of sixteen summers."[16] Luckily, the recipient of this gift failed to follow her friend's final instruction, to "rub this [message] out with India Rubbers—."

The dissemination of English-opera music throughout American culture illustrates the appeal of the Seguins' repertory to a wide strata of society. It contributes little firsthand information, however, to an understanding of the makeup of the audiences that actually attended. Performances by vocal stars attracted mixed audiences, however, and nothing suggests that the popular segment of the audience became disaffected with such artists as the Seguins during the 1840s. The diary of one young Philadelphia bookkeeper, in fact, strongly indicates the opposite. The diarist, identified only as N. Beekley, kept a succinct account of his daily activities during 1849. Although hardly a wealthy individual (he records being paid $500 a year, the 1992 equivalent of roughly $8,385), he attended lectures, concerts, and theatrical performances on a regular basis, sometimes as often as three or four times per week.[17] The catholicity of his taste in amusements makes the diary read like a compendium of American theatrical offerings of the period: he attended concerts, a series of lectures by the American naturalist Spencer Fullerton Baird, magic shows, performances by a minstrel troupe, dramatic works (including such varied fare as *The Hunchback, Guy Mannering, Lady of Lyons,* Shakespeare's *Macbeth* and *Much Ado About Nothing,* and sundry "good comedies," "amusing farces," and other unnamed entertainments), and opera performances by the Seguins (including *The Bohemian Girl,* Mercadante's *The Bravo, The Daughter of the Regiment, Don Giovanni,* and *Norma*—the latter twice in one week). Beekley's activities clearly suggest that he—and probably others like him—considered the Seguins and their repertory an ordinary part of theatrical entertainment at midcentury.

It is even more significant, however, that the Seguins also continued to attract wealthy and fashionable auditors throughout the 1840s. This is notable in view of the efforts made by the elite during the late 1840s and 1850s to appropriate Italian opera for themselves and define foreign-language opera as the only fashionable operatic entertainment. Information about audiences at the Seguins' performances clearly suggests that, even in the late 1840s, the division of the American audience into adherents of Italian (fashionable) and English (unfashionable) opera—a fissure beginning to be apparent in New York in the 1840s—was, for the most part, still in the future.

The Seguins were widely regarded as vocal stars for most of the 1840s, but they also served an important transitional role in the history of English opera performance in the United States. During the late 1840s and early 1850s—on their watch, figuratively speaking—vocal-star troupes gradually disappeared, replaced by full-sized English opera companies. The Seguins themselves were, at different times, members of each. By the mid 1840s their entourage was referred to occasionally as an "operatic troupe" or the "Seguin Operatic Company"—recognition, no doubt, that the bass and soprano toured regularly with four, five, or six other performers (Figure 39).[18]

By 1847, this shift of identity—from vocal stars to featured artists of an English opera company—was eminently desirable. In that year,

Howard Athenæum!

THOMAS FORD,   LESSEE.

W. L. AYLING,   STAGE MANAGER.

BENEFIT OF

MR. SEGUIN !

AND LAST NIGHT BUT FOUR OF THE

Seguin Operatic Troupe,

MRS. SEGUIN,
MISS E. LICHTENSTEIN,
(PUPIL OF MRS SEGUIN.)
MR. ARTHURSON,
MR. F. MEYER,
MR SHRIVAL,
AND MR. SEGUIN.

Friday Evening, November 5th, 1847

Will be presented 1st act of ROSSINI'S Comic Opera the

BARBER OF SEVILLE,

WITH ALL THE ORIGINAL MUSIC.

COUNT ALMAVIVA		MR SHRIVAL
DOCTOR BARTOLO		MR SEGUIN
FIGARO		MR MEYER
ROSINA		MRS SEGUIN
Basil	Mr Sauer | Notary	Mr Adams
Fiorello	Mr Roberts | Marcellina	Miss Roberts

Programme of Songs, Duetts and Choruses.

CHORUS—Piano, Pianissimo,	
SERENADE—" Come shining forth, my dearest."	Almaviva
CHORUS—" Many thanks sir,"	
SONG—" Oh, I am a barber." &c.	Figaro
DUET—" Oh, the Sound of chinking money"	Almaviva and Figaro
SONG—" Tyrant, soon,"	Rosina
DUET—" Thought enchanting"	Rosina and Figaro
SONG—" Yes, detraction !"	Bazil
GRAND FINALE—" Hollo ! house here" Rosina, Almaviva, Bartolo, Figaro, &c.	

39. Portion of a playbill from the Howard Athenaeum in Boston for a performance by the Seguins on 5 November 1847. The performers here are identified as the Seguin Operatic Troupe. (American Antiquarian Society)

the entire arena of operatic performance in the United States changed significantly. The Seguins were faced with their first serious competition in years, not only from the Havana Opera Company (which arrived in April) and the Astor Place troupe (its first performances were in November), but also from the British soprano Anna Bishop. Bishop performed operas in New York and Boston in August and September and then organized an English opera company, embarking on a tour of the United States in October.

All of these newly arrived or newly organized companies performed for significant lengths of time outside of New York, and all—especially the Italians—were really companies: modern, glamorous, self-sufficient, and featuring new (to Americans) celebrities. The Havana Company in particular had an overwhelming impact on the familiar and rather shopworn appeal of the Seguins who, after all, were throwbacks to an earlier era. In Boston, where they had enjoyed unchallenged popular success since 1838, the Seguins were simply outclassed by the Italians. As Clapp later observed, "Marti's Operatic Company . . . [eclipsed] all the glories of former dramatic vocalists, and consigned English opera to neglect" (376).

In 1847 and 1848, in an attempt to shed their old-fashioned vocal-star image and counter the new high-powered competition, the Seguins transformed themselves into a true, albeit small, English opera company. They accomplished this alteration primarily by adding to their entourage a chorus borrowed from the Park Theatre in New York.[19] The attempt to shed their vocal-star identity worked; henceforth the troupe was known almost universally as the Seguin Opera Company. It soon became clear, however, that the expansion itself was futile. As Clapp explained, although the Seguins returned to Boston—the scene of their former triumphs—numerous times after 1847, the huge audiences of earlier years had disappeared; the magnetic appeal of the Havana Company "made all lesser lights dim" (439).

The increase in troupe size did not have the desired effect, so the Seguins reverted to form and resumed their heavy dependence on stock companies for both dramatic and musical support. They kept their new identity as the Seguin Opera Company, but their ensemble once again became an extended vocal-star troupe. That this was indeed the case is indicated fairly conclusively by a letter Edward Seguin wrote to the manager of the theater in Buffalo in 1850. Inquiring about the possibility of an engagement during August, Seguin queried, "what are your capabilities regarding chorus, orchestra, dancers, &c, &c."[20] Clearly, after more than a decade of successfully performing in small, easy-to-manage, vocal-star ensembles, the Seguins were reluctant—or unable—to take on the added burdens inherent in the management of even a small opera company. The transition would have complicated their lives by several degrees of magnitude, and to no avail. Although the Seguins continued to perform until 1852, and although other groups of singers toured as extended vocal-star troupes in the late 1840s and early 1850s, the heyday of opera performances by vocal-star troupes in the United States had come to an end by 1848 or 1849.[21]

The Seguins' repertory was strikingly uniform all over the country, although they tended to limit American premieres to New York or Philadelphia. It also was consistent for the entire duration of their American careers. Many operas in which they performed in the early 1840s were the same works they appeared in ten years later; by the mid 1840s, they were being criticized (especially in New York) for their "dull, repetitive repertory."[22] At the same time, however, it is only fair to point out that they were responsible for a remarkable number of North American premieres. In addition to *The Bohemian Girl,* the singers introduced—all in English—Donizetti's *Don Pasquale* on 9 March 1846 in New York; Wallace's *Maritana* on 9 November 1846 in Philadelphia; Mercadante's *The Bravo* on 2 October 1849, also in Philadelphia; and Balfe's *The Enchantress* on 26 March 1849 in New York.[23] They also gave the first American performances in English of four other works already performed here in their original languages: Adam's *Le Brasseur de Preston* on 23 March 1846 in New York; Donizetti's *Anna Boleyn* (translated by Fry) on 11 April 1844 in Philadelphia; Bellini's *I Puritani* on 11 November 1845, also in Philadelphia; and *The Israelites in Egypt,* Rophino Lacy's combination of Handel's *Israel in Egypt* with Rossini's *Mosè in Egitto,* on 31 October 1842 in New York.[24]

In addition to these nine European works, the Seguins were responsible for the premieres of three "native operas." Charles Edward Horn's *The Maid of Saxony* was given its first performance in New York on 23 May 1842 (and presumably its last four days later), and C. Jarvis's *Luli* was performed three times in Philadelphia after its premiere there on 16 December 1846—after which it, too, sank without a trace.[25] The third American work was William Henry Fry's *Leonora,* the most historically significant of the three and the opera with which the Seguin Company has been closely associated by scholars of American music. Fry's work, a full-blown, three-act opera in English (but Italian in style), was the first American-composed grand opera actually to be produced.[26]

Leonora was based on Edward Bulwer-Lytton's popular *Lady of Lyons* to a libretto by Fry's brother, Joseph. The title role was written for Anne Seguin.[27] The opera was given a lavish production at the Chestnut Street Theatre in Philadelphia on 4 June 1845; the orchestra and chorus are variously reported to have numbered between fifty or sixty and seventy or eighty, respectively.[28] Critics and audience alike noted that the music was strongly influenced by contemporary Italian composers. "Many of the leading themes [of the opera] are too evidently copied from Bellini, which throws a doubt upon the originality of the piece," wrote Joseph Sill in his diary on 5 June 1845 after witnessing the second performance. "Still," he concluded, "there is enough left to stamp Mr. Fry as a man of great musical genius and to yield him the credit of being the first author of an American Opera." Several New York critics, who had traveled to Philadelphia for the performance, had a field day gleefully trashing the work, but it had a successful run of twelve performances and the Seguins revived it for an additional four at the Walnut Street Theatre in December 1846.[29] One critic mildly suggested that the work's apparent popularity with the Philadelphia public was "tolerably conclusive proof that it must possess merits— for we hold it as an indisputable fact that the public will not crowd dramatic representations which do not possess intrinsic value."[30] Francis Wemyss, a Philadelphian, later accused New York audiences and critics of sour grapes because the opera had been premiered in Philadelphia rather than in New York. "The whole United States would have teemed with [Fry's] praises," he wrote in his reminiscences, if the composer had not sinned by "daring to present the first lyrical drama ever composed in America to the citizens of Philadelphia for judgment, before the New Yorkers had an opportunity of passing upon its merits."[31]

Although *The Bohemian Girl* was one of the Seguins' most successful vehicles, their performances were by no means limited to works of English origin. Their repertory consisted, for the most part, of foreign-language works translated and "adapted" for the English stage by such composers as Michael Rophino Lacy and Sir Henry Rowley Bishop (chapter 6).[32] From 1841 through 1852, the Seguins appeared in slightly more than thirty different operas, including French, Italian, and English works and one of German origin. Statistics on the frequency of performance are unavailable, but some works were included in the repertory year after year (Table 16): *Cinderella, The Elixir of Love, Norma, La Sonnambula, Fra Diavolo, Der Freischütz, The Postillion of Longjumeau* (Adam), and *The Bohemian Girl*. All except *The Bohemian Girl* were operas from the older vocal-star repertory; four of the eight were Italian.

The repertory itself is revealing. A tabulation of all the titles, for example, strongly suggests a movement away from a rather even balance of English, French, and Italian works and toward a repertory more clearly dominated by Italian opera. From 1841–42 through 1845–46, the breakdown of opera titles (excluding the solitary German work,

Table 16. Repertory Performed by the Seguins in the United States, 1841–52.

1841–42	1842–43	1843–44	1844–45
Amilie*			Amilie
	Acis & Galatea		
		Anne Boleyn	
The Barber of Seville	The Barber of Seville	The Barber of Seville	
		The Bohemian Girl	The Bohemian Girl
The Bronze Horse			
Cinderella	Cinderella	Cinderella	
	Crammond Brig		
	The Elixir of Love		
Faint Heart			
	The Marriage of Figaro		The Marriage of Figaro
Fra Diavolo	Fra Diavolo	Fra Diavolo	Fra Diavolo
	Der Freischütz		
La Gazza Ladra			
		Gustavus III	
	The Israelites in Egypt		
	John of Paris		John of Paris
		Leonora	Leonora
			Love in a Village
	Massaniello		Massaniello
Maid of Saxony			
		Maritana	
Norma		Norma	Norma
	No Song No Supper		
	Olympic Revels	Olympic Revels	
The Postillion of Longjumeau	The Postillion of Longjumeau	The Postillion of Longjumeau	The Postillion of Longjumeau
	Rob Roy		
La Sonnambula	La Sonnambula	La Sonnambula	La Sonnambula
	Stabat Mater		
The Waterman	The Waterman		
Zampa	Zampa		

Table 16. Continued

1845–46	1846–47	1847–48	1848–49
Amilie			
	The Barber of Seville		
		Bayadere [?]	
The Bohemian Girl	The Bohemian Girl	The Bohemian Girl	The Bohemian Girl
			The Bravo
The Brewer of Preston	The Brewer of Preston		
	Cinderella [?]	Cinderella	
			The Daughter of the Regiment
			Don Giovanni
Don Pasquale	Don Pasquale		Don Pasquale
			The Enchantress
The Elixir of Love	The Elixir of Love	The Elixir of Love	The Elixir of Love
	The Marriage of Figaro		
Fra Diavolo	Fra Diavolo	Fra Diavolo	Fra Diavolo
	Der Freischütz	Der Freischütz	
		La Gazza Ladra [?]	
		Guy Mannering	
Luli			
	Maritana	Maritana	Maritana
	Massaniello	Masaniello	Masaniello
	The Mountain Sylph		
Norma	Norma	Norma	Norma
		Olympic Revels	
The Postillion of Longjumeau	The Postillion of Longjumeau	The Postillion of Longjumeau	
I Puritani			
Rob Roy	Rob Roy		
La Sonnambula	La Sonnambula	La Sonnambula	La Sonnambula
		The Waterman	
	Zampa		

Table 16. Continued

1849–50	1850–51	1851–52
		Amilie
	Bayadere	
The Bohemian Girl	The Bohemian Girl	The Bohemian Girl
The Bravo		
	Cinderella	
The Daughter of the Regiment	The Daughter of the Regiment	
Don Giovanni		
The Enchantress		
The Elixir of Love		
Fra Diavolo	Fra Diavolo	
	Der Freischütz	Der Freischütz
La Gazza Ladra	La Gazza Ladra	
Gustavus III		
	Israelites	Israelites
		Linda of Chamounix [?]
Norma	Norma	Norma
Olympic Revels		
	La Sonnambula	La Sonnambula

* Announced for performance in New Orleans.

Der Freischütz) yields ten English, ten Italian, and eight French. From 1846–47 through 1851–52, on the other hand, the singers appeared in nine English, twelve Italian, and six French works. This pattern is consistent with other information about contemporary opera performance, including the ever-increasing popularity of Italian melody and the growing numbers of Italian companies. The dominance of Italian operas in the Seguins' repertory is even more clearly marked in the final three years of their American career. From 1849–50 through 1851–52 the troupe performed four English titles, two French, and nine Italian, abandoning numerous French and English operas in favor of an increasingly Italian repertory.[33]

Between 1841 and 1852, Anne and Edward Seguin performed as members of an extended vocal-star troupe—an in-between ensemble that served as a transition from the small vocal-star companies of the 1830s and mid 1840s to the larger English opera troupes of the late

1840s and 1850s. Their overall repertory and continuation of the trend toward the performance of more Italian operas are also transitional. By keeping the older portion of this repertory before American audiences during the 1840s, they preserved and handed on to later English companies the performance tradition of the vocal stars. By updating and adding occasional newer compositions (many by Italian composers) to their corpus of works and by performing a repertory increasingly dominated by Italian operas, however, they also perpetuated a trend already visible in the repertories of vocal stars, a trend that would in turn be maintained by English opera companies of the late 1840s and 1850s. The suggestion, however, that the Seguins simultaneously kept alive an older repertory and contributed to a trend toward Italian operatic dominance might, in fact, be a case of misplaced credit. They were, after all, in the entertainment business and gave the public what it demanded. The patterns obvious from their repertory simply reveal that the American operatic and theatrical audience of the 1840s had both progressive and conservative tendencies. Americans increasingly wished to hear new Italian operas and at the same time continued to attend performances of older works, many of which had been in the repertory since the 1830s.

The Songbirds: Anna Bishop and Anna Thillon

Two of the most successful English opera companies active in the United States during the late 1840s and early 1850s were troupes assembled to support the British sopranos Anna Bishop and Anna Thillon. Some contemporary critics complained that neither "prima donna" was worthy of the name. Bishop, who had an agile and flawless but relatively weak voice, was deemed better suited to the concert hall than the operatic stage; Thillon, although a talented and beautiful actress, was but a passable vocalist. Both singers, however, attracted huge American audiences mesmerized by Bishop's "fine form," magnificent gowns, and fabulous jewels and by Thillon's dramatic ability and sheer beauty. Both women enjoyed great artistic and pecuniary success in the United States; thousands attended their concerts, and thousands more witnessed performances mounted by the English opera companies they assembled.

Anna Rivière Bishop (1810–84), the estranged wife of the British composer Sir Henry Rowley Bishop, arrived in New York in July 1847. In her party were the bass William Brough, returning once again to the scenes of his earlier success with Jane Shirreff, John Wilson, and other vocal stars, and the French harpist, composer, and convicted forger Robert-Nicholas-Charles Bochsa (1789–1856), the man for whom the soprano had abandoned her husband and three children in 1839.[34] According to the London *Musical World,* Bishop was enticed to the United States by visions of wealth: an American agent had approached her in the midst of a tour of Britain and offered such a "splendid and substantial" engagement in the United States that it would have been "little short of madness [for her] to refuse."[35] She sailed for America almost immediately.[36]

Bishop must have seriously considered an American tour even before agreeing to the agent's irresistible offer. Her experience as an itinerant musician—even before her arrival in the United States—was extraordinary. During her first concert tour, which commenced in 1839 and lasted six years, she and Bochsa performed in Denmark, Sweden, Russia, Moldavia, Austria, Italy, Hungary, and Bavaria—almost everywhere in Europe, in fact, except France, where there was a standing warrant for Bochsa's arrest.[37] Her experience as a prima donna was at the San Carlo Theatre in Naples, where she gave 327 operatic performances over the course of twenty-seven months during 1845, 1846, and 1847.[38]

Bishop's voice, a high soprano of great range, agility, and reliable intonation, was sweet and pure. Described as brilliant, exquisite, and virtuosic, and frequently likened to a bird or a flute, it was not powerful but otherwise conformed perfectly with the mid-nineteenth-century conventions of soprano vocal beauty.[39] Her concert repertory—both in Europe and in the United States—consisted of arias and scenes from contemporary operas (*Tancredi, La Gazza Ladra, Romeo e Giulietta, Anna Bolena, La Sonnambula, Lucia di Lammermoor, L'Ambassadrice, Il barbiere di Siviglia*), often performed in costume. She also included occasional ballads ("The Last Rose of Summer," "John Anderson, My Jo," "On the Banks of the Guadalquiver," "Auld Robin Gray") and works for harp, usually Bochsa's own virtuosic fantasias ("La Moderne Italie," described as a "Grand Capriccio di Bravura, introducing a melody from *Norma* and Motivo from *L'Elisir d'amore*" or "Mosaique musicale," according to the playbill, a "solo for the harp, composed by Bochsa, introducing a theme by Bellini, an Irish melody, and a motive from Donizetti").[40] Throughout Europe concert audiences were wildly enthusiastic about Bishop, foreshadowing the reaction of Americans.[41]

Although Bishop's concert tours of the United States were quite successful, she seems to have preferred to perform in opera. Over the course of her American career she did so by three different methods: as a visiting star with prominent East Coast theaters (in New York or Boston, for example); as the featured artist around which a resident opera company was assembled at the Metropolitan Theatre in San Francisco; and as the star of her own opera troupes. Although she traveled around North America with several English companies between 1848 and 1854, none survived even a single tour; several concert tours, in fact, commenced upon the collapse of one or another opera troupe. Like the various Seguin companies and many of the Italian ensembles, her troupes—all known as the Anna Bishop Opera Company or some slight variation on that sobriquet—formed anew for each tour.

Compared to her English-opera competition, Anne and Ned Seguin and their familiar band of vocalists, Bishop enjoyed some obvious advantages. Hers was a new face and a new voice; even more to the point, she was a beautiful woman and a glamorous celebrity, famous for accolades won in the capitals of Europe. Her route to American success, however, was not automatic or without setbacks. In 1847 Bishop's competition was not just the Seguins, it was also the San-quirico-Patti troupe, the Havana Company, and the Astor Place troupe, all performers of Italian opera. Bishop's arrival coincided with the development of a new and fashionable enthusiasm among many music lovers in Boston and New York for Italian opera in Italian. The fervor had taken both towns by storm earlier in the spring and continued unabated throughout the summer and into the fall and winter. As a consequence, during her engagements in the Northeast in the fall of 1847, the growing conflict between the proponents of Italian and English opera—a conflict that had been virtually nonexistent earlier in the 1840s—began to emerge as a major issue.

On 31 July, the *Spirit* expressed the hope that "the rage for Italian opera will not prejudice the revival of [opera in] our mother tongue" by Bishop and her companions (272). In fact, the soprano (along with her supporting cast of William Brough, Charlotte Bailey, and other members of the stock company) drew large audiences during her first engagement at the Park Theatre in August.[42] When she, Brough, and Bochsa went to Boston in late August for two and one-half weeks of performances at the Howard Athenaeum, however, they drew but indifferent houses (Figure 40). Her engagement, the correspondent to the *Spirit* reported on 4 September, was too early in the season to attract large audiences. More important, the operatic scenes with which she commenced the engagement were of limited interest to the Boston "fashionables," who were "all looking forward with anxiety for the Italian troupe"—the Havana Company was scheduled to open at the Athenaeum in September (332).

The singers returned to New York at the conclusion of the Boston engagement in mid-September. It was not until then that Bishop formed a real opera company, with which she intended to tour the United States.[43] The Anna Bishop English Opera Company included, among other singers, Mrs. George Alexander Macfarren (contralto), William

HOWARD ATHENAEUM.

W. H. Chippendale, ... Acting Manager.
W. L. Ayling, ... Stage Manager.

FIRST NIGHT OF
MADAME
ANNA BISHOP!

Primà Donna Assoluta di Cartello of the San Carlo, Naples,

On this occasion, MADAME ANNA BISHOP, will offer to the Public, an

Operatic Entertainment!
IN COSTUME,—IN THREE PARTS!

On the plan of those she gave at Vienna, Stockholm, St Petersburg, Munich Rome
Naples, and lately at the Park Theatre, New York, including some of her
most favourite

SCENAS IN ITALIAN & ENGLISH

☞The Free List, with the exception of the Public Press, will be suspended
during the engagement of Madame ANNA BISHOP.

PART FIRST,
THURSDAY EVENING, AUGUST 26TH, 1847.

The performance will commence with the laughable, and much admired farce, called

GRETNA GREEN

Jenkins . . .	. . . Mr Hadaway	Larder	. . . Mr Cunningam
Lord Lovewell . . .	. . . Mr Lelavor	Emily	. . . Miss Roberts
Mr Tompkins . . .	. . . Mr Jaggon	Betty Finnikin . . .	. . . Mrs Ayling

After which a GRAND SCENA from Balfe's serious Opera at the

MAID OF ARTOIS !

Composed expressly for Mdme A. Bishop, by Mr Balfe on the occasion of her debut at Drury Lane, London
last October.

RECIT,—" *My thought, which forth had wander'd.*"
CAVATINA.—" *The heart that once hath fondly teem'd.*"

ISOLINE, ... MADAME ANNA BISHOP

ARGUMENT—Isoline, the Maid of Artois, betrothed to Jules de Montagne, has been seperated from
him by a Parisian Nobleman, the Marquis of Chateauvieuf, who loving Isoline, detains her in his palace.
The above Scena depicts the sorrows of Isoline, (who is discovered on a couch awaking from a painful
dream,) and her desire to see her betrothed. Epoch, 1630. Place, Paris.

GRAND OVERTURE,   FULL ORCHESTRA.

To which will be added, a Comedy Scene from

Il Barbiere di Siviglia !

CAVATINA.—*Una voce poca fa.*"

ROSINA, ... MADAME ANNA BISHOP

PART SECOND,

The admired comedy, in 2 acts, entitled

NAVAL ENGAGEMENTS!

Admiral Kingston	. . . Mr Chippendale	Short	. . . Benson
Lieut Kingston	. . . Ayling	Mrs Pontifex . . .	. . . Mrs Maywood
Dennis	. . . Lelavor	Mary Mortimer . . .	. . . Mrs Ayling

After the first act of the Comedy, the First Scene of the Second Act of Donizetti's

LINDA OF CHAMOUNI

Introducing the favourite

CAVATINA—" *Oh light of all my Joys.*"
And the admired ballad
" *On the Banks of Guadalquiver.*"

ARGUMENT—Linda of Chamouni gone to Paris with a number of Savoyard Boys and Girls who
yearly leave their home to try their fortune in great cities, has been unexpectedly separated
from her friends—the Viscount of Sirval, who under the name of Carlo and disguised as a painter, had
won in Chamouni Linda's love, finds her in Paris, and brings her to his mother's house, in the hope that
the latter will at last give her consent to his marriage with the Maid of Chamouni ; in the meantime the
Viscount of Sirval has surrounded Linda with all the luxuries of life.

PART THIRD,
THE SECOND ACT OF THE COMEDY.

The whole to conclude with the Grand Scena and Cavatina from

TANCREDI,

O PATRIA—DI TANTI PALPITI, SUNG BY MME A. BISHOP,
In the Costume of Tancredi.

Parquet Boxes $1,—Parquet & Boxes 50 Cts.,—2d Circle 25 Cts.,
The Box Office will be open at 10 o'clock, A. M., for the delivery of Tickets.

Doors open at 7, performance to commence at a 1-4 before 8 o'clk

40. Playbill from one of Anna Bishop's Operatic Entertainments at Boston's Howard Athenaeum on 26 August 1847. The program included a farce and a comedy performed by the stock company, as well as an overture and scenes (performed in costume) from operas by Balfe, Rossini, and Donizetti. (American Antiquarian Society)

H. Reeves (tenor), Miss Mathilde Korsinsky (contralto), Signor Attilio Valtellina (bass), William Brough (bass), and Giuseppe de Begnis (bass buffo). The troupe's first engagement at the Park was brilliantly timed to fall midway between the departure of the Havana troupe and the opening of the Astor Place House; as a result, it was "very successful," according to the *Spirit* of 6 November 1847. Perhaps as a compromise to the prevailing enthusiasm for Italian opera, the company sang in Italian and English on alternate nights. Each performance concluded with a selection from the soprano's concert repertory — a "disembodied scene" from another opera (during this engagement *Tancredi* and *L'Elisir d'amore*) performed in costume.[44]

When Bishop's troupe appeared in Boston, their performances (now that the Havana Company had left) met with "great success"; in November the *Spirit* reported that the houses "have been in a continual jam."[45] By the time the company returned to New York in December, however, they found themselves in direct competition with the Astor Place troupe, and their fortunes plummeted. As the critic for the *Spirit* observed on 1 January 1848, "the rage for the Italian opera, where a better opportunity is afforded to display costly dresses and study the fashions of the *bon ton,* as the subscribers are termed, withdrew from Madame [Bishop] the patronage to which she was entitled by superior ability." Bishop and her company left New York in late December after a series of performances that, according to the same source, was "short and by no means profitable."

The troupe's next stop was in Philadelphia, where with no competition they were well received. Then, in early January, Bishop took her entourage, slightly pared down, on a southern tour that was to include stops in Charleston, Savannah, New Orleans, Mobile, and points further west. The company attracted large audiences in Charleston and "created immense sensations" in both New Orleans and Mobile. The original one-night engagement in Savannah also evidently drew large crowds, for it was extended twice for a total of four performances.[46] The troupe continued to perform in both Italian and English. In Mobile, for example, Bishop appeared in *Norma* "in its original Language (Italian)" on 7 March; *Linda of Chamounix*, "translated into the English language expressly for Madame Anna Bishop" on 9 March; and *La Sonnambula* (Figure 41) "in the English Language (Except the GRAND FINALE, that in Italian)" on the tenth.[47]

Until the Mobile engagement, the Bishop Company apparently had experienced no significant difficulties. At the final performance in that city, however, the troupe encountered some serious problems; the incident itself may provide a clue about Americans' covert attitudes toward the foreign-born performers appearing with ever-increasing fre-

41. Anna Bishop as Amina in Vincenzo Bellini's *La Sonnambula*. Taken from an engraving on a sheet-music publication, "Anna Bishop's March, founded on Bellini's celebrated Rondo finale from *La Sonnambula*," arranged by
N. C. Bochsa (New York: Pond, Firth & Co., 1849). (Music
Division, Library of Congress)

quency in the United States. On 8 April 1848, the *Literary Excelsior*, which had been following the progress of the Bishop Company, reported that Bochsa had gotten himself "into a scrape with the Mobilians." The audience had called for an encore of the finale to *Linda of Chamounix*, and Bochsa refused. What the audience found inexcusable was not so much the refusal, but rather the contemptuous manner with which Bochsa had given it. As a consequence, he was "soundly hissed." This occurrence was more than a minor incident, for the *Spirit* of the same date reported that the Bishop troupe had abruptly fallen apart in Mobile.[48] A month later, two of the erstwhile members of the company (Brough and Reeves) returned to New York City. They informed the *Spirit* on 6 May that the troupe had dissolved not because Bochsa had broken his arm as had been reported, but because of the Frenchman's arrogance and "untoward conduct . . . not only to the artists, but to the public generally, which drew especially from the Mobilians, their disapprobation" (132).[49]

Evidently, Bishop and Bochsa learned the hard way that foreign artists—especially those who advertised their foreignness by performing operas in their original languages rather than in translation—had to take care not to tread on the sensibilities of proud and wary American audiences. By the late 1840s, audiences in large cities—especially on the East Coast—were quite familiar with Italian opera in Italian. The aristocratic segments of these audiences, in fact, had begun to demonstrate a preference for—or, at least, a willingness to patronize performances of—the more fashionable Italian opera. Elsewhere, however, opera in a foreign tongue was a novelty, and performance of it—coupled with behavior that could be interpreted as arrogant or patronizing—could easily summon forth latent hostilities toward foreigners that touring European artists had to be careful not to rouse.[50]

When her company dissolved in midtour, Bishop reverted to form and embarked with Bochsa on a concert tour that lasted some five months, during which she appeared in "all the large cities and towns from New Orleans to Quebec." They returned to New York in October 1848.[51] After a lengthy and very successful farewell tour that lasted until early January 1849 ("Madame Bishop," reported the *Spirit* on 13 January, "has given her very-positively-never-to-be-repeated-and-eternal-farewell-concert, for the sixth time"), they left the United States for Mexico, not to reappear until July 1850.[52]

Over the course of the next decade Bishop returned to North America on numerous occasions, performing, for the most part, on concert tours in 1850, 1851–52, 1853, and 1859–60. In November 1852 she and Bochsa formed another opera company at Niblo's Theatre in New York, and after a successful run of performances there and in Philadelphia (performing Flowtow's *Martha, Linda of Chamounix, Lucia di Lammermoor,* and *La Sonnambula*), embarked on another tour to the South. The fate of this company, however, was similar to the fate of the previous one. By the time they reached Washington, D.C., in early February (after performances in Philadelphia and Baltimore), the *Spirit* reported on 5 February 1853 that the company "is completely scattered, never perhaps to be reorganized" (82). The reasons for the disintegration of the troupe are unknown. Bishop's most successful American operatic engagements during the 1850s were in New York and in San Francisco; in the latter city she performed from February 1854 through at least March 1855 with a company organized by the Metropolitan Theatre there.[53]

In the early 1850s, Anna Bishop was faced with a new competitor: in the autumn of 1851, another English "songbird," Anna Thillon (1812–1903, Figure 42), arrived in the United States. Thillon sang in concert less frequently than did Bishop; most of her appearances were in opera. But the troupe with which she traveled for the three years she spent in North America (1851–54) was, like the Seguin companies of the 1840s, quite small. In some ways, it was more akin to a vocal-star troupe than to an opera company. Despite its size, her company, like the later troupes of the Seguins, was referred to almost universally in the press as the "Thillon Opera Company."

Thillon came to the United States at the instigation of the New York theater and pleasure-garden manager, owner, and impresario William Niblo, who had frequently experimented with opera performances at his Manhattan establishments during the 1840s. In the spring of 1850, he engaged the Havana Company for a run of four-and-one-half weeks and was quite pleased by the large crowds the troupe attracted. His experiences with opera, reinforced by the vivid example of Jenny Lind's phenomenally successful 1850–51 American tour, convinced Niblo that opera performances would attract large, paying audiences. Consequently, he sent to Europe for a prima donna—the soprano Anna Thillon.[54]

Thillon was accompanied to North America by her French husband Claude Thillon, a violinist who had once served as Louis Jullien's concert master, and by James Hudson, an Irish vocalist and light comedian who was making his second visit to the United States.[55] Her American visit commenced with a month-long engagement at Niblo's; over the course of the next three years her troupe would return to that establishment for lengthy visits on a fairly regular basis. In true vocal-star fashion, at Niblo's as elsewhere, Thillon and Hudson were assisted by stock-company players. Thillon's husband acted as the

42. Portrait of the beautiful Anna Thillon. (*Gleason's Pictorial Drawing-Room Companion*, February 1852)

director of the opera when the troupe performed in New York; elsewhere, he also served as the conductor of the orchestra.[56]

When not engaged at Niblo's, the Thillon Opera Company performed in Philadelphia, Baltimore, and Boston. In 1853 the troupe made an extensive trip to the South and West, mounting opera seasons in New Orleans, Mobile, Memphis, St. Louis, Cincinnati, and Pittsburgh and giving concerts in Detroit, Chicago, and elsewhere (Appendix D, note 26). In late 1853 the singers set out for the Far West. Traveling to California via Nicaragua, they reached San Francisco on 31 December, shortly before the arrival of Anna Bishop.[57] Thillon and Hudson mounted operas with a company assembled by the management of the Metropolitan Theatre in San Francisco from January through early April and again in May 1854. They also embarked on an unsuccessful concert tour to the California mountains in late April and early May.[58] The California correspondent to the *Spirit* gave conflicting information about Thillon's success in the West. On 18 March 1854, for example, he claimed that she and Hudson had made $10,000 for their first eight performances; two months later, however, he reported that the visitors had attracted only two good houses during the course of their entire engagement.[59] On the other hand, the *Musical World* noted in July that the singers had made a fortune during their six months on the West Coast. "During her residence in California," the periodical reported, "Madame Anna Thillon has made from $20,[000] to $30,000."[60]

Anna Thillon's repertory was small. During the three years she spent in North America, she performed in fewer than a dozen operas. The critic for the *American Musical Review* described her repertory as "French opera Anglicized," but the works she preferred and appeared in with overwhelming frequency were standards of the English-opera repertory: *The Bohemian Girl* and *The Enchantress* (Balfe); *The Black Domino* and *The Crown Diamonds* (Auber); and *The Daughter of the Regiment,* which had been premiered in Paris in 1840 as *La fille du regiment.*[61] Thillon and Hudson also appeared occasionally in such other very familiar operas as *La Sonnambula, Cinderella,* and *Fra Diavolo* and in one that was not a standard, *Amilie.* Thillon's adaptations of these operas evidently were even more truncated than the usual English versions. In 1852, a critic for the *Spirit* referred to her *Crown Diamonds* as "a light version" of the opera. Later, another critic wrote that the same work, as performed by Thillon, was an "opera cut down to a drama [with songs]," and in July 1853 the *Spirit* noted that Thillon's repertory consisted of operas that had been "very much cut and slashed . . . [so that] the music [is] rendered accessory to the acting."[62]

These drastically pared-down versions of operas apparently were more suited to Thillon's vocal abilities than were the original works.

Many considered her not particularly well equipped for the role of prima donna. After her New York debut at Niblo's Garden in September 1851, one critic wrote that her voice, which was of "moderate compass, and well under her command; of small volume, but sweet and flexible," was more suited to "the drawing room or concert hall . . . than [to] the 'grand opera.' "[63] John Sullivan Dwight on 30 October 1852 characterized her performing style as "slender, but graceful singing" (32).

Thillon's lack of a large voice, however, did not impede her popularity. The *Spirit* reported on 1 November 1851 that for her first engagement at the Chestnut Street Theatre, she had "set the Philadelphians almost crazy by her warblings and personal beauty; the demand for seats was so great as to render an advance of price necessary" (444). Two months later a correspondent to that periodical wrote from Boston, "it appears [that] our fashionable society are entirely satisfied with [Thillon], as the house is densely crowded with brilliant audiences on the nights of her performances."[64] At the soprano's benefit in early January 1852, the theater attracted one of the most fashionable audiences seen in Boston since the engagement of Maretzek's Astor Place Company eight months earlier.[65] The *Spirit* reported on 21 February at the end of her run in Boston that Thillon had just completed "one of the most successful engagements that any *one* theatrical artiste has ever fulfilled in our city, at least for the past fifteen years" (1).

In the midst of this abundance of media enthusiasm over the "fashionable" and "brilliant" character of the Boston audiences, however, a reminder might be in order that a full house at the Howard Athenaeum and elsewhere, no matter how "brilliant" the description in the press, also included individuals of the middle and working classes. A playbill from one of Thillon's performances in Boston quietly belies the overall impression of a wealthy and exclusive house. It clearly states that although private boxes at the theater cost a prohibitive $5, one could be admitted to the dress circle and parquette for 50 cents, to the family circle or second tier for 25 cents, and to the third circle for only 12.5 cents. A legend on the playbill also reads "Colored Persons admitted to the Third Circle only." Numerous other similar playbills are extant (Figure 43).[66]

Thillon's attraction, it should be clear, was not her voice. What she lacked in vocal power, however, she more than made up with histrionic ability and sheer beauty; "her chief power," observed a critic for the *Spirit* on 23 July 1853, "lays in the seductive style of her dramatic acting" (276). The *Musical World* agreed. "Of course, nobody with ears sensitive to musical tone listens to Madam [Thillon] for the music that she affords," pointed out a critic for that periodical on 15 July. Rather, "one looks at her as an uncommonly pretty woman, who

43. Top portion of a playbill from the Howard Athenaeum showing the wide range of ticket prices and the reminder "Colored people admitted only to the Gallery." (American Antiquarian Society)

addresses herself to the eye and the taste of the auditor more than to
the ear" (126). The private, written comments of some of her auditors
confirm this assessment and also strongly hint at her appeal to the men
in her audience. John Hill Martin, who attended several of her performances in Philadelphia in October 1851, observed afterward in his
diary,

> I went to the Chestnut to *see* [Martin's emphasis] Madame Anna Thillon
> in the Opera of the "Crown Diamonds." She could not sing well. She
> was the loveliest woman I ever saw. She was graceful and fascinating,
> her perfect beauty of face and figure drew crowds to see her. Her form
> was a model of female perfection. . . . Her skin was a white as snow.
> She wore her dark brown hair in a profusion of ringlets, which fell
> over an exquisite pair of shoulders and perfect neck and bosom, in the
> style of Marie Antoinette, whose portrait she resembled very
> much. . . . Her . . . tenor was an English light-comedian called Hud-
> son. . . . Tenors are always the lovers in an Opera on the stage, [and]
> the world said that he was the lover both on and off the stage—if he
> was I know several who envied him. (1:118)

Carolyn White, a young Bostonian who occasionally attended operas
with her husband, Frank, was even less restrained in her comments.
"Frank and I went to see the beautiful handsome Anna Thillon this
eve," she wrote on 24 December 1851. "*I think I never saw so handsome
a face as hers before in my life—and her every motion is perfect grace.
So arch—so fascinating—so bewitching—you can scarce withdraw
your gaze from her—her singing is fine—her acting exquisite—Frank
is in raptures.*"[67] Her husband, White mentioned, went to see Thillon
three times while the beguiling singer was performing in Boston.

The success of Anna Bishop and Anna Thillon speaks to several
Garden during the summer of 1854. By that time, the soprano had
become an established theatrical attraction in Manhattan. During this
final engagement, she and Hudson performed three times a week,
alternating nightly with the Ravel Family, an extraordinarily popular
group of acrobats and pantomimists; both groups were regulars at
Niblo's.[68] The audiences that flocked to performances evidently did
not consider this juxtaposition to be in any way anomalous. "Niblo's
continues to be crowded nightly," the *Spirit* observed on 22 July 1854,
"it seeming to make no difference to its audience whether opera or
pantomime is the attraction" (276).

The success of Anna Bishop and Anna Thillon speaks to several
issues related to the performance of English opera in the United States
in the late 1840s and early 1850s. The most obvious is that glamour
and beauty, although not important enough to substitute for musical
ability, were nevertheless strong attractions in a prima donna. In Oc-

tober 1848 the critic Henry Watson commented that it was worth a visit to the theater just to see Anna Bishop's costumes and jewels.[69] Two years later a critic for the *Spirit,* after noting on 7 September 1850 that the orchestral music of a Bishop production was "excellent, and the chorus department is very effective," added admiringly that "the dresses, scenery, and every other requisite, are rich and gorgeous" (348). Perhaps more important, however, is the realization that to many Americans of the 1850s, opera performances—like dramatic performances of all types—clearly continued to be entertainment. Both Bishop, with her attractive figure and expensive gowns, and Thillon, with her beauty and dramatic ability, attracted huge audiences for concert and operatic performances. Americans had not yet been taught that opera was supposed to be edifying, educational, and uplifting, or that opera was art, not entertainment. Operatic artists who appeared before American audiences of the early 1850s were not yet practitioners of an esoteric art form. Rather, they were practical entertainers in search of fame, fortune, and large audiences, and they gave the American public what it was willing to pay for.

English Companies of the Middle and Late 1850s

During the middle and late 1850s, English opera companies—although not so plentiful as the ever-increasing numbers of Italian troupes—continued to be a potent force in the United States. To a certain extent, performers of English opera lost ground to the Italians during this time. Americans continued to be attracted to Italian opera, and melodies from works by Donizetti, Bellini, and Verdi in particular increasingly permeated American musical culture. In addition, more and more Italian singers of international reputation visited and performed in the United States during the decade, and these performers often won new converts to their art. Finally, Italian opera companies, especially concert troupes, took advantage of marked improvements in the American transportation system and extended their itineraries to include sections of the country that would have been unthinkable five or ten years earlier. As a consequence, individuals in many cities and towns in the American interior had the opportunity to hear opera in Italian for the first time. Many were eager to see and hear their favorite operas sung by famous European stars in the language in which the operas had been written.

In other ways, however, English opera and English opera companies made great strides during the decade. The performance of opera by Italian companies was not the only way that the appetite for Italian melody could be sated; as in previous decades, many Americans were perfectly satisfied to hear their favorite Italian operas sung in English. Theater managers, especially those in New York, were aware of this appeal and continued to import English operatic stars. Late in the decade, growing support in London for the permanent establishment of English opera (aided, to a great extent, by Louisa Pyne and William Harrison after their three-year visit to this country) had positive repercussions on the status of English opera here. Finally, the increased and deliberate appropriation of Italian opera by the wealthy, especially in urban areas of the Northeast, exacerbated by the growing perception that going to Italian operas was an elite pastime, fueled the debate over Italian versus English opera. In many ways, this increased the appeal of the latter to middle-class Americans and to Americans who lived away from the cultural centers on the East Coast.

The most prominent English troupe to visit the United States during the 1850s performed here in the middle years of the decade. The Pyne and Harrison Opera Company, which toured the country from 1854 through 1857, did much to promote the performance of opera in English in North America. Louisa Pyne, in the words of George Odell, became "one of the most popular singers known to the American stage." She was the first English soprano to tour the United States widely and for extended periods in a full-sized English opera company complete with secondary singers, chorus, and orchestra director (chapter 6).[70] Various other English opera troupes, however, also toured widely in the United States during and after the visit of the Pyne and Harrison Company. The activities of three of these troupes—the Durand, Escott, and Cooper opera companies—illustrate the fate, and document the influence, of English opera troupes during the second half of the decade.

The Lyster and Durand English Opera Company, comprised primarily of singing actors and actresses, first appeared as a troupe performing at the Holliday Street Theatre in Baltimore in March and April 1855.[71] During the next four years the company was known variously as the Durand English Opera Company, the New Orleans English Opera Company, the Lyster Opera Company, and Crisp's Opera Company. In April 1859 the entire troupe traveled to San Francisco, where they were engaged by theater manager Tom Maguire for performances at the Maguire Opera House (Figure 44); there they were known variously as the Lyster English Opera Company, the New Orleans English Opera Troupe, or, in 1860, the Lyster Grand Italian Opera Company. William Lyster was the troupe manager.[72] After 1860, as a combined English and Italian troupe, the ensemble became "a regular feature on the San Francisco scene," according to Russell Hartley.

The stars were the soprano Rosalie Durand and the baritone Fred-

44. Playbill from a performance of the vintage ballad opera *The Beggar's Opera* by the Durand Opera Company at Maguire's Opera House in San Francisco, 26 July 1859. (San Francisco Public Library)

erick Lyster; some of the other singers closely associated with the troupe had sung with the Seguins in earlier years.[73] The personnel of the company fluctuated from year to year, as was typical of most opera troupes active in the United States. Also typical of both English and Italian companies was the seeming interchangeability of singers. In particular, many English performers moved from troupe to troupe, accepting work where and when it was available. At various times, for example, the Durand Company included numerous former members of the Pyne and Harrison troupe of 1855–56; in addition to Frank Trevor and Fred Lyster these included Joseph Stretton, Frank R. Swan, G. H. Warre [or Warrie], Frank Boudinot and the Pyne Company's orchestra conductor, Anthony Reiff, Jr. Many singers named as members of the Durand Company also performed, at one time or another, with the Bishop, Thillon, and Seguin opera troupes. In late 1859, the singers Lucy Escott and Henry Squires of the Escott English Opera Company traveled to San Francisco to join forces with the Durand troupe at Maguire's Opera House.[74]

The principal—and important—difference between the Durand Company and the Pyne and Harrison troupe was the absence in the former of well-known musical celebrities. Most vocalists associated with Durand and Lyster were singing actors and actresses based in New York; many, in fact, had been members of stock companies there. More important than the rank-and-file members, however, were the name singers of the troupe. Rosalie Durand, although having a "very sweet voice of good compass . . . a fine figure, handsome face, keen black eyes, and a winning, pleasant expression when she sings," had neither the name-recognition or popular appeal of Anna Bishop or Anna Thillon—or, for that matter, any of the prominent Italian prima donnas connected with companies in the United States.[75] Indeed, she arrived in this country with no prior musical reputation at all. She spent much of her first year in America as an actress in New York theatrical companies.[76]

The inaugural performances by the Durand Company were in Baltimore in March and April 1855 and in Philadelphia in June. The following 27 October, *Dwight's* reported (29) that "Rosalie Durand and company" were performing an adaptation of Boieldieu's *John of Paris* at Burton's Theatre in New York. In fact, Durand and Lyster were at the time members of Burton's stock company; reports of activity by this operatic "troupe" in the autumn of 1855 are inaccurate. In March 1856, several thousand miles from New York, one W. H. Crisp, who had managed theaters in Savannah, Georgia, for several years, was engaged by the owners of the Gaiety Theatre in New Orleans to take over management of that house.[77] The theater, which opened in November 1856 under the name Crisp's Gaiety, featured a new stock company. According to a playbill from the theater, the "distinguished artistes" engaged in the "operatic department" of the troupe included an assortment of familiar names from Burton's Theatre: Frazer, Stretton, Lyster, Trevor, Durand, and Hodson.[78] The singers, who probably had been lured away from New York as an ensemble, performed at Crisp's Theatre during November and December 1856. They appeared in musical works and operas like *The Bohemian Girl, Der Freischütz,* and *Rob Roy* and assisted the dramatic company in the performance of such fare as John Brougham's burlesque *Pocahontas* (the title role of which Georgina Hodson had created at Wallack's Theatre in New York the previous December) and a dramatization of Walter Scott's *The Lady of the Lake.*[79]

Lyster, Durand, and the others used the New Orleans engagement to solidify their own ensemble. By February 1857 the same half-dozen individuals were at the People's Theatre in St. Louis, performing as Crisp's Opera Company.[80] Between 1857 and 1859 they acted as a true itinerant company, traveling widely around the country and performing in various theaters before becoming something of a house company at Maguire's in San Francisco in 1859.

The Durand Company, as was typical of English troupes, traveled without an orchestra. For their engagement at the New Walnut Street Theatre in Philadelphia in 1859 the management noted that "an augmented orchestra" had been engaged "expressly for the occasion"; in September 1857 the *Detroit Tribune* reported that the local theater had engaged the Detroit City Band to supplement the instrumental efforts of the house orchestra.[81] The company's repertory was monotonously typical of that of English troupes, although the usual operas (*Cinderella, Fra Diavolo, Daughter of the Regiment, The Bohemian Girl, The Crown Diamonds, Der Freischütz, The Barber of Seville,* and *La Sonnambula*) were supplemented more frequently than usual by works from the older vocal-star repertory (*John of Paris, Rob Roy,* and *The Beggar's Opera*). This slant is probably a reflection of the stock-company origins of many of the troupe's singers. At the same time, however, the company attempted to keep up with current operatic taste; by 1859 they had incorporated into their repertory translations of more recent Italian works, including *Lucrezia Borgia* and *Il Trovatore.*[82] The frequency with which they performed the latter opera (as *The Troubadour*) is suggested by John Sullivan Dwight, for this is one of the numerous troupes he referred to during the summer of 1859 as "Trovatopera" companies.[83]

From June 1857 through April 1859 the troupe, known generally as the New Orleans English Opera Company, toured widely all over the eastern half of the United States, performing in the Southeast and South in Richmond, Baltimore, Charleston, Savannah, Macon, and Columbus, and in the West in Nashville, St. Louis, Louisville, Cincinnati, Pittsburgh, Chicago (Figure 45), and Detroit. The company did not appear in either Boston or New York during these two years, and the American musical press, based primarily in those two cities, ignored it almost entirely. Consequently, both the full extent of the singers' travels and their reception by American audiences is unknown.[84]

The two remaining English troupes active in the United States during the waning years of the decade did not suffer the same fate at the hands of the American musical and theatrical press. The activities of both the Cooper and the Escott English opera companies were recorded fairly systematically in *Dwight's,* the *Musical World,* and less often in the *Spirit* throughout 1858, 1859, and 1860. The companies shared a number of similarities: both arrived in the United States in the autumn of 1858, imported by the managers of New York theaters (Cooper by Wallack's, Escott by Burton's); both fared poorly during their first engagements in Manhattan; both enlisted the services (at different times) of some of the same singers; and both traveled widely throughout eastern North America from 1858 through 1860, introducing opera to new audiences in towns and cities further and further away from the beaten track and, at the same time, avoiding New York and, for the most part, Boston.[85]

The Cooper Opera Company was the more successful and long-lived of the two ensembles. Henry C. Cooper was the company's musical director and orchestral conductor; he was described in the musical press as a "celebrated violinist" and on playbills as the "late leader of the [London] Philharmonic, Italian Opera, &c."[86] His wife Annie Milner, who had a fair complexion and light hair, was the company's prima donna. She performed in concerts in New York and Boston in 1857 and 1858 before attempting roles in opera; as the critic for the *New York Tribune* explained in 1858, "hitherto [she] has been known only in the concert-room, but during some months [past] she has been studying hard for the stage." This same critic (Fry?) described her voice as a "fresh, beautiful soprano, with great facility in the upper notes, much flexibility, and capabilities for [both] a sustained slow movement [and] equally [for] rapid, florid passages"; she also had a "great aptitude for the theatre," including an "artistic style, and an unaffected manner."[87] Although the company could not boast of any striking individual members beyond Milner and Cooper, the troupe's other singers performed well together. "The ensemble is very good," noted the critic of the *Boston Musical Times* on 25 February 1860, "the artists are unanimous—the effect is pleasant"; he also commented that he had

45. McVicker's Theatre in Chicago. Lithograph by Jeune and Almini. Published in Chicago in 1866. (Chicago Historical Society)

not heard such good English opera since the days of the Seguins (11). The critic for the *New York Times* was more enthusiastic, although one suspects from his comments that he had not been attending many of the performances by the numerous Italian companies active in New York City. "A finer quartet it has not been our good fortune to hear for many years," he wrote. "The voices are perfectly fresh, of good quality, and in some instances of very superior cultivation."[88] Most of the singers of the company performed, at one time or another, with other English opera troupes and with theatrical companies (mostly in New York) during the late 1840s and 1850s. Several also had once been members of operatic burlesque companies like the Ethiopian Serenaders and Palmo's Ethiopian Opera Company.[89]

The makeup of the Escott Opera Company was similar to that of the Cooper troupe. The company could boast of two notable singers. The soprano Lucy Escott was described as a "superior vocalist, with a pure, fresh voice, [who] sings with great expression, [is] always accurate, [with] each note full toned and each word thoroughly articulated."[90] The tenor Miranda, who joined the troupe in 1859, was described by the same critic as a "thorough artist" and an "excellent tenor [with] tones [that] are very full and sweet." When Miranda first performed in New York with the Cooper Company, the critic for the *Times* wrote, "we have had no such voice in this city for very many years. . . . [Miranda's] voice is manly, clear, sympathetic, and of unusual power"; even Dwight called him "a really good singer."[91] The other members of the company were singers who, again, had performed with other English opera troupes and with theatrical stock companies.[92]

The Cooper Opera Company first appeared in this country in successive engagements in New York at Wallack's Theatre on 6–18 September and in Boston at the Athenaeum from 20 September through 10 October. The Escott troupe opened in New York at Burton's Theatre on 4 October while Cooper and Milner were in Boston (Appendix D notes). At the time of the Cooper Company's New York performances, no English troupe had mounted productions of opera in New York since the last appearances of the Pyne and Harrison Company during the spring of 1857. The *Spirit*—which tended to favor opera in the vernacular—welcomed the Cooper troupe to Manhattan when they opened at Wallack's. "There is little difference in cost between a first-rate dramatic company and a troupe of English singers," the critic observed on 11 September 1858, "and there is little reason why a small company like Cooper's shouldn't work" (580). The same reasoning undoubtedly applied to the Escott Company. Both troupes, however, ran into serious trouble during their inaugural engagements in New York.

The New York correspondent to *Dwight's* reported on 18 September that the Cooper Company was "really quite good." The critic for the *Spirit* on the same date, however, assessed the situation differently. He observed that the singers were drawing only small audiences and further maintained that this response by the public was "justly so" (594). He went on to explain that the company's principal singers and chorus (of about twelve) were adequate but inexperienced; furthermore, the eighteen-piece orchestra was bad.[93] The company's two-week engagement at Wallack's was not renewed; after this unsuccessful (albeit not disastrous) run, the troupe headed north to try its luck in Boston. Two weeks after the Cooper Company closed at Wallack's, the Escott troupe opened at Burton's, unfortunately, to much severer criticism and a harsher fate. Their engagement—described after the fact as "another unsuccessful attempt 'to permanently establish' English opera" in New York—was an utter failure. After just six performances of *The Bohemian Girl* and *The Troubadour,* manager William Burton abruptly terminated his engagement with the opera singers.[94]

The rapid failure of two English opera companies within three weeks did not bode well for the future of vernacular opera in New York. The critic of the *Musical World* placed the blame for the Escott troupe's failure squarely on manager Burton's shoulders. "So recently have the artists of the Lucy Escott troupe arrived in this country, and so sudden has been their eclipse that we scarcely know where to begin," he wrote. The singers had barely set foot on American ground, he pointed out, when they found themselves already in front of an audience. They had been given little time to recover from the rigors of a transatlantic voyage and little—if any—time to rehearse. Furthermore, they also had to put up with the "insufficient orchestra and . . . miserable chorus" that Burton had engaged for their support. This reviewer, who probably strongly disagreed with the opinion of the *Spirit*'s critic that there was little difference in cost between an English company and a small dramatic troupe, contended that there was a world of difference in how the two types of company should be handled. "The day is passed," he argued on 16 October 1858,

> when operatic matters can be managed with the loose hand of dramatic enterprise. It is no longer practicable to use a company of singers as an individual "star," that can be driven through its repertoire without taking a breath. . . . For the simple reason that theatrical managers know nothing whatever of the requisites of opera, it follows that opera under their auspices invariably fails. . . . The conjuror who has a booth at a country fair makes more preparations for the public than does the average theatrical manager for English opera. (658)

The cause of the Escott troupe's precipitous failure may have been inadequate preparation by Burton. There were, however, even more serious and deep-rooted problems besetting English opera in New York during the fall of 1858. Odell, who described the city that autumn as "a town suffering from too much opera," suggested that the two English troupes failed because of the serious competition they faced from Italian companies. During the Cooper Company's engagement, and overlapping some with the Escott troupe's run, both the Strakosch and the Maretzek opera companies were in town competing with each other—the former at Burton's Theatre, the latter at the Academy of Music. Furthermore, not only was Strakosch's troupe scheduled to reopen at Burton's for a week starting 16 October, but the Ullman Opera Company was set to occupy the Academy of Music for six weeks starting on the twentieth (Appendix C). Maretzek, Ullman, and Strakosch soon discovered that there were hardly enough opera lovers in New York to support all of their companies simultaneously. The Maretzek troupe soon left for Havana, and Strakosch took his company on an extended trip to the West. The two English companies, both seriously outclassed by their competition, simply got lost in the shuffle.

Even worse than being outclassed and ignored, however, were the overt attacks the two English troupes suffered from critics. At issue were not only the woefully inadequate resources of the smaller troupes, but also the very operas they chose to perform. Critics in both cities took the Cooper Company severely to task over its choice of repertory in the autumn of 1858. After opening in New York with the "inevitable" *Bohemian Girl,* the singers quickly moved on to English versions of the currently popular Italian operas: *Il Trovatore* (the American premiere in English), *Lucia di Lammermoor, L'Elisir d'amore,* and (the also inevitable) *La Sonnambula.* All, with the exception of *Il Trovatore,* were well known to American opera audiences and had been performed in English adaptations for years. By 1858, however, especially in the major cities on the East Coast, these operas, and many others, were well known in their original Italian versions. The English adaptations, as a result, did not sit well any more — at least with the critics.

The decision on the part of the Cooper Company to perform a repertory of adapted Italian works, wrote one critic, "is altogether a mistake. No one wishes to see the Italian repertoire mauled, and [adaptations] amount to this and no more." Instead of translations of Italian operas, he suggested in the *Spirit* on 18 September, it would make more sense for English companies to perform selections from German operas and "from the light works of the French school — works that are heard here only in English" (594). The company suffered from similar criticism in Boston. "English opera, as it is called, or the Italian opera in English, which it usually and actually is," wrote John Sullivan Dwight on 25 September 1858, during the troupe's engagement, "is such a queer compound of incongruous things, half serious, more than half burlesque, with ingredients variously proportioned of everything, from the almost sublime to the quite ridiculous, that it is difficult, almost impossible, to write about it seriously and earnestly." Boston opera lovers, he continued, are "accustomed . . . to the conventional recitative of the Italian stage." As a consequence, "no one can help smiling, at least, when the musical thread of the drama is so harshly snapped by the intervention of the spoken dialogue." Many auditors, he continued, are not amused at all, but rather consider the "substitution of spoken dialogue in the English version, for the recitative of the Italian opera" to be nothing short of "ridiculous" (207).

To a certain extent, this negative attitude toward translated opera — a performance style that, after all, had been seen on the American stage for decades — was musical in origin. There is always a slight jarring when dialogue and singing alternate, and by 1857 East Coast lovers of foreign-language opera were used to hearing these operas sung throughout. But many of the bon ton who supported Italian opera companies had an ulterior motive in considering "the substitution of spoken dialogue . . . for recitative" to be "ridiculous": sung recitative was part of the mystique that set "their" opera apart from standard theatrical fare. If the comments by the *Spirit*'s critic are any indication, the supporters of foreign-language opera, fashionables and music lovers alike, had made a great deal of progress by the late 1850s in their campaign to define foreign-language opera as the "correct," fashionable style and translated versions of "their" repertory as vulgar, ridiculous, and fit only for the *canaille*.

The fate of these two troupes clearly indicates that in the late 1850s—at least in New York and Boston, where performances by large, polished troupes were no longer a rarity—English opera as mounted by a small company in a regular theater, especially if done so in a rather haphazard manner, was no longer satisfactory. Entirely aside from the issue of fashion was the reality that individuals who had attended performances by specialized companies now demanded much more; opera performance by inferior troupes with only two or four real singers was no longer acceptable.

The criticism leveled at the Cooper and Escott companies, however, was limited principally to Boston and New York. In marked contrast, elsewhere in the country audiences generally welcomed English opera companies with unreserved enthusiasm. Many music lovers outside of Boston and New York were grateful for any kind of opera performances. Most had little experience with large, polished opera companies and thus little basis for comparison; they were both easier to please and less eager to criticize. The exception to this generalization, as usual, was New Orleans, where audiences were quite experienced with opera performed in Italian but still enjoyed Italian opera in English. This was the result of two factors: the unique position of opera in the city's cultural fabric and the fierce, long-lived rivalry between the French- and English-speaking segments of the population, each of which continued to support the performance of opera in its own tongue (chapter 3).

Because English troupes like the Cooper and Escott companies found themselves unwelcome and financially unsuccessful in major cities of the Northeast, they increasingly set out for the interior of the country during the last few years of the decade. There they found a growing demand for opera performances. Their enthusiastic reception, and the expanded transportation system, made extended tours away from the big cities of the Northeast—and even away from the Ohio-Mississippi River system—both feasible and profitable. Consequently, both the Cooper and the Escott troupes, like the Pyne and Harrison Company before them, expanded their itineraries to include cities not previously visited by opera companies. In Worcester, Massachusetts, for example, the Cooper Company gave on 11 October 1858 what was advertised as the "first opera ever given in this city"—a performance of the English

version of *Il Trovatore; or, The Gipsy's Vengeance!* (Figure 46).[95] In
1859 the Escott and Miranda Company visited Peoria, Illinois, much
to the astonishment and delight of Peorians, who could scarcely believe
that an opera troupe of any reputation whatsoever would "come to a
place like ours." They were delighted with the company's performances
and acknowledged afterward that the merit of the troupe "could no
longer be questioned."[96] The following year, the Cooper Opera Company conducted a tour of New England that included performances
in Hartford, New Haven, Providence, Rochester, and Albany. Although
several of these towns already had enjoyed visits from opera companies
in the preceding years, as well as numerous performances by operatic
concert troupes, none could be considered to be on the beaten track
during the 1850s.

Audiences in smaller towns were much easier to please than were
the more experienced and discriminating audiences of Boston and New
York. In 1859, for example, the Cooper Company visited Milwaukee.
Before their arrival the troupe claimed to be "the largest and most
complete opera company that ever visited Milwaukee." It was a false
boast, however, for the much-larger Arditi Company had performed
there in November 1853. The English troupe also advertised that they
would be assisted by a "complete orchestra and chorus." In fact, during
this particular visit the company was quite pared down; the chorus
was comprised of only three men, and the company performed with
an "orchestra" of one pianist and H. C. Cooper on the violin.[97] Nevertheless, the Milwaukeans, although at first disappointed and angry
because of the fraudulent advertising, attended the troupe's performances in large numbers. As a correspondent later wrote to the *Musical
World,* the chorus, although small, "was really good," and the so-called
orchestra "accompanied with much taste and effect." After residents
"got over the first deception," he reported on 6 August, they "liked
the company very well, as the full houses abundantly testified" (3). The
impressions of a woman who heard the same company in 1859 may
be typical. A resident of Ann Arbor, she attended a performance of
Il Trovatore while visiting Detroit. "Last evening I went to an Opera!"
she wrote to a friend at home. She continued, "I was delighted, and
what is more strange, not disappointed. Of course, it was on a small
scale—but I could imagine how it might be in perfection, and it opened
a new world to me— . . . I was delighted and entranced . . . it was like
a story!" Although Verdi's music was new to the letter-writer, she
judged it to be "very fine." She planned to attend another performance
that evening, of *The Child of the Regiment,* and anticipated this performance with delight. Donizetti's work, she confided, "will be the
more interesting, as I have heard much of the music."[98] Even in Cin-

46. Playbill from a production billed as the "First Opera Ever Given" in Worcester, Mass. The opera was presented by the Cooper English Opera Company, 11 October 1858. (American Antiquarian Society)

cinnati—hardly an operatic or theatrical backwater—audiences were inclined to appreciate a company's performances despite its drawbacks. A critic for the *Enquirer,* writing on 27 December 1858 about a Cooper Company performance, for example, complained gently that one of the operas in the troupe's repertory, *La Sonnambula,* was "rather old-hackneyed, one might say." He was quick to add, however, that "we are too happy to get any opera to quarrel about its age."[99]

In some cities away from the Northeast, audiences preferred English opera over Italian even when both were readily available. In 1859, audiences in Montreal and Toronto heard performances by two troupes, the Parodi Italian Opera Company and the Cooper English Opera Company, and the latter was clearly the more successful of the two. In Toronto, a city familiar with Italian opera, a *La Traviata* performance by Parodi attracted but a meager audience to the Lyceum Theatre in August 1859. In contrast, three months later the Cooper Company mounted an English-language version of the same work and attracted overflowing houses.[100] One factor in the differing receptions may have been the time of year the companies chose to visit Toronto. The Parodi Company's performances in August were undoubtedly before the beginning of the regular theatrical season, which would have diminished the size of their potential audience. Nevertheless, the Cooper troupe dominated the operatic "market" in both that city and in Montreal from 1858 through 1860, despite several visits by the Parodi Company. As Dorith Cooper concluded in her study of opera performance in those two Canadian cities, "the Coopers' enormous success, especially in Toronto, indicated that Italian grand opera rendered in English could indeed draw a large audience, and was therefore an increasingly important factor which purely Italian ensembles (such as Parodi's) had to bear in mind" (133).

In the late 1850s—and into the 1860s and later—more and larger Italian troupes followed in the footsteps of the English companies (and of Italian troupes like the Arditi Company of 1853 and 1854) and expanded their itineraries to encompass all parts of the country (chapter 3 and Appendix C). As larger and more polished Italian companies visited more and more American cities and towns, even opera audiences in the hinterland became more discriminating and demanding. At the same time that Italian troupes reached out for audiences all over the country, however, English companies grew larger and more polished. In spite of the inroads that the Italians made, there continued to be a large audience for opera in English in North America. By the late 1850s, this audience was growing, fueled both by the efforts of Louisa Pyne and William Harrison to establish English opera at Covent Garden in London and by a backlash against Italian opera, which was becoming more and more entrenched in the American mind as entertainment for the wealthy.

The English opera companies that toured North America in the 1850s, although somewhat overshadowed by their Italian competitors, had a long-range impact on the performance of opera in the United States. On the foundations that these troupes laid was erected a substantial English opera movement in the United States—a movement that espoused "opera for the people," that featured fabulously successful companies headed by such American prima donnas as Emma Abbott and Clara Louise Kellogg, and that constituted an important aspect of American opera production during the second half of the nineteenth century.

6

The Pyne and Harrison English Opera Company, 1855–56

If the great mass of the American people accustomed to attend concerts were asked, after hearing opera in both [English and Italian], "which do you prefer?" we feel sure that, setting aside the influence of "snobbery," and "*id omne genus*," an overwhelming majority would vote for music in the language they speak and understand.[1]

By the middle of the 1850s the American opera audience was well established and expanding by leaps and bounds. Increasing numbers of Italian opera companies and Italian operatic concert troupes such as the Parodi-Strakosch Company plied the constantly expanding American theatrical circuit, demonstrating clearly that many Americans were happy to take opera as presented by the foreign-language troupes, lock, stock, and barrel.

At the same time, however, a rather sizable portion of the audience stubbornly resisted the allure of the glamorous foreigners. Despite a seemingly insatiable hunger to see and hear European musical "stars" (instrumental as well as vocal) and a desire to be "cultured," educated, genteel, and—above all—fashionable, many middle-class Americans were at the same time staunch adherents of the principles of egalitarianism. They resented anything that smacked of Old World aristocratic (or New World upper-class) snobbery. The growing identification of Italian opera as an elite pastime alienated many theater-goers and music lovers, especially when this was combined with the negative image of the foreign opera stars, whose numerous and well-publicized foibles continued unabated throughout the decade. Many of these Americans, as the success of the Cooper, Escott, and Durand companies attested, wanted performances of opera, but they also wanted to be able to understand what was happening on the stage. As one music critic put it in 1857, "a good English opera is, after all, the only one which can give entire satisfaction to the great mass of our people."[2]

The increased demand for English-language opera in the United States coincided with an English opera revival underway in Great Britain at the same time. Louis Jullien's attempt to establish English opera at Drury Lane in 1847–48 had ended in failure; his bankruptcy had thrown his conductor, Max Maretzek, out of work and freed Maretzek to accept the "engaging offer" made by Edward Fry of New York. The next concerted effort to establish English opera permanently in London, at Covent Garden from 1857–64, also had transatlantic connections. The principal movers behind the effort were two British singers, the soprano Louisa Pyne (1832–1904) and William Harrison (1813–68), a tenor, who spent three years before their London venture catering to the demand for English opera in the United States.[3] The Pyne and Harrison English Opera Company was the most successful English troupe to perform in North America during the 1850s (chapter 5). Their triumph—which paved the way for their London success—clearly demonstrates the demand for English-language opera in the United States during the decade.

The Pyne and Harrison English Opera Company

Louisa Pyne and William Harrison were both well-established English singers before they teamed up in 1853 as the Pyne and Harrison Opera Company. Pyne (Figure 47), almost twenty years Harrison's junior, was ten when she made her concert debut at the Queen's Concert Rooms, Hanover Square; her operatic debut, at Boulogne, was in 1849 as Amina in *La Sonnambula*. American music lovers first heard about her that same year, when the New York periodical *Message Bird* noted on 15 November that she had "received an enthusiastic reception" as Amina at the Princess' Theatre in London (135). Prior recognition among the American public, if only by name, was important if a singer hoped for a successful tour of the United States, and Pyne was off to a good start. *Saroni's* helped out a year later on 1 June 1850 by reprinting from "an English publication" a rave review of another performance at the Princess' Theatre. "With the purity of a Lind—with the sweetness of a Sontag," gushed the critic, "she stood like an angel warbling strains of comfort and resignation, totally unconscious, as it appeared, of any listening audience. . . . The vocal feats she accomplishes are perfectly marvelous in one so young, and nothing can exceed the captivating ease with which she performs her miracles of musical precocity" (425).

47 and 48. Louisa Pyne, soprano and William Harrison, tenor. The picture of Harrison is from an engraving by D. J. Pound; the source of Pyne's portrait is unknown. (George C. D. Odell Collection, Columbia University)

The soprano's first big professional break came in 1851, when she was called to the Royal Italian Opera, Covent Garden, to substitute for an indisposed singer in the part of Queen of the Night in *The Magic Flute*. Her performance in the difficult role took everyone by surprise and "quite eclipsed that of her predecessor." The American musical press noted her success and commented approvingly: "This young lady . . . is rising among the singers of European reputation, steadily and surely."[4]

Pyne's partner William Harrison (Figure 48) made his operatic debut at Covent Garden in 1839, where his success was "brilliant and decided."[5] A popular singer on the English stage, he had a voice of "remarkable purity and sweetness" as well as a reputation as an excellent actor. After his debut in 1839 in Rooke's opera *Henrique; or, The Love Pilgrim*, Harrison's performance was lauded. "His style," wrote a critic, "[is] distinguished by great power, pathos, and dramatic energy, holding, as it were, the 'mirror up to Nature,' whether representing the peasant or the king, and also by a peculiarly clear and distinct enunciation, a quality rarely to be met with in a singer."[6]

Harrison built his career around English opera. Before his arrival in the United States he created the tenor roles in William Vincent Wallace's *Maritana* (1845), Julius Benedict's *Brides of Venice* (1844) and *The Crusaders* (1846), and—significantly, in view of Americans' fondness for this opera—Michael Balfe's *The Bohemian Girl* (1843).[7] Despite a strong reputation in Great Britain, however, Harrison apparently was not well known to the American public before his arrival. Critical reaction to his singing and acting in the United States would be, at best, mixed.

The singers teamed up in England with a baritone named Borrani sometime early in 1853. They took their company on the road almost immediately, performing in Balfe's *The Enchantress* at the Theatre Royal in Liverpool in March of that year.[8] There is no news of the troupe in the American musical-theatrical press for the rest of 1853 or the first half of 1854. The singers must have stayed together as a company and performed in the provinces, however, for the following summer Thomas Barry, who was in Europe recruiting for New York's Broadway Theatre (Figure 49), signed the ensemble for a visit to the United States. On 5 August 1854, *Dwight's* noted Barry's return to New York and mentioned that he had "engaged the following singers for the Broadway Theatre:—Opera, Miss Louisa Pyne, Mrs. [*sic*] Pyne, first and second prima donnas; Mr. Harrison, tenor; M. Bassoni [*sic*] (basso)" (143).[9] On 23 August 1854, the four singers (Susan Pyne, Louisa's older sister, was a mezzo-soprano) left Liverpool for the United States, arriving on 4 September. Harrison was accompanied by his wife; the Misses Pyne had the companionship of their parents.[10]

The American debut of the new English company in *La Sonnambula* was at the Broadway Theatre on Monday, 9 October 1854. This first engagement in New York was not as a full-fledged opera company, but as a vocal-star troupe; supporting parts in *La Sonnambula* and subsequent operas mounted during the engagement (*The Bohemian Girl, Maritana, The Crown Diamonds,* and *Fra Diavolo*) were filled by members of the Broadway stock company.[11] The opening performance was auspicious. "English Opera was inaugurated last Monday evening at the Broadway by the debut of Miss Louisa Pyne, her sister, Mr. W. Harrison, and Mr. Borrani," announced the *Musical Review and Choral Advocate* on 12 October. The lengthy, favorable critique also included a detailed description of each singer's voice and concluded that "we may now congratulate ourselves on having the best English Opera company that has visited New York for many years" (355).

During the company's first year in the States their performances were limited almost entirely to the large East Coast cities: Philadelphia, New York, and Boston (Appendix D). By November the regular troupe included three additional singers: Frederick Meyer (bass), William H. Reeves (tenor), and Joseph Whiting. All had been active in this country before the arrival of the Pynes and Harrison.[12] For their engagements in Boston in November and in Philadelphia in November, February,

49. Broadway Theatre in New York, the house at which
the Pyne and Harrison Company first performed in the
United States. (George C. D. Odell Collection, Columbia
University)

and March, the English singers apparently maintained some kind of
business relationship with E. A. Marshall, the manager of the Broadway.
Thomas Barry, who had actually recruited the singers for the Broadway,
had in the autumn of 1854 assumed management of the new Boston
Theatre (the Federal Street Theatre had burned in 1852).[13] That Barry
also maintained close business connections with his old colleague Marshall is suggested by the fact that when Harrison, the Pynes, Whiting,
Reeves, and Meyer arrived for performances at the Boston Theatre
they brought, according to a playbill, "a largely increased Orchestra,
and a powerful Chorus of 49 voices."[14] Other playbills were more
specific: the "Powerful and Talented Chorus" of the Boston Theatre,
one announced, was to be augmented with "additional choristers from
New York"; the orchestra, according to another, was to be under the
direction of Signor La Manna "by permission of E. A. Marshall, Esq."[15]
When the Pynes and Harrison appeared in Philadelphia, furthermore,
it was at the Walnut Street Theatre, which was under the management
of the same E. A. Marshall who controlled the Broadway.[16] The increasing syndication of theatrical management in the United States

during the 1850s certainly made it easier for opera companies to move from city to city, especially on the East Coast.

Critics described the company as one of the best to visit the United States. Praise for Louisa Pyne, in particular, was almost universal. John Dwight's comments from 2 December 1854 are typical:

> We were delighted, as was every one, with Miss LOUISA PYNE. Short in stature, blonde, blue-eyed, with an ingenuous, pleasing English face, ease and dignity of movement, perfect self-possession, perfect understanding of her part, and a plenty of pretty archness, she was all one could desire. . . . Her voice, not very powerful, is musical and sweet and flexible and evenly developed, and she executes the most florid music . . . with an ease and liquid evenness and finish that remind one of [Henriette] Sontag. . . . There can be no doubt that she will prove a great favorite here as she has elsewhere. (69–70)

The other principal singer of the company, however, did not meet with such universal acclaim. "Mr. Harrison," wrote one critic, "is a tenor of great physical as well as vocal strength."

> In some airs he is very successful, in others, his intonation is uncertain and his voice uneven. He sometimes allows himself the production of hard unpleasant chest-tones in the upper region of his voice, too nearly resembling a yell, while at others, the same notes are taken in a pure resonant chest voice, and beautifully diminished into the falsetto without break, in a manner worthy of [Giovanni Mateo] Mario himself. The fact that he can sometimes do so difficult a thing well, leaves him without excuse for not always doing it so.

This same critic finished with a prophecy that would be readily fulfilled: "with great excellencies and great defects, radical differences of opinion will, of course, exist in reference to [Harrison], but amid them all, he will have many admirers."[17] Indeed, Harrison's performances garnered both praise and severe criticism from American reviewers. Dwight noted, again on 2 December, that the tenor's singing was "hard in quality and false continually in pitch, except when he sang occasionally in falsetto, where his tones grew singularly sweet and fine, as well as true" (70). Others were not so kind and complained that Harrison could neither sing nor act.[18] Later, when on tour in the American interior, Harrison elicited significantly less criticism and more praise. His intonation problems, however, and later his treatment by a physician for vocal difficulties, were cause for comment in the American musical-theatrical press for the entire length of his stay in this country.[19]

The baritone Borrani, although praised by some as a singer "of excellent taste, and good vocal power and compass," also was the target of criticism: "Borrani's medium tones please — upper tones, unpleas-

ant—lower tones, too weak" wrote a New York critic in 1854.[20] Susan
Pyne, the remaining member of the original foursome, generally fared
well as the seconda donna of the company. She was, however, rarely
mentioned in reviews, undoubtedly because in the repertory performed
by the company the part of the *seconda donna* is not particularly
significant. Finally, the troupe's orchestra and chorus usually drew
praise. After their first appearance in Boston, Dwight described the
chorus—"unusually large, numbering over forty voices"—as "well-
blended and euphonious; there was no excessive loudness or harshness,
but really a musical blending of voices;—a thing almost unprecedented
on our stage." He similarly praised the orchestra, noting in the same
review on 2 December that it "played neatly, but scarcely with enough
power for the [Boston Theatre]; a most rare fault and on the right
side!" (69).[21] The reviewer for the *Musical Gazette* agreed. "The chorus
and orchestra are very good," he wrote on 25 November, "the former
especially seems to have been carefully and thoroughly trained and
instructed" (17).

The company's popular reception during 1854–55—even in New
York—was gratifyingly enthusiastic. "The English Opera now at the
Broadway," wrote a critic in the *Musical World* on 21 October 1854,
"is a living proof of the success of an entertainment in music and
English words—the language the unsophisticated and untraveled folk
understand" (90). In December a critic for the same periodical expressed
amazement at the success of the English opera performers, especially
in view of the competition: the Italian opera superstars Giulia Grisi
and Giovanni Mateo Mario were performing at the Academy of Music.
"We wonder [that] English opera is able to sustain itself at all," he
wrote on 16 December. "That it is able to do so, is, in our opinion,
a favorable symptom for English operatic performance" (190).

In Philadelphia, the English opera had "been the rage" during the
company's appearances; their engagement overall had been "most successful."[22] Comments on 25 November by the same critic shed some
light on the mixed nature of the company's audience, for he expressed
bewilderment that performances of the old-fashioned *Beggar's Opera*
had drawn two full houses; the plot of the work, he sniffed, "is about
as instructive in morals as [is the melodrama] 'Jack Sheppard.'" His
explanation for the ballad opera's popularity was simple: "the applause
came generally from the upper tiers; showing," he concluded, "that it
did not meet the approbation of the intelligent portion of the audience"
(154). In Boston, the management attempted to raise prices during the
first week and the public balked; *Dwight's* on 9 December described
the turnout for the troupe's initial performances as "rather less than
average" (78). After the management "came to its senses and restored

the original prices," however, the engagement proved quite successful; during the second week the theater was "thronged every evening."[23] This reaction is revealing, especially because a little over a month later the Boston public mobbed performances by the Italians Grisi and Mario despite even higher admission prices than those attempted for the English company. A critic for the *Spirit*, apparently disgusted with the behavior of the Bostonians, noted this apparent contradiction. "A few weeks ago," he wrote on 27 January 1855, "the management attempted to raise the prices from 50 cents to $1, and the public screamed bloody murder. Now the management leases the theatre to someone from outside of Boston [James Hackett, for performances by Mario and Grisi], who raises the prices to $2, and the audience flocks to the theatre, lining the pockets of outsiders" (589). Clearly, Bostonians still viewed English opera as normal theatrical fare and hence not worthy of raised prices. The performance of Italian opera by big-name European stars, on the other hand, was sufficiently unusual that the management could successfully increase prices significantly.

The Pyne and Harrison Company spent its first summer in the United States at Niblo's Theatre in New York (Figures 50, 51), where they performed for more than five months under the direction of the American composer and conductor George Frederick Bristow (1825–98).[24] On 27 September 1855, the troupe mounted the world premiere of Bristow's *Rip van Winkle,* which met with considerable critical acclaim. It was performed nightly through October 6 and three times a week thereafter, for a total of eighteen performances.[25] The overall success of the company during this lengthy engagement clearly indicates the continued appeal of English opera, even in New York. The troupe performed six nights a week for most of the summer (the engagement lasted from the end of May until the first week of November), giving an impressive total of 125 performances. In his study of Niblo's Garden, John Blair pointed out that before this highly successful run the only company able to sustain such a lengthy season at Niblo's had been the Ravel troupe, a family of French acrobats and dancers who were "successful entertainers in a popular form." The Pynes and Harrison, Blair claimed, were the first artists to "attempt to create an audience in a serious genre." Perhaps Blair's preconceived notions about opera as a serious art form colored his conclusions, however. Evidence strongly suggests that the operatic fare performed by the Pynes and Harrison was also popular entertainment.[26]

In early November, the Pyne and Harrison Company closed its engagement at Niblo's, and the singers announced their intentions to "head South for the winter." The six-month tour was to be the troupe's first venture away from the well-trodden East Coast circuit, and the

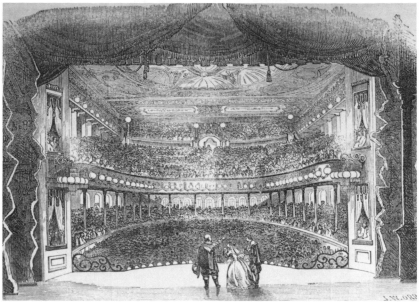

50 and 51. The interior of the theater at Niblo's Garden. (*Gleason's Pictorial Drawing-Room Companion*, February 1855 and May 1853)

singers were obliged to engage a business agent, a more-or-less permanent chorus, secondary singers, and a musical director. In other words, the Pynes and Harrison surrounded themselves with a full-fledged traveling English opera company. William Harrison served as the troupe's "managing director," but the singers were astute enough to hire William Brough to be their agent. The former vocal star had been since the late 1840s a "man of business" and "manager of operatic and musical performances generally."[27] Brough was familiar with the myriad details of itinerant performing in the United States (chapters 1 and 2). Furthermore, he had traveled extensively as a singer and a manager, was well known to both theater managers and the general public, and was a popular and congenial fellow.[28]

Also signing on for the tour were four singers who had performed with the Pynes and Harrison at Niblo's during the summer—G. H. Warre [or Warrie], Mr. Atkins, Frank R. Swan, and Henry Horncastle— as well as the newcomers Frederick Lyster, Mr. Gohr, Frank Boudinot, and George Atherton. The English bass-baritone Joseph Stretton, who had been hired to sing the role of Rip in Bristow's opera, replaced Borrani as one of the principal singers.[29] Horncastle had long been familiar on American stages (chapters 1, 2, and 5); most of the other singers would be members of either the Durand or the Cooper opera companies (or both) in the late 1850s (chapter 5).[30] Finally, a native New Yorker, Anthony Reiff, Jr., a sixteen-year-old violinist and keyboard player, was lured away from his job as conductor of the Bowery Theatre orchestra to serve as musical director and conductor of the company. Reiff, whose active and very successful musical career belies the widespread stereotype that Americans of the nineteenth century could not support themselves as musicians, served an important historical function on the tour of 1855–56: he kept a journal. Although his comments and observations are mostly social in nature (he rarely mentions performances), they nevertheless provide interesting and useful insights into the musicians' daily experiences.[31]

The Tour to the American South and West

In an issue dated 17 November, the following notice appeared in the *Boston Musical World:* "The Pyne & Harrison opera company, now playing for a few nights at Providence to crowded houses, will pay us a flying visit on Thursday, the 15th inst., and give a farewell concert, on which occasion they will give selections from the new and successful American opera of Rip Van Winkle, by Bristow, with full chorus" (337). Business agent Brough also had a local advertisement printed by the *Boston Post* on 13 November, two days before the concert: "The Pyne

& Harrison English Opera Company Respectfully announce that they will give, on Thursday, November 15th, 1855, A Grand Farewell Concert, at the Music Hall, Being positively their last appearance here this season, previous to their departure for the Western and Southern Cities."

The troupe already was well known to the Boston public, having performed in two different extended engagements there in November and December 1854 and April and May 1855. On this visit, however, their only performance was an operatic concert, the first half of which was comprised of numbers from Bristow's opera. According to local reports the concert was a success; the hall, filled with a "large and enthusiastic audience," was "as full as we have seen it this season," according to the *Boston Evening Transcript* of 16 November. Another favorable review that also appeared on the sixteenth in the *Boston Chronicle* expressed regret that the singers could give only the one concert and wished them godspeed on their tour: "We heartily commend the troupe to our musical friends at the South and West, and bespeak for Miss Louisa Pyne and her assistants the most complete success."

The company left Boston for New York on Friday, 16 November, performed there in a benefit concert for their agent William Brough, and the following Monday commenced a season of ten nights at the Holliday Street Theatre in Baltimore.[32] John Ford, the theater's manager, advertised in the *Baltimore Clipper* on 19 November that the troupe had been engaged at "enormous expense" and promptly doubled his admission prices. It was not unusual for theater managers to raise their prices for an engagement by a popular star or company — dramatic, operatic, or otherwise — especially if the attraction had recently enjoyed a great deal of success elsewhere. This was a judgment call, however, and did not always work; an attempt to do the same thing in Boston the previous November failed. But in the intervening year the fame of the Pyne and Harrison Company had grown; their unprecedented engagement at Niblo's had worked wonders for their reputation, and Ford made sure to exploit that fact. "The Pyne & Harrison English Opera Troupe," read one of the Baltimore theater's playbills, will be "aided by a Powerful Chorus! Associated with them during the recent unparalleled engagement of one hundred and twenty six nights at Niblo's Theatre, N. Y."[33] The raised admission in this case did not deter the public.[34] On the contrary, the *Baltimore Clipper* reported on 19 November that during the first week the theater "was always full" of audiences "composed of the elite of Baltimore society"; furthermore "the demand for seats was so great that in some instances [performances] were engaged several nights ahead." During the second week, reporters commented in the *Daily Republican* on 22 November that the "rush for seats . . . continues unabated, and throngs are turned away nightly." Although Baltimore was hardly a theatrical backwater, even as late as the mid 1850s opera troupes did not visit nearly as often as they did in Boston, for example. As a result, opera-loving Baltimoreans, and residents of other towns like it, were apt to be more ebullient and effusive about visiting troupes than were theater-goers in Boston, Philadelphia, or New York. One local critic, in fact, enthusiastically observed that the engagement of the Pyne and Harrison Company was "an era in the history of the opera in Baltimore." In contrast, the Bostonian John Dwight had expressed complimentary but much less effusive sentiments about the same company's performances there. "This is not GRISI and MARIO," he wrote, "but may [the Pyne and Harrison Company] not possibly prepare the way for that!"[35]

During their two-week engagement, the company mounted ten performances of nine operas: *The Crown Diamonds* (Auber), *The Bohemian Girl* (Balfe), *The Daughter of the Regiment* (Donizetti), *Maritana* (Wallace), *Fra Diavolo* (Auber), *The Beggar's Opera* (Gay-Rich), *The Love Spell* (Donizetti's *L'Elisir d'amore*), *The Barber of Seville,* and *Sonnambula* (twice); they also gave a matinee concert. The practice of changing operas nightly would be the predominant pattern throughout the company's entire tour (Table 17).

On 30 November, the troupe performed one night in Philadelphia, then the musicians packed their costumes and music and headed west (Figure 52). During a one-week engagement in Pittsburgh the theater was "crowded with one of the largest and most fashionable audiences ever inside the building" for performances of *La Sonnambula, The Bohemian Girl, The Daughter of the Regiment, Maritana,* and *The Crown Diamonds,* according to the *Pittsburgh Post* of 1 December. After the Pittsburgh engagement, the group traveled by river and rail to Cincinnati, intending to proceed from there to points further west and south. Throughout this entire tour the company—like most other performing troupes of the time—traveled by steamboat or railroad. By the mid 1850s the transportation network in the eastern United States was extensive; the travel by stage that had so fatigued Jane Shirreff and John Wilson some twenty years earlier—and had equally horrified Charles Dickens—was outdated, at least east of the Mississippi.

The Pyne and Harrison Company's engagement at the National Theatre in Cincinnati commenced on 12 December. The advertising excitement had started the previous week, with the *Cincinnati Enquirer* announcing on 8 December that "the celebrated Pyne and Harrison Opera Company will commence an engagement at the National on Monday next, when our musical epicures may feast themselves at one

Table 17. Itinerary and Repertory of the Pyne and Harrison Opera
Company, Nov. 1855–May 1856

Boston:

| 15 Nov. | Concert |

New York:

| 17 Nov. | Concert |

Holliday Street Theatre, Baltimore:

19 Nov. (Monday)	*The Crown Diamonds*
20 Nov.	*The Bohemian Girl*
21 Nov.	*The Daughter of the Regiment*
22 Nov.	*Maritana*
23 Nov.	*La Sonnambula*
24 Nov.	*Fra Diavolo*
26 Nov. (Monday)	*The Beggar's Opera*
27 Nov.	*The Love Spell*
28 Nov.	Grand Operatic Concert (afternoon)
	The Barber of Seville (evening)
29 Nov.	*La Sonnambula* (Pyne benefit)

Philadelphia:

| 30 Nov. | Concert |

Pittsburgh Theatre, Pittsburgh:

3 Dec. (Monday)	*La Sonnambula*
4 Dec.	*The Bohemian Girl*
5 Dec.	*The Daughter of the Regiment*
6 Dec.	*Maritana*
7 Dec.	*The Crown Diamonds*

National Theatre, Cincinnati:

10 Dec. (Monday)	Postponed
11 Dec.	*The Bohemian Girl*
12 Dec.	*The Crown Diamonds*
13 Dec.	Harrison ill; no performance
14 Dec.	*The Daughter of the Regiment*
15 Dec.	*La Sonnambula*
17 Dec. (Monday)	*Maritana*
18 Dec.	*Fra Diavolo*
19 Dec.	*The Crown Diamonds*
20 Dec.	*Maritana*
21 Dec.	*Cinderella*
22 Dec.	*Cinderella*
24 Dec. (Monday)	*Cinderella*
25 Dec.	*Cinderella*
26 Dec.	*Cinderella*

Table 17. Continued

27 Dec.	*Cinderella*
28 Dec.	*La Sonnambula*
29 Dec.	*The Barber of Seville* (Pyne benefit)

Louisville Theatre, Louisville:

31 Dec. (Monday)	*The Crown Diamonds*
1 Jan.	*Maritana*
2 Jan.	*The Daughter of the Regiment*
3 Jan.	*Fra Diavolo*
4 Jan.	*The Bohemian Girl*
5 Jan.	*La Sonnambula* (Pyne benefit)

St. Charles Theatre, New Orleans:

24 Jan.	*The Crown Diamonds*
25 Jan.	*Maritana*
26 Jan.	*The Bohemian Girl*
28 Jan. (Monday)	*The Bohemian Girl*
29 Jan.	*The Bohemian Girl*
30 Jan.	*Cinderella*
31 Jan.	*Cinderella*
1 Feb.	*Cinderella*
2 Feb.	*Cinderella*
4 Feb. (Monday)	*Cinderella*
5 Feb.	*Cinderella*
6 Feb.	*La Sonnambula* (Harrison benefit)
7 Feb.	*The Daughter of the Regiment* (Pyne benefit)
8 Feb.	*The Daughter of the Regiment* [?]

Odd Fellows' Hall, Mobile:

12 Feb.	Gems from *La Sonnambula* (concert)
14 Feb.	Gems from *The Bohemian Girl* (concert)
15 Feb.	Gems from *The Crown Diamonds* (concert)
18 Feb. (Monday)	Concert

Gaiety Theatre, New Orleans:

20 Feb.	*La Sonnambula*
21 Feb.	*The Crown Diamonds*
22 Feb.	*The Bohemian Girl*
24 Feb. (Monday)	*The Barber of Seville*

St. Louis Theatre, St. Louis:

10 March (Monday)	*La Sonnambula*
11 March	*The Bohemian Girl*
12 March	*The Crown Diamonds*
13 March	*Maritana*
14 March	*The Daughter of the Regiment*

Table 17. Continued

15 March	*The Crown Diamonds*
17 March (Monday)	*Guy Mannering*
18 March	*The Barber of Seville*
19 March	*Maritana*
20 March	*The Bohemian Girl*
21 March	*The Love Spell*
22 March	*The Daughter of the Regiment*
24 March (Monday)	*Cinderella*
25 March	*Cinderella*
26 March	*Cinderella*
27 March	*Cinderella*
28 March	*Cinderella*
29 March	*Cinderella*
31 March (Monday)	*The Crown Diamonds* (Bateman benefit)

Mozart Hall, Louisville:

2 April	Concert
3 April	Concert

Burnet House, Cincinnati:

4 April	Concert

Holliday Street Theatre, Baltimore:

9 April	*Cinderella*

National Theatre, Washington:

14 April (Monday)	*La Sonnambula*
15 April	*The Crown Diamonds*
16 April	*Maritana*
17 April	*The Daughter of the Regiment*
18 April	*The Bohemian Girl*
19 April	*The Barber of Seville* (Pyne benefit)

Richmond Theatre, Richmond:

21 April	Opera postponed; Harrison ill
22 April	*La Sonnambula*
23 April	*The Crown Diamonds*
24 April	*The Bohemian Girl*
25 April	*Maritana*
26 April	*The Daughter of the Regiment* (Pyne benefit)
29 April	Concert (Metropolitan Hall)

National Theatre, Washington:

30 April	*The Crown Diamonds*
1 May	*Cinderella*
2 May	*Cinderella*
3 May	*Cinderella*

Table 17. Continued

Holliday Street Theatre, Baltimore:

5 May (Monday)	*Cinderella*
6 May	*Cinderella*
7 May	*Cinderella*
8 May	*The Crown Diamonds*
9 May	*La Sonnambula*
10 May	*Cinderella* (matinee)
	Guy Mannering (evening)
12 May (Monday)	*Maritana*
13 May	*The Daughter of the Regiment*
14 May	*The Bohemian Girl* (Harrison benefit)
15 May	*The Crown Diamonds*
16 May	*Maritana*
17 May	*The Barber of Seville* (Pyne benefit)

National Theatre, Washington:

19 May (Monday)	*The Bohemian Girl*
20 May	*Cinderella*
21 May	*Maritana*
22 May	*Guy Mannering*
23 May	*The Daughter of the Regiment*

of the richest musical banquets ever spread before them." More restrained paid advertisements for forthcoming or current performances by theatrical, operatic, and instrumental performers appeared in the "Amusements" column of the classifieds. Notices like the preceding example, however, were not unusual and appear masquerading as news in the columns of the papers. These enthusiastic notices might actually reflect the attitudes of an editor or critic; many, however, were advertising puffs, reflecting surreptitious—or even nonsurreptitious—payments by the performers' agent.

Newspaper advertisements, broadsides, placards, and playbills were the responsibility of both the company's agent—in this case, Brough—and the manager of the theater in which the troupe was to perform. The usual financial arrangement, even in the mid-fifties, was for the performer to receive a percentage of the proceeds over and above an agreed-upon amount as well as a portion of the take from one or more benefits (chapter 2). As a consequence, it was in the best interests of a theater manager to promote his current engagement to the fullest extent. Many theaters apparently had regular accounts with the local newspaper, for their advertisements appeared in the same format and often on the same page every day, week after week.

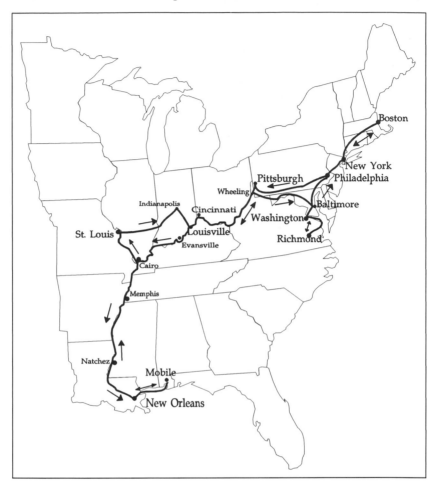

52. Map of the Pyne and Harrison English Opera Company tour to the American South and West, November 1855-May 1856. The arrows indicate the direction of their travels. (Map by Brewer Eddy, College of William and Mary)

Company managers and agents themselves, however, also took on some of the responsibilities for advertising their charges. For example, in 1856 Henry Warren, who managed theaters in Buffalo and Rochester, received a letter from Peter Richings, an actor and the manager of the Richings Opera Company, a vocal-star ensemble that later became an English opera troupe featuring the elder Richings's adopted daughter Caroline. Richings requested that Warren have a local print shop run off "one hundred copies each of the portraits of self and Miss R." to be used for advertising purposes. Richings intended to pick up the bills on his way through Buffalo to Rochester and entreated Warren to "have the kindness not to disappoint, as I am in need of them, or rather shall be at that time."[36] Another extant managerial letter was written by Nicholas Bochsa, Anna Bishop's manager, in June 1848. In the missive, which was addressed to Messrs. Peters and Field of Cincinnati, Bochsa mentioned that he had already sent local newspapers notices announcing Bishop's forthcoming visit.[37] By June 1848, however, Bishop's first English opera company had already disbanded, and she and Bochsa were concertizing. Because they were hiring halls rather than contracting with theaters, the responsibility for advertising details naturally fell on Bochsa's shoulders. Managers of opera companies would have had to do the same when arranging for occasional concert performances by their troupes, however, and they undoubtedly took an active part in advertising matters even when the company was engaged to perform in a theater. Later in the Pyne and Harrison Company tour, in fact, the *New Orleans Daily Picayune* noted on 17 February 1856 the receipt of a "telegraphic dispatch" from William Brough announcing forthcoming performances.

Despite the *Cincinnati Enquirer*'s preliminary bombast about the Pyne and Harrison troupe, the company at first drew poorly. On 16 December the critic for that newspaper complained, "[this] is, without a doubt, the best opera troupe that ever visited Cincinnati, and yet they have performed but to houses half filled. What is the matter? Parodi, Strakosch, and Madame Strakosch alone . . . drew nearly $4,000 within the walls of Smith & Nixon's Hall in three nights, and here we have a full opera troupe, with choruses and all complete, who don't appear to draw one-third of the money."

Parodi and the Strakosches were, of course, another version of the same concert troupe that had vexed Max Maretzek in Charleston in 1851. This ensemble, which played leap-frog with the Pyne-Harrison troupe during much of their 1855–56 tour, is a perfect example of the type of Italian-opera concert companies that became increasing prevalent during the 1850s. Had the Pynes and Harrison continued to draw only "one-third of the money" of the Parodi-Strakosch troupe, the evidence would have suggested that Italian opera was much more popular than English in the Queen City. This, however, was not the case. Somehow, the English troupe managed to overcome the audience's initial inertia and lure Cincinnatians to the theater. For the remainder of their stay, in fact, there were no further complaints or scoldings in the press, only reviews full of rapturous praise coupled with descriptions of the singers' enthusiastic reception by the Queen City's music lovers.

Some overly enthusiastic newspaper reviews also fall into the category of puffs, for they likewise were a result of payments to a local journalist. Unless the review contains some criticism along with praise, it is sometimes difficult to separate honest reviews from those that were purchased. Some of the more uncritical and enthusiastic reviews also represent the work of inexperienced critics, for few newspapers in this country (especially in the interior) could justify employing a full-time music or theater critic in the 1850s.[38] The fact that newspapers reviewed the Pyne and Harrison Company's performances in 1855–56 is significant, for it indicates that the visit of an opera company, like the visit of an important dramatic star, was a newsworthy event of interest to the community at large.

Puffs or no, the Cincinnati critics and public alike seem to have been genuinely taken with the Pyne and Harrison Company; even Harrison was praised for his "clear enunciation and impressive acting."[39] The reviewer for the *Enquirer,* who was of the flowery school of criticism, was consistent in his praise of the troupe in general and of Louisa Pyne in particular. He described the soprano's "seraphic notes, floating around and about like the warbling of a celestial melody" and pronounced Pyne's success to be absolute and unconditional. "The die is cast," he wrote on 20 December, "the fiat has gone forth, and from this time the name of Louisa Pyne will stand forth chronicled in the hearts of the denizens of the Queen City of the West as par excellence the 'queen of song.' "

The audience apparently shared his sentiments. The company remained in Cincinnati for a full three weeks, mounting sixteen performances of eight operas. On 21 December they introduced *Cinderella,* a smash hit, and performed it for six consecutive nights (Table 17.) On 27 December the *Enquirer* announced Louisa Pyne's benefit and reported that some admirers had attempted to arrange an extra benefit concert for the prima donna. This proved to be impossible, however, because "the engagements of the company positively preclude their remaining in the city" any longer than 29 December.

The troupe's next engagement was in Louisville, Kentucky, a short steamer trip down the Ohio River. They performed in the Louisville Theatre from 31 December through 5 January, mounting their usual repertory for the usual full houses. Despite an enthusiastic reception— at one performance "every seat was taken, and the aisles and lobby were crowded with persons standing"—there was no question of an extended engagement.[40] Travel conditions were worsening daily. The entire country was in the grip of a severe cold spell, and the Ohio River—the principal transportation conduit to the south—was freezing. William Brough, responsible for delivering the troupe to the St. Charles Theatre in New Orleans by 14 January, must have read the increasingly dismal newspaper reports with growing alarm. On 3 January the river reports were pessimistic: "The last boats from below [Cincinnati] encountered heavy running ice and several sustained considerable injury—the ice being heavy and sharp enough to cut their bows," read the "River and Steamboat News" in the *Cincinnati Daily Commercial.* On Saturday, 5 January the Ohio was still open at Louisville, but the *Daily Louisville Times* warned that "the river yesterday and last night was filled with floating ice. . . . The impression was general last night that [it] would be frozen over by morning." Undaunted, the company boarded the steamer *Thomas Swan* after concluding its last performance on Saturday night. "About midnight," the *Cincinnati Daily Commercial* reported on 9 January, "[the *Swan*] started for New Orleans, having awaited the close of the theatre to take the English Opera Troupe, who are engaged to perform at New Orleans next Monday night. The boat will hardly get out of the river in time, unless the weather moderates."

The weather did not moderate, and the steamer made painfully slow progress downriver; they did not reach Evansville, Indiana (normally a fifteen-hour trip) until Monday the seventh, almost two days later.[41] That evening the crew had to repair the paddle wheel, which had been badly damaged by the ice. On Tuesday the vessel continued to shove through the dangerous floes until about noon, when the captain decided that proceeding was too dangerous and ordered the crew to lay up. They were stuck fast in the ice.[42]

Anthony Reiff found the situation both entertaining and amusing. "It seems as if we were like 'Arctic Explorers' Ice Bound—visiting the Natives Ashore," he wrote in his journal on 10 January. "We are completely cut off from all communication with the world—nothing but Ice on one side and Forest on the other." The New Yorker, along with some of his more adventurous opera company friends, humorously dubbed themselves the "Arctic Exploring Committee" and went ashore several times to tramp around in the sparsely inhabited and frozen Kentucky woods. The young musician's descriptions—here and throughout the trip—vividly portray the near-wilderness through which the group traveled. "Nothing but a magnificent Forest to be seen," he wrote. "The Trees [are] very large . . . fill'd with most magnificent Birds . . . and abounding in Wild Grape Vines." When the musicians happened upon some of the "Natives," they discovered them to be living in "Log Cabins—made of Logs and Clay—[with] a rude sort of Chimney at back." One cabin, he wrote, "was rude in the extreme—two beds—but made cheerful by an immense Fire—in the capacious Fireplace"; another residence was "a much more dignified looking Cabin." Many of the passengers, he reported on 9 January, went out hunting in the woods, shooting at the plentiful "Deer, Birds, Possum, Squirrel &c."

Those passengers who chose to remain on the marooned steamer amused themselves in less strenuous pursuits: gambling, storytelling, and political discussions. "Any quantity of Gambling going on board the vessel," reported a scandalized Reiff, "even the Pynes & Harrison [and] Stretton." One night two passengers who were amateur musicians—a fiddler and a guitarist—teamed up with Reiff (who was made "Floor Master") and organized a dance; the following evening, 9 January, the opera company's stars gave in to the demands of the other passengers and "sang some Glees" for their entertainment. "Many jokes are cracked at night," recorded Reiff on 10 January, "some will ask where you are going to spend the Evening—one suggests the opera, another Niblo's, [and all] promise to wind up at Shelly's."[43]

After the *Thomas Swan* had been stuck for five full days the captain decided to try to break free. "At twelve noon we started through the Ice," Reiff wrote on 12 January.

> [It] was really dreadful. The Engineer—says he has been running on this river—twenty years—and never saw anything like it before. A man is continually stationed in the Hold—at the Bow to watch for any smash that may occur—I was all through the Hold today—The ice crashing against the Vessel—sounds like Artillery . . . [It is] a Foot thick! some places (in narrow passes) it was piled up Three & Four Feet. . . . An Old Captain who has been running on this river Sixteen years is quite nervous—The Ice Cakes sometimes will not break—but go under— you can then feel it rub against the keel the entire length of the Boat.

Reiff thought it all very exciting but cheerfully admitted to his own ignorance. "[Henry] Horncastle, an old Traveler [was] much frightened . . . [but] I stood on the extreme Bow of the vessel—thinking [about] what we would have for supper—'Where ignorance is bliss, 'tis folly to be wise' 'twas so with me, I did not fear any danger." The steamer managed to get through, but was one of the last boats to make it down the river to New Orleans until after the cold spell broke. The *Thomas Swan* and its passengers indeed were fortunate. On 28 February the *Memphis Daily Appeal* reported that some thirty flatboats, ten steamboats, and "the beautiful steamer Jacob Strader" had been lost to the ice at Cincinnati; ten other boats had sunk at Louisville.

By the time they reached the Mississippi River, the Covent Garden stars William Harrison and Louisa Pyne must have seriously questioned their own sanity in undertaking this trip to the American West. After breaking free of the ice at Evansville, the steamer was twice more damaged enough by ice floes to require unscheduled stops for repairs.[44] Furthermore, the proximity to the lawless frontier must have been unnerving. In Cairo, Illinois, a notorious town plagued by river pirates and situated at the junction of the Ohio and Mississippi rivers, several of the troupe members went ashore, only to discover the body of a man who had just been shot to death. "It is said that no one's life is safe at 'Cairo,'" Reiff wrote on 15 January. "Our Engineer says he never thinks of going into [town] without his revolver."

Even on board the steamer Harrison and Brough had to intervene to save a member of their own troupe — Reiff — from being shot. The young conductor had managed to get himself into a dispute with another passenger and "spoke rather excitedly to him"; as a result, he found himself presented with "the Gentleman's Card (Colonel Young — of California) [and] the request *that I would meet* him after Dinner — *With a friend* . . . [to] settle our dispute." Reiff later confessed that the prospect left him "somewhat nervous . . . for [Colonel Young] was too big for me to *pummel* and being a graduate of West Point I thought possibly a better Shot [than I] — as I have not fired a Pistol Six times in my life." Luckily, Reiff's colleagues Stretton, Swan, Harrison, and Brough all came to the rescue. In the subsequent discussion with his potential assailant, Reiff discovered that the underlying basis for the dispute had been his challenger's animosity toward foreigners. "The Colonel," he wrote on 14 January, began to lecture him "about the Customs in the Country (quite a crowd being now about us and he evidently taking me for an Englishman). [He] said [that] he was a New Yorker by birth. He was quite nonplussed when I told him that I was a native of New York — and as good an American as he was."

Eighteen days after they left Louisville, on a trip that usually took slightly more than five, the *Thomas Swan* and the opera company finally landed back in civilization at New Orleans.[45] On 23 January the *Daily Picayune* heralded their arrival:

> THE PYNE TROUPE ARRIVED. — By the "Thomas Swan," from Louisville, detained by the ice ten days over her time, there arrived here this morning our old friend Brough, with the whole of the celebrated operatic troupe, of which Miss Louisa Pyne . . . is the prima donna. . . . Our welcome friend Brough tells us that the troupe [will] open at the St. Charles theatre on Thursday evening, either in the "Crown Diamonds" of Auber, or the "Bohemian Girl" of Balfe. Their stay with us will probably extend through three weeks to come, during which several of the most popular and favorite English operas will be produced in the most attractive style.

This was the troupe's first visit to New Orleans, and they were welcomed with open arms. "The lovers of truly good music, rendered in the vernacular," commented the *Daily Picayune* on 25 January, "have now a 'feast of fat things' provided for them, in the engagement of the Pynes and Messrs Harrison and Stretton, at the St. Charles theatre.

Never, since the days of the Woods, have we had so perfect an English troupe of opera singers as this."

The company's reception in America's southern operatic capital apparently was even more ebullient than it had been in New York. The enthusiasm of New Orleanians for opera of all kinds and languages had not diminished in the 1850s, and audiences—especially of the English-language theaters in the city's American sector—were still extremely diverse socially. The company attracted houses described as "full and fashionable," although this description, as usual, is somewhat misleading. According to the historian Joseph Roppolo, "the ladies, the gentlemen, and the distinguished visitors" of New Orleans audiences "formed only a thin circle of elegance between the masses in the pit and the galleries" (Figure 53).[46] In part, the emphasis of papers like the *Daily Picayune* on the "fashionable and elite" nature of the audience may have been a deliberate attempt by the American press to irk their French-speaking journalistic counterparts. Profit-conscious theater managers catered increasingly in the 1850s to the tastes of all of New Orleans society. As one theater historian has explained, Benedict DeBar, the manager of the St. Charles, made sure to "dot his seasons with light musical entertainments, opera, melodrama, spectacles, ballet, and variety fare in order to appeal to a wide spectrum of the New Orleans populace."[47]

The audiences attracted by this varied fare at the St. Charles, observed Roppolo, "were as diverse, representative, and romantic as the city of New Orleans itself." In addition to the fashionable and elite, the audiences included "segments of the French, Spanish, Italian, German, Negro, and American populations; they included the housewives, clerks, salesmen, shopkeepers, prostitutes, vagabonds, and drunks; and they included the colorful (and often profane) longshoremen and steamboaters, the quadroons (usually in boxes of their own and frequently more glittering than the ladies), and the slaves, male and female, armed with passes from their masters so they could ignore the eight o'clock curfew cannon."[48]

The Pyne and Harrison Company packed them all in. "The box office at the St. Charles theatre," reported the *Picayune* on 31 January, "was yesterday besieged from the moment of its opening until its close, by people anxious to obtain seats for the first performance of 'Cinderella,' by the Pyne troupe; and at night the house was crowded from pit to ceiling." In addition to *Cinderella,* which they performed six times, the company mounted *The Crown Diamonds, Maritana, The Bohemian Girl, La Sonnambula,* and *The Daughter of the Regiment* over the course of fourteen performances. As usual, the stock company also presented a farce as part of each evening's performance.[49]

53. Audience scenes from the French Opera House in New Orleans from
shortly after the Civil War. Top: "A Creole Family at the Opera"; bottom
left: "Loge Grilles"; bottom right: "The Negro Gallery." *Every Sunday,* 15
July 1871. (The Historic New Orleans Collection, Museum/Research Center)

The repertory that the company performed—at least on this tour—
was rather circumscribed, at least by nineteenth-century standards.
According to reports published shortly after their arrival in the United
States, the English singers were to appear in some thirty different operas
during their visit to this country; in reality, however, this estimate was
somewhat high.[50] Over the course of their three years in the United
States the Pynes and Harrison sang in twenty-two operas: English-
language works by William Vincent Wallace (*Maritana*), Michael Balfe
(*The Daughter of St. Mark, The Bohemian Girl,* and *The Rose of Castile*),
John Baldwin Buckstone (*Queen of a Day*), John Barnett (*The Mountain
Sylph*), Sir Henry Rowley Bishop (*Guy Mannering*), and George Frederick Bristow (*Rip van Winkle*), and the ballad opera *Beggar's Opera,*

as well as works in translation by Auber (*Fra Diavolo, Masaniello,* and *The Crown Diamonds*), Halévy (*Le val d'Andorre* as *The Valley of Andorre*), Bellini (*La Sonnambula*), Rossini (*The Barber of Seville* and *Cinderella,* the latter still in the Lacy version), Donizetti (*The Daughter of the Regiment, The Love Spell,* and *Lucia di Lammermoor* as *Lucy of Lammermoor*), Mozart (*Le Nozze di Figaro* as *The Marriage of Figaro*), Flotow (*Martha*), and Victor Massé (*Les noces de Jeannette* as *The Marriage of Jeanette*). During the 1855–56 tour the company used only eleven of these operas as their warhorses (Table 17). Of these, they relied overwhelmingly on six: *La Sonnambula* and *The Daughter of the Regiment* (twelve performances each), *Maritana* (thirteen), *The Bohemian Girl* (fourteen), *The Crown Diamonds* (fifteen), and *Cinderella* (twenty-seven). Of a total of 108 opera performances, 93 (87 percent) were of these half-dozen works. Italian operas were still unquestionably the favorite of Americans: half of the performances on the company's 1855–56 tour, fifty-nine, were Italian. It is also obvious that *La Sonnambula* and *Cinderella,* both perennial favorites with American audiences for more than twenty years, were still crowd-pleasers in the mid–1850s.

The Pyne and Harrison troupe mounted a reasonable number of English operas on this tour, but a majority of their repertory was "opera with English words."[51] Their performance of adaptations and translations—and their success in doing so—fueled the continuing conflict in the American musical press over opera in English versus opera in the original language. Most "so-called English opera troupes," groused one critic, perform only "effusions of Auber, Bellini, and Donizetti, wedded to English words."[52] Another journalist was more vehement. "When professing to give us English opera," he complained in 1854, "why not give it, instead of treating us to French opera, and Italian opera, with balderdash translations?"[53] Some critics believed that it was unwise for English companies to perform adaptations of Italian operas already familiar to American audiences in the original language, for by doing so their performances "suffered . . . from comparison with great [Italian] artists with whose rendition of [these operas] the New York public are so familiar."[54] Although this particular critic referred specifically to New York audiences, as the 1850s wore on and increasing numbers of Italian troupes widened their itineraries, his comments about Americans' familiarity with Italian-language opera became more and more applicable to audiences elsewhere.

A number of critics who protested the English-opera repertory of adaptations and translations did so on more pragmatic grounds. The *Musical Review and Choral Advocate* complained in October 1854 that Louisa Pyne's pronunciation, "like most English singers . . . is indistinct," and the *Musical Gazette* agreed on 12 October (355). "Miss Louisa's pronunciation," wrote a critic for the latter periodical on 23 December, "is very disagreeable, [for] we find it impossible to catch more than a word or two here or there, either in her recitative, dialogue, or cavatina" (51). Even some critics who welcomed English translations complained of this problem. A journalist for the *National Intelligencer* in Washington expressed delight on 14 April 1856 that the Pyne and Harrison troupe's performances there would "afford our citizens an excellent opportunity to hear the 'gems of the great masters' warbled in the English tongue." After a performance of *The Barber of Seville*, however, he admitted disappointment. "It is exceedingly difficult to adopt the remarkably rapid music of this opera to expression in English," he conceded on 21 April 1856. "The notes are nearly all very vivacious, following each other so rapidly as to make it utterly impossible for any singer to utter them in English words so as to be comprehended." Another reviewer was more blunt. "The greatest farce in modern days," he wrote in the *Spirit* on 14 August 1847, "is the *English* opera; for were it not so written down, from all I heard last evening, the opera might as well have been sung in 'illigant Irish,' or the pure Choctaw" (296).

Despite the numerous complaints, opera in English was welcomed by many, especially those who lived away from the urban centers of the East Coast. "The people demand [translated] operas," wrote a critic for the *Spirit* on 21 August 1847, "and care not about hearing them in any other language but the vernacular; they want to listen *understandingly* to the *story*, and get all, or at least as much of the original music as can be adapted to English words" (308). That this general sentiment had not changed by the mid–1850s is demonstrated clearly by the success of the Pyne and Harrison troupe; as the *Musical World* pointed out on 4 June 1859, "English opera is popular with a large class of our citizens" (3).

English Adaptations in the Pyne Company Repertory

The people who adapted operas to the English stage during the first half of the nineteenth century tended to be musicians connected with the theater. The adapted works in the Pyne Company's repertory, in fact, represent the efforts of a large number of British musicians, many of whom had some association with the London stage.[55] But the adaptation of foreign-language operas for English-speaking audiences was not limited to musicians who lived in Great Britain. It was a commonplace activity on this side of the Atlantic as well. Theater orchestra directors, opera company managers, and even performers constantly tinkered with versions of their favorite operas, tailoring them to suit their own needs or the needs of their companies. For example, Charles Edward Horn (chapter 1), who was the musical director at the Park Theatre in New York in the 1830s, made adaptations of Rossini's *La Cenerentola* and Mozart's *Die Zauberflöte*.[56] Anna Bishop's manager and companion Bochsa also tried his hand at arranging; in the soprano's repertory was an opera titled *Judith,* which was described as a potpourri of selections from Verdi's operas "as assembled by Bochsa."[57] Furthermore, the *Spirit* reported on 16 October 1852 that a newly formed Anna Bishop Opera Company planned to mount a production of Donizetti's *Lucia di Lammermoor,* "the whole opera [as] arranged by the indefatigable Bochsa, to suit the English version" (420). Thomas Comer (1790–1862), for many years the music director and orchestra leader of the Boston Theatre, made an arrangement of *La Cenerentola* that was performed there in December 1850. Henry Drayton, later the manager of the Drayton Parlor Opera Company, arranged Halévy's *La Juive* for a performance in 1854; George Loder (1816–68), a conductor of various American theater orchestras and later musical director for the Anna Bishop and Lyster companies, arranged Auber's *L'Ambassadrice* for a performance in New York in 1851; and the vocal star John Wilson made an arrangement of Adolphe Adam's *The Postillion of Longjumeau* in the 1830s.[58] Henry Horncastle made at least one operatic adaptation of Auber's *La Bayadere* (chapter 1), and *The Beggar's Opera* as performed by the Pyne and Harrison Company was "adapted to the Modern Stage by Mr. W. Harrison" himself.[59]

By far the two most important adaptors of works for the English and American stage during the period were the British musicians Michael Rophino Lacy and Sir Henry Rowley Bishop. Lacy (1795–1867), a violinist, playwright, actor, and leader of the ballet orchestra at the King's Theatre in London, was responsible for the adapted versions of numerous operas, including *Ivanhoé* (a pasticcio of numbers from Rossini operas), *Il Turco in Italia, Der Freischütz, The Israelites in Egypt, La Sonnambula,* and *Lucia di Lammermoor*.[60] Better known, however, were his versions of *Fra Diavolo* and *La Cenerentola,* which he renamed *Cinderella; or, The Fairy Queen and the Little Glass Slipper*.[61] Published libretti and newspaper advertisements confirm that the latter two works were the versions the Pyne and Harrison Company used during their American tour.[62] Henry Rowley Bishop (1786–1855), the dominant theatrical composer in England during the second and third decades of the nineteenth century, served at various times as the director of music at both Covent Garden and Drury Lane theaters. He had a hand in some 125 works presented on the London stage between 1805 and 1840. Some twenty-five were adaptations, including *John of Paris, The*

Libertine (after Mozart's *Don Giovanni*), *The Barber of Seville*, *The Marriage of Figaro*, *Der Freischütz*, *William Tell*, and *La Sonnambula*.[63] During the antebellum period, many English opera troupes, including the Pyne and Harrison Company, used Bishop's well-known and easily obtained versions of these operas.[64]

Italian and French operas, when translated and adapted for the English stage, were essentially transformed into English comic operas (chapters 1 and 2). Recitative, where present, was replaced with spoken dialogue (although some French operas such as *Fra Diavolo* already had spoken dialogue). Solos, duets, and some choruses were acceptable, but long concerted pieces often were replaced with shorter, simpler songs, sometimes strophic. A song that could be published separately as sheet music with the tag "as sung by the celebrated [favorite prima donna] to immense applause at [famous] theatre" was an obvious goal. Some adaptors added music and dances not in the original score and occasionally tinkered with the text itself. The changes depended to a great extent on the opera, but the result was closer to a play with many songs and ensemble numbers than to an opera as performed at La Scala, the Royal Italian Opera in London, or the Astor Place Opera House in New York. Of course, many eighteenth- and nineteenth-century operas were based on plays, which under the theatrical conventions of the time were performed with generous amounts of music. The operatic adaptations by Lacy, Bishop, and their compatriots can thus be thought of as plays regenerated from operas. These "reclaimed" dramatic works had more characteristics of the latter than the former, however, for the adapted operas included significantly more, and higher quality, music than had the original versions.

Henry Bishop's adaptations used music by the original composer of the opera (changed and unchanged), music by other composers, and pieces of his own composition. He automatically turned the recitative into spoken dialogue. This, however, should not be considered a simplification or a technique of "adaptation," but rather a perfectly normal change under prevailing theatrical conventions; furthermore, it did not significantly alter the musical content of the work. In his adaptation of *The Marriage of Figaro*, however, there was significant alteration: Bishop added ten songs and six dances of his own composition. He also introduced a character (Fiorello from Rossini's *Barber of Seville*) to sing Almaviva's music because the actor engaged for the part of the Count at the Covent Garden premiere was not a singer.[65] The alterations that Bishop made to *Don Giovanni* were also significant, but consisted primarily of modifications to Mozart's music, omission of some numbers (especially the complex finales), and shuffling of the order of numbers. The first act of Bishop's version is arranged as follows:

OVERTURE (to *Don Giovanni*)

1. "Come Shining Forth My Dearest" (Deh vieni alla finestra)
   Canzonetta (Don Giovanni)
   (from Mozart's *Don Giovanni*, number 16, from act 2)
2. "Leave Me, Forever Leave Me" (Fuggi, crudele, fuggi!)
   Duet (Donna Anna and Don Octavio)
   (*Don Giovanni*, number 2)
3. "Pretty Lasses Lover's Summer Remember" (Giovinette, che fatte all'amore)
   (Zerlina, Masetto, chorus)
   (*Don Giovanni*, number 5)
4. "Now Place Your Hand in Mine, Dear" (La ci darem la mano)
   Duet (Zerlina and Don Giovanni)
   (*Don Giovanni*, number 7)
5. "Pray Behold, Ma'am" (Madamina, il catalogo è questo), (Leporello)
   (*Don Giovanni*, number 4)
6. "Strangers, Pray This Way Bend You"
   (Leporello, Donna Anna, Donna Maria, Don Octavio)
   (from the minuet in *Don Giovanni*, number 14)
7. "Chide Me, Chide Me, Dear Masetto" (Batti, batti) (Zerlina)
   (*Don Giovanni*, number 13)
8. "Tremble, Traitor!" (Trema, trema, scelerato) septetto
   (from *Don Giovanni*, number 14)

Bishop's version included much less music than Mozart's; the complex finale has also been eliminated. (Some simplifications may have been absolute necessities; a contemporary listener might justifiably blanch at the imagined results of an attempt by the standard nineteenth-century American theater orchestra to negotiate the three-orchestra, three-rhythm section in the act 1 finale, for example.) Bishop also inserted into his second act a duet from *Die Zauberflöte*: "The Purest Flame This Bosom Warming" (Bei Männern, welche Liebe fühlen).[66]

In his adaptations, Bishop apparently left the original composer's music intact whenever possible. This was true even for sheet-music publications of arias. An example is his treatment of scene 3 of Bellini's *La Sonnambula*. The scene commences with a recitative ("Care compagne"), then proceeds to an aria ("Come per me serena") followed by the cabaletta "Sovra il sen la man mi posa"; both of the latter are sung by the character Amina. The soprano's two sections are separated by a chorus ("Sempre, o felice"); she is also supported by the chorus during the cabaletta. For sheet-music purposes, this scene consists of two songs separated by a chorus, which is precisely how Bishop dealt with the work: the recitative is omitted, the first cavatina is treated as a separate song, "Oh Love Me for Thy Power," and the second becomes another song, "While the Heart Its Joy Revealing."[67] Each song was published separately, and also together as a scena. In the latter version, a piano interlude connects the two, for which Bishop uses the accompaniment to the choral section. What is interesting about Bishop's "adaptation" is that the music is almost identical with Bellini's. Bishop transposes the songs into a key that is lower and easier to sing (F major, from the original A-flat major). Aside from that, however, the melody is all Bellini's; it is not "simplified" at all.[68]

Rophino Lacy's version of *Fra Diavolo,* as another example of an adaptation, is fairly close to the original. *Opéra comique,* of course, lends itself well to translation: the original versions have spoken dialogue rather than recitative, and the airs are more "tuneful" and less florid than the arias of Italian bel canto opera. Lacy leaves the plot of *Fra Diavolo* almost unchanged and uses most of Auber's music, although he substitutes shorter works for the several extended ensembles (the three finales) in the original. His sheet-music publications of some of the numbers, however, like Bishop's, are almost identical with Auber's versions. A note-by-note comparison of a nineteenth-century publication of one aria, "On Yonder Rock Reclining" (Voyez sur cette roche) with a modern piano-vocal score reveals fewer than a dozen insignificant changes in the popular romanza. All of the modifications, furthermore, are in the piano accompaniment, which is itself an arrangement from the orchestral score. The song itself is completely unaltered.[69]

Lacy's *Cinderella; or, The Fairy Queen and the Little Glass Slipper,* on the other hand, is vastly different from Rossini's *La Cenerentola* in both text and music.[70] Rossini's libretto omits two of the elements most familiar in the old fairy tale — the fairy godmother and the glass slipper — substituting an advisor to the prince for the former and a bracelet for the latter. Lacy's version keeps the prince's advisor, reinstates the godmother (now called the fairy queen), and returns the glass slipper to its place of prominence. He astutely draws attention to these alterations by the subtitle he added to his work.[71]

Cinderella was immensely popular and was sung for decades all over the country. Although some companies later altered even Lacy's version (dropping some of the ensemble pieces and interpolating different songs), others continued to use his adaptation, unaltered, as late as the mid 1860s.[72] *Cinderella* was far better known to American opera-goers than was *La Cenerentola;* it was also better liked, even by some members of the musical elite. When Marietta Alboni's Opera Company mounted a production of *La Cenerentola* in Boston in 1853, for example, no less a musical luminary than John Sullivan Dwight complained on 5 February that "the plot of this Rossini 'Cenerentola' was extremely meagre; it was emptied of all the charm of the nursery story; it had not even half the interest of the English version of Rophino Lacy; we missed the pieces of fine music which he combined into it from other operas, and which form the most abiding charm of the thing as we remember it in the days of the Woods and the Seguins" (143).

The "pieces of fine music" to which Dwight alludes represent Lacy's other abiding change in *Cenerentola*. Because of the alterations he had made, Lacy had to find or write additional music. He kept as many of the *Cenerentola* numbers as possible; although little of Rossini's version remains in Lacy's act 3, his acts 1 and 2 retain much of the original music. For the other numbers, however, Lacy chose a variety of arias from other operas by Rossini: *Maometto II, Armida,* and *Guillaume Tell.* His version, then, is an operatic pasticcio, but entirely of music by Rossini.[73]

A majority of the Pyne and Harrison Company's repertory consisted of these adaptations and translations. The troupe, however, took great pains to advertise that the operas they performed were "without abridgment or curtailment," "complete," "with the original music," or "given with the Whole of the Original Music."[74] Critics all over the country regularly commented on this aspect of the Pyne-Harrison troupe's performances. They were contrasted favorably, for example, with unnamed "second class artists [who] emasculate" certain operas, "retaining only that portion which has suited their limited capabilities" and with other "English and Italian artists" who produce "mutilated and garbled portions" of operas.[75] Music lovers were encouraged to attend performances by the Pynes and Harrison, for their troupe supposedly presented "complete opera[s] . . . intact" and offered the opportunity to hear "for . . . the first time" certain operas "without mutilation."[76] The "second class artists" may have been an oblique reference to Anna Bishop and Anna Thillon. Bishop tended to perform disembodied scenes from operas in her concerts; Thillon generally appeared in versions of operas that were so drastically pared-down as to be plays with songs. In comparison, the works that the Pyne and Harrison Company performed, although adapted and changed, would have seemed "intact" and "complete."

Originally scheduled for a three-week run at the St. Charles Theatre in New Orleans, the Pyne and Harrison Company performed there for a little more than two. The singers' arrival had been delayed for over a week, and the theater's manager Benedict DeBar did what he could to accommodate them. He had contracts of his own to honor, however, and the next performer—the actor James K. Murdoch—was scheduled to commence his engagement on 9 February.[77] The company's success in opera-happy New Orleans had been so great (one scholar of the

New Orleans stage called their engagement "an outstanding attraction" and their performances of *Cinderella* an "overwhelming success") that the singers were reluctant to leave.[78] The other English theater in town, the Gaiety, was a variety house that offered fare including comedy, vaudeville, farce, and ballet deliberately chosen to not compete directly with the productions of the St. Charles Theatre.[79] The management of the Gaiety had recently changed hands, however, and the new actor-manager Dion Boucicault had both a redecorated theater and a full thirty-piece orchestra at his disposal. As a consequence, although he was reluctant to compete with the St. Charles, when William Brough approached him about engaging the Pynes and Harrison he expressed interest, especially if the other theater could not accommodate the company. The Gaiety, however, had available in its schedule only a portion of a week, and that started on 20 February, twelve days hence. If the singers wanted to avail themselves of the chance to mount opera for a few additional nights in New Orleans, they had to find something else to do in the interim.

Brough's next move is a good example of the type of scheduling improvisation typical of itinerant companies. He presumably shot off some telegrams to the nearest large town, Mobile, Alabama. Brough discovered that although the Mobile Theatre and its orchestra were booked, it was possible to engage the Odd Fellows' Hall for four evenings.[80] The receipts from four concerts looked much better than the receipts from lying idle for a week, so on 6 February he left for Mobile to arrange for the company's appearances there. The troupe followed him two days later, traveling by rail and steamboat.[81]

Mobile was an important theater town in antebellum America, with good facilities and a reputation for supporting opera. Brough had performed there numerous times on his various travels as a singer; the local newspaper described him as a "gentleman . . . well known to our musical citizens from years past."[82] When the Pynes and Harrison troupe announced that they intended to perform only in concert, the local critics expressed resigned disappointment. "This evening the far-famed . . . Pyne and Harrison Troupe, will make their first appearance in Mobile at the Odd Fellows' Hall, in a Concert and Operatic Entertainment—the latter being selections from the well-known opera of 'Sonnambula.' Much as we regret that we cannot hear the entire opera (especially as we hear the present party are the best that has appeared in this country), yet, we must feel content with the installment offered to us."[83]

Despite the city's reputation, Reiff was not impressed with either Mobile (he called it "a miserable dirty hole") or the hall in which the company performed, which he described as "nearly square—with a small staging backed by an Arch—through the back of which the performers enter—the Hall . . . has rather too much reverbera-tion . . . [it] will seat between Six and Seven hundred . . . there are no galleries" (11–12 February 1856). Reiff found the countryside, how-ever—especially Mobile Bay—to be unlike anything he had ever seen. He marveled at the natural beauty and constantly expressed delight at being outside in shirtsleeves in February. He also made numerous friends among the townspeople, many of whom were eager to entertain a visiting celebrity. The owner of the city's music store, according to Reiff, was "very anxious for me to come here to teach" (11 February 1856). While in Mobile, he witnessed his first slave auction (which he thought "absolutely horrible") and was again mistaken for a foreigner—this time in church, by a minister who "preached a sort of Know Nothing sermon and once when he said Foreigner . . . he pointed *at me*" (18, 17 February 1856).[84]

The four performances in Mobile were billed as "Concerts and Operatic Entertainments." Advertisements, reviews, and notices like the one quoted mention only that the first half of each performance was a "concert of miscellaneous vocal music," and the second half "gems" from an opera, sung "in character costume," according to the *Daily Advertiser.* The general public crowded the hall in gratifyingly large numbers. Although some Mobilians were disappointed that the company did not mount any operas, the sentiment expressed by the editor of the *Daily Advertiser*—that a concert was better than noth-ing—evidently was shared by many. The Mobile critic, who obviously preferred to hear operatic selections in English, wrote favorably of the troupe's performances. "There was no attempt at display," he pointed out on 15 February, "no assumptions of foreign manners or style—but we had the good old English all the way through." On 19 February he sent the artists on their way back to New Orleans with "the best wishes of our musical community."

Half-way through their tour, the Pyne and Harrison Company was enjoying a financially successful trip; the troupe had attracted large audiences wherever they performed. Perhaps as a reflection of this wealth, their accommodations en route were, if not first class, certainly more than adequate. The *Thomas Swan,* on which they had traveled to New Orleans, was a first-class steamer, and the stars of the company (if not the entire troupe) had lodged at the tony St. Charles Hotel during their stay in that city, according to the *Daily Picayune* of 23 January. The singers traveled back to New Orleans from Mobile by way of "a very fine vessel," the steamer *Cuba.* Their luxurious state-rooms, according to young Reiff, were "the most complete things of the kind I ever saw"; his was equipped with a marble-topped washstand, small sofa, chairs, two berths, and a looking glass (19 February 1856). The stars—Harrison, the Pynes, Horncastle, and Stretton—usually stayed in first-class hotels, while the rest of the troupe was lodged at boardinghouses. When Reiff mentioned accommodations, however, his comments were always favorable.[85] Evidently, Brough took care of all travel and lodging details; some individual musicians, but probably not the stars, were responsible for their own trunks.

Back in New Orleans, the company performed for four evenings at the Gaiety, a theater Reiff described as "not as wide as Niblo's but about as deep—having but Two Tiers of Boxes—[it] is beautifully filled up—good seats and well lighted" (23 January 1856). The admission was a uniform 75 cents to all parts of the house, according to the *Picayune* of 20 February; the next day (the day after the troupe's opening performance) the paper noted, "this beautiful theater was tested as an opera house last evening for the first time, and the result was auspicious." After four performances, the company headed north in late February; they were already booked into the St. Louis Theatre for an engagement in March. As usual, Brough left several days earlier than the rest of the troupe.

Heading North and Back East

The trip by steamer from New Orleans to St. Louis is a long one— almost 1,200 miles—and Brough intended to break it up by having the company give concerts in Natchez and Memphis. Neither town was large enough to warrant a full opera season, but cities of such size could usually be counted upon to supply a large crowd for a concert or two.[86] On 7 February, the *Daily Picayune* reported that the Parodi-Strakosch concert company had just completed "a tour of most successful concerts in Baton Rouge, Vicksburg, Jackson, Natchez, &c, where, at double our New Orleans prices, they had [attracted] crowded rooms every night they performed." The citizens of Memphis were intensely interested in a proposed concert by the Pynes and Harrison. On 2 March the *Daily Appeal* trumpeted an announcement: "Our readers will be pleased to learn that [the] Pyne and Harrison celebrated Opera Troupe will visit our city. . . . We feared our city would not offer sufficient inducements to make it profitable for them to visit us, but it appears that we are, so prepare, ladies and gentlemen for the great operatic entertainment. Due notice will be given of their arrival." Unfortunately for Brough's well-laid plans and fairly tight schedule, Louisa Pyne fell ill in New Orleans. The *Daily Picayune* announced on 26 February that "Miss Louisa Pyne, the charming vocalist, remains quite ill, at the St. Charles Hotel in this city, and the troupe of which she is the chief feature are obliged, in consequence, to postpone their western engagements."

Feigned illness was often used as a weapon by Italian vocal stars in both their struggles with the management and their squabbles with each other. During this period, however, there were no English companies in the United States large enough to hire rival prima donnas, and the spectacular fights in which the Italian artists so often engaged were almost unknown among English singers. Real illness, however, was a constant danger that stalked all itinerant performers. Both Louisa Pyne and William Harrison had been sick in Cincinnati, necessitating a postponement of their first performance there and the cancellation of another. According to Reiff, Pyne often came down with a cold or fever of one kind or another, and she was not alone. Early in the tour on 19 January he commented laconically on the general health of the troupe's stars: "Stretton sick with a slight touch (I reckon of Fever and Augue)—Susan Pyne somewhat recovering from her Neuralgia and Harrison from his Boil—Louisa Pyne laid up with Boils—and Horncastle going about with an enormous stye in his eye. Good party." Reiff betrayed youthful confidence in his own good health at this point, but he did not always feel so well himself. On 12 February in Mobile he complained of feeling "very ill with a severe Colic and Bilious attack," and on 17 February was "very unwell—costive and bilious." Later in May, when the company performed in Baltimore and Washington, he complained for two weeks of feeling "very unwell." On several days he was sick enough to necessitate staying in bed; after one rehearsal his friend Atherton told Reiff that he had been "very Morose in the Orchestra this morning" (13, 17 May 1856).

In addition to sickness and ill-health, itinerant performers also had to face the danger of accidents so common to steamboat travelers. Explosions and fires—with resultant loss of life—were very real events, and the Pyne and Harrison troupers had several moments of excitement. When the company left New Orleans for St. Louis, for example, they headed into a serious storm; the pilot had difficulty keeping his steamer on course, for "the wind was blowing a perfect gale, the rain came down in torrents, and the vessel shook terrifically." Furthermore, sparks came out of the smokestacks "in myriads" and were blown all about the boat. "Many of the passengers," Reiff noted on 26 February, "were much frightened"; the singer Gohr advised him not to go to bed, "for we are in imminent danger" of blowing up. The fear on this occasion came to nothing, but the troupe's other adventure could have been a calamity. The steamer *Cuba,* on which the company had traveled from Mobile back to New Orleans, was evidently also a packet boat, for during their transit it carried a large quantity of cotton. The bales,

Reiff noted on 19 February, were "so piled that it is almost impossible to get about on the mail deck—small passages are left—through which only *one man* at a time can go—" Such overloading was not uncommon and presented no real hazard—except that cotton is flammable, and sparks tend to fly from steamers' smokestacks. As Reiff recounted their experience,

> [Frank] Swan and I (just after Sundown) were sitting in the Bow, on some Cotton Bales . . . when we were aroused by smelling something burning, upon looking around we saw the Cotton was on *Fire!* Just inside the doors—(which shut out the forward part of the Vessel)—some men were pulling a Bale from the inside—they got it upon the outside—but were unable to throw it overboard in consequence of its being so *much* on Fire. Swan made a terrific *dash* [up] the stairs . . . in the shortest space of time—he dashed through the Cabin, into his State Room—the Passengers, seeing [him], some of them bolted out—and we had quite a panic on the "forward" part of the Vessel—I was only for an instant a little nervous—it was when I look'd to see how near Land we were—in one direction only could I see land and that was almost imperceptible from the distance it was away—my next glance [was] at the laden Vessel (Cotton, Cotton, and only two small Boats to save us)—However [the nervousness] was only momentarily, for I thought [the fire] would get put out *somehow*—.

Luckily, Reiff was correct. The fire was extinguished, and disaster was averted.

The company's St. Louis engagement was to commence on 10 March, and despite the prima donna's illness Brough was unable—or unwilling—to postpone it. St. Louis was an important theater town in antebellum America; in the South it was ranked second only to New Orleans.[87] None of the company members wanted to risk a repeat of their New Orleans scheduling problems, and Pyne's prolonged illness was cause for alarm, for it both complicated the travel arrangements and jeopardized the announced concerts in Natchez and Memphis. The citizens of the latter city remained optimistic but became increasingly apprehensive, especially when the stars did not show up for the scheduled performance on 4 March (the rest of the troupe was already in town), according to the *Daily Appeal* of 5 March. "We trust our citizens will not be disappointed," the local editor had written hopefully on 4 March, "and that the troupe will be able to meet their engagement." That the company could not perform without Louisa Pyne clearly indicates the troupe's overwhelming dependence, like many other companies, on its star singer or singers. When Pyne still did not appear on 5 March—the last date on which a concert could be given—the rest of the troupe left. The *Daily Appeal* lamented this development on 6 March: "An unavoidable disappointment.—Owing to the sickness of Miss Louisa Pyne, attached to the Opera Troupe of Pyne & Harrison, no concert was given last night. Having exhausted the time allowed for their stay in Memphis, the Troupe took its departure up the river yesterday afternoon. The public regret this."[88]

The Pyne and Harrison Company arrived in St. Louis on Saturday, 8 March 1856. To everyone's relief Louisa Pyne rejoined them that weekend, and they were able to commence their engagement on schedule the following Monday. Simultaneously engaged at the St. Louis Theater was the Montplaisir Ballet Troupe, an ensemble of French dancers. As was the case with Maretzek's company, the larger Italian troupes sometimes engaged dancers to add luster and variety to performances. Few of the smaller companies—and no English troupes—had the resources required for this additional attraction. It was not unusual, however, for the paths of itinerant opera and dance troupes to cross on the American theatrical circuit. When this happened, the two companies often teamed for joint performances, as did the Pyne-Harrison and Montplaisir troupes.[89] On several nights in St. Louis the dancers performed after the opera: the ballet "Capricious Widow" followed *Daughter of the Regiment* on Friday, 14 March, and a "Grand Pas de Deux" was performed after *Maritana* on the nineteenth. On other evenings the dancers were featured as part of the opera performances. Mme. Clocca, for example, danced a grand pas de deux during the first act and a Bohemian polka during the second act of *The Bohemian Girl* on 11 March.[90]

According to newspaper advertisements, the Pynes, Harrison, and their entourage were engaged in St. Louis for only one week. The company, however—to the surprise of no one—was "re-engaged" at the conclusion of the first six days. This standard policy of "re-engagement" was a conventional managerial ruse designed to increase attendance. It was also possible for a company to leave "prematurely" without disgrace if audiences were small.[91] As such it was similar to other familiar managerial techniques: the false or misleading announcements of "final" performances, for example, or the much bally-hooed, endless "farewell" engagements and tours. The company did prove to be popular in St. Louis and was reengaged a second time, for a total visit of three weeks' duration. The critics, as expected, were complimentary. The *Daily Democrat* gushed that "such music was never before heard in our city" and concluded that the company "are fully equal to that fame which has preceded them." The engagement of the troupe, the critic wrote, "has produced great interest among the public here, whose fine musical taste is well known. Not only do the large and fashionable audiences attest how decided an impression has been created, but the prevailing topic of the day is the beautiful vocalization of Miss Louisa Pyne."[92]

Evidently, music lovers even in such a remote western city as St. Louis were aware of the current controversy about English versus Italian opera. The same critic attempted to disarm any possible negative re-action to the troupe's English performances. "To our mind — or, better, ear," he wrote on 13 March,

> it makes but little difference whether the opera we hear is English or Italian, so far as the mere words are concerned; and after all, we cannot pretend to say which of the texts is the more intelligible. . . . The troupe then, now performing at the St. Louis Theater gains nothing in our affections by being an *English* Opera Troupe. Miss Pyne would sing in any tongue as divinely as in her native accent. Her voice in no wise depends upon the vocabulary of any particular people. Let her sing in what phrase she will, her voice would always to us retain its smoothness, its sweetness, its extraordinary power to sweep the heart strings, and linger in the memory like the poetry of a beautiful dream.

The company finally packed up its costumes and headed east via rail on 31 March. Reiff's descriptions give glimpses of the vast stretches of near-frontier that separated the pockets of urban culture where the opera singers performed. "In the Woods," he wrote on 1 April, "[we] passed a cluster of very primitive looking Log huts — the children and women about them were dressed in the rudest, rustic, most wild manner possible." The next day, in Indiana, he described a "dense Forrest — of Beach (or Beech) Poplars — and some Sycamores — occasionally a few acres are cleared and some few common Log Huts or Cabins meet the view." En route from Louisville to Cincinnati, he wrote at length on 4 April:

> the [railroad] has only been through here a short time — yet villages are springing up all along — the first one we came to will serve as an ex-ample — in the midst of the Forrest was about two acres cleared — that is to say the Trees cut down for the stumps still remained in the ground — and the general "debris" had not been taken away — a store was erected and three houses — all entirely new — not a particle of paint — no fences — nothing in fact — yet this may be the commencement of a large town — Stretton remarked in 25 years I *might* be giving a concert here. The Rail Road builders — in making this road have cut down an *immense* quantity of the largest Trees — which lie rotting — it seems quite shock-ing — Horncastle says he cannot bear to look at it — (the prodigal waste of wood) — it seems *too* bad — Occasionally we pass some Cabins —.

The troupe gave two "Grand Operatic Entertainments" at Mozart Hall in Louisville, and the next day traveled to Cincinnati and gave a "Grand Farewell Operatic Concert" that evening.[93] The local hall, Smith and Nixon's, was otherwise engaged, so the singers performed in the dining room of the Burnet House Hotel, which was fitted up as a "concert saloon."[94] Despite the makeshift surroundings, the concert by Cincinnati's acclaimed "favorite Opera Troupe" was a success. More than four hundred tickets had been sold two days before the performance, and on the evening of the singers' appearance the room was "crowded to its utmost capacity."[95] Following this concert the performers had a well-earned weekend off, allowing them to relax and to bask in the plentiful adulation the local citizens bestowed on the visiting celebrities.[96] By this time the troupers had been on the road for four and a half months. Reiff noted on 5 April that he was "quite a happy man"; the next day, however, he was not sure, commenting "I begin to feel anxious to get home." The company, however, had yet another six weeks to go.

On 7 April the performers boarded the side-wheeler *Pittsburgh* for their return trip up the Ohio. Most of their fellow passengers, according to Reiff, were a "rough-looking set—western all over—they 'reckon, mighty smart, thar and bar'—to an awful extent." The members of the opera troupe stood out in such company. "Stretton's dignified mustache, Horncastle's portly form, and my impudent manner—combined with the fact that we are more fastidious and give more trouble than any one else," Reiff noted humorously on 7 April, "established the fact that *we were the people!*" William Brough had left the troupe in Cincinnati the previous week and by 5 April was already in Baltimore busily arranging for the company's next series of engagements.[97] His charges, separated from their agent for almost a week, quickly missed his sure managerial hand and encountered transportation difficulties when they arrived at Wheeling, Virginia. Reiff was dismayed by the prospect of having to cross the mountains at night, although his reasons are unclear. More significant was the fact that there were not enough seats on the train for all the troupe. The only alternative was for the company to wait until the next day, which was impossible because they had a performance scheduled in Baltimore on Thursday evening. Both Horncastle and Reiff were very angry, but there was little they could do. The part of the company that could secure passage did so (Reiff took the last seat in the last car) and left the rest—including the bass Joseph Stretton and some of the choristers—behind. They were to follow on Thursday.[98]

The company traveled all night across the Allegheny Mountains. On 9 April Reiff described scenery that was "wild and rude in the extreme." He continued, "rude cabins are met with, built in all sorts of extraordinary places—on the steep sides of a hill, on the banks of streams—or in a hollow—the very children belonging to these Cabins seem to partake of the wildness of their Houses—and no wonder for they are completely shut out from the world." As the musicians progressed eastward, however, the surroundings became more familiar. "We are now running along the Potomac River," he wrote that same day, after leaving Cumberland, Maryland. "The face of the Country is large hills . . . frequently farms—looks more eastern—no Cabins."

As the tour neared its end, the pace of travel became increasingly hectic. The train deposited the company in Baltimore on 10 April, and the performers rehearsed all afternoon and presented *Cinderella* the same evening. The missing choristers made a difference in the performance, for a critic complained in the *Daily Republican* on 11 April that "the chorus lacked somewhat both in numbers and melody." After this rather uncommon brief engagement (one-night stands usually were devoted to operatic concerts), the company traveled to Washington, D.C., the next day to commence an engagement at the National Theatre on Monday, 14 April. A Washington newspaper, the *National Intelligencer,* reported on 12 April that "a number of carriages passing up [Pennsylvania] Avenue conveying baggage labelled 'Pyne and Harrison Opera Troupe,' herald the approach of that unrivaled company." At the National the troupe performed six different operas from their standard repertory (Table 17).[99] The company found itself competing once again with the Parodi-Strakosch concert troupe, which was performing at Odd Fellows' Hall. As before, however, the English opera company held its own against the Italians.[100] The critic for the *National Intelligencer* was rather self-congratulatory in his comments on 21 April. "It is a somewhat remarkable occurrence that in this city, at a season of frequent social entertainments and festivities, two great musical enterprises should experience such decided success; but the import of this popular verdict is that both are eminently worthy of the popular favor. Both indeed were triumphs, and both, or rather each, will at any future time be gladly welcomed back to our city."

Earlier that week the *Evening Star* had reported that "Parodi, with Patti and other members of her troupe" attended the English company's performance of *Maritana*. The Italians, the critic noted approvingly on 17 April, "testified their generous appreciation of the merits of the performance by repeated applause." That same evening, according to Reiff, President Franklin Pierce "visited the opera."

Saturday morning, 20 April, found the weary travelers again on the road. They gathered up their trunks, costumes, and music and boarded the steamboat *Baltimore* to travel down the Potomac to Aquia Creek, then by rail to Richmond, Virginia. The pressure was beginning to wear on some of the performers. On the way down to Richmond the singers Proctor Kemble, G. H. Warre, and Henry Horncastle got "horribly drunk." Reiff noted on 20 April that he and another singer, Mr. Gohr, "were almost obliged to carry Horncastle to the Broad Street House, by which means my baggage was locked up and I could not get it until next morning."

The pressures of constant traveling, coupled with those generated by nightly performances and close contact with the same people over a long period, had predictably disastrous consequences for opera troupes. Hints of discord between Jane Shirreff and Edward Seguin had surfaced in their small vocal-star ensemble's tour (chapter 2), and numerous examples exist of abortive Italian companies that fell apart under the pressure of financial difficulties or simple internal dissension (chapter 3). English opera troupes were not immune from such problems. Both of the opera companies that Anna Bishop attempted disbanded after several months on the road. Less is known about other English troupes, except that the musical-theatrical press occasionally announced that a particular singer had left the folds of one company and had either joined another or had struck off on his or her own.

For all its outward appearances of harmony, at least on this tour, the Pyne Company's performers had their share of squabbles and strife. In New Orleans the troupe lost its second tenor, who subsequently had to be replaced.[101] In the midst of the tour, furthermore, Reiff mentioned that Louisa Pyne and Harrison had a disagreement (he referred to the two as "Pocahontas and Smith"). In the same entry he noted that "some words occurred between Harrison and Susan [Pyne;] she gave him fits."[102] Reiff himself, something of a hothead, managed to get into a scuffle with Mr. Atkins, a singer, over some derogatory remarks the latter made about Americans. A knock-down, drag-out fistfight was averted only when Joseph Stretton intervened and kept Reiff company for the entire evening.[103] Despite their occasional problems, however, the Pyne and Harrison Company presented a remarkably harmonious front to the public, especially compared with the combative Italians. This no doubt contributed to their phenomenal success.

The company performed operas for a week in the Virginia capital, presenting almost precisely the same repertory as the previous week in Washington.[104] They ended their engagement on Tuesday, 29 April with a grand musical entertainment—an operatic concert—at the Metropolitan Hall. The performance was given at the request of "many of our most influential ladies, who, with others, were prevented from attending the operas at the Theatre, and who are most desirous of hearing Miss Louisa Pyne and her talented troupe of vocalists ere they leave our city," according to the *Richmond Enquirer* of 29 April. Some music lovers—even those not barred from theaters for religious reasons—preferred the potpourri of an operatic concert to the more rigorous structure of an opera. One critic, for example, had explained in the *New Orleans Daily Picayune* on 23 January that "in the concert room" Louisa Pyne was "unhampered by the requisitions of the opera [and furthermore] she [could] make such selections from her repertoire as [to] enable her to display to the fullest extent the wondrous witchery of her powers." Italian and English performers alike were well aware of this bias on the part of some of their audience, and so occasionally chose operatic concerts for their benefit performances, thus attracting as large a crowd as possible. Because concerts were less expensive than were operas, profits to the beneficiaries increased.

The "stars" had yet another technique for "displaying to the fullest extent their powers": adding extra songs to the evening's entertainment, a common practice with all singers during the period. The principal singers of most English companies—like vocal stars or prima donnas of Italian troupes—either interpolated songs into the opera itself or sang them after the opera, between acts, or between the opera and a farce. The extra music was an expected part of the evening's performance, and the songs often were mentioned in advertisements or on playbills. For example, an advertisement in the 19 November 1855 *Baltimore Clipper* for a Pyne and Harrison Company performance of *The Daughter of the Regiment* noted that "in the course of the opera a choice selection of Songs, Chorusses, Duets, &c" would be sung. Sometimes specific tunes were named: a list of those performed by the Pyne and Harrison troupe indicates that American taste had not changed much since the days of the Shirreff/Wilson/Seguin Company tour in 1838–39. The songs tended to be favorite arias from other operas, songs from the popular repertory ("Home, Sweet Home" was a favorite, as were Irish or Scottish songs), or virtuosic songs designed to bedazzle the audience with the star's vocal skills. William Harrison usually chose "Then You'll Remember Me" or "Tis Sad to Leave Our Father Land," both from Balfe's *The Bohemian Girl;* "The Bay of Biscay" from John Davy's 1805 ballad opera *Spanish Dollars;* or the ballad "Oh! Whisper What Thou Feelest!," allegedly written for him by the English pianist Henry Brinley Richards. Louisa Pyne almost always sang "Lo! Here the Gentle Lark" by Henry Rowley Bishop; a vocal version of Pierre Rode's *"Air varié pour le violon,"* known colloquially as "Rode's Variations"; or a song that became her trademark, "The Skylark" by the English opera composer Julius Benedict. The three songs were all typical of the showy fare that touring prima donnas generally chose.

Benedict's composition, which inspired Pyne's American nickname "The English Skylark" (a counterpart, of course, to Jenny Lind's sobriquet "The Swedish Nightingale"), was published in New York in 1850 as "The Skylark, a Morning Song, as Sung by Miss Louisa Pyne at her Concerts in America."[105] It is a strophic setting of two innocuous verses and obviously designed as a vehicle for the virtuosic display of a soprano voice. Although not particularly complex harmonically, the work is not dull. What harmonic activity there is adequately supports and adds interest to the vocal part.

The notated melody itself is remarkably free of decoration, but the song, by its very nature, calls for birdlike trills and other embellishments. One of the several copies in the collection of the Library of Congress has embellishments written in pencil on the score; most of them are markings for trills. Of particular interest are repeated instructions to perform trills on notes an octave higher than written and uniformly pianissimo. A performance of such a song, con spirito, with numerous embellishments, and sung in places pianissimo, would have been stunning.

Pyne's performance had precisely this effect on many of her listeners. Her delicate voice—flexible, even, and true of intonation—was perfect for the performance of such a composition. "The appetite for Louisa Pyne's singing," a critic wrote in the *New Orleans Daily Picayune* on 3 February 1856, "especially of Bishop's [sic] Skylark Song, grows by what it feeds on. We have never known a more decided sensation made upon our audiences than that produced by her performance of this song." Her rendition moved some effusive admirers to compare her favorably with that midcentury paragon of soprano beauty, Jenny Lind. "Louisa Pyne's rendering of the 'Sky Lark,'" wrote one critic in the *Washington Evening Star* on 19 April 1855, "equalled that of Jenny Lind in similar pieces, if the taste and delicacy with which its wonderful passages were executed by Miss P. did not surpass the execution of the Lind in her Echo Song. [Pyne] has not the Lind's power of voice, but her execution of such passages of music as are the gems of the 'Sky Lark' touch the heart and charm the ear of a cultivated taste far more than Jenny Lind ever did in rendering her songs of that class." The *Cincinnati Enquirer*'s critic was even more assured of the superiority of the English Skylark. "Whatever may have been said of Jenny Lind and the whole cage of canaries that warbled in her trills," he wrote on 20 December 1855, "we defy the Swedish or any other nightingale to hear such notes as Miss Louisa Pyne gave last night in [Rode's Variations] without growing mute with astonishment, or 'pining with grief,' if not dying with envy, at being so far surpassed."

After their final grand concert in Richmond, the Pyne and Harrison troupe left Virginia for Washington on 30 April. For the next three weeks they alternated engagements in Washington and Baltimore. Their performances attracted some of the "largest and most fashionable audiences . . . ever seen" at the Holliday Street Theatre, according to the *Baltimore Clipper* of 6 May 1856. Another critic was particularly eloquent about the audience one evening. "The dress circle of the Holliday Street Theatre last night," he wrote on 10 April 1856 in the *Daily Baltimore Republican,* "presented one of the finest conventions of fashion and loveliness ever seen within the time-honored walls of that ancient temple of the drama. The variegated tissues, the rainbow-hued silks, the charming headdresses, and the gleaming, glittering jewelry with which the array of loveliness was enshrined and ornamented, presented more the semblance of a fairy garden than a mere matter of fact assembly of operatic admirers."

Anthony Reiff, however, confirms that such audiences also included ordinary Baltimoreans. The boardinghouse where he lodged during the troupe's Baltimore engagement was run by a Miss Emily, a "perfect precise affable Old Maid." Reiff gave tickets to her and to another woman who lived there. "Miss Emily was much pleased," Reiff recorded on 15 May 1856, "and Mrs. H. was almost crazy with delight—said she could scarcely restrain herself from jumping on the stage and kissing Miss Pyne—she wants to go to the Opera every night."

The final performance of the tour was on Friday, 23 May. The next day the travelers rose at 4:30 in the morning to catch a northbound train at 6. Twelve hours later, the musicians were back in their American home base, New York City, the trip finally over. Anthony Reiff recorded his jubilation by writing one word on the final page of his journal: "Hurrah!"

The Pyne and Harrison Company had been on the road for slightly more than six months. They had traveled close to six thousand miles and performed almost nightly, for a total of 108 opera and twelve concert appearances. Often they played to full houses and enthusiastic audiences. They performed in the increasingly developed and cultured cities of the East Coast, where they successfully challenged those who claimed that opera in Italian was the only viable form. More important, the English singers also took opera to the American interior—to cities that were growing and prospering yet were still very close to wilderness and frontier. They introduced many Americans to opera and also fulfilled a need and desire already there. Their very popularity clearly indicates that even Americans who lived in new cities but a short remove from the frontier loved music and theater.

The pattern established by Louisa Pyne, William Harrison, and other singers associated with them did not cease with the completion of the tour. After a brief rest in New York and performances at Niblo's and at the Athenaeum in Brooklyn, they left again—headed even further out into the American interior—north and west for engagements in

54. Louisa Pyne from the cover of a contemporary piece of sheet music (New York: Cook & Brothers, n.d.). The inscription "To Miss Louisa Pyne" is an indication of the adulation in which the soprano was held by the conclusion of the 1855–56 tour. The portrait—of a simple and modest-looking, yet attractive, woman— would have appealed to Americans who were increasingly suspicious of the pretentiousness of Italian prima donnas. (Music Division, New York Public Library)

NIBLO'S GARDEN
Monday, Sept. 3d, 1855,

THE

PYNE
AND

HARRISON
COMPANY.

In Donizetti's Comic Opera, in 2 acts,

DAUGHTER
OF THE

REGIMENT

MARIE, Vivandiere of the Regiment
MISS LOUISA PYNE

MARCHIONESS de BERKENFIELD
.... **MISS PYNE**

SERJEANT SULPIZIO...... **MR. BORRANI**

HORTENSIUS, Intendant to the Marchioness
.... **MR. HOLMAN**

Corporal Spontine.... } of the 23d. { **Mr. Chambers**
Corporal Grenadi .... } { ......**Mr. Hayes**
Notary..**Mr. Paul**
First Peasant ....**Mr. Jones**

TONIO ----- **MR. W. HARRISON**

Ladies, Gentlemen, Soldiers of the 23d,
Peasants, Servants, &c

The action is in the Tyrol. during the period of its invasion by the French

Act I. Mountain Pass overlooking the Plains,
Act II. A Splendid Sa'oon in the Chateau of the Marchioness de Berkenfold

Between the 1st and 2nd acts an Intermission of 20 minutes will be given for Promenade.

Books of he Opera for sale in the Garden.

☞ NO FREE LIST ☜
The Press Excepted.

The same system of careful supervision, which has obtained for this establishment its present high popularity, will be rigidly followed to ensure the comfort of the audience, maintain good order and prevent the intrusion of objectionable characters.

SPECIAL NOTICE

The Parquet, Dress Circle and Boxes will be thrown open to the Public without reservation of Seats, at a Standard uniform price

Tickets - - Fifty Cents
The only Seats that can be secured in advance, are

Orchestra Seats.............. ......One Dollar Each
Private Boxes...................Five Dollars Each

Box Office open from 8 A. M., till 3 P. M., for the Sale of Tickets and securing Orchestra Seats an Private Boxes only.

Doors open at seven: Performances commence at 8.
Curtain will rise at eight o'clock precisely

Tuesday, Bellini's Grand Opera of

Sonnambula
By the Harrison Opera Company

Due notice will be given of the next performance of the Grand Romantic Opera of

CINDERELLA

55. Playbill from a Pyne and Harrison performance of Gaetano Donizetti's *The Daughter of the Regiment* at Niblo's Garden in New York, 3 September 1855. At the bottom of the playbill the troupe typically advertised future performances, in this case mentioning two of their most popular works, Bellini's *La Sonnambula* and the Rossini/Lacy version of *Cinderella*. (American Antiquarian Society)

Montreal, Chicago, Detroit, and elsewhere.[106] During their three years in the United States the group took English opera all over the eastern half of the country, as far west as Madison, Wisconsin, and as far north as Montreal and Quebec. During their American visit they gave more than five hundred performances and more than a hundred concerts.[107] The very success of the Pyne and Harrison Company during their three years in North America—both on the East Coast and in the middle of the continent—slowed the progress of the upper-class attempt to limit the definition of opera to foreign-language performances with aristocratic overtones. Their success helped to foster a popularity of the genre among ordinary Americans; it also ensured that opera in most places in the country remained a normal part of the theatrical repertory. Finally, their success, like the success of so many other companies, indicates a great deal about the importance of opera within the musical culture of the antebellum United States. Completely forgotten today, the Pyne and Harrison Company was a force to be reckoned with in the North America of the 1850s.

Epilogue

[I] had intended to go to the Opera this evening, but it was so rainy and stormy that I concluded it would be more desirable to stay in the house, as we had a comfortable fire to sit by.[1]

In the late 1850s, the New York correspondent to *Dwight's* submitted a report about Max Maretzek's new Academy of Music opera troupe. After describing the various stars of the company, the orchestra, the manager, the conductor, and so on, he mentioned the troupe's practice of mounting afternoon performances. "A Matinée," he wrote on 5 June 1858, "is a very nice place to while away a leisure hour—so convenient to just drop in if you are out shopping, such a charming place for a little innocent flirting, and all that sort of thing" (78).[2] The American author and journalist Nathaniel Parker Willis, in a work of fiction written about the same time, expressed remarkably similar sentiments. "I was disappointed in the luxury I had allotted to myself for the evening," spoke one of the characters in his novel *The Convalescent*. "The promised opera was interrupted by the illness of the prima donna; and so my three hours of effortless recipiency—that deliciously reversed process to the day's weary givings-out of thought, talk, and action—were to be otherwise disposed of" (304).[3]

These contemporary descriptions of opera performances as pleasant and diverting activity sum up the attitudes of most antebellum Americans toward the genre: it was theater; it was entertainment. "The theatre in the first half of the nineteenth century," Lawrence Levine has explained, "played the role that movies played in the first half of the twentieth: [as] a kaleidoscopic, democratic institution presenting a widely varying bill of fare to all classes and socioeconomic groups."[4] It is in this context that opera in antebellum America can best be understood.

This proposition is supported not only by the prominent place of opera within the theatrical repertory of the time, but also by the American public's fascination with celebrities and by the pervasiveness of operatic music within American culture. The first is easy to document and has been discussed in earlier chapters. The techniques used by antebellum opera managers to advertise their performances, however, reveal Americans' infatuation with stars and are much like promotional techniques used on behalf of popular rock, cinematic, or "art-music" celebrities in the twentieth century. "Up and down Broadway," wrote a critic in the *Boston Musical Times* in March 1860, "we have portraits of [Adelina] Patti . . . and inside our hats and neck-ties her name [will] soon [appear]." A month later a correspondent from Baltimore reported to the same journal: "The success of the Opera at the Holliday St., Baltimore, was a glorious triumph. Nothing was talked of but 'Patti'; 'Patti hats,' 'Patti segars,' while one enthusiastic restaurant-keeper advertised 'Oyster-Pattis.' "[5] The celebrity nature of a company's stars was of paramount importance to the success of an opera troupe; this factor goes a long way toward explaining the popular appeal of opera performances. "The Opera is the rage," pointed out the *Spirit* on 19 February 1853. "Alboni is THE STAR in whose glory all other stars, however bright they may be 'on their own hook,' cannot help paling. Nobody seems to know a thing about the Opera—it's all Alboni—so [long as] SHE sings, it's the same to the listeners whether the Opera is 'Marie' or 'Cene'-something, which is the Italian for Cinderella" (1).

Walt Whitman—the former implacable foe of imported European opera, who by the 1850s had become a true convert to performances by Italian companies—described the same phenomenon, about the same artist:

> The best songstress ever in America was Alboni.—Her voice is a contralto of large compass, high and low—and probably sweeter tones never issued from human lips. The mere sound of that voice was pleasure enough.—All persons appreciated Alboni—the common crowd quite as well as the connoisseurs.—We used to go in the upper tiers of the theatre, (the Broadway), on the nights of her performance, and remember seeing that part of the auditorium packed full of New York young men, mechanics, "roughs," etc, entirely oblivious of all except Alboni, from the time the great songstress came on the stage, till she left it again.[6]

Completely aside from the allure of the stars, however, was the popularity—and familiarity—of the music being performed. In March 1847 George Templeton Strong, who only two months earlier had finally overcome his moral scruples about dramatic presentations, witnessed his first performance of *Il barbiere di Siviglia* at Palmo's. "Pleasant evening, rather," he wrote on the twenty-first. "Most of the music I'd heard before in some shape or other, and the music is perfect of its kind—lively, sparkling, and thoughtless, like the gabble of a French *soirée*."[7] That Americans who did not attend the theater were more than passing familiar with operatic music is clear. Extant published programs from concerts held in the United States during the nineteenth century almost invariably include a large number of operatic compositions, and these programs accurately reflect a reality of American concert life during the antebellum period. Concerts by opera singers, of course, were full of operatic music, but so, too, were instrumental presentations by touring orchestras, pianists, and violinists. Many of the concerts given by the Germania Musical Society (Figure 56) were in conjunction with such operatic stars as Jenny Lind, Adelaide Phillipps, Henriette Sontag, and Catherine Hayes, and as a consequence were heavily dominated by operatic music.[8] Extant programs, however, suggest that even their purely instrumental concerts were of a similar bent. Of eleven works presented during a "Grand Instrumental Concert" given in 1851, for example, seven were operatic in origin: the overtures to *Der Freischütz* and *Martha;* an "Introduction and Variations Brilliants, for Flute, on a Favorite Thema from Sonnambula"; a "Tergetto [*sic*] and Finale to the 2d Act of the Opera, 'Lucrezia Borgia,' Arranged for Orchestra"; a "Romanza, from the Opera 'Eclair' [*sic*] for Corno and Flute"; an "Aria, from the Opera, 'Favorita Spirito Gentil' " [*sic*]; and the "Grand Finale to the Opera, 'Maritana.' "[9]

Furthermore, the repertories of three European virtuoso pianists who toured the United States during the 1840s and 1850s—Leopold de Meyer (1816–83), Henri Herz (1803–88), and Sigismund Thalberg (1812–71)—were full of operatic transcriptions and fantasies on *Lucia di Lammermoor, Norma, I Puritani, Lucrezia Borgia,* and numerous other well-known and favorite operas.[10] These works were not only heard by thousands in concert halls, but they were also disseminated widely as sheet-music publications. "The Thalberg fantasies were all the rage for a time," remembered George Upton in 1908. "Every little piano thumper tackled them."[11] Other instrumentalists such as guitarists and flutists also had their choice of operatic arrangements (Figure 57). The reams of this type of sheet music still found today in libraries, museums, used bookstores, antique shops, and the attics of private residences across the country clearly demonstrate the former popularity of operatic compositions among American amateur musicians.

Anecdotes abound about amateur performances of operatic music; copies of arias and other tunes in sheet-music collections often show evidence of use. One example is a copy of Henry Bishop's version of "Sounds so Joyful" from *La Sonnambula* in the collection of the Library of Congress. A former owner has written the Italian text above the printed English words, presumably for her own performance ease. Charles Hamm has persuasively described this facet of American musical culture. In a discussion of sheet-music publications of numbers from

CITY HALL

The LAST Grand

INSTRUMENTAL

CONCERT!

THE

GERMANIA

MUSICAL SOCIETY.

Consisting of 23 Instrumental Solo Performers,

Respectfully announce to the Ladies and Gentlemen of Worcester and vicinity, that they will give

Only ONE More

CONCERT

On FRIDAY Evening, Oct. 3d,

AT THE

CITY HALL.

PROGRAMME.

PART I.

I. EXCELSIOR MARCH, by - - - J. STRAUSS.
II. OVERTURE TO THE OPERA WILLIAM TELL, - ROSSINI
III. DUBLIN WALTZ (introducing the air "the Last Rose of Summer.") LABETZKY
IV. INTRODUCTION & VARIATIONS BRILLANTS, for the Violin, on the Air "Je suis le petit Tambour," executed by MR. SHULTZE, DAVID
V. GRAND FINALE from Lucia de Lammermoor, - - DONIZETTI

PART II.

VI. OVERTURE to Shakspeare's Midsummer Night's Dream, (by request) MENDELSSOHN
VII. The Celebrated BIRD SONG, as sung by Mad'lle Jenny Lind, at her Concerts in the United States—arranged for the Orchestra by Mr. CARL BERGMANN, TAUBERT
VIII. LOVE POLKA, (Ach und Krach.) - - - BERGMANN
IX. DUETTO, from the Opera Belisaria—for Clarionett and Oboe DONIZETTI
X. SOUNDS FROM HOME, (by request,) Styrian National Melodies, performed by Mr. SCHULTZE.
XI. GRAND POTPOURRI, from the Opera The Daughter of the Regiment, - - - - DONIZETTI

TICKETS 50 CENTS EACH.

For Sale at the Hotels, Book Stores, and at the Door.

Doors open at 7—Concert commences at 8 o'clock.

Printed by Chas. Hamilton,—Palladium Office,—Worcester.

56. Broadside from two concerts given by the Germania Orchestra at City Hall in Worcester, Mass., 2–3 October 1851. The repertory illustrates the preponderance of operatic music, even on instrumental concert programs. (American Antiquarian Society)

Cinderella, he observes that "all evidence insists that [this music] was indeed performed in the American parlor and that these operatic songs became part of the popular song repertory. They were printed and sold in the same form, by the same publishers, in quantities equal to and even greater than earlier successful songs."[12]

A contemporary observer further supports this assertion. Lady Emmeline Stuart-Wortley, who published an account of a trip to the United States in 1849–50, described New Englanders as "generally a very quiet people, and very fond of music: we hear them playing and singing a great deal. Some of them sing exceedingly well, too, airs out of Italian operas."[13] The sound of this music became part of American consciousness; as early as 11 March 1826 the *New-York Mirror* pointed out that "we have only to call to our minds many favorite tunes, (and which are familiar and pleasing, because furnished with English words,) and we shall find they have been taken from *Italian opera!*" (262-63). "Italian melody," wrote Hamm, "became the most pervasive musical influence in America since Thomas Moore's *Irish Melodies.*"[14]

The pervasiveness of operatic—especially Italian—music was hardly limited to concerts, informal soirées, or the music racks of parlor pianos. Band concerts, for example, were full of operatic works. In 1857 John Sullivan Dwight described a series of Promenade Concerts in Boston that featured performances by military bands. The works offered, he wrote on 8 August, included overtures and "operatic arrangements" such as "the Trio from *Lucrezia Borgia,* the 'Miserere' from *Il Trovatore,* and endless potpourris from fashionable operas . . . &c. &c." (149–50, Figure 58). Music that bands performed at the mineral-springs resorts of Virginia included favorite works from the operatic stage; one visitor to Salt Sulphur Springs in 1856, for example, reported that the string band that entertained guests who were lounging and strolling about the grounds played "gems from the operas."[15] During the 1840s, the Marine Band's repertory included a "balance of musical styles represented by polkas, waltzes, quickstep arrangements of popular songs, and especially opera selections." Furthermore, operatic arrangements made by Francis Scala, the leader of the band from 1855 to 1871, included works by Auber, Bellini, Boieldieu, Donizetti, Flotow, Gounod, Meyerbeer, Offenbach, Rossini, Verdi, and von Weber.[16] Finally, the music that orchestras and bands played for dances—the most popular form of social recreation in the nineteenth century—was likewise heavily operatic. Although dance cards or programs from the antebellum period are scarce, the plentiful samples of such items from the 1870s, 1880s, and 1890s indicate clearly that arrangements from the musical stage—including operas—usually comprised more than half (and sometimes significantly more) of the music performed at such

57 and 58. Portions of the title pages of two sheet-music publications that illustrate some of the numerous arrangements for various instruments of operatic arias disseminated during the antebellum period. Top: "La Sonnambula Quickstep" as performed by the Boston Brass Band (Boston: Oliver Ditson, 1836). Bottom: "My Boyhood's Home," from Michael William Rooke's *Amilie,* as arranged for Spanish guitar (Philadelphia: G. Willig, 1840). (Music Division, Library of Congress)

functions.[17] Furthermore, countless arrangements of operatic music in the form of quadrilles, quick steps, waltzes, and other dances were published as sheet music during the antebellum years.[18]

A communication from Stephen Massett to the *Spirit* in 1852 reveals yet another method of disseminating operatic music. Writing about the forthcoming premiere of the opera *Peri* by the American theater musician James Maeder, he observed on 20 November that "three weeks after its production, the popular airs will be heard from every barrel-organ in the country" (480). The premiere of the popular *Bohemian Girl* in 1845 had created a raft of tunes that soon were "established favorites . . . whistled by every boy . . . and ground by every hand organ," according to the *New-York Mirror* of 29 April 1845. Twelve years later, on 14 February 1857 (156), the New York correspondent to *Dwight's* discoursed at length—and revealingly—about "popular street-organ music":

> Often, at night, when the streets are still and quiet, on returning from the opera your ear will catch the distant tones of some air you have just heard warbled by Lagrange or Parodi, floating from afar, like a sweet echo. At one corner the death-song in *Lucia* is wasting its sweetness on the desert air of Broadway, while in the next block the *Miserere* of *Trovatore* brings back memories of Brignoli or Tiberini. . . . Then the next moment we hear the *Casta Diva,* and as we pass on it merges into some of Verdi's passionate arias, till frequently a night walk in Broadway is one continued concert. . . .
>
> There is one air, however, without which a street organ would no more be a street organ than a man without a head would be a man. After Verdi and Donizetti, the street organs fall back upon the inevitable "Mira Norma," of Bellini, as if it were their *normal* condition. . . . when you hear the tones of a street organ in the distance, but too far off to distinguish the melody, you may be certain that it is "Mira Norma." As a distinguished poet aptly remarks:
>> Be weather clear, or damp, or stormy,
>> They're always playing, "Hear Me, Normy."

Another example of the ubiquity of operatic music in antebellum America is also about New York and from the pages of *Dwight's.* "Up in the belfry of Trinity," the correspondent wrote on 10 January 1857,

> the chimes are ringing out their welcome to Eighteen Hundred and Fifty-Seven, and their first song is . . . the sweet, familiar tones of "Home, sweet home." Let us stand there in front of the church and listen; all is still save that sweet music. . . . Soon, the melody changes, and the "Sicilian Mariner's Hymn" rings out more gladly . . . but even these fade, as with wild joy the belfry chimes ring out merrily the Brindisi from *Lucrezia,* and banish all sad thoughts, drive back the starting tear, bring a smile upon the cheek, and reminds us of the many happy, as well as

sad moments, the past year had brought us, and of the many happy plans we have formed for the New Year. (115–16)

A final—but very important—guise in which operas and operatic music became known was through the profusion of operatic burlesques seen and heard on the American stage. Starting in the late 1830s and continuing unabated through the 1850s and later, parodies with such titles as *Amy Lee [Amilie], The Bohea-Man's Girl, He Fries and Shoots! or, The Seven Charming Pancakes, Herr Nanny [Ernani], Lucy Did Sham Amour [Lucia di Lammermoor], Mrs. Normer, The Roof Scrambler [La Sonnambula], The Virginian Girl [The Bohemian Girl], Schinder El'ler,* and *Lend Her the Sham Money [Linda di Chamounix]* were performed in New York—and, slightly later, by itinerant burlesque opera and minstrel troupes—all over the rest of the country.[19] Contemporary criticism and the published examples that survive suggest that much of the original music was left intact. The humor was in the juxtaposition of familiar operatic music and lyrics with the ridiculous words and absurd situations of the burlesques. "The travesties on the Italian opera by the Ethiopian company at Palmo's," explained the *Spirit* on 5 July 1845, "give the entire musical features of a piece, although rendered grotesque by a slight distortion not exactly of notes but of the vocalists' countenances" (224). Another critic writing in the same periodical on 1 July 1854 described the music performed in a burlesque of *Cinderella* as "in a great measure very faithful to the original, although as relief bits, two or three of the favorite negro melodies are interspersed" (240). According to Vera Lawrence, a version of *The Bohea-Man's Girl* performed that same year included "vocal satire" such as a song titled "I Dreamt I Had Money to Buy a Shawl," a parody of the popular "I Dreamt I Dwelt in Marble Halls."[20] Another parody of this same *Bohemian Girl* perennial, arranged in four-part harmony with the tune intact and only the words changed (Figure 59), can be found in *The Ethiopian Glee Book,* an 1848 songster of "Popular Negro Melodies, Arranged for Quartett Clubs."[21] The unabashedly racist lyrics, in crude dialect but maintaining the rhyme scheme of the original, closely parody Balfe's song. The original lyrics are given first:

> I dreamt that I dwelt in marble halls,
> With vassals and serfs at my side,
> And of all who assembled within those walls,
> That I was the hope and the pride.
> I had riches too great to count, could boast
> Of a high ancestral name
> But I also dreamt, which pleas'd me most
> That you lov'd me still the same.

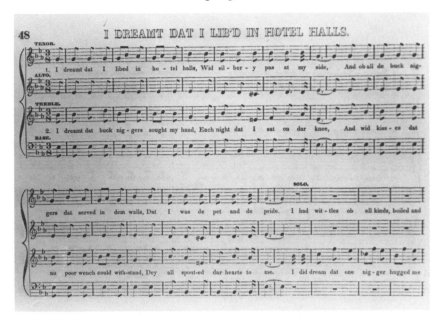

59. First page of a burlesque arrangement (in four-part harmony) of the extremely popular "I Dreamt that I Dwelt in Marble Halls," from Michael Balfe's *The Bohemian Girl*. This example, from *The Ethiopian Glee Book: A Collection of Popular Negro Melodies* (Boston: Elias Howe, 1848), is one of many burlesque arrangements of operatic arias found in mid-nineteenth-century American songsters. (Music Division, Library of Congress)

> I dreamt dat I libed in hotel halls,
> Wid silbery pans at my side,
> And ob all de buck niggers dat served in dem walls,
> Dat I was de pet and de pride.
> I had wittles of all kinds, boiled and roast,
> And dishes too many to name
> And I also dreamt, what charmed me most
> Dat I loved Coon still de same.[22]

Another songster, published in 1850 and also in the collection of the Library of Congress, included tunes "sung by the New Orleans Serenaders" and has another, less obvious, operatic parody: the barcarolle "Agnes la jouvencelle" from Auber's *Fra Diavolo,* retitled "Young Sue," arranged in four-part harmony and preserving the melody in the tenor voice. Furthermore, one of the few extant pieces of sheet music from an operatic burlesque—"The Phantom Chorus" (Figure 60), a parody on the chorus "A fosco cielo" in Act 1 of *La Sonnambula*—also

60. "The Phantom Chorus," from *La Sonnambula,* as arranged by Edwin
Pearce Christy (New York: C. Holt, Jr., 1848). (American Antiquarian Society)

preserves, but in a humorous manner, the sentiment of the aria as well
as the entire melody.[23]

If parodies of this nature were simply perpetuations of a shallow
stereotype of opera in general or opera singers in particular, then the
fact that such examples are widespread in the songster repertory would
suggest nothing more than Americans' knowledge of the stereotype.
The familiar modern image of a female opera singer as a heavyset
woman wearing a horned helmet, for example, hardly suggests that

late twentieth-century Americans are conversant with the operas of Richard Wagner or have any knowledge whatsoever of the character Brünnhilde. But mid-nineteenth-century operatic "dis-arrangers" clearly took great care with their parodies, often choosing a text that closely paralleled (or punned upon) that of the aria. Furthermore, the arrangers generally maintained the original rhyme scheme rigorously, at least of arias that were familiar in English or in English translation, as is illustrated by the parody of "I Dreamt" quoted previously. These carefully crafted burlesques were much more than simple, shallow, and stereotypical humor. The close alignment between original and parody made the burlesque versions more complex, sophisticated, and vastly more amusing. But the humor was predicated on the audiences' familiarity with the original material. This familiarity was crucial to the success of an operatic parody; as a writer for the *Spirit* casually mentioned on 31 March 1849, "the Christy Minstrels will forthwith proceed to burlesque the 'Enchantress' as a matter of course." He continued, "as soon as the songs of that opera become popular in the streets, she will come before the audience in a very neat Ethiopian costume" (72).

Operatic burlesques also sometimes went far beyond parodies of the music, the story, or song texts. Playbills suggest that the name of the composer, the names of characters, and the names of well-known operatic stars were also fair game. In 1845, according to Lawrence, the singers of the Ethiopian Burlesque Opera Company appeared under such aliases as Madame Pico (Rosina Pico), Madame McBuckwheat (Amalia Majocchi), Signor Aint-a-ninny (Antognini), and Signor De Big-Knees (de Begnis).[24] Again, one can conclude from such detailed parody only that intended audiences were quite familiar with operatic performances in the original versions.

The makeup of the audience at Mitchell's Olympic, and at other burlesque houses, is also revealing. Not only were the working and middle classes attracted to such spoofs, but so were the "fashionable and elite." On 6 March 1841 the *Spirit* remarked, "it is not a little singular that the audience in the dress circle of [the Olympic Theatre] is quite the most fashionable that can be collected at any theatre in this city." Ten years later, the enthusiasm had not abated. On 22 March 1851 a manager of a burlesque house announced in the *Spirit* that "the manager begs to state that the immense encouragement given to his celebrated Concerts, every evening for the last eleven months, by the elite and fashion of this great metropolis, has induced him to engage artists of the very first talent, to produce Burlesque Italian Opera Scenes, Burlesque Concerts and Ballets, in a style equal to the originals produced at the Italian Opera, of this city" (60). The *New-York Mirror,* at one point, claimed that the audience seen at the Italian opera on any one night was remarkably similar to that seen at Mitchell's Olympic the next.

The ubiquity of operatic music in the United States—and the variety of forms in which it appeared—demonstrate clearly that most Americans did not consider it as the chosen preserve of the musical and social elite. It was music that was simultaneously cultivated and vernacular, to use H. Wiley Hitchcock's apt terms. But although these terms might be appropriate for the discussion of music in the late-nineteenth and (especially) early-twentieth centuries, their use in reference to music of the antebellum period is problematical. Several scholars have recently argued that during the 1830s, 1840s, and 1850s there was indeed a nascent proselytizing movement—the goal of which was the elevation of certain genres and styles of music into "classical" forms (and in so doing to isolate them from the more plebeian "popular" styles).[25] But despite this trend, operatic music of the antebellum period obstinately defies such neat classification—in part because the categories themselves were just beginning to form. In this respect, then, opera and operatic music were of a piece with the rest of American culture of the period: it was heterogeneous, varied, jumbled, wonderfully exciting, and stubbornly resistant to the categorization so characteristic of Western culture in the twentieth century.

An example of a similar blurring of the lines between the cultivated and the vernacular—but in another art—are recent scholarly findings about the place of Shakespeare's works in American society of the nineteenth century. Lawrence Levine has shown that the playwright's works were known to and loved by ordinary antebellum Americans to a degree unfathomable today, and to an extent almost precisely analogous to the pervasiveness of opera in the same society.[26] "From the large and often opulent theaters of major cities," Levine writes, "to the makeshift stages in halls, saloons, and churches of small towns and mining camps, wherever there was an audience for the theater, there Shakespeare's plays were performed prominently and frequently."[27] The playwright's works, like operas, were parodied and burlesqued. His characters and situations, like wafts of Italian melody from a church steeple or an organ-grinder, were part of the public consciousness. Well-read copies of his plays, like piles of sheet-music arias, could be found in countless homes all over the United States. To most Americans, neither Shakespeare's works nor those of Bellini, Rossini, Donizetti, or Verdi, were solely Art. They were also an integral part of popular entertainment, an everyday part of popular culture.

The removal of opera from the domain of the popular theater eventually succeeded. So did the similar removal of Shakespeare. Both developments were part of a massive change in American culture that took place gradually over the course of the second half of the nineteenth century; this development has been described by Levine.[28] Culture was broken down into segments; parts of it continued to function as "popular" culture, other segments became Culture and, hence, no longer "popular." The theater, which early in the century had functioned as a social microcosm, presenting widely divergent bills of fare to all ranks of society, gradually became more specialized. Different houses were established to cater to different audiences; drama, dance, farce, acrobatics, melodrama, and opera increasingly were viewed as unrelated and separate. Music, which once had subsumed under its umbrella all sorts of widely divergent styles, likewise was divided into popular music and art music. It was vernacular or cultivated, but rarely both.

This quantum change in the function of music was part of a larger cultural process at work in American society. It is also further evidence of a significant movement occurring in Europe at the same time: the transformation of music from a utilitarian craft into an Art. This shift, a long and gradual process, was one of the principal achievements of the Romantic period. By midcentury, the process in America was inextricably bound up with the appearance of a musical elite, a group that wholehartedly embraced the philosophy and the music of the German Romantics, the leaders in this movement. An examination of this change is not the function of this study. Although the process began in this country in the antebellum period, it did not really occur, for the most part, until after 1860. But in order to understand the development of American musical culture during the nineteenth century, and through it to better understand the changes that took place in American society as a whole, it is important to understand thoroughly musical culture of the antebellum period as well. In order to know where we are going, we must know where we have been.

During the period under discussion, one of the great musical forms of western culture was part of the blood of average Americans. Writers on opera refer to "golden ages" in the history of opera in the United States—meaning the turn of the twentieth century or the heyday of the New York Metropolitan Opera in the 1940s. During a much earlier historical period, however—from the 1830s to the 1850s (and later) for English-language opera and from the mid 1840s through the 1860s and beyond for opera performed in Italian—opera was important to Americans to an extent difficult to fathom now. As such, the antebellum period also deserves to be considered such a golden age.

Appendix A
Personnel of Italian Opera Troupes, 1833–47

MONTRESOR COMPANY
New York and Philadelphia: 6 Oct. 1832–11 May 1833:
  Madame Brichta, Giuseppe Corsetti (bass), Signora Fabbrica (contralto), Luciano Fornasari (bass), Signor Manetti (tenor), Lorenza Marozzi (soprano), Giovanni Battista Montresor (tenor), Ernesto Orlandi (buffo), Adelaide Pedrotti (soprano), Alessandro Pedrotti (tenor), Giuliano Placci (bass), Emilia Saccomani (contralto), Francesco Sapignoli (tenor), Enrichetta Salvioni, Albina Stella (soprano),Teresa Verducci (soprano), Antonio Bagioli (orchestra director), Michele Rapetti (orchestra leader), Carlo Salvioni (chorus director), Giacomo Montresor (company director).
  Sources: Schiavo 1947, 42; *Spirit,* 4 Aug. 1832; Odell 1970, 3:642–45.

RIVAFINOLI OPERA COMPANY
New York and Philadelphia: 18 Nov. 1833–July 1834:
  A. Bazzani, M. Bazzani, Louisa (or Luigia) Bordogni (mezzo-soprano), Antonio de Rosa (bass), Gianbattista Fabj (or Fabi) (tenor), Clementina Fanti (soprano), Rosina Fanti (soprano), Adelaide Ferrero (dancer), Stefano Ferrero, Tomaso Manetti, Cl. Marozzi, Lorenza Marozzi (soprano), Signora Maroncelli, Ernesto Orlandi (buffo), Antonio Porto (bass), Luigi Ravaglia (tenor), Signor Richaud, Carlo Salvioni, Francesco Sapignoli (tenor), Amelia Schneider-Maroncelli (contralto), Luigi Volta, Piero Maroncelli (chorus director), Michele Rapetti (orchestra leader).
  Sources: Schiavo 1947, 54–55; *New-York Daily Mirror,* 21 Sept. 1833, 94; Odell 1970, 3:690–94.

PORTO-SACCHI COMPANY
New York and Albany: 10 Nov. 1834–May 1835:
  Clementina Fanti (soprano), Rosina Fanti (soprano), Gianbattista Fabj (or Fabi) (tenor), Stefano Ferrero, Monterasi, Antonio Porto (bass), Francesco Sapignoli (tenor), Luigi Ravaglia (tenor), Julia Wheatley, Antonio Porto and Signor G. A. Sacchi (directors).
  Sources: Schiavo 1947, 57; *AMJ,* Dec. 1834, 42; Odell 1970, 4:40–41.

MONTRESOR OPERA COMPANY
New Orleans: 6 March 1836–31 May 1837:
  Antonio de Rosa (bass), Lucia Gadenghi, Signor Manetti (tenor), Lorenza Marozzi (soprano), Giovanni Battista Montresor (tenor), Ernesto Orlandi (buffo),

Adelaide Pedrotti (soprano), Luigi Ravaglia (tenor), Enrichetta Salvioni, Francesco Sapignoli (tenor).
Source: Kendall 1968, 136.

DE ROSA OPERA COMPANY
New Orleans: 4 Dec. 1836–27 Feb. 1837:
Antonio de Rosa (bass), Signor Manetti (tenor), Lorenza Marozzi (soprano), Ernesto Orlandi (buffo), Luigi Ravaglia (tenor), Mme. Thielmann.
Source: Kendall 1968, 143.

HAVANA OPERA COMPANY
New Orleans: 4 April–6 June 1837 (St. Charles Theatre), 10 June–14 July (Théâtre d'Orléans):
Cerilo Antagnini (tenor), Federico Badiali (tenor), Pietro Candi (bass), Cassati, Paolo Ceresini, Cerroni, Clorinda Corradi-Pantanelli (contralto), Gianbattista Fabj (or Fabi) (tenor), Luigi Fornasari (bass), Garganti, Grandi, Lazzarini, Tomaso Manetti, Marcucci, Martinelli, Signora Papanti, Elisa Rossi, Teresa Rossi (soprano), Signor Rossi, Francesco Sapignoli (tenor), Sorcini, Tartarini, Francis Brichta (manager), Luigi Gabici (conductor).
Sources: Kmen 1966, 151–58; Kendall 1968, 143–44.

HAVANA OPERA COMPANY
New Orleans: 22 Feb.–10 March 1842 (St. Charles Theatre), 16 March–18 April 1842 (Théâtre d'Orléans):
Signor Albertazzi, Signora M. Albertazzi, Cerilo Antagnini (tenor), Federico Badiali (tenor), Marietta Barbetti, Louisa Balgarelli, Alessandro Cecconi (bass), Alberto Lozzi (bass), Lorenza Marozzi (soprano), Adolfo Montegri (bass), F. Morians (tenor), Signora Pantanelli, Signora Papanti, Arunta Pardinni (soprano), Luigi Perozzi (tenor), Arabella Ober de Rossi (soprano), Signora Rossi (second one), Celestino Salvatori (bass), Arribal Statutti (bass), Emelina Fantoin Sutton (soprano), Bartolomeo Thames, Lauro Rossi (director and composer), Michele Rapetti (orchestra director), A. Beckerim (apundator [prompter?]), Ester Mencer (director of sastreria [?]), Francisco Marti y Torrens (impresario).
Sources: Belsom 1955, 73–88; New-York Daily Mirror, 5 March 1842, 32; Spirit, 12 March 1842; Smither 1944.

HAVANA OPERA COMPANY
Itinerary:
New Orleans, 17 April–17 May 1843; Cincinnati, 8–21 June; Pittsburgh, 30? June–3? July; Philadelphia, 15–31 July; (whereabouts unknown in August); New York (Niblo's Garden), 15 Sept.–23 Oct.; Philadelphia, 13–24 Nov. (in Schiavo, 15–25 November); Baltimore, Dec.; New Orleans (American Theatre), 13 Dec. (Kendall 1968, 233).

Personnel:
New Orleans: Cirillo Antognini, Francesco Calvet, Ester Corsini (soprano), Gioacchino Gussinie, Amalia Majocchi, Lorenza Marozzi, Signora Marozzi, Luigi Perozzi (tenor), Bartolomeo Thames, Attilio Valtellina, Felice Vittoria.

Cincinnati: Calvetti, Ester Corsini, Gioacchino Gussinie, Amalia Majocchi, Lorenza Marozzi, Luigi Perozzi, Bartolomeo Thames, Attilio Valtellina.

Philadelphia: M. Albertazzi, Ph. Albertazzi, Todoro Brotolone, Francesco Calvet, Ester Corsini, Gioacchino Gussinie, Amalia Majocchi, Lorenza Marozzi, Luigi Perozzi, Bartolomeo Thames, Attilio Valtellina.

New York: Cirillo Antognini, Francesco Calvet, Coadi [Coad?], Ester Corsini, Amalia Majocchi, T. Maggiori (bass), Paul Salomini (tenor), Bartolomeo Thames, Attilio Valtellina.

Luigi Gabici and Signor La Manna (orchestra leaders).

Sources: Belsom 1955, 98, 101; Wilson 1935; Wolz 1983.

PALMO'S OPERA HOUSE COMPANY

Personnel:

3 Feb.–25 March 1843 (First season): Albani, Matilda Albertazzi, Philippo Albertazzi, Cirillo Antognini, Daniele Benetti, Eufrasia Borghese, Madame Boulard, Giuberneau (bass), Majocchi, Mayer, Naldi, Luigi Perozzi (tenor), Salmonski.

29 April–10 June (under de Begnis): Matilda Albertazzi, Philippo Albertazzi, Daniele Benetti, Eufrasia Borghese, Guiseppe de Begnis (buffo), Louis Martini (buffo), Luigi Perozzi, Antonio Sanquirico (buffo).

30 Sept.–19? Oct. 1843; 18 Nov. 1843–25 Jan. 1844; fall 1844: Cirillo Antognini, Eufrasia Borghese, Luigi Perozzi, Rosina Pico (contralto), Signor Tomasi (bass).

Attilio Valtellina (general director), Michele Rapetti (orchestra leader), Mr. Etienne (chorus master), Mr. Wells (stage manager), Guiseppe de Begnis (second season director).

Sources: Schiavo 1947, 66–67, White 1882, 874–76; *Spirit,* 4 May 1844, 118, 16 Nov. 1844; Lawrence 1988.

SANQUIRICO-PATTI COMPANY

New York: Palmo's

First Season (4 Jan.–31 March 1847): Clotilde Barili (soprano), Caterina Barili-Patti (soprano), Sesto Benedetti (tenor), Daniele Benetti, Ferdinando Beneventano, Madame Boulard (soprano), Luigi Martini (bass), Salvatore Patti (tenor), Rosina Pico (contralto), Harriet Phillips, Antonio Sanquirico (buffo), Benetti Riese.

Second Season (7 April–7 June 1847): Clotilde Barili, Caterina Barili-Patti (Schiavo includes her, but no other sources do so), Sesto Benedetti, Daniele Benetti, Ferdinando Beneventano, Madame Boulard, Luigi Martini, Benetti Riese.

Salvatore Patti, Antonio Sanquirico, C. Pogliani (managers), Antonio Barili (maestro and stepson of Salvatore Patti), Michele Rapetti (orchestra leader), H. C. Beames (chorus director), Barozzi (prompter), Benetti Riese (stage manager).

Sources: Spirit, 21 Nov. 1846, 468; Schiavo 1947, 69; Lawrence 1988, 425.

HAVANA OPERA COMPANY, 1847

Itinerary:

New York (Park Theatre), 15–16 April, concert on 17 April; Boston (Athenaeum) 19 April–4 June; New York (Park Theatre) 9 June–8 July (12 performances), 9 July grand soirée musicale (concert); Philadelphia (Walnut Street Theatre), 12 July–6 Aug.; New York (Castle Garden), 18 Aug.–17 Sept.; Boston, 21 Sept.–1 Oct.; New York, farewell concert at Tabernacle, 15 Oct.

Personnel:

(72 artists; by July numbered 83): Federico Badiali (tenor), Luigi Battaglini (bass), Pietro Candi (bass), Luigi di Vita (baritone), Luigia Caranti di Vita (soprano), Teodolinda Gerli, Sofia Marini, M. Marini, Pietro Novelli (bass), Natale Perelli (tenor), Luigi Perozzi (tenor, former Palmo's member), Giuseppe Piemontesi (tenor), Teresa Ranieri (soprano), Signor Ranieri, Juan B. Severi (tenor), Fortunata Tedesco (mezzo soprano), F. Badiali (general director), Jose Villarino (tour manager), Luigi Arditi and Giovanni Bottesini (codirectors).

Sources: Odell 1970, 5:263, 266, 403; *Spirit,* 17 April 1847; Armstrong 1884, 54; Lawrence 1988, 434–35; 438, 445–46; *BMG,* 25 Oct. 1847.

ASTOR PLACE OPERA COMPANY, 1847–48

F. Albertazzi, Attilio Arnoldi, Antonio Avignone (baritone), Avogadro, Francesco Bailini (principal tenor), Caterina Barili-Patti (new member), Antonio Barili (bass), Clotilda Barili (soprano), Sesto Benedetti (returns on 15 Dec. after resolution of monetary dispute), G. V. Beneventano (baritone), Eliza Biscaccianti (soprano, three-month engagement), Claudio Bonzanini (bass), Felix Genovesi, Angiolina Morra, Signor Morra, Amalia Patti, Salvatore Patti, Giuseppe Piamontesi, Giuseppina Lietti Rossi (contralto), Settimo Rossi (principal bass), Antonio Sanquirico (buffo), Severo Strini, Teresa Truffi (soprano), Adelino Vietti (principal tenor), A. Sanquirico and S. Patti (general managers), John Sefton (acting manager), Antonio Barili (maestro-director), Michele Rapetti (orchestra leader), Biondi (stage manager), Ravaglia (costumer).

Sources: Odell 1970, 5:381–82; Schiavo 1947, 77–79; Lawrence 1988, 457, 466, 500.

Appendix B
Itinerant Opera Companies Active in the United States, 1841–48

The table should be read from top to bottom; entries in concurrent columns represent opera companies active during the same time period. Under the Astor Place Opera Company (No. 19), the entries within brackets represent branches of the parent company.

The following abbreviations and short titles are used in this table:

Amer	American Theatre	Holli	Holliday Street Theatre
Astor	Astor Place Opera House	Phila	Philadelphia
Athen	Athenaeum Theatre	NO	New Orleans
Balt	Baltimore	NYC	New York City
B'way	Broadway Theatre	OC	Opera company
Castle	Castle Garden	St. Chas	St. Charles Theatre
Ches	Chestnut Street Theatre	Tremt	Tremont Street Theatre
con	concert	Wal	Walnut Street Theatre
Fed	Federal Street Theatre		

1841

SEGUIN OC (1)
Boston
  (Tremt)   27 Sept-8 Oct
Phila (Ches)   Oct? Nov?
Richmond   22-30 Nov
Charleston   7-16 Dec
Augusta   Dec (1 night)

1842

NO (St. Chas) 5 Jan-
                -5 Feb   **HAVANA OC (2)**
Mobile (Royal
  St)   10-28 Feb   NO (St. Chas) 22 Feb-
                                   -10 Mar
Charleston   12-29 Mar   NO (Théâtre 16 Mar-
NYC (Park)   25 Apr-   d'Orléans)   -18 Apr
                -7 June

SEGUIN OC (3)
NYC (Park)   29 Oct-
                -26 Nov
Phila (Ches)   5 Dec-

1843

                -18 Feb
Charleston   3-18 Mar
Savannah   21 Mar-
                -6 Apr

1843 (con't)

		HAVANA OC (4)		FRENCH OC OF NO (5)	
Charleston	10-27 Apr	NO	17 Apr-	NYC (Niblo)	19 May-
unknown	May-		-17 May		
	-June	Cincinnati	8-21 June		
		Pittsburgh	30? June-		
Cincinnati	1 July		-3? July		
	-14 July	Phila	15 July-		
St. Louis	31 July-		-31 July		
	-12 Aug	unknown	Aug		-2 Aug
				Toronto	10-21 Aug
				Canada?	Sept?

SEGUIN OC (6)		NYC (Niblo)	6-11? Sept		
unknown	Sept	NYC (Niblo)	15 Sept-	Phila (Ches)	14 Sept-
Balt (Holli)	11-30 Oct		-23 Oct		-21 Oct
		Phila	13-24 Nov		
		Balt	Dec		
		NO	13 Dec		

1844

Mobile (Co-rinthian)	2 Jan
NO (Amer)	4? Jan-
	-3 Feb

		PALMO'S OC (7)	
Mobile	14-20 Feb	NYC	3 Feb-
Charleston	7-11 Mar		-20 Mar
Phila (Ches)	1-23 Apr	NYC	29 Apr-
NYC (Park)	25 Apr-		
	-11 May		
Phila	28? May-4? June		-10 June
To England	Summer		
		NYC	30 Sept-
			-19? Oct

SEGUIN OC (8)

NYC (Park)	25 Nov-	NYC	18 Nov-
	-14 Dec		
Phila	20 Dec-		

1845

	-11 Jan		
NYC	13-18 Jan		-25 Jan
Charleston	29 Jan-		
	-15 Feb		
pass thru Mobile	27 Feb		
NO (St. Chas)	3-15? Mar	ITALIAN OC (9)	
		NO	3 Mar-
Mobile (Royal St)	17-26 Mar		
unknown	Apr		
NYC (Park)	28 Apr-		
	-17 May		-2 May

1845 (con't)

SEGUIN CO (con't)

Phila (Ches)   19 May-

               -1 July

FRENCH OC OF NO (10)
NYC (Park)   16 June-

               -15 Aug
NYC (Niblo)   25 Aug-

BROUGH-DELCY OC (11)
NYC (Park)   15 Sept-
                              -24 Sept
SEGUIN OC (12)   -3 Oct   Phila (Ches)   29 Sept-
Boston   27 Oct-   Phila (Ches)   13 Oct-   -11 Oct
                                     -25 Oct
               -1? Nov   Phila (Ches)   10 Nov-
                                           -22 Nov   NYC (Park)   17 Nov-
Balt (Holli)   1?-13? Dec   -3 Dec
NYC (Park)   22 Dec-

1846
               -6 Jan
Boston
  (Athen)   ? Jan-13? Feb
NYC (Park)   9-31 Mar
Boston (con)   14 Apr
Phila (Ches)   27 Apr-
               -8 May
Long Island   June

SEGUIN OC (13)
Boston (Fed)   28 Sept-
               -16 Oct
unknown   late Oct
Phila (Wal)   2-27 Nov
Phila (Wal)   8-16? Dec

1847
               -Jan?   **SANQUIRICO-PATTI OC (14)**
Boston (Fed)   22? Jan-5 Feb   NYC (Palmo's)   4 Jan-
Charleston   22 Feb-
               -6 Mar
Savannah   8-20 Mar

                              -31 Mar   **HAVANA OC (15)**
Phila (Ches)   5 Apr-   NYC (Palmo's)   7 Apr-   NYC (Park)   15-16 Apr
                                                        Boston
                                                          (Athen)   19 Apr-
                                                                     -4 June
               -5 June   -7 June   NYC (Park)   9 June-
                                                                        -8 July
London   July   Phila (Wal)   12 July-

SEGUIN OC (16)   **ANNA BISHOP OC (17)**
Montreal   Aug-
                       NYC (Park)   4-18 Aug   -6 Aug
                       Boston   26 Aug-   NYC (Castle)   18 Aug-
                                -10? Sept   -18 Sept
               -Sept
Boston   21 Sept-?

1847 (con't)

SEGUIN OC (con't)		ANNA BISHOP OC (con't)		MANVERS OC (18)	
				NYC (Park)	4-5 Oct
Phila (Wal)	11-26 Oct	NYC (Park)	21 Oct-	Albany	
				(con)	21 Oct
Boston					
(Athen)	4 Nov-		-6 Nov	Michigan	when?
	-19 Nov	Boston (Fed)	? -18 Nov	**ASTOR PLACE OC (19)**	
		Phila (Wal)	22 Nov-	NYC (Astor)	2 Nov-
			-7 Dec		
		NYC (B'way)	13-24 Dec		
NYC					
(con)	26 Dec	Phila (Wal)	27 Dec-		

1848

unknown	Jan-			[Boston	
			-6 Jan	(Athen)	5 Jan-
		Charleston	12-24 Jan		
		(cons)	28-29 Jan		-28 Jan]
		Savannah	31 Jan-		
			-5 Feb		
	-Feb	NO (St. Chas)	14 Feb-		-18 Feb
				Phila (Ches)	19 Feb-
			-2 Mar		
Richmond	17-31 Mar	Mobile	6-21 Mar		-24 Mar
Petersburg					
(con)	early Apr?			NYC (Astor)	27 Mar-
NYC					
(Bowery)	13 Apr-				
					-28 Apr
	-7 May	NO	May	Phila	May
Balt (Holli)	May ?-			Boston	29 May-
	-10? June			[Phila (Ches)	6-13 June]
					-26 June

Commentary and Sources

1. Seguin Opera Company. During 1841 and 1842, the Seguins traveled with Charles Manvers. In Charleston, the company was reported to consist of Mr. and Mrs. Seguin, Mr. and Mrs. Manvers, Miss Manvers, and Miss Coad. Coad and Miss Manvers evidently remained in Charleston when the Seguins left for New Orleans, for in January they are reported among the cast of the Charleston Theatre rehearsing for a performance of *Figaro*. In New Orleans, the troupe consisted of the Seguins, Richardson, Manvers, and Mr. Archer; see Kendall (1968) for a description of the stock company's role in opera performances. In Mobile, the troupe is identified as the "St. Charles Opera Company"; other performers named (besides Manvers) included Mr. Archer, Mr. Verity, Mr. Brunton, Mad. Thielman, Mr. Hodges, and Mrs. Richardson. In New York in April, the "name" singers included the Seguins, A. Andrews, Mrs. Knight, Mary Taylor, and Charles Manvers. Sources: *Boston: Spirit*, 23 Oct. 1841; Playbill, Tremont Theatre, 1 Oct. 1841, NN; *Mirror*, 2, 9, 16 Oct. 1841; *Philadelphia: Spirit*, 23 Oct. 1841; *Richmond: Spirit*, 20 Nov. 1841; *Charleston:* Hoole 1946, 114; Massett 1863, 42–43; *Spirit*, 18, 25 Dec. 1841, 26 March 1842; *Mirror*, 22 Jan. 1842; *Augusta: Spirit*, 25 Dec. 1841; *New Orleans: Spirit*, 25 Dec. 1841; 15, 22 Jan., 5, 19

Feb. 1842; Kendall 1968, 183–84; *Mirror,* 22, 29 Jan., 12 Feb., 5 March 1842; Smither 1944; *Mobile:* Bailey 1934, 92, 298–300; *Mirror,* 26 Feb. 1842, 21; Duggar 1941, 111–12; *New York: Spirit,* 23, 30 April, 7, 13, 28 May 1842; *Mirror,* 30 April 1842, 87; Odell 1970, 4:544–45.

2. Havana Opera Company. Sources: Belsom 1955, 73–88; *Mirror,* 5 March 1842, 32; *Spirit,* 12 March 1842; Smither 1944.

3. Seguin Opera Company. According to Odell, this was the worst theatrical season financially in the history of New York theatricals (1970, 4:603). During this season the Seguins opened with three weeks of the Rossini/Lacy *Israelites in Egypt,* then resumed their standard fare. In Philadelphia during the winter the Seguins lost two of their children to scarlet fever. For information about the role of stock companies in St. Louis, see Carson 1949. The Seguins performed with the following singers: *New York:* Thomas Archer, Mr. Boulard, Charlotte Bailey, Mrs. Hoskins, Mrs. Knight, Mr. Plumer, and Mr. Shrival; *Philadelphia:* Bailey, Coad, Plumer, Richings, and Shrival; *Charleston:* Archer, Coad, and Shrival; *Savannah:* Archer, Coad, H. Phillips, and Shrival; *Cincinnati:* Bailey and Shrival; *St. Louis:* Archer and Shrival. Sources: *New York:* Odell 1970, 4:610–11; *Spirit,* 29 Oct., 5, 26 Nov. 1842; *Philadelphia: Spirit,* 10, 24 Dec. 1842; Armstrong 1884, 42; Wemyss 1847, 379–80; Playbill, Chestnut Street Theatre, 6 Feb. 1843, Theatre Division, PP; Wilson 1935; *Mobile:* Bailey 1934, 324; *Charleston:* Hoole 1946, 46, 116; *Savannah:* Dorman 1967, 167; Green 1971, 391; *Cincinnati:* Wolz 1983; *Spirit,* 8 July 1843; *St. Louis:* Carson 1949, 229–31; *Spirit,* 19 July 1843.

4. Havana Opera Company. Sources: *New Orleans:* Belsom 1955, 98, 101; Kendall 1968, 233; *Cincinnati:* Wolz, 1983, 50; Wyrick 1965, 113; *Philadelphia:* Wilson 1935; Armstrong 1884, 47; Schiavo 1947; *New York:* Lawrence 1988, 216–18; Odell 1970, 4:694–95; *Baltimore: Spirit,* 9 Dec. 1843; Kaufman worklist, Baltimore. See also chapter 3.

5. French Opera Company of New Orleans. Sources: *New York:* Odell 1970, 4:689–94; 5:67; Lawrence 1988, 213–16; *Spirit,* 20 May 1843, 27 May 1843; *Philadelphia:* Wilson 1935; Armstrong 1884; Curtis t.s., 309; *Toronto, Canada:* Cooper 1984, 65–69; Lawrence 1988, 216.

6. Seguin English Opera Company. It is unclear just when the Seguins left for England, or how long they stayed. They are last mentioned in the spring of 1844, singing in concert in New York on 31 May 1844 (Odell 1970, 5:73–74). During the 1843–44 season, the Seguins performed with the following singers: *Baltimore:* Archer, Bailey, Richings, and Shrival; *Mobile:* Archer, Mrs. Richardson, and Shrival. Secondary singers included Misses Verity, Jones, Warner, and Hally, Mrs. Bowman, Mr. Van Pragg, Solomon, A'Beckett, Walters, Bowers, Milto, Bowman, and Sig. Paladine; *Charleston:* A'Beckett and Shrival; *Philadelphia:* Frazer and Shrival; *New York:* Andrews, Coad, Knight, and Shrival. Sources: *Baltimore:* Kaufman worklist, Baltimore; *Spirit,* 28 Oct. 1843; *Mobile:* Bailey 1934, 324, 326; Duggar 1941, 132–34; *New Orleans: Spirit,* 6 Jan., 17 Feb. 1844; *Charleston: Spirit,* 16 March 1844; Hoole 1946, 48, 118; *Philadelphia:* Wilson 1935; Armstrong 1884, 48; *New York: Spirit,* 16, 23 March, 20, 27 April, 4, 11 May 1844; Odell 1970, 5:15–16; Lawrence 1988, 267–69; *England:* Lawrence 1988, 267; *Spirit,* 23 March 1844.

7. Palmo's Opera Company. Under this heading appeared three companies. All the troupes performed only in New York over the course of three seasons. For more information on the troupes, see chapter 3; for information on company members, see the Appendix A. Sources: Schiavo 1947, 66–67; White 1882, 2:874–76; *Spirit,* 4 May 1844, and 16 November 1844; Lawrence 1988, 355.

8. Seguin Opera Company. After spending the summer in England, the Seguins brought back to the United States a new tenor (a Scotsman named James Frazer) and Balfe's *The Bohemian Girl.* The *Spirit* reported on 25 Jan. 1845 that Frazer, the Seguins, and others had sailed for New Orleans. In February, the company passed through Mobile en route to New Orleans; it is not clear whether or not they performed (*Spirit,* 15 March 1845). The Seguins sang with the following singers: *New York:* Andrews, Frazer, Knight, and Pearson; *Charleston:* Andrews, Frazer, and Miss Moss; *New Orleans:* Andrews, Coad, and Frazer; *Mobile:* Andrews and Frazer; *New York:* Frazer. Sources: *New York:* Odell 1970, 5:92–93; *Spirit,* 30 Nov., 7, 14 Dec. 1844; 18, 25 Jan. 1845; 26 April, 12, 17 May 1845; Odell 1970, 5:101; Lawrence 1988, 267; *Philadelphia:* Armstrong 1884; Wilson 1935; Wemyss 1847,

401; *Charleston:* Hoole 1946, 48, 120; *Spirit*, 8 Feb. 1845; *Mobile:* (February): *Spirit*, 15 March 1845; (later season): Bailey 1934, 49, 330; *Spirit*, 5, 12 April 1845; Duggar 1941, 140; *New Orleans:* Playbills, St. Charles Theatre, 3–8, 12, 15 March 1845, HTC.

9. Italian Opera Company. This troupe represents the remnants of Palmo's Company (chapter 3). Sources: Kaufman worklist, New Orleans.

10. French Opera Company of New Orleans. Sources: *New York:* Odell 1970, 5:103, 158; Lawrence 1988, 329–34; *Spirit*, 14 June 1845, 188; 28 June, 30 August, 320; 13, 20 Sept. 1845. *Philadelphia:* Wilson 1935; Armstrong 1884, 51; Curits n.d., 340.

11. Brough-Delcy English Opera Company. This was a short-lived extended vocal-star troupe. In New York, the company included Miss Catherine Delcy (the daughter of Michael Rophino Lacy), the tenor F. Gardner, William Brough, and Miss Moss. Lacy, who accompanied his daughter from England, served as musical director and conductor. According to Curtis, in Philadelphia the company included Delcy, Gardner, Owens, Coad, Mrs. Hughes, Mr. Eberle, Mr. Shaw, Mr. Dunn, and Mr. Stevens. How many of these individuals were members of the Chestnut Street stock company is unknown. In November in New York, the company mounted the American premiere of the English version of Donizetti's *Lucia di Lammermoor.* Sources: *New York: Spirit*, 13, 20, 27 Sept. 1846; Odell 1970, 5:167, 170; *Spirit*, 15, 22, 29 Nov., 6 Dec. 1845; Lawrence 1988, 335–36; *Philadelphia:* Curtis n.d., 343; Armstrong 1884, 52; Wilson 1935.

12. Seguin English Opera Company. During the 1845–46 season the Seguins sang with the following performers: *Boston:* Mrs. Rosenthal, Mrs. Burrowes, Mr. Van Pragg, Mr. Benetti, and Mr. Schnepff (all advertised as from the Park Theatre); *Philadelphia* (Nov.): Seguins, Frazer, and Delavanti; *Baltimore:* Bailey and Frazer; *New York* (Dec.): Delavanti, Frazer, and Moss; *Boston:* (Jan.): Frazer and Meyer; *New York* (March): Frazer, F. Meyer. Sources: *Boston:* Playbill, Howard Athenaeum, 29 Oct. 1845, MWA; *Spirit*, 24 Jan., 14, 21 Feb. 1846; notice of concert on 14 April in *BMG*, 27 April 1846, 54; Clapp 1969, 435ff; *Philadelphia:* Wilson 1935; Armstrong 1884, 52–53; Curtis n.d., vol. 2, 346; *Spirit*, 15 Nov. 1845, 452, 2, 9, 16 May 1846; *Baltimore: Spirit*, 6, 13 Dec. 1845; *New York:* Odell 1970, 5:172–73, 179–80; *Spirit*, 20, 27 Dec. 1845, 3 Jan. 1846, 7, 14, 21, 28 March 1846; *Boston:* Playbills, Boston Athenaeum, 6, 11, 13 Feb. 1846, NN; Playbill, Boston Athenaeum, 9 Feb. 1846, Rare Books, MB; (summer): *Spirit*, 20 June 1846.

13. Seguin English Opera Company. In January 1847 Seguin and Frazer leased the Chestnut Street Theatre in Philadelphia, then rented it out, "until their return from the South on the 1st of March (*Spirit*, 9 Jan. 1847). During the 1846–47 season the Seguins performed with the following singers: *Boston:* Frazer and Meyer; *Philadelphia:* Frazer; *Boston* (Jan.-Feb.): Frazer, Holman, Meyer, and Phillips; *Charleston:* Frazer, G. Holman, Meyer, Adelaide Phillips, and full chorus from the Park Theatre in New York; *Savannah:* Frazer, Holman, Meyer, and Phillips; *Philadelphia* (April): Frazer. Sources: *Boston:* Playbills, Federal Street Theatre, 28 Sept., 9, 12, 17 Oct. 1846, NN; Playbill, Federal Street Theatre, 16 Oct. 1846, MWA; Playbill, Federal Street Theatre, 28 Sept. [1846], Rare Books, MB; *Spirit*, 26 Sept., 17, 24 Oct. 1846; Clapp 1969, 389; *Philadelphia:* Wilson 1935; *Spirit*, 7, 14 Nov. 1846; December engagement: Armstrong 1884, 53; *Spirit*, 9 Jan. 1847; Lawrence 1988, 488; *Boston* (1847): Playbills, Federal Street Theatre, 25 Jan., 5 Feb. 1847, NN; Playbill, Federal Street Theatre, 22, 29 Jan., 1 Feb. 1847, Rare Books, MB; *Charleston:* Hoole 1946, 50, 124; *Spirit*, 6 March 1847; *Savannah:* Dorman 1967, 167; Green 1971, 421; *Spirit*, 27 March 1847; *Philadelphia:* Wilson 1935; *Spirit*, 10 April, 22 May 1847; *London: Spirit*, 19 July 1847, 236.

14. Sanquirico-Patti Italian Opera Company. For more information on this troupe, see chapter 3; for a list of company members, see Appendix A. Sources: *Spirit*, 21 Nov. 1846, 468; Schiavo 1947, 69; Lawrence 1988, 425.

15. Havana Opera Company. For more information on this troupe, see chapter 3; for a list of company members, see Appendix A. Sources: Odell 1970, 5:263, 266; *Spirit*, 17 April 1847; Armstrong 1884, 54; Lawrence 1988, 434–35, 438.

16. Seguin English Opera Company. In May, William H. Reeves, who had been with the Bishop Company, joined the Seguins when Bishop's troupe disintegrated in April (*Literary Excelsior and Musical World*, 27 May 1848). During the 1847–48 season, the Seguins performed with the following singers: *Montreal:* Arthurson; Miss Lichtenstein, Meyer, Shri-

val, and chorus; *Boston* (Nov.): Arthurson, Lichtenstein, Meyer, and Shrival; *Richmond:* Gardner, Lichtenstein, and Mr. Sauer; *New York* (April): Gardner, Lichtenstein, Phillips, Sauer, and Miss Turnbull; *Baltimore:* Reeves. Sources: *Montreal: Spirit,* 4 Sept. 1847, 332; Cooper 1984, 56–58; *Philadelphia:* Wilson 1935; *Literary Excelsior,* 30 Oct. 1847; Armstrong 1884, 47; *Boston: Spirit,* 6 Nov. 1847, 440; Playbills, Boston Athenaeum, 4, 12, 19 Nov. 1847, NN; *Literary Excelsior,* 13 Nov. 1847; Playbill, Boston Athenaeum, 5 Nov. 1847, MWA; *New York:* Odell 1970, 5:314 (report of concert) 5:350–51 (April-May); Lawrence 1988, 524; *Richmond:* Stoutamire 1960, 179; *Literary Excelsior,* 25 March, 15 April 1848; *Spirit,* 18 March, 1 April 1848 (*Spirit* gives the last night as 23 March, but Mrs. Seguin gave a concert that evening; Stoutamire gives the last night as 31 March); *Petersburg: Literary Excelsior,* 15 April 1848; *Baltimore: Spirit,* 3 June 1848, 180; *Literary Excelsior,* 10 June 1848.

17. Anna Bishop English Opera Company. Bishop's departure from England was reported in the *Spirit* on 12 June 1847. Her American operatic debut was on 4 Aug. 1847 at the Park Theatre. (See also the note to number 2 in Appendix D.) Bishop appeared with the following singers in 1847–48: *New York City* (Park): Mrs. Bailey, William Brough, James Frazer, Sidney Pearson (member of Park Theatre Company), and T. Y. Chubb (in charge of the orchestra); *Boston* (Aug.): Brough; *New York* (Oct.): Brough, de Begnis, Giubilei, Korsinsky, Macfarren, Reeves (debut), Valtellina, Bochsa (director), and R. Benetti (chorus director); *Boston* (Nov.): Benetti [Biennetti], Brough, de Begnis, Giubilei, Macfarren, and Reeves; *Philadelphia* (Nov.): Brough, Korsinsky, Reeves, and Valtellina; *New York* (Dec.): Brough, MacFarren, Reeves, and Valtellina; *Philadelphia* (Dec.): A'Beckett, Andrews, Mary Barton, Benetti, Brough, Korsinsky, Macfarren, and Reeves; *Charleston:* Andrews, Barton, Benetti, Brough, Reeves, Korsinsky, and Valtellina; *Savannah:* Barton, Brough, Korsinsky, Meighen, Reeves, and others (some perhaps from the Charleston Theatre); *New Orleans* (Feb.): Barton, Benetti, Brough, Korsinsky, Reeves, and Watson; *Mobile:* Benetti, Brough, Korsinsky, Reeves, and Valtellina. Sources: *New York: Spirit,* 12 June, 17, 24, 31 July, 7, 14, 21 Aug. 1847; Odell 1970, 5:321–22, 324–25; *Spirit,* 16, 23, 30 Oct., 6 Nov. 1847; *Literary Excelsior,* 23, 30 Oct., 13 Nov. 1847; third engagement: Odell 1970, 5:336; Playbills, Broadway Theatre, 13, 14, 16, 18, 20–23, 25? Dec. 1847, Bishop Collection, MB; *Spirit,* 18, 25 Dec. 1847, 1 Jan. 1848; Lawrence 1988, 470, 473; *Boston:* Playbill, Howard Athenaeum, 26 Aug. 1847, MWA; Playbill, Howard Athenaeum, 31 Aug. 1847, Rare Books, MB; Clapp 1969, 451; *Spirit,* 4, 18 Sept. 1847; *BMG,* 13 Sept. 1847, 134; second engagement: Playbills, Federal Street Theatre, 17–18 Nov. 1847, Rare Books, MB; *Spirit,* 20 Nov. 1847, 464; *Philadelphia:* Wilson 1935; *Spirit,* 4 Dec. 1847; Armstrong 1884, 57; Curtis t.s., vol. 2, 386; second visit: Playbills, Walnut Street Theatre, 27–31 Dec. 1847, 1, 3–6 Jan. 1848, Bishop Collection, MB; Armstrong 1884, 57; Curtis t.s., vol. 2, 386; *Spirit,* 8 Jan. 1848; *Charleston:* Hoole 1946, 52, 126; Playbills, Charleston Theatre, 12–14, 17–18, 21 (concert), 22, 24, 28–29 Jan. 1848, Bishop Collection, MB; *Spirit,* 5 Feb. 1848; *Savannah:* Green 1971, 429; Playbills, Savannah Theatre, 31 Jan., 1, 3, 5 Feb. 1848, Bishop Collection, MB; *New Orleans:* Playbills, St. Charles Theatre, 14–15, 17–18, 20–21, 23–24, 28–29 Feb., 2 March 1848, Bishop Collection, MB; *Spirit,* 26 Feb. 1848; *Literary Excelsior,* 18 March 1848; *Mobile:* Bailey 1934, 104; Playbills, Mobile Theatre, 6–7, 9–11, 13–15, 17–18, 20–21 March 1848, Bishop Collection, MB; *Literary Excelsior,* 8, 15 April 1848; *Spirit,* 8 April 1848.

18. Manvers Opera Company. According to Lawrence (1988), Eliza Brienti was incapacitated by nerves on opening night; the performance also coincided with Anna Bishop's second concert, and consequently was a financial disaster. The season closed after the second performance. The company included the following singers: *New York* (Oct.): Charles Manvers, Eliza Brienti, August Giubilei, Mrs. Grary, and Mr. Andrews; *Albany:* Manvers, Brienti, and Giubilei; *Michigan:* Manvers and Brienti; *New Orleans:* Brough and Brienti. Sources: *New York: Spirit,* 19 Oct. 1847, 392; Odell 1970, 5:324; Lawrence 1988, 472–73; *Albany: Spirit,* 30 Oct. 1847, 428; *Michigan:* Teal 1964, Appendix C; *New Orleans:* Kendall 1968, 269.

Appendix C

Itineraries of Italian Opera Companies in America, 1847–60

This table is arranged chronologically, from top to bottom. Entries in concurrent columns represent opera companies active during the same time period. The number after the name of each troupe refers to additional information about the company to be found in the Notes section following the table. The entries in parentheses (for example, under entry number 2) indicate splinter groups from the parent company.

The following abbreviations are used in this table:

Aca	Academy of Music	Ches	Chestnut Street Theatre
Amer	American Theatre	con	concerts
Astor	Astor Place Opera House	Holli	Holliday Street Theatre
Athen	Athenaeum Theatre	Maguire	Maguire's Opera House
Balt	Baltimore	McVicker	McVicker's Theatre
B'way	Broadway Theatre	Metro	Metropolitan Theatre
Castle	Castle Garden	Nat	National Theatre
		Niblo	Niblo's Theatre

NO	New Orleans	St. Chas	St. Charles Theatre
NYC	New York City	Var	Varieties Theatre
OC	Opera Company	Wal	Walnut Street Theatre
Phila	Philadelphia		
SF	San Francisco		

1847

SANQUIRICO-PATTI OC (1)
NYC (Palmo) 4 Jan-
            -31 Mar
        7 Apr-
            -7 June

ASTOR PLACE OC (2)
(Sanquirico & Patti, mgrs)
NYC (Astor) 22 Nov-

1848

            -18? Feb

Boston
(Athen) 5? Jan-

1848 (con't)

ASTOR PLACE OC (con't)

Phila (Ches)	19 Feb- -28? Jan
NYC (Astor)	27 Mar- -24 Mar
Phila (Patti- Barili)	May -28 Apr
Boston	29 May-
(Phila [Ches]	6-13 June) -4 June
	-26 June
NYC (Park)	9 June- -8 July
Phila (Wal)	12 July- -6 Aug
(Phila	14-26 Aug)
NYC (Castle)	18 Aug- -17 Sept
NYC (Niblo)	4-15 Sept
Boston	21 Sept- -1 Oct
Phila (Ches)	5-28 Oct
NYC (Tabernacle)	15 Oct

HAVANA OC (3)

NYC (Park)	15-17 Apr
Boston (Athen)	19 Apr-

LOMBARDI OC (4)

Boston	May

ASTOR PLACE OC (2A)
(Edward Fry, mgr)

NYC (Astor)	1 Nov-

ASTOR OC (BRANCH) (2B)

Phila	5-31 Dec,

1849

Boston	18 Jan- 5 Jan

ASTOR PLACE OC (5)
(Max Maretzek, mgr)

NYC (Astor)	19 Mar- -2 Mar -12 Apr -4 Apr

TEDESCO OC (6)

Charleston	14-15 Mar

GRAND ITALIAN OC (7)

Savannah?	7 Aug

1849 (con't)

ITALIAN OC (8)
NYC (B'way) 13 Aug- -15 Sept

UNKNOWN OC (9)
Pittsburgh 6-10 Oct

ADAMS OC (11)
Savannah 19-29 Nov

ASTOR PLACE OC (10)
(Maretzek, mgr)
NYC (Astor) 1 Nov-

ASTOR OC (BRANCH) (10a)
Phila 9 Dec- -20 Jan

1850
Boston 12 Mar- -7 Mar
-3 May

HAVANA OC (12)
Charleston 26 Mar- -2 Apr
NYC (Niblo) 11 Apr- -8 May
Boston (Athen) 13-31? May
NYC (Astor) 3 June- -5 July
NYC (Castle) 8 July- -7 Sept
Phila (Ches) 10-24 Sept
Havana (Tacon) 10 Oct

ASTOR PLACE OC (13)
NYC (Astor) 21 Oct-

ASTOR OC (BRANCH) (13a)
Phila (Ches) 10 Dec- -20 Jan

1851
Boston (Athen) 17 Feb- -23 Feb
Phila (con) 4 Mar -8 Mar
Balt (Holli) 23 Jan- -12 Feb

PELLEGRINI OC (14)
SF (Adelphi) 12 Feb-

1851 (con't)

ASTOR PLACE OC (con't)

Charleston	21 Mar-
	-12 Apr
Augusta	14-21 Apr
Charleston	22 Apr
Boston	29 Apr-
	-30 May
NYC (Astor)	3-14? June
NYC (Castle)	16 June-
	-19 Sept

NYC (Astor)	3 Nov-
	-22 Dec

1852

NYC	19 Jan-
	-early Mar

ASTOR PLACE OC (16)

NO	31 Mar-
	-19 Apr
Mexico	Apr-

ASTOR OC (13b)
(SOUTHERN BRANCH)

Phila	22 Sept-
	-13 Oct
Richmond	29 Oct-
	-4 Nov
Charleston	10 Nov-
	-13 Dec
Savannah	17-31 Dec

ARTISTS' UNION
ITALIAN OC (15)

NYC (Niblo)	12 Jan-
	-12 Feb
Boston	16 Feb-
(Theatre)	-8 Mar

PELLEGRINI OC (con't)

-8 Apr

STRAKOSCH OC (17)

NO	23-30 Apr

CARNCROSS OC (18)

Columbus, Ga   Sept

SONTAG OC (19)

NYC (con)   27 Sept

1852 (con't)

ASTOR PLACE OC (con't)

1853

-Mar

GRAND COMBINATION <------ [Alboni Co. merges]
OC (23)
NYC (Niblo) 28 Mar-

 -7 May

MARETZEK OC (27)
 (including Sontag)
NYC (Castle) 11 July-

 -23 Aug
NYC (Niblo) 19 Sept-

ALBONI OC (20)
NYC (B'way) 27 Dec-

Boston   -28 Jan
(Athen) 31 Jan-
      -18 Feb
Phila (Wal) 28 Feb-
(Maretzek, cond) -11 Mar

STEFFANONE OC (24)
Charleston 10-12 May
Richmond 18 May

SONTAG OC (con't)
con tour Nov-Dec

NYC (Niblo) 10 Jan-

     -18? Mar

Phila (Nat) 28 Mar-

    -16 Apr

Boston
(Athen) 19 Apr-

    -27 May
Worcester 29-30 May

ARDITI ITALIAN OC (26)
Montreal 20 June-
     -4 July
Toronto 8 July
Buffalo 11-22 July
Cincinnati 27 July-
     -6 Aug
Louisville 9-20 Aug
Cincinnati 23-29 Aug
St. Louis 26 Sept-
    -2 Oct
Chicago 27-31 Oct
Milwaukee 2-5 Nov

LORINI OC (21)
Lima, Peru Feb-
     -Mar

DUMBOLTON'S OC (25)
Michigan when?

PELLEGRINI OC (22)
SF (Adelphi) Feb-

?

    -Apr

1853 (con't)

MARETZEK OC (con't)

-19? Dec

1854

To Havana   Jan

HENRIETTE SONTAG (CONCERT TOUR) (29)
Mobile   20-24+ Feb
NO (St. Chas) 6-31 Mar

SONTAG OC (30)
leave NO   1 Apr
Mexico City   12 Apr-
           -June

HAYES OC (31)
SF   29 May?
         -8 July

MARETZEK OC (32)
NYC (Castle)   30 June-
         -25 Aug

ARDITI OC (con't)
Chicago   7 Nov
Detroit   9-16? Nov
Pittsburgh   18 Nov-
           -2 Dec
Balt (Front)   5-14 Dec
Washington   19-31 Dec

ARDITI OC
(aka DEVRIES OC)
Richmond   2-14 Jan
Charleston   18-19 Jan
(con)   24 Jan-
Savannah   -3 Feb
Augusta   6-10 Feb

JOINT WITH SONTAG
Mobile   20-24+ Feb
NO (St. Chas) 6-31 Mar

ARDITI OC (con't)
where?   1-9 Apr
NO   10-13 Apr
Memphis   22, 24 Apr
St. Louis   1-22 May
Nashville   26 May-
           -5 June
Louisville   12 June-
           -3 July
Cincinnati   5-22 July
Cleveland   25-29 July
Buffalo   31 July-
           -5 Aug
Toronto   9-12 Aug
Rochester   14-19 Aug

STEFFANONE OC (28)
NO to
Havana   Jan

Havana   Feb-
           -Mar

Mexico City   Apr

1854 (con't)

MARETZEK OC (con't)
Phila (Ches) 28 Aug--16 Sept

GRISI & MARIO OC (33)
NYC (Castle) 4-29? Sept
NYC (Aca) 2 Oct-
-29 Dec

1855

WARDEN'S OC (37)
Louisville 2-19 Jan

ACADEMY OF MUSIC OC (38)
NYC (Aca) 19 Feb-
-2? Mar
(aka MARETZEK OC)
NYC (Aca) 12 Mar-
-18 May
Boston 21 May--9 June
NYC (Aca) 11-18 June

LAGRANGE OC (40)
NYC (Niblo) 8 May
NYC (Aca) 21 May--8 June
Boston 11-18 June
NYC (Aca) 21-29 June

WARDEN'S OC (37)
Phila (Wal) 2, 5, 6 Jan
Balt 9 Jan
Washington (Nat) 8 Jan
Phila (con) 10 Jan
NYC (con) 11 Jan
Boston 15 Jan-
-11 Feb

ACADEMY OF MUSIC OC (38)
NYC (Metro) 13-20 Feb

ARDITI OC (con't)
Chicago 11 Oct, Nov
Chicago (con) 17 Nov
Nashville (con?) Dec

METROPOLITAN OC (39)
Chicago (Warner Hall) 22 Feb

LORINI OC (35)
Chicago (con) 11 Oct, 7 Nov
St. Louis 16 Oct-
-15 Nov
Cincinnati 22 Nov--1 Dec

UNKNOWN OC (34)
Boston 26 Aug--?
-23 Dec

BARILI-THORNE OC (36)
SF (Metro) 15 Nov-
SF (Metro) Jan-
-Feb
SF (Amer) 18-25 Mar
SF (Ital OC) May
S America August

1855 (con't)

ACADEMY OF MUSIC OC (41)
NYC (Aca)   1 Oct-

VESTVALI OC (42)
Mexico   20 Oct-

GARBATO OC (43)
SF   1855?

PARODI OC (44)
Michigan   1855-56

1856
Baltimore ?	-4 Jan	
Phila (Wal)	?	
NYC (Aca)	14-16 Jan	
Boston	18 Jan (1 perf)	
	21 Jan-	
	-22 Feb	
Phila (Wal)	20 Feb-	
	-6 Mar	-Mar?
NYC (Aca)	12 Mar-	
	-7 Apr	
NYC (Aca)	16 Apr-	
	-13 June	
	Boston	4-19 June
	to Mexico	Sept
	Mexico City	17 Oct

ACADEMY OF MUSIC OC (45)
NYC (Aca)   1-30 Sept
Boston   20 Oct-
                 -8 Nov

MARETZEK OC (46)
NYC (Aca)   10 Nov-
                 -11 Dec ---> to Havana   Dec
to Havana

1857

ACADEMY OF MUSIC OC (47)
NYC (Aca)   21 Jan-
                 -13 Feb
                 Charleston   16-17 Feb
NYC (Aca)   23 Feb-   25 Feb-
                 -20 Mar
                 Phila (Aca)

VESTVALI OC (48)
NO   7 Apr-
                             -11 Apr
NYC (Niblo)   13 Apr-
                 -8 May

D'ANGRI OC (49)
Charleston   11 May

1857 (con't)

MORELLI OC (50)
NYC (Aca)   18, 20, 22 May
NYC (Aca)   4-5? June

LAGRANGE OC (52)
Cincinnati (con)   June
NYC (Aca)   29 June-   -20 July

ACADEMY OF MUSIC OC (54)
NYC (Aca)   7 Sept-   -10 Oct
NYC (Aca) (aka ULLMAN OC)   2-20? Nov
NYC (Aca)   30 Nov-

1858
Phila (Aca)   22 Jan-   -15 Jan
NYC (Aca)   22 Feb-   -16 Feb
-1 Apr

MARETZEK OC (59)
NYC (Aca)   30 Aug-   -11 Oct

MARETZEK OC (con't)   Phila (Aca)   11-25 May
Boston   8 June-   -4 July

MARETZEK OC (55)
Phila (Aca)   5-21 Oct
Havana   early Nov-

Charleston   2-6 Mar   -Mar
Phila (Aca)   20 Mar-   -1 May

NYC (Aca)   31 May-   -30 June

STRAKOSCH OC (60)
NYC (Burton) 14 Sept-   -1 Oct
Boston   5-9 Oct

VESTVALI OC (con't)   -29 May
St. Louis   13-26 June
Cincinnati   2 July
Pittsburgh   22-27 July
tour to Mexico and Cuba   leave 9 Nov-
Cuba   Nov-
-Mar
ITALIAN OC (57)   NYC (Burton) 10-15 May
UNKNOWN OC (58)   Balt (Front)   May?

ST. JOHN'S OC (51)
Savannah   19-20 June

BURTON'S OC (53)
NYC (Burton) 17 Aug-   -? Aug

STRAKOSCH OC (56)
Louisville   19-22 Jan

1858 (con't)

MARETZEK OC (con't)

Baltimore	Oct?
Washington	Oct?
Charleston	Nov?
Havana	Nov-

1859

VESTVALI OC (63)

Boston (Theatre)	?-18 June	-18 June

STRAKOSCH OC (con't)

Providence	11-13? Oct	
Boston	14 Oct	
NYC (Burton)	16-22? Oct	
Balt (Holli)	23-28? Oct	
Phila (Aca)	1 Nov-	17? Dec
Louisville	26-29 Jan	
St. Louis	31 Jan-	-19 Feb
Chicago (McVicker)	21 Feb-	-11 Mar
Cincinnati (Pike's)	15 Mar-	-13 Apr
Pittsburgh (Nat)	15-21 Apr	
NYC (Aca)	4 May-	-Apr
Hartford	early June	

ULLMAN OC (61)

NYC (Aca)	20 Oct-	-7 Dec
Boston	9 Dec-	-4 Jan
NYC (Aca)	6-13 Jan	
Phila (Aca)	14-29 Jan	
Balt (Holli)	2-5 Feb	
Phila (Aca)	10 Feb	
NYC (Aca)	11-12 Feb	-19 Feb
NO	3 Mar-	-21 Mar
NYC (Aca)	11-30 Apr	
Phila (Aca)	6-11 May	
Phila (Theatre)	19 May-	-11 June
Worcester	14 June	
Boston (Theatre)	15 June-	-2 July

PARODI OC (62)

Louisville (Mozart Hall)	11-13 Jan	
St. Louis	31 Jan-	

BIANCHI OC (64)

SF	May-	-Sept

PARODI OC (con't)

Buffalo	Aug	
Rochester	Aug	
Cincinnati	24 Aug-	-3 Sept
Louisville (Mozart Hall)	7-15 Sept	

1859 (con't)

MARETZEK OC (65)

NYC (Aca)	12 Sept-	
	-1 Oct	
to Havana	16 Nov-	

ULLMAN-STRAKOSCII OC (66)

Boston (Theatre)	3-15 Oct	
NYC (Aca)	17 Oct-	
	-3 Dec	
Phila (Aca)	5-23 Dec	
NYC (Aca)	21-30 Dec	

1860

Boston (Aca)	2-27 Jan	
NYC (Aca)	6 Feb-	
	-3 Mar	
Phila (Aca)	5-10 Mar	
Balt (Holli)	12-17 Mar	
Washington	19-24 Mar	
Balt (Holli)	26-31 Mar	
Phila (Aca)	2-4 Apr	
	-26 Mar	
NYC (Aca)	9 Apr-	

NYC (Winter Garden) 11 Apr-

-19 May

-2 June?

PARODI OC (con't)

St. Louis	15 Sept-	
	-10 Oct	
Cincinnati (Pike)	17-28? Oct	
Detroit	21? Nov-	
	-2 Dec?	
Chicago (Metro)	5-10 Dec	
St. Louis (Var)	19-21 Dec	
St. Louis (Opera Hse)	27 Dec-	
	-7 Jan	
Nashville	18?-28? Jan	
Savannah (Athen)	13-18 Feb	
Augusta	late Feb	
Charleston (Theatre)	20 Feb-	
	-3? Mar	
Charleston	12-14 Mar	
Macon	late Mar	
Columbus, Ga	26-31 Mar	
Mobile (Ampi-theatre)	April	
NO	23 Apr-	
	-4? May	

CORTESI OC (68)

left Havana	early Feb	
Matanzas, Cuba	Mar	
Porto Principe, Cuba	Mar	
Charleston	14-15 May	
Boston (Theatre)	28 May-	
	-2 June	
NYC (Aca)	4-19 June	
Boston	20-27 June	

ANSCHUTZ OC (67)

NYC (Niblo)	12-17 Dec

Commentary and Sources

1. Sanquirico-Patti Opera Company. For a detailed discussion of this company, see chapter 3.

2. Astor Place Opera Company. For a detailed discussion of this company, see chapter 3.

2a. Astor Place Opera Company. For a brief discussion of this company, see chapter 4.

2b. Astor Place Opera Company (Detachment).

3. Havana Opera Company. For a detailed discussion of this company, see chapter 3.

4. Lombardi Opera Company. An unknown company; see *MW*, 27 May 1848.

5. Astor Place Opera Company. Max Maretzek's first (partial) season as manager of the Astor Place Company. For a brief discussion of this company, see chapter 4.

6. Tedesco Opera Company. This troupe is perhaps a remnant of the Havana Opera Company (see Hoole 1946, 127).

7. Grand Italian Opera Company. According to a single surviving playbill, this company was comprised of thirty-five artists, including a chorus and a full orchestra. Performances in Mobile, Charleston, and New Orleans also are mentioned; there is no mention of personnel or repertory. Playbill in Special Collections, University of Georgia (cited in Mahan 1967).

8. Italian Opera Company. This company included the soprano Fortunata Tedesco; it was formed from parts of the Astor and Havana troupes (Lawrence 1988, 573).

9. Unknown Opera Company. This unnamed company is mentioned by Fletcher (1931). The company's repertory included *Lucrezia Borgia* and *La fille du regiment*.

10. Astor Place Opera Company. Max Maretzek's first full season as the manager of the Astor Place Company. For a brief discussion of this company, see chapter 4.

10a. Astor Place Opera Company (detachment).

11. Adams Opera Company. This troupe also is identified as the Biscaccianti Opera Company (Green 1971, 437).

12. Havana Opera Company. This company also was referred to as the Arditi Opera Company. According to Hoole (1946), the troupe numbered more than ninety performers when it arrived in Charleston; by the time it reached Philadelphia six months later, it claimed on a playbill to be 110 strong. This company is discussed briefly in chapter 4. Information for the itinerary of the 1850 Havana Opera Company is from the following sources: *Charleston:* Hoole 1946, 55, 128; *New York:* Odell 1970, 5:563, 575, 590; appropriate issues of the *Spirit, Saroni's,* and the *Message Bird; Boston: Message Bird,* 15 May 1850, 335; 1 June 1850, 346, 351; 15 June 1850, 351; Kaufman worklist; *Philadelphia:* Playbill, Chestnut Street Theatre, 11 Sept. 1850, Opera Programs, 1836–59, MWA; *Figaro,* 14 Sept. 1850; *Prompter's Whistle,* 28 Sept. 1850, 89, 91; Curtis n.d.; *Havana: Message Bird,* 1 Nov. 1850, 515.

13. Astor Place Opera Company. For an extended discussion of the 1850–51 Astor Place Opera Company, see chapter 4.

13a. Astor Place Opera Company.

13b. Astor Place Opera Company (detachment). Maretzek split his 1851–52 Astor Place Opera Company into two branches. The northern half was to perform in New York until the end of their New York engagement, then planned to meet the southern half, which had proceeded south in a more leisurely fashion, performing en route, in New Orleans. From there, the reunited forces would proceed to Havana for a lengthy engagement. In *C&Q,* Maretzek reveals that the southern branch was under the charge of "an agent" (identified in the *Savannah Republican* as Bernard Ullman). The company experienced some difficulties in Charleston (Maretzek writes that Ullman "had got into serious troubles with the vocalists placed under his charge") and subsequently fell apart in Savannah. Hoole (1946) reports two different companies for the Charleston engagement: the Max Maretzek Opera Company (which performed 10–29 Nov.) and the Don Giovanni Italian Opera Company

(1–13 Dec.). The singers for the two companies are the same, however, suggesting that the company split up before it reached Savannah. For an amusing account of events in the south, see *C&Q*, 193–99; the *Savannah Republican* is cited in Green 1971, 457. The Philadelphia engagement is reported in Curtis (n.d.) and Armstrong (1884) as well as in the appropriate issues of *Spirit*, the *Message Bird*, and *Saroni's*. Curtis (461) gives the terminal date of the engagement as 4 Oct., but Armstrong (who mis-identifies the company as the "Havana Opera Company") gives it as 13 Oct. (69). According to Stoutamire, this troupe was the first to give complete performances of Italian opera in Richmond (1960, 180). In-formation on Charleston is from *Saroni's*, 29 Nov. 1851, 61 and Hoole 1946, 57; for Savannah, see Green 1971, 457.

14. Pellegrini Opera Company. The first Italian opera mounted in San Francisco was *La Sonnambula*, performed by the Pellegrini troupe on 12 Feb. 1851. This was the first opera performance of what would be a fifty-five night season in 1851. According to an uncited interview with the company's bass Alfred Roncovieri, the troupe arrived in San Francisco from Chile; their California appearances were the end of a six-month tour that had encompassed twenty-five thousand miles (Samson n.d.; McMinn 1941, 374–75; Hartley t.s.; Estavan 1939, 10–13; Gagey 1950, 32; Lengyel 1939, 122; and Gaer 1970).

15. Artists' Union Italian Opera Company. This was a splinter group from the Astor Place Company of 1851–52. The Artists' Union Company performed at Niblo's in direct competition with Maretzek, an event that precipitated an operatic price war that left both groups broke. The Artists' Union then went to Boston, where (according to Maretzek) they per-formed for two weeks before disbanding (*C&Q*, 205). The troupe also was known as the Bosio Opera Company and the Italian Artists' Union Opera Company. See *Spirit*, 21 Feb. 1852, and Kaufman worklist, Boston.

16. Astor Place Opera Company. At the conclusion of his second New York engagement at the Astor Place Opera House, Maretzek took the remnants of his troupe to New Orleans and Mexico. The company had been severely crippled by the loss of numerous singers to the Artists' Union Italian Opera Company. Furthermore, according to Maretzek, the operatic war between the two companies during January and February had all but ruined him financially. As a consequence, his only recourse was to "carry that portion of the company which had remained faithful to my fortunes to Mexico, where I felt confident that it must make money" (*C&Q*, 202–5, 221). For information on the engagement in New Orleans and Mexico, see Kaufman worklist, New Orleans; *Saroni's*, 10 April 1852, 357; *AMR*, June 1852, 89; *C&Q*, 221ff. The company's arrival back in New York in March 1853 is reported in *Spirit*, 12 March 1853.

17. Strakosch Opera Company. See Kaufman worklist, New Orleans.

18. Carncross Opera Company. This was a small troupe comprised of three women and four men; the troupe reportedly sang opera in English and Italian (Mahan 1967, 35–36). Nothing further is known about it.

19. Sontag Opera Company. The German-born Henriette Sontag (1806–54) was a first-rank soprano. She had appeared to great acclaim in Vienna, Berlin, Paris, and London (where she and Malibran had a friendly rivalry) before marrying a Sardinian ambassador, Count Carlo Rossi, and retiring from the stage in 1830. She resumed her operatic career in 1848, making several tours of England, then came to the United States at the behest of Bernard Ullman. For information on her career, see Pleasants 1981, 192–97; Slonimsky 1978; and Lerner 1970, 64–73. See also White 1882, 4:39–40. Sontag made her American debut in concert on 27 Sept. 1852; between 14 Oct. and mid-Dec. she appeared in concerts in Philadelphia twice and in Boston, New York City, Balti-more, and Washington. Her operatic debut was at Niblo's Garden in New York on 10 Jan. 1853 (Lerner 1970, 71; *Dwight's*, 8 Jan. 1853, 111; *AMR*, Jan. 1853, 10–11). Information on the New York opera season can be found in the appropriate issues of *Spirit*, *MW*, and *AMR*; see also Odell 1970, 6:240–42. For her Philadelphia engagement, see Curtis n.d., 491 and Armstrong 1884, 76–77. The Boston information is from Kauf-man worklist, Boston; Lerner 1970, 78; and *Spirit*, 28 May 1853. The Worcester appearance was a concert performance only (Playbill, 29 May 1853, Worcester City Hall, MWA).

20. Alboni Opera Company. Marietta Alboni (1826–94), a mezzo-soprano, was another highly successful European singer. She had studied

with Rossini as his only pupil and had a "sumptuous and flawless" voice (Pleasants 1981, 223); Dwight described her as the "greatest contralto in the world" (*Dwight's*, 15 May 1852, 46). She arrived in this country in June 1852 (*Spirit*, 26 June 1852, 228) and performed in concert in various cities until Dec. 1852, when she formed an opera company under the management of Le Grand Smith (*Spirit*, 12 March 1853). By the time of her Philadelphia engagement, Max Maretzek, who had been in Mexico with his company, was serving as her orchestra conductor. Shortly thereafter, her company and Maretzek's joined forces for performances at Niblo's Garden in New York (*Spirit*, 12 March 1853, 48). See also note 21, below. About Alboni's career, see Pleasants 1981, 223–24. For comments on her voice, see White 1882, 3:35–39. Information on her itinerary is from the following sources: Dec. 1852 through March 1853 issues of *Dwight's*, *Spirit*, and *MW*; Odell 1970, 6:186–89; Kaufman worklist, Boston; Playbills, Walnut Street Theatre, 28 Feb., 2, 4, 5 March 1853, Theatre Collection, PP; Curtis n.d., 469; and Armstrong 1884, 75–76.

21. Lorini Opera Company. In March 1853 Eliza Biscaccianti was reported to be on her way to join Domenico Lorini's Opera Company in Lima, Peru. According to Waddington (1947, 49), the Lorini Company also was known as the Garbato Opera Company, and it performed in San Francisco sometime in 1853. Lorini's troupe presumably disbanded during the winter or early spring of 1854, for he joined the Arditi Opera Company in New Orleans in April 1854 (*Spirit*, 5 March 1853; Kaufman 1986–87, 45).

22. Pellegrini Opera Company. See Estavan 1939, 10–13; Waddington 1947, 49.

23. Grand Combination Opera Company. This troupe was a combination of the Alboni and Maretzek opera companies, the latter recently returned from Mexico. At the end of this engagement Marietta Alboni returned to Europe; she left on 1 June 1853. For more information, see Odell 1970, 6:242; and note 20.

24. Steffanone Opera Company. This was a company formed around the soprano Balbina Steffanone, a former prima donna with the 1850 Havana Opera Company. See Hoole 1946, 133; Stoutamire 1960, 180; and White 1882, 3:31.

25. Dumbolton's Opera Company. See Teal 1964, Appendix C.

26. Arditi Italian Opera Company. For a full description of this company's tour, see Kaufman 1986–87. Other sources for the Arditi-DeVries Company's itinerary include: *Cincinnati*: Wolz 1983, 64; *Spirit*, 13 Aug. 1853; *Louisville*: Weisert 1955; *St. Louis*: *MW*, 13 May 1854, 19; 20 May 1854, 25; 27 May 1854, 42; *Dwight's*, 3 June 1854, 71; Playbill, Varieties Theatre (St. Louis) 8, 12 May 1854, HTC; *MR&CA*, 25 May, 8 June 1854; *Chicago*: Hackett 1913, 32; *Detroit*: Teal 1964, Appendix C; *Baltimore*: *Spirit*, 10 Dec. 1853, 516; *MW*, 23 Dec. 1853; *Washington*: *MW*, 14 Jan. 1854, 19; *Richmond*: *MW*, 21 Jan. 1854, 28; Stoutamire 1960, 180; *Savannah*: *MR&CA*; 17 Aug. 1854, 292; Green 1971, 466; *Augusta*: *MW*, 11 Feb. 1854, 65; *New Orleans*: *MW*, 22 April 1854, 190; *Dwight's*, 15 April 1854, 15. Sources for the Arditi Company's itinerary between 12 June-Dec. 1854: *Louisville*: *MW*, 17, 24 June, 1, 8, 15 July; *Cincinnati*: Wolz 1983, 67; *Spirit*, 22 July 1854; Playbill (Cincinnati) National Theatre, 19 July 1854, HTC; *MW*, 8 July 1854; *Cleveland, Buffalo, Toronto*: Kaufman 1986–87; *Rochester*: *MR&CA*, 17 Aug. 1854, 292 and 31 Aug. 1854, 207; *MW*, 26 Aug. 1854, 203; *Chicago*: *MG*, 2 Dec. 1854, 25; Sherman 1947, 258; Upton 1847–81, vol. 1, Nov. 1854; *Nashville*: Davenport 1941, 139.

27. Maretzek Opera Company. Maretzek's company performed at New York's Castle Garden during the summer of 1853. The troupe's prima donna during July and August was Henriette Sontag, who left the company after the close of the Castle Garden engagement. In September Maretzek's troupe took up residence at Niblo's Garden because the Astor Place house had been closed. His prima donna was Balbina Steffanone; she and several other members of the company (Lorenzo Salvi and Ignazio Marini) were left over from the great Havana troupe of 1850. See Odell 1970, 6:270–71, 314–15. See also Sept.-Dec. issues of *MW*, *AMR*, *Dwight's*, and *Spirit*. For information on the singers, see Schiavo 1947, 75 and White 1882, 3:31–32. On 5 Jan. 1854, Maretzek and his company were reported to be on their way to Havana by the *MR&CA*.

28. Steffanone Opera Company. This troupe was also known as the Salvi Opera Company. It included among its members Carolina Pico-

Vietti and her husband, Adelindo Vietti, who left this troupe and joined the Arditi Company in New Orleans in April 1854 (Kaufman 1986–87, 45). Information on the company's itinerary is from *MW*, 18 March 1854, 121; *Dwight's*, 15 April 1854, 15; and *MR&CA*, 19 Jan. 1854, 16 Feb. 1854.

29. Henriette Sontag (concert tour). Between 17 Sept. and mid-Oct. 1853 Henriette Sontag concertized extensively, performing in Philadelphia, Boston, Worcester, Buffalo, Baltimore, and elsewhere. According to Kaufman, she and her manager Bernard Ullman made their way south to New Orleans via the Ohio and Mississippi rivers, presumably concertizing en route. Lerner provides no information on this tour. Sontag gave a series of concerts in New Orleans between 13–17 Feb. (her competition was the concert troupe of Maurice Strakosch], then joined the Arditi-DeVries Opera Company in Mobile (Kaufman 1986–87, 44, 50; Lerner 1970, 83; Playbill, 5 Dec. 1853, Worcester City Hall, MWA.

30. Sontag Opera Company. For information on Sontag's Opera Company in Mexico, see *MW*, 18 March 1854; *MR&CA*, 11 May 1854, 157; and *Dwight's*, 15 April 1854, 15. In June, while the company was en route from Mexico City to Vera Cruz, Sontag and several members of her troupe contracted cholera. Sontag, Pozzolini, and Rossi all died of the disease; Badiali and others recovered. Pozzolini's death is reported in *MR&CA*, 3 Aug. 1854, 277; Rossi's death is reported in *MW*, 5 Aug. 1854, 158 and *MR&CA*, 17 Aug. 1854, 292. Sontag died on 17 June 1854 (*MW*, 1 July 1854, 97).

31. Hayes Opera Company. Catherine Hayes (1820–61) performed with a company assembled for her at the Metropolitan Theatre in San Francisco; it included Signor Leonardi, Stephen Leach, and George Loder. This was not a traveling company, but rather a troupe assembled to assist a visiting star. Hayes left for Australia on 8 July 1854. See *Spirit*, 20 May 1854 and 3 June 1854; Estavan 1939, 39. A biography of Hayes appears in Lengyel 1939, 30–39.

32. Maretzek Opera Company. According to Odell, this troupe consisted of an "almost entirely new group of singers" from the previous year; it was "the most undistinguished [aggregation] that had been in New York for years" (1970, 6:336). Information on the Philadelphia

engagement is from Curtis n.d., vol. 2; see also the June-Sept. issues of *Dwight's*, *MR&CA*, *MW*, and *Spirit*.

33. Grisi and Mario Opera Company. Giulia Grisi (1811–69) and her husband Giovanni Matteo Mario (1810–1883) were two of the very best European singers during their prime. Their brief visit to the United States in 1854 was both historic and lucrative. American critics and audiences alike, however, expressed disappointment. Mario tended to be frequently indisposed, and Grisi was past her prime. Their company performed at the inaugural season of the New York Academy of Music. While in the United States the two singers were under the management of James H. Hackett, an actor and sometime theatrical manager. Luigi Arditi was the orchestra director for this troupe, the other singers of which were recruited in the United States. For information on the singers, see Pleasants 1981, 178–84 and White 1882, 4:193–97. *Dwight's*, *MG*, and *MW* are full of commentary about them from Sept. 1854-Feb. 1855. Information about their itinerary is also from the following sources: *Philadelphia:* Armstrong 1884, 83; *Washington: Dwight's*, 13 Jan. 1855, 116; *Baltimore: MW*, 14 April 1855, 177 and Kaufman worklist, Baltimore; *Boston: MG*, 20 and 27 Jan. 1855; *MW*, 3, 10, and 17 Feb. 1855.

34. Unknown Opera Company. See *MR&CA*, 31 Aug., 14 Sept. 1854.

35. Lorini Opera Company. The Lorini Opera Company also is referred to as the Garbato Opera Company and the Lorini-Vietti Opera Company. When performing in Cincinnati the troupe was small; Wolz reports that it consisted of only eight performers. Information on the troupe's itinerary is from the following sources: *St. Louis: Spirit*, 14 Oct. 1854; *MG*, 18 Nov. 1854, 9; Kaufman worklist, St. Louis; Jennings worklist, St. Louis (Jennings's terminal date for the St. Louis engagement is 10 Nov.); *Cincinnati:* Wolz 1983, 68; Playbill, Cincinnati Lyceum Theatre, 26–27 Nov. 1854, HTC; *Chicago:* Upton 1847–81, vol. 1, 29.

36. Barili-Thorne Opera Company. The Barili-Thorne troupe reportedly was from New York. They stopped for a short engagement in San Francisco on their way to Guayaquil, Ecuador, and Lima, Peru. The company, however, did not go south at the completion of their engagement in San Francisco in December 1854, for they are reported performing in that city during Jan. and Feb. 1855. See *Spirit*, 16 Dec. 1854,

13 and 20 Jan. 1855; Playbills, San Francisco Metropolitan Theatre, 8, 18, 23 Dec. 1854, 31 Jan. 1855, HTC; Playbills, Metropolitan Theatre, 2 Feb, 1 March 1855, CSf; McMinn 1941, 403–4; MW, 24 Feb. 1855; Estavan 1939, vol. 7, 90; Hartley t.s.; Hixon 1980, 18–19, 33. On 8 Sept. 1855 *Dwight's* reported that the troupe had left California and was en route to Callao, a port city west of Lima, "with the design of making a professional visit to all the principal South American cities" (181). Madame Clotilde Barili-Thorne died in Lima sometime in late Aug. or early Sept. 1856 (*Dwight's*, 13 Sept. 1856, 191).

37. Warden's Opera Company. Unknown company that performed in Mozart Hall, Louisville (Weisert 1962).

38. Academy of Music Opera Company. During its first season the Academy of Music Opera Company was under the joint management of Ole Bull, Maurice Strakosch, and Max Maretzek. Bull was general manager and lessee of the academy, Strakosch went to Europe to recruit, and Maretzek conducted the orchestra (*Dwight's*, 6 Jan. 1855, 111; *MW*, 3 Feb. 1855, 37). The enterprise collapsed within two weeks but then reopened under the management of Maretzek (*MR&CA*, 15 March 1855, 90–91; *Dwight's*, 10 March 1855, 180–81, 188). For Maretzek's account of the affair, see *S&F*, 16–17. In early May the LaGrange troupe was engaged at Niblo's, and William Niblo arranged that the two troupes perform jointly. Odell reports, however, that the joint season was a failure. The singers did not get along, and the LaGrange Company performed only once during this period. For accounts of the singers' squabbles, see Odell 1970, 6:395; *NYMR&G*, 19 May 1855, 162; *Dwight's*, 19 May 1855, 55; and *MW*, 19 May 1855. For an account of the final season in New York City, see Odell 1970, 6:395. For information on the Boston engagement, see Kaufman worklist, Boston; Tompkins 1908; and Playbills, Boston Theatre, 21 May–9 June 1855, Rare Books, MB.

39. Metropolitan Opera Company. Unknown company that performed for one week (Sherman 1947, 281).

40. LaGrange Opera Company. During the LaGrange Company's engagement in Boston they performed only one opera (on 18 June); the rest were concerts (Tompkins 1908, 33; Kaufman worklist, Boston; Playbill, Boston Theatre, 18 June 1855, Rare Books, MB; *Dwight's*, 9, 16, 23 June 1855). For New York, see Odell 1970, 6:395–96, and the appropriate issues of *Dwight's*, *NYMR&G*, and *MW*.

41. Academy of Music Opera Company. The 1855–56 Academy of Music Company was under the management of W. H. Payne; Maretzek was conductor. The troupe is also referred to as the Maretzek Opera Company, the LaGrange Opera Company, and the Italian Opera Company. Sources: *New York:* Odell 1970, 6:476–77, 477–78; *Dwight's* and *MW* (Oct. 1855–June 1856); *Philadelphia:* Armstrong 1884, 85; *Baltimore:* *Dwight's*, 19 Jan. 1856, 127; *Boston:* Kaufman worklist, Boston; Playbills, 21 Jan.–22 Feb., Boston Theatre, Rare Books, MB; Tompkins 1908, 40–41.

42. Vestvali Opera Company. This troupe was named for the soprano Felicita (or Teresa) Vestvali; it also is identified as the Roncari (or Ronconi) Opera Company. It was reportedly performing in Mexico in late Oct. 1855; the troupe included an orchestra of forty and a chorus of thirty-six (*MW*, 15 Dec. 1855, 385 and 1 March 1856, 97; *Dwight's*, 27 Oct. 1855, 29 and 29 March 1856, 205). For Boston performances, see Tompkins 1908, 44; Playbills, Boston Theatre, 4–18 June, Rare Books, MB. For information on travel to Mexico in the fall of 1856, see *MW*, 6 and 20 Sept., 15 Nov. 1856. For information on Vestvali, see White 1882, 4:197–98.

43. Garbato Opera Company. See Estavan 1939, 13.

44. Parodi Opera Company. This troupe was the company of the soprano Teresa Parodi (Teal 1964, Appendix C). For information on Parodi, see chapter 4.

45. Academy of Music Opera Company. The Sept. season of the Academy of Music Company was under the direction of Max Maretzek. This troupe is referred to variously as the LaGrange, Maretzek, and Academy of Music opera companies; the prima donna was Anna de LaGrange. The fall season in New York came to an abrupt end as the result of a disagreement between Maretzek and the Academy of Music stockholders, and Maretzek took the troupe to Boston. The subsequent New York season of 10 Nov.–11 Dec. nominally was under the management of Baron Stankovitch, LaGrange's husband. Under the arrangement Stankovitch had made with the stockholders (masterminded by

Maretzek) Maretzek was not permitted to conduct, yet he did so anyway after a large audience at the academy gave an obviously staged demonstration in his favor. For Maretzek's account of the story, see *S&F*, 21–25; see also Odell 1970, 6:573–74; *MW*, 4 Oct. 1856, 465 and 25 Oct. 1856, 529; *NYMR&G*, 15 Nov. 1845, 353; and *Dwight's*, 11 Oct. 1856, 15. For information on Boston, see Kaufman worklist, Boston; Playbills, 20 Oct.–8 Nov., Boston Theatre, Rare Books, MB; Tompkins 1908, 48. The second New York season (under Stankovitch) came to an abrupt halt in early Dec. when the entire company accepted an engagement at the Tacon Theatre in Havana (*Dwight's*, 6, 13, and 20 Dec. 1856).

46. Maretzek Opera Company. Maretzek stayed in Havana for two months, then brought his troupe back to the United States in Feb. 1857 with the intention of opening the new Philadelphia Academy of Music. By the time the company reached Charleston its prima donna, Anna de LaGrange, had left and was concertizing in New Orleans; she was replaced in Philadelphia by the soprano Marietta Gazzaniga. For Maretzek's account of his company's adventures in Havana, see *S&F*, 26–32. See also *Dwight's*, 7 Feb. 1857, 151 and 21 Feb. 1857, 167, and Hoole 1946 for dates of performances in Charleston. For Philadelphia information, see Armstrong 1884, 88–89; Playbills, American Academy of Music, 6 March–23 May, American Academy of Music Scrapbook, Music Department, PP; *MW*, 7 March 1857, 150, and issues from 23 May–6 June 1857; *Dwight's*, 11 April 1857, 14–15. For information on the New York (Niblo's) engagement, see Odell 1970, 6:563–64; *Dwight's*, 11 April, 2 May; and *MW*, 9 May 1857, 290. For the two-night "season" at the New York Academy of Music in June, see *MW*, 13 June 1857, 371 and *Dwight's*, 6 June 1857; Odell does not mention these appearances. Boston information is from Kaufman worklist, Boston; *Dwight's*, 13, 20, and 27 June 1857; *MW*, 20, 27 June and 4 July 1857; Playbills, Boston Theatre, 13, 15 June 1857, MWA.

47. Academy of Music Opera Company. The Academy of Music Company of Jan.–March 1857 (also known as the Strakosch Opera Company) was a completely different troupe from that of the previous fall, for Maretzek had taken most of the singers in the former company to

Havana in Dec. 1856. The New York company, whose prima donna was Teresa Parodi, was under the management of Maurice Strakosch. Since her New York debut under Maretzek during the 1850–51 season, Parodi had toured the United States extensively in concert troupes with Strakosch. The company mounted two seasons in New York; at the close of the second, the academy was dark until mid-May. See Odell 1970, 6:575–76; *MW*, weekly issues 31 Jan.–21 March 1857; and *Dwight's*, weekly issues 24 Jan.–21 March 1857. For information on Parodi, see chapter 4.

48. Vestvali Opera Company. This company also is identified as the Corradi-Setti Opera Company. Information on the troupe's itinerary is from the following sources: *New Orleans*: Kaufman worklist, New Orleans; *St. Louis*: Kaufman worklist, St. Louis; Jennings worklist, St. Louis; *Cincinnati*: Wolz 1983, 71; Playbill, Wood's Theatre, 2 July 1857, HTC; *Pittsburgh*: Fletcher 1931. When she was not managing her own opera troupes (which generally performed in Central or South America), Felicita Vestvali performed in the companies of others. In late Aug. 1857 she was part of a troupe that performed at Burton's Theatre in New York, and in Sept. and Oct. of that year was a member of the Academy of Music company during its first 1857–58 season (Odell 1970, 6:529, 7:62). By 21 Nov. she was reported to have sailed for Matanzas, Cuba, with the rest of her own troupe. The following April Dwight reported that she had been "reaping laurels and dollars in Havana" (*MW*, 21 Nov. 1857, 721; *Dwight's*, 3 April 1858, 7).

49. D'Angri Opera Company. This unknown company featured the soprano Elena D'Angri. It performed *Il barbiere di Siviglia* on 11 May 1857 at the Charleston Theatre; whether it was the entire opera or just scenes is unknown. The troupe included in its ranks Theodore Thomas (see Hoole 1946).

50. Morelli Opera Company. The New York Academy of Music was opened for three performances under the management of P. Morelli to give the young New York singer Cora de Wilhorst a chance to perform in opera before she left for more training in Europe (Odell 1970, 6:573–74; *Dwight's*, 6 June 1857, 78).

51. St. John's Opera Company. This company is mentioned in the

Savannah Daily Morning News on 15 June 1857; no repertory or other information is provided (Green 1971, 504).

52. LaGrange Opera Company. The Cincinnati visit is mentioned in *MW*, 20 June 1857, 389. Information on the season at the academy is in Odell 1970, 6:576–77; *MW*, 18 July 1857, 455; and *Dwight's*, 4 and 11 July 1857.

53. Burton's Opera Company. The Burton troupe was not intended to be an itinerant troupe, and it performed only in New York during Aug. 1857. It seems to have functioned in part as a temporary job for a number of singers (including Vestvali, Brignoli, Amodio, Coletti, and Luigia Caranti) who were in between engagements (Odell 1970, 6:529).

54. Academy of Music Opera Company. The dates Lerner gives (1970, 136–37) for the 1857–58 Academy of Music seasons are only partially correct. The company was managed jointly by Ullman, Thalberg, and Strakosch; the troupe also was known as the Ullman-Strakosch Opera Company. The star singers were Erminia Frezzolini, Anna de LaGrange, and Edouard Gassier (baritone); the conductor was Carl Anschitz. According to Lerner, the troupe numbered 150 members, including a corps de ballet (130–31). The Philadelphia information is from *Dwight's*, 30 Jan., 13 Feb. 1858; Armstrong 1884, 92. The great German bass Carl Formes (1815–89) made his American operatic debut with the Ullman Company early in the season that commenced 30 Nov. 1857. As usual, the manager (Ullman) was beset with a variety of difficulties during the season, including a strike by the male chorus on 8 Jan. (Odell 1970, 7:63–65; *MW*, 5, 19, and 26 Dec. 1857; *Dwight's*, 16 Jan. 1858, 322). For information on Formes, see White 1882, 4:204; for Formes's account of his adventures with the Ullman Company, see his memoirs (1891, 188ff). For information on the first Philadelphia engagement, see Armstrong 1884, 92; *Dwight's*, 30 Jan. 1858, 351, and 13 Feb. 1858, 306. For the second New York engagement, see Odell 1970, 7:65; *Dwight's*, 20 Feb.–3 April 1858.

55. Maretzek Opera Company. During its Philadelphia engagement, the Maretzek Opera Company was also known as the Marshall Opera Company, or the Marshall-Maretzek Opera Company; E. A. Marshall was the lessee of the Philadelphia Academy of Music (*S&F*, 41; *Dwight's*,

26 Sept. 1857, 207; *MW*, 10 Oct. 1857, 647). Later the troupe also was identified as the Havana Opera Company. For information about the Philadelphia engagement, see Armstrong 1884, 91; *Dwight's*, 3 Oct. 1857, 215; 17 Oct. 1857, 231. At the beginning of the engagement at the Tacon Theatre, Maretzek had in his company both Marietta Gazzaniga (the successful prima donna of the previous year) and Erminia Frezzolini, apparently stolen from the Ullman-Strakosch New York Academy of Music Company. By February, Frezzolini had left the Havana Company and was performing in New Orleans with Maurice Strakosch (*S&F*, 32–34; *Dwight's*, 13 Feb. 1858, 367). For information on the Charleston engagement, see Hoole 1946, 146; about the second Philadelphia engagement, see Armstrong 1884, 95–96; weekly issues of *Dwight's*, 10 April–15 May 1858; Playbills, American Academy of Music, 8, 23, and 24 April 1858, Academy of Music Scrapbook, PP; and Playbills in Scrapbook vol. 5 (Academy of Music), PPL. At the conclusion of the season in Philadelphia the company broke apart in the midst of "pecuniary difficulties, intrigues, plots and counterplots, quarrels, and many other concomitant features of this peculiar and sensitive institution" (*Dwight's*, 15 May 1858, 53). When Maretzek's company returned from its travels to the South and commenced an engagement at the New York Academy of Music, the troupe was referred to as the Academy of Music Opera Company, the Maretzek Opera Company, or (in honor of the prima donna) the Gazzaniga Opera Company (Odell 1970, 7:66; *Dwight's*, 5 June–17 July 1858; *MW*, 22 May–19 June 1858).

56. Strakosch Opera Company. According to Lerner (1970, 137), Strakosch broke off his partnership with Ullman during the second Academy of Music season (2–20 Nov. 1857) and headed into the hinterland with Frezzolini. Frezzolini, however, is reported to have gone to Havana with Maretzek's company. Strakosch probably took a group of singers on a concert tour; he later met up with Frezzolini in New Orleans (see note 55). The Louisville information is from Weisert 1962.

57. Italian Opera Company. Dwight identified this company as a fragment of the Philadelphia Academy of Music Company (the Maretzek Opera Company and the Havana Opera Company). They performed in Burton's Theatre (formerly Palmo's Opera House) for a week (*Dwight's*,

15 May 1858, 55; Odell 1970, 7:16–17). Giorgio Ronconi and Anna de LaGrange both sang with this short-lived troupe. According to Dwight (22 May 1858, 63), they both left for Europe on 19 May 1858.

58. Unknown Opera Company. This mysterious company is identified in MW of 24 April 1858 (258) as belonging to Max Maretzek. In the 15 May issue, however, this connection is denied (305). According to the latter report, "a Mr. Stuart" was the operatic speculator managing the company. Originally the season was to commence on 21 April; apparently it started on 8 May. Marietta Gazzaniga was somehow connected with the troupe.

59. Maretzek Opera Company. For information on the New York season, see Odell 1970, 7:156, and Dwight's, 4 Sept. 1858, 182; general information about the season can be found in the weekly issues of Dwight's, 18 Sept., 2, 9, and 16 Oct.; a summary of the season is in 23 Oct., 236–37. See also MW for the same period. Just before the end of the season in New York, Maretzek learned that the Tacon Theatre, where his company had planned to start an engagement in November, had been severely damaged in an explosion. This caused much sympathetic hand-wringing on the part of the MW's editorial staff. There was speculation that Maretzek's company would have to be broken up and that many of the singers would return to Europe. They would have difficulty finding employment in the United States, the editor pointed out, because there was "such a plethora [of singers] at present" in the country. Maretzek left immediately for Havana and secured a lease for another theater. He and his troupe reportedly left New York on 16 Nov. 1858. See MW, 23 Oct. 1858, 674, and 6 Nov. 1858, 707. A playbill from the Holliday Street Theatre in Baltimore announced in advance that the Havana Opera Company (Maretzek's troupe) planned a short series of four performances in that city, followed by "two or three in Washington," en route to Charleston and Havana (15 Oct. 1858, Rare Books, MB). However, no evidence of these performances has come to light. The damage to the Tacon Theatre delayed the troupe's departure from New York by two weeks, and it is likely that the company took the most direct route to Havana so as not to delay the opening of their season there. How long the Havana engagement lasted is unknown, although apparently it went

well. By 9 April Dwight reported that the return of Maretzek's company to New York was "expected at any time" (22 Jan. 1859, 341; 9 April 1859, 14).

60. Strakosch Opera Company. Strakosch opened his New York season at Burton's Theatre in direct competition with Maretzek at the academy. According to Dwight, the season was to be short and to be followed by a "provincial tour" (18 Sept. 1858, 197; see also Dwight's, 2 and 9 Oct. 1858; Odell 1970, 7:113). For Boston and Providence information, see Kaufman worklist, Boston; Dwight's, 9–23 Oct; Tompkins 1908, 72. For New York information, see Odell 1970, 7:114, and MW, 23 Oct. 1858. An advertisement that appeared in the playbills of Baltimore's Holliday Street Theatre during October informed patrons of the imminent arrival of "Strakosch's Celebrated N. York Italian Opera Company." According to the advertisement, the troupe numbered thirty performers (Playbills, Rare Books, MB). See also Kaufman worklist, Baltimore. For Philadelphia information, see Armstrong 1884, 99, and Dwight's, 13 Nov.–25 Dec. 1858. After the conclusion of the Philadelphia engagement in December, Strakosch and his troupe headed south and west for a tour. In Cincinnati the company opened the brand-new Pike's Opera House. They chose for the opening performance Flotow's Martha, and according to Wolz (1983, 74), the public of the Queen City was outraged that the company inaugurated their new Italian opera house with a non-Italian opera. The information on the itinerary is from the following sources: Louisville: Weisert 1955; St. Louis: Kaufman worklist, St. Louis; Chicago: Upton 1847–81, vol. 1, 54; Hackett 1913, 51; Sherman 1958, 428; Cincinnati: Wolz 1983, 74; Dwight's, 23 April 1859, 30; Playbills, Pike's Opera House, 15–23 March 1858, HTC; Pittsburgh: Fletcher 1931. When the Strakosch Company returned to New York, they reopened at the New York Academy of Music following the conclusion of the Ullman Company's engagement on 30 April. Strakosch now had in his ranks Ullman's former star, Maria Piccolomini (see note 61), whose "farewell engagement" lasted from 4–31 May. When she left, Strakosch introduced a new soprano, Adelaide Cortesi. According to Dwight, a part of Strakosch's troupe performed in Hartford, Connecticut in early June (11

62. Parodi Opera Company. This troupe also is referred to variously as the Strakosch Opera Company, the Grand Opera Company, and the Italian Opera Company. Their travels have not been thoroughly researched and undoubtedly were much more extensive than indicated here. Dwight reports that the company numbered forty performers in August 1859, and when they appeared in Columbus, Georgia, in March 1860 the troupe also is described as forty in number. The information given here is from the following sources: *Louisville:* Weisert 1962; *St. Louis:* Hoole 1917, 30; Jennings worklist, St. Louis; Kaufman worklist, St. Louis (according to Kaufman, the Dec.-Jan. engagement ended on 5 January); *Buffalo and Rochester: Dwight's,* 20 Aug. 1859, 166; *Cincinnati:* Wolz 1983, 84; *Dwight's,* 3 Sept. 1859, 183; *MW,* 5 Nov. 1859, 5 (both *MW* and the *Cincinnati Enquirer* [quoted in Wolz] indicate that the troupe was not well received in Cincinnati); *Detroit:* Teal 1964, Appendix C; *Chicago:* Upton 1847–81, vol. 1, 61; *Spirit,* 14 Jan. 1860, 304; *Nashville: Spirit,* 18 Feb. 1860, 384; Davenport 1941, 142; *Savannah:* Green 1971, 541; *BMT,* 25 Feb. 1860, 7; *Charleston:* Hoole 1946, 151; *BMT,* 25 Feb., 7 and 10 March 1860, 28; *Augusta:* Steinhaus 1973, 124; *Macon: BMT,* 7 April 1860, 63; Steinhaus 1973, 124; *Columbus:* Mahan 1967, 105; *Mobile: BMT,* 21 April 1860, 79; *New Orleans: BMT,* 5 May 1860, 95; Kendall 1968, 484.

63. Vestvali Opera Company. See Playbill, Boston Theatre, 18 June 1859, MWA.

64. Bianchi Opera Company. Information about this troupe is fairly scattered. The company may have performed intermittently from May through September; it may also have mounted several successive seasons. Information is from the following sources: Hixon 1980, 20, 48, 64; Gaer 1970; Estavan 1939, 90; Commanday, unpublished research notes; California; Verdi, *Il Trovatore* 1859 (includes list of members of the Bianchi Company).

65. Maretzek Opera Company. Maretzek's was the first company to perform at the Academy of Music during the 1859–60 season; Dwight refers to this engagement as a "preliminary season" (3 Sept. 1859, 183). Lerner states (1970, 157–58) that Maretzek and Ullman were business partners in this venture, but he provides no evidence to support this

June 1859, 88). For information on the New York season, see *Dwight's,* 7 May 1859, 45; Odell 1970, 7:161–62; *Dwight's,* 14 May–18 June 1859.

61. Ullman Opera Company. Bernard Ullman's troupe took over the New York Academy of Music after Maretzek and his company vacated the premises to go to Havana in early October 1858. According to *MW,* Ullman's company had a chorus of eighty and an orchestra of sixty, the latter led by Carl Anschütz. The troupe's two stars were the bass Carl Formes and the soprano Maria Piccolomini; the latter became an immense favorite with American audiences (*MW,* 23 Oct. 1858, 674). About Piccolomini, see White 1882, 4:205–6. The information on the New York engagements is from Odell 1970, 7:156–60; *Dwight's* (23 Oct.–4 Dec. 1858; *MW* (23 Oct.–11 Dec. 1858). Kaufman's Boston worklist gives 3 Jan. as terminal date for that engagement; Dwight reports 4 Jan. See also *Dwight's,* 8 Jan. 1859, 326–27 and Tompkins 1908, 72. For the Philadelphia engagement the troupe was called the Piccolomini Opera Company (Armstrong 1884, 100–101; *Dwight's,* 15 Jan.–5 Feb. and 26 Feb.). For Baltimore, see Kaufman worklist, Baltimore; also Playbills, Holliday Street Theatre, 2–5 Feb. Rare Books, MB. Before heading South the troupe stopped for one additional performance in Philadelphia and two in New York. Odell mentions only one performance in Manhattan, on 11 Feb., but both Dwight and *MW* report two (Odell 1970, 7:160; *Dwight's,* 26 Feb., 381; *MW,* 19 Feb. 1859, 115). After the final New York performance, Ullman probably formed a smaller company for operatic and concert performances. According to Lerner, the troupe toured the West, stopping in Cincinnati and other places en route to New Orleans (1970, 154; Kaufman worklist, New Orleans). When he returned from the south, Ullman reopened at the Academy of Music minus his two major stars, Piccolomini and Formes. According to Lerner, the soprano had defected to the camp of Maurice Strakosch because Ullman had bungled her appearance in New Orleans (1970, 154–55; *Dwight's,* 2 April–7 May 1859; Odell 1970, 7:161). For Philadelphia, see Armstrong 1884, 103–4; Playbills, American Academy of Music, 16–17 May 1859, Academy of Music Scrapbook, PP; *Dwight's,* 14 and 21 May 1859. For Boston, see Kaufman worklist, Boston; *Dwight's,* 28 May–18 June, 2 July 1859. For Worcester, see *Dwight's,* 11 June 1859, 7.

contention. Furthermore, Maretzek's unceasing and extremely negative references to Ullman in C&Q make any kind of amicable partnership between the men seem highly unlikely. Odell suggests that the season was managed by Ullman, and Maretzek was the conductor (1970, 7:256–57). However, the personnel of Maretzek's company was quite different from that of the Ullman-Strakosch troupe (whose engagement at the Boston Theatre overlapped Maretzek's New York run slightly), which suggests that there were two different and distinct companies. Reference to the sailing date to Havana is in *Wilke's Spirit*, 22 Oct. 1859, 112. The terminal date of the Havana season is reported in *MW*, 10 March 1860, 5. In early Feb., *MW* reported that there had been a rift in Maretzek's company, and that his former prima donna Adelaide Cortesi was now "marching under her own banner" (25 Feb., 10 March 1860). For his Winter Garden Company, Maretzek featured as his new prima donna Inez Fabbri, a German. The Winter Garden, formerly the Metropolitan Theatre, had been refurbished, renamed, and reopened to the public in Sept. 1859 (Odell 1970, 7:215–16; Ireland 1968, 2:700–702; *BMT*, 2, 16 June 1860).

66. Ullman-Strakosch Opera Company. The Ullman-Strakosch Company opened its fall campaign in Boston; the orchestra conductors of the troupe were announced as Carl Anschütz and Theodore Thomas. The real winter opera season of the New York Academy of Music opened on 17 Oct., after Maretzek's troupe had left. The company in residence was jointly managed by Ullman and Strakosch; Muzio was the conductor. This season was almost a disaster, for several of the stars Strakosch imported from Europe failed completely. Only the fortuitous operatic debut of Strakosch's sixteen-year-old sister-in-law, Adelina Patti—and her phenomenal success—saved the season. At the conclusion of the season Maurice Strakosch formed another concert company and toured the country extensively with Adelina Patti, performing "an almost endless series of farewells" (*BMT*, 19 May 1860, 103). Information about the itinerary of the company is from the following sources: *Boston*: Kaufman worklist, Boston; Playbills, Boston Theatre, 4–15 Oct., Rare Books, MB; Tompkins 1908, 78–79; *Wilke's Spirit*, 22 Oct. 1859, 112; 14 Jan. 1860, 304; 21 Jan. 1860, 308; Playbills, Boston Academy of Music, 7, 14, 20 Jan. 1860, NN; Playbills, Boston Academy of Music, 11, 14, 21 Jan. 1860, MWA; *NYMR&G*, 21 Jan., 4 Feb. 1860; 18 Feb. 1860 has a summary of the fall season in New York, see *Wilke's Spirit*, 10 Dec. 1859, 224; 31 Dec. 1859, 272; *NYMR&G* and *MW*, 8 Feb.–10 March 1860, 14 April and 26 May 1860. For Philadelphia, see Armstrong 1884, 105, 109; *BMT*, 21 April 1860, 78. For Baltimore: Kaufman worklist, Baltimore; *BMT*, 10 March and 7 April 1860; Playbills, Holliday Street Theatre, 20 March 1860, HTC. For Washington: *BMT*, 24 March and 7 April 1860.

67. Anschütz Opera Company. This company was a nontraveling troupe formed of "second-choice" singers from the Academy of Music under the direction of Carl Anschütz (Odell 1970, 7:249).

68. Cortesi Italian Opera Company. This was a splinter group from Maretzek's Havana Opera Company, headed by Adelaide Cortesi. The formation of the new troupe (and information concerning its plans to perform in Matanzas and Porto Principe in March) was reported in the *Charleston Courier* on 14 Feb. 1860 and reprinted in *BMT*, 25 Feb. 1860. The Charleston engagement was reported in the same periodical on 19 May 1860; Hoole (1946) does not mention the company. For Boston information, see Kaufman worklist, Boston; *NYMR&G*, 9 June 1860, 183; *BMT*, 2 and 16 June 1860. For New York, see Odell 1970, 7:263. Odell states that the season ended on 20 June, but both Kaufman and *BMT* report that the troupe opened in Boston on that date.

Appendix D

English Opera Companies, 1847–1860

The table should be read from top to bottom; entries in concurrent columns represent opera companies active during the same time period. Dates in square brackets indicate that although a secondary source has located a company somewhere at a particular time, this is probably an error.

The following abbreviations and short titles are used in this table:

Aca	Academy of Music		Fed	Federal Street Theatre
Amer	American Theatre		Holli	Holliday Street Theatre
Astor	Astor Place Opera House		Maguire	Maguire's Opera House
Athen	Athenaeum Theatre		McVicker	McVicker's Theatre
Balt	Baltimore		Metro	Metropolitan Theatre
B'way	Broadway Theatre		Mscl Fund	Musical Fund Hall
Ches	Chestnut Street Theatre		Nat	National Theatre
con	concert		New Wal	New Walnut Street Theatre

Niblo	Niblo's Theatre	
NO	New Orleans	
NYC	New York City	
OC	Opera company	
Phila	Philadelphia	
SF	San Francisco	
St. Chas	St. Charles Theatre	
Var	Varieties Theatre	
Wal	Walnut Street Theatre	

1847

SEGUIN OC (1)	ANNA BISHOP OC (2)	MANVERS OC (3)
Montreal Aug-	NYC (Park) 4-18 Aug	
	Boston 26 Aug-	
		-10? Sept
Boston -Sept		
21 Sept-?		NYC (Park) 4-5 Oct
Phila (Wal) 11-26 Oct	NYC (Park) 21 Oct-	Albany (con) 21 Oct
Boston 4 Nov-		Michigan when?
(Athen) -19 Nov	Boston (Fed) ?- -6 Nov	
	Phila (Wal) 22 Nov- -18 Nov	
		-7 Dec
	NYC (B'way) 13-24 Dec	
NYC 26 Dec (con)	Phila (Wal) 27 Dec-	

1848

SEGUIN OC (con't)		ANNA BISHOP OC (con't)		MANVERS OC (5)	
unknown	Jan-		-6 Jan	NYC (Astor)	18? July
	-Feb	Charleston	12-24 Jan		
		(con)	28-29 Jan		
		Savannah	31 Jan-		
			-5 Feb		
Richmond	17-31 Mar	NO (St. Chas)	14 Feb-		
Petersburg	early Apr?		-2 Mar		
(1 con)		Mobile	6-21 Mar		
NYC (Bowery)	13 Apr-				
	-7 May	NO	May		
Balt (Holli)	May ?-				
	-10? June				
		ANNA BISHOP OC (4)			
SEGUIN OC (6)		NYC	July		
Phila (Wal)	25 Sept-				
	-12 Oct	NYC (Park)	4-28 Oct		
NYC (B'way)	11-21? Oct	(scenes)			
Phila (Wal)	26? Nov	Phila (Arch)	31 Oct-	Cincinnati	6 Nov?
		(scenes)	-8 Nov		
Charleston	7-16 Dec	NYC	23, 27 Dec,	NO	Dec?
Savannah	18-30 Dec	(con)	early Jan		
1849		Boston	Dec-		
Charleston	1-6 Jan		-6? Jan		
Richmond	23 Jan-	Phila	17 Jan, 3 Feb	NO (St. Chas)	29 Jan-
	-6 Feb	[Charleston	6-24 Mar]		-4 Feb
unknown	Feb-Mar				
NYC (B'way)	26 Mar-			St. Louis	Apr? (con)
	-17 Apr				

1849 (con't)

SEGUIN OC (con't)

Phila (Wal)	23 Apr-
	-5 May
Boston (Athen)	4?-8 June
[Phila (Barnum)	20 May-15 June]

SEGUIN OC (7)

Phila (Wal)	18-29? Aug
Phila (Wal)	1-13? Oct
Balt	22-26 Oct
NYC (B'way)	12-24 Nov
Phila (Wal)	26 Nov-
	-8 Dec
Charleston?	Dec?

1850

Boston	7-? Jan
NYC	Feb
Balt (Holli)	4-26 Mar
Providence	Apr

MANVERS OC (con't)

Cincinnati (Melodeon)	18-27 Apr (con)
Pittsburgh	14-18? May
Toronto	20 June-
	-10 July

MANVERS OC (8)

Richmond	Nov
Petersburg (operatic soirees)	
unknown	Dec
Savannah	late Dec
	31 Dec-
unknown	-11 Jan
(NO?)	Jan-
Mobile (operatic entertainments)	-Feb
unknown	Feb
	Mar-
	-Apr
St. Louis	27 May-
	-8 June
Milwaukee	July
Chicago	29 July

UNKNOWN OC (9)

Savannah	?- -21 Mar

1850 (con't)

SEGUIN OC (10)

Albany	July- -Aug
unknown	Sept-
NYC	-Oct? Nov-

1851

Phila (Barnum)	-Jan 10 Feb- -1 Mar
Balt (Holli)	7-15 Mar
St. Louis (Bates)	14 Apr- -3 May
Louisville	12-28 May
Cincinnati (Nat)	2-21 June

SEGUIN OC (16)

Boston (Athen)	27 Oct- -1 Nov
Phila (Wal)	1-6? Dec
Washington	8 Dec-

ANNA BISHOP OC (11)

Charleston	July (con?)
NYC (Astor)	20-23 Aug
NYC (B'way)	2-12? Sept
Michigan	when?
Phila (Wal)	Feb
Charleston	Apr- -May
Chicago	Aug (con)

ANNA BISHOP OC (15)

| Newark (con) | 22 Oct |
| NYC (con) | Oct- -Dec |

MANVERS OC (12)

| Buffalo (Eagle St) | 2-7 Sept |
| Pittsburgh? | 26 Nov- -18 Dec |

UNKNOWN OC (13)

| Milwaukee | Dec- -Jan |
| Chicago | 24 Feb- -8 Mar |

ANNA THILLON OC (14)

NYC (Niblo)	18 Sept- -18? Oct
Phila (Ches)	22 Oct-
Balt (Holli)	-15? Nov
unknown	17-22? Nov early Dec
Boston (Athen)	24 Dec-

1852

SEGUIN OC (con't)

Phila	Feb?-	-Jan?
unknown	late Feb-	
Balt (Holli)	22 Mar-	-Mar
Washington	5?-16? Apr	-2? Apr
Phila (Wal)	22 May-?	
NYC (B'way)	7-19? June	
vacation	July-	-Aug

CARNCROSS OC (21)

Columbus, Ga   Sept

CAROLINE RICHINGS OC (22)

Phila (Wal)	25 Oct-	-6 Nov
NYC (B'way)	13-24 Dec	

1853

Phila (Wal)   Jan?
on tour (con?)

UNKNOWN OC (24)

Boston (Athen)   Jan

BISHOP OC (con't)

Balt (Holli)	10-22 Jan	
Columbus, Ga	May	
Charleston	June (con)	
Phila	June con?	

ANNA BISHOP OC (23)

NYC (Niblo)	1 Nov-	-2 Dec
Phila (Wal)	6 Dec	
Balt	Jan	

THILLON OC (con't)

Phila (Ches)	Feb-	-11 Feb
NYC (Niblo)	15 Mar-	-5? Mar
		-9 June

ANNA THILLON OC (20)

Michigan	16 July con	
NYC (NY Theatre)	30 Aug-	-? Sept
NYC (Niblo)	8-16 Sept	
Boston (Athen)	18 Oct-	-26 Nov
NYC (Niblo)	6-21 Dec	
Phila	29 Dec?	

RICHINGS OC (17)

Phila (Wal)	9 Feb-	-21 Feb

UNKNOWN OC (19)

Phila (Ches)	5 Apr-	-5 June

UNKNOWN OC (18)

Balt	16-18 Feb	

1853 (con't)

BRAHAM'S OC (25)

Balt	Feb- -Mar

ANNA BISHOP OC (con't)

Washington	Feb- (2 con)
Charleston (con)	Apr
Richmond (con)	late Apr
Augusta (con)	Apr-May
Savannah (con)	May
NYC (Niblo)	15, 17 Nov

ANNA THILLON OC (con't)

NO (St. Chas)	26? Feb- -? Mar
Mobile	Mar?
Memphis?	when?
St. Louis (Var)	23? Mar- -7? Apr
Cincinnati (Bates)	18-30 Apr
Pittsburgh	6-11? May

ANNA THILLON OC (26)

NYC (Niblo)	6 July- -2 Sept
Boston (Athen)	3-26 Oct

DUMBOLTON'S OC (27)

Michigan	when?

RICHINGS OC (28)

Boston	Oct
Cleveland (Foster)	16 Dec

ANNA BISHOP OC (29)

Phila (Wal)	6?-29? Dec
SF (Metro)	arrive 2 Feb / 7 Feb (con) 16? Jan-
SF (con't)	30 Apr-
(gave 10 seasons)	
hinterlands (con)	Apr- -? Apr 16
SF (Metro)	-May ?-26? May

1854

Cincinnati	20-25 Feb
Detroit	22? May- -3? June

1854 (con't)

DE MARGUERITES OC (30)
Phila (Ches)   12-14 June

PYNE & HARRISON OC (31)
NYC (B'way) 9 Oct-
                        -28 Oct
Phila (Wal) 30 Oct-
                        -18 Nov
NYC (B'way) 20-23 Nov
Boston   27 Nov-
                        -16 Dec
NYC (B'way) 18 Dec-

ANNA BISHOP OC (con't)
(Sf, con't)
                        -Nov

ANNA THILLON OC (con't)
mountains   June (con)
NYC (Niblo) 4 July-
                        -8 Aug

RICHINGS OC (32)
Chicago   2 Oct
(con)

NAU OC (33)
NYC (Niblo) 20 Nov-

BARILI-THORNE
OC (34)
SF (Metro)   Nov-
                        -Dec

WARDEN'S OC (36)
Louisville   2-19 Jan

1855

Phila   19? Feb-
                        -17 Feb

NYC (Niblo) 2, 9 Apr
(con)
NYC (Brook- 5, 10 Apr
lyn) (con)
Boston   16 Apr-
(Theatre)
Providence   May?   -5 May

PYNE & HARRISON OC (39)
NYC (Niblo) 23 May-
                        -3 Nov

To Australia   Aug

ANNA BISHOP OC (35)
SF (Metro)   Jan-
                        -Mar

Charleston   16-20 Jan
                        -3 Jan

METROPOLITAN OC (37)
Chicago (War- 19?-24? Feb
ner Hall)

DURAND OC (38)
Balt (Holli)   26 Mar-
                        -27 Apr

Phila (City   11-29? June
Museum)

DURAND OC (40)
NYC (Burton) Oct

Cincinnati   26 Feb-
                        -9 Mar

1855 (con't)

PYNE & HARRISON OC, con't

Providence	12?-16? Nov
Boston	15 Nov (con)
NYC	17 Nov (con)
Balt (Holli)	19 Nov-
	-29 Nov
Phila (con)	30 Nov
Pittsburgh	3-7 Dec
Cincinnati	
(Nat)	11 Dec-
	-29 Dec
Louisville	31 Dec-

1856

NO (St. Chas)	24 Jan-
	-5 Jan
	-8 Feb
Mobile	12, 14-15, 18 Feb
NO (Gaiety)	20-22, 24 Feb
St. Louis	10 Mar-
	-31 Mar
Louisville	
(con)	2-3 Apr
Cincinnati	
(con)	4 Apr
Balt	9 Apr
Washington	14-19 Apr
Richmond	21-29 Apr
Washington	30 Apr
	-3 May
Balt (Holli)	5-17 May
Washington	19-23 May
NYC (Niblo)	26, 28 May (con)
Montreal	June

PYNE & HARRISON OC (44)

Detroit	11-16? Aug
Chicago	18, 27 Aug (con)
Buffalo	17 Sept (con)

ANNA BISHOP OC (41)

Sydney, Aus	Dec

AMERICAN OC (42)

Phila (Mscl Fund) (con)	Apr

RICHINGS OC (43)

St. Louis	22 May

1856 (con't)

PYNE & HARRISON OC (con't)

Boston (Athen)	Oct? Nov?
New Beford	Nov?
NYC (con)	15 Nov
Washington	10-14 Nov
Balt (Holli)	17 Nov
	-1? Dec
NYC (Niblo)	15 Dec-

1857

	-27 Jan
Richmond	23?-28 Feb
Pittsburgh	9-14 Mar
NYC (Burton)	14 Apr-
	-1 May
(con)	1, 7 May
Boston (Music Hall) (fare-well con)	18 May

1858

COOPER OC (49)

Louisville	10-15 Jan

DURAND OC (45)

NO (Gaiety)	Nov-
	?
	-Dec

St. Louis (People's)	2-14 Feb

KNEASS OC (46)

Michigan	1856 or 57?

DURAND OC (47)

Richmond	June
Balt	8-24 June
Phila (Nat)	29 June-
	-4 July
Detroit	7?-12? Sept
Cincinnati	10 Oct
Richmond	1 Nov

ST. JOHN'S OC (48)

Savannah	19-20 June

Savannah	4-16 Jan
Charleston	18 Jan-
	-6 Feb
Macon	24 Feb

RICHINGS OC (50)

Phila (Wal)	8 Jan-

1858 (con't)

COOPER OC (con't)

| NYC (Wallack) | May |
| Washington | 10 June-? |

COOPER OC (52)

NYC (Wallack)	6-18 Sept
Boston (Athen)	20 Sept-
	-10 Oct
Worcester	11 Oct
Detroit	15-19 Nov
St. Louis	29 Nov-
	-11 Dec
Cincinnati	27 Dec-

DURAND OC (con't)

Columbus, Ga	12-24 Mar; 3-19 Apr
Nashville	29 Apr-?
Cincinnati	17-29 May
Louisville	31 May-
	-12 June
Memphis	17-26 June
St. Louis	30 June-
	-7 July

NEW ORLEANS OC (51)

Cincinnati	16-28 Aug
Louisville	30 Aug-
	-11 Sept
Chicago (McVicker)	27 Sept-
	-8 Oct
Pittsburgh	13-27 Oct
Richmond	1-6 Nov
Petersburg (con)	Nov
Lynchburg	15-20 Nov
Charleston	Nov?-
	-4 Dec
Savannah	6 Dec-
	-24 Dec
Macon	late Dec- -Jan

RICHINGS OC (con't)

| | -26 Apr |

ESCOTT OC (53)

| NYC (Burton) | 4-9 Oct |
| Hartford | Nov |

1859

COOPER OC (con't)

	-4 Jan
unknown	Jan-Feb- -Mar
Louisville	22 Mar- -1 Apr
Chicago (Nat)	11-23 Apr
Detroit	25? Apr- -7? May
Pittsburgh	23-31 May
Canada?	June?
Detroit	July (6 perf)
Chicago (Metro)	11-17 July
Milwaukee	18-23? July
Cincinnati	1-14 Aug

COOPER OC (55)

Pittsburgh	30 Aug- -10 Sept
Toronto	early Oct
Montreal	17? Oct- -1 Nov

NEW ORLEANS OC (con't)

Columbus	10? Jan
Augusta	Jan?
Columbia, SC	Jan?
Savannah	28 Jan- -22 Feb
Charleston	28 Feb- -8 Mar
Phila	21 Mar-
(New Wal)	-2 Apr

LYSTER GRAND ITALIAN OC (54)

Sailed for Calif	20 Apr
Arrived	16 May
SF (McGuire)	27 May- -26 June
Sacramento	29 June- -9 July
SF	13? July- -13? Aug

ANNA BISHOP OC (56)

return to US	Aug
NYC (con)	Sept
Sacramento	when?
Marysville	Sept
Mining camps	4 Sept
SF (Amer)	late Sept- -4 Oct
Stockton, CA	26 Oct- -3 Nov
Newark	21, 23 Oct; 7-8, 21 Nov

ESCOTT & MIRANDA OC (57)

Newark	2 Nov
Buffalo	21? Nov

RICHINGS OC (59)

Buffalo	?-18 Nov
Cincinnati	21-24 Nov

1859 (con't)

COOPER OC (con't)		DRAYTON PARLOR OC (58) NYC, fall		BISHOP OC (con't)		ESCOTT & MIRANDA OC (con't)		RICHINGS OC (con't)	
						Detroit (Metro)	late Nov	Pittsburgh?	Nov?
Buffalo	Dec					Chicago (McVicker)	5-17 Dec		
				Worcester (con)	16 Dec			Balt (Holli)	12-31 Dec
Pittsburgh	27-31 Dec					Peoria	26-31 Dec		
1860									
unknown	Jan	Phila (Concert Hall)	?-			Cincinnati	9 Jan	unknown	Jan-
Balt (Holli)	13-14 Feb		-18 Feb	Savannah	Feb	Cincinnati	2 Feb-		
Phila (Aca)	16? Feb- -3 Mar	Balt (Maryland Institute)	Mar	Texas	Feb-Mar?		-18 Feb		
Hartford (1 perf)	pre-10 Mar	Hartford	22-24 Mar						-Mar
New Haven (2 perfs)	Mar							Memphis (con?)	
Boston (Museum)	5-17 Mar							Louisville	Apr
Providence (Pine St)	19-23? Mar							Cincinnati	Apr
Boston	24 Mar								30 Apr- -7 May
Albany	26 Mar?- -7? Apr	Boston (Melodeon)	2-? Apr						
Montreal	9? Apr-?								
Toronto	?- -19 May								
Rochester	22-26? May								
Albany	28?-30? May			St. Louis (con)	24-25 June				

Commentary and Sources

1. Seguin English Opera Company. In May: "Mr. Reeves, late of the Bishop company, has joined the Seguins" (*Literary Excelsior*, 27 May 1848). Sources: *Montreal: Spirit*, 4 Sept. 1847, 332; Cooper 1984, 56–58. *Philadelphia:* Wilson 1935; *Literary Excelsior*, 30 Oct. 1847; Armstrong 1884, 47; *Boston: Spirit*, 6 Nov. 1847, 440; Playbills, Boston Athenaeum, 4, 12, 19 Nov. 1847, NN; *Literary Excelsior*, 13 Nov. 1847; Playbill, Boston Athenaeum, 5 Nov. 1847, MWA; *New York:* Odell 1970, 5:314 (report of concert); 5:350–51 (April–May); Lawrence 1988, 524; *Richmond:* Stoutamire 1960, 179; *Literary Excelsior*, 25 March, 15 April 1848; *Spirit*, 18 March, 1 April 1848 (*Spirit* gives the last night as 23 March, but Mrs. Seguin gave a concert on that date; Stoutamire gives the last night as 31 March); *Petersburg: Literary Excelsior*, 15 April 1848; *Baltimore: Spirit*, 3 June 1848, 180; *Literary Excelsior*, 10 June 1848.

2. Anna Bishop English Opera Company. Bishop's departure from England is reported in the *Spirit* on 12 June 1847. About her own travels, Bishop told Seilhamer (1881): "After leaving the Park, I made a tour of the country, appearing in all the principal cities, both in concert and opera. For several years I repeated my visits to the chief towns annually, and even extended my journeyings to Havana and Mexico, and finally to California. From California I was induced to visit the Australian colonies." Sources: *New York: Spirit*, 12 June, 17, 24, 31 July, 7, 14, 21 Aug. 1847; Odell 1970, 5:321–22, 5:324–25; *Spirit*, 16, 23, 30 Oct., 6 Nov. 1847; *Literary Excelsior*, 23, 30 Oct., 13 Nov. 1847; third engagement: Odell 1970, 5:336; Playbills, Broadway Theatre, 13, 14, 16, 18, 20–23, 25? Dec. 1847, Bishop Collection, MB; *Spirit*, 18, 25 Dec. 1847, 1 Jan. 1848; Lawrence 1988, 470, 473; *Boston:* Playbill, Howard Athenaeum, 26 Aug. 1847, MWA; Playbill, Howard Athenaeum, 31 Aug. 1847, Rare Books, MB; Clapp 1969, 451; *Spirit*, 4, 18 Sept. 1847; *BMG*, 13 Sept. 1847, 134; second engagement: Playbills, Federal Street Theatre, 17–18 Nov. 1847, Rare Books, MB; *Spirit*, 20 Nov. 1847, 464; *Philadelphia:* Wilson 1935; *Spirit*, 4 Dec. 1847; Armstrong 1884, 57; Curtis t.s., vol. 2, 386; second visit: Playbills, Walnut Street Theatre, 27–31 Dec. 1847, 1, 3–6 Jan. 1848, Bishop Collection, MB; Armstrong 1884, 57;

Curtis t.s., vol. 2, 386; *Spirit*, 8 Jan. 1848; *Charleston:* Hoole 1946, 52, 126; Playbills, Charleston Theatre, 12–14, 17–18, 21 (concert), 22, 24, 28–29 Jan. 1848, Bishop Collection, MB; *Spirit*, 5 Feb. 1848; *Savannah:* Green 1971, 429; Playbills, Savannah Theatre, 31 Jan., 1, 3, 5 Feb. 1848, Bishop Collection, MB; *New Orleans:* Playbills, St. Charles Theatre, 14–15, 17–18, 20–21, 23–24, 28–29 Feb., 2 March 1848, Bishop Collection, MB; *Spirit*, 26 Feb. 1848; *Literary Excelsior*, 18 March 1848; *Mobile:* Bailey 1934, 104; Playbills, Mobile Theatre, 6–7, 9–11, 13–15, 17–18, 20–21 March 1848, Bishop Collection, MB; *Literary Excelsior*, 8, 15 April 1848; *Spirit*, 8 April 1848.

3. Manvers Opera Company. In Toronto, the company gave "operatic soirées." See also note 18 in Appendix B. Sources: *New York: Spirit*, 19 Oct. 1847, 392; Odell 1970, 5:324; Lawrence 1988, 472–73; *Albany: Spirit*, 30 Oct. 1847, 428; *Michigan:* Teal 1964, Appendix C; *New Orleans:* Kendall 1968, 269; *Toronto:* Cooper 1984, 70.

4. Anna Bishop Opera Company. From the time the company broke up until her return to New York City, Bishop, Bochsa, and Valtellina made their way north on a "concert tour," with Bishop presenting her "disembodied opera scenes" and Bochsa his "spectacular harp solos" (Lawrence 1988, 524). On their return to New York City, Bishop was "added to the Park forces" and sang scenes from numerous operas to supplement the Park's dramatic fare (Odell 1970, 5:413–14). Sources: *New York (arrival): Spirit*, 5 Aug. 1848, 288; Odell 1970, 5:413–14; *New York (concert):* Lawrence 1988, 543–44; *Philadelphia:* Curtis t.s., vol. 2, 416–17; *Charleston:* Hoole 1946, 127 (probably a mistake).

5. Manvers English Opera Company. William Niblo rented the Astor Place Opera House for his summer campaign. This was the house troupe; it performed some operas but was not really a company. In October the group was reported headed south to New Orleans for an engagement that was to commence in early December (*Spirit*, 21 Oct. 1848). In New Orleans, the company consisted of Manvers, Brienti, and Brough. In Cincinnati, the performances were "operatic entertainments" with no chorus and no orchestra; accompaniment was on piano. Sources: *New*

York: Odell 1970, 5:385; *Cincinnati: Spirit*, 18 Nov. 1848; *Spirit*, 12 May 1849, 144; Wolz 1983, 56; *New Orleans: Spirit*, 21 Oct. 1848; Playbills, St. Charles Theatre, 29 Jan.–4 Feb. 1849, HTC; *St. Louis: Spirit*, 12 May 1849, 144; *Pittsburgh:* Fletcher 1931; *Mobile:* Duggar 1941, 161; *Toronto:* Cooper 1984, 70–74.

6. Seguin English Opera Company. In New York and Philadelphia in the spring the company produced Balfe's *The Enchantress* for long periods. During this season the company included the following singers: *New York:* Reeves, the Seguins, George Holman, Stephen Leach (his New York debut), Mrs. H. Phillips, and G. H. Andrews; *Charleston:* Holman, Reeves, Phillips, and Leach; *New York* (spring 1849): Leach, Holman, and Reeves; *Philadelphia:* Leach, Holman, and Reeves. Sources: *Philadelphia:* Wilson 1935 (terminal date is 12 Oct.); *Spirit*, 7 Oct. 1848, 396; second engagement: Armstrong 1884, 63; third engagement: Wilson 1935; Armstrong 1884, 62–63; Curtis t.s., vol. 2; Playbill, Walnut Street Theatre, 24 April 1849, Theatre Division, PP; *Spirit*, 5 May 1849, 132; *New York:* Odell 1970, 5:419–20, 425–26; *Spirit*, 21, 28 Oct. 1848; 31 March 1849, 72; 7, 14, 21 April 1849; *Charleston:* Hoole 1946, 127; *Savannah:* Green 1971, 434; Dorman 1967, 167; *Richmond:* Stoutamire 1960, 179; *Boston:* Playbill, Howard Athenaeum, 8 June 1849, Rare Books, MB; *Philadelphia* (May–June): Curtis t.s. (there is nothing about this in either Armstrong 1884 or Wilson 1935).

7. Seguin English Opera Company. In mid-September the *Message Bird* reported that Brienti, Manvers, and the Seguins were back in New York City. According to Curtis, the Seguin Company brought dancers to Philadelphia, at least on one of their trips (Curtis t.s., vol. 2, 429). Before the Baltimore engagement, the troupe gave several costume concerts at Carroll Hall of selections from *The Barber of Seville* and *The Postillion of Lonjumeau*. The company was reported in New York in Feb. 1850, but there is no record of performances there, and they probably were just passing through (*Message Bird*, 15 Feb. 1850, 240). In Providence, the company reportedly performed at the Museum. The troupe consisted of the following singers: *New York:* Rosa Jacques, Reeves, and the Seguins; *Baltimore:* Jacques, Seguin, and Reeves (Meyer was added in

March). Sources: *Philadelphia:* Wilson 1935; *Message Bird*, 15 Oct. 1849, 103; 1 Nov. 1849, 118; 1 Dec. 1849, 151, 160; Curtis t.s., vol. 2; *New York:* Odell 1970, 5:515–16; *Spirit*, 17 Nov. 1849, 468; 24 Nov. 1849; *Saroni's*, 24 Nov. 1849, 100; 1 Dec. 1849, 112; *Message Bird*, 15 Sept. 1849, 64; *Charleston: Saroni's*, 22 Dec. 1849, 148 (however, there is no mention in Hoole, so this is perhaps an error); *Boston: Saroni's*, 19 Jan. 1850, 196; *Message Bird*, 1 Jan. 1850, 185; *Baltimore:* Kaufman worklist, Baltimore; Playbill, Holliday Street Theatre, 23 March 1850, HTC; *Baltimore Olio*, March 1850, 35; *Providence: Spirit*, 20 April 1850, 108.

8. Manvers English Opera Company. There was a report in mid-September that Brienti, Manvers, and the Seguins were back in New York City, then Holman and Brienti evidently left the Seguins. In November, *Saroni's* reported that the "Manvers Company" was en route to Richmond, where they intended to give a "series of operatic representations." The same periodical reported in December that the troupe was giving successful operatic soirées in Petersburg, Va. In St. Louis, the company, according to playbills, was "Assisted by the Dramatic Corps and an Augmented Orchestra." This troupe gave the first operatic performance in Chicago on 29 July 1850; just before the second performance the theater burned. For a description, see Davis 1965; see also Farwell and Darby 1915, 169–70. By spring, the Leatis evidently had left the Manvers Company, for they were reported performing in "costume concerts" in Toronto from 11–27 June 1850 (Cooper 1984, 74). The Manvers troupe consisted of the following singers: *Petersburg:* Manvers, Brienti, and the Leatis; *St. Louis:* Brienti, Manvers, and Giubilei. Sources: *New York: Message Bird*, 15 Sept. 1849, 64; *Richmond: Saroni's*, 24 Nov. 1849, 100; *Petersburg: Saroni's*, 22 Dec. 1849, 148; *Savannah:* Green 1971, 438; *Saroni's*, 12 Jan. 1850, 185; *Mobile: Saroni's*, 2 March 1850, 267; *St. Louis:* Playbills, St. Louis Theatre, 24 May, 27 May–8 June, HTC; Jennings worklist, St. Louis; *Milwaukee:* Schleis 1974, 38–39; *Chicago:* McVicker 1884, 69; Davis 1965, 36–37; Hackett 1913, 16.

9. Unknown Opera Company. The only source for this troupe is a playbill for the Savannah Theatre dated 21 March 1850, HTC.

10. Seguin English Opera Company. The *Message Bird* reported in September that the troupe was giving operatic scenes in costume in Albany

(1 Sept. 1850, 446). The same month, the *Prompter's Whistle* mentioned that they were about to disembark on a tour to the West (14 Sept. 1850, 43). This report was premature, however, for both Edward Seguin and Meyer performed in New York with Anna Bishop in a production of *The Mount of Olives* on 3 Nov. 1850 and *The Creation* on 17 Nov. 1850. They also appeared in a benefit performance on 10 Dec. 1850 for T. D. Rice. Both of the Seguins also performed at the Broadway Theatre in late Dec. and early Jan. 1851 and at a benefit for Brough on 23 Jan. 1851 (Odell 1970, 6:8, 68, 90–91). The company included the following singers: *Philadelphia*: the Seguins, Meyer, Bailey, and Gardner; *Cincinnati*: Coad, Meyer, Bernard, and Mehen; *Baltimore*: the Seguins, Gardner, and Bailey. Sources: *Albany*: *Message Bird*, 1 Sept. 1850, 446; *New York City*: Odell 1970, 6:8, 60, 90–91; *Philadelphia*: Wilson 1935, *Spirit*, 1 March 1851, 24; Armstrong 1884, 69; Curtis t.s., vol. 2 (Curtis gives terminal date of 1 March; Wilson gives terminal date of 28 Feb.); *Message Bird*, 15 April 1851, 45; *Baltimore*: Kaufman worklist, Baltimore; *St. Louis*: Kaufman worklist, St. Louis; *Louisville*: Weisert 1955, 35–36; *Cincinnati*: *Spirit*, 14 June 1851, 204; Wolz 1983, 60.

11. Anna Bishop Opera Company. Bishop was in Mexico during part of 1849 and 1850; the *Baltimore Olio* (March 1850, 35) and *AMR* (May 1850, 36) reported her return to the United States in April 1850. She performed in *Judith* at the Astor Place House in Aug.; business was not good, so the company moved to the Broadway Theatre in Sept. There she was assisted by Novelli, Mlle Adeline, Mueller, and Beutler; they also performed scenes from operas. The Charleston performances were at Hibernian Hall. Sources: *Charleston*: *Baltimore Olio*, July 1850, 83; Hoole 1946, 57; *New York*: Odell 1970, 6:2–3, 61–62; *Saroni's*, 31 Aug. 1850, 578; *Michigan*: Teal 1964, Appendix C; *Philadelphia*: *Spirit*, 8 Feb. 1851, 612; *Chicago*: Upton 1847–81, vol. 1, 14.

12. Manvers Opera Company. This company in Buffalo consisted of Manvers, Brienti, and Giubilei. Sources: *Buffalo*: *Prompter's Whistle*, 14 Sept. 1850, 42; *Pittsburgh*: Fletcher 1931.

13. Unknown Opera Company. The *Spirit* reported that a company performed *Cinderella* every night for two weeks in Milwaukee. Another (the same?) company performed *Cinderella* and *Rob Roy* in Chicago slightly later. These may have been performances by theatrical stock companies. Sources: *Milwaukee*: *Spirit*, 11 Jan. 1851, 564. There is no information about this troupe in Schleis (1974); *Chicago*: Rice 1851–57, Account Book, 23.

14. Anna Thillon Opera Company. Thillon made her U.S. debut at Niblo's on 18 Sept. 1851 in a company that included Mr. and Mrs. Holman, Meyer, Hudson, and Mary Taylor; it was directed by Claude Thillon, and Signor La Manna conducted. During this engagement (on 18 Sept. 1851), she gave the American premiere (in English) of Auber's *The Crown Diamonds*, which (according to advertisements put out by Niblo), was written for Thillon. Her Philadelphia company included Hudson and Meyer. *Saroni's* mentions that in Boston she was "well supported by Mr. Hudson and the talented stock company of the Howard [Athenaeum]" (27 Dec. 1851, 125). At Niblo's from March through June, her company sang three times a week, alternating with the stock company. The troupe included Andrews, Moorehouse, Julia Daly, Wharton, Trevor, Roberts, and Williams (presumably many from Niblo's stock company) (Blair 1982, 68). Sources: *New York* (Sept.–Oct.): Odell 1970, 6:163–64; Blair 1982, 68, 74; *Spirit*, 20 Sept. 1851, 372; 27 Sept. 384; 11 Oct. 408; (March–April): *Saroni's*, 28 Feb. 1852, 261; 27 March 1852, 325; 17 April 1852, 373; *AMR*, April 1852, 57; *Spirit*, 13 March 1852, 48; 20 March 1852, 60; 27 March, 72; 3 April, 84; 10 April, 96; 17 April, 108; 1, 15 May, 1 June 1852; *Dwight's*, 1 May 1852, 28; Odell 1970, 6:165–66; *Philadelphia*: *Spirit*, 1 Nov. 1851, 444; 15 Nov. 1851; Armstrong 1884, 71; *Baltimore*: Playbill, Holliday Street Theatre, HTC; *Boston*: *Spirit*, 20 Dec. 1851, 528; 10 Jan. 1852, 564; 17 Jan., 576; Clapp 1969, 461; *Saroni's*, 14 Feb. 1852, 236, 244; Playbills, Howard Athenaeum, 31 Dec. 1851, 7 Jan., 11 Feb. 1852, Rare Books, MB; Playbill, Howard Athenaeum, 14 Jan. 1852, MWA; *Spirit*, 21 Feb. 1852, 1; *AMR*, Feb. 1852, 25; *Chicago*: Upton 1847–81, vol. 1, 19; *Detroit*: Teal 1964, Appendix C

15. Anna Bishop Opera Company. The engagement in Georgia lasted one week. This tour was billed as a "Farewell Tour." According to *Dwight's* of 5 June 1852, Bishop had visited thirty or forty towns and given 120 concerts. In Baltimore the troupe was reported to be comprised

of Jacques, Braham, Strini, Leach, and Rudolf. Sources: *Newark*: Kaufman 1974; *New York*: Odell 1970, 6:90–92; *Baltimore*: Kaufman worklist, Baltimore; *Columbus*: Mahan 1967, 54; *Charleston*: *Dwight's*, 5 June 1852, 70; *Philadelphia*: *Saroni's*, 3 July 1852, 98; *Toronto*: Cooper 1984, 92.

16. Seguin English Opera Company. The troupe performed in Philadelphia in May with the dancer Mad. Celeste. During June, the Seguins were associated with the stock company at the Broadway Theatre in New York, jointly with Mad. Celeste. They were reported to be on vacation during the summer of 1852 (*Spirit*, 17 July 1852, 264 and 14 Aug. 1852, 312). In the fall of 1852, Edward Seguin joined the stock company at Wallack's Theatre in New York as an actor and as primo buffo. He made his final appearance on 10 Sept. and died of consumption on 12 Dec. 1852 at the age of forty-three. He had been ill for some time (Odell 1970, 6:215, 217; *Dwight's*, 18 Sept. 1852, 372). In Boston the company included: Mr. Bishop, Mrs. Bailey, Julia Turnbull, and Miss Price. By 1852 the only singers named (besides the Seguins) were Bishop and Caroline Richings. Sources: *Boston*: *Spirit*, 1 Nov. 1851, 444; 8 Nov. 1851; White Diary, MWA; Playbill, Howard Athenaeum, 27 Oct. 1851, Rare Books, MB; Clapp 1969, 460; *Philadelphia*: *Spirit*, 29 Nov. 1851, 492; Armstrong 1884, 71; *Spirit*, 28 Feb. 1852, 14; Armstrong 1884, 72; *Washington*: *Spirit*, 29 Nov. 1851, 492; 3 Jan. 1852, 552; 10 April 1852, 96; *Saroni's*, 17 April 1852, 374; *Baltimore*: Playbill, Holliday Street Theatre, 24 March 1852, HTC; *Spirit*, 13 March 1852, 48; 3 April 1852, 84; *Saroni's*, 10 April 1852, 357; *New York*: Odell 1970, 6:120; *Spirit*, 12 June 1852, 204, 19 June 1852, 216; Playbills, Broadway Theatre, 7, 14[?] June 1852, Theatre Division, PP; Playbills, Broadway Theatre, 18 June 1852, MWA.

17. Caroline Richings Opera Company. Caroline Richings (1827–82), a British-born soprano and the adopted daughter of the veteran actor Peter Richings, made her operatic debut in Philadelphia on 9 Feb. 1852 as Marie in *The Daughter of the Regiment*. She probably performed with the stock company of the Walnut Street Theatre, with which her stepfather was associated. The two later toured the country, performing in dramatic works and operas; this may have been an early version of such

a troupe. Sources: Wilson 1935; *Saroni's*, 14 Feb. 1852, 237; Bailey 1986.

18. Unknown Opera Company. Source: Kaufman worklist, Baltimore. The members of the troupe included: Bregel[?], Braham, Strepel[?], Jacques, and Leach. Perhaps this was the Seguin Company, whose whereabouts in February 1852 are unknown.

19. Unknown Opera Company. This might be the Seguin Company, which performed in Philadelphia during May 1852. The repertory appears to be the Seguins'. It included: *Norma, Fra Diavolo; The Postillion of Longjumeau, La Sonnambula, Maritana, The Brewer of Preston, The Bohemian Girl, Don Pasquale, Masaniello, Cinderella, The Elixir of Love, The Marriage of Figaro, Der Freischütz, Zampa,* and others. Source: Wilson 1935.

20. Anna Thillon Opera Company. During the fall of 1852, the company's schedule at Niblo's was "confused and sporadic" (Blair 1982, 90). In Dec., the schedule was more regular; they performed weekly, on Monday, Wednesday, and Friday. The company included: *New York*: Meyer, Leach, Lyster, Thillon, Hudson, Alleyne, Beutler, Mueller, Rea, G. Howard, Convers, Mrs. Convers, M. Nesbitt, and others; *Boston*: Thillon, Hudson, and Meyer (Thillon as manager and director). Sources: *Michigan*: Teal 1964, Apppendix C; *Chicago*: Upton 1847–81, vol. 1, 19; *New York*: Odell 1970, 6:243–44, 239–40; *Spirit*, 4 Sept. 1852, 348; Blair 1982, 90; *Boston*: *Dwight's*, 30 Oct. 1852, 31; 6 Nov. 1852, 39; *Spirit*, 23 Oct. 1852, 421; 30 Oct. 1852, 444; 4 Dec. 1852, 499; *Philadelphia*: Armstrong 1884, 75; *New Orleans*: Kendall 1968, 281; *Spirit*, 26 Feb. 1853, 24; *Mobile*: *Spirit*, 26 March 1853, 72; *Memphis*: *Spirit*, 19 March 1853, 60; *St. Louis*: Playbills, Varieties Theatre, 29 March, 7 April 1853, HTC; *Spirit*, 16 April 1853, 108; *Cincinnati*: Wolz 1983, 64; *Spirit*, 30 April 1853, 132; *Pittsburgh*: Fletcher 1931.

21. Carncross Opera Company. This opera company is totally unknown and reportedly consisted of three women and four men; they performed in English and Italian (Mahan 1967, 35–36).

22. Caroline Richings Opera Company. On 9 July 1853, the *Spirit* reports that Richings and his daughter succeeded "beyond their expectations" in their operatic representations (252). Peter Richings had performed with the Seguins and with Anna Bishop. The company in Phil-

adelphia included: Richings, Miss E. Reed, Mr. T. Bishop, Mr. Rohr, Mr. Richings, Mr. A'Beckett, and Mr. Cunnington (the music director). Sources: *Philadelphia:* Playbills, Walnut Street Theatre, 25–28 Oct., 6 Nov. 1853, Theatre Division, PP; *Spirit,* 9 July 1853, 252; *New York:* Odell 1970, 6:200; *Philadelphia: MW,* 5 Feb. 1853, 62.

23. Anna Bishop Opera Company. The formation of "Bishop's Opera Company" was much discussed during summer of 1852. As early as July 1852 *Dwight's Journal* noted that a company was being planned and would consist of Braham, the Seguins, Bishop, and others; the whole troupe was to be under the direction of Bochsa. In October *Dwight's* named the company: Rosa Jacques, Mrs. Barton Hill, Bishop, Signors Guidi, Leach, Strini, and Henry Phillips. The reviews of the first performances named Jacques, Guidi, Strini, Leach, Rudolph, Augustus Braham, La Manna, and Bochsa. The company gave the North American premiere of Flotow's *Martha* on 1 Nov. 1852, in which Augustus Braham made his American operatic debut. By the time the troupe reached Baltimore, Guidi had left the ranks. In Washington, the singers were still referred to as "Bishop and her troupe," but evidently by now the company had disbanded. *MW* reported the dissolution of the company in its issue of 5 Feb. 1853 (82). After the troupe dissolved, Bishop and Bochsa embarked on a "concerting jaunt southward" (*Spirit,* 26 Feb. 1853, 24); both the *Spirit* and the *AMR* covered her concertizing activities in Charleston, Richmond, Augusta, and Savannah (*Spirit,* 9 April 1853, 96; 23 April 1853, 120; 30 April 1853, 132; *AMR,* May 1853, 75). Sources: *New York: Dwight's,* 24 July 1852, 127; 2 Oct. 1852, 206; *Spirit,* 2 Oct. 1852, 396; 16 Oct. 1852, 420; 6 Nov. 1852, 456; 13 Nov. 1852, 468; 4 Dec. 1852, 504; Odell 1970, 6:239–40; *MW,* 6 Nov. 1852, 150; Blair 1982, 94; *Philadelphia:* Armstrong 1884, 75; *Baltimore: MW,* 22 Jan. 1852, 59; *Washington: Spirit,* 19 Feb. 1853, 3.

24. Unknown English Opera Company. This troupe, probably a theatrical company, performed *The Bride of Lammermoor* at the Athenaeum. Singers named: Mrs. Mowatt and Mr. W. R. Goodall. Source: Playbill, Howard Athenaeum, 7 Jan. 1853, NN.

25. Braham's Opera Company. The *Spirit* reported on 26 Feb. 1853 (24) that Braham's Opera Company "has been delighting the Batimor-

eans." The troupe included Rosa Jacques. By March, the company had disbanded (*Spirit,* 5 March 1853, 36).

26. Anna Thillon Opera Company. The New York company sang in the fall of 1853 on Mondays, Wednesdays, and Fridays at Niblo's; the troupe included Thillon, Hudson, Maeder, Julia Miles, Leach, Martin, Lyster, H. Eytinge, Meyer, Rea, Russell, Frazer, and La Manna. In Boston, the company included Frazer, Leach, Meyer, Hudson, Julia Miles, and others. Thillon performed at Niblo's in Nov. 1853 with Leach, Hudson, and Maeder. Thillon left for California with Hudson via Nicaragua and arrived on 31 Dec. 1853. They attempted a tour of the interior in May 1854 and failed (Estavan 1939, 49–50). The company returned east in June 1854. The San Francisco engagement started 23 Jan. 1854, according to the *Spirit,* 18 Feb. 1854; however, a clipping in the S.F. Chronology file gives the third performance on 20 Jan., which suggests that she started 16 Jan. Thillon performed at the Metropolitan Theatre in a series of engagements from January through April; in April and May she performed in the interior (for example, Marysville and Grass Valley, Calif.). In New York City in July and Aug. 1854, the company included Fred Lyster, Frazer, Meyer, Reynolds, Andrews, and Maeder (Blair 1982, 135). Sources: *New York:* Odell 1970, 6:243; Blair 1982, 108 (gives terminal date of the season as 21 Aug.); *Spirit,* 9 July 1853, 252; 16 July 1853, 264; 23 July 1853, 276; 30 July 1853, 288; 6 Aug. 1853, 13 Aug. 1853, 312; 20 Aug. 1853, 324; 3 Sept. 1853, 348; *AMR,* Aug. 1853, 122; Nov. engagement: Odell 1970, 6:315; *Spirit,* 12 Nov. 1853, 468; 19 Nov. 1853, 480; *AMR,* Dec. 1853, 186; July 1854 engagement: Odell 1970, 6:316; *Spirit,* 7 July 1854, 252; 15 July 1854, 264; 22 July 1854, 276; *Dwight's,* 5 Aug. 1854, 143; *MW,* 15 July 1854, 126; Blair 1982, 135; *Boston:* Playbills, Howard Athenaeum, 10, 17, 26 Oct. 1853, MWA; *Spirit,* 8 Oct. 1853, 408; 22 Oct. 1853, 432; 29 Oct. 1853, 335; *San Francisco:* S.F. Chronology file; *MR&CA,* 2 March 1854, 75; *MW,* 18 Feb. 1854, 78; *Spirit,* 28 Jan. 1854, 589; 18 Feb. 1854, 7; 18 March 1854, 55; 8 April 1854, 92; 20 May 1854, 159; 3 June 1854, 185; 1 July 1854, 230; Playbills: Metropolitan Theatre, 1, 24 Feb., 1, 8, 17, 21 March, 17, 19 May 1854, HTC; Gaer 1970; Archives, CSfCP.

27. Dumbolton's Opera Company. Unknown opera company (Teal 1964, Appendix C).

28. Richings Opera Company. Sources: *Boston: Spirit,* 8 Oct. 1853, 408; 29 Oct. 1853, 435; *Cleveland: Gaiser* 1953; *Cincinnati:* Wolz 1983, 67; *Detroit: MW,* 3 June 1854, 50; 10 June 1854, 62.

29. Anna Bishop Opera Company. Bishop traveled to California via Panama. In San Francisco, she started with concerts, but failed, for her prices were too extravagant even for California. The California correspondent to the *Spirit* (Stephen Massett) wrote: "The great mistake which stars labor under in coming to California is, that every dream of the golden land *must be realized*—they anticipate too much at first, and learn a lesson by their disappointment" (18 March 1854, 55). Bishop's production at midsummer of *Der Freischütz* was called the "most outstanding event of 1854" (McMinn 1941). The theater featured an orchestra of thirty-three, with Bochsa as musical director. The company included Bishop, Mengis, and Julia Gould. Sources: *San Francisco:* Waddington 1947; Estavan 1939, 41; McMinn 1941, 403–6; Playbill, American Theatre, 3 March 1854, HTC; Playbills, Metropolitan Theatre, 30 April 1854, 7 May 1854, 22 July 1854, 25 Nov. 1854, HTC; *Spirit,* 18 March 1854, 55; 8 April 1854, 92; 3 June 1854, 185, 188; 1 July 1854, 230; 2 Sept. 1854, 338; 4 Nov. 1854, 446; 18 Nov. 1854, 470; *MW,* 1 July 1854, 98; Commanday RN.

30. De Marguerites English Opera Company. Unknown company. According to the *Spirit,* the troupe proved to be a failure and closed after its second performance. The members who were named included Madame de Marguerites, A. Gernville, Prof. Rohr, Mrs. King, E. Warden, Mrs. Altemus, and Severino Strini; the musical conductor was Charles Mueller. Sources: Curtis t.s., vol. 2, 503; Sill Diaries, vol. 10, 511; *Spirit,* 10 June 1854, 204; 17 June 1854, 216; 24 June 1854, 228; Armstrong 1884, 78.

31. Pyne and Harrison English Opera Company. The company at the Broadway Theatre included Borrani, Harrison, L. Pyne, S. Pyne, and Reeves; other roles were filled by Broadway stock and some other singers. In Philadelphia the company included Borrani, Harrison, Meyer, the Pynes, and Reeves; Mr. Sefton was the stage manager. The troupe stopped in New York in November for four performances at the Broadway Theatre, en route from Philadelphia to Boston. The company at the Broadway (Dec. 1854–Feb. 1855) included Harrison, Borrani, Meyer, Reeves, and Whiting. Sources: *New York:* Odell 1970, 6:343–44; *MR&CA,* 3 Aug. 1854, 277; 12 Oct. 1854, 355; 26 Oct. 1854, 371; *MW,* 14 Oct. 1854, 79; 21 Oct. 1854, 90; 28 Oct. 1854, 102; *Spirit,* 14 Oct. 1854, 420; 21 Oct. 1854, 432; 28 Oct. 1854, 444; 4 Nov. 1854, 456; *Dwight's,* 14 Oct. 1854, 14. Second engagment: Odell 1970, 6:344; *Dwight's,* 25 Nov. 1854; *MG,* 25 Nov. 1854, 17; *Spirit,* 18 Nov. 1854, 480; 25 Nov. 1854, 492. Third engagement: Odell 1970, 6:345; *MG,* 30 Dec. 1854, 57; 6, 27 Jan. 1855; *MW,* 23 Dec. 1854, 202; *Spirit,* 23 Dec. 1854, 540; 30 Dec. 1854, 552; 6 Jan. 1855, 564; 27 Jan. 1855, 600; *Dwight's,* 6 Jan. 1855, 111; concerts: Odell 1970, 6:415, 421; *MG,* 7 April 1855; *MW,* 14 April 1855, 170; *Philadelphia: Dwight's,* 4 Nov. 1854, 37; *MG,* 18 Nov. 1854, 9; *MW,* 18 Nov. 1854, 142; 25 Nov. 1854, 154, 155; Armstrong 1884, 79; *Spirit,* 25 Nov. 1854. Second engagement: Armstrong 1884, 84–85; *MG,* 10 March 1855; *MW,* 10 March 1855, 111; *Boston:* Playbills, Boston Theatre, 14–15 Dec. 1854, MWA; Playbills, Boston Theatre, 27 Nov.–16 Dec. 1854, Rare Books, MB; *Dwight's,* 9 Dec. 1854, 78; 16 Dec. 1854; *MG,* 25 Nov. 1854, 17; 2 Dec. 1854, 25; 9 Dec. 1854, 36; 16 Dec. 1854, 44; 23 Dec. 1854, 51; *MW,* 9 Dec. 1854, 179; 16 Dec. 1854, 190; *Spirit,* 2 Dec. 1854, 504; 16 Dec. 1854, 517; 23 Dec. 1854, 535; Tompkins 1908, 27–28; second engagement: *Dwight's,* 21 April 1855, 21; 5 May 1855, 39; 19 May 1855, 55; Playbills, Boston Theatre, 25 April, 2 May 1855, Playbill Collection, NN; Playbills, Boston Theatre, 17 April–5 May 1855, Rare Books, MB; *NYMR&G,* 19 May 1855, 165; *MG,* 28 April 1855, 197; Tompkins 1908, 31; *Providence:* Blake 1971, 261–63. For further information on the Pyne and Harrison Company, see chapter 6.

32. Richings Opera Company. The Cincinnati engagement was primarily theatrical. Only two operatic works were performed. Sources: *Chicago:* Upton 1847–81; John Rice Account Book, ICHi; *Cincinnati:* Wolz 1983, 69.

33. Nau Opera Company. Also known as Niblo's English Opera Troupe. The troupe was brought to the United States by William Niblo

to replace the Pyne and Harrison Company. Dolores Nau was a native of Baltimore and was educated in France. The company consisted of A. St. Albyn (U.S. debut), Eliza Brienti, Allan Irving, George Harrison (U.S. debut), and Horncastle; the conductor was Thomas Baker. The chorus was not very skilled; the orchestra, however, was reported to be good. The company went south under the direction of Mr. Corbyn (MG, 13 Jan. 1855, 73). There is no mention of them after Charleston. Sources: New York: Blair 1982, 147; Odell 1970, 6:380-81; MG, 11 Nov. 1854, 3; 25 Nov. 1854, 18-19; 9 Dec. 1854, 30 Dec. 1854, 57; NYMR&G, 23 Nov. 1854, 402; 7 Dec. 1854, 419; 21 Dec. 1854, 438; Spirit, 4 Nov. 1854, 456; 25 Nov. 1854, 492; 9 Dec. 1854, 516; 16 Dec. 1854, 528; Dwight's, 4 Nov. 1854, 37; 25 Nov. 1854; MW, 4 Nov. 1854, 114; 16 Dec. 1854, 190; 23 Dec. 1854; Charleston: Hoole 1946, 138; MG, 27 Jan. 1855, 89.

34. Barili-Thorne Opera Company. Nothing more is known about this troupe. They may have sung in Italian. Emily Thorne returned to New York from California in Oct. 1855, and joined the stock company at Burton's Theatre. Sources: Gaer 1970; Odell 1970, 6:432, 433.

35. Anna Bishop Opera Company. In March Bishop performed with the Barili-Thorne Company in San Francisco. Her farewell concert there was on 27 Aug. 1855, then she sailed for Australia on 30 Aug., arriving in Sydney on 3 Dec. 1855. Sources: San Francisco: Playbills, Metropolitan Theatre, 16 Jan., 13 Feb., 8 March 1855, HTC; Australia: Estavan 1939, 43.

36. Warden's Opera Company. It is unclear whether this company performed operas or operatic concerts (Weisert 1962).

37. Metropolitan Opera Company. This unknown company performed for one week in Chicago (Sherman 1947, 81).

38. Durand English Opera Company. Also known as the Lyster and Durand English Opera Company. The troupe consisted of Rosalie Durand, Frederick Meyer, Miss Mary Gannon, Miss E. Morant, Mrs. G. H. Allen, Fred Lyster, and Mr. Herbert. William H. Reeves was scheduled to replace James Frazer on 7 April. Philadelphia Company: Durand, Reeves, and Lyster. Sources: Baltimore: MW, 7 April 1855, 159; 14 April 1855, 178; 5 May 1855; Philadelphia: Armstrong 1884, 84; Wilson 1935.

39. Pyne and Harrison Opera Company. The company had a triumphant summer season under the musical direction of George Bristow. They commenced with a falsely claimed American premiere of The Daughter of the Regiment ("from the original score"). The season's engagement also included performances of The Daughter of St. Mark (Balfe), Queen of a Day (Buckstone-Fitzwilliam), and Bristow's Rip van Winkle (premiere, 27 Sept.), among other standard works. The company included Borrani, Horncastle, Holman, Stretton, and Swan, and the season lasted 125 nights. Sources: New York: Odell 1970, 6:381-82; 469-70; Dwight's, 2 June 1855, 68; 6 Oct. 1855, 6; MW, 3 Nov. 1855, 313; 10 Nov. 1855, 325; 16 June 1855, 80; 23 June 1855, 92; 30 June 1855, 102; 11 Aug. 1855, 169; 25 Aug. 1855; 15 Sept. 1855; 29 Sept. 1855, 253; 13 Oct. 1855, 278-79; NYMR&G, 19 May 1855, 165; 2 June 1855, 177; Providence: MW, 17 Nov. 1855, 337; Boston: Dwight's, 17 Nov. 1855, 54; MW, 17 Nov. 1855, 337; New York (concert): MW, 17 Nov. 1855, 337; Odell 1970, 6:508; Baltimore: Playbill, Holliday Street Theatre, 19 Nov. 1855, HTC; Philadelphia (concert): Dwight's, 8 Dec. 1855, 76; New Orleans: Daily Picayune, 25 Jan. 1856, 9 Feb. 1856; Mobile: Mobile Daily Advertiser, 12-19 Feb. 1856; New York (May): Odell 1970, 6:505; Montreal: Dwight's, 21 June 1856, 95. For the company's itinerary from 3 Dec. 1855-23 May 1856, see chapter 6.

40. Durand English Opera Company. Lyster and Durand were part of the stock company at Burton's in Sept. 1855. Sources: Odell 1970, 6:431, 433; Dwight's, 27 Oct. 1855, 28.

41. Anna Bishop Opera Company. Bishop and Bochsa reached Sydney, New South Wales, in Dec. 1855; they reportedly were performing in Melbourne in June. Bochsa died in Sydney in Jan. 1856. Sources: Australia: Estavan 1939, 43; Dwight's, 17 Sept. 1856, 207; Walker 1962, 141.

42. American Opera Company. This is an unknown opera company, perhaps only a concert troupe. The members of the troupe included Miss Henriette Behrend, Mr. H. Millard, and Mr. Borrani (from the Pyne and Harrison troupe) (NYMR&G, 5 April 1856, 103).

43. Richings Opera Company. Richings and Company performed Daughter of the Regiment. How much of the troupe's repertory was

dramatic and how much operatic is unknown (Kaufman worklist, St. Louis).

44. Pyne and Harrison Opera Company. According to Teal 1964, the company gave a six-night season in Detroit, which was the longest held in that city up to that point. The company at Niblo's in Dec. 1856 included Horncastle, Reeves, Guilmette, Harrison, the Pynes, and Mrs. Reeves. Sources: *Detroit: MW*, 30 Aug. 1856, 405; Teal 1964, Appendix C; *Chicago: MW*, 13 Sept. 1856, 421; Upton 1847–81, vol. 1, 35; Sherman 1947, 305; *Buffalo: NYMR&G*, 20 Sept. 1856, 290; *Boston: MW*, 1 Nov. 1856, 343; 22 Nov. 1856, 625; *New Bedford: MW*, 22 Nov. 1856, 625; *New York: MW*, 22 Nov. 1856, 625; *Washington: MW*, 22 Nov. 1856, 625; Kaufman worklist, Washington; *Baltimore: MW*, 6 Dec. 1856; Kaufman worklist, Baltimore; *New York:* Odell 1970, 6:563; *MW*, 13 Dec. 1856, 697; 20 Dec. 1856, 721; 17 Jan. 1857, 35; *NYMR&G*, 27 Dec. 1856, 403; *Dwight's*, 24 Jan. 1857, 132; 31 Jan. 1857, 141; Blair 1982, 193; *Richmond:* Playbill, Richmond Theatre, 28 Feb. 1857, HTC; Stoutamire 1960, 179; *Pittsburgh:* Fletcher 1931; *New York (April–May):* Odell 1970, 6:525, 598; *Dwight's*, 18 April 1857, 21; 2 May 1857, 39 (according to Odell, the troupe gave concerts on 1 and 7 May; according to Blair [1982, 204], their final performance was on 1 May); *Boston: Dwight's*, 16 May 1857, 55; *MW*, 23 May 1857, 324.

45. Durand English Opera Company. The company included Durand, Hodson, Stretton, Frazer, Lyster, Trevor, and Marie Duckworth. According to Kaufman, the company (in St. Louis) consisted of the following performers: Durand, Hodson, Frazer, Trevor, Lyster, and Stretton. Sources: *New Orleans:* Playbill, Crisp's Gaiety Theatre, 14 Nov. 1856, HTC; *Dwight's*, 20 Dec. 1856, 95; Kendall 1968, 365–66; *St. Louis:* Kaufman worklist, St. Louis.

46. Kneass Opera Company. Source: Teal 1964, Appendix C.

47. Durand Opera Company. This company also was known as Crisp's Opera Company (for Crisp's Gaiety Theatre in New Orleans), the Lyster and Durand Opera Company, the New Orleans English Opera Company, and the Great English Opera Company. According to Kaufman (worklist, Baltimore), in Baltimore the troupe included Durand, Hodson, Trevor, and Lyster. The company performed in Detroit for "an unheard-of two-

week opera season" (Teal 1964). Hoole names the members of the troupe when performing in Charleston as Fred Lyster, H. Warton, Frank Trevor, Rosalie Durand, Ada King, Georgia Hodson, and Anthony Reiff. In Savannah, the company included Hodson, Durand, Lyster, Trevor, F. B. Swan, and Reiff. For St. Louis, Jennings's terminal date is 6 July; Kaufman and Reiff both report 7 July. Sources: *Richmond:* Stoutamire 1960; *Baltimore:* Kaufman worklist, Baltimore; *Philadelphia:* Playbills, National Theatre, 29 May–4 July 1857, Theatre Division, PP; *Detroit:* Teal 1964, Appendix C; *Savannah:* Green 1971, 510; *Charleston:* Hoole 1946, 146; *Macon:* Steinhaus 1973, 53; *Columbus:* Mahan 1967, 37; *Nashville:* Davenport 1941, 142; *Cincinnati:* Wolz 1983, 239, 73; Reiff 1905; *Louisville:* Weisert 1955; *Memphis:* Reiff 1905; *St. Louis:* Jennings and Kaufman worklists, St. Louis; Reiff 1905.

48. St. John's Opera Company. Unknown opera company, cited in Green 1971, 504. No repertory or other information is available.

49. Cooper Opera Company. Annie Milner, Perring, Guilmette, and Henry Cooper performed at Wallack's Theatre in New York in May 1858. The *Musical World* of 29 May 1858 (337) mentioned a "new English Opera Company, organised by Dr. Guilmette of this city" that included Milner, Frazer, and Mr. Rudolpsohn. The periodical reported that they planned to open in Washington on 10 June 1858, followed by appearances in Baltimore and New York. See *MW*, 29 May 1858, 337. Sources: *Louisville:* Weisert 1962; *New York:* Odell 1970, 7:27.

50. Richings Opera Company. These may have been operatic performances by the stock company of the Walnut Street Theatre, featuring Carolyn Richings as a vocal star. The Richings Opera Company itself was not founded until 1859 (see note to number 59, below). During this run, the Walnut Street Theatre Company mounted performances of *The Daughter of the Regiment*, in "Miss Richings' popular adaptation, in 2 acts." Source: Playbills, Walnut Street Theatre Company, 8 Jan., 5 March, 26 April 1858, PPL.

51. New Orleans English Opera Company. This is the Durand Opera Company under another name. According to Reiff (1905), the troupe temporarily disbanded after the close of their season in St. Louis. William and Fred Lyster, Hodson, Durand, and Trevor headed north to Canada

for a reprieve from the heat of the summer of 1858; Reiff went home to New York. The company regrouped in Cincinnati on Sunday, 15 August and commenced their new season there the next evening. For a fascinating and engaging firsthand account of this company's adventures, see Reiff 1905. In Savannah the troupe included J. Arnold, Boudinot, Fred Lyster, F. R. Swan (Upton names F. B. Swan), Trevor, G. H. Warrie, Rosalie Durand, G. Hodson, A. King. William S. Lyster (the manager), and Reiff (the conductor). The troupe consisted of many of the singers from the Pyne and Harrison Company. In Charleston the company included Hodson, Durand, Lyster, Trevor, and Reiff. Sherman erroneously has the terminal date as 9 Oct, which was a Sunday. The company sometimes was known as the Hodson and Durand English Opera Company (in addition to all its other names). Sources: *Cincinnati:* Wolz 1983, 239; Reiff 1905; *Louisville: Dwight's,* 19 June 1858, 96; Weisert 1955; Reiff 1905; *Chicago:* Upton 1847–81, vol. 1, 51; Hackett 1913, 42; Sherman 1947, 396; Reiff 1905; *Pittsburgh:* Fletcher 1931; Reiff 1905; *Richmond:* Stoutamire 1960; Reiff 1905; *Savannah:* Green 1971, 511, 521; Reiff 1905; *Macon:* Reiff 1905; *Augusta and Columbia:* Reiff 1905; *Columbus, Ga.:* Mahan 1967, 37; Reiff 1905; *Charleston:* Hoole 1946, 149; Reiff 1905; *Philadelphia:* Playbills, New Walnut Street Theatre, 21 March–2 April 1859, Theatre Department, PP; Reiff 1905.

52. Cooper Opera Company. By September the company had jelled and was known as H. C. Cooper's Opera Troupe (at least according to Odell, who reports that they "came in" to Wallack's Theatre in September). The artists included Mr. and Mrs. Holman, D. Miranda (a new tenor), Annie Milner (Mrs. Cooper), Charles Guilmette, and F. Rudolphsohn; Cooper was the conductor. Dwight incorrectly claimed that the company was performing at Niblo's. According to Odell, the Ravels had sole possession of the latter theater for all of Sept. and Oct. (1970, 7:54). The troupe, at least by late Dec. 1858, was also known as the Annie Milner Opera Company and was identified as such in Cincinnati and Louisville. Wolz has the dates of their engagement in Cincinnati as 10 Dec. 1858–4 Jan. 1859 and says the company was comprised of secondary singers drawn from the New York theaters. By April 1859 the troupe included the following singers: Brookhouse Bowler, Ansley Cook, Annie Milner, Rudolphson, Andrews, Prof. Hoffman (the pianist), Miss C. T. Smith, Miss H. Payne, Miss J. Payne, Mr. Sobatzy, and others (named in Upton). In Detroit, the company included Cooper, Milner, Holman, Mrs. Holman, Fiske, Guilmette, Miranda, and Rudolphsen. Sources: *New York:* Odell 1970, 7:29; *MW,* 11 Sept. 1858, 580; 18 Sept. 1858, 594; *Dwight's,* 4 Sept. 1858, 182–83; 18 Sept. 1858, 197–99; *Boston:* Playbill, Howard Athenaeum, 27 Sept. 1858, Brown Vertical File, Music Department, MB; *Dwight's,* 25 Sept. 1858, 207; *Worcester:* Playbill, Worcester Theatre, 11 Oct. 1858, MWA; *Montreal and Toronto:* Cooper 1984, 133–37; *Detroit:* Teal 1964, Appendix C; *St. Louis:* Jennings worklist, St. Louis; *Dwight's,* 1 Jan. 1859, 317; *Cincinnati:* Wolz 1983, 73, 83, 240; *Dwight's,* 1 Jan. 1859, 317; *Louisville:* Weisert 1962; *Chicago:* Sherman 1947, 449, 452; Upton 1847–81, vol. 1, 57–59; *Detroit: MW,* 21 May 1859; Teal 1964, note 190 and Appendix C; *Pittsburgh:* Fletcher 1931; *Canada:* Teal 1964, Appendix C ("after leaving Detroit in early May they embarked upon a Canadian tour and then returned to Detroit for six nights in July."); Cooper 1984, 139; *Detroit:* Teal 1964, Appendix C; *Milwaukee: MW,* 6 Aug. 1859, 3.

53. Escott English Opera Company. This company was named for the English soprano, Lucy Escott. It first appeared in New York. There the company consisted of Lucy Escott, Miss White, Emma Heywood, Charles Durand, Henry Squires, Aynsley Cook, Hayes, and Gledhill. Most or all were new. Brookhouse Bowler made his U.S. debut with the company on 6 Oct. 1858. The company was a failure in New York. Escott performed variously in New York City in stock companies in May and June 1858. See Odell, 1970, 7:119, 152, 159, 194, 200. Sources: *New York:* Odell 1970, 7:113–14; *Dwight's,* 4 Sept. 1858, 182; 9 Oct. 1858, 221, 223; 16 Oct. 1858, 231; *Hartford: Dwight's,* 4 Dec. 1858. The report from Hartford is dated 27 Nov. 1858.

54. Lyster Grand Italian Opera Company (Durand Opera Company). This was another name for the Durand Company. Under the name "Lyster Grand Italian Opera Company," the troupe left for California on 20 April 1859 and arrived on 16 May. They were imported by Tom Maguire, a theater manager in San Francisco, for performances at his Opera House and gave four seasons during 1859. *Dwight's* reported in Aug. that the

company included Rosalie Durand, Georgia Hodson, Ada King, Frederick Lyster, Francis Trevor, and Frank Boudinot. The troup also included Alicia Mandeville, Frederick Meyer, Stephen Leach, G. H. Warre, William Reeves, and James J. Frazer. Escott and Squires sailed for San Francisco in April 1860 to join them. Reiff's account (1905) includes details of their travel to California and information about their activities there until May 1860. Sources: *Departure for California: BMT*, 7 April 1860, 63; Reiff 1905; *San Francisco: Dwight's*, 20 Aug. 1859, 166; Gagey 1950, 92; McMinn 1941, 419; Commanday RN; Estavan 1939, 13, 26; Playbill, Maguire's Opera House, 26 July 1859, CSf; Reiff 1905; *Sacramento:* Reiff 1905; *Stockton:* Noid 1968, 226–27; Reiff 1905; *Marysville:* Reiff 1905; *Mining camp:* Reiff 1905.

55. Cooper English Opera Company. The company included Annie Milner, Bowler, Rudolphsen, Cook, Cooper, and others. The troupe in Baltimore (Feb. 1860) included Arnold, Barton, Bowler, Boudinot, Cook, Collins, Cooper, Gillespie, Hurlie, Kemp, Mandeville, Milner, Mikens, Payne, and Warrie. The company's business agent was T. Allston Brown. In Philadelphia (Feb. 1860) the troupe included Milner, Bowler, Cook, Boudinot, Warrie, Sudgen, Ryley, Miss H. Payne, Mrs Burroughs, Mr. Neale, and Mr. Bell; Cooper was the musical director. The company failed in Philadelphia. In Nov. 1860, the company performed in Charleston, in front of "small, disinterested audiences," and the manager of the theater curtailed the engagement (Hoole 1946, 63). According to the *BMT* (3 Nov. 1860), "Charleston, although said to be a musical city, is now under too much political excitement to prove a profitable place for amusements until after the election. I question whether the best stars in the musical world would attract here now." In Savannah in Dec. Annie Milner inserted into a performance of *Fra Diavolo* a "southern call to arms," with "words adapted and respectfully dedicated to the MINUTE MEN OF THE SOUTH" (Playbill, Savannah Theatre, 15 Dec. 1860, HTC). Sources: *Pittsburgh:* Fletcher 1931; *Montreal: Wilkes's Spirit*, 22 Oct. 1859, 112; Cooper 1984, 149–52; second engagement: *BMT*, 21 April 1860, 74; *Toronto: Wilkes's Spirit*, 22 Oct. 1859, 112; *Buffalo: MW*, 31 Dec. 1859, 4; *Wilkes's Spirit*, 31 Dec. 1859, 272; *Baltimore:* Playbills, Holliday Street Theatre, 13–14 Feb. 1860, HTC; *Philadelphia:* Playbills,

Academy of Music, 18, 21 Feb. 1860, Scrapbooks, PPL; *BMT*, 25 Feb. 1860, 7, 11; *MW*, 10 March 1860, 4; *Boston: BMT*, 10 March 1860, 5, 22; *NYMR&G*, 17 March 1860, 86; Playbills, Boston Museum, 5–17 March 1860, MWA; *MW*, 31 March 1860, 5; *Providence: BMT*, 25 Feb. 1860, 12 (reports that the company was to commence a short season on 5 Nov.—apparently erroneously); *BMT*, 10 March 1860, 44–45; 24 March 1860, 44; *MW*, 31 March 1860, 5; *Albany: MW*, 31 March 1860, 5; *NYMR&G*, 31 March 1860, 103; 14 April 1860, 26 May 1860, 161; *Hartford: BMT*, 10 March 1860, 41; *New Haven: BMT*, 24 March 1860, 45; *Toronto and Montreal: BMT*, 19 May 1860, 103; Cooper 1984, 152–57; *Rochester: BMT*, 19 May 1860, 103.

56. Anna Bishop Opera Company. Bishop returned to the United States for her second visit in September 1859 (Seilhamer 1881, 109). Although the troupe was billed as the Anna Bishop Opera Company, most of these performances probably were concerts. The *BMT*, for example, noted on 25 Feb. 1860 that Miss Bishop was meeting with "marked success" on her tour of the South and that the local newspapers "speak of her concerts as being attractive novelties" (3). Sources: *New York:* Odell 1970, 7:295; *Newark:* Kaufman 1974; *Worcester:* Playbill, Mechanic's Hall, 16 Dec. 1859, MWA; *Savannah: BMT*, 25 Feb. 1860, 7; *Texas: MW*, 28 April 1860, 4; *St. Louis:* Kaufman worklist, St. Louis.

57. Escott and Miranda Opera Company. Escott and Miranda were associated with Niblo's Theatre during June 1859 (Odell 1970, 7:152 and *MW*, 4 June 1859, 3) and sang in opera (presumably with members of the stock company) at the Boston Museum on 18–19 July (Playbill, Boston Museum, 18–19 July 1859, MWA). On 29 Oct., *MW* announced that Miranda was forming an opera company "to give performances in the West during the autumn and coming winter" (5). In Buffalo the company reportedly included Escott, Annie Kemp, Miss Duckworth, Boudinot, Mr. Ross Frank, Miranda, Mayer, M. Boudinot, Miss Dunn, and Mme. Shinfie; in Chicago, the members named were Escott, Kemp, Frazer, Boudinot, Duckworth, Miss Ross, Miranda, Frank R. Swan, Mr. Myers, Miss Boudinet, Miss Derm, and others. On 24 March 1860, *MW* reported that Miranda and Escott were back in New York after completion of their western tour and were looking for work (4). In April,

Miranda was reported to have been hired by Maretzek for Italian opera (BMT, 21 April 1860, 79). Escott joined the Durand Opera Company in April 1860 (BMT, 7 April 1860, 63). Sources: Newark: Kaufman 1974; Buffalo: Spirit, 26 Nov. 1859, 192; MW, 3 Dec. 1859, 5; Detroit: Teal 1964, Appendix C; Chicago: Sherman 1947, 445; MW, 17 Dec. 1859, 4; Upton 1847–81, vol. 1, 61; Peoria: Marine 1972, 180; Cincinnati: Wolz 1983, 88.

58. Drayton Parlor Opera Company. It is unclear exactly what these performances were like, although they probably were costume concerts. The MW noted on 3 March 1860 that "those who are ... opposed to theatrical or operatic performances, find in these entertainments an extremely agreeable and entirely unobjectionable substitute" (4). According to Odell, the company performed "theatrical proverbs" in New York (1970, 7:212, 264). They invented their "parlor operas" at Hope Chapel in New York in Nov. 1859 (Odell 1970, 7:265, 292); they also called their productions "Parlour Operas and Lyric Proverbs" (Odell 1970, 7:299; Spirit, 17 Dec. 1859, 240, 256). Sources: New York: Spirit, 17 Dec. 1859, 240, 256; Odell 1970, 7:212, 264, 265, 292, 299; Philadelphia: BMT, 25 Feb. 1860, 7; MW, 3 March 1860, 4; 17 March 1860, 5; 24 March 1860, 3; Baltimore: BMT, 10 March 1860, 28; Hartford: BMT, 24 March 1860, 41; Boston: NYMR&G, 14 April 1860, 118; BMT, 10 March 1860, 7; 7 April 1860, 58.

59. Richings Opera Company. According to Bailey (1986), Peter and Caroline Richings founded the Richings Opera Company in 1859. Sources: Buffalo: Spirit, 26 Nov. 1859, 192; Cincinnati: Spirit, 26 Nov. 1859, 192; Wolz 1983, 92, 240; Baltimore: Playbills, Holliday Street Theatre, 12–31 Dec. 1859, HTC; Memphis: MW, 21 April 1860, 5; Louisville: MW, 28 April 1860, 4.

Notes

Abbreviations Used in the Notes and Bibliography

AG	*The New Grove Dictionary of American Music* (ed. Hitchcock and Sadie)
ALS	Autograph letter, signed
AMJ	*American Musical Journal*
AMS	American Musicological Society
AMT	*American Musical Times*
ATC	*American Theatre Companies, 1749–1887* (ed. Durham)
AMR	*American Monthly Musical Review*
BMT	*Boston Musical Times*
BMG	*Boston Musical Gazette*
C&Q	*Crotchets and Quavers* (Maretzek)
Ca&S-CJ	*The Choral Advocate and Singing-Class Journal*
CSf	San Francisco Public Library
CSfCP	Society of California Pioneers
DAB	*Dictionary of American Biography*
DG	*Don Giovanni*
DNB	*Dictionary of National Biography*
DLC	Library of Congress
Figaro	*Figaro, or Corbyn's Chronicle*
Grove's Dictionary	*A Dictionary of Music and Musicians* (ed. Grove)
HTC	Harvard Theatre Collection
ICHi	Chicago Historical Society
ICN	Newberry Library, Chicago
MB	Boston Public Library
MdHi	Maryland Historical Society, Baltimore
MG	*Musical Gazette*
Mirror	*New-York Mirror*
MOC	Maretzek Opera Company Playbills, 1850–51, MB
MR	*Musical Review*
MR&CA	*Musical Review and Choral Advocate*
MR&G	*Musical Review and Gazette*
MW	*Musical World*
MW (London)	*Musical World*, London
MWA	American Antiquarian Society, Worcester, Mass.

NA&USG	*North American and United States Gazette* (Philadelphia)
NHi	New-York Historical Society
NG	*The New Grove Dictionary of Music* (ed. Sadie)
NN	New York Public Library
NNM	Museum of the City of New York
NYMR	*New York Musical Review*
NYMR&G	*New York Musical Review & Gazette*
PHi	Historical Society of Pennsylvania
PP	Free Library of Philadelphia
PPL	Library Company of Philadelphia
RN	Research Notes
S&F	*Sharps and Flats* (Maretzek)
Saroni's	*Saroni's Musical Times*
WM	*World of Music*

Prologue

1. *Mirror,* 10 Dec. 1836, 190.
2. Mates 1985, 24.
3. Hamm 1979, 81.
4. Mates 1985, 24.
5. Mates 1985, 22.
6. Rich, Yellin, and Hitchcock 1986.
7. For his excellent study of antebellum American theater and culture, Grimsted compiled several lists, using figures from secondary sources, of the most frequently performed theatrical works in Philadelphia, Charleston, New Orleans, and St. Louis from 1831 to 1851. Of the top twenty-two titles on his list of "Feature Plays," six (almost 37 percent) are operas. Furthermore, as Grimsted points out, "opera's position on these lists is a little low because [one of the secondary studies] for New Orleans excludes operatic performances" (1968, 108, 254–55). Because New Orleans was a major operatic center in antebellum America, this omission is significant.
8. The production of opera by dramatic companies continued throughout the period from 1825 to 1860, despite the increasing numbers of itinerant opera troupes better equipped to handle the repertory. Although this was especially true of theaters located in cities on the frontier (to which opera troupes, at least at first, did not travel), opera also remained in the stock repertories of theaters in such cities as New York and New Orleans, where itinerant troupes visited regularly. The performance of opera by theatrical stock companies, however, does not fall within the boundaries of this study (except for performances that were in conjunction with vocal stars); this tradition, as a consequence, will not be discussed except in passing. It is important to note, however, that American theatrical companies did continue to stage opera during the entire antebellum period.
9. Ireland 1968, 1:329.

10. Odell 1970, 3:14, 64; Ireland 1968, 1:331.

11. Lawrence 1988, 15n. According to the *Mirror,* he also was popular because he had the foresight (or good fortune) to program in his concerts the still relatively unknown—but soon-to-be exceedingly popular—songs of Thomas Moore (3 Jan. 1835). See also Ireland 1968, 1:330; Odell 1970, 2:499; and Hamm 1979, 70.

12. Bernheim 1932, 5.

13. Odell 1970, 2:348. For a lucid—and welcome—description of the development of the star system in the United States, see Porter 1991, 14, 196–202.

14. Odell 1970, 2:309.

15. In the 1830s and 1840s the United States had two dominant theatrical centers: New York and New Orleans. Both cities had their own spheres of influence. For New Orleans, this included Mobile and Baton Rouge and, slightly later, Nashville and St. Louis; in New York's sphere were Philadelphia, Boston, and Baltimore. Itinerant performers visited each city. In the late 1830s the two circuits still were fairly independent of each other. Only in the early 1840s did traveling actors and singers begin to include both cities (and sometimes cities in their circuits) on their tours on a regular basis. It was not until the 1850s that visits to each became expected; this occurred in the later decade after such long-distance tours were made economically feasible by the construction of a viable transportation network and the establishment of permanent theaters in towns and cities along the Ohio-Mississippi River network.

16. Bernheim 1932, 29. Traveling opera troupes, especially self-sufficient companies such as the large Italian troupes of the 1840s and 1850s, were precursors of the combination system.

1. Vocal-star Troupes

1. Wemyss 1847, 125.

2. Wemyss 1847, 64, 67.

3. Information about salaries earned by antebellum performers is rather scarce, especially in published sources. Satirical accounts are one source of information about motives. The article quoted here, "The Way to Give Concerts in America," is one such source (*MR,* 27 Oct. 1838, 243–45).

4. Wemyss 1847, 67, 74–75.

5. The nature of Sharpe's voice is described in the *Mirror* (July 1832, 22).

6. Odell 1970, 3:180.

7. Odell 1970, 445, 447, 603, 605, 180, 232, 383.

8. Ireland 1968, 1:464; Odell 1970, 3:381–82, 444, 546.

9. Odell, 4:338.

10. Kendall gives her Christian name as Eliza, but according to both Ireland and Lawrence, it was Mary Ann (Kendall 1968, 49; Lawrence 1988, 44; Ireland 1968, 1:511).

11. Quoted in Odell 1970, 3:304.

12. Ireland 1968, 1:511–12.

13. Kmen 1966, 128, 148; Kendall 1968, 49, 61–62, 79–80, 88, 98, 105.

14. Ireland, 1968, 1:511; Odell 1970, 3:240, 304.

15. Brooks 1986, "Austin."

16. Wemyss 1847, 123.

17. Brown says that her debut was at the Walnut Street Theatre, and Wemyss, in his *Chronology,* erroneously gives the date as 18 December (Brown 1870; Wemyss 1852, 21).

18. Wemyss 1847, 130.

19. *Mirror,* Sept. 1831; Ireland 1968, 1:546; Hamm 1979, 71. For information on Elizabeth Austin and on several other singers and impresarios discussed in this book I am indebted to William Brooks, who generously gave me research notes to the articles he wrote on them for *AG.*

20. Kendall 1968, 80; Kmen 1966, 129–30.

21. Ireland 1968, 1:546; Odell 1970, 3:624; *AMJ,* April 1835, 114–15. The North American premiere of *Fra Diavolo* (in French) was in Philadelphia on 16 Sept. 1831 by the New Orleans French Opera Company; this company sang the opera in New York one month later, 17 Oct. 1831. The version in which Austin performed was an English adaptation by the English singer/ actor/adaptor Thomas Reynoldson, who also acted in the premiere (Belsom 1955, 24; Odell 1970, 3:590, 624; Lawrence 1988, 15n, 25n). The American premiere of *La dame blanche* (in French) took place in New Orleans on 6 Feb. 1827; the New York premiere (by the New Orleans French Opera Company) was on 24 Aug. 1827. According to Mattfeld, the Drury Lane version in which Austin appeared had different characters than Boieldieu's opera, but was based on the same story. Also according to Mattfeld, the real New York premiere of the English version was on 21 May 1832. Austin appeared in that performance as well (Belsom 1955, 13; Odell 1970, 3:316, 557; Mattfeld 1927, 47). The U.S. premiere of *Le Calife de Bagdad* (in French) was in New Orleans on 25 Dec. 1805; New York's first hearing had to wait more than twenty years, until 27 Aug. 1827. The English version in which Austin performed in 1829 was an adaptation by J. T. Dibdin (Kmen 1966, 63; Mattfeld 1927, 44; Chevalley 1955, 32; Odell 1970, 3:444). Odell (3:382) claims that Austin performed in the North American premiere of Weber's *Oberon,* but Lawrence (p. 154) suggests that this was not the case.

22. Hamm 1979, 71–72. According to Durham, *Cinderella* was produced fifty times its first season at the Park Theatre, eighty times during the subsequent (1831–32) season, and "regularly for years thereafter" (1986, 398). For more information about Lacy's version of *Cinderella,* see chapter 6.

23. *AMJ,* April 1835, 115, 116.

24. Playbill, 15 Oct. 1831, HTC; Playbill, 25 May 1833, PPL. From sheet music in the collection of the Music Division of the Library of Congress we learn that "Cupid Hear Me," arranged by one T. Cooke, was from an opera by an unknown composer named Balduci (a badly misspelled Boieldieu?); "The Arab Steed" and "Savourneen Deelish" were traditional tunes published as broadsides; and "Away to the Mountain's Brow" was by the English composer George Alexander Lee (1802–51). "Strike for Tyrol and Liberty," a song from Henry Bishop's opera *Hofer, the Tell of the Tyrol,* was set to the well-known melody from the overture to Rossini's *William Tell.*

25. Durang 1868, 2:54, 12 July 1857. "We're a Noddin'," called a "favorite glee," was included in the *Boston Glee Book* compiled by Lowell Mason and George Webb (Boston: J. H. Wilkins, 1838). Today it is best known as "The Dodger" in Aaron Copland's *Old American Songs.*

26. The disparaged songs, "Over the Water to Charlie" and "Bluebonnets," were both broadside tunes of a political nature: both were Scots loyalist songs. My thanks to Wayne Shirley for pointing this out.

27. Quoted in Grimsted 1968, 52.

28. Some theaters built after 1840 had a two- rather than a three-part division of the house (by the omission of the gallery, or the transformation of the pit into a more genteel "parquet"), but the triple division remained the most common arrangement of American theaters throughout the entire period (Grimsted 1968, 52). As late as the old Metropolitan Opera House in New York, this remained true of the highest gallery. It was also true of the unremodeled Carnegie Hall, although less blatantly.

29. Curtis n.d., 273.

30. Kmen 1966, 138.

31. In the mid–1840s the Chestnut Street Theatre in Philadelphia instituted a "colored gallery" in an attempt to attract lower-class audiences. At New York's Park Theatre during that same decade, according to Durham, "half the gallery was filled with boys, servants, and sailors, half with seating for blacks" (Fielder 1986, 198; Durham 1986, 397; Grimsted 1968, 52–53).

32. Curtis n.d., 273; Chamberlain 1835–40, 1:14 Sept. [1835?].

33. Grimsted 1968, 52–55.

34. Whitman and *Ladies' Port-Folio,* both quoted by Grimsted 1968, 55 and 53.

35. Grimsted 1968, 55. According to Joseph Sill (8 April 1847), the management of the Chestnut Street Theatre created a "Parquette" in 1847. The new section featured "backs & arms to the Seats, which renders that part of the house very pleasant, as it is by far the best place for seeing & hearing." He further commented on the fact that "Ladies occupied both the Boxes and the Parquette," lending to the theatre a "gay & handsome appearance." The Astor Place Opera House, which opened in New York in 1847, also had such a section.

36. *Spirit,* 2 April 1836; *AMJ,* Oct. 1835, 260; *Gentleman's Vade-Mecum,* 7 May 1836.

37. Wemyss 1847, 258.

38. Hamm 1979, 71; Odell 1970, 3:657–58. Paton made her London stage debut as Susanna in *The Marriage of Figaro* in October 1822; that same year she also appeared as Rosina in *The Barber of Seville,* Polly in *The Beggar's Opera,* and Mandane in *Artaxerxes.* In 1824 she enjoyed a great deal of success in *Der Freischütz,* and two years later created the role of Reiza in *Oberon* (Husk 1904; Grove 1879–83).

39. Brooks, 1986, "Wood"; Brooks, RN Wood.

40. Wemyss 1847, 258.

41. By rights, the role of Cinderella "belonged" more to Mary Anne Paton

than to Elizabeth Austin, for Lacy had the former singer in mind when he created his adaptation. Paton introduced the role in the London premiere of Lacy's version on 13 April 1830. For information on Lacy's *Cinderella,* I am indebted to John Graziano for the loan of an unpublished paper on the subject.

42. Although the performance of *La Sonnambula* was the North American premiere of the work, the performance of *Norma* was the premiere only of the English version, this one a translation (not an adaptation) by Joseph Reese Fry, brother of the composer William Henry Fry. The premiere of the original version of *Norma* had taken place in New Orleans five years earlier, on 1 April 1836 (Belsom 1955, 32).

43. Hamm 1979, 74. For information on the continued popularity of these operas through the 1850s, see chapters 5 and 6. One measure of *La Sonnambula*'s popularity is the fact that it was the first opera to be performed in Chicago (on 29 July 1850, in English, by the Manvers English Opera Company) and in San Francisco (on 12 Feb. 1851, in Italian, by the Pellegrini Italian Opera Company) (Hackett 1913, 16–17; Gagey 1950, 32; Estavan 1939, 87).

44. Seven years later, Sill still enjoyed the opera. On 8 April 1847 he wrote that the vocal stars James Frazer, Anne Seguin, and Edward Seguin "played & sung very effectively & [*La Sonnambula*] was well done—the repetition of it always affords me pleasure."

45. James 1968, 568, 572–74, 588–91, cited in Brooks RN Wood.

46. Clapp 1969, 326, 331; Durham 1986, 484.

47. Quoted in Odell 1970, 4:446.

48. Quoted in Odell 1970, 3:657; Husk 1904.

49. Quoted in Odell 1970, 4:446; Clapp 1969, 317.

50. Seilhamer 1881, "Mary Ann Horton." Euphrosine Parepa(-Rosa) (1836–74) was a successful Scottish soprano of the mid-nineteenth century. She made tours of the United States from 1865 to 1867 and in 1872, appearing in concert and opera, during the first tour as the star of the Parepa-Rosa Opera Company (Rosenthal 1982).

51. *Mirror* critic quoted in Odell 1970, 3:657.

52. Brooks 1986, "Wood." For information on the aborted New Orleans engagement, see the *Spirit* of 6 March 1841 for a published copy of the letter Joseph Wood wrote to James Caldwell, manager of the St. Charles Theatre in New Orleans, explaining why he and his wife suddenly cancelled their already scheduled engagement at his theater.

53. Odell 1970, 3:304. Horn played an important part in the development of music in the United States during the antebellum period. When he arrived in America he had already established a reputation as a composer of operas and songs and as an adaptor of the operas of other composers, including Mozart and Rossini. In 1832 he became the musical director at the Park Theatre; he later served as the conductor of Boston's Handel and Haydn Society; was active as a music publisher and the owner of a music store in New York; and participated in the founding of the New York Philharmonic

Society in 1842 (Temperley 1986, "Horn"; *Albion,* 20 Oct. 1827; *Spirit,* 15 Sept. 1832; *AMJ,* 1 Oct. 1834, 23).

54. Odell 1970, 3:385; critic quoted by White 1882, 1:696.

55. Ireland 1968, 1:564. Francis Wemyss, who described Feron as "really fat, fair, and past forty," wrote that she returned home "mortified with her reception [here], with no very exalted opinion of the American taste for music" (1847, 163).

56. Odell 1970, 3:385.

57. Ireland 1968, 2:50.

58. Odell 1970, 3:621; *Spirit,* 2 May 1840.

59. Odell 1970, 4:51.

60. Seilhamer 1881, "Seguin."

61. It is almost impossible to divine from playbills which of the subordinate parts of an opera were sung and which were read. Critics are of little help, for they generally limit their specific comments to the visiting stars, with an occasional passing mention of a performance by only the most prominent members of the stock company.

62. According to Fielder, although Philadelphia's Chestnut Street Theatre company continued to operate throughout the 1830s as "a typical stock company," the troupe nonetheless emphasized productions of operas, spectacles, and pantomimes, as these were its most profitable works. In 1835, for example, the troupe had sixty operas or operettas in its repertory (1986, 194).

63. Curtis n.d., 346.

64. Seilhamer 1881, "Horton."

65. Not until the advent of larger itinerant Italian companies in the 1840s and 1850s did opera troupes begin to travel with their own orchestras. In 1836, the Italian Opera Company connected with James Caldwell's St. Charles Theatre in New Orleans and traveled to Louisville, where they performed in the American Theatre (also operated by Caldwell) from Aug.–Oct. Although at least some of the St. Charles orchestra members accompanied the singers to Kentucky, this troupe cannot be considered a true itinerant company on tour (chapter 3). Apparently the first truly itinerant troupe to travel with its own orchestra in this country was the Havana Opera Company of 1843 (chapter 3).

66. Playbills from MWA and NN.

67. The only theater with a comparable (or larger) orchestra than those maintained by these four houses was the Théâtre d'Orléans in New Orleans, where performances were in French. This house also supported a resident opera company. For both of these reasons, the establishment did not engage performers of English opera, and as a consequence it is excluded from this discussion.

68. Clapp 1969, 265.

69. Kmen 1966, 139.

70. Kmen 1966, 138–40.

71. *Mirror,* 3 Jan. 1835, 211; Playbill, Seguin Opera Company, 16 April 1841, MWA.

72. Compared to these several American theater orchestras, the instrumental ensemble of Drury Lane Theatre in London for 1841 numbered forty-one musicians. In 1829 Fétis ranked the orchestras of both Drury Lane and Covent Garden theaters far below those of the Variétés Théâtre and the Théâtre de Madame in Paris. How the Drury Lane orchestra compared with the ensembles of other European theaters in the late 1830s or early 1840s is unknown (Carse 1948, 201, 199). For a very useful discussion of American theater orchestras of earlier in the century, see Porter 1991, 361–405.

73. Armstrong 1884, 48.

74. Blake 1971, 224.

75. *Mirror,* 2 Oct. 1841; uncited newspaper quotation in Hoole 1946, 44.

76. Wemyss 1847, 236.

77. By the 1830s, theatrical supremacy of the East Coast had shifted from Philadelphia to New York; consequently, the managers most responsible for importing new stars from England were the managers of Manhattan's theaters.

78. Ireland 1968, 1:343, 2:229.

79. Lawrence 1988, 40.

80. Odell 1970, 4:211.

81. During the 1850s, Horncastle would be associated with the Nau English Opera Troupe (in 1854) and the Pyne and Harrison Opera Company (in 1855–56). For further information on Horncastle's activities from 1838 to 1840, see chapter 2; for his activities with the Pyne and Harrison Company, see chapter 6.

82. Odell 1970, 4:212.

83. Lawrence 1988, 40.

84. Odell 1970, 4:219; Lawrence 1988, 40.

85. Odell 1970, 4:191.

86. Odell 1970, 4:194; Ireland 1968, 2:218.

87. White 1882, 2:865; *Musical Reminiscences of an Old Amateur* (1827), quoted by White, 2:866.

88. Quoted by Lawrence 1988, 15.

89. Odell 1970, 4:204, 208; Lawrence 1988, 44.

90. Lawrence 1988, 45; Odell 1970, 4:208. The following theatrical season (on 14 Jan. 1839) Allan, along with Brough, Bailey, Hughes, and Jones, would participate in another American premiere—of the English version of *La Gazza Ladra* (Odell 1970, 4:282). The opera had first been heard in North America in French in New Orleans at the Théâtre d'Orléans on 30 Dec. 1828; the East Coast premiere, again in French, was by John Davis's French Opera Company of New Orleans in Philadelphia, on 30 Dec. 1828 (Belsom 1955, 18). The North American premiere of the Italian version was by the Rivafinoli Company on 18 Nov. 1833. Lawrence erroneously suggests that Caradori-Allan's success at the Park Theatre during the 1837–38 season was hampered by the unprecedented triumph of the vocal stars Shirreff, Wilson, and Seguin at the National Theatre. This trio of stars did not arrive in the United States until the beginning of the 1838 season. They did, however, have a deleterious effect on the fortunes of the Park Theatre during the 1838–39 season (Lawrence 1988, 45). For additional information, see chapter 2.

91. *MR,* 16 Feb. 1839, 380.
92. Ireland 1968, 2:275.
93. Odell 1970, 4:342.
94. *Corsair,* 14 Sept. 1839, 426, quoted in Lawrence 1988, 59; Odell 1970, 4:343.
95. Ireland 1968, 2:298; Odell 1970, 4:342.
96. Ireland 1968, 2:299; Odell 1970, 4:342.
97. *Evening Star,* 10 Sept. 1839, quoted in Lawrence 1988, 59.
98. Ireland 1968, 2:299.
99. Ireland 1968, 2:299; Lawrence 1988, 60.
100. White 1882, 2:873–874.

2. Jane Shirreff and John Wilson

1. Odell 1970, 4:212, 290.
2. Schiavo 1947, 1:50, 54. For more information about the construction of the Italian Opera House, see chapter 3.
3. Brown 1903, 1:240–41.
4. Ireland 1968, 2:229.
5. Both Henry and James had made their American debuts twenty years earlier, in 1818 (Ireland 1968, 1:341, 375).
6. William Michael Rooke (1794–1847), an Irish composer and violinist, is best known as the teacher of the British opera composer Michael William Balfe. Rooke was a well-known theater musician, first in Dublin and later in London. He served as chorus master at Drury Lane and orchestra leader under Bishop at Vauxhall Gardens in the 1830s. *Amilie,* Rooke's first opera, had been composed in 1818, and thus was not new at the time of its premiere on 9 Dec. 1837. Husk and Flood 1982; *Athenaeum,* 9 Dec. 1837, 900.
7. *Athenaeum,* 9 Dec. 1837, 900; *MW* (London), 8 Dec. 1837, 203.
8. Husk and Flood 1982.
9. Phillips made a concert tour of the United States in 1844, which he detailed in his memoirs, published in 1864. The *Athenaeum* review of the premiere performance of *Amilie* also mentions two other singers who later toured the United States, Charles Manvers and Joseph Stretton (9 Dec. 1837, 900). Manvers was among the troupe of vocalists that Edmund Simpson of the Park Theatre recruited for his 1839–1840 season (chapter 5). For further information on Stretton, see chapters 5 and 6.
10. For more information about Wood, see chapter 1; for Pyne, see chapter 6.
11. Shirreff Collection. The Shirreff Collection includes volumes of playbills from her London career as well as documents pertinent to her American tour, for example, a financial ledger, playbills, clippings, a journal kept by Mary Blundell, and a pocket diary. The New York Public Library is unable to supply information concerning the provenance of the collection.
12. At Covent Garden, for example, she appeared as Isabel in that theater's premiere (in 1832) of Meyerbeer's *Robert le Diable,* as adapted by Michael Rophino Lacy; as the page Oscar in the London premiere of Auber's *Gustavus*

III (1833); as Zerlina in Mozart's *Don Giovanni* (1834); and in Hérold's *Le Pre aux Clercs* (1834) and Auber's *Lestocq* (1835), both as adapted by Thomas Cooke. During this time she performed with an impressive number of other Covent Garden singers who, at one time or another, would appear in the United States: Miss Inverarity (who would appear at the Park in 1839 as Mrs. Martyn), Thomas Reynoldson, John Braham, Henry Phillips, Theodore Victor Giubilei, and William Harrison (Rosenthal 1958, 40, 42, 46–50). For more about William Harrison's tour of the United States in an opera company with Louisa Pyne, see chapter 6.

13. Husk 1898; Stratton and Brown 1971; *Boston Morning Post,* 7 Nov. 1838; *Knickerbocker,* Nov. 1838, 470.

14. William Armstrong, writing forty-five years after the fact, disagreed, claiming that Shirreff was "young and good looking, had an agreeable voice, and sang well," but that she "could not be compared with Mrs. Wood as an artist" (1884, 45).

15. *Knickerbocker,* Nov. 1838, 470; *Gazette* quoted in *MR,* 19 Jan. 1839.

16. *Pennsylvanian,* 21 Jan. 1839; *Boston Morning Post,* 26 Nov. 1838.

17. *Corsair,* 16 May 1839, 13; *Boston Morning Post,* 7 Nov. 1838. The earnest cultivation of an image of moral purity was something to which many prima donnas and actresses paid close attention, for the American theatrical public could be damning in its condemnation of those who did not live up to its high standards. Francis Wemyss, for example, relates that during Elizabeth Austin's first engagement in Philadelphia in 1828 no women were in the audience because of an "unmanly attack" on the soprano's morals (concerning the propriety of her relationship with her manager F. H. F. Berkeley) in a local newspaper before her arrival in Pennsylvania (1847, 135). Ten years later, the actress and singer Eliza Vestris (1797–1856), who married her lover Charles Mathews (rather belatedly) just before their arrival in America, suffered for not measuring up to what Vera Lawrence calls "the rigid standards of morality exacted from theatre folk by an aggressively bigoted American public." The Mathews' American engagement was disastrous, and the couple returned to England somewhat bitter about their failure here (Lawrence 1988, 47; Odell 1970, 4:272–73). This American tendency to judge women performers on the basis of private morality was still an issue as late as 1850. Jenny Lind paid such careful attention to the cultivation of her image during her American tour of 1850–52 that "she became something of a symbol" in the popular mind (Brooks 1986, "Lind"). That Americans by this time were slowly becoming more tolerant of the private lives of women performers, however, is suggested by the professional triumph of the English soprano Anna Bishop, who seems to have suffered no audience repercussions when she arrived here in 1847, despite open knowledge that she had abandoned her husband and children to travel and perform with her lover, Nicholas Bochsa (chapter 5).

18. Curtis n.d., 249.

19. Stratton and Brown 1971, 452.

20. Ireland 1968, 2:278; Stratton and Brown 1971, 452; *Philadelphia National Gazette,* 15 Jan. 1839.

21. Stratton and Brown 1971; *Quebec Gazette,* 9 July 1849.

22. Tawa 1986; Husk 1911.

23. *New York Times,* 25 Aug. 1888; Tawa 1986; Husk 1911. Tawa describes Seguin's voice as a soprano; Odell (1970, 4:297) states that she had "a contralto voice of superb quality, produced with all the elegance and finish of the English school." She seems, however, to have sung primarily soprano roles.

24. *Spirit,* 17 Feb. 1844; *Mirror,* 30 April 1842, 87; Tawa 1986.

25. In England, Mr. Seguin was known as Arthur; in the United States, he adopted his middle name, Edward (Tawa 1986).

26. Ireland 1968, 2:276.

27. Odell 1970, 4:292–93; Ireland 1968, 2:242. A week's engagement at the National Theatre consisted of six performances, one every evening, excluding Sundays (Shirreff playbills, 30–31 Oct. 1838).

28. *MW* [London], 8 Dec. 1837, 203; *Boston Morning Post,* 7 Nov. 1838. The Library of Congress has a bound piano-vocal score of *Amilie.* A detailed description of the plot and musical numbers can be found in the *Boston Morning Post,* 7 Nov. 1838 and numerous individual sheet-music selections from the work (ten arias, several with recitatives, one chorus, and the overture) and several copies of the opera's libretto are in the collection of the Music Division, DLC.

29. Hamm 1979, 142; Cockrell 1986.

30. Hamm 1979, 142, 76.

31. The immutable reality that performers had to leave a theater at the end of their allotted time—even though they might be at the height of a theatrical triumph—was one of the most obvious failings of the star system. Odell refers to this method of operation as "that wretched system of short engagements" (4:55). Excepting only the performance on Monday, 19 Nov., when John Wilson chose to play in *Guy Mannering* and *The Waterman* for his benefit. See Playbill, Tremont Street Theatre, 19 Nov., 1838, Shirreff Collection, NN.

32. *Washington National Intelligencer,* 27, 28, 29 Dec. 1838; *Baltimore Sun,* 5 and 10 Jan. 1839.

33. See, for example, "The Beauties of *Amilie; or, The Love Test,*" containing the whole of the songs, duetts, choruses, etc., arranged in four books as brilliant divertimentos for the pianoforte by Charles M. King (New York: Firth & Hall, n.d.); "Quadrilles, Selected from Rooke's Celebrated Opera of *Amilie,*" arranged by J. Weippert (Baltimore: J. Cole, n.d.); "My Boyhood's Home," arranged for Spanish Guitar (Philadelphia: George Willig, n.d.); "When Morning First Dawns," arranged as a waltz for piano (New York: Firth & Hall, n.d.); and "Quadrilles Selected from W. M. Rooke's Celebrated Opera of *Amilie*" as performed at the Light Guard Soirée, New York (New York: Hewitt & Jacques, n.d.), all in the collection of the Music Division, DLC; and "The Most Popular Melodies of W. M. Rooke's Opera *Amilie,*" arranged for flute by E. Manuel (Philadelphia: Fiot, Meignen & Co., n.d.) in the collection of the Music Department, MB.

34. The vocal-star troupe mounted the North American premiere of the

English version of Adam's opera (as translated by J. B. Phillips) in New York during the subsequent theatrical season, on 30 March 1840 (*New York Sun*, 30 March 1840; Loewenberg 1978, 783). The North American premiere of the opera (in French) had been at the Théâtre d'Orléans in New Orleans two years earlier on 19 April 1838 (Belsom 1955, 48).

35. *Pennsylvanian*, 24 Jan. 1839; *Philadelphia National Gazette*, 21 April 1840.

36. As an example, *Fra Diavolo* was introduced in Philadelphia during the third week of the troupe's first engagement there. On 29 January 1839 the house took in $730; for the subsequent four performances, the takes were $570, $520, $362, and $481 (Saturday night), according to Shirreff's financial ledger.

37. Wemyss 1847, 305; Wilson 1935, 198.

38. The critic for the *National Gazette*, however, was not convinced. He wrote that he much preferred the vocal-star troupe's second novelty, Adolphe Adam's *The Postillion of Longjumeau*, and referred to *Amilie* as a "bald eruditie" (23 April 1840).

39. *Pennsylvanian*, 31 Jan. 1839; Shirreff financial ledger, 21 Jan. 1839.

40. Ireland 1968, 2:274; Shirreff playbills. Extra performers did not appear with Shirreff and Wilson during their last-minute engagement at the Providence Theatre, which suggests that the troupe's other engagements in Philadelphia, Boston, Washington, and Baltimore had been arranged ahead of time, possibly by Wallack. The fact that the singers performed works exclusively from the older repertory in Providence also indicates that they functioned there as a true vocal-star troupe, relying entirely upon the local stock company for support.

41. *American and Commercial Daily Advertiser*, 25 Dec. 1839; *Washington National Intelligencer*, 24 Dec. 1838; Shirreff playbills.

42. Information about casts is gleaned from a variety of sources, including playbills in the Shirreff Collection and from advertisements in numerous newspapers, including the following: Boston: *Evening Transcript* and *Morning Post* (5–23 Nov. 1838); Baltimore: *American and Commercial Advertiser* and *Daily Advertiser* (31 Dec. 1838–13 Jan. 1839); Philadelphia: *Pennsylvanian*, *North American*, and *Gazette* (14 Jan.–9 Feb. 1839); Washington: *National Intelligencer* (24–29 Dec. 1839). Information on the 1838–39 stock companies of the New York and Philadelphia theaters is from Ireland 1968, 2:274; Odell 1970, 4:334 (National Theatre); and Wilson 1935, 103 (Chestnut Street Theatre).

43. No details of Wallack's management or of contractual agreements between the manager and the troupe have survived, thus any statements about management practices are conjectural. Little is known about theatrical or musical management during this period. The closest study that exists is Bernheim's (1932). Although the thrust of Bernheim's study is theater in the late-nineteenth and early-twentieth centuries, he does include a survey of colonial and antebellum theatrical practices. Another useful study, which concentrates on sectional theatrical developments, is by Dormon (1967). For information

on theatrical management during the colonial and federal periods, Porter's study (1991) is invaluable. Some management issues are also dealt with in various studies of individual theatrical managers: for example, Carson's excellent works (1932, 1949), which both deal with the careers of Sol Smith and Noah Ludlow; James (1968), which is based on the daily account books of William Wood's Chestnut Street Theatre; Wilt (1923); and Nugent (1967). The area of musical management is even less well documented. Lerner (1970) is a useful start but unfortunately contains many errors. A more recent and quite valuable contribution, however, is Lott (1986), part of which covers some of the same ground attempted by Lerner.

44. Letters, Davis Collection; ALS, Bochsa to Peters and Field, 19 June 1848; Correspondence, Ford Theatre Collection.

45. Shirreff playbills, 5–9 Feb. 1839. Shirreff's attempts to continue to perform—for whatever the reason—contrast with the behavior of Italian prima donnas of the late 1840s and 1850s. These singers had a reputation among Americans for feigning illness. In fact, despite her obvious illness, at least one of Edward Seguin's supporters believed that the soprano was shirking her duty, for she mentions in her diary receiving "a most impertinent anonymous letter respecting my not playing Seguin's [benefit] night" (9 Feb. 1839).

46. Shirreff kept detailed financial accounting, including her terms of engagement, the total gross receipts, and her shares, for the period from December 1838 to May 1840. For the period from October through December 1838 she noted only her earnings.

47. In Baltimore, for the vocal stars' engagement, the theater's figure was $150; the Chestnut Street Theatre in Philadelphia was guaranteed $250, as was the National in New York for the company's engagements in October and December 1838 and in February and March 1839. In October 1839, however, the National was guaranteed $300 of each evening's receipts; undoubtedly this reflected the singers' success.

48. Singers usually agreed to one benefit per engagement, but occasionally there were extra joint benefits and extra solo benefits. For a long engagement, the number of benefits increased. Performers sometimes also agreed to sing for a benefit for the manager, the orchestra director, the stage manager, or for certain members of the stock company, such as an old actor or actress who was retiring. These latter, however, generally were special events and not part of a performer's contract (*Spirit,* 27 April 1839; Odell 1970, 4:30; Shirreff financial ledger 25 March 1839; Shirreff playbills).

49. Figures based on 1992 equivalent sums (Greene 1987, 48).

50. Latham made his American debut at the Park on 3 Sept. 1834, as Figaro in *The Barber of Seville.* He performed widely with the stock companies of both the Park and the National theaters. Although apparently not a regular member of the National's stock company during the 1838–39 season, he had appeared with the Shirreff/Wilson/Seguin forces during the season, as Lord Allcash in *Fra Diavolo* (5 Dec. 1838) and as Basilo in *The Barber of Seville* (11 Feb. 1839) (Odell 1970, 4:2, 295, 297; Ireland 1968, 2:99).

51. For example, the Seguins gave grand vocal concerts in Montreal on 21

and 23 August, the week before Shirreff and Wilson were to appear in that city (*Montreal Gazette*, 20, 22 Aug. 1839).

52. It was not unusual for singers and other performers to travel with other members of their families. As Baker points out in his study of nineteenth-century actors, "while the stock system predominated, acting was essentially a family affair. The family unit was central to almost all companies, large and small; indeed among the smallest troupes a single family might comprise . . . the whole company" (*The Rise of the Victorian Actor*, quoted in Bloom 1986, 93–94). The same could be said for itinerant musical performers. Many, like the Seguins, were married to each other. It is difficult to document family relationships, however, for newspaper or periodical accounts almost never mention them. For example, the bass Theodore Victor Giubilei was probably married to the dancer Mme. Proche Giubilei, for the two often appeared in the same engagements, in New York and elsewhere around the country (Ireland 1968, 2:299, 300). No newspaper confirmation of this, however, has come to light. Many others—actors, dancers, singers—were related. The baritone Charles T. Martyn was married to the soprano Miss Inverarity, who at least henceforth had the consideration—for future historians—to be known as Mrs. Martyn. Later in the century, Caroline Richings, a soprano vocal star, would travel around the United States with her adoptive actor-father, Peter; the actress and singer Charlotte Cushman was married to James G. Maeder, a theater musician and composer; and the Ravel family, a renowned troupe of dancers and acrobats, was indeed a family. Nontheatrical family members— spouses, parents, siblings, and children—are almost never mentioned in the print media of the early nineteenth century. Barring a handful of chance references, one would assume that itinerant performers did not have families— or that they were tucked away back home somewhere, safe and sound. References to Shirreff's mother are limited to the list of passengers who arrived on the steamer *Great Western* from London on 24 September 1838, to her diary, and to the journal kept by her friend, Mary Blundell; Mary Wilson and the Seguins' children are likewise officially mentioned only in passenger lists, although Miss Shirreff does refer to "the Wilsons" and to "Mary" in her diary. The presence in the United States of the Seguin children is confirmed elsewhere by the death in 1843 of two of them of scarlet fever in Philadelphia while the Seguins were performing there (Sill, 11 Jan. 1843). Whether the three Seguin children normally traveled with their parents or whether the family made its home in Philadelphia is unknown.

53. Diary, 11, 17 July 1839; Blundell 1838–40, 161–72.

54. Wemyss 1847, 327; Shirreff playbills, Sept. 1839; *Pennsylvanian*, 16 Sept. 1840.

55. Shirreff playbills [Baltimore], Oct. 1839; *Baltimore American and Commercial Daily Advertiser*, 30 Sept. 1839.

56. Carson 1949, 15.

57. Ireland 1968, 2:315.

58. Bloom 1986, 91.

59. *Morning Herald,* 11 Nov. 1839, 21 Nov. 1839.

60. Copies of these compositions can be found in the collection of the Music Division, DLC.

61. These selections were performed on the following dates: Rossini: Albany, 8 July 1839 and Baltimore, 30 Jan. 1840; Balfe: Albany, 8 July 1839, Baltimore, 27 Jan. 1840, and New York City, 15 Nov. 1839; Bellini: Albany, 1 July 1839; Donizetti: Baltimore, 1 Feb. 1840; Adam: Baltimore, 1 Feb. 1840; and Hérold: New York City, 15 Nov. 1839.

62. The quotations are taken from the following pieces of sheet music, all of which can be found in the collection of the Music Division, DLC: "The Rapture Dwelling" (New York: Atwill, 184?); "The Flowers of the Forest" (New York: Millett Music Saloon, n.d.); and "Proudly and Wide" (New York: Atwill, n.d.). These publications are typical.

63. The U.S. premiere of Sir Henry Rowley Bishop's version of *The Marriage of Figaro* had been in New York in 1824. For information on the popularity of *Cinderella* and *La Sonnambula,* see chapter 1. Thomas Reynoldson's adaptation of Auber's *Fra Diavolo* was premiered in New York in June 1833 by Elizabeth Austin (chapter 1). On 19 November 1833 the Woods premiered a "new arrangement" of the opera, presumably the adaptation made by Michael Rophino Lacy (Odell 1970, 6:661). It, too, continued to be popular on the American stage, at least through the mid-1850s. *Cinderella, La Sonnambula,* and *Fra Diavolo* all were staples in the repertory of the Pyne and Harrison English Opera Company on their American tours from 1854 through 1857 (chapters 5 and 6).

64. *Mirror,* 15 Dec. 1832; *Spirit,* 3 July 1847, 224. The first quote was in reference to *Il Pirata;* the second is a description of *La Sonnambula.*

65. Wilson sang "John Anderson" at almost every performance that included songs, including in New York (27 Oct. and 19 Dec. 1838), Washington, D.C. (27 Dec. 1838), Baltimore (4 Jan. 1839), and Philadelphia (21 Jan.). He sang the others less frequently (Shirreff playbills).

66. These examples are from concerts performed in New York City (20 Dec. 1839), Washington, D.C. (Dec. 1838), and Baltimore (11 Jan. 1839) (Shirreff playbills).

67. Seguin performed the *Figaro* aria on the following dates: 4 Jan. 1839 (Baltimore), 27 Oct. 1838 (New York City), 27 Dec. 1838 (Washington, D.C.), and 21 Jan. 1839 (Philadelphia). The aria from *The Magic Flute* appears on a Philadelphia playbill dated 6 Feb. 1839 (Shirreff playbills).

68. Seguin performed the aria from *La Sonnambula* on 27 Oct. 1838 (New York City); the *Amilie* aria was included in concerts on 8 Jan. 1839 (Baltimore), 6 Feb. 1839 (Philadelphia), and 9 Feb. 1839 (Philadelphia) (Shirreff playbills).

69. *Philadelphia Public Ledger and Transcript,* Jan. 1839; *Pennsylvanian,* Feb. 1839.

70. Playbill, 20 Dec. 1838, NN.

71. Playbill, Baltimore Holliday Street Theatre, 8 Jan. 1839, NN.

72. Blundell 1838–40, 182–99.

3. Italian Opera Companies

1. *Dwight's,* 23 Oct. 1858, 235.

2. The first resident opera company in the United States, a French troupe, was established in 1806 at the St. Peter Street Theatre in the French Quarter of New Orleans (Kmen 1966, 73–74).

3. Francis 1858; Nelson 1976, 24–25.

4. Odell 1970, 2:209; Durham 1986, 387–91.

5. Nelson 1976, 82–88; Durham 1986, 390–91.

6. Mattfeld 1927, 18.

7. Lawrence 1988, xliv.

8. *Harmonicon,* 1830, 248, quoted in Mattfeld 1927, 17–18.

9. Mattfeld 1927, 18.

10. Mattfeld 1927, 18; Lawrence 1988, xlv.

11. Odell 1970, 3:174.

12. Tawa 1986; Nelson 1976, 126–27.

13. Quoted in Mattfeld 1927, 20.

14. Rossini's *Il barbiere,* a four-act French version, had been performed in New Orleans in 1823 (Belsom 1955, 12).

15. For a day-by-day accounting of the troupe's performances, see Nelson 1976, 316–20.

16. Lawrence 1988, l.

17. *Mirror,* 3 Dec. 1825, quoted in Mattfeld 1927, 14; *New York American,* 30 Nov. 1825, quoted in Lawrence 1988, xlviii. For other descriptions of the "elegant and fashionable" audience, see Lawrence 1988, xlviii-l; Nelson 1976; Odell 1970, 3:183–84; Mattfeld 1927, 13–14; Teran 1974; and Hamm 1979, 64–66.

18. Advertisement from the *New York American,* quoted in Odell 1970, 3:182.

19. Lawrence 1988, xlviii.

20. McConachie 1988, 182.

21. Quoted in Lawrence 1988, l.

22. *New York Literary Gazette and Phi Beta Kappa Repository,* 17 Dec. 1825, quoted in Mattfeld 1927, 15.

23. Lawrence 1988, li-lii; Tawa 1986.

24. Madame Malibran remained in New York for another year, eking out an existence—and further acquainting New York audiences with Italian melody—by singing in concerts and in English-language operas at the Bowery Theatre. Her final performance in New York was on 27 Sept. 1827, after which she returned to Europe, leaving her husband behind (Mattfeld 1927, 22).

25. Odell 1970, 3:410–11; Curtis n.d., 109; Wemyss 1847, 172.

26. Mattfeld 1927, 26; Odell 1970, 3:458; Porter 1988, 106–7.

27. *Spirit,* 4 Aug. 1832. For da Ponte's own explanation of his motives, see the forward ("To the Citizens of Philadelphia") to the libretto of *Il Pirata,* published in Philadelphia in 1833. A copy is in the collection of the Music Department, PPL.

28. *Spirit,* 4 Aug. 1832; Odell 1970, 3:642.

29. Schiavo 1947, 1:44. In New York, they performed 6 Oct.–27 Dec. 1832 at the Richmond Hill Theatre, and 10 April–11 May 1833 at the Bowery Theatre; in Philadelphia, 23 Jan.–13 March 1833 at the Chestnut Street Theatre.

30. Curtis n.d., 164. The surprise move by the board seems to have been the result of political intrigue; Rivafinoli apparently was something of a wheeler-dealer. He managed to convince the powers that be that under his management the opera house would earn large amounts of money, whereas under Montresor's tutelage the Italian Opera Association members would lose their collective shirts (Schiavo 1947, 45–49).

31. Mattfeld 1927, 31–32; White 1882, 1:702; Schiavo 1947, 50–53; Odell 1970, 3:691–92.

32. McConachie 1988, 183.

33. Ireland 1968, 2:95.

34. The company's seasons were as follows: in New York: 18 Nov. 1833–21 Feb. 1834, 24 Feb.–4 April 1834, and 24 May–sometime in July 1834; in Philadelphia: 8 April–19 May 1834 (Schiavo 1947, 55; Curtis n.d., 191; Odell 1970, 3:695). *La Gazza Ladra* had been performed in French in Philadelphia (1827), New Orleans (1828), and New York (1830), and *La Donna del Lago* likewise had been produced in French in both New Orleans (1829) and New York (1829). The Rivafinoli Company's productions of both these operas were the first in Italian in the United States (Belsom 1955, 18–19; Loewenberg 1978, 655, 665).

35. Schiavo 1947, 56. For a reproduction of Rivafinoli's account ledger, see Ritter 1883, 211–12.

36. 11 Nov. 1835, quoted in Mattfeld 1927, 34.

37. Quoted in Mattfeld 1927, 34.

38. Phelps 1880, 187. Albany had a population of approximately thirty thousand in 1835. See U.S. Bureau of the Census, 1832, 37, and U.S. Bureau of the Census, 1841, 93.

39. Schiavo 1947, 88.

40. Schiavo 1947, 43; Kmen 1966, 140.

41. Schiavo 1947, 63. Brichta's relationship to the female vocal star of the same name (Frances Brichta) is unknown; their names, however, are suspiciously similar.

42. Brichta at this point decided to go to Italy to recruit another company, and by July 1835 he had secured a troupe of fifty, including instrumentalists and choristers, and was en route back to Havana, where he had a three-year contract to manage an opera company (Schiavo 1947, 63).

43. Kmen 1966, 140.

44. Members of the New Orleans Montresor troupe who had been in the New York company included Francesco Sapignoli, Adelaide Pedrotti, Enrichetta Salvioni, Lorenza Marozzi, Signor Manetti, Ernesto Orlandi, and G. B. Montresor. Of these, Sapignoli, Salvioni, Marozzi, Manetti, and Orlandi had sung with Rivafinoli; the two singers Montresor hired who had come to the

United States for Rivafinoli were Antonio de Rosa and Luigi Ravaglia (Kmen 1966, 136; Schiavo 1947, 42, 55; *Spirit,* 4 Aug. 1832; Odell 1970, 3:644, 690–94; *Mirror,* 21 Sept. 1833, 94).

45. The U.S. premiere of *Il Pirata* had been in New York on 5 Dec. 1832 by the earlier troupe of the same name (Belsom 1955, 32; Loewenberg 1978, 709).

46. Kmen 1966; Kmen 1961, 408–11.

47. Kmen 1961, 408, 411; Belsom 1955, 31, 34.

48. According to John Kendall, Caldwell claimed to have lost money on the Italians; although he did lose money during the last half of his season, the deficits were not due to the productions of Italian opera (Kendall 1968, 137).

49. Kmen 1966, 73–83; Belsom 1955, 4.

50. Quoted in Kmen 1966, 142.

51. Kmen 1966, 141.

52. Kmen 1966, 143; *Spirit,* 22 Oct. 1836; Kendall 1968, 143; *Louisville Daily Journal,* 1 Aug.–21 Oct. For a list of the company personnel—including instrumentalists—see the *Daily Journal* of 29 July 1836.

53. Kendall 1968, 136, 142–43.

54. Kmen 1961, 412–15. The "real" Montresor troupe—or at least Montresor himself—was reported to have been in Mexico during 1836 (Armstrong 1884, 23). By 1840 he was once again back in Havana, as the conductor of the Italian company at the Tacon Theatre (J. G. 1840).

55. Kendall 1968, 143.

56. Kmen 1966, 151; Kendall 1968, 144.

57. Reported in *Boston Musical Journal,* 30 May 1838, 21.

58. U.S. premieres: *I Capuleti e I Montecchi,* 4 April 1836; *Caritea, Regina di Spagna* (as *Donna Caritea*), 26 April; *Semiramide,* 19 May; and *Chiara di Rosembergh,* 3 May; New Orleans premieres: *Parisina,* 4 June and *Tancredi,* 12 May (Belsom 1955, 36, 39, 40, 45; Kmen 1961, 418). For information on repertory in various cities I am indebted to Thomas G. Kaufman of Boonton, N.J., who generously gave me copies of his research notes for a book on operatic premieres in the United States.

59. *New Orleans Picayune,* 23 May 1837, quoted in Belsom 1955, 41–42 and Kmen 1966, 154.

60. Kmen 1966, 151–57.

61. *New Orleans Picayune,* 6 June 1837; *Le Courrier de la Louisiane,* 12 June 1837, quoted in Belsom 1955, 46.

62. Belsom 1955, 73; *Spirit,* 26 March 1842. According to Schiavo, however, the Havana company was under the direction of Lauro Rossi from 1835 through 1844 (1947, 423–24). Perhaps Lauro was Marti's acting manager.

63. "Sayings and Doings in New Orleans," *Spirit,* 26 March 1842.

64. Kendall 1968, 184–85; *Spirit,* 26 March 1842; *Mirror,* 5 March 1842, 32.

65. Belsom 1955, 79; Kendall 1968, 185.

66. The troupe's engagements in New Orleans were 22 Feb.–10 March 1842 at the St. Charles, and 16 March–18 April 1842 at the Théâtre d'Orléans.

67. U.S. premieres: *Marino Faliero* on 22 Feb. 1842, *Beatrice di Tenda* on 5 March, *Il Furioso nell' Isola di San Domingo* on 28 March, and *Belisario* on 15 April 1842 (not in 1843 in Philadelphia as cited by Loewenberg 1978, 776); New Orleans premieres (in Italian): *L'Elisir d'amore* and *La Sonnambula* (Belsom 1955, 73, 77, 81, 84).

68. Belsom 1955, 101–8. The premieres were of *I Puritani* on 17 April, *Gemma di Vergy* on 22 April, and *Lucrezia Borgia* on 11 May (Belsom 1955, 99, 103, 107).

69. Belsom 1955, 100–101; Schiavo 1947, 65–66.

70. Cincinnati *Gazette,* 2 June 1843, quoted in Wyrick 1965, 112.

71. Quoted by Wolz 1983, 50. The orchestra and the chorus must have been small because the total size of the company was only thirty. Perhaps only a nucleus of each—to be filled out by locals—traveled with the troupe.

72. Wolz 1983, 50; Wyrick 1965, 113; *Daily Gazette,* 10 June 1843, cited in Wolz 1983, 50.

73. Schiavo 1947, 65; Belsom 1955, 106.

74. Wilson 1935; Armstrong 1884, 47.

75. Kaufman worklist, Baltimore.

76. Odell 1970, 4:694; Lawrence 1988, 216.

77. Odell 1970, 4:694; Lawrence 1988, 217.

78. Ireland 1968, 2:404; Loewenberg 1978, 740, 763.

79. Schiavo 1947, 65; Armstrong 1884, 47.

80. *Spirit,* 9 Dec. 1843; Kaufman worklist, Baltimore; Kendall 1968, 233.

81. Schaivo 1947, 66.

82. Lawrence (1988, 251–53) gives the capacity of the theater as 1,100–1,200, but both Brown (1870, 1:337–39) and Klein (1986, 134) give the total seating as eight hundred.

83. Quoted in Lawrence 1988, 253.

84. Lawrence 1988, 254; Schiavo 1947, 259–61.

85. *Spirit,* 3 Feb. 1844; Lawrence 1988, 255.

86. Loewenberg 1978, 750, 765, 776; Odell 1970, 5:52.

87. Quoted in Lawrence 1988, 253.

88. Lawrence 1988, 257.

89. Odell 1970, 5:52.

90. Lawrence 1988, 260.

91. *Anglo American,* 23 March 1844, 526, quoted in Lawrence 1988, 260. Currency equivalences based on Greene 1987.

92. *Anglo American,* 6 April 1844, 573, quoted in Lawrence 1988, 260.

93. Odell 1970, 5:53.

94. Loewenberg 1978, 730, 743.

95. Lawrence 1988, 263.

96. Farwell and Darby 1915, 125; Lawrence 1988, 264.

97. For an eye-witness description, see *Spirit,* 19 Oct. 1844.

98. Loewenberg 1978, 686, 735, 756.

99. For a detailed—and fascinating—account of the entire Palmo's fiasco, see Lawrence 1988, 250–67, 325–28. Although Palmo was financially ruined

by his venture, it apparently did not embitter him, even though he went to work as a cook and subsequently was forced to depend on the generosity of friends and other Italians in New York for sustenance. According to the editor of an Italian-language newspaper (*Eco d'Italia*), Palmo continued to be serene, cheerful, and generous for the rest of his life; he maintained a "philosophical indifference [to] both prosperity and undeserved adversity" (quoted by Schiavo 1947, 389).

100. *Spirit,* 8 Feb. 1845; Odell 1970, 6:147–48; Lawrence 1988, 355.

101. Kaufman worklist, New Orleans.

102. Lawrence 1988, 355.

103. By June 1847 Palmo's house had been taken over by a dramatic company, and in July 1848 it became Burton's Theatre (Odell 1970, 5:302, 377, 429–30).

104. For information on the effect of Palmo's company on the construction of the Astor Place house, see Lawrence 1988, 430n.

105. Sanquirico was still in New York as late as 12 May 1845, for he participated in a concert at Castle Garden on that date (Lawrence 1988, 302; *Spirit,* 29 Aug. 1846).

106. *Spirit,* 29 Aug. 1846, 21 Nov. 1846.

107. Both singers were members of Max Maretzek's 1850–51 Astor Place Opera Company (chapter 4). In addition, Salvatore Patti (1800–1869) was the patriarch of a musical family of great importance to the development of musical culture in the United States of the mid-nineteenth century. He married Caterina Barili (?–1870), an Italian soprano, former prima donna, and the widow of the composer Francesco Barili. Several of Caterina Barili's children were musicians who appeared on European and American stages, including Clotilda Barili (d. 1856) and her three brothers Ettore (1829–85), a baritone; Nicola (d. 1878), a basso cantante; and Antonio (1820–76), a bass and conductor (*Dwight's,* 13 Sept. 1856, 191; Lawrence 1988, 425; Schiavo 1947, 238–42). The union of Salvatore and Caterina Barili-Patti produced one son, Carlo (1842–73), a violinist and conductor, and three daughters: Carlotta (1836–89), a soprano; Amalia (1831–1915), a contralto; and Adelina (1843–1919), a soprano (Brooks, RN Strakosch and RN Maretzek; Brooks 1986, "Strakosch," "Maretzek"; Lawrence 1988; Schiavo 1947, 394–407).

108. Lawrence 1988, 425; *Courier & Enquirer,* 5 Jan. 1847, quoted in Lawrence 1988, 427; White 1882, 2:877.

109. Lawrence 1988, 428; *Herald,* 19 Jan. 1847, quoted in Lawrence 1988, 429. One other company member new to New York was Ferdinando Beneventano (bass-buffo). The troupe filled out its ranks with other singers already in the United States, including Rosina Pico, Daniele Benetti, Madame Boulard, Harriet Phillips, and Benetti Riese; Antonio Sanquirico sang bass roles.

110. Lawrence 1988, 429.

111. Lawrence 1988, 432.

112. Lawrence 1988, 434; *C&Q,* 149–58. The theater is still standing, although it has been much modified over the years. Today it serves as the

National Theatre of Cuba; it was renamed (after the Revolution of 1959) the Teatro García Lorca (Pride 1973, 96).

113. Other important members of the troupe who had been recruited around the same time included the sopranos Fortunata Tedesco and Luigia Caranti di Vita; the tenors Natale Perelli, Juan Severi, and Luigi Perozzi (a member of the first Palmo company); and the basses Pietro Candi and Luigi Battaglini. Many of these singers would appear in the early 1850s on the rosters of a variety of other Italian companies that toured the United States, and several settled permanently in this country.

114. Their appearances were as follows: New York (15–16 April, concert on 17 April); Boston (19 April–4 June); New York (Park Theatre, 9 June–8 July, concert on 9 July); Philadelphia (12 July–6 Aug.); New York (Castle Garden, 18 Aug.–17 Sept.); Boston (21 Sept.–1 Oct.); and New York (farewell concert at the Tabernacle, 15 Oct.).

115. Playbill, Boston Athenaeum, 5 May 1847, MWA; Lawrence 1988, 445.

116. Quoted in Lawrence 1988, 434.

117. *BMG*, 25 Oct. 1847; *Spirit*, 12 June 1847.

118. Lawrence 1988, 442.

119. *Mosè in Eggito* was also performed in Boston as a opera.

120. *BMG*, 25 Oct. 1847. Many Americans of the nineteenth century regarded theatrical entertainment as immoral, in part because some religious denominations taught that all play-acting was basically lying and, hence, inherently corrupt and evil. Others chose not to be associated with a style of entertainment presented by individuals of dubious reputation, or to patronize a place where prostitution was often openly solicited.

121. Lawrence 1988, 438.

122. Lerner claims that Ullman had a revolutionary and eye-opening role in the history of opera performance in the United States, because he emphasized in 1853 the "total unity of the ensemble performance of Italian opera," as opposed to the use of opera simply to "showcase the prima donna" (Lerner 1970, 75–78). It is obvious, however, that American audiences and critics were strongly impressed by the ensemble of the 1847 Havana Company, a full six years before Ullman's "significant" activities as the manager of Henriette Sontag's Opera Company. Lerner also claims that Ullman was an innovator because he hired an orchestra and chorus to travel as part of the Sontag Company. This, notes Lerner, was "extraordinary for nineteenth century America. Usually, only the principals travelled, while if an orchestra or chorus were used at all, they would be recruited as needed en route from the ranks of available local musicians, whatever their quality." This was not the case with the Havana Company of 1847, nor was it the case for the troupe that Marti would send to this country in 1849 or 1850. In fact, the Havana Company of 1843 also had traveled with an orchestra, albeit a small one. Furthermore, the Astor Place companies of 1848–49 (under the management of Fry), as well as Maretzek's first two Astor Place troupes, the companies of 1849–50 and 1850–51, both traveled with chorus and orchestra (chapter 4).

123. White 1882, 2:879; Schiavo 1947, 77.

124. *Herald,* 25 March 1847, quoted by Lawrence 1988, 454.

125. The newcomers to the United States were Caterina Barili-Patti, a soprano, the mother of Clotilda Barili, and Salvatore Patti's wife; Teresa Truffi, a soprano; Giuseppina Lietti Rossi, a contralto; Settimo Rossi, a bass; Antonio Avignone, a baritone; and the tenors Adelindo Vietti and Francesco Bailini. The troupe members from the previous Sanquirico-Patti company included Clotilda Barili, G. F. Beneventano, S. Patti, A. Sanquirico, and Antonio Barili. The star tenor of the previous season, Sesto Benedetti, was embroiled in a wage dispute with the management but finally joined the troupe about a month into the season (Lawrence 1988, 466). The management also engaged— for three months—another potential star, Eliza Biscaccianti (née Ostinelli), a Boston-born soprano who had studied and performed in Italy. Biscaccianti (1824–96) was the granddaughter of the American composer James Hewitt and the daughter of Sophia Hewitt and the Italian violinist Louis Ostinelli, who had emigrated to the United States sometime before 1822. Biscaccianti would enjoy a respectable career in both opera and concert performances, especially in California during the 1850s (Lawrence 1988, 454, 462; Schiavo 1947, 254–56).

126. *Courier & Enquirer,* 25 Nov. 1847, quoted by Lawrence 1988, 460.

127. Lawrence 1988, 455–56; *Albion,* 27 Nov. 1847, quoted in Lawrence 1988, 455; White 1882, 2:881. In fairness, the chandelier problem was probably the result of architectural incompetence rather than deliberate elitist callousness.

128. Teran 1974, 19.

129. Quoted by Young 1973, 1:112.

130. White 1882, 2:880. Lawrence states that the Astor Place House had a capacity of between 1,500 and 1,800 (1988, 455). Fry, however, gives the following information on seating in that house: parquet, 308; two stage-boxes, 28; first-tier balcony and boxes, 277; second-tier private and open boxes, 246; third tier or amphitheatre, 600; total seating for "nearly 1500 persons" (1856, 116).

131. Lawrence 1988, 457.

132. Quoted in Lawrence 1988, 456.

133. Lawrence 1988, 504.

134. Lawrence 1988, 466.

135. Odell 1970, 5:382–83.

136. Lawrence 1988, 505; Wilson 1935; Curtis n.d., 393.

137. Curtis n.d., 393.

138. *Spirit,* 6 May 1848; Lawrence 1988, 505.

139. Odell 1970, 5:383.

140. *Literary Excelsior and Musical World,* 6 May 1848; Lawrence 1988, 505.

141. Armstrong 1884, 60; Curtis n.d., 393; Wilson 1935.

142. Curtis n.d., 393.

143. Playbill, 29 May 1848, MWA; Kaufman worklist, Boston.

144. Odell 1970, 5:406.

145. According to the *Democratic Review,* Clotilda Barili had been engaged (at the princely salary of $500 per month) for the entire season but by March had appeared only four or five times. Caterina Barili-Patti had been engaged for a month (at $800) but had refused to sing after only two performances— possibly because of the shameful treatment to which she had been subjected by the New York critics (Lawrence 1988, 497; *Democratic Review,* March 1848, quoted in Lawrence 1988, 503).

146. Quoted in Lawrence 1988, 459.

147. By the mid–1840s, more than a hundred thousand immigrants (mostly Irish and German) entered the United States annually; by 1847 the number climbed to more than two hundred thousand (Morris 1976, 653–54).

148. Quoted in Faner 1951, 39.

149. Many of the Italian performers, of course, contributed to this negative image themselves by their constant bickering and fighting.

150. An excellent full-length study of the social and cultural pressures that led to the Astor Place Riot is found in Buckley 1984.

151. I should point out that McConachie (1988) does not claim that New York opera audiences during this time were exclusively aristocratic. The goal of his article was not to describe the overall socioeconomic makeup of the audience, but rather to examine the various means employed by the New York aristocracy to make "operagoing" into an elite pastime.

152. *MW,* 1 March 1852, 171; *MG,* 17 March 1855. Many contemporary sources clearly suggest that the United States had a reputation as a performers' goldmine; see, for example, *Saroni's,* 17 Nov. 1849, 86.

153. Russell 1969, 11–25; Thomas 1905, 1:25.

154. For information on the tours made by Sontag, Alboni, de la Grange, and Vestvali, see the entries and accompanying notes on their companies in Appendix C. Most of the other singers named performed at various times in the Havana, Astor Place, Academy of Music, Maretzek, Ullman, or Strakosch Opera companies (Schiavo 1947; *C&Q; S&F*).

155. *MR,* 1 March 1855, 31 Aug. 1854, 306.

156. The Astor Place House witnessed its last performances of Italian opera in March 1852. In early January 1852, the company, managed by Max Maretzek, literally broke in half, and the disaffected singers formed their own troupe, the Italian Artists' Union. This group performed at Niblo's Theatre in direct competition with the remnants of the Astor Place Company. The brief operatic war that ensued crippled both companies economically (Odell 1970, 6:165; *Saroni's,* 10 Jan. 1852, 156). The Astor Place Company subsequently went south to New Orleans, and then to Mexico. The Italian Artists' Union had a brief engagement in Boston and then dissolved (*AMR,* April 1852, 57 and June 1852, 89; *MW,* 15 April 1852, 154; *C&Q*). The Astor Place house reopened as a theater in August 1852 but closed its doors forever two months later (Odell 1970, 6:243–44).

157. Kolodin, Perkins, and Sommer 1986.

158. Brooks 1986, "Ullman"; Lerner 1970, 93, 97–98; Lott 1986.

159. Brooks 1986, "Strakosch."

160. Brooks, RN Strakosch.

161. Opera troupes that operated out of the Philadelphia or the New York Academies of Music almost invariably were referred to as simply the "Academy of Music Company," which compounds the confusion associated with the ambiguous names of opera companies.

162. Brooks 1986, "Maretzek."

163. Horner-Lott 1986.

164. Kaufman 1986–87, 39–52.

4. Max Maretzek and His Astor Place Company

1. Kolodin, Perkins, and Sommer 1986.

2. The term *season* as used during this period does not always have the implication of longevity that it now does. Although the original meaning of the term was the same as the modern meaning (i.e., roughly from fall of one year to the spring of the subsequent year), during the nineteenth century a "season" was more like a modern "run." An operatic season might last five months, or it might last no longer than a week. The term was also sometimes used with the modern meaning.

3. Schiavo 1947, 81.

4. Haywood 1968, xix.

5. Ireland 1968, 2:544; Maretzek 1968, *C&Q*, xxii.

6. Lawrence 1988, 508–9.

7. Maretzek 1968, *C&Q*, 21; Lawrence 1988, 508–9, *AMT*, 17 June 1848, 16. The editor of the *American Musical Times* incorrectly identified the purchaser of the opera company properties as William Henry Fry.

8. Newman 1960, 456–57; Haywood 1968, xxii. According to Rosselli (1984, 63), the opera industry in Italy was dealt a series of severe blows first by the depression of 1847, then by the wars and revolutions in 1848–49; the industry did not fully recover until the mid–1850s.

9. Maretzek 1968, *C&Q*, 25.

10. Maretzek 1968, *C&Q*, 13.

11. Odell 1970, 5:243, 384–85.

12. Lawrence 1988, 510.

13. Maretzek 1968, *C&Q*, 21. Krehbiel (1980) disparagingly described E. R. Fry as a man "who came from the counting house to a position of which he can have known nothing more than what he could acquire from attendance upon opera, of which he was fond, and association with his brother." This glib assessment is not entirely correct. As Chase points out (1987, 305), Edward had served as general manager for his brothers' (Joseph and William Henry) successful production of *Norma* in Philadelphia in January 1841. Furthermore, he had written several opera librettos and had assisted his brother in adaptations of operas (Schiavo 1947, 77–80; Maretzek 1968, *C&Q*, 25). For two engaging accounts of the 1848–49 season, see *C&Q* and Lawrence 1988, 510–22.

14. Maretzek 1968, *C&Q*, 148.

15. Maretzek 1968, *C&Q*, 74.

16. *Message Bird*, 1 Oct. 1849, 83. The season in the spring of 1849 lasted only four weeks, from 19 March–12 April. During the subsequent theatrical year (1849–50), Maretzek's company performed at the Astor Place House from 1 Nov.–7 March and in Boston from 12 March–4 May (Odell 1970, 5:481, 570–73; Ireland 1968, 2:544; *Saroni's*, 16 March 1850, 290; Howard Athenaeum (Boston) Playbills, 15 and 16 April 1850, MWA). In the summer of 1849, William Niblo and James Henry Hackett leased the Astor Place House for theatrical performances. During this period the managers had the misfortune to engage the British actor William Charles Macready, and on 9 May the infamous Astor Place Riot occurred.

17. Maretzek 1968, *C&Q*, 82.

18. Maretzek 1968, *C&Q*, 98.

19. Odell 1970, 5:573; *Saroni's*, 2 Feb. 1849. For other information on the success of the opera season, see *Spirit*, 23 Feb. 1850, and 4 May 1850; Maretzek 1968, *C&Q*, 107; and Rieck 1922, 6.

20. *Message Bird*, 15 June 1850, 351; *Saroni's*, 17 Aug. 1850, 556. According to Rosselli (1984, 36–37, 137–48), by the 1840s operatic agencies were well established in Italy. An impresario or a theater manager could visit or write to an agency office (Milan was the center for most agents, but offices also were located in Venice, Florence, Rome, Naples, and elsewhere) to engage solo and chorus singers, instrumentalists, dancers, stage hands, or prompters. The businessman also acted as a forwarding agent for music rental or costume purchases. In the 1840s, Alessandro Lanari (1787 or 1790–1852), one of Italy's leading impresarios, supplied singers for companies in European cities and for "the fast developing American market, especially Havana and New York."

21. Maretzek 1968, *C&Q*, 82.

22. Maretzek 1968, *C&Q*, 83. Apparently, the wonders of the 1848 Havana Opera Company were but distant memories by 1850. Maretzek does not mention those singers; of course, he had not been in the United States at the time.

23. Brooks 1986, "Lind." One indication that Americans were aware of Lind's impending arrival was the response to an announcement in the *New York Daily Tribune* in August for a contest to furnish lyrics for a special song to be sung by Miss Lind. Several hundred poems, from all over the United States, were submitted (Ware and Lockard 1980, 5, 14–15).

24. The Havana Company's run in New York was at Niblo's from 11 April–8 May (*Spirit*, 20 April, 11 May, 1850); at the Astor Place Opera House from 3 June–5 July (*Prompter's Whistle*, 15 June 1850, 31–32; *Saroni's*, 15, 29 June, 6 July 1850; *Message Bird*, 15 July 1850, 351); then at Castle Garden from 8 July–7 September (Odell 1970, 5:592). The company stopped for performances in Philadelphia during September on its way back to Havana (*Prompter's Whistle*, 28 Sept. 1850, 89, 91; *Message Bird*, 1 Nov. 1850, 515).

25. Maretzek 1968, *C&Q*, 156.

26. See *Message Bird*, 15 May 1850, 330, and 15 June 1850, 351; *Saroni's*, 11 May 1850, 386; *Spirit*, 20 April 1850, 108; *Figaro*, 31 Aug. 1850; *Prompter's*

Whistle, 31 Aug. 1850, 21; *AMR,* Sept. 1850, 60. Giovanni Bottesini was still the orchestra leader of this much-touted company, which by 1850 numbered 110 artists, had an orchestra of forty, and a chorus of thirty (Playbill, Chestnut St. Theatre, 11 Sept. 1850, MWA). The principal singers included sopranos Angiolina Bosio, Balbina Steffanone, and Fortunata Tedesco; tenors Lorenzo Salvi and Domenico Lorini; basses Ignazio Marini and Pietro Novelli; and baritones Cesare Badiali and Luigi Vita (Schiavo 1947, 75–76). Although the reputations of few of these singers have survived, many were well known and highly respected artists in the middle of the nineteenth century. Angiolina Bosio (1830–59), a soprano with a "pure, silvery" voice that was "remarkably alike for its penetrating quality and for its charm so fine and delicate that it seemed almost intellectual" (White 1882, 3:34), was in her prime when she sang in New York, although her European reputation was not made until 1852 (Krehbiel 1980, 61; Lahee 1898, 89). Balbina Steffanone, another soprano, was described as "a fine artiste, an admirable singer, and a powerful actress" (*Albion,* 13 April 1850, quoted in Odell 1970, 5:564). Fortunata Tedesco, although not a great artist, could pour out "floods, or rather gusts of rich, clear sound" using a voice that was "so copious and so musical that she could not be heard without pleasure" (White 1882, 2:879). She was well received in this country (Odell 1970, 5:263, 266–67, 563). According to Maretzek, Salvi, Marini, and Badiali—long before their appearances in the United States—had established European reputations "as artists of the very first class" (*C&Q,* 156). White describes Salvi's voice as "divine" (1882, 3:31); Odell calls him "one of the most golden-voiced tenors in the history of opera" (1970, 5:565); and Schiavo refers to him as "one of the greatest tenors of the nineteenth century" (Schiavo 1947, 75). Ignazio Marini, according to Maretzek, was known in London as "the greatest Italian basso who had ever sung there," with the single exception of Louis Lablache (*C&Q,* 157).

27. Arditi 1977, 9.

28. Maretzek 1968, *C&Q,* 149–54.

29. It is possible that the Havana troupe of 1849–51 was one of the companies sent out by the impresario Lanari. It was not unusual for his agency to dispatch troupes on two-year contracts. By the late 1840s, Lanari was in partnership with one Lorini, an agent who "specialized in American business." A singer in the Havana Company was named Domenico Lorini (Rosselli 1984, 187, note 69).

30. Maretzek 1968, *C&Q,* 155–58; Odell 1970, 5:591.

31. Maretzek 1968, *C&Q,* 157.

32. Maretzek 1968, *C&Q,* 157.

33. Odell 1970, 5:159; Maretzek 1968, *C&Q,* 170; Playbill, MOC, 18 July 1851.

34. Odell 1970, 5:560.

35. Lawrence 1988, 3.

36. Hone Diary, 23 May 1845, quoted in Lawrence 1988, 304.

37. *Spirit,* 17 Aug. 1850, 312; *Saroni's,* 13 July 1850, 494.

38. *Spirit,* 17 Aug. 1850, 312; 20 July, 3 Aug. 1850; *Saroni's,* 13 July 1850, 494.

39. Quoted in *AMR*, Sept. 1850, 60.

40. Odell 1970, 6:83. It is only fair to point out here that Americans—especially those living in the major cities on the East Coast—were not quite the gullible, unsuspecting, and naive musical ignoramuses that some chroniclers of Lind's American tour have implied (Ware and Lockard 1980; Barnum 1970, 281–82). The first-rank singers of the Havana Opera Company (including Bosio, Badiali, Marini, and Salvi), after all, had just recently performed in front of audiences in Boston, New York, and Philadelphia. Furthermore, residents of the latter two cities also had heard performances by the incomparable Maria Malibran, albeit twenty-five years earlier. It is unjust, then, to suggest that American audiences had never heard singers of Lind's caliber. Furthermore, the implication (by Barnum and Ware and Lockard, for example) that her fame in the United States was entirely the result of Barnum's publicity is incorrect. Lind's friend, the British composer Julius Benedict, who accompanied her on the U.S. tour, later wrote that the impression Lind had made in Europe had "excited the greatest interest among lovers of music in the United States," and this demonstrated interest had given Barnum the idea for the tour (Benedict 1881, 127).

41. Ware and Lockard 1980, 19, 26.

42. Ware and Lockard 1980, 20–21, 27.

43. Odell 1970, 6:83–91.

44. Brooks 1986, "Lind."

45. Maretzek 1968, *C&Q*, 122–23.

46. Maretzek 1968, *C&Q*, 124. Although Maretzek was quick to point out in his memoirs that this was "the first, and I am proud to say, the only time" he used Barnum's puffing tactics, several years later he was referred to in a music periodical as "the Barnum of the opera" (*MW*, 2 Feb. 1852, 152).

47. The sopranos included Teresa Truffi, Amalia Patti, Apollonia Bertucca-Maretzek, and T. Avogadro; the tenors were Giuseppe Forti, Salvatore Patti, and Domenico Lorini; the baritones were Antonio Avignone and G. F. Beneventano; and the basses were August Giubilei, Settimo Rosi (or Rossi), Antonio Sanquirico, and Pietro Novelli. Teresa Truffi was the company's leading light. White (1882, 2:880) observed that Truffi "was not a great singer. She had not even a great voice, as Tadesco [*sic*] had. But there was that nameless something in the tone of her voice . . . which enabled her to move her hearers when many a more finished vocalist would leave them as untouched as by the piping of a bulfinch. Her voice was noble, if not perfect . . . her style was both admirable and charming. . . . She bore her audience away and aloft on a high tide of emotion. It must be confessed that this was partly due to her magnificent beauty and to her acting. . . . She had much influence upon the taste of the generation that saw her. After her, they . . . could not easily tolerate frivolous and vulgar artists, even when they were accomplished singers and pretty women."

48. In his memoirs, Maretzek describes the 1848–49 Astor Place Company orchestra as consisting of "about thirty-six performers on their individual instruments" (*C&Q*, 15). In this he evidently was mistaken, unless Fry had

greatly exaggerated the extent of his instrumental forces in the newspaper advertisement that ran just before the beginning of the season. This latter seems unlikely, however, for the advertisement lists by name each member of the chorus and orchestra (*New York Tribune,* 1 Nov. 1848).

49. Rosi, according to White, was a favorite in New York. He was "handsome, strong, and manly," and he sang "always well, always correctly, and always in good taste" (1882, 2:881).

50. *Message Bird,* 14 Sept. 1850, 462; *Spirit* 19 Oct. 1850. Lorini first sang in New York with the Havana Company as early as the summer of 1847; he returned to the United States with Marti's troupe during the spring of 1850. He was, however, only a second tenor with the Havana Company; Lorenzo Salvi was the first (Odell 1970, 5:317, 563).

51. Maretzek 1968, *C&Q,* 123.

52. Maretzek 1968, *C&Q,* 123.

53. Playbills, MOC, 21, 23 Oct. 1850.

54. *Figaro,* 26 Oct., 2 Nov. 1850.

55. The U.S. premiere of *Lucia di Lammermoor,* in French, had been in New Orleans, by Eugene Prévost's company at the Théâtre d'Orléans on 28 May 1841, not on 28 Dec. as reported by Loewenberg (1978, 772). The New York premiere (in Italian) was two years later on 15 Sept. 1843, presumably by the Havana Company (Belsom 1955, 65–70; *Spirit,* 13, 16, 23 Sept., 7, 28 Oct. 1843). The U.S. premiere of *Ernani* had been on 15 April 1847 at the Park Theatre in New York, also by the Havana Company (Loewenberg 1978, 838; Odell 1970, 5:263; Mattfeld 1927, 30).

56. Maretzek 1968, *C&Q,* 124.

57. Quoted by Schiavo 1947, 394.

58. Maretzek 1968, *C&Q,* 126.

59. Tickets for the company's performances before Parodi's arrival cost $1.50 for reserved parquet or box seats and 25 cents for seats in the amphitheater (gallery). For performances starting 4 Nov., the night of Parodi's debut, the same seats cost $2.50, $2, and $1 (Playbills, MOC, 1 and 4 Nov. 1850).

60. Maretzek 1968, *C&Q,* 127.

61. Teresa Parodi (b. 1827) was a native of Genoa; her training likewise took place in the north of Italy, under Felice Ronconi in Milan and Giuditta Pasta in Como. Her identification as a "singer of the south" refers to her participation (with her brother) in the insurrection at Palermo in 1848. Evidently, she sang in a carnival in that city in the midst of the revolution and aroused such a frenzy of excitement that, according to an account in the *Boston Daily Evening Transcript* (13 Feb. 1851), "the whole people seemed to have gone mad for the beautiful *cantatrice*" (*Message Bird,* 2 Dec. 1850, 541–42). The soprano subsequently was obliged to take refuge on a Sardinian ship for more than three weeks. Americans of this period were remarkably sympathetic toward all sorts of revolutionary movements, and Parodi's identification as the heroine of an embattled populace was a calculated attempt to appeal to these emotions. Her appearance in this country also struck a

sympathetic chord with Italian immigrants. When she first arrived, according to Schiavo, "a flock of Sicilian refugees in New York welcomed her as their elder sister" (1947, 393–94).

62. The North American premiere of *Norma* had been in New Orleans in April 1836 by the Montresor Company. The East Coast premiere (in Italian) was in Philadelphia in Nov. 1843 by the Havana Company (chapter 3). Hamm referred to the arrival of this opera in the United States as "one of the central musical events of the entire nineteenth century" (1979, 78).

63. Pleasants (1981, 204) related the horror of the English critic Henry Chorley at Lind's failure in the role in London. Her rendition, Chorley wrote, was "something as entire, as aimless as it is possible for so remarkable an artist to make. The actress and the play had no agreement."

64. *New York Tribune*, 31 Oct. 1850.

65. *Albion*, 16 Nov. 1850, quoted in Odell 1970, 6:63–64.

66. *Spirit*, 30 Nov., 14 Dec. 1850. The critics never explain just what about Parodi's singing and acting was so controversial. It is possible that Parodi was a better Lucrezia than she was a Norma (the two roles, of course, are extremely different) and that the negative comments were from critics who considered Norma to be the final test of a singer. It is also possible that the dispute centered on Parodi's dramatic (rather than her musical) abilities and that she was an adherent of the older, exceedingly melodramatic school of acting rather than the newer, more natural and quieter style. This change, which caused a great deal of controversy, took place gradually over the century. A good example of the contrast is the difference in style between Junius Brutus Booth (1796–1852) and his son Edwin (1833–93) (Levine 1984, 56–58). A critic for the *Boston Courier*, in a generally positive review on 28 Feb. 1851, admitted that Parodi "may sometimes slightly exaggerate, or sometimes fail to come up with the freshness of reality"; he defended her acting, however, by adding that "this can be no justification to detract from her merits as an artist." A reporter for *Harper's* described Parodi as "not without dramatic talent, although prone to exaggeration" (February 1851, 417), and George Upton later wrote in his *Musical Memoirs* that she "was often intensely energetic and 'ranted,' if I may apply that dramatic term to singing" (quoted by Schiavo 1947, 394). Another Boston critic, who compared performances by Parodi and Angiolina Bosio, later wrote that Bosio's interpretation of Lucrezia was "as a whole, the best personation of that character we have ever had. It was far less ambitious than Parodi's, but more natural and effective" (*Evening Transcript*, 8 May 1851).

67. Loewenberg seconds the claim that this was the U.S. premiere. The actual North American premiere, however, had been in New Orleans on 4 June 1837, by the Havana Company (Belsom 1955, 45). Loewenberg also gives an incorrect date (20 Oct. 1850) for the New York premiere of the opera (751).

68. Playbill, MOC, 22 Nov. 1850.

69. Playbill, MOC, 6 Jan. 1851.

70. It is difficult to determine with any degree of certainty the precise

number of repetitions of these various operas. Information about scheduled performances can be obtained from playbills and newspaper advertisements; neither source, however, is reliable. As Odell observed about the repertory performed by the Havana Opera Company during the summer of 1850: "I warn the reader . . . that my record is from the advertisements in the *Herald;* but the *Albion* expressly complains that the programme was frequently changed at the last moment, and on some occasions no performance was given" (1970, 4:591). Only the review of an actual performance confirms that an opera had been given as advertised, and most newspapers in New York reviewed opera performances sporadically.

71. *MW,* 1 Jan. 1853, 2.

72. That this practice of cutting, adding, and altering was a normal occurrence in Europe is exemplified by a comment Hector Berlioz made in an essay about this same Rossini opera: "Ruthless cuts have been made in the present score," he wrote of *William Tell* in 1834. The French composer, however, evidently disagreed with Dwight's verdict on the choice of deleted material, for he continued, "those who make cuts know only how to cut out the good things; [as] in castrating, it is precisely the noblest parts that are removed" (reprinted in Strunk 1950, 813). The widely accepted practice of wholesale alteration is also suggested by the numerous changes made to operas written for Italy but performed in Paris. One of the most obvious examples is the transformation of Verdi's *I Lombardi,* which was so thoroughly rewritten for its 1847 production at the Paris Opéra that the new version, *Jérusalem,* can be considered a separate opera. My thanks to H. Robert Cohen for directing me to the Berlioz quote.

73. *Dwight's,* 11 June 1859, 88; *MW,* 31 Jan. 1857, 68; letter published in *Dwight's,* 28 May 1859, 71; *BMT,* 3 Nov. 1860, 296. None of these complaints, however, shed much light on what was performed; the answer to that question must await further research.

74. Playbill, MOC, 10 Dec. 1850.

75. *NA&USG,* 27 Nov. 1850.

76. The U.S. premiere of this opera had been in New Orleans (by the Havana Company) on 22 April 1843, not in New York on 2 Oct. 1843 (presumably by the same company) as reported by Loewenberg and Mattfeld (Belsom 1955, 103).

77. Maretzek 1968, *C&Q,* 167; *New York Tribune,* 2 Dec. 1850.

78. MOC, Astor Place Opera House, 5 Dec. 1850. This performance, and the one that was to take place on Saturday, evidently were extras and not part of the subscription series.

79. Odell 1970, 6:65.

80. Maretzek 1968, *C&Q,* 98–99.

81. According to an article in *MW* (28 Nov. 1857, 733), in 1857 the choral and orchestral members of the opera company at the Academy of Music in New York were paid $15 a week ($225 a week in 1992 dollars), a pittance when compared with the amounts the stars took home (Greene 1987, 48). If one or more performances during a week were cancelled, the week's pay was adjusted accordingly.

82. *MW,* 11 July 1857, 437. Information about salaries paid to singers during this period is difficult to find. Newspapers or periodicals occasionally printed the reported salaries of various individual artists, but usually there is no means to verify the authenticity of these data. Because the figures often were given in articles expressing editorial outrage over the exorbitant salaries paid to opera singers, the figures themselves are suspect. On 17 March 1855, *MG* published an article on Maretzek's company, which was performing at the New York Academy of Music. Rather than listing the supposed salaries paid to the stars of the company, the author gave figures that he felt represented "the highest sum which [these particular singers] can be worth per month to any impresario, either in Europe or America." The figures he supplied included monthly salaries of $500 (approximately $7,485 in 1992 dollars), $400 ($5,990), $300 ($4,491), $200 ($2,994), $150 ($2,245), and $100 ($1,497) (Greene 1987, 48).

Presumably, these suggested figures were significantly lower than the amounts that Maretzek's stars were actually paid, for the same article reports that one individual (who deserved, in his opinion, a monthly salary of no more than $150) had been paid $600 a month the previous season. Although actual dollar amounts mentioned in periodicals may be suspect, there is no question that Italian singers were paid more in the United States than they earned at home (Rosselli 1984, 50, 59). The figures reported in *MG* represent monthly salaries, but stars often were hired and paid for a certain number of performances. On 7 May 1853, for example, an article in the *Spirit* on the sudden collapse of the Alboni Opera Company noted that the tenor Lorenzo Salvi had been hired at a large salary for thirteen performances. He had been paid in advance, and at season's end had appeared only seven times. His behavior, according to the *Spirit,* had helped to bring about the downfall of the troupe (144). If a singer refused to live up to his or her commitments, the manager's only recourse was generally to take the offending individual to court for breach of contract. For one example of litigation between a manager and a star, see *Saroni's,* 6 July 1850, 484.

83. Letter published in *Dwight's,* 17 July 1852, 114.

84. Reprinted in *MW,* 21 May 1853, 59–60.

85. Quoted in Wolz 1983, 109.

86. Pre-season advertisements that appeared in newspapers and periodicals often included lists of the name singers expected to appear during the engagement. Most such enumerations, however, turn out to be inaccurate. The list that appeared in the *North American and United States Gazette* on 27 Nov. 1850 before the commencement of the Philadelphia season, for example, is incorrect on two counts. It included a singer (Benedetti) who did not perform in either New York or Philadelphia, and it also neglected to mention five vocalists who did appear in the latter city. (Benedetti did serve as a conductor in Philadelphia.) Newspaper advertisements also occasionally have inaccurate casts listed for individual opera performances. In an attempt to sort out which of the company's singers were in Philadelphia and which were in New York on particular days during the simultaneous engagements, I compared news-

paper advertisements from both cities with extant playbills. For six different performances, for which there are no playbills, newspaper advertisements from both cities claim some of the same singers. Presumably, the Philadelphia advertisements were correct, for they were newer. Apparently the New York advertisements were recycled from earlier in the season, and cast corrections had not been made.

87. It is possible that Maretzek delegated some of the legwork to his assistants, such as his brother Albert (who often worked as his agent) or Edward Walker. But because the company was Maretzek's, and the responsibility for its economic well-being his, he probably made a majority of the decisions.

88. *NA&USG,* 11 Dec. 1850; *Public Ledger,* 14 Dec. 1850. But Curtis (n.d., 10 Dec. 1850) writes that the first performance by the troupe drew a poor house, the result of high prices, cold weather, and the recent appearance of Jenny Lind.

89. Martin 1841–57, 1:103.

90. Playbills, MOC, 17 and 20 Dec. 1850.

91. *NA&USG,* 27 Dec. 1850.

92. Playbill, MOC, Chestnut Street Theatre, 28 Dec. 1850.

93. *NA&USG,* 30 Dec. 1850.

94. This arrangement apparently was a last-minute affair prompted by the success of Saturday's performance, for the dancers' second appearance, which is announced in the newspaper, is not mentioned on the playbill distributed for that evening's performance (*NA&USG,* 30 Dec. 1850; Playbills, MOC, 28 and 30 Dec. 1850).

95. The 1847–48 Astor Place Company had mounted the U.S. premiere of *Il Giuramento;* the work was performed by the 1848–49 company, but not by Maretzek's troupe of 1849–50 (Mattfeld 1927, 31). *La Favorita* had most recently been performed at Castle Garden by the Havana Company during April 1850 (Odell 1970, 5:565, 566).

96. Playbill, MOC, 2 Jan. 1851 MB.

97. *NA&USG,* 4 Jan. 1851.

98. As with drama (or with movies today), however, Sill exercised caution in his choice of which operas he took the children to see. After his first hearing of *Don Giovanni* by the Seguins in 1841, he wrote on 5 May that "the moral of the Play is shocking, and hardly tolerable," and when he attended the Astor Place Company's presentation of this work on 14 Jan. he went alone. During this same engagement, however, Sill took his daughter Mary to see Parodi in *Lucrezia Borgia,* an opera he had described on first hearing in 1847 as "of course unpleasant in the story, & bloody in the end" (29 Nov. 1847).

99. "Fine Arts," *Graham's Magazine,* Aug. 1850.

100. Playbills, MOC, 4, 5, 17, 18, 20 Jan. 1851. Maretzek undoubtedly returned to Philadelphia for the performance on 20 Jan., which was his benefit (Playbill, MOC, 17 Jan. 1851).

101. Strakosch 1850; Loewenberg 1978, 888.

102. The libretto and six pieces of sheet music (New York: William Hall & Son, 1851) are in the collection of the Music Division, DLC.

103. It is impossible to ascertain just how financially successful the opera was. No information about attendance is available beyond that the newspapers report, and critics' descriptions of houses as "crowded and brilliant" are notoriously unreliable. The opera was performed four times in New York before being withdrawn. It was not performed by the company anywhere else during 1850–51; whether or not it has been mounted since is unknown.

104. Kreutzer also had been associated with Maretzek's 1849–50 troupe as orchestra leader (Odell 1970, 5:571). Nothing more is known about him.

105. Evidently, ethnic conflicts of this nature, although rarely mentioned in histories of music in the United States, were not unprecedented. In May 1858, for example, a small unnamed opera company that was performing in Baltimore had to postpone a performance because, according to *MW* on 15 May, "the German elements of the orchestra [would not] amalgamate with the Italian." After a "violent quarrel" sprang up between the local (German) musicians and the director (an Italian), the musicians left the hall en masse, and "all the eloquence of a veteran music-publisher, or the threats of the manager, could not prevail on them to return to duty" (305). The manager had to import an orchestra from Philadelphia before the performances could proceed.

106. Maretzek 1968, *C&Q*, 158.

107. Odell 1970, 5:571.

108. *Baltimore Sun*, 27 and 28 Jan. 1851.

109. *Baltimore Sun*, 28, 24 Jan., 12 Feb., 27–28 Jan. 1851.

110. "Communication from Baltimore," dated 27 Oct. 1851, in *Saroni's*, 8 Nov. 1851, 11–12.

111. The Germania Musical Society, an orchestra comprised of some twenty-five young German instrumentalists, toured the United States from 1848 to 1854. The goal of the society was to introduce the instrumental music of Germany to audiences in the United States. The orchestra toured widely in the eastern part of the country and in Canada. Their final tour (1854) included visits to such western cities as Pittsburgh, Cincinnati, Louisville, St. Louis, Chicago, Minneapolis, Cleveland, and Milwaukee. While in the United States, the musicians performed in some nine hundred concerts; many of these were in conjunction with instrumental soloists (Ole Bull, Camilla Urso, and Alfred Jaell) or operatic stars (Jenny Lind, Henriette Sontag, Catherine Hayes, Adelaide Phillips, and Teresa Parodi). The Germanians spent most of the winter of 1850 in Baltimore. They returned to that city in early 1851 and performed there with the Baltimore branch of Maretzek's company. For further information, see Johnson 1953 and Johnson 1986.

112. This was Parodi's final appearance in New York with the Astor Place Company during this season, but it was hardly her final appearance in the city. Although New York journalists widely announced that she was shortly to return to Europe, she did not do so until 1853, when she went to France to sing with the Paris Opera (1853–54). At the conclusion of her contract

with Maretzek in March 1851, she formed a concert troupe with Strakosch, Amalia Patti, the baritone Antonio Avignone, and several other artists. They toured in the South from March through June, appearing in Richmond, Charleston, Mobile, Louisville, and New Orleans, among other cities. Parodi was back in New York with the Astor Place Company for part of the 1851–52 season, and she, Patti, and Strakosch (occasionally with other artists) toured widely throughout the United States during 1852 and, after her return from Europe, in 1855 and 1856. In 1857, the soprano appeared with both the Maretzek and the Strakosch Opera companies, and in 1859 and 1860 she formed her own opera troupe and took it on tour (Appendix C). Her activities after 1860 are unknown.

113. *New York Tribune,* 18 Feb. 1851; Greene 1987, 48.

114. *Message Bird,* 1 March 1851, 642.

115. *Boston Courier,* 11 Feb. 1851.

116. The García troupe included in its ranks a set designer, and Giacomo Montresor brought from Italy as part of his company a scene painter and three assistants (chapter 3). I have located no other references to scene painters as members of itinerant companies.

117. *Boston Courier,* 13 Feb. 1851.

118. Durham 1986, 80.

119. *Boston Evening Transcript,* 11 Feb. 1851, italics added.

120. *Boston Courier,* 17 Feb. 1851.

121. *Message Bird,* 1 March 1851, 643; Greene 1987, 48.

122. For other evidence of Boston audience enthusiasm, see the *Courier* of 20 and 22 Feb. and the *Evening Transcript* of 22 and 27 Feb. 1851.

123. It was not coincidental that Hauser and Strakosch were in Boston. Their concert company with Parodi commenced performing almost immediately following the conclusion of her engagement with the Astor Place Company on 3 March. The Strakosch and Parodi Company must have left Boston immediately, for they appeared at the Chinese Museum and the Musical Fund Hall in Philadelphia on 6 and 8 March, respectively (*Boston Evening Transcript,* 22 Feb. 1851). In Philadelphia, the troupe included Hauser, Strakosch, Amalia Patti, Parodi, Avignone (a baritone who had sung with the Astor Place Company in Philadelphia and Baltimore), and a Mr. Waldtenfel (probably Waldteufel) (*Philadelphia North American,* 6 March 1851).

124. Ware and Lockard 1980, 38.

125. *Boston Evening Transcript,* 10 March 1851.

126. *Charleston Daily Courier,* 19 March 1851.

127. *Charleston Mercury,* 20 March 1851.

128. The *Daily Courier* carried the following announcement on 17 March 1851: "Subscribers to the Opera, will please call at the Box Office, between the hours of 9 and 12 o'clock on This Day and receive their tickets for this season, which will be in readiness."

129. Radford 1979, 347.

130. Pred 1980, 12; *Seventh Census of the United States. Appendix,* 339.

131. Passenger list, *Charleston Daily Courier,* 19 March 1851.

132. Playbills, MOC, Charleston Theatre; *Charleston Daily Courier,* 21 March 1851. Maretzek's presence in Charleston is confirmed by the appearance of his name on the passenger list of the *Southerner,* which appeared in the *Daily Courier* on 19 March 1851.

133. These singers included the soprano Mrs. Garrett, bass Domenico Locatelli, and tenor Napoleone Parozzi. Parozzi was listed as a chorus member of the 1848 Astor Place Company. During the 1850–51 season he performed in name roles regularly in Philadelphia; he also was a member of the Baltimore branch of the company. Mrs. Garrett had performed in name roles twice in New York and once in Boston in January and February 1851. Locatelli had been featured twice in Philadelphia and once in Baltimore (Playbills, MOC).

134. Her name appears on none of the playbills from this season, but it shows up on the passenger list from the *Southerner.*

135. Vietti, a contralto, was a member of Marti's Havana Opera Company, which had recently concluded its season at the Tacon Theatre. Vietti and Fortunata Tedesco, another of Marti's former singers, had arrived in Charleston on 11 March, according to the passenger list of the *Isabel* (*Charleston Daily Courier,* 12 March 1851). Whiting's mother probably remained with the company for as long as her daughter was engaged (*Charleston Daily Courier,* 28 March 1851). If so, the soprano would not have been the only member of the troupe to have the company of family in Charleston. The singers Beneventano, Garrett, Locatelli, Parozzi, and Truffi all traveled with their spouses (Truffi and Benedetti were married) (*Charleston Daily Courier,* 19 March 1851). As these were all "name" singers, it appears that the troupe's stars were permitted to bring their spouses on tour but the members of the chorus and orchestra were not.

136. *Charleston Mercury,* 20 March 1851.

137. Nevins 1850.

138. *Charleston Daily Courier,* 14 March 1851.

139. *Charleston Daily Courier,* 2 April 1851. According to the *Message Bird,* the troupe was described before a concert in Richmond, Virginia, as consisting of Strakosch, Hauser, and the "principal performers of the Astor Place Opera Troupe" (1 March 1851, 643).

140. The Parodi-Strakosch troupe arrived only one day before the first scheduled performance, which under any circumstances was cutting the schedule a little close (*Charleston Daily Courier,* 2 April 1851).

141. *Charleston Mercury,* 3 April 1851.

142. Playbill, MOC, 1 April 1851.

143. Of this total population, 4,718 were slaves. According to the *Seventh Census of the United States,* population statistics were not available for the city of Augusta. Local officials, however, took a census of their own in 1852, and these figures were included on page 366 of the Census Appendix Report published in 1853.

144. Playbill, MOC, Augusta Concert Hall, 15 April 1851.

145. Playbill, MOC, Charleston Theatre, 22 April 1851.

146. Maretzek 1968, *C&Q,* 158, 157.

147. Maretzek 1968, *C&Q*, 158.

148. They arrived on the *Isabel* from Cuba and Key West on 25 March, according to the *Charleston Daily Courier*, 26 March 1851. Undoubtedly, Maretzek was not pleased with the arrival of one of his rivals, Maurice Strakosch, several days later.

149. In addition to Bosio, Vietti, and Marini, these singers included the tenors Timoleon Barratini (or Baratini), Geremia Bettini, and Domenico Lorini (who had left the Havana company earlier in the year and had appeared with Maretzek's troupe in February), and the bass Domenico Coletti.

150. *Daily Evening Transcript*, 19 April 1851; *Boston Courier*, 29 April 1851.

151. Playbill, MOC, Federal Street Theatre, 29 April 1851; *Boston Courier*, 14 Feb. 1851.

152. The company gave eighteen performances of eight operas during this engagement. The following works were mounted: *Lucrezia Borgia* (twice), *Il barbiere di Siviglia*, *Romeo e Giuletta*, *La Favorita* (three times), *Ernani* (three times), *Il Giuramento*, *Lucia di Lammermoor* (three times), and *Don Giovanni* (four times). The troupe also gave four concerts, all on Saturdays. See playbills, MOC, Federal Street Theatre, and *Boston Courier* and *Evening Transcript*.

153. All of Maretzek's "new" singers had performed in Boston with the Havana Company earlier in the year. Their first performances, consequently, were "first" only for the season, with the company, or in a particular role in Boston. There were no real debut performances, and Maretzek was careful to observe this distinction. Maretzek was a master in the art of concocting slightly misleading playbills, and the troupe's advertisements for its three productions of *Ernani* illustrate his tactics well. Maretzek used the company's opening-night performance of *Ernani* on 9 April to herald Ignazio Marini's first appearance. On 9 May, the troupe mounted the same opera again, but this time—according to the playbill—it was for the "last time this season." In fact, it was the last time that *Marini* would perform in *Ernani* that season. The company, however, presented Verdi's opera once more on 29 May for Truffi's benefit, this time announcing boldly the "first appearance of/Signor Bettini!/in Ernani!" It was Bettini's third appearance, but his first in that opera. See Playbills, MOC, 9 and 29 May 1851.

154. Greene 1987, 48. The company's second concert (on 10 May), however, was only "thinly attended" (*Daily Evening Transcript*, 12 May 1851).

155. Maretzek 1968, *C&Q*, 127.

156. Maretzek 1968, *C&Q*, 158.

157. Maretzek 1968, *C&Q*, 170.

158. Maretzek 1968, *C&Q*, 158.

159. Maretzek 1968, *C&Q*, 164–69. Rosselli (1984, 96–99) explains that impresarios in Italy, as Maretzek implied, turned to civil authorities when faced with disciplinary problems with singers. A vocal star who feigned illness and thereby broke his contract was arrested and kept in jail or under house arrest and delivered to the opera house each night in time for the performance. This was the case in Mexico as well, according to Maretzek (1968 *C&Q*, 256–60).

160. Maretzek 1968, *C&Q*, 158.

161. Maretzek 1968, *C&Q*, 171; Greene 1987, 48. Maretzek also blamed small audiences at Castle Garden for contributing to the collapse of his company. Reviews published in the *New York Herald* and *New York Tribune*, however, consistently comment on the large crowds in attendance at the opera that summer. (See, for example, reviews that appeared on 7 and 22 June, 12, 14, 24, and 26 July, 21 Aug., and 2 Sept. 1851 in the *Herald* and throughout July and August in the *Tribune*.) This apparent discrepancy between reportedly large and enthusiastic audiences during a season and almost invariable financial distress and failure at its conclusion was fairly commonplace; the issue was the target of much editorial commentary during the 1850s.

162. *Dwight's*, 23 Oct. 1858, 235, reprinted from the *Boston Courier*.

163. *AMR*, Nov. 1853, 170; *MR&G*, 3 May 1856, 132; *MW*, 24 Sept. 1853, 27.

164. *Dwight's*, 2 Oct. 1858, 214.

5. English Opera Companies, 1841–60

1. Bernheim 1932, 28.

2. Tawa 1986; Husk 1982; Legge.

3. According to Odell, the period 1839 to 1848 was "perhaps the very worst" of times for theaters during the entire nineteenth century (1970, 4:339).

4. English vocal stars continued to visit the United States during the 1840s, but none seemed to catch the imagination of American audiences to the extent of earlier singers such as Austin, Wood, Shirreff, or the Seguins. The English tenor John Braham (1774–1856) performed in this country from October 1840 through January 1843, but his activity did nothing to challenge the Seguins' domination. Although he was one of the leading vocalists on the English stage, by the time he arrived in the United States he was sixty-eight, and many believed that he was past his prime. Braham appeared in both operas and concerts but was thought by many critics to be better suited to the concert hall than the operatic stage (Hamm 1986; Lawrence 1988, 178; *WM*, 23 Nov. 1840, 60).

5. Wemyss 1847, 379.

6. Hoole 1946, 46.

7. Hoole 1946, 46.

8. Hoole 1946. For information on the Seguins' various tours, see the notes to Appendix B. In view of these frequent, lengthy, and far-ranging trips, it should be clear that the Seguins' ensemble was truly an opera company of the United States. Lawrence's implication, perhaps unintentional, that theirs was a New York-based company that took an "occasional time out [from performances in New York] for a tour" is incorrect (1988, 328).

9. As discussed in chapter 3, the only performances of Italian opera in Italian in the United States during this period, excepting the Havana Company visits in 1842 and 1843, were in New York City. The important exception to any general statement about opera performances in the United States during the antebellum period is New Orleans, where a resident French opera troupe

performed at the Théâtre d'Orléans. The French Opera Company of New Orleans also embarked upon several East Coast tours in 1844, visiting New York, Montreal, and Philadelphia, and in 1845 performed in St. Louis, New York, and Philadelphia.

10. *Spirit,* 18, 25 Dec. 1841; 5, 19 Feb. 1842.

11. Quoted by Bailey 1934, 92.

12. Evidence of reference to the Seguins as vocal stars is found on numerous playbills, which are widely scattered in various collections. See, for example, the following playbills: Chestnut Street Theatre, 15 May 1841 and 6 Feb. 1843, Theatre Department, PP and 27 May–21 June 1841, PPL; St. Charles Theatre, New Orleans, 3 March 1845, HTC; Tremont Street Theatre (Boston), 1 Oct. 1841, NN; Federal Street Theatre (Boston), 1 Feb. 1847, Federal Street Theatre Collection, Rare Books Department, MB. Occasionally during the 1841–42 tour, the Seguins and Manvers enlisted the help of the better actors and singers of some of the particularly strong stock companies and, as a temporarily expanded troupe, made short tours to nearby cities. During January and February 1842, for example, the trio apparently struck a bargain with James Caldwell, the manager of New Orleans' St. Charles Theatre, that was similar to the arrangement that Shirreff, Wilson, and Seguin had made with James Wallack two years earlier. In this case, the vocal stars performed with the stock company of the St. Charles Theatre for a month, then went to Mobile for a two-week engagement, accompanied by about a half-dozen singers from Caldwell's New Orleans company. Several of the performers named in a review published in the *Mobile Advertiser and Chronicle* were members of the stock company at the St. Charles (Bailey 1934, 92; Kendall 1986, 181).

13. *Spirit,* 19 Feb. 1841; Hoole 1946, 46.

14. *Spirit,* 6 Dec. 1845, 488; 6 March 1847, 24; 22 May 1847.

15. Sill Diary, 27 April 1846, 28 April 1848, 5 June 1848.

16. This particular piece of sheet music, "The Music of the *Bohemian Girl,* Consisting of Six Songs and Three Pieces" (Philadelphia: E. Ferrett and Company, 1845) can be found in the collection of the Music Division, DLC. An indication of the lasting popularity of melodies from *The Bohemian Girl* is the inclusion of five numbers from the opera in a collection of popular songs titled *Heart Songs* published early in the twentieth century.

17. Greene 1987, 48.

18. Playbill, Howard Athenaeum, 11 Feb. 1846, NN; Playbills, Howard Athenaeum, 9 Feb. 1846 and Federal Street Theatre (Boston), 1 Feb. 1847, Rare Books Department, MB. A playbill from a performance by the Seguins, Mr. Frazer, and five other singers ("from the Park Theatre, New York") at the Howard Athenaeum in Boston on 29 Oct. 1845 (MWA) refers to the musicians as an "Operatic Troupe." A year later, *Spirit* described them on 17 Oct. 1846 as the "Seguin troupe."

Although it is clear that the Seguins did maintain a small, somewhat fluctuating company during this period, it is almost impossible to discover very much about the troupe: how large it was at any one time or in any one location, how long the associations lasted, or even if management engaged the various singers individually or as a group.

19. Their appearances in Charleston in February and March 1847 featured a "full chorus from the New York Park Theatre"; in August of that same year the stars performed for two weeks in Montreal, again assisted by a chorus from the Park (Hoole 1946, 50; Cooper 1984, 56–58; *Spirit*, 4 Sept. 1847, 332).

20. ALS, Seguin to Messrs Carr & Warren, 23 May 1850, Davis Collection, ICHi.

21. Edward Seguin disbanded the troupe in 1852 due to his own ill health; he died in December 1852. Anne Seguin retired from the stage when the company was disbanded and subsequently taught voice in New York until shortly before her own death in 1888 (Husk 1982; Legge; *BMT*, 21 April 1860, 87; *Spirit*, 12 June 1852, 204; Playbill, Broadway Theatre [New York], 18 June 1852, MWA).

22. Lawrence 1988, 418.

23. Mattfeld 1927, 49–50; Loewenberg 1978, 852; Wilson 1935; Armstrong (1884, 63) gives the date for *The Bravo* as 2 Oct. 1848.

24. Mattfeld 1927, 43, 58; Loewenberg 1978, 728, 798.

25. Armstrong 1884, 53; *Spirit*, 9 Jan. 1847.

26. It was this opera (translated into Italian) that the composer's brother Edward Fry wanted the first Astor Place Company to mount; their failure to do so led to his ill-fated attempt to manage that troupe during 1848–49.

27. Lawrence 1988, 336.

28. Lawrence 1988, 336; Hitchcock 1988, 98.

29. Lawrence 1988, 336–42; Armstrong 1884, 53; Hamm 1983, 204.

30. *Albion*, 14 June 1845, 228, quoted in Lawrence 1988, 341.

31. Wemyss 1847, 401.

32. During this time, opera in English was the norm; there is little controversy to be found in the American musical or theatrical press over the relative merits of English versus Italian opera before 1847 or 1848.

33. A simple title inventory of this nature is inevitably misleading because each work in the company's repertory is given equal weight whether performed once, twice, or forty times. This type of tabulation, in fact, is biased in favor of the English titles rather than the French or Italian ones because the operas that the Seguins premiered (and performed only several times, such as *The Maid of Saxony* and *Luli*) were English works. If it was possible to weight titles based on frequency of performance, then, the dominance by Italian works would be even more obvious.

34. *Spirit*, 18 June 1847, 188; Slonimsky 1978; Weidensaul 1970, 4–7; Walker 1962, 135–36.

35. Reprinted in the *BMG*, 2 Aug. 1847.

36. The *Musical World* reported that Bishop planned to return to England in the spring; in fact, she did not return until September 1858 (Northcott 1920, 93).

37. Seilhamer 1881, 105; Walker 1962, 137–38; Weidensaul 1970, 6–7.

Bishop's globe-trotting habits did not end with her visit to North America. Between 1847 and 1876, she performed in Mexico, California, the Utah Territory, Australia, New Zealand, Chile, Brazil, Argentina, the Sandwich Islands (Hawaii), Manila, Hong Kong, Singapore, Calcutta, Ceylon, India, and South Africa. Over the course of her three decades of traveling she collected numerous extraordinary (and sometimes apocryphal-sounding) tales. In 1849 in Mexico, for example, she and Bochsa (and their private escort of ten *cavalleros*) were held up by thieves. The banditti, so the story goes, did not wish to murder their victims and steal their gold and jewels; they wanted instead for Bishop, accompanied by Bochsa, to sing a Mexican song titled "La Pasadita." After listening to a somewhat nervous performance, the outlaws exclaimed their appreciation, thanked the prima donna, then "mounted their horses, and dash[ed] off at full speed" (*Message Bird,* 15 Aug. 1850, 424). Nicholas Bochsa either wrote the satirical song "La Pasadita" or transcribed and published it (Philadelphia: A. Fiot, 1850) under his name, with a lithograph of Anna Bishop in Mexican costume on the cover, in an attempt to capitalize on the publicity that the story generated. Another adventure, even more fantastic, occurred in 1866 when Bishop was en route from Honolulu to Hong Kong. The ship on which she was a passenger was caught in a hurricane and wrecked. She and several others, who were marooned on an uninhabited desert island in the South Pacific, survived for three weeks on provisions salvaged from the wreck, then made their way, in an open boat, to the Ladrone Islands some 1,400 miles distant (Northcott [quoting Bishop extensively] 1920, 94–96; Walker 1962, 141).

38. Seilhamer 1881, 105; Walker 1962, 137–38.

39. For an assortment of contemporary descriptions of Bishop's voice, see the *Albion,* 7 Aug. 1847, quoted in Odell 1970, 5:321 and the various accolades quoted by Lawrence (1988, 469ff).

40. From playbills in the Bishop Collection.

41. Walker 1962, 137, 140–41. For a summary and contemporary accounts of Bishop's reception in New York, see Lawrence 1988, 469–73, 524–27.

42. Lawrence's suggestion (1988, 469) that Bishop formed an actual troupe for her performances at the Park Theatre is incorrect. Bishop herself fails to mention forming a company for this engagement; furthermore, when she appeared in Boston in late August and early September, Brough was the only other singer mentioned in the press or named on playbills (Seilhamer 1881, 109; *Spirit,* 24 July 1847, 260; 18 Sept. 1847, 356; Playbill, Boston Athenaeum, 31 Aug. 1847, MB). If the singers who performed with the soprano at the Park had been part of a Bishop Company, they would have accompanied her north to Boston.

43. *Literary Excelsior,* 23 Oct. 1847, 8 Jan. 1848.

44. *Literary Excelsior,* 23 Oct. 1847; *Spirit,* 16 Oct. 1847, 404; the quote is from Lawrence 1988, 474.

45. *BMG,* 13 Sept. 1847, 134; *Spirit,* 20 Nov. 1847, 464.

46. Hoole 1946, 52; *Spirit,* 8 April 1848, 84; Playbills, Savannah Theatre, 31 Jan., 1, 3, 5 Feb. 1848, Bishop Collection.

47. Playbills, March 1848, Bishop Collection.

48. *Spirit,* 8 April 1848, 84; report confirmed by the *Literary Excelsior,* 15 April 1848.

49. I have been unable to unearth any more details about this incident. The reporter for the *Mobile Register and Journal* only alludes to this occurrence, which probably took place on the evening of the troupe's final performance, 21 March. On 22 March 1848, the newspaper reported the close of the opera season and the reviewer commented that the troupe, which had created "more intense [excitement] than we remember," left behind pleasant memories. He praised various company members then added, "the veteran Bochsa, too, though perhaps of the genus *irritable* is made up of the soul of music. The little specks of over-appreciation, which jar a little on the scene, are lost in the contemplation of his greatest attainments."

50. Before returning north, Brough and Reeves gave a number of concerts in small southern towns (*Spirit,* 25 March 1848). In May, Reeves joined the Seguin Opera Company and sang with that troupe throughout the 1848–49 season (*Literary Excelsior,* 17 May 1848; see also Appendix B, no. 16). After leaving the Bishop Company, Brough joined the Manvers Opera Company and toured with them during 1848–49 and 1849–50 (Appendix B).

51. Lawrence 1988, 526.

52. As an example of her success, a New York concert on 30 Dec. 1848 attracted an audience of five thousand. For additional information on the tour to Mexico, see Walker 1962, 141; *Baltimore Olio,* March 1850, 35; *AMR,* May 1850, 36.

53. Bishop's repertory in San Francisco was rather extensive and included the following operas: *Don Pasquale, Lucrezia Borgia, Lucia di Lammermoor* (as *Lucy of Lammermoor,* adapted by Bochsa), *La Favorita, Maria di Rohan* (all by Donizetti), *La Sonnambula, Der Freischütz, Martha,* Meyerbeer's *Robert-le-Diable* (as *Robert the Devil*), *The Barber of Seville, La Gazza Ladra, Nabucco,* and *Judith* (Verdi, as adapted by Bochsa). She also sang in Haydn's *The Creation* and Rossini's *Stabat Mater.* Estevan 1939, 41; McMinn 1941, 403–6; Waddington 1947; Playbills: American Theatre (San Francisco), 3 March 1854 and Metropolitan Theatre (San Francisco), 30 April, 7 May, 22 July, 25 Nov. 1854, HTC; *Spirit,* 18 March 1854, 55; 8 April 1854, 92; 3 June 1854, 185, 188; 1 July 1854, 230; 2 Sept. 1854, 338; 4 Nov. 1854, 446; 18 Nov. 1854, 470; *MW,* 1 July 1854, 98. For some of the information on Bishop's activities in San Francisco I am indebted to Robert Commanday, who generously allowed me to consult his research notes for a projected book on the history of opera in that city.

54. In 1851 and 1852, Niblo put his theory about the appeal of opera to American audiences to the test: over the course of that season he engaged not only the Thillon troupe, but also the Artists' Union Italian Opera Company (the spin-off group from Maretzek's Astor Place troupe) and the French Opera Company of Madame Fleury-Jolly and Monsieur Menehard. According to Blair (1982, 84), who analyzed the productions at Niblo's Garden Theatre from 1849 through 1862, both the French company and the Thillon-Hudson troupe were very successful at Niblo's.

55. Wolz 1983, 64; Ireland 1968, 2:550.

56. Blair 1982, 69; Playbills, Howard Athenaeum (Boston), 3 Nov. 1852, 26 Oct. 1853, MWA; Playbill, St. Louis Theatre, 29 March 1853, HTC; Wolz 1983, 64.

57. Hartley n.d., 50.

58. *Spirit,* 18 March, 55; 8 April, 92; 20 May, 159; 3 June, 185; 1 July 1854, 230.

59. *Spirit,* 18 March 1854, 20 May 1854.

60. *MW,* 1 July 1854, 98. Translated into 1986 dollars, this figure of $20,000–$30,000, if accurate, would be the equivalent of an astonishing $310,400–$465,600 (Greene 1987, 48).

61. *AMR,* Feb. 1852, 25. Blair (1982, 68) incorrectly repeats Niblo's assertion that *The Crown Diamonds* performance was the North American premiere (in English) of this work. In fact, Charles Manvers's vocal-star troupe had mounted the opera in New York in July 1848 (Loewenberg 1978, 791).

62. *Spirit,* 20 March 1852, 60; 16 Dec. 1853, 517; 23 July 1853, 276.

63. *Albion,* 20 Sept. 1851, quoted in Odell 1970, 6:164.

64. *Spirit,* 10 Jan. 1852, 564; 17 Jan. 1852, 576.

65. *Spirit,* 10 Jan. 1852, 564.

66. Playbill, Howard Athenaeum, 3 Nov. 1852, MWA.

67. White 1851–52, vol. 3, emphasis in the original.

68. Blair 1982, 135.

69. *Mirror,* 11 Oct. 1848, quoted in Lawrence 1988, 526.

70. Odell 1970, 6:343.

71. *MW,* 7 April, 159; 14 April, 178; 5 May 1855.

72. Gagey 1950, 92; Estavan 1939, 7, 13; Noid 1968, 226–27, 229–30; McMinn 1941, 419; Playbill, Maguire's Opera House, 26 July 1859, CSf; Reiff 1905.

73. The troupe members were Georgina (or Georgia) Hodson (contralto), Ada King, Alicia Mandeville, Francis (Frank) Trevor (tenor), Frederick Meyer (bass), Stephen Leach, G. F. Warre (tenor), Frank Boudinot (bass), William Reeves (tenor), and James J. Frazer; the latter two had been associated with the Seguins (Frazer only briefly). Reiff 1905; Playbills, New Walnut Street Theatre, 21 March–2 April 1859, PP.

74. Hoole 1946, 146; Green 1971, 521; Playbill, Crisp's Gaiety Theatre (New Orleans), 14 Nov. 1856, HTC; Reiff 1905; George E. Barnes, *Bulletin,* 7 March 1896, quoted in Estavan 1939, 26. In addition to the already mentioned associations with the Seguins and the Pyne and Harrison troupes, Fred Lyster appeared with Anna Thillon at Niblo's during the summers of 1852 and 1853 (Odell 1970, 6:240, 316). James Frazer, in addition to his appearances with the Seguins in 1844 through 1846, sang with Bishop during her first New York engagement in the autumn of 1847 and with Thillon during the summers of 1853 and 1854 (Lawrence 1988, 267–69, 469, 473; Odell 1970, 6:243, 316). Meyer performed with the Seguins from 1846, with Anna Thillon at Niblo's in 1851, and with the Pyne and Harrison Company at the Broadway Theatre in New York in Dec. 1854 (Lawrence 1988, 418; Odell 1970, 6:163ff, 345–

46). Reeves appeared with Anna Bishop in 1848 (Lawrence 1988, 473–74; *Literary Excelsior,* 30 Oct. 1847) and toured with the Seguins in 1848 and 1849 (Lawrence 1988, 524, 588; Cooper 1984, 56–58). For other sources on the Seguin Company, see the notes to Appendix B.

75. *MW,* 5 May 1855, 8.

76. Durand made her American debut in New York in June 1855; she was a member of the acting company at Burton's Theatre during the autumn of 1855 and moved to Laura Keene's Varieties in January 1856 (Ireland 1968, 2:630; Odell 1970, 6:431ff, 452ff). Lyster was a member of the company at Brougham's Lyceum in New York; during the 1852–53 season he sang at Laura Keene's, and in 1855–56 at Burton's Theatre (Odell 1970, 6:48–49ff, 214ff, 431ff).

77. Kendall 1968, 362.

78. Kendall 1968, 165–66; Playbill, Crisp's Gaiety Theatre, 14 Nov. 1856, HTC.

79. Kendall 1968, 366; Odell 1970, 5:443. For a thorough discussion of the burlesque *Pocahontas,* see Brooks 1984.

80. Kaufman worklist, St. Louis; Jennings worklist, St. Louis.

81. Playbills, 21 March–2 April 1859, PP; 9 Sept. 1857, quoted in Teal 1964, Appendix C.

82. Cooper 1984, 229–30; Weisert 1955; Program, McGuire's Opera House [1859] benefit performance, Archives of the Performing Arts, CSf; Reiff 1905.

83. *Dwight's,* 4 June 1859, 20 Aug. 1859, 166.

84. In 1992, a manuscript written by Anthony Reiff surfaced; it was purchased by Swem Library at the College of William and Mary. This document, which Reiff wrote in 1905, is evidently a manuscript copy of a book he was writing about his adventures as the musical director of various itinerant opera companies. The extant section consists of chapters 4–10 and covers the activities of the Lyster and Durand Opera Company from May 1858 through May 1860. Reiff discusses the company's singers, repertory, performance practices, itinerary, and travel adventures; he also mentions audience reactions to the performances. The document is another extremely valuable source of insight into the travels and reception of English opera companies active in the late 1860s. See Reiff 1905.

85. According to Weisert (1962), the Cooper Company performed in Louisville in Jan. 1858. This information is incorrect, however. Henry Cooper arrived in this country in September of that year, and the troupe was not organized until then. D. Miranda, a tenor who made his American debut with the Cooper troupe, joined the Escott Company in 1859. The troupe subsequently was called the Escott and Miranda Opera Company. John Brookhouse Bowler (tenor) and Aynsley Cook (bass), both of whom came to this country with the Escott Company, joined the Cooper troupe in 1859 (see notes to Appendix D).

86. *MW,* 29 May 1858, 337; Playbills, Boston Museum, 5–17 March 1860, MWA.

87. Reprinted in *Dwight's,* 18 Sept. 1858, 197. In 1857, Milner toured with

an entourage identified as the "Ullman Opera Troupe," and in November she was singing with them in concerts in New York. She also performed in Boston in oratorios in the spring of 1858 (*Dwight's*, 21 Nov. 1857, 269; 25 Sept. 1858, 207).

88. Reprinted in *Dwight's*, 18 Sept. 1858, 199.

89. Other members of the company included, at various times, Charles Guilamette (baritone), George Holman (tenor), Harriet (Phillips) Holman, Annie Kemp (contralto), D. Miranda (tenor), G. H. Warre, Mr. F. Rudolphsen (bass), Aynsley Cook (bass), Brookhouse Bowler (tenor), and others. It was the Holmans who had performed in burlesque companies (Odell 1970, 5:133–34, 233, 244–45; Lawrence 1988, 524).

90. *MW*, 17 Dec. 1859, 4. Escott was a native of Springfield, Massachusetts. She had been educated in Europe, made her operatic debut in Italy, and later organized an English opera company; in June 1858 this troupe was reported performing in towns located in the British provinces (Limerick, Cork, Plymouth) (Ireland 1968, 684; Wolz 1983, 88; *Dwight's*, 5 June 1858, 78). The Escott Company had some reputation in the United States before their arrival here; the 10 July 1858 issue of *Frank Leslie's Illustrated Newspaper* contained an announcement that the "Lucy Escott English opera company" was planning to come to the United States (87).

91. *New York Times* critic quoted in *Dwight's*, 18 Sept. 1858, 199 (Dwight quotation on 198).

92. The other members of the company included Emma Heywood, Charles Durand, Henry Squires, Aynsley Cook, Brookhouse Bowler, a Miss White, Mr. Gledhill, and Mr. Hayes.

93. *Spirit*, 11 Sept. 1858, 580; 18 Sept. 1858, 594; Odell 1970, 7:29.

94. Burton, who had been growing dissatisfied with theatrical management, permanently closed his theater and returned to the stage after canceling the Escott contract (*MW*, 16 Oct. 1858, 658; Odell 1970, 7:113–14). Although the Escott Company had been drawing poorly, he evidently was not particularly interested in fixing whatever ailed the troupe.

95. Playbill, Theatrical Programs, 1831–34, MWA.

96. *Peoria Daily Transcript*, 29 Dec. 1859, quoted in Marine 1972, 180.

97. The Cooper English Opera Company apparently fluctuated in size. For its visits to the West (including Detroit and Milwaukee) in 1858 and 1859, the company did not travel with a chorus. In 1860, however, the troupe was closer in size to the Pyne and Harrison Company and included at least the core of a chorus (Teal 1964, Appendix C, note 190; Playbills, Baltimore Holliday Street Theatre, 14 Feb. 1860, HTC; *BMT*, 10 March 1860, 41).

98. Quoted in Teal 1964, Appendix C, note 190.

99. Quoted in Wolz 1983, 73.

100. Cooper 1984, 124–33.

6. The Pyne and Harrison English Opera Company

1. *AMR*, July 1853, 104.

2. *MW*, 11 July 1857, 437.

3. Hurd 1981, 307–29; Rosenthal 1962, 16–18.

4. Rosenthal 1982; *CA&S-CJ*, Sept. 1851, 55. The most complete source of information on Louisa Pyne's English career is Clayton, *Queens of Song*. Because the book was published in 1863, however, the coverage of Pyne's career ends with the early 1860s.

5. Harrison printed material, HTC.

6. Harrison printed material, HTC.

7. Grove 1879–83, "Harrison."

8. Massett 1863, 162.

9. As Susan Pyne is elsewhere consistently referred to as "Miss Pyne," it appears that this reference to her as "Mrs." is erroneous.

10. *New-York Daily Times*, 5 Sept. 1854; Clayton 1863, 399. Anthony Reiff, the musical director of the Pyne and Harrison Company during their 1855–56 tour, also frequently mentioned in his journal the presence of Mrs. Harrison.

11. Odell 1970, 6:343–44.

12. Odell 1970, 6:345; Playbill, Boston Theatre 14–15 Dec. 1854, MWA. Frederick Meyer, a German actor and singer, had appeared in concert and opera performances in and around New York since at least 1842 (Lawrence 1988, 150, 166, 168, 170, 216–17, passim). William H. Reeves was the brother of John Sims Reeves, a prominent English tenor active during the middle and second half of the nineteenth century. William sang in Edinburgh and elsewhere in the provinces before making his way to the United States where, according to his brother, he appeared "with great success" (Reeves 1889, 6). In 1847 Reeves was a member of Anna Bishop's first American opera company; when that troupe collapsed he joined the Seguin troupe (*Spirit*, 21 Oct. 1847, 25 March 1848, 6 May 1848; Lawrence 1988, 473–74, 524, 588; Appendix B). Meyer and Reeves later sang with the Lyster and Durand company in 1857 (chapter 5). Joseph Whiting (1842–1910) was a singer active around 1852 (Brown 1870).

13. Durham 1986, 93–94, 99; Odell 1970, 6:341.

14. Playbill, 14 Dec. 1854, MWA.

15. Playbill, 27 Nov. 1854, Rare Books Department, MB; Playbill, 16 Dec. 1854, MWA. According to the *MW*, during the company's performances in Philadelphia in November the orchestra likewise had been led "by our old friend, Signor La Mana" (18 Nov. 1854, 142). The ubiquitous but historically elusive La Manna had conducted the 1843 Havana Opera Company when that troupe appeared in Philadelphia (chapter 3). His name appears occasionally in connection with various concerts and theaters in New York and, more rarely, Philadelphia. According to Schiavo (1947, 347–48) and Odell (1970, 6:341), La Manna was the orchestra leader at the Broadway during the 1854–55 season; he also is named as the "Musical Conductor" on a playbill from the Broadway Theatre from 31 Jan. 1855 (MWA). That La Manna was well known to New York audiences is suggested by the fact that he is mentioned prominently in a spoof of the popular (traditional?) tune "Rosin the Bow" in John Brougham's fabulously successful burlesque *Pocahontas*. In the song,

La Manna is described in the verse as "that harmonious Italian"; the chorus proceeds: "La Manna, come rosin your bow, oh, oh, / La Manna, come rosin your bow, / We aint got no forte-piano, / Old beeswax, come rosin your bow." *Pocahontas* was popular in New York and elsewhere; it opened at William Mitchell's Olympic Theatre in New York in December 1855 (Brooks 1984, 31).

16. Burge 1986, 121–22; Fielder 1986, 534–35, 539.

17. *MR&CA,* 12 Oct. 1854, 355.

18. *MG,* 23 Dec. 1854, 50, 10 March, 1855; *NYMR,* 7 Dec. 1854, 419.

19. It is somewhat surprising that there is no hint in the secondary sources on Harrison of the serious vocal problem that plagued him for most of his American visit.

20. *MR&CA,* 12 Oct. 1854, 355; *NYMR,* 7 Dec. 1854, 419.

21. The Pyne and Harrison Company was the first opera troupe to perform in the new Boston Theatre, which had opened on 11 Sept. 1854 (Young 1973, 117).

22. *MW,* 18 Nov. 1854, 142; *MW,* 25 Nov. 1854, 154.

23. *MG,* 9 Dec. 1854, 36; *Dwight's,* 16 Dec. 1854.

24. Eight playbills from the Pyne and Harrison Company's engagement at Niblo's have been located; three name no conductor, and five (18 June, 30 Aug., 8 and 27 Sept., and 2 Nov.) name Bristow. The playbills are in NN, NNM, the Music Division of DLC, and MWA. In his dissertation on Bristow, Rogers notes (1967, 111) that at Niblo's during the summer of 1855 the composer conducted other operas between performances of his own, and concluded that this experience "seemingly was the extent of his role as an opera conductor." No other biographical sources on Bristow mention that he was engaged as a conductor at Niblo's on a regular basis, as seems to have been the case (Rogers 1986; Gombert 1977; Rieck 1925, 3, 19).

25. Rogers 1967, 107.

26. Blair 1982, 155–70.

27. *Baltimore Clipper,* 14 May 1856; *Spirit,* 2 Oct. 1852, 396; *Mobile Daily Advertiser,* 8 Feb. 1856.

28. In the 1 Aug. 1840 issue of the *Spirit,* Brough was described as "a favorite wherever he wanders, both off and on the stage"; Francis Wemyss wrote that he was a "good-natured friend" (1847, 262); and Joseph Sill referred to him in a diary entry dated 13 Oct. 1845 as "our old friend Brough." Portions of Brough's American career have been discussed in earlier chapters. Apparently, his first stint at managing was as the agent and business manager for Anna Bishop's first American opera company (Lawrence 1988, 469; *Spirit,* 6 May 1848). Evidently, Brough also served in some sort of managerial capacity for the Italian soprano Marietta Alboni, for the *Spirit* reported in the summer of 1852 that he was "at Niagara, discoursing with Alboni as to their future movements, so as to 'head off' Sontag" [their competition] (14 Aug. 1852, 312).

29. Reiff 1855–56; Playbills: (Baltimore) Holliday Street Theatre, 19 Nov. 1855, 5 May 1856, HTC; 23, 26, 28 Nov. 1855, MdHi; Odell 1970, 6:470; Blair 1982, 165.

30. Although the company must have included some women choristers as well, Reiff evidently did not spend time socializing with female members of the troupe, for they are not mentioned in his journal. James Henry Horncastle (1801–69) sang at Drury Lane and the Dublin and Liverpool theaters before crossing the Atlantic. He came to this country in 1837 as a vocal star at the behest of James Wallack; his American debut was in September 1837 as Elvino in *La Sonnambula* at the National Theatre. Subsequently, he had an active career as a singer, appearing in vocal-star companies with the Seguins, Brough, Shirreff, and others; in various English opera troupes; and in the stock companies of Niblo's and the Olympic theaters in New York. He also was the author of works for the stage; in 1840 he collaborated with George Loder, then the music director at the Olympic Theatre, on a burlesque of Rossini's *La Gazza Ladra* and later adapted Auber's *La Bayadere* for the English stage (Brown 1870; Odell 1970, 4:211–12; "Horncastle, Henry," *National Union Catalogue*). Atkins performed in *Rip* as the Spirit of Hendrick Hudson, hence, he must have been a baritone (Playbill, Niblo's Theatre, 27 Sept. 1855, Music Division, DLC). The previous April (1855) he had appeared with Louisa Pyne, Harrison, Horncastle, and Borrani in a concert at the Brooklyn Athenaeum (Odell 1970, 6:421).

31. Anthony Reiff, Jr. (1840–1916) evidently started his professional career as a member of Jenny Lind's orchestra at Castle Garden, according to his obituary in the *New York Times* on 7 Oct. 1916. By his own admission, he "commenced [an] engagement with [A. H.] Purdy," presumably at the National Theatre in New York, in February 1852, and subsequently moved to the Bowery Theatre, where in 1854 he was conductor of the orchestra (Reiff 1855–56, 9 Feb. 1856; Bryon 1986, 376; Playbill, Bowery Theatre (New York), 10 Nov. 1854, MWA). Following his six-month tour with the Pyne and Harrison Company in 1855–56, Reiff taught piano, violin, and voice in New York and led the orchestra at the New Olympic Theatre there (*MW*, 27 June 1857, 409; Odell 1970, 6:585). He subsequently was musical director of a number of opera troupes, including the New English Opera Company, the Lyster English Opera Company, Maguire's Italian Opera Company, and the Clara Kellogg and Teresa Parepa-Rosa opera companies (Playbill, New English Opera Company, Walnut Street Theatre, 21 March 1859, PP; Reiff 1905; Playbill, Maguire's Opera Company, Academy of Music, 30 May 1865, San Francisco History Room, CSf). He traveled to Australia with the William Lyster Opera Company, which arrived in Melbourne on 1 March 1861 and subsequently performed in various other towns, including Sydney. Reiff remained in Australia until September 1863, when he apparently left for Europe. (For this information I am indebted to Adrienne Simpson, a research fellow at the National Library in Wellington, New Zealand.) Reiff also was associated with the first American Gilbert and Sullivan Company (*New York Times*, 7 Oct. 1916). Reiff's father was a bassoonist and clarinettist of German birth who was active in New York during the 1830s, 1840s, and 1850s. In 1843, the elder Reiff was a member of the group of New York musicians that formed the New York Philharmonic; he was elected the orchestra's first vice president (Shanet 1975, 82). Six years later, in 1849, Reiff, Sr., was named one of the

vice presidents of the newly formed American Musical Fund Society (Lawrence 1988, 610). The younger Reiff, who studied violin with U. C. Hill and piano with the conductor and pianist Henry C. Timm, became a violinist in the Philharmonic in 1857; he later served as vice president, chairman of the Board of Trustees, and chairman of the Music Committee of the Orchestra (Erskine 1979, 10; Wielich 1914, 26). He also served at least two terms as president of the Musical Mutual Protective Union in New York (Reiff 1905).

32. *MW,* 17 Nov. 1855, 337. The "grand farewell concert," featuring the full troupe and entire chorus, was held at the Brooklyn Athenaeum. It was not unusual for managers to stipulate a benefit performance as part of a contract. Brough's wish to have his benefit in New York, and at the beginning of the tour (while local enthusiasm generated by the singers' successful Niblo's engagement was still high) demonstrates the agent's astute business sense (*New York Daily Times,* 16 Nov. 1855).

33. Playbill, 20 Nov. 1855, HTC.

34. Admission to the troupe's performances in St. Louis and Pittsburgh also was raised (*St. Louis Daily Missouri Democrat,* 5–31 March 1856; *Pittsburgh Post,* 7 Dec. 1855). Admission cost to performances in Cincinnati, Louisville, New Orleans, and Washington, however, was not increased.

35. *Baltimore Clipper,* 19 Nov. 1855; *Dwight's,* 2 Dec. 1854, 70.

36. ALS, Richings to Carr and Warren, 4 Nov. 1856, Davis Collection, ICHi.

37. ALS, Bochsa to Peters and Field, 19 June 1848, Manuscript Collection, ICHi.

38. For two examples of naive criticism, see the reviews of Maretzek's company in Charleston cited in chapter 4. American musical criticism of the antebellum period has been the subject of some scholarly investigation, but these studies have been limited almost entirely to critics working on the East Coast. There are no studies of prewar musical criticism in any American interior cities, for example, in Pittsburgh, St. Louis, or Cincinnati, or even in New Orleans. Two dissertations deal with criticism in New York and Boston, and Upton has discussed William Henry Fry's work as a music critic in New York and Philadelphia; the first volume of Lawrence's treatment of George Strong's diaries is invaluable for its information on New York critics (Lebow 1969; McKnight 1980; Upton 1954; Lawrence 1988). Feldman's dissertation (in progress) on George P. Upton will just barely touch on criticism in the antebellum period in Chicago. The article on musical criticism in *AG* likewise reflects the current state of research, and for the antebellum years deals only with Boston, New York, Philadelphia, and (briefly) Chicago (Downes and Rockwell 1986).

39. *Cincinnati Daily Commercial,* 17 Dec. 1855.

40. *Daily Louisville Times,* 5 Jan. 1856.

41. *Cincinnati Daily Commercial,* 10 Jan. 1856, report from Evansville dated 8 Jan.

42. Reiff 1855–56, undated entry, Jan. 1856.

43. New York city directories from 1855–59 fail to mention any establishments called "Shelly's"; Reiff probably referred to a tavern or saloon.

44. Reiff 1855–56, 13, 15 Jan. 1856.

45. Haites, Mak, and Walton 1975, 68.

46. *Daily Picayune,* 8 Feb. 1856; Roppolo 1950, 2:125.

47. Pinkston 1986, 437.

48. Roppolo 1950, 126.

49. Nugent 1967, 70–71.

50. *NYMR,* 12 Oct. 1854, 355.

51. *NYMR,* 19 May 1855, 165.

52. *MG,* 30 Dec. 1854, 59.

53. *NYMR,* 23 Nov. 1854, 402.

54. *NYMR,* 23 Nov. 1854, 402.

55. The lesser-known among these musicians were William Hawes (1785–1846), musical director of the English Opera House in the 1820s; Henry Brinley Richards (1819–85), prominent nineteenth-century English pianist; T. H. Reynoldson; George A. A'Beckett; Thomas Attwood (1765–1838), English organist, prolific composer of operas, and one of Mozart's students; W. McGregor Logan; and Thomas Simpson Cooke (1782–1848), singer, music director, and conductor of the orchestra at both Drury Lane and Covent Garden theaters and later musical manager of Vauxhall Gardens (Husk-Rainbow 1982; Edwards 1982; Temperley 1982; Carr 1982).

56. Horn also made a number of other adaptations while he was still in England (Temperley 1982; Hipsher 1927, 31).

57. *Saroni's,* 10 Aug. 1850, 543.

58. Playbill, Boston Theatre, Dec. [?] 1850, MWA; Loewenberg 1978, 766, 786; Temperley 1982; Middleton, *DNB;* Lawrence 1988, 99.

59. Playbill, Holliday Street Theatre, 26 Nov. 1855, MdHi. Harrison also adapted Victor Massé's *Les noces de Jeanette* for a performance in New York by his company in April 1855 (Loewenberg 1978, 905). The adaptation that William Henry Fry and his brother Joseph made of Bellini's *Norma* in 1840 was entirely different from the usual. Fry's intention was simply to translate the work, not to adapt it to the popular stage. Consequently, he followed Bellini's music quite closely, made no cuts, and added no extraneous music (Upton 1954, 25–27).

60. Husk and Carr 1982; Lawrence 1988, 335.

61. "B.," *Mirror,* 19 Feb. 1831, 259.

62. Lacy 1854, 1855; *New Orleans Daily Picayune,* 30 Jan. 1856. Copies of these libretti are in the collections of the Music Division, DLC (*Fra Diavolo*) and the Museum of the City of New York (*Cinderella*).

63. Temperley 1982; Carr 1981, 290–91; Carr 1982, "Bishop" Worklist.

64. There are a large number of libretti to Bishop's adaptations in the collections of various archives and libraries in the United States, including (among others) DLC, NN, MWA, MB, ICN.

65. Northcott 1920, 33, 48.

66. Northcott 1920, 33. The numbers of Mozart's opera are as in the C. F. Peters edition, as reprinted by Dover (1974). I am much indebted to Bruce Carr of the Pittsburgh Symphony Orchestra for sharing information on Bish-

op's version of *Don Giovanni.* Carr examined Bishop's score at the British Museum while working on a dissertation (in progress) titled "The Theatrical Music of Sir Henry Rowley Bishop."

67. Bellini n.d.

68. Bellini 1901. The published version of the scena does not mention Bishop, but the two songs ("Oh Love Me for Thy Power" and "While the Heart Its Joy Revealing"), as "adapted by Henry Bishop," were published individually (Philadelphia: Fiot, Meignan & Co., n.d.); these versions are identical to those published as the scena. All the sheet music examples are from the Music Division, DLC.

69. Auber n.d.; Auber 1925. This particular tune is the "big hit" from *Fra Diavolo.* Lacy surely realized that tampering with it was asking for trouble. But this does not negate my point that many adaptations retained much of a work's original music. In fact, it further supports the contention that a great deal of operatic music was quite familiar to Americans, even in its original form.

70. Much of the following information on *Cinderella* is from Graziano 1983.

71. Graziano 1983, 1, 5.

72. Hamm (1979, 72) compared a libretto of *Cinderella* used by the Caroline Richings Opera Company in 1867 to Lacy's original and discovered that the two were precisely the same.

73. Graziano 1983, 14.

74. Playbill, Holliday Street Theatre, 19 Nov. 1856, HTC; *Daily Richmond Enquirer,* 19 April 1855; Playbill, Boston Theatre, 27 Nov. 1854, Rare Books Department, MB; Playbill, Niblo's Garden Theatre, 21 Sept. 1855, MWA.

75. *Daily Richmond Enquirer,* 26 April 1856; *Cincinnati Enquirer,* 19 Dec. 1855.

76. *Cincinnati Enquirer,* 19 Dec. 1855; *Washington Evening Star,* 16 April 1856.

77. Kendall 1968, 305; *New Orleans Daily Picayune,* 9 Feb. 1856.

78. Nugent 1967, 100, 102.

79. The Gaiety, or Varieties, Theatre was operated along the lines of William Mitchell's popular and very successful Olympic Theatre in New York. In 1856 William H. Crisp took over management, renamed the house Crisp's Gaiety, and recruited Frederick Lyster, Rosalie Durand, and a number of other opera singers from New York to form the "operatic department" of his company (Pinkston 1986, 501–6). See also chapter 5.

80. *Mobile Daily Advertiser,* 11–15 Feb. 1856.

81. *New Orleans Daily Picayune,* 6 Feb. 1856; Reiff 1855–56, 9 Feb. 1856.

82. Kendall 1968, 85; *Mobile Daily Advertiser,* 8 Feb. 1856.

83. *Mobile Daily Advertiser,* 12 Feb. 1856.

84. By the early 1850s, the xenophobia of American society had reached a peak of sorts with the development of the Know-Nothing movement. The genesis of this political movement was complex, but overt opposition to foreigners was a major party issue. Know-Nothings emerged as a political

force around 1852; four years later the party fielded a presidential candidate in the person of Millard Fillmore who, although unsuccessful, garnered 22 percent of the total presidential vote. Reiff himself expressed typically American anti-foreigner sentiments in numerous comments about French New Orleans. "Nearly every person in the Market," he wrote, "seem'd to be talking at once—the chattering of these French people—would do credit to an Army of Monkees" (27 Jan. 1856). He seemed astonished that there were people living in the United States who could speak only French or German. "The children in [the French Quarter] speak French as if it was their Native Language," he marveled, "and English an acquired one"; even the Negroes "speak French" (22, 23, 24 Jan. 1856). He attended services at the Cathedral with George Atherton one Sunday morning, but the two musicians left prematurely: "Atherton and myself presuming that possibly the Sermon would do us but little good (being in French) got disgusted with these Foreigners—and evaporated—" (3 Feb. 1856).

85. About their Mobile lodgings, Reiff wrote: "Put up at Mrs. Ackerman's Boarding House—on St. Louis St—The House stands back from the street about fifty feet—with a fine door yard—it is three stories high—and a garret—with three verandahs in front—which can be enclosed with green blinds—the whole giving the establishment a country aspect—" (11 Feb. 1856).

86. In 1856 Memphis probably had a population of around 15,000; according to the 1850 census the town's population was 8,841, but by 1860 it had more than 22,000 residents (Pred 1980, 26, 94).

87. Dormon 1967, 223.

88. Reiff's reaction to this development is unknown, for about thirty days' worth of his journal is missing (28 Feb.–26 March). The missing section covered the troupe's movements between New Orleans and St. Louis and a majority of the company's stay in the latter city.

89. At Niblo's Theatre in 1852, for example, the Thillon Opera Company and the Caroline Rousset Ballet Troupe performed on alternate evenings; opera nights were Monday, Wednesday, and Friday, ballet nights were Tuesday, Thursday, and Saturday (Niblo's Theatre Playbill, 19 May 1852, MWA). For further information on the Montplaisir Troupe and on the other major ballet-acrobatic troupe, the Ravel Company, see Brown 1870. Ballet companies (most of them itinerant) are another important aspect of the eighteenth- and nineteenth-century musical stage that has been almost entirely neglected by music, theater, and dance historians.

90. *Daily Democrat*, 5–31 March 1856.

91. In his study of the Rice Theatre of Chicago, Wilt noted that although performers at that house were always "re-engaged" for the second week, the theater's account books leave no doubt that the performers had been hired for a two-week engagement from the start (1923, 5–6).

92. *Daily Democrat*, 11, 12 March 1856.

93. *Daily Louisville Times*, 1–3 April 1856.

94. *Cincinnati Enquirer*, 30 March 1856.

95. *Cincinnati Daily Commercial,* 4, 5 April 1856.

96. Reiff 1855–56, 5 April 1856.

97. Reiff 1855–56, 5 April 1856.

98. Reiff 1855–56, 9 April 1856; *Daily Baltimore Republican,* 8–10 April 1856.

99. *Washington Evening Star,* 14–19 April 1856.

100. In Washington, the other members of the concert troupe were Amalia and Maurice Strakosch, and a Sig. Leonardi. The troupe had just returned from its successful tour of the South; they had been in New Orleans and Mobile around the same time as the Pyne and Harrison Company engagement in those two towns (*Washington National Intelligencer,* 11 April 1856).

101. *New Orleans Daily Picayune,* 29–31 Jan. 1856. Reiff does not mention this, and the identity of the singer is unknown, as are any details about why he left the troupe.

102. This reference to Smith and Pocahontas, coupled with the comment "gave him fits," is interesting in an arcane way, for it strongly suggests that Reiff was more than passing familiar with John Brougham's *Pocahontas* (as mentioned previously in relation to Signor La Manna). The two main characters of the spoof are Pocahontas and John Smith; furthermore, one of the tunes in the burlesque has a chorus the text of which is "Give him fits." That Reiff would know Brougham's work even before its premiere performance (24 Dec. 1855) is perfectly plausible given the nature of the small New York musical community of which he was a born-and-bred member.

103. "Up very late with dear Joe and slept very little," Reiff wrote on 18 April. "Adkins [*sic*] sat in the next room purposely to annoy us."

104. Harrison was ill and unable to perform on 21 April; consequently, there were only five opera nights in Richmond, and *The Barber of Seville* was not performed (*Daily Richmond Enquirer,* 21–29 April 1856).

105. Benedict 1850.

106. Odell 1970, 6:505; *Wasington Evening Star,* 24 May 1856; Upton 1847–81, 1:35; *MW,* 30 Aug. 1856, 290; *MR&G,* 1 Nov. 1856, 343.

107. Harrison printed material, HTC.

Epilogue

1. Beekley Diary, 2 Oct. 1850.

2. The fact that the *Dwight's* correspondent probably was being deliberately condescending does not invalidate the implication of his remarks. Americans did regard a matinee performance of an opera as a popular form of entertainment.

3. My thanks to Stephen Nissenbaum of the University of Massachusetts (Amherst) for this reference.

4. Levine 1984, 40.

5. *BMT,* 10 March 1860, 23; 7 April 1860, 56.

6. Quoted in Faner 1951, 59.

7. Quoted in Lawrence 1988, 432.

8. Johnson 1986.

9. Program, Worcester, Mass. City Hall, 2 Oct. 1851, MWA.

10. Lott 1986, 37, 191, 193, 250, 328.

11. Quoted in Lott 1986, 328.

12. Hamm 1979, 76.

13. Stuart-Wortley 1851, 43.

14. Hamm 1983, 198. Hamm also discerns a clear influence of Italian melody on American composers of the antebellum period (1983, 182, 235).

15. Quoted in Kidd 1953, 88.

16. Kirk 1986, 57.

17. For a discussion of the pervasiveness of music from the stage (including opera) in late-nineteenth-century American life, see Preston 1992.

18. For example, see "A Set of Quadrilles, Selected from the Celebrated Italian Opera La Sonnambula, Arranged for the Piano Forte by Bellini" (New York: F. Riley, ca. 1840) and "Waltz from the Opera of La Somnambula [sic] Arranged for the Piano Forte by S. Knaebel" (Boston: Charles H. Keith, 1836), both (along with numerous other examples) in the collection of the Music Division, DLC.

19. These titles have been extracted from a wide variety of sources, some secondary, some primary. The sources include: Lawrence 1988; Spirit, 15 July 1854, 264; 22 Feb. 1845, 613; 15 March 1845, 32; 7 Nov. 1840; 22 April 1843; Playbills: Adelphi Theatre (New York), 10 Feb. 1848, NN; Chestnut Street Theatre, 5 April 1845 and 26 March 1845, PP; Armstrong 1884, 41; Odell 1970, 4:403, 404, 503–4; 5:127, 160, 432.

20. Lawrence 1988, 328.

21. Chaff 1848, title page. My thanks to Wayne Shirley of the Music Division of the Library of Congress for pointing me in the direction of several of these songster examples. An in-depth scholarly study of nineteenth-century American songsters is much needed and long overdue. Such a study, if undertaken by a scholar familiar with popular mid-nineteenth-century operatic melodies, will undoubtedly unearth many such operatic parodies.

22. The same parody of "I Dreamt" can be found in other midcentury songsters, including My Old Dad's Wooly Headed Screamer (1844) and Negro Melodies No. 4—Christy's (1865), both in the R. W. Gordon Collection of Nineteenth-Century Songsters at the Library of Congress.

23. A copy of "The Phantom Chorus" can be found at the American Antiquarian Society. Kathryn Reed-Maxfield, who is studying the music of minstrel-show composers, has found that the published minstrel-show songs often include phrases borrowed from operas, but usually not in any systematic fashion. Their technique apparently was much the same as that used by James Maeder in his arrangement of music for the burlesque Pocahontas (Brooks 1984). Unless scores, parts, libretti, or prompt-books from an opera-burlesque production turn up, we will probably never know just how much of the original music was left intact and how much it was changed. According to Lawrence, most of the operatic travesties performed at William Mitchell's Olympic Theatre in New York were arranged by George Loder and "closely adhered to the originals." Her source for this information, however, is not

revealed; later she claims that the supposed adherence to the original scores was "a highly unlikely supposition" (Lawrence 1988, 135, 342).

24. Lawrence 1988, 342.

25. See Paul Charosh, "Popular and Classical Music in the Mid-Nineteenth Century," *American Music* 10 (Summer 1992): 117–35; Michael Broyles, "The Musical Canon in Europe and America: Differences and Implications," paper presented to the American Musicological Society, Chicago, November 1991; and Broyles, *"Music of the Highest Class": Elitism and Populism in Antebellum Boston* (New Haven: Yale University Press, 1992).

26. Levine 1984, 40.

27. Levine 1984, 40.

28. Levine 1988.

Bibliography

Much of the information in this book came from music and theater periodicals published in the United States during the period from 1823 through 1860. No single collection contains complete runs of all the American theater and music periodicals I wished to examine. I was able to find a majority of extant issues, however, in four repositories: the Library of Congress, the New York Public Library, the American Antiquarian Society in Worcester, Massachusetts, and the Newberry Library in Chicago. Several reference works on periodicals were indispensable: Carl Stratman, *American Theatrical Periodicals, 1798–1967: A Bibliographical Guide* (Durham, N.C.: Duke University Press, 1970); Charles Wunderlich, "A History and Bibliography of Early American Musical Periodicals, 1782–1852," Ph.D. diss., University of Michigan, 1962; and Mary Veronica Davison, "American Music Periodicals 1853–1899," Ph.D. diss., University of Minnesota, 1973. I was able to find almost every newspaper that I wished to examine in the excellent nineteenth-century newspaper collection of the Library of Congress.

I also relied heavily on other primary materials, in particular sheet music, libretti, playbills, concert programs, and manuscript letters and diaries. Material of this nature proved to be extremely valuable for firsthand information about performances themselves and for providing insights into nineteenth-century Americans' reactions to operatic performances and performers. Such material is surprisingly plentiful in libraries across the country, but it often is classified as ephemera and as a consequence is more difficult to access than are books, newspapers, or periodicals. I deliberately limited my research to libraries located in areas of the country that were of particular importance to operatic production in the antebellum period (such as Boston, New York, San Francisco, Philadelphia, and Chicago) or to repositories likely to have materials from all over the country (the Library of Congress, the Harvard Theatre Collection, and the American Antiquarian Society). I did not examine materials in several important cities, for example, New Orleans, Cincinnati, or St. Louis, because of the availability of reliable secondary-source studies concerning operatic and theatrical productions there. Of particular value to research of this nature are collections in the following libraries: playbills, sheet music, and libretti at the American Antiquarian Society and in the Music and Rare Books Divisions of the Library of Congress; playbills, scrapbooks, and the Engravings and Illustrations Collection at the Harvard Theatre Collection; playbills and scrapbooks at the Library Company of Philadelphia and the Billy Rose Theatre Collection of the New York Public Library; playbills, scrapbooks, and concert programs in the Rare Books and Music Departments of the Boston Public Library; playbills and libretti at the Museum of the City of New York; libretti and sheet music at the Newberry Library; libretti, playbills, and concert programs in the Music and Theatre Departments of the Free Library of Philadelphia; and playbills at the Chicago Public Library, the San Francisco History Room and the Archives for the Performing Arts of the San Francisco Public Library, and the Society of California Pioneers (in San Francisco), and the Maryland Historical Society. For diaries, letters, and other primary materials, the Manuscript Collections in the following repositories are particularly fruitful: the American Antiquarian Society, the New York Public Library, the New-York Historical Society, the Library of Congress, the Chicago Historical Society, and the Historical Society of Pennsylvania. Finally, the Special Collections of the Louisiana State University Library and the Federal Theatre Project Archives at George Mason University in Fairfax, Virginia, have valuable materials.

Periodicals

Numerous theater and music periodicals were published in the United States from 1823 to 1860. I examined all available extant issues of the periodicals in the following list. Years for which issues are extant are indicated in parentheses. Alternate titles are indicated by square brackets. Periodicals are listed in chronological order, by year of establishment.

The New York Mirror (1823–42)
The Critic (1828–29)
Theatrical Censor and Musical Review (1828)
Dramatic Mirror (1829)
The Spirit of the Times [*Porter's Spirit of the Times, Wilke's Spirit of the Times*] (1831–60)
The Euterpiad (1830–31)
The American Musical Journal (1834–35)
The Family Minstrel (1835–36)
Gentleman's Vade-Mecum (1835–36)
The Musical Magazine (1835–36)
The Musical Library (1835–36)
Boston Musical Gazette (1838–39)
The Musical Review (1838–39)
The Musical Magazine (1839–42)
The American Journal of Music and Musical Visitor [*Musical Visitor, Boston Musical Visitor*] (1840–46)
The World of Music [*Moore's World of Music*] (1840–43)
The Musical Reporter (1841)
The Musical Cabinet (1841–42)
The Dramatic Mirror and Literary Companion (1841–42)
Lady's Musical Library (1842–45)
The Orpheus (1843)

The World of Music (1843–48)
The Boston Musical Review (1845)
The Broadway Journal (1845–46)
The Boston Musical Gazette [*Musical Gazette*] (1846–50)
The American Musical Times (1847–49)
The Literary Excelsior and Musical World (1847–48)
Philharmonic Journal (1848–49)
The Musical Times [*Saroni's Musical Times*] (1849–52)
The Musical World [*The Message Bird. A Literary and Musical Journal; The Message Bird. Journal of the Fine Arts; Journal of the Fine Arts and Musical World; Musical World and Journal of the Fine Arts; Musical World and New York Musical Times; New York Musical World*]
Figaro, or Corbyn's Chronicle (1850–51)
The Lorgnette (1850)
The Prompter [*The Prompter's Whistle*] (1850)
The New York Weekly Review [*The Choral Advocate and Singing-Class Journal, Musical Review and Choral Advocate, New York Musical Review and Choral Advocate, New York Musical Review and Gazette, Musical Review and Musical World*]
The American Monthly Musical Review [*The American Monthly Musical Review and Choir Singers' Companion; The American Musical Review*] (1850–52)
The Baltimore Olio, and American Musical Gazette (1850)
Journal of Music (1852–60)
Dwight's Journal of Music (1852–60)
The Boston Musical Journal (1853–54)
The Musical Gazette [*New York Musical Review and Choral Advocate, New York Musical Review and Gazette, New York Weekly Review*] (1854–55)
The Musical Pioneer [*New York Musical Pioneer and Choristers' Budget, New York Musical Pioneer*] (1855–60)
The Lorgnette (1859–60)
The Musical Times (1860)

Many literary magazines from the period also contain a wealth of information about music and the theater. The following periodicals proved to be useful for certain years but were not examined as thoroughly as were the music and theater journals.

Boston Weekly Magazine (1839–40)
Frank Leslie's Illustrated News Paper (1855–59)
Gleason's Pictorial Drawing-Room Companion (1851–54) [*Ballou's Pictorial Drawing-Room Companion* (1855–59)]
Godey's Magazine and Ladies' Book
Graham's Magazine
Harper's New Monthly Magazine
The Knickerbocker Magazine

Newspapers

Newspapers, although not always reliable, are nevertheless an essential source of information in a study of this nature. I used information from newspapers throughout the book, but relied on this source to a much greater extent for chapters 2, 4, and 6 than for chapters 1, 3, and 5. Because the former three chapters concern particular performers with specific itineraries, newspapers were invaluable in corroborating and amplifying information. Only those newspapers that were examined extensively are listed. In general, I consulted issues published several weeks before an engagement, during the engagement, and for several days afterward.

Albany, N.Y.: *Evening Journal* (1839), *Daily Albany Argus* (1839); Augusta, Ga.: *Tri-Weekly Chronicle* (1839), *Daily Chronicle and Sentinel* (1839–40, 1851), *Daily Chronicle* (1839–40); Baltimore, Md.: *American and Commercial Advertiser* (1838–39, 1850–51), *Daily Advertiser* (1838–39), *Daily Republican* (1855–56), *Republican* (1838–39), *Sun* (1839, 1850–51, 1855–56), *Clipper* (1850–51, 1855–56); Baton Rouge, La.: *Daily Advocate* (1856); Boston, Mass.: *Daily Courier* (1851), *Daily Evening Transcript* (1838, 1851), *Morning Post* (1838), *Post* (1851, 1855–56); Charleston, S.C.: *Mercury* (1851), *Southern Patriot* (1839–40), *Daily Courier* (1839–40, 1851); Cincinnati, Ohio: *Commercial* (1855–56), *Enquirer* (1855–56), *Volksfreunde* (1855–56); Detroit, Mich.: *Daily Advertiser* (1839), *Daily Free Press* (1839), *Democratic Free Press* (1839); Hartford, Conn.: *Courant* (1839), *New England Weekly Review* (1839), *Patriot and Democrat* (1839), *Weekly Times* (1839); Indianapolis, Ind.: *Daily State Sentinel* (1856); Jackson, Miss.: *Semi-Weekly Mississippian* (1856); Kansas City, Mo.: *Weekly Enterprise* (1856); Kingston, Ont.: *Chronicle and Gazette* (1839), *Spectator* (1839), *Political Reformer* (1839); Louisville, Ky.: *Louisville Daily Journal* (1836); *Daily Louisville Times* (1855–56); Memphis, Tenn.: *Daily Appeal* (1856); Mobile, Ala.: *Daily Advertiser* (1856); Montreal, Quebec: *Gazette* (1839), *Transcript* (1839); Natchez, Miss.: *Daily Courier* (1856); New Haven, Conn.: *Columbia Weekly Register* (1839); New Orleans, La.: *Courier* (1855–56), *Daily Picayune* (1845, 1855–56), *Daily Advocate* (1855–56), *Louisiana Courier* (1855–56); New York City: *Daily Tribune* (1850–51), *Daily Express* (1839), *Evening Mirror* (1850–51), *Evening Post* (1850–51), *Herald* (1851), *Morning Herald* (1838), *New Era* (1840), *Sun* (1839–40), *Times & Evening Star* (1839); Philadelphia, Pa.: *Freeman* (1839), *National Gazette* (1839, 1840), *North American and United States Gazette* (1850–51), *Pennsylvanian* (1839, 1840), *Public Ledger* (1839, 1850–51), *Transcript* (1839, 1840); Pittsburgh, Pa.: *Daily Union* (1855), *Daily Morning Post* (1855), *Daily Dispatch* (1855); Providence, R.I.: *Daily Journal* (1851), *Daily Post* (1851), *Herald* (1839–40); Quebec City: *Gazette* (1839, 1849); Richmond, Va.: *Daily Richmond Enquirer* (1856); Savannah, Ga.: *Daily Republican* (1839–40), *The Georgian* (1839–40); Springfield, Mass.: *Weekly Republican* (1839); St. Louis, Mo.: *Daily Missouri Democrat* (1856); Toronto, Ont.: *Patriot* (1839), *Upper Canada Gazette or American Oracle* (1839); Troy, N.Y.: *Daily Whig* (1839); Utica, N.Y.: *Oneida Whig* (1839), *Observer* (1839); Washington, D.C.: *Evening Star* (1856), *National Intelligencer* (1838, 1840); Worcester, Mass.: *Weekly Argus* (1839), *Massachusetts Spy* (1839).

Other Materials

A number of individuals—friends, acquaintances, and even several strangers—generously gave or lent to me data and research notes they had amassed for their own related projects. This information, which was of inestimable value in the research and writing of this book, is cited throughout as the unpublished "RN" (research notes) or worklists of these various individuals. I have photocopies or precis (on computer disk) of much of this material. The individuals to whom I am indebted for this information are: William Brooks (University of Illinois) for notes compiled for articles he wrote for *AG* on Austin, the Woods, Strakosch, and other singers and impresarios; Bruce Carr (Pittsburgh Symphony Orchestra) for information on Sir Henry Rowley Bishop, in particular on that composer's adaptations of Italian operas for the English stage; Robert Commanday (*San Francisco Chronicle*) for data he has collected on the history of opera in San Francisco; Harlan Jennings (Michigan State University) for information on the history of opera in the West; Thomas Kaufman (Boonton, N.J.) for worklists of repertories and itineraries of opera companies that he compiled for his book *Verdi and His Major Contemporaries: A Selected Chronology of Performances with Casts* (New York: Garland, 1990) and that he allowed me to use prior to publication; and Kathryn Reed-Maxfield (University of Michigan) for information related to minstrel-troupe burlesques of Italian operas.

Albrecht, Otto E. 1979. "Opera in Philadelphia, 1800–1831." *Journal of the American Musicological Society* (Fall):499–515.

Anonymous Diary, New York City. 1844. Manuscript Division, New York Public Library.

Arditi, Luigi. 1977. *My Reminiscences.* New York: Dodd, Mead, 1896; reprint New York: Da Capo Press.

Armstrong, William G. 1884. *A Record of the Opera in Philadelphia.* Philadelphia: Porter & Coates.

Auber, Daniel Francois-Esprit. 1925. *Fra Diavolo.* Leipzig: C. F. Peters.

———. n.d. "On Yonder Rock Reclining." In *Select Pieces from Auber's Popular Opera Fra Diavolo, as Sung by the Pyne Opera Troupe.* Cincinnati: W. C. Peters & Sons.

"B." 1831. "Lacy's Version of Cinderella, and the Lyric Drama." *New-York Mirror,* 19 Feb., 259.

Bailey, Dee. 1986. "Carolyn Richings." In *AG,* ed. Hitchcock and Sadie.

Bailey, Frances Margaret. 1934. "A History of the Stage in Mobile, Alabama from 1824–1850." Master's thesis, State University of Iowa.

Barnum, Phineas T. 1970. *Struggles and Triumphs.* Hartford: J. B. Burr, 1869; reprint New York: Arno.

Barriskill, James M. 1955. "An Index for *Record of the Boston Stage* by W. W. Clapp, Jr." Typescript. American Antiquarian Society, Worcester, Mass.

Beale, Thomas Willert. 1890. *The Light of Other Days Seen Through the Wrong End of an Opera Glass.* 2 vols. London: Richard Bentley and Son.

Beekley, N. 1849. Diary. Manuscript Collection, American Antiquarian Society.

Bellini, Vincenzo. n.d. " 'Oh Love for Me Thy Power' and 'While This Heart Its Joy Revealing' as Sung by Madame Malibran & Mrs. Wood in the Opera of La Sonnambula. As Adapted by Henry Bishop." Baltimore: Geo. Willig Jr.

———. *La Sonnambula*. 1901. New York: G. Schirmer.

———. n.d. " 'Sounds so Joyful,' a Cavatina from Bellini's Opera La Sonnambula. Adapted by Henry R. Bishop." Philadelphia: Fiot, Meignen.

Belsom, John. 1955. "Reception of Major Operatic Premières in New Orleans during the Nineteenth Century." Master's thesis, Louisiana State University.

Benedict, Julius. 1881. "Jenny Lind." *Scribner's Monthly*, May.

———. 1850. " 'The Skylark,' a Morning Song, as Sung by Miss Louisa Pyne at her Concerts in America." New York: Firth, Pond.

Bergstrom, Lois Mildred. 1930. "The History of McVicker's Theatre: 1857–1861." Ph.D. diss., University of Chicago.

Berlioz, Hector. 1950. "Rossini's *William Tell*." *Gazette musicale de Paris*, 1834; reprint in *Source Readings in Music History*. Edited by Oliver Strunk. New York: W. W. Norton, 813.

Bernheim, Alfred L. [1932]. *The Business of the Theatre: An Economic History of the American Theatre, 1750-1932*. New York: Benjamin Blom.

Betterton, William F. 1963. "A History of Music in Davenport, Iowa, before 1900." Ph.D. diss., University of Iowa.

Bishop, Anna. Collection of Playbills. Music Department, Boston Public Library.

Bittner, Robert E. 1950. "The Concert Life and the Musical Stage in New Orleans up to the Construction of the French Opera House." Ph.D. diss., University of Wisconsin.

Blair, John Purdy. 1982. "Productions at Niblo's Garden Theatre, 1849–1862." Ph.D. diss., University of Georgia.

Blake, Charles. 1971. *An Historical Account of the Providence Stage: Being a Paper Read Before the Rhode Island Historical Society, October 25th, 1860*. Prividence, R.I.: G. H. Whitney, 1868; reprint New York: Benjamin Blom.

Bloom, Arthur W. 1986. "The Jefferson Company, 1830–1845." *Theatre Survey: The American Journal of Theatre History*, nos. 1-2 (27):89–153.

Blundell, Mary. 1838-40. "Journal in America." In Shirreff Collection, NN.

Bochsa, Nicholas. 1848. ALS to Messrs Peters and Field, Music House, Cincinnati, 19 June. Manuscript Division, Chicago Historical Society.

Bonner, Aletha. 1942. *Music and Musicians of Tennessee*. Nashville: Lellyett & Rogers.

Boyce, Monique Davis. 1957. "The First Forty Years of the Augusta, Georgia Theatre." Master's thesis, University of Georgia.

Boyer, Robert Downer. 1963. "A History of the National Theatre in Washington, D.C." Master's thesis, University of Maryland.

Brooks, William. 1986. "Elizabeth Austin." In *AG*, ed. Hitchcock and Sadie.

———. 1986. "Jenny Lind." In *AG*, ed. Hitchcock and Sadie.

———. 1986. "Joseph Wood." In *AG*, ed. Hitchcock and Sadie.

―――. 1986. "Bernard Ullman." In *AG*, ed. Hitchcock and Sadie.

―――. 1986. "Maurice Strakosch." In *AG*, ed. Hitchcock and Sadie.

―――. 1986. "Max Maretzek." In *AG*, ed. Hitchcock and Sadie.

―――. 1984. *"Pocahontas: Her Life and Times." American Music* (Winter):19–48.

Brown, Lilla Jean. 1947. "Music in the History of Dallas, 1841–1900." Master's thesis, University of Texas.

Brown, T. Allston. 1870. *A History of the American Stage*. New York: Dick & Fitzgerald.

―――. 1903. *History of the New York Stage from the First Performance in 1732 to 1901*. New York: Dodd.

Broyles, Michael. 1991. "The Musical Canon in Europe and America: Differences and Implications." Paper read at the American Musicological Society annual meeting, Chicago.

―――. 1992. *"Music of the Highest Class": Criticism and Populism in Antebellum Boston*. New Haven: Yale University Press.

Bruner, Robert Russell. 1964. "A History of Music in Cedar Rapids, Iowa, before 1900." Ph.D. diss., University of Iowa.

Buckley, Peter George. 1984. "To the Opera House: Culture and Society in New York City, 1820–1860." Ph.D. diss., State University of New York at Stony Brook.

Bull, Sara C. 1883. *Ole Bull: A Memoir*. Boston: Houghton Mifflin.

Bunn, Alfred. 1840. *The Stage: Both Before and Behind the Curtain, from "Observations Taken on the Spot."* London: Bentley.

Burge, James. 1986. "Broadway Theatre Stock Company." In *ATC*, ed. Durham.

Byron, George B. 1986. "[Purdy's] National Theatre Company." In *ATC*, ed. Durham.

Carr, Bruce. 1981. "Theatre Music: 1800–1834." In *The Romantic Age, 1800–1914*, ed. Nicholas Temperley. *The Athlone History of Music in Britain*, vol. 5. London: Athlone Press.

―――. In progress. "The Theatrical Music of Sir Henry Rowley Bishop." Ph.D. diss., State University of New York at Buffalo.

―――. 1982. "Thomas Simpson Cooke." In *NG*, ed. Sadie.

―――. 1982. "Worklist, Henry Rowley Bishop." In *NG*, ed. Sadie.

Carse, Adam. 1948. *The Orchestra from Beethoven to Berlioz*. Cambridge: W. Heffer & Sons.

Carson, William G. 1949. *Managers in Distress: The St. Louis Stage, 1840–1844*. St. Louis: St. Louis Historical Documents Foundation.

―――. 1946. *St. Louis Goes to the Opera 1837–1941*. St. Louis: Missouri Historical Society.

―――. 1932. *The Theatre on the Frontier: The Early Years of the St. Louis Stage*. Chicago: University of Chicago Press.

―――, ed. 1945. *Letters of Mr. and Mrs. Charles Kean Relating to Their American Tours*. St. Louis: Washington University.

Chaff, Gumbo. 1848. *The Ethiopian Glee Book; a Collection of Popular Negro Melodies, Arranged for Quartett Clubs*. Boston: Elias Howe.

Chamberlain, Thomas. 1835–40, 1840–61. Diaries. Vols. 1 and 2. Manuscript Division, New York Public Library.

Charosh, Paul. 1992. "Popular and Classical Music in the Mid-Nineteenth Century." *American Music* 10 (Summer): 117–35.

Chase, Gilbert. 1987. *America's Music: From the Pilgrims to the Present.* 3d ed. Urbana: University of Illinois Press.

Chevalley, Sylvie. 1951. "La Première Saison Theatrale Francaise de New-York." *The French Review* (May):471–79.

———. 1955. "Le Théâtre D'Orléâns en Tournée dans les Villes du Nord, 1827–1833." In *Comptes Rendus de l'Athénée Louisianais,* 27–71. New Orleans.

Christy, Edwin P. 1848. "The Phantom Chorus: A Parody from La Sonnambula as Arranged and Sung by the Christy Minstrels." New York: C. Holt Jr.

Clapp, William W., Jr. 1969. *A Record of the Boston Stage.* Boston: James Monroe, 1853; reprint New York: Greenwood Press.

Clay, Lucille N. 1930. "The Lexington, Kentucky, Theatre from 1800–1840." Master's thesis, University of Kentucky.

Clayton, Ellen Creathorne. 1863. *Queens of Song: Being Memoirs of Some of the Most Celebrated Female Vocalists Who Have Appeared on the Lyric Stage, From the Earliest Days of Opera to the Present Time.* London: Smith, Elder.

Cockrell, Dale. 1986. "Rainer." In *AG,* ed. Hitchcock and Sadie.

Cole, Ronald F. 1975. "Music in Portland, Maine from Colonial Times Through the Nineteenth Century." Ph.D. diss., Indiana University.

Colee, Norma Weathersby. 1948. *Mississippi Music and Musicians.* Magnolia, Miss.: Prescott's Printery.

Cone, John Frederick. 1983. *First Rival of the Metropolitan Opera.* New York: Columbia University Press.

Cooper, Dorith R. 1984. "Opera in Montreal and Toronto: A Study of Performance Traditions and Repertoire." Ph.D. diss., University of Toronto.

Cowell, Joseph. 1844. *Thirty Years Passed among the Actors and Actresses of England and America.* New York: Harper & Bros.

Crews, Emma Katherine. 1961. "A History of Music in Knoxville, Tennessee, 1791–1910." Ph.D. diss., Florida State University.

Curtis, John. n.d. "One Hundred Years of Grand Opera in Philadelphia." Typescript. 7 vols. The Historical Society of Pennsylvania, Philadelphia.

Da Ponte, Lorenzo. 1929. *Memoirs of Lorenzo da Ponte.* Translated by Elisabeth Abbott. Edited by Arthur Livingston. Philadelphia: J. B. Lippincott.

Davenport, Francis Garvin. 1943. *Ante Bellum Kentucky: A Social History, 1800–1860.* Oxford, Ohio: Mississippi Valley Press.

———. 1941. *Cultural Life in Nashville on the Eve of the Civil War.* Chapel Hill: University of North Carolina Press.

Davidge, William. 1866. *Footlight Flashes.* New York: American News Company.

Davis, Ronald L. 1965. *A History of Opera in the American West.* Englewood Cliffs, N.J.: Prentice-Hall.

Davis, William James. Collection. Manuscript Division, Chicago Historical Society.

Davison, Mary Veronica. 1973. "American Music Periodicals 1853–1899." 2 vols. Ph.D. diss., University of Minnesota.

Dickey, Judy Ruth. 1968. "The Music of a Louisiana Plantation Family." Master's thesis, Louisiana State University.

Dictionary of American Biography.

Dictionary of National Biography.

Dix, William S. 1946. *The Theatre in Cleveland, 1854–1875.* Chicago: University of Chicago Press.

Dorman, James H., Jr. 1967. *Theater in the Ante Bellum South: 1815–1861.* Chapel Hill: University of North Carolina Press.

Downes, Edward, and John Rockwell. 1986. "Criticism." In *AG,* ed. Hitchcock and Sadie.

Duggar, Mary Morgan. 1941. "The Theatre in Mobile, 1822–1860." Master's thesis, University of Alabama.

Dunn, Esther Cloudman. 1939. *Shakespeare in America.* New York: Macmillan.

Dunston, Carolyn. 1856. Diary. Vol. 1. Manuscript Division, New York Public Library.

Durang, Charles. 1868. *History of the Philadelphia Stage, Between the Years 1749–1855.* 6 vols. Philadelphia: *Sunday Dispatch.*

Durham, Weldon B., ed. 1986. *American Theatre Companies, 1749–1887* [*ATC*]. Westport Conn.: Greenwood Press.

———. 1986. "Park Theatre Company." In *ATC.*

———. 1986. "Tremont Theatre Company." In *ATC.*

Edwards, Owain. 1982. "(Henry) Brinley Richards." In *NG,* ed. Sadie.

Ernst, Alice. 1961. *Trouping in the Oregon Country.* Portland: Oregon Historical Society.

Erskine, John. 1979. *The Philharmonic-Symphony Society of New York: Its First Hundred Years.* New York: Macmillan, 1943; reprint in *Early Histories of the New York Philharmonic,* ed. Howard Shanet. New York: Da Capo.

Estavan, Lawrence, ed. 1939. *San Francisco Theatre Research: History of Opera in San Francisco.* Vol. 7: *History of Music in San Francisco Series,* ed. Cornel Langyel. History of Music Project, WPA: Northern California, San Francisco. Federal Theatre Project Archives, George Mason University.

Faner, Robert D. 1951. *Walt Whitman and Opera.* Carbondale: Southern Illinois University Press.

Farkas, Andrew. 1985. *Opera and Concert Singers: An Annotated International Bibliography of Books and Pamphlets.* New York: Garland.

Farwell, Arthur, and W. Dermont Darby. 1915. *Music in America.* Vol. 4: *The Art of Music,* ed. Daniel Gregory Mason. New York: National Society of Music.

Federal Theatre Project. Archives. George Mason University.

Feldman, Mary Ann. In progress. "The Collected Writings of George P. Upton:

A Half Century of Chicago Musical Criticism." Ph.D. diss., University of Chicago.

Ferguson, James Smith. 1970. "A History of Music in Vicksburg, Mississippi, 1820–1900." Ph.D. diss., University of Michigan.

Fielder, Mari Kathleen. 1986. "[Old] Chestnut Street Theatre Stock Company." In *ATC*, ed. Durham.

———. 1986. "[Third] Walnut Street Theatre Company." In *ATC*, ed. Durham.

Fletcher, Edward Garland. 1931. "Records and History of Theatrical Activities in Pittsburgh, Pennsylvania from Their Beginnings to 1861." Ph.D. diss., Harvard University.

Ford, John T. Theatre Collection. Correspondence. Manuscript Division, Library of Congress.

Ford, Tom. 1850. *A Peep Behind the Curtain, by a Boston Supernumerary.* Boston: Redding.

Formes, Karl. 1891. *My Memoirs.* San Francisco: James H. Barry, Printer.

"Forty Years a Manager." 1887. *New York Times,* 11 Oct., 5:2.

Foster, Lois. n.d. *Annals of the San Francisco Stage.* Part 1: *1850–1860.* Typescript. Research Department of the San Francisco Theatre Project, WPA. Federal Theatre Project Archives, George Mason University.

Francis, John Wakefield. 1858. "The Garcias and da Ponte." *Dwight's Journal of Music,* 1 May, 35–36.

———. 1971. *Old New York; or, Reminiscences of the Past Sixty Years.* New York: W. J. Widdleton, 1865; reprint, New York: B. Blom.

Freedley, George. 1936. *Theatre Collections in Libraries in Museums.* New York: Theatre Arts.

———. 1958. "The Twenty-Six Principal Theatre Collections in American Libraries and Museums." *New York Public Library Bulletin* (July):319–29.

Fry, William Henry. 1856. "The Opera in New York." *Dwight's Journal of Music,* 12 Jan., 116; 19 Jan., 123–24; 26 Jan., 131–32.

Gaer, Joseph, ed. 1970. Rev. ed. *The Theatre of the Gold Rush Era in San Francisco.* New York: Burt Franklin, 1932.

Gafford, Lucille. 1932. *A History of the St. Charles Theatre in New Orleans, 1835–1843.* Chicago: University of Chicago Press.

Gagey, Edmund McAdoo. 1950. *The San Francisco Stage: A History.* New York: Columbia University Press.

Gaiser, Gerhard. 1953. "The History of the Cleveland Theatre from Its Beginning to 1854." Ph.D. diss., University of Iowa.

Gallegly, Joseph. 1962. *Footlights on the Border: The Galveston and Houston Stage Before 1900.* The Hague: Mouton.

Gohdes, Clarence. 1967. *Literature and Theatre of the States and Regions of the United States of America: An Historical Bibliography.* Durham, N.C.: Duke University Press.

———. 1965. "The Theatre in New York: A Tentative Checklist." *New York Public Library Bulletin* (April):232–46.

Gombert, K. E. 1977. "*Leonora* by William Henry Fry and *Rip Van Winkle* by George Frederick Bristow: Examples of Mid-Nineteenth Century American Opera." Ph.D. diss., Ball State University.

Grau, Robert. 1909. *Forty Years of Observation of Music and the Drama*. New York: Broadway.

Graziano, John. 1983. *"Cinderella, or the Fairy and the Little Glass Slipper."* Paper read before a meeting of the Sonneck Society for American Music, Keele, England, July.

Green, Elvena M. 1971. "Theatre and Other Entertainments in Savannah, Georgia, 1818–1865." Ph.D. diss., University of Iowa.

Greene, Gary. 1987. "Understanding Past Currency in Modern Terms." *Sonneck Society Bulletin* (Summer):48.

Greenfield, Mildred Albert. 1953. "An Early History of the Theatre in Baltimore." Master's thesis, Johns Hopkins University.

Greiner, Tyler. 1977. "A History of Professional Entertainment at the Fulton Opera House, Lancaster, Pennsylvania, 1852–1930." Master's thesis, Pennsylvania State University.

Grimsted, David. 1968. *Melodrama Unveiled: American Theatre and Culture, 1800–1850*. Chicago: University of Chicago Press.

———. 1963. "A Mirror for Nature: American Theatre 1800–1850." Ph.D. diss., University of California at Berkeley.

Grove, George, ed. 1879–83. *A Dictionary of Music and Musicians* [*Grove's Dictionary*]. London: Macmillan.

Hackett, Karleton. 1913. *The Beginnings of Grand Opera in Chicago (1850–1859)*. Chicago: Laurentian Publishers.

Haites, Erik F., James Mak, and Gary M. Walton. 1975. *Western River Transportation: The Era of Early Internal Development, 1810–1860*. Baltimore: Johns Hopkins University Press.

Hall, Lillian Arville. 1930. *Catalogue of Dramatic Portraits in the Theatre Collection of the Harvard College Library*. 4 vols. Cambridge: Harvard University Press.

Hamil, Linda Virginia. 1976. "Study of Theatrical Activity in Natchez, Mississippi, 1800–1840." Master's thesis, University of Mississippi.

Hamm, Charles. 1986. "Braham, John." In *AG*, ed. Hitchcock and Sadie.

———. 1983. *Music in the New World*. New York: W. W. Norton.

———. 1966. *Opera*. Boston: Allyn and Bacon.

———. 1979. *Yesterdays: Popular Song in America*. New York: W. W. Norton.

Harris, Geraldine. 1937. "A History of the Theatre in Ohio, 1815–1850." Master's thesis, Ohio State University.

Harrison, Gabriel. 1884. *A History of the Progress of Drama, Music, and the Fine Arts in the City of Brooklyn*. Brooklyn: Privately Published. Reprinted from *Illustrated History of Kings County*, ed. H. R. Stiles. Brooklyn: W. W. Munsell, 1884.

Harrison, William. Unidentified printed material, Harrison folder. Engravings and Illustrations Collection. Harvard Theatre Collection.

Hartley, Russell. n.d. "Opera in San Francisco." Typescript. San Francisco Archives of the Performing Arts, San Francisco Public Library.

Haywood, Charles. 1968. Introduction to Maretzek, *Crotchets and Quavers* and *Sharps and Flats*.

Heart Songs: Dear to the American People. 1909. Boston: Chapple Publishing.

Hebron, Dorothy. 1940. "Sir Walter Scott in New Orleans, 1833–1850." Master's thesis, Tulane University.

Heintze, James R., ed. 1984. *American Music Studies: A Classified Bibliography of Master's Theses*. Detroit: Information Coordinators.

Henderson, Myrtle. 1934. *A History of the Theatre in Salt Lake City*. Evanston, Ill.: Published privately.

Hester, Wyline. 1930. "The Savannah Stage." Master's thesis, Alabama Polytechnic Institute.

Hill, Benjamin. Benjamin Hill Collection. Vol. 1: "The Early Drama in Worcester, 1787–1854." Manuscript Collection, American Antiquarian Society.

Hindman, John Joseph. 1971. "Concert Life in Ante Bellum Charleston." Ph.D. diss., University of North Carolina.

Hines, James Robert. 1973. "Musical Activity in Norfolk, Virginia, 1680–1973." Ph.D. diss., University of North Carolina.

Hipsher, Edward Ellsworth. 1927. *American Opera and Its Composers*. Philadelphia: Presser.

Hitchcock, H. Wiley. 1988. *Music in the United States: A Historical Introduction*. 3d ed. Englewood Cliffs, N.J.: Prentice-Hall.

Hitchcock, H. Wiley, and Stanley Sadie, eds. 1986. *The New Grove Dictionary of American Music [AG]*. 4 vols. New York: Macmillan.

Hixon, Don L. 1980. *Verdi in San Francisco, 1851–1899: A Preliminary Bibliography*. Irving, Calif.: Published privately.

Hoole, W. Stanley. 1946. *The Ante Bellum Charleston Theatre*. University: University of Alabama Press.

———. 1937. "Two Famous Theatres of the Old South." *South Atlantic Quarterly* (July):233–37.

Hornblow, Arthur. 1919. *A History of the Theatre in America*. 2 vols. Philadelphia: Lippincott.

Horner, Keith, and R. Allen Lott. 1986. "Luigi, Arditi." In *AG*, ed. Hitchcock and Sadie.

Hunter, Alexander, and J. H. Polkinhorn. 1855. *The New National Theatre, Washington, D.C.: A Record of Fifty Years*. Washington, D.C.: R. O. Polkinhorn & Son.

Hurd, Michael. 1981. "Opera: 1834–1865." In *The Romantic Age, 1800–1914*, ed. Nicholas Temperley. *The Athlone History of Music in Britain*, vol. 5. London: Athlone Press.

Husk, W. H. [Revised by Bruce Carr.] 1982. "Michael Rophino Lacy." In *NG*, ed. Sadie.

———. 1898. "Jane Shirreff." In *Grove's Dictionary*.

———. 1904. "Mary Anne Paton." In *Grove's Dictionary*.

———. 1911. "Seguin." In *Grove's Dictionary*.

———. 1982. "Seguin." In *NG*, ed. Sadie.

Husk, H. W., and W. H. Grattan Flood. 1982. "William Michael Rooke." In *NG*, ed. Sadie.

Husk, W. H., and Bernarr Rainbow. 1982. "William Hawes." In *NG*, ed. Sadie.

Hutton, Laurence. 1875. *Plays and Players*. New York: Hurd and Houghton.

Ireland, Joseph N. 1968. *Records of the New York Stage from 1750 to 1860*. 2 vols. New York: T. H. Morrell, 1866–67; reprint New York: Burt Franklin.

J. G. ("on the U. S. ship 'Warren,' off Cuba, March 1, 1840"). 1840. "Theatricals in Havana." *Spirit of the Times*, 4 April.

James, Reese D., ed. 1968. *Old Drury of Philadelphia: A History of the Philadelphia Stage 1800–1835, Including the Diary or Daily Account Book of William Burke Wood, Co-Manager with William Warren of the Chestnut Street Theatre, Familiarly Known as Old Drury*. Philadelphia: University of Pennsylvania Press, 1932; reprint New York: Greenwood Press.

Johnson, Claudia D., and Vernon E. Johnson. 1982. *Nineteenth-Century Theatrical Memoirs*. Westport, Conn.: Greenwood Press.

Johnson, H. Earle. 1979. *First Performances in America to 1900: Works with Orchestra*. Detroit: Information Coordinators.

————. 1986. "Germania Musical Society." In *AG*, ed. Hitchcock and Sadie.

————. 1953. "The Germania Musical Society." *The Musical Quarterly* 39 (January): 75–93.

Jones, Jane E. 1932. "A History of the Stage in Louisville, Kentucky, from the Beginning to 1845." Master's thesis, University of Iowa.

Kaufman, Charles Howard. 1974. "Music in New Jersey, 1655–1860." Ph.D. diss., New York University.

Kaufman, Thomas G. 1986–87. "The Arditi Tour: The Midwest Gets Its First Real Taste of Italian Opera." *Opera Quarterly* (Winter):39–52.

Kendall, John S. 1968. *The Golden Age of the New Orleans Theatre*. Baton Rouge: Louisiana State University Press, 1952; reprint Westport, Conn.: Greenwood Press.

Kennedy, Robert Allen. 1960. "A History and Survey of Community Music in Mobile, Alabama." Ph.D. diss., Florida State University.

Kidd, James R. 1953. "The History of Salt Sulphur Springs, Monroe County, West Virginia." Master's thesis, West Virginia University.

Kirk, Elise K. 1986. *Music at the White House*. Urbana: University of Illinois Press.

Klein, Daniel A. II. 1986. "Burton's Stock Company." In *ATC*, ed. Durham.

Kmen, Henry A. 1966. *Music in New Orleans: The Formative Years, 1791–1841*. Baton Rouge: Louisiana State University Press.

————. 1961. "Singing and Dancing in New Orleans: A Social History of the Birth and Growth of Balls and Opera, 1791–1841." Ph.D. diss., Tulane University.

Kolodin, Irving, Francis D. Perkins, and Susan Thiemann Sommer. 1986. "New York. 4. Opera and Musical Theater." In *AG*, ed. Hitchcock and Sadie.

Krehbiel, Henry Edward. 1980. *Chapters of Opera*. New York: Henry Holt, 1909; reprint New York: Da Capo.

————. 1887. "Da Ponte in New York." New York *Tribune*, 28 Aug.

Lacy, M. Rophino. 1855. "*Cinderella; or, The Fairy [Queen] and Little Glass*

Slipper . . . as performed by the Pyne and Harrison Troupe at the Broadway Theatre." Libretto. New York: French.

————. 1854. "*Fra-Diavolo; or, The Inn of Terracina* . . . as performed by the Pyne and Harrison Troupe, at the Broadway Theatre . . . by M. Rophino Lacy." Libretto. New York: French.

Lahee, Henry C. 1898. *Famous Singers of To-Day and Yesterday.* Boston: L. C. Page.

————. 1912. *The Grand Opera Singers of Today.* Boston: Page.

Langley, William Osler. 1937. "The Theatre in Columbus, Georgia from 1828 to 1878." Master's thesis, Auburn University.

Langworthy, Helen. 1952. "The Theatre in the Frontier Cities of Lexington, Kentucky and Cincinnati, Ohio, 1797–1835." Ph.D. diss., University of Iowa.

————. 1926. "The Theatre in the Lower Valley of the Ohio, 1797–1860." Master's thesis, State University of Iowa.

Lawrence, Vera Brodsky. 1988. *Strong on Music: The New York Music Scene in the Days of George Templeton Strong, 1836–1875.* Vol. 1: *Resonances, 1836–1850.* New York: Oxford University Press.

LeBow, Marcia W. 1969. "A Systematic Examination of the *Journal of Music and Art,* Edited by John Sullivan Dwight: 1852–1881, Boston, Massachusetts." Ph.D. diss., University of California at Los Angeles.

Legge, Ronald Humphrey. "Seguin." In *DNB.*

Lengyel, Cornel, ed. 1939. *History of Music in San Francisco Series.* Vol. 1: *Music of the Gold Rush Era.* History of Music Project, WPA: Northern California, San Francisco. Federal Theatre Project Archives, George Mason University.

Leonard, James M. 1971. "The Letters of William Duffy, Albany Theatre Manager, 1830–1835." Ph.D. diss., Cornell University.

Lerner, Lawrence. 1970. "The Rise of the Impresario: Bernard Ullman and the Transformation of Musical Culture in Nineteenth Century America." Ph.D. diss., University of Wisconsin.

Leuchs, Frederick. 1928. *The Early German Theatre in New York, 1840–1872.* New York: Columbia University Press.

Levine, Lawrence W. 1988. *Highbrow, Lowbrow: The Emergence of Cultural Hierarchy in America.* Cambridge: Harvard University Press.

————. 1984. "William Shakespeare and the American People: A Study in Cultural Transformation." *American Historical Review* (Feb.):34–66.

Lincoln, Jean. 1939. "Music in Michigan before 1860." Master's thesis, Michigan State University.

Linscome, Sanford Abel. 1970. "A History of Musical Development in Denver, Colorado, 1858–1918." Ph.D. diss., University of Texas.

Litto, Fredric M. 1969. "Edmund Simpson of the Park Theatre, New York, 1809–1848." Ph.D. diss., Indiana University.

Loewenberg, Alfred. 1978. *Annals of Opera 1597–1940.* 3d ed. Totowa, N.J.: Rowman and Littlefield.

Logan, Olive. 1870. *Before the Footlights and Behind the Scenes: A Book about "The Show Business."* Philadelphia: Parmelee.

Lott, R. Allen. 1986. "The American Concert Tours of Leopold de Meyer, Henri Herz, and Sigismond Thalberg." 2 vols. Ph.D. diss., City University of New York.

Ludlow, N. M. 1880. *Dramatic Life as I Found It.* St. Louis: G. I. Jones.

Luttrell, Wanda M. 1951. "The Theatre of Memphis, Tennessee from 1829–1860." Master's thesis, Louisiana State University.

Mackinlay, M. Sterling. 1908. *Garcia the Centenarian and His Times.* New York: S. Appleton.

Madeira, Louis C. 1896. *Annals of Music in Philadelphia.* Philadelphia: Lippincott.

Mahan, Katherine H. 1967. "A History of Music in Columbus, Georgia, 1828–1928." Ph.D. diss., Florida State University.

A Man about Town. 1835. "The Orchestras. New-York—Boston—Philadelphia—Baltimore." *New-York Mirror,* 3 Jan., 211.

Mandeville Family. Papers. Special Collections, Louisiana State University.

Marco, Guy A. 1985. *Opera: A Research and Information Guide.* New York: Garland.

Maretzek, Max. 1968. *Revelations of an Opera Manager in Nineteenth Century America.* Reprint (2 vols. as one) of *Crotchets and Quavers* (1855) and *Sharps and Flats* (1890). Introduction by Charles Haywood. New York: Dover.

Maretzek Opera Company. 1850–51. Playbills. Brown Collection, Music Department, Boston Public Library.

Marine, Don. 1972. "A History of Professional Stage Theatricals in Peoria, Illinois Before the Civil War." Ph.D. diss., Tulane University.

Marion, John Francis. 1984. *Within These Walls: A History of the Academy of Music in Philadelphia.* Philadelphia: Academy of Music.

Marshall, Thomas F. 1961. "Beyond New York: A Bibliography of the Nineteenth-Century American Stage from the Atlantic to the Mississippi." *Theatre Research* 3, no. 3, 208–17.

Martin, John Hill. [1841–57.] Papers and Diary. Manuscript Division, Historical Society of Pennsylvania.

Mason, Lowell, and George Webb. 1838. *Boston Glee Book.* Boston: J. H. Wilkins.

Massett, Stephen. 1863. *"Drifting About"; or, What "Jeemes Pipes of Pipesville" Saw-and-Did.* New York: Carleton.

Mates, Julian. 1985. *America's Musical Stage: Two Hundred Years of Musical Theatre.* Westport, Conn.: Greenwood Press.

———. 1971. "American Musical Theatre: Beginnings to 1900." In *The American Theatre: A Sum of Its Parts,* ed. Henry B. Williams. New York: Samuel French.

Mattfeld, Julius. 1927. *A Hundred Years of Grand Opera in New York: 1825–1925.* New York: New York Public Library.

McConachie, Bruce A. 1988. "New York Operagoing, 1825–50: Creating an Elite Social Ritual." *American Music* (Summer):181–92.

McCurdy, Evelyn M. 1953. "A History of the Adelphi Theatre, San Francisco, California." Master's thesis, Stanford University.

McDavitt, Elaine Elizabeth. 1935. "A History of the Theatre in Milwaukee, Wisconsin, up to 1865." Master's thesis, Northwestern University.

McDermott, Douglas. 1974. "Touring Patterns on California's Theatrical Frontier, 1849–59." *Theatre Survey* (May):18–28.

McGlinchee, Claire. 1940. *The First Decade of the Boston Museum.* Boston: Bruce Humphries.

McKee, Edna H. 1959. "A History of Theatrical Entertainment in Jackson, Mississippi from August 1839 to April 1860." Ph.D. diss., Florida State University.

McKnight, Mark C. 1980. "Music Criticism in the *New York Times* and the *New York Tribune,* 1851–1876." Ph.D. diss., Louisiana State University.

McMinn, George Rupert. 1941. *The Theatre of the Golden Era of California.* Caldwell, Idaho: Caxton Printers.

McVicker, J. H. 1884. "The Theatre; Its Early Days in Chicago." Paper read before the Chicago Historical Society. Chicago: Knight & Leonard.

Meggett, Joan M., ed. 1978. *Music Periodical Literature: An Annotated Bibliography of Indexes and Bibliographies.* Metuchen, N.J.: Scarecrow Press.

Middleton, Lydia Miller. "George Loder." In *DNB.*

Minnegerode, Meade. 1924. *The Fabulous Forties: 1840–1850.* New York: Putnam's Sons.

Moehlenbrock, Arthur H. 1941. "The German Drama on the New Orleans Stage." Ph.D. diss., University of Iowa.

Moore, Lester. 1966. "A History of Professional Theatre in Newark, New Jersey, 1847–1867." Ph.D. diss., Columbia University.

Morley, Malcolm. 1962. "Maurice Strakosch." In *Enciclopedia della Spettacolo.* Rome: Casa Editrice le Maschere.

Morris, Richard, ed. 1976. *Encyclopedia of American History.* 5th ed. New York: Harper & Row.

Mott, Frank Luther. 1930. *A History of American Magazines, 1741–1850.* New York: Appleton.

Nelson, Molly. 1976. "The First Italian Opera Season in New York, 1825–1826." Ph.D. diss., University of North Carolina.

Nevins, Elizabeth West [Mrs. Charles Lawrence Perkins]. 1850. Diary. Manuscript Division, New-York Historical Society.

Newman, Ernest, trans. and ed. 1960. *Memoirs of Hector Berlioz from 1803–1865.* New York: Alfred A. Knopf, 1932; reprint New York: Dover.

Noid, Benjamin. 1968. "A History of the Theatre in Stockton, California, 1850–1892." Ph.D. diss., University of Utah.

Noole, Alfred Henry. 1917. "The German Drama on the St. Louis Stage." *Americana Germanica, No. 32.* Philadelphia: University of Pennsylvania.

Northall, William K. 1851. *Before and Behind the Curtain; or, Fifteen Years Observations Among the Theatres of New York.* New York: Burgess.

Northcott, Richard. 1920. *The Life of Sir Henry R. Bishop.* London: Press Printers.

Nugent, Beatrice L. 1967. "Benedict DeBar's Management of the St. Charles Theatre in New Orleans, Louisiana 1853–1861." Master's thesis, Louisiana State University.

Odell, George C. D. 1970. *Annals of the New York Stage.* Vols. 2–7. New York: Columbia University Press, 1927–31; reprint New York: AMS Press.

O'Shea, Joseph James. 1964. "A History of the English-Speaking Professional Stage in Milwaukee, 1842–1876." Ph.D. diss., Northwestern University.

Perry, Ted, ed. 1977. *Performing Arts Resources.* Vol. 3. New York: Drama Book Specialists.

Petty, Fred Curtis. 1971. "Italian Opera in London, 1760–1800." Ph.D. diss., Yale University.

Phelps, H. P. 1880. *Players of a Century: A Record of the Albany Stage.* Albany: Joseph McDonough.

Phelps, John W. March 1849–Sept. 1850. Diary. Manuscript Division, New York Public Library.

Phillips, Henry. 1864. *Musical and Personal Recollections During Half a Century.* London: C. J. Skeet.

Pinkston, C. Alex, Jr. 1986. "Varieties Theatre Stock Company." In *ATC,* ed. Durham.

Pleasants, Henry. 1981. *The Great Singers: From the Dawn of Opera to Caruso, Callas and Pavarotti.* New York: Simon & Schuster.

Porter, Andrew. 1988. "Musical Events." *New Yorker,* 24 Oct., 106–7.

Porter, Susan. 1977. "Performance Practice in America Opera at the Turn of the Nineteenth Century as Seen in *Children in the Wood,* a Representative Musical Entertainment." Ph.D. diss., University of Colorado.

——. *With an Air Debonair: Musical Theatre in America, 1785–1815.* Washington, D.C.: Smithsonian Institution Press.

Pred, Allen. 1980. *Urban Growth and City-Systems in the United States, 1840–1860.* Cambridge: Harvard University Press.

Preston, Katherine K. 1992. *Music for Hire: Professional Musicians in Washington, D.C., 1877–1900.* New York: Pendragon Press.

Price, Robert Bates. 1977. "A History of Music in Northern Louisiana until 1900." Ph.D. diss., Catholic University of America.

Pride, Leo B., ed. and comp. 1973. *International Theatre Directory: A World Directory of the Theatre and the Performing Arts.* New York: Simon & Schuster.

Pugh, Donald Wagner. 1970. "Music in Frontier Houston, 1836–1876." Ph.D. diss., University of Texas.

Radford, John P. 1979. "Race, Residence, and Ideology: Charleston, South Carolina in the Mid-Nineteenth Century." In *Geographic Perspectives on America's Past,* ed. David Ward. New York: Oxford University Press.

Reeves, J. Sims. 1889. *My Jubilee; or, Fifty Years of Artistic Life.* London: London Music Publishing.

Reiff, Anton (Anthony). 1855–56. Journal. Special Collections, Louisiana State University.

Reiff, Anthony. 1905. Manuscript account of activities of Lyster English Opera Company, 1858–60. Manuscripts and Rare Books Department, Swem Library, College of William and Mary, Williamsburg, Va.

Reines, Philip. 1970. "A Cultural History of the City of Winston-Salem, North Carolina, 1766–1966." Ph.D. diss., University of Denver.

Rice, John Blake. 1851–57, 1858–72. Account Book and Daybook for Rice's Theatre, Chicago. Manuscript Division, Chicago Historical Society.

Rich, Maria F., Victor Yellin, and H. Wiley Hitchcock. 1986. "Opera." In *AG,* ed. Hitchcock and Sadie.

Rickert, Alfred. 1967. "The History of the Theatre in Oswego, New York from the Beginning to 1875." Ph.D. diss., University of Denver.

Rieck, Waldemar. 1922. "Max Maretzek—Impresario, Conductor and Composer." *Musical Courier,* 22 June, 6.

———. 1925. "When Bristow's Rip Was Sung at Niblo's Garden." *Musical America,* 5 Dec., 3, 19.

Rietz, Louise Jean. 1939. "A History of the Theatre of Kansas City, Missouri to 1900." Ph.D. diss., State University of Iowa.

Ritchie, Anna Cora Ogden Mowatt. 1980. *Autobiography of an Actress; or, Eight Years on the Stage.* Boston: Ticknor, Reed, and Fields, 1854; reprint, New York: Arno Press.

Ritter, Charles C. 1957. "The Drama in Our Midst—the Early History of the Theatre in Memphis." *Western Tennessee Historical Society Papers,* 5–35.

———. 1956. "The Theatre in Memphis, Tennessee from Its Beginning to 1859." Ph.D. diss., University of Iowa.

Ritter, Frederic Louis. 1883. *Music in America.* New York: Charles Scribner's Sons.

Rodecape, Lois Foster. 1941–42. "Tom Maguire, Napoleon of the Stage," *California Historical Society Quarterly,* Dec., March, June, Sept.

Rogers, Clara Kathleen. 1919. *Memories of a Musical Career.* Boston: Little, Brown.

Rogers, Delmer D. 1986. "George Frederick Bristow." In *AG,* ed. Hitchcock and Sadie.

———. 1967. "Nineteenth-Century Music in New York City as Reflected in the Career of George Frederick Bristow." Ph.D. diss., University of Michigan.

Rogers, Francis. 1915. "America's First Grand Opera Season." *Musical Quarterly* 1 (Jan.): 93–101.

Roorbach, Orville Augustus. 1939. *Bibliotheca Americana: Catalogue of American Publications, Including Reprints and Original Works, from 1820 to 1852, Inclusive; Together with a List of Periodicals Published in the United States.* 4 vols. New York: O. A. Roorbach, etc., 1849–61; reprint New York: Peter Smith.

Roppolo, Joseph Patrick. 1950. "Audiences in New Orleans Theatre, 1845–1861" In *Tulane Studies in English,* vol. 2, 121–35. New Orleans: Tulane University Press.

Rosenthal, Harold. 1982. "Euphronsyne Parepa(-Rosa)." In *NG,* ed Sadie.

———. 1962. "Opera in English." *Music and Musicians* (Sept.):16–18.

———. 1982. "Pyne." In *NG,* ed. Sadie.

———. 1958. *Two Centuries of Opera at Covent Garden.* London: Putnam.

Rosselli, John. 1984. *The Opera Industry in Italy from Cimarosa to Verdi: The Role of the Impresario.* Cambridge: Cambridge University Press.

Rourke, Constance. 1928. *Troupers of the Gold Coast; or, The Rise of Lotta Crabtree*. New York: Harcourt, Brace.

Russell, Theodore Caskey. 1969. "Theodore Thomas: His Role in the Development of Musical Culture in the United States, 1835–1905." Ph.D. diss., University of Minnesota.

Sablonsky, Irving. 1986. *What They Heard: Music in America, 1852–1881*. Baton Rouge: Louisiana State University Press.

Sadie, Stanley, ed. 1982. *The New Grove Dictionary of Music* [NG]. 20 vols. London: Macmillan.

Samson, Blake Anthony. n.d. "Opera in San Francisco—the Starting Years." *San Francisco Opera Magazine*.

San Francisco Chronological File. n.d. In the Archives of the Performing Arts, San Francisco Public Library.

Scharf, J. Thomas, and Thompson Westcott. 1884. *A History of Philadelphia 1609–1884*. Philadelphia: L. H. Everts.

Schiavo, Giovanni Ermenegildo. 1947. *Italian Music and Musicians in America*. New York: Vigo Press.

Schick, Joseph. 1939. *The Early Theatre in Eastern Iowa: Cultural Beginnings and the Rise of the Theatre in Davenport and Eastern Iowa, 1836–1863*. Chicago: University of Chicago Press.

Schilling, Lester. 1961. "A History of the Theatre in Portland, Oregon, 1846–1959." Ph.D. diss., University of Wisconsin.

Schleis, Thomas Henry. 1974. "Opera in Milwaukee, 1850–1900." Master's thesis, University of Wisconsin.

Schoberlin, Melvin. 1941. *From Candles to Footlights: A Biography of the Pike's Peak Theatre, 1859–1876*. Denver: Old West Publishing.

Seilhamer, George. 1881. "Mary Ann Horton (Mrs. Charles Horn)," "Anne Sequin," and "Anna Bishop." In *An Interviewer's Album*. New York: Alvin Perry.

Sellen, Maxine, ed. 1983. *Ethnic Theatre in the United States*. Westport, Conn.: Greenwood Press.

Shanet, Howard. 1975. *Philharmonic: A History of New York's Orchestra*. New York: Doubleday.

Sherman, John K. 1958. *Music and Theatre in Minnesota History*. Minneapolis: University of Minnesota Press.

Sherman, Robert L. 1947. *The Chicago Stage: Its Records and Achievements*. Chicago: Published privately.

Shirreff, Jane. Collection: Diary, Financial Ledger, Playbills. Billy Rose Theatre Collection. New York Public Library.

Sill, Joseph. 1836–54. Diaries. Manuscript Division, Historical Society of Pennsylvania.

Slonimsky, Nicholas. 1978. *Baker's Biographical Dictionary of Musicians*. 6th ed. New York: Schirmer Books.

Smith, Sol. 1868. *Theatrical Management in the West and South for Thirty Years*. New York: Harper & Bros.

Smither, Nellie. 1944. *A History of the English Theatre in New Orleans*. New York: Benjamin Blom.

Sonneck, Oscar G. 1915. *Early Opera in America.* New York: Benjamin Blom.

Southworth, Henry C. May 1850-July 1851. Diary. Manuscript Division, New-York Historical Society.

Sparks, Andrew H. 1940. "A History of the Theatre in Savannah, Georgia, 1800–1836." Master's thesis, University of Georgia.

Steinhaus, Walter E. 1973. "Music in the Cultural Life of Macon, Georgia, 1823–1900." Ph.D. diss., Florida State University.

Stolzenbach, Norma F. 1954. "The History of the Theatre in Toledo, Ohio from Its Beginning to 1893." Ph.D. diss., University of Michigan.

Stone, Henry Dickinson. 1873. *Personal Recollections of the Drama; or, Theatrical Reminiscences.* Albany, N.Y.: Benthuysen.

Stoutamire, Albert. 1960. "A History of Music in Richmond, Virginia, 1742–1856." Ph.D. diss., Florida State University.

———. 1972. *Music of the Old South: Colony to Confederacy.* Teaneck, N.J.: Fairleigh Dickinson University Press.

Strakosch, Maurice. 1850. *Giovanna Prima di Napoli.* Libretto. New York: Published for and sold at the box office of the [Astor Place] Opera House.

Stratman, Carl. 1970. *American Theatrical Periodicals, 1798–1967: A Bibliographical Guide.* Durham, N.C.: Duke University Press.

———. 1965. *Bibliography of the American Theatre, Excluding New York City.* Chicago: Loyola University Press.

———. 1963. "The New York Stage: A Checklist of Unpublished Dissertations and Theses." *Bulletin of Bibliography* (Sept.–Dec.):41–44.

———. 1966. "The Theatre in New York: Addenda." *New York Public Library Bulletin* (June):389–407.

Stratton, Stephen S., and James D. Brown. 1971. *British Musical Biography: A Dictionary of Musical Artists, Authors, and Composers Born in Britain and Its Colonies.* Birmingham: Stratton, 1897; reprint New York: Da Capo.

Strunk, Oliver, ed. 1950. *Source Readings in Music History.* New York: W. W. Norton.

Stuart-Wortley, Emmeline. 1851. *Travels in the United States, etc, during 1849 and 1850.* New York: Harper & Brothers.

Sturtevant, Catherine. 1930. "A Study of the Dramatic Productions of Two Decades in Chicago, 1847–1857 and 1897–1907." Ph.D. diss., University of Chicago.

Sturtevant, John T. 1835–1905. Diary (Reminiscences). Manuscript Division, New York Public Library.

Taber, Louise E. n.d. *Gold Rush Days.* San Francisco: Albert S. Samuels.

Tanner, H. S. 1845. *New Universal Atlas.* Philadelphia: Carey & Hart.

Tawa, Nicholas. 1986. "Seguin." In *AG,* ed. Hitchcock and Sadie.

Taylor, Rosser. 1942. *Ante Bellum South Carolina: A Social and Cultural History.* Chapel Hill: University of North Carolina Press.

Teal, Mary Evelyn. 1964. "Musical Activities in Detroit from 1701 through 1870." Ph.D. diss., University of Michigan.

Temperley, Nicholas. 1986. "Charles Edward Horn." In *AG,* ed. Hitchcock and Sadie.

————. 1982. "Thomas Attwood," "Henry Rowley Bishop," "George Loder." In *NG*, ed. Sadie.

Teran, Jay R. S. 1974. "The New York Opera Audience: 1825–1974." Ph.D. diss., New York University.

Thomas, Theodore. 1905. *A Musical Autobiography.* Ed. George P. Upton. 2 vols. Chicago: A. C. McClurg.

Tolan, Robert. 1968. "A History of the Legitimate Professional Theatre in Ft. Wayne, Indiana from 1854 to 1884." Ph.D. diss., Purdue University.

Tompkins, Eugene. 1908. *The History of the Boston Theatre, 1854–1901.* New York: Houghton, Mifflin.

Tracy, Charles. 1856. Diary. Vol. 1. Manuscript Division, New-York Historical Society.

Turner, Vivian. 1929. "The Stage in New Orleans, Louisiana, after 1837." Master's thesis, State University of Iowa.

U.S. Bureau of the Census. 1832. *Fifth Census or Enumeration of the Inhabitants of the U.S. as Collected at the Department of State, 1830.* Washington, D. C.: Duff Green, 37.

————. *Seventh Census of the United States: An Appendix Embracing Notes upon the Tables of Each of the States, etc.* 1853. Washington, D.C.: Robert Armstrong, Public Printer.

————. 1841. *Sixth Census or Enumeration of the Inhabitants of the U.S. as Collected at the Department of State, 1840.* Washington, D.C.: Blair and Rives, 83.

U.S. Government. 1941. District of Columbia Historical Records Survey. *WPA Bio-Bibliographical Index of Musicians in the United States of America since Colonial Times.* Washington, D.C.: Music Division, Pan American Union.

Upton, George P. 1847–81. "Attractions in Chicago." 6 vols. Manuscript Division, Chicago Historical Society.

————. 1908. *Musical Memories, My Recollections of Celebrities of the Half Century, 1850–1900.* Chicago: A. C. McClurg.

Upton, William Treat. 1954. *William Henry Fry, American Journalist and Composer-Critic.* New York: Crowell.

Varnardo, Alban F. 1947. "A History of Theatrical Activity in Baton Rouge, Louisiana, 1819–1900." Master's thesis, Louisiana State University.

Verdi, Giuseppe. 1859. *Il Trovatore.* Libretto. San Francisco: Towne and Bacon.

Waddington, Peter. 1947. "Musical Beginnings of the City of St. Francis." *Opera and Concert* (Sept.):48–59.

Wagstaff, Julie A. 1829–1907. Diary. Manuscript Division, New York Public Library.

Walker, Frank. 1962. *The Man Verdi.* New York: Alfred A. Knopf.

Ward, Genevieve, and Richard Whiting. 1918. *Both Sides of the Curtain.* London: Cassell.

Ware, W. Porter, and Thaddeus C. Lockard, Jr. 1980. *P. T. Barnum Presents Jenny Lind: The American Tour of the Swedish Nightingale.* Baton Rouge: Louisiana State University Press.

Watson, Margaret. 1964. *Silver Theatre: Amusements of the Mining Frontier in Early Nevada, 1850–1864.* Glendale, Calif.: Clark.

Webb, Dorothy. 1970. "An Early History of the Arch Street Theatre, 1828–1834." Ph.D. diss., Indiana University.

Weichlein, William J. 1970. *A Checklist of American Music Periodicals 1850–1900.* Detroit: Information Coordinators.

Weidensaul, Jane. 1970. "Bochsa: A Biographical Sketch." *American Harp Journal* (Fall): 4–7.

Weinstock, Herbert. 1987. *Rossini: A Biography.* New York: Limelight Editions.

————. 1980. *Vincenzo Bellini: His Life and His Operas.* New York: Alfred A. Knopf.

Weisert, John J. 1958. *The Curtain Rises: A Checklist of Performances at Samuel Drake's City Theatre and Other Theatres at Louisville from the Beginning to 1843.* Louisville: Published privately.

————. 1955. A Large and Fashionable Audience: A Checklist of Performances at the Louisville Theatre, 1846–1866. Louisville: Published privately.

————. 1962. *Mozart Hall: 1851–1866: A Checklist.* Louisville: Published privately.

Wemyss, Francis C. 1852. *Chronology of the American Stage, 1752–1852.* New York: Taylor.

————. 1847. *Twenty-Six Years of the Life of an Actor and Manager.* New York: Burgess, Stringer & Co.

White, Carolyn B. 22 Sept. 1851–7 July 1852. Diary. Vol. 3. Manuscript Collection, American Antiquarian Society.

White, Richard Grant. 1882. "Opera in New York." *The Century Magazine* (March):686–703; (April):865–82; (May):31–43; (June):193–210.

Wielich, Ludwig. 1914. "The Philharmonic Society's Early Days." *Opera Magazine* (Feb.):26–28.

Willard, George O. 1891. *History of the Providence Stage, 1762–1891, Including Sketches of Many Prominent Actors Who Have Appeared in America.* Providence: Rhode Island Company.

Williams, Grier M. 1961. "A History of Music in Jacksonville, Florida, 1822–1922." Ph.D. diss., Florida State University.

Willis, Nathaniel Parker. 1859. *The Convalescent.* New York: Scribner.

Wilmeth, Don B. 1978. *The American Stage to World War I: A Guide to Information Sources.* Detroit: Gale.

————. 1982. *Variety Entertainment and Outdoor Amusements: A Reference Guide.* Westport, Conn.: Greenwood Press.

Wilson, Arthur Herman. 1935. *A History of the Philadelphia Theatre, 1835–1855.* Philadelphia: University of Pennsylvania Press.

Wilson, John. n.d. *Wilson's Edition of the Songs of Scotland.* London: Published privately.

Wilt, James Napier. 1923. "History of the Two Rice Theatres in Chicago from 1847 to 1857." Ph.D. diss., University of Chicago.

Woestemeyer, Ina Fae, and J. Montgomery Gambrill. 1939. *Reprints of Source Materials on the Cultural Frontier.* New York: Appleton-Century.

Wolz, Peter D. 1983. "Opera in Cincinnati Before 1920." Ph.D. diss., University of Cincinnati.

Wood, Maude A. 1926. "The Early History of Grand Opera in Chicago." Ph.D. diss., University of Chicago.

Wood, William Burke. 1855. *Recollections of the Stage.* Philadelphia: Baird.

Wunderlich, Charles Edward. 1962. "A History and Bibliography of Early American Musical Periodicals, 1782–1852." Ph.D. diss., University of Michigan.

Wyrick, Charles R. 1965. "Concert and Criticism in Cincinnati, 1840–1850." Master's thesis, University of Cincinnati.

Yocum, Jack H. 1955. "A History of the Theatre in Houston, 1831–1954." Ph.D. diss., University of Wisconsin.

Young, William C. 1973. *Documents of American Theatre History.* Vol. 1: *Famous American Playhouses 1716–1899.* Chicago: American Library Association.

Index

KATHERINE K. PRESTON has degrees from The Evergreen State College, Olympia, Washington, the University of Maryland at College Park, and the Graduate School of the City University of New York. She teaches music history at the College of William and Mary in Williamsburg, Virginia. She has published book and record reviews, articles in periodicals and books, and has contributed to *The New Grove Dictionary of American Music* and *The New Grove Dictionary of Opera*. She is also the author of *Music for Hire: A Study of Professional Musicians in Washington, D.C., 1877–1900.*

Paul Hindemith in the United States
Luther Noss

"My Song Is My Weapon": People's Songs, American Communism,
and the Politics of Culture
Robbie Lieberman

Chosen Voices: The Story of the American Cantorate
Mark Slobin

Theodore Thomas: America's Conductor and Builder
of Orchestras, 1835–1905
Ezra Schabas

"The Whorehouse Bells Were Ringing" and
Other Songs Cowboys Sing
Guy Logsdon

Crazeology: The Autobiography of a Chicago Jazzman
Bud Freeman, as Told to Robert Wolf

Discoursing Sweet Music: Brass Bands and Community Life
in Turn-of-the-Century Pennsylvania
Kenneth Kreitner

Mormonism and Music: A History
Michael Hicks

Voices of the Jazz Age: Profiles of Eight Vintage Jazzmen
Chip Deffaa

Pickin' on Peachtree: A History of Country Music in Atlanta, Georgia
Wayne W. Daniel

Bitter Music: Collected Journals, Essays, Introductions, and Librettos
Harry Partch; edited by Thomas McGeary

Ethnic Music on Records: A Discography of Ethnic Recordings
Produced in the United States, 1893 to 1942
Richard K. Spottswood

Downhome Blues Lyrics: An Anthology from
the Post-World War II Era
Jeff Todd Titon

Ellington: The Early Years
Mark Tucker

Chicago Soul
Robert Pruter

That Half-Barbaric Twang: The Banjo in American Popular Culture
Karen Linn

Hot Man: The Life of Art Hodes
Art Hodes and Chadwick Hansen

The Erotic Muse: American Bawdy Songs
Second Edition
Ed Cray

Barrio Rhythm: Mexican American Music in Los Angeles
Steven Loza